ALSO BY CHRISTOPHER LEONARD

The Meat Racket: The Secret Takeover of America's Food Business

KOCHLAND

THE SECRET HISTORY OF KOCH INDUSTRIES AND CORPORATE POWER IN AMERICA

CHRISTOPHER LEONARD

Simon & Schuster

NEW YORK   LONDON   TORONTO   SYDNEY   NEW DELHI

Simon & Schuster
1230 Avenue of the Americas
New York, NY 10020

First Simon & Schuster hardcover edition August 2019

SIMON & SCHUSTER and colophon are registered trademarks
of Simon & Schuster, Inc.

For information about special discounts for bulk purchases,
please contact Simon & Schuster Special Sales at 1-866-506-1949
or business@simonandschuster.com.

The Simon & Schuster Speakers Bureau can bring authors to your
live event. For more information or to book an event, contact
the Simon & Schuster Speakers Bureau at 1-866-248-3049
or visit our website at www.simonspeakers.com.

Manufactured in the United States of America

1   3   5   7   9   10   8   6   4   2

Library of Congress Cataloging-in-Publication Data is available.

ISBN 978-1-4767-7538-8
ISBN 978-1-4767-7540-1 (ebook)

This book is for my mother, Victoria Brigham Leonard,
who taught me to think about the other person.
Thank you.

CONTENTS

PART 3: GOLIATH

The Fighter

(1967–2019)

On May 18, 1981, four Wall Street bankers traveled to Wichita, Kansas. They went there to make an offer to Charles Koch, the CEO of an obscure, midsize energy company. The bankers, from Morgan Stanley, wanted to convince Koch to take his family's company public, offering shares for sale on the New York Stock Exchange. Their deal was squarely in line with the conventional wisdom of corporate America at the time. Going public was seen as a natural progression for companies like Koch Industries, offering them access to big pools of money and promising enormous paydays for the existing team of executives. All it required from the CEO was to surrender control. Morgan Stanley, in return, would collect a small fortune in fees.

Charles Koch was forty-five years old. He had run Koch Industries since he was thirty-two, when his father died suddenly. He was trim, tall, and had an athlete's build. He spoke quietly in meetings and seemed almost passive. The bankers laid out their plan to take Koch public. They revealed what, to most executives, at least, might have been the most significant detail: if Charles Koch agreed to the deal, he could earn $20 million overnight. The bankers seemed incredulous when they prepared a confidential memo about Koch's reaction.

"He does not want this cash," the memo reported.

Charles Koch calmly explained to them why their offer made no sense. His company was breathtakingly profitable. It operated in vital, deeply complex corners of the American energy industry. During the 1980s, Koch Industries was the largest purchaser and transporter of US crude oil. It owned an oil refinery. It employed teams of commodities traders who bought and sold a wildly diverse menu of raw materials and financial products, from gasoline to paper futures contracts. This might have encouraged most CEOs to take their company public. Koch Industries, however, did not want outsiders to know how much money its traders were earning. Taking the company public would expose too many of its secrets.

"Certain of [Koch's] commodity traders are particularly worried that their high salaries, once disclosed to the public, would be used against them by their trading partners," the memo said.

Secrecy was a strategic necessity for Koch Industries. Charles Koch did not want to surrender it. He also didn't want to surrender control. He had a specific, clear vision of how to run his company, and he didn't need Wall Street investors to interfere.

If the bankers expected Charles Koch to go along with the conventional wisdom of their time, then they, like so many outsiders, did not understand him. Beneath his low-key veneer, Charles Koch was, at his core, a fighter. He had unmovable ideas about how things should be, and he did not back down when challenged. When he was challenged by his own brothers for control of Koch Industries, he fought them in a bitter legal battle that lasted decades. When he was challenged by members of a powerful labor union during his first years as CEO, he fought them even as they committed an act of industrial sabotage that nearly destroyed Koch's oil refinery. When the FBI and the US Department of Justice launched a criminal investigation into Koch Industries' oil gathering business, Charles Koch fought them with every legal and political tool at his disposal. When a liberal Congress and President Barack Obama sought to impose regulations on the fossil fuel industry to control greenhouse gas emissions, Charles Koch fought them in ways that changed US politics.

In each of these fights, Charles Koch prevailed.

When Charles Koch dismissed the bankers in 1981, it was just a small skirmish in the larger war to control Koch Industries. After prevailing in that fight, he created a company that was true to his vision. He avoided the snares that entangled many publicly traded companies that report their financial results to investors every three months. Koch Industries didn't have to think quarter to quarter. The company thinks year to year. An internal think tank and deal-making committee, called the development group, will sometimes think through a business deal on a timeline measured in decades. This long-term view made Koch nimble where other companies stumbled. In 2003, for example, Koch Industries bought a group of money-losing fertilizer plants when no publicly traded company was willing to take the risk. Today those plants are as profitable as a broken ATM machine that spews out cash around the clock. Unlike publicly traded companies, Koch Industries does not pay out rich dividends to investors. Charles Koch insists on reinvesting at least 90 percent of the company's profits, fueling its constant expansion.

This strategy laid the foundation for decades of continuous growth. Koch Industries expanded continuously by purchasing other companies and branching out into new industries. It specialized in the kind of businesses that are indispensable to modern civilization but which most consumers never directly encounter. The company is embedded in the hidden infrastructure of everyday life. Millions of people use Koch's products without ever seeing Koch's name attached. Koch refines and distributes fossil fuels, from gasoline to jet fuel, on which the global economy is dependent. Koch is the world's third largest producer of nitrogen fertilizer, which is the cornerstone of the modern food system. Koch makes the synthetic materials used in baby diapers, waistbands, and carpets. It makes the chemicals used for plastic bottles and pipes. It owns Georgia-Pacific, which makes the wall panels, beams, and plywood required to build homes and office buildings. It makes napkins, paper towels, stationery, newspaper, and personal hygiene products. Koch Industries owns a network of commodities trading offices in Houston, Moscow, Geneva, and elsewhere, which are the circulatory system of modern finance. Koch traders sell everything from fertilizer, to rare metals, to fuel, to abstract derivatives contracts. Koch Industries' annual revenue is larger than that of Facebook, Goldman Sachs, and US Steel combined.

The profits from Koch's activities are stunning. Charles Koch and his brother David own roughly 80 percent of Koch Industries. Together the two men are worth $120 billion. Their fortune is larger than that of Amazon CEO Jeff Bezos, or Microsoft founder Bill Gates. Yet David and Charles Koch did not invent a major new product or revolutionize any industry. The Koch brothers derived their wealth through a patient, long-term strategy of seizing opportunities in complex and often opaque corners of the economic system.

This book tells the history of Koch Industries and shows how the

Koch brothers' fortune was made. In doing so, it also provides a portrait of the American economy since the 1960s. Koch's operations span the entire landscape of the American economy. The company's story is the story of America's energy system, of its blue-collar factory workers, of millionaire derivatives traders, corporate lobbyists, and private equity deal makers. To examine Koch is to examine the modern American economy.

This account is based on hundreds of hours of interviews, conducted over six years, with dozens of current and former Koch Industries employees, managers, whistle-blowers, and senior executives, including Charles Koch. Also interviewed were outside regulators, prosecutors, politicians, bankers, and competitors. These verbal accounts were supplemented by internal company memos, minutes of executive meetings kept by firsthand witnesses, government documents declassified for this book, legal transcripts, regulatory filings, contemporaneous news accounts, and other documents.

Ralph Waldo Emerson famously said that an institution is the lengthened shadow of one man. This observation would seem to be particularly true of Koch Industries, which has been led by one CEO since 1967. Charles Koch's control of the company is complete. His portrait hangs in the company's lobby, and employees are trained with his videotaped speeches. Every employee must embrace Charles Koch's highly detailed philosophy called Market-Based Management. But Emerson's quote captured only half of the truth about institutions. They are shadows of people, but they are also shadows of the political and economic systems in which they exist. A large corporation in China, for example, is quite different from a large corporation based in America. The laws, culture, and economic incentives are radically different in each nation. Koch Industries, then, reflects an American system in which it grew and thrived.

When Charles Koch took control of the company, America operated under a political framework called the New Deal, which was characterized by dramatic government interventions into the private marketplace, empowered labor unions, tightly regulated energy companies, and a shackled financial industry. Charles Koch despised it. He subscribed to the philosophy of Austrian economists such as Ludwig von Mises, who believed that government intervention only created more harm than good. During Charles Koch's career, the New Deal system fell apart. The system wasn't replaced by a libertarian society, as Charles Koch might have wanted, but by a dysfunctional political economy characterized by selective deregulation coupled with a sprawling welfare and regulatory state. Charles Koch didn't just operate within this political framework. He dedicated his life to transforming it. He created a political influence network that is arguably the most powerful and far-reaching operation ever run out of an American CEO's office. Koch Industries has one of the largest, most well-funded lobbying operations in the United States. Its efforts are coupled with a nationwide army of activists and volunteers called Americans for Prosperity, along with a constellation of Koch-funded think tanks and university-based programs. Charles Koch's political vision represents one extreme pole in the ongoing debate about the role of government in markets; a view that government should essentially protect private property and do little else. Political figures on the opposite pole believe that a robust federal government should provide a safety net and contain the power of large corporations. There is currently no political consensus in support of either view.

As the argument between these visions drags on in a stalemate, the modern American economy is one that favors giant companies over the small, and the politically connected over the independent. More than anything, it favors companies that can master complexity—the complexity of interconnected and global marketplaces, and the complexity of wide-reaching, intrusive regulatory regimes.

Charles Koch frequently derides the current political era as one of "crony capitalism," but the company he built is perfectly suited to thrive in this environment. Koch Industries employs an army of legal experts to navigate the extensive legal intrusion of the state. A similarly large group of market analysts and traders navigate the fractured and byzantine markets of energy products. It is revealing that Koch Industries expands, almost exclusively, into businesses that are uncompetitive, dominated by monopolistic firms, and deeply intertwined with government subsidies and regulation.

To take just one example: Koch derives much of its profits from oil refineries. The entire economy depends on refined oil, but no one has built a new oil refinery in the United States since 1977. The industry is dominated by entrenched players who run aged facilities at near-full capacity, reaping profits that are among the highest in the world. A single refinery shutdown causes gasoline prices to spike across entire regions of the United States. The underlying cause of this dysfunction is a set of loopholes in the Clean Air Act, a massive set of regulations passed in 1963 (and significantly expanded in 1970) that imposed pollution controls on new refineries. The legacy oil refiners, including Koch, exploited arcane sections of the law that allowed them to expand their old facilities while avoiding clean-air standards that would apply to new facilities. This gave them an insurmountable advantage over any potential new competitor. The absence of new refineries to stoke competition and drive down prices meant that Americans paid higher prices for gasoline.

Koch Industries has applied its profits to maximum advantage. In 2018, the company's headquarters campus in Wichita resembled a fortified kingdom. The facility was expanded in 2014, with the addition of several thousand square feet of office space in buildings arrayed at the base of the iconic Koch Tower—a large building with black windows and gleaming dark granite. The renovation also included the installation of a tall, earthen wall surrounding the north side of the campus. A local city street was diverted around the wall, at Koch's expense, to keep passersby at a safe distance. Seldom has a company gained such deep reach into so many Americans' lives while simultaneously walling itself away into an insular community.

Koch Industries' employees arrive to work early, creating small traffic jams at entrances to the campus, under the watch of security guards. Many of them enter Koch Tower through an underground pedestrian tunnel, passing a series of photo collages that memorialize Koch's history. They reach an underground lobby and an elevator bank, where the portrait of Charles Koch hangs on the wall. It is one of those composite portraits, made of countless tiny images that combine to form a larger picture. The tiny images are of Koch's employees; the larger picture is Charles Koch. Across the lobby, employees shop at the company store, called Hot Commodities, where they can buy coffee or an audio CD relating the history of founder Fred Koch. There is a magazine rack stocked with glossy copies of the company newsletter, called *Discovery*, which regularly features columns by Charles Koch.

When each employee is hired, he or she undergoes a multiday training session to learn the tenets of Charles Koch's philosophy, Market-Based Management, or MBM as they call it. Charles Koch says the philosophy is a blueprint for achieving prosperity and freedom. It is equally applicable to business ventures, personal habits, and national government. Adherence to the creed is nonnegotiable for anyone who remains at Koch Industries. Charles Koch, in one of his books, writes that an "act of conversion" is necessary for MBM to be effective. It cannot be adopted in bits and pieces. The Ten Guiding Principles of MBM are printed and hung above cubicles throughout company headquarters. When employees get free coffee in the break room, the Guiding Principles are printed on their disposable cups. The employees learn MBM's vocabulary and speak a language among themselves that only they truly understand. They drop phrases like "mental models," "experimental discovery," and "decision rights," that instantly convey deep meaning to insiders. The employees become more than employees; they become citizens of an institution with its own vocabulary, its own incentives, and its own goals in the world. The financial success of Koch Industries only reinforces the idea that what they are doing is right and that the tenets of MBM are indeed the key to proper living.

Because this book is the biography of an institution, not an individual, many people will come and go through its pages. Readers will meet Heather Faragher, a Koch employee who blew the whistle on systematic wrongdoing inside Koch, only to face the harshest consequences. Readers will meet Bernard Paulson, a hard-driving executive who helped Koch Industries break the back of a militant labor union. They will meet Dean Watson, a rising star at Koch Industries, who embraced the teachings of Market-Based Management but whose career collapsed under the weight of his own ambition. They will meet Philip Dubose, a Koch employee who stole oil to make his bosses happy. They will meet Steve Hammond, a warehouse worker who negotiated for workers' rights against his bosses at Koch. And they will meet Brenden O'Neill, a striving middle-class man from Wichita who became a millionaire on Koch's commodity trading floors. Unfortunately, many of these people will arrive and then fall away as Koch Industries moves forward and changes with the times. This is the nature of large institutions. The people in them come and go. If it is difficult to keep track of so many individuals, readers can turn to an alphabetical directory of characters at the end of the book.

There is one person, however, who is present for the entire fifty-plus-year span of this story. He resides, almost the entire time, at the pinnacle of power at Koch Industries, driving it forward, shaping it to his vision, and reaping its great rewards. Charles Koch is the author, more than anybody, of Koch Industries' story.

Even though his influence is felt throughout Koch Industries, and throughout America's political system, Charles Koch remains a remarkably opaque figure. He prizes his privacy and cherishes secrecy. Countless people have tried to understand Charles Koch by looking at him from outside the tall walls and dark glass windows of Koch Industries headquarters. One of those people is an FBI special agent named James Elroy. He dedicated many years of his life to investigating the leadership organization of Koch Industries. Elroy was convinced, in 1988, that Charles Koch and his lieutenants were engaged in a massive criminal conspiracy.

That is why Elroy positioned himself, one day, in the middle of an Oklahoma cow pasture, holding a camera with a wide-angle lens, trying to surveil Charles Koch's employees. That is the moment where this book begins.

PART 1

THE KOCH METHOD

CHAPTER 1

Under Surveillance

(1987–1989)

FBI special agent James Elroy stood on a remote expanse of pasture-land and waited for the man from Koch Oil to arrive. Elroy had a 600-millimeter camera, a telephoto lens, and plenty of film. Perhaps most importantly, he also had a bag of feed cubes for the cattle. Elroy had arrived early at this carefully chosen spot to stake out his position. He stood at a place with a commanding view of a large, cylindrical oil tank. The tank was one of hundreds just like it that were scattered through-out the Oklahoma countryside, sitting on land that was desolate on its surface but which covered rich deposits of underground crude-oil lakes. The oil was slowly drained by unmanned pumps that bobbed up and down day and night, drawing out the crude and sending it into the big metal tanks. When those tanks were finally full, an employee from Koch Oil would arrive in a big truck, siphon out the fuel, and take it to market. Elroy planned to be ready for him.

Elroy opened the feed bag, grabbed handfuls of cubes, and scat-tered them on the ground. Soon enough, the cattle began to congregate around him, lowering their heads to sniff through the grass and pick out pieces of their unexpected meal. As he hoped would happen, Elroy was soon fully encircled by the cattle. On the flatland prairies of Oklahoma, this was about the only way to stay hidden.

For a long time, it was just Elroy out there, all alone. The nearest town was called Nowata, and it wasn't much more than a tiny grid of neigh-borhoods surrounding a strip of one-story brick buildings that passed as downtown. In Nowata, the main drag wasn't called Main Street: it was called Cherokee Avenue. Elroy was standing in "Indian Country," as out-siders called it, the Indian reservations that were home to the last rem-nants of American tribes like the Osage and Cherokee. Elroy was familiar with this country, having been an FBI agent in Oklahoma City for several years. During his time in Oklahoma, Elroy had developed a specialty in breaking open large, complicated fraud schemes—his biggest case was a massive public corruption sting in the early 1980s that netted more than two hundred convictions, including two-thirds of all the sitting county commissioners in the state of Oklahoma.

So maybe it was inevitable that Elroy would be sucked into this investigation and would find himself standing in the middle of a cattle herd, staring at a lonely oil tank. The surveillance was part of a special detail—the FBI had loaned Elroy out as a special investigator for the US Senate. Although he had a new boss, the job was a familiar one. Elroy was collecting evidence for a sprawling, complex fraud case. Elroy's new bosses in the Senate were increasingly convinced that the obscure company called Koch Oil was engaged in a conspiracy to steal millions of dollars' worth of oil from local Indians—and possibly US taxpayers, too. Elroy's job was to document whether the fraud was real. That's why he had the 600-millimeter camera at the ready.

Soon enough, Elroy spotted his target: a lone truck was coming down a narrow road that led to the oil tank. As the truck approached, Elroy was well concealed behind a wall of cattle. He raised his camera and aimed it at the truck as it pulled alongside the oil tanker and a man got out.

Elroy then trained his telephoto lens on the Koch Oil man as he went about his work, down by the oil tank. The camera went in and out of focus. Blurry, then sharp. Then Elroy could see the Koch Oil man as if he were standing just feet away. His face, his clothing, his hands as he worked. Elroy focused in.

Snap. Snap. Snap.

Elroy's photos were developed in a darkroom. The images were vague at first, but the picture clarified with each dip in a chemical bath, shapes and profiles refining and sharpening until the complete picture came into view. The Koch Oil man approaching the oil tank. Opening it. Measuring the oil within. Writing a receipt. The images were crisp and clear. Inarguable evidence. Over time, Elroy developed a stack of images like this, high-quality shots that allowed him to see the Koch Oil man perfectly. The 600-millimeter telephoto lens had done its job.

As clear as the photos were, Elroy did not plan to use them as evidence in court. They were going to be a tool for his investigation—a way to exploit human weakness.

Elroy learned how to investigate large conspiracies for the FBI during the 1980s. To break open a large conspiracy, you start at the edges. You find the most vulnerable link in the large chain of corruption, and you exploit it. That's why Elroy decided to focus on the Koch Oil employees who actually emptied the oil tanks. These were the kind of people who were very quick to start talking when an FBI agent knocked on their door. They were the working stiffs; the most visible players in what Elroy was increasingly convinced was a complex conspiracy.

Elroy wasn't the typical FBI man, with the stereotypical crew cut and shiny black shoes. When he graduated from the FBI Academy in Quantico, Virginia, in 1970, Elroy looked as much like a young corporate attorney as anything else, with a slightly shaggy mop of dark hair and a knowing smirk on his face. He knew American criminal code inside and out, was foulmouthed and well trained with a rifle. In spite of his irreverence, he was a law-and-order man through and through. He revered Director J. Edgar Hoover, whom he saw as a visionary leader rather than the bureaucratic despot that many historians judged him to be. When Elroy was told he'd be working for the US Senate, he wasn't thrilled. As a rule, Elroy thought that Senate investigations were political theater. As an FBI man, he was accustomed to operating under strict legal rules about gathering evidence to ultimately prosecute a criminal case. The Senate investigations seemed lightweight compared to that: the senators only seemed to ever want enough evidence to support a public hearing in Washington so they could have a show. But Elroy's bosses knew him well. They knew that when he was assigned to a case, he became borderline obsessed. And that is exactly what happened in the case of Koch Oil.

The Senate had gotten a tip that Koch Oil was stealing oil from Indian reservations throughout Oklahoma. These Indian lands were administrated by the federal government, so the Senate took a keen interest in the allegations. Elroy was told that the scheme was relatively simple: Koch Oil was an oil transportation company. The company would show up at the metal oil tanks, drain the oil, and then ship it to the market by truck or pipeline. But every time Koch drained the oil, it would intentionally underreport just how much it was taking. If Koch drained a hundred barrels, for example, it would say it had only gathered ninety-nine barrels. This meant that Koch was getting one barrel for free every time it bought oil.

While the alleged scheme was simple, it proved remarkably difficult to investigate. Koch Oil seemed to be built for the very purpose of avoiding outside scrutiny.

The company was owned by Koch Industries, a conglomerate based in Wichita. The company was family-owned and private. It seemed that nobody in either the Senate or the FBI had ever heard of the firm when they began investigating it in 1988. They mistook it for Coca-Cola, the soft drink maker in Atlanta, or they mispronounced the company name altogether in a way that rhymed with "watch" rather than the correct pronunciation, which rhymed with "smoke." But for all its obscurity, it turned out that Koch Industries was a sprawling and vitally important company. Senate investigators learned that Koch Oil was the single largest purchaser of crude oil in the United States. Over the decades, it had quietly bought up tens of thousands of miles of pipelines and trucking services. As a result, when oil drillers like Exxon or Chevron wanted to ship their oil from remote wells in places like Oklahoma, Koch Oil was sometimes the only buyer for their product. It was the only way to get oil from the well to market. Millions of Americans used Koch's products when they filled up their car's gas tank, but no one seemed to even know the company's name.

The only thing that was clear about Koch was that it harbored a deep antipathy toward the federal government and toward regulation in general. David Koch, one of the company's primary owners and executives, had run for vice president on the national ticket for the Libertarian Party in 1980. Its platform had called for the abolishment of everything from the US Post Office to the Environmental Protection Agency to public schooling. The company itself had tangled with federal energy regulators for years over price control laws and other matters. Koch executives consistently argued that energy companies should operate in markets untrammeled by federal regulations. Koch Industries sat at the nexus of America's energy supply, but for all its power and influence, Koch was a hidden giant. The company had somehow insinuated itself into nearly every corner of America's energy infrastructure without ever revealing its position.

How, then, could Elroy hope to prove whether the company was steal-ing oil or not? He went after the employees who drained the oil tanks, known as "gaugers" in the business. The only benefit they could possi-bly get from mismeasuring oil was their paychecks. They lived in small towns, worked hard to support their families, and some of them prob-ably didn't even fully grasp what they were doing when they took the oil. They were just doing what their bosses told them to, Elroy suspected. Elroy visited their houses in the evenings. He pulled up at the houses with a partner, walked up to the front door, and knocked. When some-one answered, Elroy identified himself as an FBI agent and asked if he could come in and talk. It was highly likely that these men had never met an FBI agent before. This gave Elroy the advantage: the Koch Oil men were confused, knocked off balance, wondering why in the world two men from the FBI were standing in their living room. He, on the other hand, was prepared with a list of specific questions and some evidence on hand to back up very serious allegations of theft.

Elroy sat down and began to run through his list of questions, asking the men about their daily jobs and the business of measuring oil. It must have been surreal for them, their minds racing, trying to figure out why the FBI was asking them about their relatively mundane days at work. Asking questions about wood-backed thermometers and oil gauges. The men must have wondered, *Did I do something wrong? Am I in trouble?*

An FBI agent is an expert at asking such questions in a way that leaves a witness to slowly ponder the terrible possibilities that might result from his answers. And then the agent, Elroy in this case, drops the ter-rible word that no one wants to hear: "Wouldn't you consider this kind of mismeasurement to be *stealing*? Aren't you basically getting oil with-out paying for it?"

To finish them off, Elroy brought out the photos taken with a tele-photo lens. He could put the crystal-clear pictures on the table, and the men would look down at them and know that they had been made. Elroy could ask them, as quietly and innocently as possible, "Isn't this *you* in this photo? Isn't this *you* measuring the oil?" And then Elroy could tell them that, in fact, he had been there as well, and he had measured the same tank of oil right after the Koch Oil man had left, and, boy, was there a difference in the measurements! Significant differences. The Koch Oil man had some explaining to do.

In this way, Elroy rolled up several witnesses who began to describe what life was like at Koch Industries and how the company went about measuring the oil that it took. Each witness statement gave him more ammunition to use against the next witness. Soon he could start asking about specific meetings, specific managers, specific directives that were sent down from management.

Over the months, Elroy would interview more than fifteen employees. He granted many of them the promise of anonymity so that they could talk openly about their employer. As he gathered their stories, a picture began to emerge.

Koch managers never told their employees to go out and steal. It was never that obvious. Instead, the company put relentless pressure on the employees to meet certain standards. Koch managers made clear to the gaugers that they were never to be "short"—meaning they reported taking more oil from the tanks than they actually delivered to Koch— on too many tanks of oil. If a gauger was short week after week, he wouldn't be working for Koch much longer. So the gaugers found ways to be perpetually "long."* That meant they were consistently under- reporting how much oil they drained from the tanks. They told the producer they were taking 100 barrels, and then they were delivering 101 barrels to Koch's pipeline. As a result, the company ran a profitable surplus every year, collecting far more oil than it paid for, at least in the state of Oklahoma.

The Koch employees told Elroy that the need to be long on oil was con- stantly drilled home to them in something called "continuous improve- ment" meetings. These meetings seemed to be the way that employees got their marching orders from Koch headquarters in Wichita. Elroy soon became convinced that Koch Oil was "a corporate-directed crimi- nal enterprise."

What wasn't clear to anyone in the government was just how far up the chain of command the control of this enterprise went. Who was put- ting the pressure on gaugers to "continuously improve"? Who was tell- ing them to fudge the numbers when they measured how much oil they were taking?

---

* Some gaugers and Koch managers used an interchangeable set of terms, saying "under" rather than "short," and "over" rather than "long."

Elroy sought to answer these questions as he roamed from living room to living room in rural Oklahoma. His efforts would bring Koch into direct confrontation with the federal government that the company so deeply disdained.

It was almost an accident that Koch Industries found itself the target of Elroy's efforts. A strange and unlikely series of events put the company in the crosshairs of US Senate investigators to begin with, and that chain of events began on a quiet Sunday morning in Phoenix.

It was the morning of October 4, 1987. Early that day, newspaper boys rode their bikes through the neighborhoods of Phoenix and threw fat copies of the *Arizona Republic* Sunday edition onto lawns and driveways. The front page was plastered with an explosive story that carried the headline "Fraud in Indian Country: A Billion-Dollar Betrayal."

The story was the first in a series that the *Arizona Republic* would publish over the next week. The series consisted of thirty stories covering several full newspaper pages, and it focused mostly on rampant corruption and incompetence at a federal agency called the Bureau of Indian Affairs, or BIA.

The front-page story on that first Sunday said that federal Indian programs were "a shambles, plagued by fraud, incompetence, and deceit and strangled by a morass of red tape that has all but destroyed their effectiveness." And that was just the first sentence.

While the central target of the stories was the federal government, the bulk of the first day's investigation focused on US oil companies that drilled on Indian lands. A headline across the front of the Sunday paper declared that the federal system allowing oil companies to drill on Indian reservations was really nothing more than a "license to loot."

The looting happened in a complicated and insidious way. The *Arizona Republic* story showed that the oil companies themselves were responsible for reporting how much oil they drilled on the Indian reservations: the companies would drill wells, pump the oil, and then report to the government how much oil they had taken out of the ground. The government was not effectively double-checking the companies' reports to verify how much oil they were actually getting from the Indian reservations. The whole thing worked on an honor system, and the *Arizona*

Republic alleged that firms were abusing it by consistently underreporting how much oil they pumped out of the ground. The stories said that oil companies were carting off at least millions of dollars in free oil every year.

The *Arizona Republic* series garnered the kind of attention, and outrage, that most reporters can only dream of. In particular, the series captured the attention of Arizona's Democratic US senator, Dennis DeConcini. He told reporters that the series was "devastating." The stories, he said, "indicate criminality as well as mismanagement."

There was something about the allegations that seemed to particularly bother DeConcini. Crime and bureaucratic mismanagement were always offensive, but it seemed especially offensive when the victims were Native Americans. DeConcini sat on a Senate committee that oversaw affairs on Indian reservations. He was intimately familiar with the fact that Native Americans in his home state were among the most beleaguered people in America. On paper, America's Indian tribes were considered sovereign nations. By the late 1980s, those nations were really nothing more than a giant, failed Socialist state. After being hounded and dislocated and, finally, penned into reservations, the tribes signed treaties that left them with land and natural resources. However, the land was held in trust by the United States and administered by the BIA, so that, in short, the treaties made the federal government a paternalistic overlord of the supposedly sovereign tribes. It seemed that every aspect of life on Indian reservations was governed by the BIA, from health care to housing, education to oil drilling.

By the late 1980s, the results of this arrangement were truly ruinous. About 45 percent of all Indians lived below the poverty line, the unemployment rate was above 50 percent, and fewer than half of Indian households had a telephone. Most of the people lucky enough to have a job earned about $7,000 a year. Town squares were boarded up, and business was booming at liquor stores; some of the villages resembled shantytowns. This squalor was all the more offensive because a tidal wave of taxpayer money washed up on the shores of Indian reservations every year. The federal government spent about $3.3 billion a year to support the BIA and Indian programs. Strangely, the entire Native American population managed to earn *less* than $3.3 billion a year even when government assistance from Indian programs was factored in. The federal bureaucracy was sucking up cash while managing to infuriate the very Indians it was supposedly helping.

The *Arizona Republic* alleged that oil companies were exploiting this toxic system. Some of the world's biggest oil drillers operated on the wide belt of federal land and reservations stretching across Oklahoma, Texas, Arizona, and surrounding states. These firms were making a killing amid all the dysfunction and poverty, collecting a steady stream of crude oil and piping it out to US and world markets. Rumors of oil theft had been circulating for years.

In Washington, the Senate Select Committee on Indian Affairs held a private meeting and voted to form a special investigative subcommittee that would look into the allegations. Senator DeConcini was selected to lead the subcommittee. He was joined by Arizona's other senator, the Republican John McCain, and by Tom Daschle, the Democrat from South Dakota.

What resulted was one of the most far-reaching investigations of its kind. DeConcini and his counterparts decided to investigate major oil companies, the BIA, local Indian schools, and even the tribal authorities themselves. DeConcini knew that he would need a top-notch investigator to run the effort. He would need someone who could manage a large team of lawyers and field agents like Jim Elroy, and someone who could oversee a sprawling and complicated chain of evidence that would be developed.

Luckily for DeConcini, there was a young lawyer who had recently gone on the job market named Ken Ballen. Ballen was on the job market because he had been a lead investigator for the Iran-Contra hearings, a nationally watched investigation of covert US arms sales to Iran. When the investigation wrapped up, Ballen was looking for a new challenge. And he was about to get it.

In the spring of 1988, Ken Ballen walked down a tree-lined sidewalk near Capitol Hill, on the way to his new job. He walked past a strip of low-slung brick buildings that were built back in Washington, DC's earliest days, when it was not much more than a sleepy little town that seemed to shut down when the legislature was not in session. Just across from these quaint buildings was the imposing nine-story structure where Ballen was headed, an edifice that evoked the new age of Washington and all of its power. This was the Hart Senate Office Building, where Ballen had just recently started work as the lead investigator for the Senate's investigation into potential criminal conduct on Indian reservations.

The front of the Hart Building was a grid of rectangular, black windows, bordered by a façade of white marble. This was the face of the Senate bureaucracy. Ballen hustled into the main entrance of the Hart Building along with the usual crowd of Washington workers. While it is nondescript from the outside, the interior of the Hart Building is magnificent. It's the kind of place that makes a person feel important, even powerful, just by the mere fact of working there every day. Even in the bathrooms, the partitions between urinals are made from slabs of white marble, giving every corner of the space a feeling of quiet authority.

Ballen certainly had considerable authority in his new position. He oversaw a large team of investigators who had recently been given full reign over the ninth floor of the Hart Building, the top story that contained a warren of cubicles and offices. He was just thirty-three years old in 1988 and not too long out of law school. But even at that young age, he had already played a major role in one of the biggest investigations in the US Senate. That's how he caught the eye of Senator DeConcini. Ballen took the job when DeConcini offered it because he believed that the new subcommittee was dedicated to uncovering the truth and, just as importantly, because the Senate would be willing to give him the resources he needed. Ballen wasn't disappointed on this front. As he entered the Hart Building and took an elevator to the ninth floor, he walked into an entire suite of offices that were now dedicated to his effort.

Early in the investigation, Ballen knew that he needed a lead investigator in the field, and the Senate turned to the FBI to find one. The request was sent to Oliver "Buck" Revell, who, at that time, was the FBI's associate deputy director in charge of all investigative operations. When Revell got the request, he only had one agent in mind: Jim Elroy. Revell had worked with Elroy back when the two of them were based in Oklahoma, and he thought Elroy would be the perfect agent to head a complex and difficult investigation. "I think Jim's the best investigator I ever ran into at the FBI. And I ran into thousands," Revell said many years later.

Elroy agreed to take the assignment, and soon he and Ballen were talking back and forth about Elroy's plans to lead the fieldwork out in

Indian Country. One of the first items of business was dealing with the oil companies.

In the beginning, Ballen decided that his primary target would be the biggest oil companies—the majors, as they were called—such as Exxon and Mobil. The *Arizona Republic* articles insinuated that these firms were the prime offenders of oil theft. Ballen approached the companies with the same prosecutorial zeal he'd applied to witnesses of the Iran-Contra affair. He sent them a series of subpoenas demanding that they hand over documents that would otherwise be confidential and closely held; documents that showed exactly how the firms bought and sold the oil that was drilled on Indian reservations.

With his subpoenas, Ballen was able to breach the wall of corporate secrecy that reporters at the *Arizona Republic* could never penetrate. He used the full authority of the federal government to compel them to turn over the records that would show, in black and white, what they were doing.

Not surprisingly, the phone calls started coming in soon after. And the callers were not happy. Ballen began to get inquiries from the top lawyers for the oil companies; the highly paid Washington insiders who represented Exxon, Mobil, or Phillips. The attorneys told Ballen that the subpoenas were onerous and complying with them would require untold hours of labor and expense. Why was he casting such a wide net? What was he looking for? Ballen didn't back off, and eventually the boxes of documents started arriving at the Hart Senate Office Building. Ballen's team began digging through them and compiling numbers.

Ballen's team did not find what it expected. The picture that developed, in fact, was downright shocking. It was also deflating. The companies, it turned out, were not stealing at all. Their own records proved it.

The large oil purchaser Kerr-McGee, for example, was actually taking away *less* oil than it paid for in the state of Oklahoma for the years 1986, 1987, and 1988. The company was short every year, to use the industry term. During that same period, Conoco was also short for one year, and the other two years, it was long, or over, by only a tiny margin. Conoco took 351 extra barrels in 1986 and 375 barrels in 1988. The overage was tiny, negligible. The same pattern held for Sun Oil.

It appeared that the *Arizona Republic* had gotten its facts wrong. But as his team was compiling the records, Ballen kept getting phone calls from top oil company lawyers. And they told him there was more to the story than he was seeing. They informed him, in confidence, what was really going on, and their admissions would never be made public over the ensuing years.

"Everyone operating on Indian territory told us one thing and one thing only: 'We're not stealing oil, but we'll tell you who is: Koch Industries,'" Ballen recalled. "And they all told me that Koch was taking one to three percent. And I said, 'Why don't you do something about it?' And first of all, they said, 'It's just more trouble than it's worth to fight with them.'"

The oil companies also pointed out another compelling reason: Koch Industries had too much market power to be trifled with. It was risky to make the company mad. The oil wells in question were hardly the best wells. They were scattered across the countryside and were hardly gushers. The wells barely broke even for the producers, and Koch Oil was the only firm willing to take the oil and ship it, and the producers like Exxon and Mobil didn't want to aggravate Koch Oil more than they had to.

And the oil companies said something else. If Ballen's team was willing to look into the matter, he could count on the oil majors for help. This was a highly unlikely alliance. Oil companies held a unique role in the American economy in 1988 and that role made them politically toxic. They were both a villain and an indispensable part of life. Everybody depended on the oil companies, but nobody seemed to like them. This wasn't a new thing—one of the first major US oil companies was also one of America's most hated firms. The Standard Oil Company was operated by John D. Rockefeller, the most famous of the robber barons of the late 1800s. Rockefeller amassed a fortune by cleverly using a network of secret "trusts," or shell companies, to build an unrivaled monopoly in the oil business. Rockefeller controlled supplies, put competitors out of business, and cut secret sweetheart deals with railroads. His business became the poster child for the "antitrust" movement, which was aimed squarely at breaking up the kind of opaque and powerful business enterprises that he'd spent his life creating. The government eventually split Standard Oil into multiple competing firms.

But all the bad blood over Rockefeller seemed to have dissipated by the 1960s. At that time, the United States was the nation of the oil gusher. America was the biggest oil producer and seemed to have a limitless supply of the geological treasure. Oil was the primary energy source of America's industrial economy, and it became the raw material of its economic growth. Dark crude oil was an embodiment of America's special place in the world and its unrivaled economic supremacy. During this era, the United States developed a deep dependency on its oil companies. The well-being of the economy itself and the price of oil became intertwined. Ten of the eleven recessions after World War II were preceded by a spike in oil prices. This dependence, predictably, created deep resentments. Public sentiment turned against the oil industry decisively in the 1970s, but this time it wasn't necessarily the fault of a robber baron like Rockefeller.

This time the villain was the public demand itself, coupled with an unprecedented exercise of power by oil-producing nations in the Persian Gulf. Demand for oil in the United States had quietly surpassed the level of available supplies, leaving the nation reliant on imports to make up the difference. In 1973, a cartel called the Organization of Petroleum Exporting Countries, or OPEC, imposed an embargo that unleashed unprecedented chaos in oil markets. By the time the whole mess had settled in 1974, oil prices had risen from $3 a barrel to $12 a barrel.

Oil prices would fall again during the 1980s, but the psychological wound never healed. Americans knew that their economy was now held hostage by oil. The stability of the 1950s and 1960s was gone. Oil prices could spike overnight, a concept that no one had ever really thought of before. The concept of oil price spikes would soon become embedded in Americans' vocabulary, and with it a new way of seeing oil companies. These firms were now seen as predatory. The well-being of oil companies and the American people were at odds by 1988. Oil companies embodied the opposite ideal of the old maxim, which claimed that "what was good for our country was good for General Motors, and vice versa." Instead, what was good for oil companies came at the expense of everyone else.

Most people suspected that the oil companies were screwing them in one way or another, so it only made sense that oil companies would be the central target of Ken Ballen's investigation. This was a message that was delivered to Ballen in no uncertain terms by Senator Daniel Inouye of Hawaii, who was chairman of the Senate Indian Affairs Committee and a friend of Senator DeConcini's. As chairman of the committee, Inouye had authority over the special investigative team that DeConcini had put together. Inouye therefore had some measure of authority over Ballen, and he made it clear to Ballen that the investigation was meant to uncover wrongdoing on behalf of the oil majors like Exxon or Mobil. Instead, Ballen found himself working with the oil majors in order to entrap Koch Industries, which no one had ever heard of. It was a politically risky move, in Ballen's eyes, but that's where the evidence in the case was leading him.

Ballen's case grew stronger after he took a trip to Boston. He'd received a tip that there was a whistle-blower in Boston who might be able to shed light on Koch Oil's alleged theft. The whistle-blower was in a good position to know about it. His name was William "Bill" Koch, and he was brothers with Koch Industries' CEO.

Ballen learned that Koch Industries was a family-controlled company, founded in 1940 by a man named Fred Koch in Wichita, Kansas. Fred Koch had four sons. Three of the sons worked for the family company until 1967, when Fred Koch died. At that point, all hell broke loose. The second-oldest son, Charles, was left in charge of the firm. In that role, he oversaw his younger twin brothers, David and Bill. It became clear that Bill didn't want to take orders from his older brother Charles, and so Bill left the company in 1983. Then he sued David and Charles, claiming that they had ripped him off by underpaying him for his share of the family business.

What interested Ballen was what Bill did next. Bill launched a private investigation into the very behavior that Ballen had stumbled upon: Koch Oil's alleged theft of oil from remote wells. After arriving in Boston, Ballen met with Bill Koch for two hours in a conference room. He listened carefully while Bill Koch laid out detailed allegations that matched what the oil majors were already saying: Koch Oil practiced widespread theft, Bill Koch confirmed. He should know, because it was happening while he worked there.

The story was convincing, but it also made Ballen uneasy. Bill Koch's testimony was tainted by the fact that he was suing his brothers. For that reason, he would not make a great witness at a public hearing, or in a courtroom.

Ballen went back to Washington and met with his team. He told them that there was only one path to follow: they would subpoena Koch Oil just as they had subpoenaed the other oil companies. And they wouldn't proceed unless the company's documents compelled them to.

Then Koch's documents began to arrive. The parcels of internal company papers were hauled up to the ninth floor and opened by Ballen's team, who began to tabulate them.

Ballen's team narrowed its subpoenas to examine oil sales in the state of Oklahoma. This made it easier for the companies to comply with the request and made it easier for Ballen's investigators to sift through the documents once they arrived. The financial results from Koch's records were stark. They were so stark it seemed unbelievable. The numbers were checked, and checked again. And even then, they told the same story: In 1988, Koch Oil had taken 142,000 barrels of oil without paying for them and cleared pure profit on each of those barrels when it sold them. In 1986 and 1987, the other years that Ballen's team investigated, Koch was over by 240,680 and 239,206 barrels, respectively. The second-highest overage of any other company in those years was the Phillips Petroleum Company's overage of 2,181 barrels in 1987, still just 0.009 percent of Koch's overage that year.

The set of numbers was the only clear thing that the Senate team could determine about Koch. As investigators dug further into the company, they discovered an organization that seemed built to obscure its very existence. There was a reason that no one had heard of Koch Oil, even though the company operated huge pipeline networks and two major oil refineries (one in Corpus Christi, Texas, and the other just outside of Minneapolis, Minnesota).

To begin with, Koch made the rare decision to remain privately owned rather than selling shares of the company on the stock market. Most firms go public after they reach a certain size because doing so gives them access to an almost limitless amount of money they can use to expand and fund their operations. The downside of this decision is that when a company goes public, it is required to disclose a lot of information to the public, so that investors know what they are buying. Publicly traded firms need to publish the salaries of their CEOs, the value of their debt, the amount of money they make or lose every quarter, and any risks that might be in store for investors who bought their stock. Koch had apparently decided that getting money from Wall Street wasn't worth the headache of making such information public.

Even more confusingly, the firm was an intricate web of interlocking subsidiaries and divisions. Its pipeline unit, for example, had done business under different names over the years, such as Matador, without using the name of its parent company. Without the kind of public filings that most companies released to public investors, it was difficult for Ballen's investigators to even puzzle out exactly what Koch owned and where. And Koch clearly made no effort to build its brand. The company didn't even put a sign on some of the buildings where it operated, let alone invest in advertising to build a good reputation with customers. Koch clearly preferred being a dark box.

Koch was a difficult target to go after, but Ballen was convinced that the evidence was persuasive enough to warrant the effort. Ballen worked with FBI agent Jim Elroy to draw up a plan to build the case against Koch Oil. They came up with an audacious idea: Elroy and a team of experienced oil workers would arrive at oil tanks before Koch Oil employees were scheduled to get there, and Elroy's team would measure how much oil was in the tanks. Then they would lay in wait until the Koch Oil man arrived and drained the tank. The Koch Oil employee would leave a document behind, called a run ticket, that stated how much oil Koch had carted off. If the firm was really taking as much oil as it appeared to be, the run tickets should show a smaller amount of oil than Elroy and his team had measured. That's how Elroy ended up surrounded by cattle, secretly photographing the Koch Oil gaugers.

But there were two big obstacles to making this plan work. The first was the fact that the oil tanks were all located on private property—property owned by oil drillers like Exxon and Mobil. Elroy couldn't just trespass on the land to take oil measurements. The second obstacle was figuring out when Koch Oil was due to arrive and drain the tanks. It would be cost prohibitive to have Elroy stake out the company around the clock for weeks at a time.

Ballen turned to the oil majors for help. While none were willing to attack Koch publicly for taking oil from them, they were more than happy to help Ballen behind the scenes. Their assistance was never publicly disclosed, even as videotape of the surveillance was shown publicly during a later Senate hearing. The companies gave Elroy permission to enter their property and to measure their oil. They also told Ballen's team when the Koch Oil truck was scheduled to arrive, so that Elroy could be there to observe it.

With the secret help of the oil majors, Ballen and Elroy were ready to build the case against Koch. They had copius amounts of documentation and photographic evidence. They had the testimony of Koch's own oil gaugers, whom Elroy had interviewed.

But Ballen knew that they needed more. So the Senate issued subpoenas to senior Koch Industries executives in Wichita—subpoenas that would compel the men to answer questions under oath. Then Ballen bought a plane ticket to Wichita. There he would question one of the men he had just subpoenaed. It was the man who had ultimate control over this enterprise: the chief executive, Charles Koch.

It is almost awe-inspiring to fly into the Wichita airport. During the daytime hours, airplane passengers can look out the window and see the Kansas prairie stretching away toward the horizon like an impossibly long tabletop covered in green. Wichita itself seems minuscule and stranded within this wide expanse, a small jewel of white buildings surrounded by residential neighborhoods and factories. Outside the city limits, the emptiness looked like the far edge of America.

Ken Ballen arrived in Wichita with his assistant attorney, Wick Sollers, in late April of 1989. They had a grueling schedule ahead of them.

On April 24, the two Washington attorneys drove to Koch Industries headquarters. They were scheduled to depose, or interview under oath, eleven of the company's senior executives and employees. As they drove to the headquarters, Ballen and Sollers might have thought they'd been given wrong directions. One of the largest and most profitable companies in Wichita wasn't located in a skyscraper downtown. Instead, Ballen and Sollers kept heading west on Thirty-Seventh Street, away from the city center, until they reached the far northeastern corner of Wichita's city limits. On the north side of Thirty-Seventh, the city ended and gave way to a limitless horizon of tall prairie grass. On the south side of the street was their destination: a squat office building of steel and glass with darkened windows.

They arrived early in the morning. Their first deposition would take place just after nine o'clock, and it was arguably their most important: they would start the day by interviewing Charles Koch.

Lower-level investigators like Jim Elroy became convinced that Charles Koch must have been aware that his firm was taking far more oil than it paid for from oil wells throughout the Midwest. It seemed that the behavior was so widespread that it must have been directed from the top. It was almost inconceivable that Koch would not be aware of it. Now Ballen would have the chance to question Charles Koch directly.

But first, they had to get into the building. This turned out to be no easy task. Ballen and Sollers were stopped at a security checkpoint, where security guards asked them to show their identification. They passed through a metal detector. Then they walked down a hallway into the center of the building and came to yet another security checkpoint. They showed their identification for a second time and once again passed through a metal detector. They walked down yet more hallways, twisting and turning through the labyrinthine interior of the building. Then another security checkpoint. It seemed to Ballen that they went through concentric rings of security as they progressed deeper and deeper into the complex. The setup reminded him of traveling to CIA headquarters in Langley, Virginia.

Eventually, Ballen and Sollers were led into a windowless conference room. They sat down at a table and were joined by four attorneys representing Koch Industries. Two of the attorneys were from Washington, and the other two were in-house Koch lawyers based in Wichita. The contingent of attorneys was clearly led by Don Cordes, a vice president at Koch Industries and the company's top lawyer.

When Charles Koch entered the room, it became clear almost instantly that this man was the master of this domain. The people around him treated Charles Koch with deference—a deference that seemed to go deeper than simple respect for a boss. Sollers and Ballen had no way of knowing that Charles was not, in fact, just the boss of the company. He was its leader. Charles Koch did not order people around him to do what he said. He inspired them to do so. He had a command of the people around him that was difficult for outsiders to understand. Visitors like Ballen and Sollers couldn't have known that Charles Koch had spent decades building up the loyalty and admiration of the people who worked for him. They didn't know about his management seminars, the classes and lectures that he held to impart his philosophy.

But what they could see clearly was that Charles Koch's authority was complete. He was trim and, at fifty-three, still had an athletic build. He had thick blond hair, a square jaw, and bright blue eyes. He sat down at the table across from Ballen and Sollers and he looked at the two of them, these Washington lawyers. Whatever he might have thought about them, it was impossible to say. But it was clear that he was not intimidated.

"Could you please state your full name for the record?" Ballen began.

"Charles de Ganahl Koch."

"Sir, what is your position with Koch Industries?" Ballen asked.

"I am chairman and chief executive," Koch replied.

Chairman and chief executive. This was much more than a job title. It was a statement that there was no higher authority within Koch Industries than Charles Koch. And this authority was greater than most CEOs' because Koch Industries was privately held. Charles Koch and his brother David were the primary shareholders; they'd bought out any shareholders who might have challenged them. Many people could criticize Charles Koch, but it was difficult to see how anyone could actually fire him. As long as his brother David agreed with him, Charles Koch had total command over the enterprise.

Ballen didn't treat Koch with deference; he certainly wasn't inspired by Koch. There might have even been a note of disdain in his voice. As Ballen had done in many depositions and many interviews before, he began to bore in with a list of questions.

"Sir, what were the company's overall sales in 1988?" Ballen asked.

"I think about ten billion dollars."

"What was the net profit figure for the company last year?"

"It was about four hundred million."

Ballen could not have known exactly how offensive those simple questions were to Charles Koch. The CEO prized his privacy and his ability to keep Koch's financial performance concealed behind a wall of secrecy. It was privileged information to know what Koch's annual revenue was. The level of profits was considered top secret. And here was this lawyer, stomping all over Koch's secrets with total disregard.

"What percentage of the business involves crude oil—crude oil purchases?" Ballen continued.

"Percent in what sense?" Koch shot back.

Percent in what sense? Ballen gamely tried to define the word *percent*, and the sense in which he meant it.

"Of sales and profit, approximately," Ballen said.

"I would guess about ten percent of the profit and—this is a guess again—about twenty percent of sales," Koch replied.

Ballen gave Charles Koch a set of documents—the same documents that had shocked Ballen's investigators in Washington. These were Koch's own internal figures showing that Koch had taken far more oil than it paid for from oil wells. Ballen would see how Charles Koch responded to these documents. Charles Koch might say that the documents were forgeries, or that they did not actually show what they appeared to show. But Charles Koch said none of those things as he looked over the figures.

"Have you ever seen any of these documents?" Ballen asked.

"Yes, I typically see the quarterly—"

"All right," Ballen interrupted.

"—figures," Koch finished.

Charles Koch said he didn't review monthly figures that showed whether the firm was long or short on the oil it bought. But he didn't dispute the authenticity of the numbers.

Ballen pushed further. Referring to one of the documents, he asked, "And then what is indicated in the first quarter '86? What do those numbers show?"

"Well, Louisiana was about two thousand barrels long."

"And that would be long?"

"That would be long."

For a prosecuting attorney like Ballen, Charles Koch had just done two important things: he had confirmed that Ballen's evidence was authentic—that the numbers on oil sales Ballen obtained through the subpoena were correct—and Koch had also confirmed that he had been aware of those numbers, that he had known that Koch was long on its oil sales.

Ballen's line of questioning then sought to establish that Charles Koch knew what *long* really meant. That way, there would be no ambiguity about the case. Charles Koch didn't seem interested, however, in helping Ballen establish that fact. Charles Koch parsed the definition of *long* and seemed to indicate that Ballen didn't understand it. The two men went back and forth over the definition until Ballen finally asked, "So, in other words, if you purchase oil and then sell oil, if there is more oil in the inventory than sold, then you are long. Is that correct?"

"I am not sure—"

"Is that correct?"

"I am not sure I understood that."

"All right. Why don't you explain it again? What do you mean by being 'over,' or 'long,' on oil?"

"I am not sure I can do any better than I just did," Koch replied.

Around they went.

Ballen tried a different route: "If Koch purchases crude oil, purchases a hundred barrels, the actual inventory shows a hundred ten barrels, would Koch be over in that example by ten barrels?" Ballen asked.

"Did we sell any?"

"Well, why don't you try the question first," Ballen said. "Is that an accurate—"

"Well, it is an incomplete equation. I mean it is—there is no answer. You got two unknowns."

"Suppose you sold a hundred ten," Ballen pressed.

"Okay. You bought—"

"One hundred."

"And you sold a hundred ten?"

"Right."

"I am going to need my slide rule in a minute," Koch joked.

It went on like this for a long time, with the two men discussing barrels of oil, inventory levels, and even hypothetical inventory levels. The other attorneys in the room begin to interject and add their own observations and questions about hypothetical inventories.

Finally, Ballen's assistant, Wick Sollers, dove in and started asking questions. Eventually, he pushed Charles Koch into a corner, eliciting a very elegant description of just what it means to be long.

"I don't think there is such a thing as an exactly accurate measurement," Charles Koch said. "But if you just look in dollar terms, yes, we got more money than we paid for oil."

There it was: "We got more money than we paid for oil," Koch had said.

But there was something else in his statement; the idea that there was no such thing as a perfectly accurate measurement. Earlier in the interview, Charles Koch had interrupted Ballen to press this point and to make it sound as if unsophisticated oil gaugers were making mistakes out in the field that might account for the company's annual overages.

"I mean, in the oil field, as I understand it, it is—you got a lot of small tanks, you got a lot of changing conditions, and it is a very uncertain art," Charles Koch had said. "And you have people who aren't rocket scientists, necessarily," he continued. "I mean, good people. I don't mean to imply—good people, trying to do a good job, and they are always not fully trained, either."

This defense contradicted everything that Agent Elroy had been hearing in his field interviews with the Koch gaugers. Those gaugers told him that they faced constant pressure from above to be "long." They knew that if they were not long, then the consequences would be dire. They weren't making mistakes, the gaugers said; they were following orders. And these orders were apparently conveyed in meetings where Koch managers discussed the company's policy of continuous improvement. It was on this point that Ballen began to press.

Just what was continuous improvement, exactly? Ballen asked.

"How much time do you have?" Koch replied.

"How much time do *you* have?" Ballen replied.

"Continuous improvement philosophy is a philosophy developed by a man called J. Edward Deming, who is a statistician," Koch said.* "So he set up a philosophy based on statistics, how companies can improve their competitive position by improving the quality for the customer and your own productivity."

Koch went on for a long time, talking about this guy named Deming, whom Koch seemed to truly admire. Deming's ideas seemed to revolve around coming up with mathematical models for how to improve a business, and then continually driving workers to make those improvements and hold true to the plan.

"This is a long-term program," Koch said. "As [Deming] puts it: 'You never get out of this hospital.' You are going to be working at this forever."

* Charles Koch appears to have misspoken here. The statistician's name is W. Edwards Deming, and his influence on Koch Industries is discussed at length in Chapter 6.

The digressions about Deming and statistics didn't matter much to the case that Ballen was building. Charles Koch had already laid out what continuous improvement might mean for gaugers.

"What our policy is, is to be as accurate as possible and not have a loss; try to avoid losses within that," Koch had said. He denied that the company had a stated policy of stealing oil, but he supported the notion that gaugers would face pressure to be long.

When the interview was over, Charles Koch stood up and left the room, walking down the corridor. He eventually went back to the company's executive suite and his office, a large room with a wide-open view of the Kansas prairie.

Ballen kept working through the day in the building's interior. He and Sollers interviewed nearly a dozen more Koch Industries executives, slowly building a case that the investigators would soon present before the Senate, slowly gathering evidence that they would hand over to the US Department of Justice.

At the end of the long day, Ballen and Sollers packed up their papers and left. They caught a flight back to Washington and continued their work up on the ninth floor of the Hart Senate Office Building.

But even after all the time they'd spent at Koch headquarters, even after all the time they'd spent digging through boxes of Koch Industries' confidential documents, and even after all the time they'd spent interviewing Charles Koch himself, Ken Ballen and Wick Sollers were no closer to answering one of the most perplexing questions at the center of their case. It was a question that would be asked later, by Senator DeConcini himself, as the Senate panel held public hearings on Koch's alleged oil theft.

At one point during the hearings, DeConcini was questioning Agent Elroy. DeConcini stopped, as if perplexed, and asked the FBI man the most important question of them all:

"Who is Charles Koch? Can you explain that?"

CHAPTER 2

The Age of Volatility Begins

(1967–1972)

It was a Friday in mid-November, just one week before Thanksgiving 1967. A multimillionaire named Fred Koch sat in a duck blind watching the sky, his gun at the ready.

Fred Koch was a large man, and he had a forceful personality to match his physical presence. He was one of those people whom midwesterners call "larger than life," meaning that he filled a room when he entered it; one of those very rare breed of people who are unquestionably the masters of their own realm. He was an engineer, an entrepreneur, and a self-described patriot. At the age of sixty-seven, Fred Koch had built a small business empire, and as the master of this empire, Koch was the hub of so many spinning wheels: He was chairman of the board for his growing company. He was a cofounder of a right-wing political group called the John Birch Society. He was a self-published author who sold anti-Communist pamphlets through the mail for 25 cents a copy. He was also the father of four rowdy and brilliant boys, boys in whom he'd worked to instill the values that mattered most to him: intelligence, a hard work ethic, integrity, and drive.

If Fred Koch's life was a noisy one, then the duck blind where he sat that Friday in November was pristinely silent. Maybe that's why he traveled to the place, which was about a thousand miles from his home in Wichita. The duck blind was near the Bear River, just outside the small town of Ogden, Utah. The natural beauty of the place was overwhelming. When visitors turned and faced east, they saw a craggy wall of mountains rise up, the sharp and irregular peaks often painted white with snow. Turning to the west, a visitor could see where the land immediately flattened out into a hard plateau of ranchland and salt marshes. The Great Salt Lake was nearby, and the glittering marshes around it lured flocks of migrating ducks as they made their way south from Yellowstone Park and the forests of Idaho.

The ranchlands spoke to Fred Koch in a special way. He owned thousands of acres of pasture, land that he would pass on to his sons and that they would keep for decades, knowing how much it meant to their dad. A ranch was an unfettered place; a place of freedom. It was also a place of ceaseless work; a place where any enterprise, whether it be a family or a business, survived or failed based solely on the work ethic and competence of the people who ran it. Ranching was honest, and it happened in the most wide-open and most free countryside in America. Maybe Fred Koch went to Bear River to think—to make plans for his business and his life in a place where he could enjoy a little silence. His business empire was a complicated set of interlocking companies. He oversaw an oil refinery, oil pipelines, manufacturing plants, and, of course, his beloved ranches. Bear River would have been a good place to escape it all, to consider it from a distance. It was the kind of place where a man could think, where he could compose a game plan to enact when he went back home. Considering Fred Koch's life, it seems highly likely that he was considering those things as he scanned the horizon, waiting for the V-shaped flocks of ducks to come into view and start circling, looking for a place to land.

Fred Koch sat in the duck blind with a field guide who helped him handle his weapon and other provisions. According to Koch family lore, Fred Koch aimed his weapon at the sky, took a shot, and then marveled at his marksmanship when a duck came wheeling down.

Then, Fred Koch slumped over. He was unconscious, and he was very far from the nearest hospital. The gun loader must have tried to figure out what to do, but there was nothing to be done. Fred Koch died there at the foot of the mountain range, overlooking the salt marshes and ranchland.

Whatever plans he might have been considering disappeared with him in that instant. His company and his family would never hear another word of guidance from him. It would be entirely up to them to figure out how to go forward.

In one moment, the great patriarch was gone.

Fred Koch's sudden death was not the end of a story, but the beginning of one. It was the first surge of volatility in an era that would be defined by volatility for Fred Koch's family. It was only the first time that stability would disappear in an instant and leave everyone scrambling to figure out what to do. And these waves of volatility would crash primarily onto the shoulders of one person. One person, more than anyone, would have to figure out how to negotiate this era and, ultimately, how to profit from it. That person was Fred Koch's second-oldest son, Charles.

One of Charles Koch's earliest memories is of sitting in a public school classroom in Wichita, watching the teacher write math problems on the chalkboard. He was in the third grade. He would always remember how the other students were asking questions, and how the teacher kept trying to explain to them the mechanical interactions between the big white numerals and symbols.

This was puzzling to Charles Koch. He didn't understand why the other children should be confused. "I can remember that clearly. Most things back then, I can't remember at all. But I remember that clearly," he later said in an interview. "All the other kids, or most of them, were struggling. . . . *Why?* I asked myself," he recalled, and then he laughed. "The answers are obvious!"

This was when he realized that he had a gift for math and the mind of an engineer. He could clearly see a set of rules, the language of numbers. And this was a set of rules that existed perfectly within its own realm, whether people understood it or not. Math didn't change just because a person struggled with it. Math was perfect. And Charles Koch understood it.

Charles Koch was not completely surprised when his father died. Fred Koch had been ailing for many years. The end was sudden, but not unexpected.

When that terrible moment came, Charles Koch had a plan. He had been constructing this plan for years.

During the summers of his childhood, Charles Koch's family belonged to the Wichita Country Club. There was the pool and the clubhouse and the Elysian green hills of the golf course, all of it contained in a tiny oasis hidden away from the rest of the city. The Koch family's house was close enough to the country club that the Koch boys, when they were teenagers, could hear kids playing at the pool during the long summer days. This was a place where the rich kids in town whiled away their summers and charged meals to their parents' accounts. In the evenings, a teenaged Charles Koch would have been able to sneak liquor with friends at the clubhouse or organize card games in private rooms where the walls were paneled with tasteful, burnished hardwood.

But Charles Koch was denied that kind of summer while he was growing up. It was understood that he would stay away from the country club, as close as it might be to his backyard. Fred Koch felt that too much leisure time would corrupt the boy's character. So he sent Charles out west to the ranch country that Fred loved so much. As a teenager, Charles Koch learned to ride horses, which might sound nice, or even romantic. But it wasn't. For Charles Koch, learning to ride a horse was more like learning how to drive a forklift. His job was to ride on horseback for monotonous hours on end, inspecting the fence lines that kept the cattle from wandering off into the wilderness. At night, during those summers, he slept in a log cabin with other ranch hands, who had names like "Bitterroot Bob"—men who had likely never set foot in a country club.

This was the rhythm of Charles's childhood. Work, and school, and back to work again. It was the rhythm prescribed by his father. And Charles Koch rebelled against it. He got into trouble as a teenager and was sent to a military-style prep school in Indiana. He didn't straighten out until he graduated high school, when he enrolled at the Massachusetts Institute of Technology, receiving an engineering degree in 1957, just as his father had done before him.

But even then, Charles Koch rebelled. He wasn't satisfied to follow in his dad's footsteps. He didn't return to Wichita but stayed out east in Boston and got a job on his own. Fred implored Charles to come home and join the family business. The business was a complicated thing, and Fred wanted a capable son who could help him run it. The business units included Rock Island Oil and Refining Co., which held a refinery and pipelines; the Matador Cattle Company, which ran the vast expanses of ranchland; and Koch Engineering Co., which made specialized equipment for the oil refineries and chemical plants. Fred Koch wanted to pass this group of companies on to someone who could manage it well, and he made it clear that Charles was the person for the job.

But Charles resisted. He was happy making his way in the wider world. Fred Koch had been a domineering father, a forceful personality who had an unmovable set of beliefs about how the world worked and how a man should conduct himself. Charles had carved out his own life in Boston, getting a job as a management consultant with the prestigious firm Arthur D. Little. He knew that if he went back home, he'd be living in his father's shadow, always subject to his father's authority.

"I thought, *My God, I go back, he won't let me do anything, and he'll smother me*," Charles Koch recalled decades later in an interview with the *Wichita Eagle*.

When Fred Koch was unable to persuade his son to return home, he resorted to guilt. He told his son that unless Charles returned to run the firm, Fred would sell it. The patriarch knew that his health wouldn't last forever, and if Charles didn't want the company, then someone else would.

Out of a sense of guilt, or obligation, or simple duty, Charles Koch finally relented. In 1961, he came back home to join his father's company. Over the years, Fred Koch gave Charles increasing authority. Charles had originally been hired within the Koch Engineering division, and eventually Fred Koch gave up his job as president of that division and handed over the title to Charles. In 1966, Fred Koch did the same thing with the much larger division of Rock Island Oil and Refining Co., which was the main pillar of the family's fortune, making Charles president. But Fred kept his authority over Charles by remaining chairman of the board.

On Monday, November 20, 1967, Charles Koch attended his father's funeral. The services were held at the Downing East Mortuary, and Fred's remains were cremated. When prominent members of the Wichita business community dropped by to pay their respects, they tried to console the large family that Fred Koch had left behind. Most prominent in the crowd, of course, was Fred Koch's elegant widow, Mary Koch, a poised and beautiful woman who was known throughout Wichita as an energetic supporter of the arts.

And then there were the couple's children, the four boys. As they stood shoulder to shoulder, the Koch boys were an impressive sight. They were very tall, all of them, standing well above six feet. The Koch boys lived their lives looking downward during most conversations. And they were handsome on top of it, with slender, muscular frames and square jaws inherited from their father. It might have seemed natural that Frederick Koch, the firstborn, would be heir apparent to his father's company. But Frederick, or Freddie, as everybody knew him, never had a strong interest in the family business—or any commercial business, for that matter. He was interested in art, and he studied drama in college rather than engineering. Freddie drew himself away from the orbit of the family company very early on in his life. When Fred Koch died, Freddie was teaching acting classes and producing plays in New York City.

After Freddie came Charles, who adopted the role of surrogate first-born.

Then there were the youngest Koch boys, a set of fraternal twins named David and William. Both twins, like their dad and Charles, attended MIT. When their father died, David had graduated and was working as a chemical engineer in New York. He was not just tall, but also possessed the muscular physique of a star athlete. He'd played basketball at MIT and was captain of the team. During his tenure on the team, Koch averaged twenty-one points and twelve rebounds per game, allowing him to graduate as the school's top-scoring player. He set the record for most points scored during a single game, at forty-one, a record that wouldn't be broken for forty-six years. His twin, Bill, was also on the team, but he didn't have David's talents. Bill, who was slightly shorter, spent more time on the bench. When their father died, Bill was still studying at MIT, working on his PhD.

Charles was the only son working at his father's company at that time. As he stood there, at Fred Koch's funeral, he was standing alone in a very significant way. Their father's business empire—everything that Fred Koch had built during his life—all of it was suddenly left to Charles to manage. He was thirty-two years old.

It's a truism of family business. The second generation of a successful family company is destined to ruin everything. Charles Koch was painfully aware of this stigma and wanted to prove that he was a builder. When he was left alone to run the company, he arrived early every day at the office, stayed late, and worked over the weekends. It was not uncommon for Koch to call employees on a Sunday afternoon, asking them to come down to the office for a meeting.

And he didn't just work hard. He worked with an intense purpose. Even in early 1968, just a few months after his father died, it was clear that Charles Koch had a stunningly ambitious vision for the company he and his brothers just inherited. He also had a strategy for how to get there. He wasted no time in carrying out a plan of his own, a plan that would fundamentally reshape everything that Fred Koch had built during his lifetime.

The first pillar of the plan to fall into place was organizational. Almost immediately, Charles Koch set about restructuring the interlocking group of companies that Fred Koch had left behind. The confusing amalgam of corporate entities—the engineering company, the oil gathering business, the pipelines, the ranches—would soon be welded into a single entity.

The second pillar of Charles Koch's plan was physical: the company would be based in a new office complex. Before Fred Koch died, the company had offices in a downtown building that was named after him. But by a stroke of coincidence, that building was scheduled to be demolished just when Fred died, torn down in order to make way for an urban renewal project. In its place, Charles Koch oversaw the construction of new headquarters, this one on the far-northeast corner of town. The new complex included an office building and a midsize factory floor where the company would make oil refinery equipment and other products. This is where Charles Koch would start to build a new company. Over the next forty years, the office complex would expand. Parking lots would be made where the prairie grass stood in 1967, a corporate tower would be added alongside the low-slung office complex just north of the factory. The complex, located on a remote stretch of Thirty-Seventh Street, was the blank slate on which Charles Koch would draw his plans and execute his vision.

The third pillar was personal. Charles Koch surrounded himself with the smartest people in the company that his father left behind, and the people that Charles Koch could trust. The most important of these people was a man named Sterling Varner.

Varner was a tall man, like Fred Koch, and, also like Fred Koch, he had the giant personality to match his imposing physical presence. When

Varner walked through the hallways of the new Koch offices, he was known to stop and talk with employees of every rank. He was a back-slapper and a shoulder squeezer. He remembered everyone's name and always took a moment to ask how he or she was doing. He was the kind of boss who made an employee feel important, no matter their rank. "Some people get sought out—you just want to be with them and be around them. And that's just the way Sterling was," recalled Roger Williams, who worked alongside Varner at Koch for many years.

Varner was born into a poor family, and famously told stories of life growing up in the Texas and Oklahoma oil patches, working as a roughneck on the drilling rigs and sleeping in tents. A Koch employee named Doyle Barnett recalled one moment when Varner was driving through rural Oklahoma and saw a vagrant by the side of the road. Varner declared, "But for the grace of God, there goes I."

Charles Koch relied on Sterling Varner from the very beginning of his time at the head of the company, and not just for counsel. Varner provided a measure of warmth and personal charisma that Charles Koch simply lacked. Charles Koch was not imperious—he didn't demean the people who worked for him. But he didn't have the common touch. Charles Koch was quiet, almost awkward. But he seemed to recognize this shortcoming, and he kept Varner close.

While Charles Koch relied on people like Varner to help him as he laid the foundations of his new company, Koch did some of the most important work on his own. Charles Koch was intently focused on what made people tick, and he approached the subject with the mind of an engineer: he was seeking to discover discernible laws. He knew that there were laws dictating what happened in the physical world, laws that were well understood by physicists and chemists. He thought there must be similar laws that dictated affairs in the human world.

"It's an orderly world, the physical world is. It follows certain laws. And so I thought: *Well, the same thing's got to be true for how people can best live and work together*," Koch recalled. "So I started reading everything I could on the subject."

Koch read the work of Karl Marx and other socialist thinkers. He read books on history, on economics, on philosophy, and on psychology. But for all the breadth of his research, it appears that his conclusions about the world came to rest on the small patch of ideological terrain where

he was raised. As a boy, Koch's father had regaled Charles and his brothers with horror stories about his time in the Soviet Union, where he had
helped Stalin's regime build oil refineries. He had impressed upon his
boys the evils of government and the inevitable overreach that seemed to
arise when the state interfered with the activities of free people.

Charles Koch became enamored with the thinking of economists and
philosophers like Ludwig von Mises and Friedrich Hayek, two Austrian
academics who did most of their formative work during the 1930s and
1940s. In later years, Charles Koch would be described as a libertarian
or a conservative. But these were imperfect labels that didn't capture his
true world view. More than anything, he was an Austrian economist, or
a "classical liberal," as he liked to call it. Hayek, in particular, put forward
a radical concept of capitalism and the role that markets should play in
society, and his thinking had an enduring effect on Charles Koch.

In Hayek's view, even well-intentioned state actions ended up causing far more human suffering than the market-based ills that they were
meant to correct. His most famous example of this was the policy of rent
control, which was big in Hayek's hometown of Vienna. Politicians put a
cap on rent prices to help people who rented homes and apartments. But
Hayek described a long list of unintended consequences. The controls
made it unprofitable for landlords to reinvest their cash in money-losing
apartments, for example, so those apartments devolved into squalor.
Because there was no incentive to build new apartment buildings, housing shortages became perpetual. Big families were stuck in small apartments because they couldn't afford to move out of their rent-controlled
dwellings. Hayek said this proved a simple point: cutting one thread in
the tapestry of a free market—even with the goal of helping people—
only unraveled other parts of the tapestry.

Hayek was almost religious when it came to describing what the
market could do when left to its own devices. He believed that the market was more important, and more beneficial, than the institution of
democracy itself. A market was able to mediate all the wishes of everyone on earth. When people entered a market, their demands instantly
put a price on the thing they wanted. The market also put a price on the
things that they had to offer (like their labor). These prices were not dictated or set by a king. Instead, they were derived from the push and pull
of supply and demand. The prices in a free market were the most hon-

est assessment of reality that humans could ever hope to achieve. Government, on the other hand, was never really able to mediate between all the competing needs of its people. It was impossible for everyone in a large society to come to some sort of consensus that the government could then enforce through law. Laws and regulations were unworthy tools to use to deal with problems of the natural world, because the natural world was always changing. Laws were static; the world was fluid. Only the market could respond to the ways the world rapidly changed, Hayek believed.

And if markets were Hayek's religion, then entrepreneurs were his saints. He saw entrepreneurs as the lifeblood of adaptation and efficiency. They were the ones who spotted new ways of doing things. They were the ones who created new products, created new technology, established new orders when it was time for the old orders to decay.

Charles Koch believed this, too. From the very earliest days of Koch Industries, Charles Koch sought to stock his workforce full of entrepreneurs, employees who would keep their eyes open, learn constantly, and spot new opportunities on the horizon before others saw them. That's why one of the first and most important jobs that Charles Koch and Sterling Varner tackled was bringing new blood into the company.

The two of them quickly began hiring some of the smartest minds they could find.

Roger Williams was an engineer with Mobil Oil Company, based outside of Houston, Texas. Williams had worked for Fred Koch back in the early 1960s but left the company to strike out on his own as an entrepreneur. His independent business venture had failed, so he took the job with Mobil and was still happily working there in 1968. That year, Williams was in a management meeting when he got a phone call from Sterling Varner, whom he'd worked with years before. Varner said he had a job offer for Williams: he wanted him to move to Wichita and help run Koch's pipeline system. Williams politely declined. He was very happy with Mobil and felt no need to go job hopping.

Varner told him, "Well, you haven't ever met Charles." Williams remembered. It was true—he had never met Fred Koch's son. At Varner's suggestion, Williams took a trip to Wichita to meet Charles, just to talk and hear him out. Shortly after the meeting, he quit his job and moved to Kansas.

One of Williams's first assignments was to open an office in Alaska, near the North Slope region, where Koch would set up a shipping business. Charles Koch and Sterling Varner came to visit his new operation, and they invited him to come back to Wichita with them on their corporate plane. As they flew over the densely wooded mountainsides of Alaska, the three men began discussing a thorny issue: What should they name the new company? Charles and Sterling had successfully fused the many companies Fred Koch ran into one firm, but now they needed to name it. Why not call the company Koch Industries? The name would honor Charles's late father, and it was an easy enough catchall title for a group of businesses that were already very diverse.

Charles Koch wasn't wild about the idea. He seemed embarrassed by the thought of having his last name stamped on the entire company. His name would be embossed on the letterhead, emblazoned on the sign outside the company headquarters, spoken on the lips of everyone who worked for him. There was a vanity about this that seemed at odds with Charles Koch's nature. But Williams argued in favor of naming the company Koch. In his mind, the benefit of the name was that it was neutral, in the way Exxon was neutral. For many industries, neutrality was the enemy. Companies like Coca-Cola spent millions to ensure that their names weren't neutral and forgettable. But the oil industry was different because Big Oil was cast as the villain in so many economic stories.

For this reason, "Koch" was the perfect moniker for the firm. It was slippery, hard to grasp. Everybody mispronounced it when they read the name, and when they heard the name, they confused it with the much better known soft-drink maker. Koch was the perfect flag to fly for a firm that sought to grow, and grow exponentially, while simultaneously remaining invisible. In June of 1968 Charles Koch announced that his father's holdings would be consolidated into one company. And it would be named Koch Industries.

When he was in Wichita, Roger Williams met with Charles Koch and Sterling Varner in their new corporate suite. And that's where he learned about the strategy at the heart of Charles Koch's corporate reorganization.

Fred Koch's fragmented holdings would be fused into one organization, but they would be combined in a loose way that made the new Koch Industries nimble. The new company would be divided up into a set of divisions that could be more easily managed than the stand-alone companies had been. As a single entity, these divisions would be bound together with one simple goal: to grow.

Koch Industries would grow in a way that reflected Sterling Varner's approach to business. Varner was "opportunistic," in a way that Koch employees used the word, meaning that he was always looking for new deals that were connected to businesses in which he already operated. When Koch was shipping natural gas, for example, Varner pushed the company to build a specialized natural gas refinery in Medford, Oklahoma, to process the gas into liquid by-products. In this way, Koch could expand while building on the skills it already possessed. The gas refinery, or "fractionator" as they called it, became a huge moneymaker.

Varner encouraged his senior managers, like Williams, to think the same way. Williams was told that his job wasn't just to keep his head down and run his division—his job was to keep his eyes on the horizon, to scan the environment of his business for new opportunities. Even more important, Varner told Williams to pass this mentality on to everyone who worked for *him*. The pipeline employees, the engineers, the oil gaugers—all of them needed to look for new deals as they went about their daily work. Everybody was supposed to act like an entrepreneur who worked in the mergers and acquisitions department.

"When you get that idea spread among your people, then you've got gaugers out there with their eyes open. The ideas come in. If you've got a couple of thousand [employees] looking for things, you're going to get some stuff that comes in that'll be all right." Williams said.

Charles Koch and Sterling Varner held quarterly meetings to evaluate how managers like Williams were doing in this regard. Williams was expected to report on his pipeline business and also to bring up new "high-quality investments" that he had spotted in the field.

A ritual was formed at these meetings. A manager like Williams would propose the idea for some new investment. And then the questions would begin. Charles Koch's questions were relentless, seemingly never ending, and the managers understood that they must be prepared to answer all of them. If a manager didn't have the answers, the topic was dropped until he could return with them.

The rhythm of corporate life at Koch Industries began to revolve around these quarterly meetings. And the rhythm beat a steady message into every manager and every employee below them down the chain: grow.

This message would soon be felt in the farthest corners of Koch Industries, such as the bayou country in southern Louisiana, where Koch Industries was running some of its largest pipeline and oil gathering operations. The oil gathering business was still the company's foundation, handed down from Fred Koch. In Louisiana, Koch was reaping a fortune from the oil-rich land. And the ways in which Koch was reaping this fortune would soon be discovered by one of the company's newest hires: a young oil gauger named Phil Dubose.

The company directives that came out of Wichita would become a daily part of Dubose's life. And it would change him in ways that he would never be proud of. The directives also set Koch on a path that drew the attention of Kenneth Ballen and the US Senate Committee investigating oil theft on Indian land.

In 1968, Phil Dubose was working in a grocery store in rural Louisiana. His future didn't look especially bright: he was in his late twenties, had no college education, and was married with three kids. He was raised in a part of Louisiana with chronically high unemployment, where many people worked intermittently and made most of their money in cash under the table. It might seem unlikely, then, that over the next twenty years Dubose would be promoted up through the ranks of Koch Industries, into the realm of senior management, where he would find himself in charge of a surprisingly large chunk of America's energy infrastructure.

Dubose loved hard work. His mom was a hardworking farm girl who instilled in him the religion of an honest day's pay for a hard day's work. His dad was an oil company manager who considered weekends to simply be a time when he could get work done outside the office. Dubose didn't finish college because he was inspired to join the army in 1962 when he was newly married and just a year out of high school. President

John F. Kennedy's call for public service, combined with the Cuban Missile Crisis, convinced Dubose that he needed to enlist. He served in Vietnam, and then came back home in need of work. That's when he landed a job as manager of a local grocery chain.

Dubose's life changed one day when a teenager asked if Dubose could give him more shifts at the store. Dubose told the boy that he'd allow it, but only if the kid brought his report cards to work so that Dubose could make sure his grades weren't falling. This small decision changed the path of Dubose's life. The kid's father was named Don Cummings, and he was impressed to hear that a grocery store manager would care so much about his son's grades. Cummings thanked Dubose, and then he offered him a job. Cummings said Dubose could work for him at a local oil company called Rock Island Oil. Cummings made a convincing pitch. Rock Island might sound like a tiny company, but it was owned by a conglomerate out of Wichita that was owned by the wealthy Koch family.

Oil companies garnered a lot of respect in the Gulf Coast. The economy in most bayou towns was tied to the rice harvest, which ran in boom and bust cycles. But the oil business was different. The money was steady, and the pay was good. Dubose knew this because his father was an engineer with Superior Oil Company, which people in the area referred to, even in casual conversation, as *the* Superior Oil Company. In the fifties and sixties, the swamplands around Lafayette, Louisiana, were like a microcosm of the entire US oil industry. It was a place full of gushers, in other words. There were tremendous oil deposits located beneath the marshy wetlands and out in the bayous, and the landscape was covered with oil wells. Across the country, oil drilling was increasing, and the price of oil was falling slowly each year through the 1960s.

Koch Industries hired Dubose as an oil gauger. His job would be to measure the oil in each tank before Koch collected it, and then he would pump it onto a barge and take it to one of Koch's pipelines, where it would be shipped to a refinery. Dubose spent many of his days on the water, out on the bayou and river channels. He piloted a small barge that could navigate through just a few feet of water, an ideal craft for negotiating the marshy lands. He steered expertly through the fingerlike lanes, avoiding cypress stumps and rocks and muddy shallows. He went from oil well to oil well, collecting the crude that was held there in large tanks. After running a circuit of several tanks, he took the oil to one of Koch's terminals, where it was fed into a pipeline or moved onto a larger barge for shipment.

But before he could drain the tanks, Dubose had to measure just how much oil was in there. There was a regimented series of steps to taking the measurements, a kind of standardized ritual that oil gaugers around the country followed. This ritual was codified in an industry standard published by the American Petroleum Institute. These standards were voluntary, however, and Koch Industries did not follow them. Dubose said he was given a playbook for taking oil without paying for it.

The Koch method for oil measurement followed a few simple steps. First, Dubose dropped his gauge line to see how deep the oil was. If the gauge line said it was fifteen feet and two inches, Dubose would record it as fifteen feet and one inch. Already, this meant that Dubose was getting an inch worth of oil for free. This was called "cutting the top."

Then he measured the "gravity" of the oil, which determined its quality. The top-dollar crude oil fell within an API measurement of gravity between 40.0 and 44.9, so Dubose fudged the numbers to push it outside of that range. This way, Koch would pay the oil producer less for the oil, even if the quality was ideal. If the oil measured 40.0, then he would record it as 39.2, for example.

After Dubose drained the tank, he would take his final depth measurement, which was recorded to show how much oil Koch had taken. If Dubose measured that fourteen inches of oil were left, he would record it as fifteen inches. This meant he was paying for one less inch of oil than he had taken. This technique was called "bumping the bottom."

Dubose learned the Koch method by rote. He estimated that by using it, he could get about ten to twelve extra barrels of crude from each tank he drained. That was only a small fraction of the whole, but it was enough to ensure that he was over at the end of every month. And he knew that the extra oil added up over time, because all of his coworkers were doing the same thing.

Dubose's bosses measured the amount of oil that Dubose drained from each tank, and then they compared it against the amount of oil he finally delivered into Koch's pipelines or terminals. Everybody knew that those numbers probably wouldn't match up exactly, thanks to the slippery nature of oil. If a gauger was under, it meant that he delivered less oil into Koch's pipelines or trucks than he gathered. If a gauger was over, on the other hand, then the opposite was true: he'd delivered *more* oil into Koch's system than he had recorded gathering at the oil tanks. It was only possible to be over by mismeasurement because it was physically impossible for oil supplies to increase as they made their way through the supply chain.

At the end of each month, Koch tabulated its oil shipments and figured out if each was over or under. The company posted the results at the branch office where Dubose worked. If a gauger was consistently under, his manager would grill him and ask what was going wrong. If a gauger was consistently over, then he had no problems.

Dubose's boss at the time was a manager named Doyle Barnett, who later recalled the reason for encouraging employees to be over. "You wanted to keep your company operating for sure. So, I guess I'd rather be over than short if I was the company," Barnett said. His bias toward being over was widely shared by Koch managers across the country. Keith Langhofer, a Koch Oil manager overseeing Texas and New Mexico, would later tell federal investigators that he also encouraged his gaugers to be over.

"I think we probably take an aggressive approach to purchasing crude oil. We certainly don't want to be short," Langhofer said, while under oath. If an employee came up short, then he was punished or demoted. If an employee was consistently over, the company "didn't do anything to him," Langhofer said.

It was clear to Dubose that the Koch method was not the industry norm. New hires expressed shock at the company's practices. In fact, the norm was for oil companies to be slightly under overall because it was more natural for them to lose some oil along the transportation chain rather than miraculously create oil, as Koch did. Even being slightly under, these other firms made money—oil was a profitable business, after all. The new hires at Koch either adapted, or they quit.

Dubose adapted. He knew in the back of his mind that he was effectively stealing oil. But it was only a little bit at a time. He took comfort in the fact that measuring oil was an inexact science. No one ever got it perfect.

"It's a very gray area. And I think Koch saw this," Dubose said. "They saw where they could manipulate this, because it's such a gray area. And they took advantage of it."

———

Koch's oil gathering division delivered a steady flow of cash and profits into the company. This money gave Charles Koch a chance to put his management theories to the test. He encouraged his employees to look for new growth opportunities and to act like entrepreneurs. He wanted to lead by example. In his first years as head of Koch Industries, Charles Koch put together one of the most brilliant and profitable deals in the history of Koch Industries. The deal involved an oil refinery.

Since the late 1950s, Fred Koch had owned a minority share in the Great Northern oil refinery outside of Minneapolis, near the Pine Bend Bluffs natural reserve. The other shareholders in the refinery were an oil tycoon named J. Howard Marshall II and the Great Northern Oil Company. In 1969, the refinery didn't look like a gold mine. Competition in the sector was fierce, with new refineries being put into production monthly.

But the Pine Bend refinery, as everyone called it, had a secret source of profits. And this source of profits could be traced to exactly the kind of government intervention that Hayek hated most. In the 1950s, President Dwight Eisenhower capped the amount of oil that could be imported into the United States, in one of the federal government's many ploys to protect domestic oil drillers. (Imported oil was often cheaper than domestic oil, so US drillers wanted it kept out.) But there was a loophole in that law that allowed unlimited imports from Canada. As it happened, Canada was the primary source of oil processed at the Pine Bend refinery. Pine Bend was one of only four refineries in the nation that was able to buy cheaper imported oil in unlimited quantities, giving it a huge advantage over firms that were forced to buy mostly domestic oil. The four companies who benefited from this loophole received a second advantage from the government. Thanks to a complex voucher system for oil imports, companies like Koch were able to "double dip" and exchange their voucher tickets for domestic oil in a scheme that gave them a subsidy of $1.25 per barrel. This loophole boosted profits, and Fred Koch had been happy to remain a minority shareholder and enjoy the windfall.

In 1969, Charles Koch executed a secret plan that would increase those profits beyond anything Fred Koch could imagine. Charles approached J. Howard Marshall and convinced Marshall to sell his share in the refinery in exchange for shares in Charles Koch's newly created firm, Koch

Industries. When that secret deal closed, Charles Koch was a majority shareholder in the Pine Bend refinery. He then approached Great Northern, now a minority shareholder, and convinced that company to sell its ownership stake. By the end of the year, Koch Industries was the sole owner of the Pine Bend refinery. Charles Koch saw something in the refinery that others didn't see.

There was, however, one significant obstacle standing in the path of Charles Koch's plan. It was a labor union.

Workers at the Pine Bend refinery had been organized in a union since the 1950s. The union was deeply entrenched and powerful. No sooner had Charles Koch purchased the Pine Bend refinery than he learned that he could not control it. Charles Koch had almost total authority over Koch Industries, but his authority was hemmed in at the Pine Bend refinery. The union set the rules in Pine Bend, and the union set the wages. Over the years, the labor contracts in Pine Bend became so favorable to the employees that even some of the union members thought that it was a little excessive.

In the late 1960s, most CEOs considered powerful unions to be a fact of life. The New Deal included pro-union laws, passed in the 1930s, that made unions almost indomitable. It was a losing game to take on unions; their power was too great to challenge. Most companies chose to accommodate organized labor.

Charles Koch faced this same choice, and he chose to fight. The battle against organized labor at Pine Bend was the first to test Charles Koch's resolve. His first move was to find the right commander for the conflict. Charles Koch found his man in the spring of 1971, when he attended an industry conference in California and met an oil industry engineer named Bernard Paulson.

Paulson was living in Corpus Christi at the time and managing an oil refinery for Coastal Oil & Gas. Paulson was instantly impressed with Charles Koch. Like so many people who met him, Paulson was first struck by Koch's intelligence. Paulson had met a lot of impressive people in the business—self-made millionaires and wildcatters—but even when compared against such characters, Charles Koch stood apart. There was nothing of the wildcatter about Charles Koch. He was not a flamboyant man who needed to impress strangers. He was an engineer by temperament, a man who questioned more than he talked. Charles Koch also seemed taken with Paulson—the two men quickly hit it off and Koch asked Paulson if he'd like to get dinner. Paulson agreed, and they talked a long time over dinner that night. Koch described his new investment at Pine Bend. The deal made perfect sense to Paulson. They talked about the oil refining business in-depth. Refining is the kind of hyper-complicated business that only two engineers could discuss in detail over dinner, and that's what the two of them did.

After Paulson returned to Texas, Charles Koch called him. They talked more, and soon Koch offered him a job. It seemed to Paulson that he had one job qualification that was especially important: he knew how to handle unions. When Paulson was hired to run the Coastal Oil refinery in Texas, the company had narrowly avoided a vote to unionize its employees. Paulson took over the business, and a few years later there was another union vote. He worked hard to convince his employees that union membership only hurt them, and he bargained hard against unionized firms that tried to get contracting work at the refinery. When still another union vote occurred under his management, the union lost by a five-to-one margin. Paulson had proved that he was adept at keeping unions out of an oil refinery, no matter how hard they might fight to get in. During their conversations Charles Koch told Paulson how toxic the union was in Pine Bend. Koch Industries needed to regain control. Breaking the union would be a key part of Paulson's job.

Paulson was, in many ways, the perfect man for this job. He came from tough circumstances—he was raised on a small farm in Michigan and educated in a one-room schoolhouse. He wasn't sentimental about business, and he knew how to stick out a hard situation. One of Paulson's heroes was General George S. Patton, the military hero who was best known for his rousing speeches that gave soldiers the courage they needed to head into battle. Patton had famously told his recruits: "Americans, traditionally, love to fight. All real Americans love the sting of battle. . . . Americans love a winner and will not tolerate a loser. Americans play to win all the time." Paulson yearned to be a leader who had the kind of inner strength that Patton possessed.

In 1971, Paulson joined Koch Industries. He was transferred immediately to Pine Bend, where he took control as manager of the refinery.

He immediately began, in his words, "to straighten it out."

CHAPTER 3

The War for Pine Bend

(1971–1973)

Public policy concerning labor unions has, in little more than a century, moved from one extreme to the other. . . . [Unions] have become the only important instance in which governments signally fail in their prime function: the prevention of coercion and violence.

—Friedrich A. Hayek, 1960

Married life ain't hard when you got a union card,
A union man has a happy life when he's got a union wife.
Oh, you can't scare me, I'm sticking to the union,
I'm sticking to the union 'til the day I die.

—Lyrics of the folk song "Union Maid"
by Woody Guthrie, 1940

Bernard Paulson arrived for his first day on the job at the Pine Bend refinery in 1971.

As he drove to work, Paulson traveled down two-lane country roads that passed through a sparsely populated landscape of rolling corn and soybean fields. The refinery is located near the tiny town of Rosemount, Minnesota, about twenty miles south of Minneapolis and Saint Paul. Good-paying jobs were scarce in this place. The local kids were raised on farms, and when they graduated from public high school—*if* they graduated from high school—they didn't have many job options other than farming. There was a smattering of industrial plants throughout the area: an ammonia plant near Rosemount and a paper plant across the river in Wisconsin, for example. But these jobs didn't pay a lot. The best source of jobs throughout the 1960s was at the Great Northern Oil Company, which had just recently been renamed the Koch Refining Company. Jobs at the refinery were sought after. They were union jobs, with union benefits. A guy could get hired at the refinery right out of high school and soon make the kind of steady wage that supported a mortgage and a family.

The refinery played a towering role in the local economy, and it dominated the landscape as well. As Paulson drove nearer to the refinery, he would have been able to see this for himself. The refinery became visible on the horizon many miles before Paulson arrived there, and it was an arresting sight. After passing many miles of rolling hills, small farmhouses, tractors, and grain silos, the refinery came into view and looked very much like the skyline of a small city. But there was something alien, even ominous about this skyline. The towers in the skyline didn't have any windows. They spewed clouds of white steam and gas, and some of them, on the south end of the refinery, spewed columns of flame into the sky. The gargantuan torches burned so steadily that airline pilots used them as a landmark when they approached the local airport.

To reach the refinery gates, Paulson drove along a highway that ran roughly parallel to the Mississippi River, which was hidden behind a dense stand of pine and oak trees. Great Northern was smart to locate the refinery where it did, near a big, wide spot in the Mississippi called Pine Bend. In this part of Minnesota, rivers are not scenic waterways but industrial transit tools. The river afforded passage for giant barges toting mountains of grain or coal, or, when they were loaded at Koch Refining, crude oil and asphalt. The barges took these commodities down south at a much cheaper rate than either rail or road, at least when the river wasn't frozen over during Minnesota's brutal winters.

Paulson pulled off the highway onto an access road that led to the refinery's front gate. At the base of the giant towers, there was a squat office building made of beige bricks, just north of a parking lot where Paulson steered his car. This was the refinery's main office, where Paulson would work. As he drove into the lot, he noticed that the parking spots were marked by signs with employees' names on them. The spots were apparently reserved for individuals, and he saw that the best parking spot, the one nearest the sidewalk to the office door, had his name on it. Paulson had arrived early, as he always did, and most of the parking spots were empty. He pulled in to the best spot—the one marked with his name—and turned off his car.

Paulson walked down the sidewalk and into the double glass doors of the office building. One of the first things he told his assistant that first day was to get rid of the reserved parking spots.

"I said: 'If you want the best spot, you get here early.'"

Bernard Paulson often wore cowboy boots to work. They were a parting gift from his employees back in Texas, and he wore them with pride because they reminded him how well he'd gotten along with employees in the past. He considered himself a good leader, and a fair leader, even if he was tough.

He saw very quickly that Charles Koch had been correct. Paulson's leadership skills were needed, and needed desperately, at the Pine Bend refinery. Paulson saw this when he started doing the rounds at Pine Bend. Unlike most managers, he came to work on Saturdays. He arrived early on the weekends, just like he did on the weekdays, and he walked the grounds to inspect operations firsthand. What he saw often appalled him. He came across employees who were sleeping. He stopped and watched them sleep next to the large machines where superheated petrochemicals passed through pipes under extreme pressure—enough pressure to cause an explosion if a problem went undetected for too long. Paulson woke up the employees, and he didn't do it gently.

Sleeping on the job in an oil refinery is not like sleeping on the job at a car factory. The Pine Bend refinery covered seven hundred acres, and it was a landscape of winding pipes, giant tanks, and looming towers with walkways between them. This was a dangerous landscape, a massive circulatory system full of inflammable liquids under high pressure. The refinery was divided into different "units," or different machines that each had a unique function. Each unit, in turn, had a team of operators who oversaw it. There were usually three operators per unit, men who would sit for long shifts—sometimes ten-hour shifts, sometimes longer—babysitting the complex and dangerous chemical reactions happening inside the machinery. If everything went well, it was a mundane job. If things didn't go well, it could quickly turn into a disaster.

Oil arrived at the refinery by pipeline, and it was stored in giant, white tanks. This crude oil was then moved into the giant "boiler" units, which were giant furnaces that heated the oil to around 700 degrees Fahrenheit.

Running the boilers is a dangerous and vital job. When a young man named Lowell Payton was hired at the Pine Bend refinery, he noticed that there was a tall, thick wall around the boiler. He asked what that wall was for, and he remembers his boss telling him: "That's so if the boiler blows up, your body won't be found fifty miles away."

After the oil is heated up, it undergoes a series of chemical reactions that seem to border on alchemy. Oil looks like nothing more than shiny black goo, but it contains a remarkably diverse set of chemicals. The heat unwinds the chemical chains that kept these riches together and breaks free a rainbow of compounds like gasoline, butane, kerosene, propane, diesel fuel, and an almost countless array of petrochemicals that are used to make everything from clothing to lip balm and plastic building material. This chemical unwinding happens inside the most visible part of an oil refinery: the giant towers. The towers are called fractionators because they break the crude oil into fractions, or its component parts. The heated crude oil is pumped into the bottom of the towers, where it is vaporized. The oil vapors float up through the fractionating tower like smoke through a chimney. Along the way, the different components of oil are captured on a series of trays inside the tower. One tray separates out kerosene, another gasoline, and so on. Vaporized crude oil is like the apocryphal buffalo that the Plains Indians used to hunt: every piece is used, nothing is left to waste. One of the biggest skills for oil refining is figuring out how to squeeze every possible drop of every possible petrochemical out of the crude without wasting anything to evaporation.

Paulson knew this business very well, and he was obsessed with running the refinery as efficiently and profitably as possible. But he wanted order among the men who worked in the units. Paulson was tall and imposing, and when he toured the refinery grounds, he walked like a navy admiral inspecting the deck of a battleship. He was often trailed by two assistants, and he wasn't shy about barking orders or using crude language.

This might have been intimidating, or even frightening, to many employees. But the refinery employees were not afraid of Bernard Paulson. They were not afraid of anybody, in fact. They had the union to back them.

Employees at Pine Bend were organized under the auspices of a powerful labor union called the Oil, Chemical and Atomic Workers Union—

or the OCAW, for short. They belonged to a local chapter called the OCAW Local 6-662.

Men took an oath when they joined the OCAW. They raised their right hand and they pledged allegiance to the union. More specifically, they pledged their allegiance to their fellow union brothers and sisters. For these men, it was union first, company second. The OCAW men gathered for meetings in rented halls, where they held votes on union contracts and discussed their problems with certain supervisors or managers. They drank regularly at a little bar south of the refinery called the House of Coates, which was built to look like a log cabin or large hunting lodge.

The union president, Joseph Hammerschmidt, was known for drinking heroic quantities of alcohol at the House of Coates and then talking at very high volume about the refinery's management and what he planned to do to that management. Hammerschmidt was a union man down to the level of his DNA; he was a "hard case," as his fellow workers called him. Everybody at the refinery knew that it was Hammerschmidt who led contract negotiations with a nearby company called Red Wing Pottery, which also employed OCAW members. During the negotiations, Hammerschmidt refused to believe that Red Wing Pottery was really in the financial trouble it claimed to be in. Even when Red Wing showed him the company books, Hammerschmidt refused to believe the books were genuine. The OCAW couldn't reach a contract agreement with Red Wing, and Red Wing's owners were forced into bankruptcy. Hammerschmidt seemed proud of this fact. It was like a scalp on his wall. No damn company was going to boss around the OCAW.

Hammerschmidt carried himself like a provincial governor while he belted back shots of whiskey with his union friends at the House of Coates, and he had reason to act like that. Like a governor, Hammerschmidt had real power. The OCAW was a strong union in itself, but maybe even more important was the fact that the OCAW was located in a heavily unionized state. This was important: the OCAW didn't just draw power from itself; it drew power from an interlocking web of loyalty oaths with other unions in the state. The police were unionized, the truckers were unionized, the teachers were unionized, the newspaper reporters were unionized, the chemical workers were unionized. The OCAW men were loyal to their own union, and the union was, in turn, loyal to other unions in the state. If one union went on strike, the other unions would support it. Men like Hammerschmidt could put a company out of business if they felt like it. Red Wing Pottery was proof of that. And the OCAW wasn't shy about using this power to its members' benefit.

During the 1950s and 1960s, the OCAW negotiated a framework of rules at the Pine Bend refinery that did far more than provide higher pay and benefits for the union members. The rules gave the OCAW a large measure of control over the refinery's operations.

Paulson saw the fruits of this arrangement shortly after he took over as the plant manager.

When an OCAW employee found a broken valve while inspecting the refinery, for example, that employee didn't fix the valve. Instead, he sat down and radioed for help. The union had broken the workforce down by specialty skills—or by "trades," to use the union terminology—and the men only performed work that fell within their trade. When an employee found the broken valve, he called someone whose trade was insulation to come and unwrap the insulation around the pipe. Then he'd call a guy from the electrical trade to check the wiring or shut off electricity to the problem area. And these employees who came to help fix the valve had to drive a truck to the site (the refinery covered seven hundred acres, after all), and there was a union rule that prohibited any union employee from riding in a vehicle with a supervisor. To satisfy this rule, the refinery had a union guy whose job was to sit in a pickup truck and ferry people around the refinery. As the different tradesmen were called on the radio, the pickup truck driver went to collect them—first the insulation specialist, then the electrician—and take them down to the problem site. The truck driver job was one of the cushier positions that the union carved out for its members. Only after the different tradesmen were called, and were ferried down to the site, and did their work one by one, only then could the leaky valve be fixed.

There were also rules for overtime pay that even the OCAW men found amusingly absurd. One rule stated that a shift worker needed to be given at least two hours of notice if he was going to be asked to stay late and work. If he didn't get that notice, then he received a bonus payment worth two hours' work plus time and a half. Thanks to this rule, it was often hard to locate anyone at the refinery around two in the afternoon, exactly two hours before the four o'clock shift change came around. The control rooms were empty at two. Then everyone suddenly reappeared at their desks at two fifteen—available to stay late and work overtime if asked, but in need of the bonus payment to do it.

Even longtime union members recognized that these rules were too good to be reasonable. "It's crazy—I don't know how they got what they got. The union had management by the balls," recalled Ernie Tromberg, who was hired at the refinery in 1956 when he was still in his early twenties.

Paulson talked often to Charles Koch on the telephone. He told his boss what he was seeing in the refinery. This might not have been news to Charles Koch. He had seen the union operate firsthand. For at least one summer when he was younger, Charles Koch had worked at Pine Bend and must have seen the near impunity enjoyed by union bosses like Joseph Hammerschmidt. Koch couldn't have been shocked as Paulson relayed over the phone what he was seeing in the plant. The union put at risk everything that Charles Koch was hoping to build. "He told me, 'I'm worried that the union is going to take this company down,'" Paulson recalled.

Shortly after arriving at the refinery, Paulson was given his chance to fight the OCAW. The union contract was set to expire at the end of 1972. Negotiating a new contract would give Paulson, and Charles Koch, a chance to rewrite the refinery rules and make the place operate as they believed it should.

In April of 1972, Paulson made his first move. He scheduled Hammerschmidt to work on Easter Sunday.

Hammerschmidt, apparently, did not want to work on Easter. So Hammerschmidt did what was commonly done in those days. He told Paulson no. He wasn't going to work Easter Sunday.

Hammerschmidt could be forgiven if he thought that his open insubordination would not be challenged or punished, because that's how things worked at Pine Bend: if the union guys were unhappy about something—say, the disciplining of a fellow worker—they simply dropped what they were doing. They walked to the front office and took a seat until the matter was resolved, and management usually caved to their demands. It seemed that Paulson would have caved as well because he wasn't popular with the employees. The cowboy boots, the military-style inspections, waking the guys up and embarrassing them on Saturday mornings—all of it had soured the employees on Paulson. He recalls hearing what the union men were saying behind his back: "They were going to jam those boots 'down Paulson's ass and send him back to Texas.'"

When the shift began on Easter, and Hammerschmidt wasn't there, Paulson fired him immediately. In the eyes of the OCAW, Paulson had just declared war.

In the late fall and early winter of 1972, it was time for Koch Refining Company and the OCAW to negotiate a new labor contract.

There was a regular calendar and set of traditions that surrounded these contract negotiations. A labor contract is a broad agreement between a union and a company that sets out the terms of employment at the workplace, from the level of wages to the value of extra benefits like health care coverage. The contract even laid out workplace rules, like the procedures for firing a worker or the means by which an employee could file a grievance to complain about abuses by management. The labor contracts typically lasted about three years. When the contracts were set to expire, a group of Koch Refining lawyers would go into a meeting room and sit down across the table from a group of negotiators selected by the OCAW. The union negotiators were almost always refinery employees rather than lawyers or negotiating experts. When it came to bargaining with the company, the union men relied on their personal knowledge of how the refinery worked. They knew what to ask for, and they knew what they could offer in return. To get what they wanted, the union men relied on their collective willpower. They stood together, ready to walk off the job as a group if management did not agree to their requests.

During his first meeting with the OCAW team, Paulson sat down in the meeting room, flanked by his company lawyers. Across the table sat Joseph Hammerschmidt, the union president. Even though Hammerschmidt had been fired, the union insisted that he be present for the negotiations. The union had already filed a grievance over Hammerschmidt's firing, and, in the meantime, he was still a member.

After everybody was settled, Paulson presented his offer.

Koch would unilaterally rewrite all the work rules inside the refinery. The seniority system the union enjoyed would be gone. The rules that barred employees from doing work in different "trades" would be gone. The employee shuttle truck? Gone. The rule about a bonus payment for overtime without two hours' notice? Gone. And then Paulson showed the union men that there would be precious little room for negotiation. These were the new rules. This was how things would work at the refinery. End of story.

This might have seemed like a bluff; like a way for Paulson to start the contract negotiations with a Texas swagger. But after Christmas, and into the first frigid days of the new year, it became clear to the union that Paulson was not bluffing. He was not going to negotiate.

In the eyes of the OCAW men, there was no choice as to what to do next.

On January 9, 1973, at four in the afternoon, the entire unionized workforce left their stations and walked off the property grounds. They walked out through the parking lot and then through a wide gate that led outside the refinery property. As they passed through the gate, the gate became something entirely new. It became a picket line. Crossing the picket line marked a moment of no return. After they left the gate, the OCAW men became locked out of the refinery. They became locked out from their jobs. They became unemployed.

The refinery inside that gate had provided the men with everything they had: the income that fed their kids and paid down their mortgages. It made a middle-class life possible for them. And none of the men knew if they would ever get back inside or if their job would ever be open to them again. Bernard Paulson and Charles Koch had made it clear at the negotiating table: Koch Refining planned to break the OCAW. And the union men had to make it clear to Bernard Paulson and Charles Koch: the OCAW could not be broken.

This wasn't an easy thing to do. None of the OCAW men were happy about using their jobs as a bargaining chip. Joseph Quinn, for example, had a wife and five children. Quinn didn't see his kids a lot—he missed at least five Christmas mornings in a row because he'd been working at the refinery. His wife, Rita, handed out the presents without him. But through his absence, Quinn gave his kids a life that he had never known. He and Rita owned a tidy home in suburban Minneapolis, near Rosemount. Their kids went to good public schools. They didn't work long days in the farm fields under the hot summer sun, as Joseph Quinn had done growing up in western Minnesota.

But Quinn didn't question his union when the OCAW told him to walk off the job. There was a simple idea that motivated his obedience: solidarity. Solidarity encapsulated everything that the union stood for and everything that made the union strong. Quinn hadn't learned about solidarity growing up. He was raised by a farmer, so he learned about individual accomplishment and the value of hard work. Quinn's dad taught him that unions were Communist front groups and that unions encouraged laziness. But when he moved to Minneapolis, the only jobs available to Quinn were union jobs. When Quinn raised his right hand and pledged allegiance to the OCAW, he pledged solidarity to his union brothers at the refinery. But the pledge didn't sink in too deeply; Quinn just wanted the job.

Then Quinn got in trouble for the first time.

One of his jobs at the refinery was to check on the level of crude oil in the big white tanks on the south end of the plant. This was a critical job because the tanks could overflow if their levels weren't closely monitored. At the end of one shift, Quinn was unable to check on the oil in one tank because men were welding some equipment there. After the men left, he went to check the oil levels, but a fellow worker was urinating near the hatch that Quinn was supposed to check, so Quinn backed off to give him privacy. The end of his shift came, and Quinn still hadn't checked the level of that oil tank. He told his manager as much, and his manager told him not to worry about it.

"The next thing I knew, that big, beautiful white tank was black, covered completely in oil," Quinn recalled. The tank had overflowed, and it would not have done so if Quinn had checked the oil levels as he was supposed to.

Quinn was suspended without pay for three days for the transgression. The paycheck that covered his mortgage, that fed his kids, would be about one-third short of what it should be. He couldn't afford to take a financial hit like that, and he didn't think it was fair that he should need to. So Quinn filed a union grievance over the punishment. A grievance is a formal complaint that only union members can file. It is a complaint that is handled somewhat like a lawsuit, with the union acting as the employee's personal legal team. Without a union, there are no formal grievances—an employee can simply complain and he or she is on their own to persuade the boss to take their complaint seriously. With a grievance, the employee has the union on their side.

After Quinn filed his grievance, he was summoned to the refinery offices. He went into a meeting room and found a company lawyer there, who wanted to discuss Quinn's punishment. But Quinn wasn't alone. There was a representative of the OCAW sitting at the table next to him. As Quinn and the company lawyer were talking over the issue, the OCAW man kept interrupting. He kept correcting Quinn, kept interjecting new details into the story. Quinn disagreed vehemently with some of those details, even though the details skewed the story to Quinn's benefit. Quinn even started to argue with the OCAW man as the company lawyer sat there and watched. Finally, the company lawyer called an end to the meeting, seemingly in exasperation. It was hard to get a straight answer about anything with the pushy OCAW man sitting right there.

A few days after that meeting, Quinn was called to the front office once again. This time it was only his manager there. His manager pointed to the desk, where there was a check made out to Quinn in the amount of the wages he had lost from the three days he was suspended. "He told me, 'Don't take this as a victory.' But there was the victory right there on his desk!" Quinn recalled. Quinn happily took that check and cashed it.

The episode taught Quinn an important lesson. The OCAW negotiator had made the grievance process hellish for the company lawyer and had chosen to fight for just three days' wages for just one guy. Thanks to that episode, Quinn understood what solidarity meant: "I saw how things really work." When it came time to walk off the job, Quinn walked off the job. He didn't question the OCAW, because the OCAW hadn't questioned him. It was all for one and one for all.

When the strike began, Joseph Quinn helped organize the picket line. The refinery employees took scheduled shifts to picket at the refinery's three main gates to ensure that the picket line was staffed around the clock. The OCAW organized much of this activity out of a small trailer parked just outside the refinery property. Guys lounged and played cards outside the trailer. Others showed up to get picket signs that they would hold during their shift, signs bearing slogans like: "Koch For Slavery" and "OCAW LOCAL 6-662—ON STRIKE." It was Quinn's job to make sure the shifts ran smoothly and that the signs were always available.

The striking employees carried placards and signs, but the picket line was far more than a simple form of public protest. It was an economic weapon that had been employed to great effect over one hundred years of American labor struggles. The goal of the picket line was to financially strangle Koch Refining Company.

The picket line was a barricade designed to stop any truck traffic going in or out of the refinery—a barricade that would effectively shut the refinery down. A huge proportion of products made at the refinery were shipped out by big tanker trucks that took heating oil to nearby school buildings or gasoline to nearby service stations. If the trucks couldn't come and go, Koch couldn't sell its products. The OCAW aimed to starve the company out, forcing it back to the negotiating table in a weakened position.

The tanker truck drivers—and even the cops who patrolled the road outside the refinery—belonged to the Teamsters union, which meant that crossing the picket line was akin to violating their own sacred oath of solidarity. The picket line worked. On a typical day at the refinery, about two hundred tanker trucks passed through the gates to pick up fuel and ship it out. That number dropped to near zero after Quinn helped get the OCAW picketers organized and standing in shifts.

The union had cut off the oxygen supply of cash to Koch's refinery. They knew that the owner, Charles Koch, was losing enormous amounts of money for every minute the OCAW was on strike. It seemed certain that Charles Koch would have no choice but to fold. He might hold out for a week or two to save face, but there was no way Koch could hold out for long.

These union men clearly had no idea who they were dealing with.

Bernard Paulson was prepared. He had set up a cot in his office, a cot where he would sleep for most of the next nine months, rarely leaving the refinery, rarely leaving his post. He had also stockpiled food. The refinery had a large cafeteria near the office building, and when the union workers walked off the job, Paulson gave an order that the cafeteria was to be open twenty-four hours a day. A skeleton crew of nonunion workers would be living inside the refinery gates, and Paulson made sure that the cafeteria was open to them whenever they needed to eat. And they would need to eat at odd times during the strike because there weren't going to be any more eight-hour shifts. Running the refinery would now be an around-the-clock job. There wouldn't be regular mealtimes.

Paulson did more than just stockpile food. He had also quietly built the workforce he needed. Many members of this new workforce were the nonunion supervisors who worked at the refinery. They would each now do the job of two or three men, working sixteen-hour shifts. But even that wouldn't be enough. So Paulson started making phone calls back to Texas, back to the oil-patch state where Paulson had friends and employees who thought the world of him. He called these old friends and asked them to come up to Minnesota to work. Shortly after the picket line was erected outside the refinery gates, Paulson arranged for helicopters to fly these workers into the refinery. The helicopters swooped in low over the refinery fences and landed on the refinery grounds to drop off his new workers from Texas and Oklahoma and other states where unions were not only rare but widely hated. Inside the main office building, Paulson converted a large room in the basement into a barracks for the new workers.

On the picket line, the OCAW men watched as the helicopters passed over them, hovered, and landed inside, delivering the workers who would replace them. The picket line was becoming symbolic.

But even with Paulson's new workforce, it wasn't easy to keep the refinery going. Paulson needed to run giant machines called reformers, for example, which made a vital chemical for Koch's fuel products. The reformers could not be started with the simple press of a button, however. They needed tank loads of hydrogen to spark their ignition. After running out of hydrogen, Paulson knew he couldn't convince any local truckers to break the picket line and deliver more to him. So he called some old friends of his at Amoco, and they told him about a solution: he could use natural gas—which came into the refinery via pipeline—to ignite the reformers. It was a tricky, complicated process, but Paulson and his team figured out how to make it work. Soon he had all the reformers firing, and the fractionating towers were running at full steam.

On the first night of the strike, however, one of the boiler units—the large furnaces that superheated oil before it was sent to the fractioning towers—wasn't working right. The mechanical problems inside the boiler went unnoticed for many hours because the unit was understaffed. Usually the boiler was monitored by three employees, but Paulson had to run the unit with fewer. The boiler malfunction grew worse until the system collapsed with an incendiary blast. It was a small miracle that nobody was killed—the explosion tore a gaping hole in the side of the boiler. The unit was shut down in a panic, the valves were closed to stop the flow of oil and prevent a fire that could have engulfed the property. The salaried supervisors went out and inspected the boiler. It was a total loss.

A manager came into Paulson's office and told him the news. The boiler couldn't be fixed, the manager said, at least not without help from the unionized operators who ran the machines. Koch would need to bring the operators back from the picket line for the repair job. "He said, 'We've lost the strike. I want my operators back,'" Paulson recalled. "And I said to him, 'If you believe that, hit the effing road.'"

Paulson again called one of his friends in Texas, waking him in the middle of the night. He said he needed an urgent favor and told his friend about the explosion. Paulson's old friend hustled a team together and got them on a plane to Minneapolis. From there, the team was flown by helicopter into the refinery. The unit was up and running again within about a week.

At night, before he went to bed, Paulson walked around the refinery to make sure his men were doing well. He dropped into the monitoring rooms where the men were staring at screens, gaunt from spending unending hours on the job. The pressure on them was tremendous. Everyone knew that there was a potential catastrophe waiting to happen every minute of every day. The boiler explosion was proof of that. Now, with a skeleton crew overseeing them, the boilers were firing and pumping out superheated, flammable fuels throughout the refinery. It was almost reckless to run the refinery so short-staffed, when just a few minutes of inattention could get people killed. One employee quit after suffering from exhaustion and an anxiety attack that left him nearly catatonic.

When Paulson walked his rounds at night, he made sure to exude confidence to keep the spirits of his employees high. "They said it was very important, my demeanor, during that strike," Paulson recalled. "One of our salespeople, during that time, he called me Patton. He said, 'All you lack are those two ivory-handled revolvers.'"

Weeks passed. The men on the picket line kept their positions at all hours. They choked off truck traffic going into the refinery. But standing outside the refinery gates, they could see that the fractionating towers were still spewing steam, and the flare towers were still shooting out flames.

The picket line was not able to stop every truck. Paulson's workers from Texas and Oklahoma passed in and out of the refinery. Even some of the local nonunion truck drivers began to break the picket line, delivering and gathering fuel.

Ernie Tromberg, an OCAW employee who worked in one of the fractionating towers, watched the anger boil over among his coworkers as "scab" drivers approached. The union men stood in front of the trucks and waved their placards. But the scab trucks inched forward slowly, haltingly, heading into the refinery. Tromberg saw his coworkers assemble "jacks," thorny balls made of outward-facing metal spikes and nails, and throw them on the ground in front of approaching trucks. Paulson estimates that Koch spent $100,000 (or about $593,000 when adjusted for inflation in 2018), to replace truck tires in the first few months of the strike alone.

Koch Refinery hired a private company called Wackenhut to police the gates, and the private guards looked like teenagers with rented badges. They only made the picketers angrier. Tromberg was standing near a truck as it passed when he heard the unmistakable *tink* of a jack being thrown into the truck's wheel well. A young Wackenhut guard approached Tromberg from behind and accused him of throwing the jack. The guard escorted Tromberg over to a state police trooper, but the officer said there was nothing he could do because he hadn't witnessed the event. Tromberg saw that the Wackenhut guards were helpless to do much of anything, and the picketers realized it.

An atmosphere of lawlessness began to surround the picket line. When scab drivers edged closer to the gates, the union men jumped up on the running boards of the trucks and pounded on the windows. When that didn't stop the trucks, they grew more violent. "We had some pretty tough guys working there. They would open the doors and pull out drivers," recalled Lowell Payton, a unionized worker who picketed outside the gates.

When the workers got violent, Paulson seized on their mistake. He went to court and filed a motion that would bar the OCAW from picketing in front of the refinery. Paulson's lawyers argued that the OCAW's property destruction and violence went far beyond the scope of legal union activity. A local district court judge agreed with the company and handed down a temporary restraining order against the union. The restraining order didn't bar picketing outright, but it greatly limited what the union could do. The judge said the union must now be limited to having four men stand with picket signs at the refinery, where there had been dozens before. These four men would be prohibited from doing anything intimidating or violent. The unionized police officers at the site couldn't stand back and remain neutral: they had a judge's injunction to enforce. The judge's order smothered the picketing.

As the third week passed and then the fourth week, the reality of the strike began to sink in. The men at the plant still had mortgages to pay and kids to support. They sought out part-time jobs in secret, and many of them found work, but it didn't pay what the refinery had paid. As the strike dragged on, the OCAW members began to see just how easy it might be for them to fall from the middle class. They saw how easy it might be to lose their home, lose their car, endanger the economic future of their kids. And they knew who was responsible for this danger. They blamed Bernard Paulson. Many of the men began to hate Paulson and his Texas cowboy boots and his superior bearing. The men gathered at the Coates bar and drank and talked about what they might do. And their anger boiled over.

On Friday night, February 23, more than thirty union men gathered outside the refinery. Paulson and his employees had been camped inside the gates for about six weeks, and they couldn't stay inside forever. The union men knew this, and they were waiting outside when a caravan of Paulson's employees, packed inside a row of cars, drove out through the refinery gates. The union men pounded on hoods, broke car windows, and screamed at the workers inside. The picketers had been practicing a technique to tip the cars over by gathering in groups and rocking the cars from side to side. They tried this technique on the cars that passed. Someone fired gunshots into the refinery during the melee. No one was hit, and no one was able to determine who fired the gun.

Around this time, Bernard Paulson's wife was alone at the couple's home, taking care of their six children. One night a man called her house and asked if Paulson was there. She said he wasn't and asked if she could take a message. The caller said she could, and he told her the message was that soon Mr. Paulson would not be breathing anymore. Then the caller hung up, leaving Mrs. Paulson alone with her thoughts and six sleeping children.

Bernard Paulson did not bend. He kept working, sleeping on the cot in his office. He was not going to quit; he was not going to back down in the face of threats.

Whenever Paulson needed encouragement, he picked up the phone and called Wichita.

"I worked directly for Charles, and we consulted several times a day. It was with his backing," Paulson recalled. "He knew exactly what I was doing and why I was doing it."

On the night of March 15, Paulson went to his office, laid down on his cot, and pulled up the covers before drifting off to sleep. He was exhausted, and he slept soundly. While he slept, someone carried out a plan that might have killed him and every employee to whom he had just said good night.

A set of railroad tracks ran along the west side of the refinery. The tracks carried tanker cars of crude oil and ran right into the middle of the refinery complex where the trains could load and unload fuel. At night, the tanker cars and diesel engines were often parked in a small depot outside the refinery, waiting for the next day's delivery. It was common practice for railroad companies to leave the diesel engines idling throughout the night because it takes a lot of fuel to start the vehicles. Some of the refinery employees would have known this because a handful of them had once worked for the railroad. These men knew how the trains worked and knew where they were parked.

In the dark hours just after midnight on March 15, someone snuck between the train cars and engines near the refinery. The saboteur jumped up to the doorway of one of the diesel engines and climbed inside. It is unknown whether it was one person or a group of people who did this, but whoever went inside the engine knew how to operate it. They knew where to find the throttle and how to engage it. They pushed the throttle forward and leapt out of the train as it began to chug forward.

The diesel engine picked up momentum as it traveled down the track. The cab was empty, and there were no employees at the depot to spot the engine as it headed over empty cropland and gathered speed. At roughly one in the morning, the train was speeding directly toward the refinery. The tracks it rode led directly to the center of the plant, into a nest of pipes and silos and towers filled with flammable fuel.

Bernard Paulson woke up in his office to the phone ringing. He answered it and heard an employee shouting on the other end. Paulson was half asleep and trying to make sense of what he was hearing. There had been some kind of accident. A train crash. Paulson quickly dressed and ran out of his office. There were men shouting outside, and he ran toward them.

Then he saw a surreal thing. A diesel engine, lying on its side, in the middle of the refinery grounds. The giant train engine was still running.

When the train engine came hurtling through the refinery, it had been heading straight toward a large refining tower. But there were mechanisms set into the train tracks, called derailers, that acted as a safety stop to prevent damage from runaway trains. The engine hit the derailers at a high speed and the mechanisms did their job, flipping the steel engine onto its side and off the track, sending it skidding over the refinery grounds.

If the derailers had not been in place, if the train had kept going, it would have crashed directly into a series of gasoline lines, pumps and pipes. It is likely that an inferno would have engulfed the refinery and killed many of the men who were working there. Paulson could have been burned alive in his office. The wreck was roughly two hundred feet from where he'd been sleeping.

Paulson tried to absorb what he was seeing as he circled the diesel engine. One of his employees on shift at the time had worked on train lines before, and he climbed into the fallen engine and shut it off.

Paulson stared at the wreckage and thought of all the people who had just narrowly avoided death. And he thought to himself: Who could do something like that? The wreck sent a clear message. If Koch aimed to destroy the OCAW, the OCAW would destroy Koch.

The union's violence was driven in part by anger. But it was also driven by fear. The union men might have had strength in numbers, but, in many important ways, the union was not as powerful as it once had been.

The strength of modern American unions rested largely on one significant piece of New Deal legislation passed in 1935, called the Wagner Act. The law gave workers the legal right to join a union and legally obligated companies to bargain with them. The act also created a federal agency to oversee union disputes, called the National Labor Relations Board. With these new legal protections, the ranks of union membership swelled. By the 1950s, labor unions were an accepted, almost inevitable part of mainstream American life, with more than one-third of US workers belonging to a union. The impact of the unions was felt even by workers who didn't belong to them—the very presence of unions affected nonunion companies. These companies knew that their wages and working conditions had to be generous enough to ward off the threat that their employees would defect or start a union of their own. This system started to corrode during the 1960s, however, and it corroded partly from within.

Unions were formed to protect the little guy, but by the late 1960s, many unions had become bloated power structures that lost the sympathy of their own members. Union leaders became union "bosses," many of them overpaid and corrupt. Violence and thuggery became all too common hallmarks of organized labor campaigns. Public approval of unions began to plummet, according to opinion polls. At the same time, companies in heavily unionized states began to move their factories down to southern, nonunion states. Rather than negotiate with unions, these companies started sneaking out the back door.

In spite of their militancy and their arrogance, union leaders like Joe Hammerschmidt were losing their power by the early 1970s. This added an element of toxicity to their efforts and a level of desperation to their actions.

Koch Refining Co., on the other hand, acted methodically and patiently. The actions reflected the thinking of the man in charge.

Charles Koch traveled to Pine Bend, and when he arrived, he entered the refinery compound quietly. The media did not report his presence, and it appears that none of the picketers outside knew he was there.

Koch walked the grounds with Bernard Paulson and saw for himself the toll that the strike had taken. The refinery looked like a disaster site. Equipment was being run far past the required time for maintenance. The staff was minimal. Provisions were sparse. And the OCAW was not going to give up its fight.

It might have seemed unreasonable for Koch to ask Paulson to continue this fight. Paulson and his team were risking their lives each night of the strike. The refinery's previous owners, including Fred Koch, would almost certainly have surrendered and headed back to the negotiating table.

But Paulson didn't want to back down. And Paulson saw that Charles Koch didn't want to back down, either. Koch and Paulson retired to Paulson's office, which now resembled the quarters of a field general. Near Paulson's desk was the cot where he slept most nights, the telephone always nearby. The two men sat down, and together they worked through a new budget for the refinery. With pen and paper, they sketched out new projections of revenue and production for the year.

After the crash, Bernard Paulson went back to the negotiating table with the OCAW. His position had not softened, but the union's had. When Paulson sat down at the table, there was somebody missing: Hammerschmidt had been replaced by the OCAW's new local president, a man named John Kujawa. Paulson felt that Kujawa was more reasonable than Hammerschmidt had been; he was less militant, more likely to listen to Paulson's demands.

Roughly one week after the diesel train sabotage, Kujawa and Paulson began a bargaining session, overseen by a Minnesota judge who acted as a mediator. The session went on for six days. The major point of contention was not money or benefits, but work rules at the refinery. Paulson was insistent that Koch be given more control over the operations, while Kujawa and his team fought to maintain the rights the union had bargained for over the last twenty years.

At noon on March 26, the talks ended with no agreement.

On the night of April 17, an OCAW man was driving near the refinery when he pulled over to the side of the road and removed a hunting rifle from his car.

He took aim at the electrical substation of the refinery, a large patch of electrical transformers and wires that was essentially a miniature power plant that kept electricity flowing through the plant. The man opened fire. He sent several armor-piercing bullets into the substation. One of the slugs penetrated a large transformer, which began leaking oil from its punctured hull. Employees in the refinery heard the shots, and knew quickly what they were. They called police, and a witness described the parked car where they believed the shots were coming from. The rifleman got back in his car and drove away. Police soon pulled him over because he was driving erratically and appeared to be drunk. The rifle was in the backseat, and he was arrested.

On June 2, 1973, John Kujawa traveled to Washington, DC, to testify before Congress. A joint House and Senate committee was investigating national fuel shortages, and part of the inquiry examined the supply disruptions in Minnesota caused by the strike at Pine Bend. Almost six months into the strike, it appeared that Koch and the OCAW were no closer to an agreement than they were when the strike began.

Kujawa and Paulson continued to meet even though neither seemed to have faith in the process. Paulson even flew to Washington to meet with Kujawa and his team of OCAW negotiators. The two camps met at the US Department of Labor, and during their session, the US secretary of labor himself came into the room to talk with the opposing negotiators. The secretary's message was clear: "Let's work this thing out."

During the negotiations, Koch's team and the union's team were sent to separate conference rooms. A mediator shuttled back and forth between the rooms passing demands and counterdemands back and forth. The sessions went on through the night. At one point, Paulson laid down on a conference table and fell asleep while waiting for the courier to return from the OCAW's room.

It was useless. Even prodding from the labor secretary could not push the two sides to an agreement. The kernel of the dispute still remained the work rules at the refinery. It was a fight over control, and neither side would budge.

Koch Refining Company offered a $25,000 reward for information leading to the arrest of whoever had sent the diesel train crashing into the plant. But the money never induced anyone to come forth with information about the diesel engine sabotage. The reward was never collected, and an arrest was never made. And the picket line remained outside the refinery even as the employees entered their seventh month without a paycheck from Koch.

But Bernard Paulson and Charles Koch seemed to understand something intuitively. They understood that solidarity had its limits. The OCAW's cohesion was unbreakable. But the OCAW would be weaker if it stood alone. In fact, it was doubtful if the OCAW would be able to stand at all if it was alone. Isolating the union would prove to be the only way to beat it. During the summer and fall of 1973, that's exactly what happened.

At that time, Paulson needed to perform maintenance at the refinery and install new equipment. The repairs could be delayed no more. But the companies in Minnesota that could do the specialized work were largely unionized, and they would not cross the picket line to do the job. Paulson had faced this problem before, during his days in Texas. When he ran the refinery there, he often hired both union and nonunion companies to do maintenance work at the facility. During one project, Paulson had two companies—one unionized and the other nonunion—working at the refinery simultaneously. The unionized firm said it would walk off the job unless the nonunion firm agreed to let its workers organize. It was a high-pressure ultimatum, and Paulson responded by calling the union president personally.

"I knew him. I knew he'd come from Oklahoma. So I got him on the phone. I said, 'You damn Oklahoma squirrel hunter,'" Paulson recalled. "I said: 'Look. You go ahead with what you're trying to do, and I will only do one of these units at a time. I will do it nonunion, and you union guys won't even be in the plan.' So he backed down from that."

Now, in Minnesota, Paulson used a similar tactic. He let the local maintenance and repair companies know that he needed work to be done at Pine Bend, which was the state's largest refinery and an important source of work. He also let the companies know that if they refused to do this work now, when he needed it, then he would never call them again. If they refused, Koch would only use nonunion maintenance companies in the future.

The outside unions buckled. They accepted the work Paulson was offering them. Paulson built a special entrance into the refinery for these companies, one far away from the main picket line out front. The work began, and the OCAW picket line was weakened that much more.

Next, Paulson put a wedge between the Teamsters union, which handled trucking and shipping at the refinery, and the OCAW. The Teamsters still refused to cross the picket line, so Paulson arranged a cunning system that allowed the Teamsters to work with Koch Refining anyway. Paulson used a small parking lot near the refinery as a transit point. The Teamsters pulled into the lot and got out of their trucks. Nonunion truck drivers who worked for Koch Oil in the South were waiting for them there, and as the Teamsters got out of their trucks, the Koch Oil drivers got in. The Koch Oil drivers then took the trucks down the road and into the refinery, past the gauntlet of the picket line where men beat on the truck windows and threw their jacks beneath the wheels. Thanks to this arrangement, the Teamsters did business with Koch without technically violating the picket line. The oil was flowing in, the gasoline was flowing out, and support for the OCAW was ebbing away by the day.

John Kujawa, the OCAW president, did not talk about work when he got home. His wife, Martha Ann, knew very little about the negotiations he was leading with Koch Refining. John often spent the weekends and evenings drinking with his friends. When he was home, he was silent.

But Martha Ann could see the tension building in him. He was in turmoil inside. His drinking was intense.

Kujawa was in an impossible position. If he pushed for an agreement to end the strike, he would be labeled a traitor or a sellout. If he failed to

meet Koch's demands, or at least some of them, the employees he represented might never get their jobs back.

Then Bernard Paulson dropped a bombshell on Kujawa during their
negotiations. Paulson said that he was prepared to break an unwritten
agreement that refinery owners had long honored: he was prepared to
hire in nonunion replacement workers. It was exceedingly rare for any
company to make such a move, which violated all principles of collective
bargaining. Doing so would alienate Koch Refining from any unionized
worker it dealt with in Minnesota. And it would effectively destroy the
OCAW local 6-662.

As August turned to September, Kujawa began pressing his union to
end the strike. But working with his own union members was almost as
difficult as working with Paulson. Martha Ann Kujawa said internal tensions were so heated that she believed her husband might be in danger.
John never confided in her what was going on, but she saw things that
concerned her.

"I was looking out the window of the duplex that we lived in and he
was being followed home by somebody. And they were threatening him.
He was walking on the sidewalk and he started speeding up and came
to the house quickly. And I thought that was strange," she recalled. "I
wouldn't even be a bit surprised if his life was in danger."

By September 15, Kujawa had helped the union come to a tentative
agreement with Koch. The agreement caved to many of Koch's demands,
but the union leaders argued that it was the best deal the members could
get after nine months of being on strike.

On the evening of September 17, the OCAW workers gathered in a
junior high school near the oil refinery. They were presented with the
contract that Kujawa had negotiated. It was time for them to vote on
it, time to decide whether they were willing to end the strike and move
on. Kujawa pointed out that pay and benefits were not even the primary
issues in the negotiations. The main dispute was over how much control Koch's management would have over the employees. The members
voted to reject the contract, 149 to 103.

After the vote, Paulson gave the Teamsters an ultimatum: "Either you
guys start coming across [the picket line], or we are going to go non-

union with all of our deliveries. Even after this strike is over," he remembers telling them. The Teamsters came around to Paulson's rationale. In mid-September they drove across the picket line. In doing so, they broke the back of the OCAW. Even decades later, feelings were raw about that betrayal. Lowell Payton, an OCAW man who stood for months out on the picket line, was still bitter decades later when he recalled watching the Teamster-driven trucks roll past the picket line. "Teamsters are no better than an egg-sucking dog," Payton said.

On the evening of September 23, the OCAW gathered again at the junior high school to vote on the contract. They voted this time to accept the contract, by at least 140 to 100.* The contract would last sixteen months, only seven months longer than the strike itself.

Paulson felt that the OCAW had no choice but to agree to it. "They could see they were, you know, losing everything," he said.

OCAW workers like Ernie Tromberg and Joe Quinn were shocked when they returned to the refinery. The place was in terrible shape. Most of the OCAW men who went back to work remember the massive overtime payments they received as they worked long days to get the refining equipment back into good working order.

But many of the employees did not come back. The bitterness ran too deep. Tromberg said that Koch lost many of its best engineers and operators after the strike; the people who knew the Pine Bend facility most intimately. Kujawa later lost his reelection bid to be president. Joe Quinn replaced him.

Paulson retained his job as head of the plant, and he said that each new union president was more "reasonable" than the last. The days of Joseph Hammerschmidt were over. The union members knew who was truly in charge, and they knew that Charles Koch would not back down to demands as his predecessors had done.

The OCAW agreed to significant changes in its relationship with Koch Refining. The work shuttle that ferried employees around was gone. A new rule imposed mandatory overtime, meaning that a manager could simply tell a shift worker that he must stay and work late, or come

---

* At least one news report put the tally at 144 to 100.

in on a Saturday, rather than request those extra hours from him.* The work rules of old, which required that workers of certain "trades" could only work on the tasks that fit their skills, were jettisoned.

The grievance process, by which employees could appeal their boss's decision, was defanged. There would be no more cash payments if an employee won a grievance fight. There would be no more checks like the one that Joe Quinn received to compensate for lost wages or other penalties. Instead, if an employee won a grievance fight, he or she would be allotted enough overtime work to cover the amount they were owed—in other words, if an employee won a grievance, he earned the right only to work extra hours to earn back the money Koch owed him.

Employees at the Pine Bend refinery remain unionized to this day.† But the strike of 1973 broke the union's power. This fit into a pattern that was being played out across the United States between 1973 and 1993. Unions disbanded and broke apart. Solidarity became an artifact. The remaining unions became something like a shadow human resources department. They offered employment services like health insurance and credit union membership, but they seldom went on strike for better wages or working conditions.

Charles Koch won the labor battle at Pine Bend. In doing so, he took greater control over an asset that would become the fountainhead of profits for his company.

Decades later, former Koch Industries executives would refer to the Pine Bend refinery with a sense of admiration, and almost awe. Virtually all of them would use the term "cash cow" when describing the facility. The years would prove that Charles Koch was remarkably insightful—or remarkably lucky—when he purchased Pine Bend in 1969. In the 1960s,

---

* This rule cut both ways for the union. While it reduced the freedom of workers to set their own schedule, the majority of them seemed to approve of the mandatory overtime provision. There is a culture of working long shifts at the refinery, and employees enjoyed the pay bumps that overtime brought them. Most of the labor disputes about overtime at the refinery revolved around who got it and did not, rather than how much overtime work was required.

† The OCAW eventually merged with the larger United Steelworkers union, which currently represents the employees.

the refinery had profited in part by exploiting a loophole in US oil pro-grams, but even after those loopholes were closed, the refinery was in a prime position.* It was one of the few refineries in the United States that had access to a special form of Canadian oil that was very cheap, and it sold the gasoline it made into a retail market that was particularly expen-sive. Charles Koch was able to exploit this opportunity to the fullest.

But in 1973, after beating the OCAW, Charles Koch didn't have any time to celebrate.

On September 24, the St. Paul *Pioneer Press* carried a story on the front page with the headline "Employees End Koch Strike." But just a few weeks later, on November 26, that same newspaper carried a head-line that was much larger. That headline read: "Nixon Asks [for] Wide Energy Power."

For Charles Koch, the true age of volatility had just arrived.

---

* The refinery had once benefited from a special importing arrangement with Canada, outlined in the previous chapter.

CHAPTER 4

The Age of Volatility Intensifies

(1973–1975)

Within a matter of months after the OCAW strike ended, Charles Koch found himself sitting on the edge of a large hole on his family's estate in Wichita, a pit that was meant to be the foundation of a new home he was building for himself and his new wife, Liz, a local woman whose family owned a chain of department stores. But construction might have to be suspended because he feared he was running out of money. Koch Industries was suffering huge losses because of decisions he had made, and he worried the company might go out of business. "I was worried that if the company went under, this house would take me under as well," Charles Koch later wrote. He had won control over the Pine Bend refinery, only to be blindsided by market forces outside his command.

The trouble started on October 6, 1973, when Egypt and Syria launched a surprise military attack against Israel. The United States assisted Israel in its defense, causing Arab nations to retaliate in a novel way. The oil-rich nations banned oil exports to the United States entirely, while also cutting overall production by 5 percent. In every ensuing month, the Arab nations would cut an additional 5 percent of production.

It was not obvious at first just how catastrophic this retaliation would be. Up until that point, Americans had felt secure in their abundance of oil. The 1960s were the era of the all-American gusher, but the age of abundance was about to end. American demand for fossil fuels had been slowly outstripping domestic supplies. In 1968, the oil economy pivoted from surplus into scarcity as oil drilling outpaced oil supplies for the first time, by 0.07 percent. American oil drillers were essentially operating with the pedal to the metal and still were not able to entirely meet growing demand. Oil imports nearly tripled between 1967 and 1973. With US demand for imports so strong, there was virtually no cushion of extra oil supplies on global markets to help absorb a shock to supplies. The Arab embargo kept about 4.4 million barrels of oil a day off the market: 9 percent of the total supply. For the first time in its history, the United States could not make up for the loss.

The shock was unprecedented. Gasoline prices, which had hovered along at the same level year after year for decades, spiked. In some markets, crude oil prices jumped from $5.40 a barrel to $17 a barrel—a 600 percent increase in a matter of weeks. There were shortages and long lines at gas stations that were open for limited hours if they were open at all. Fist fights broke out, black market auctioneers sold gasoline at exorbitant prices, and people hoarded gas when they could find it.

The price shock caused a calamity inside Koch Industries. Charles Koch had been quietly expanding a profitable segment of the company, a shipping division that carried crude oil on oceangoing tankers. Strong demand for US oil imports created a small boom for oil tankers, and Koch Industries signed leases to carry crude around the world. The money was so good that Charles Koch decided to make a giant bet on the business by building a "supertanker" of his own. He named it after his mother, Mary R. Koch, then in her midsixties. What Charles Koch didn't realize was that he was making a giant, one-directional bet on the future of oil imports. When production plummeted, the bet left him exposed. The shipping market was plagued by crippling excess capacity, almost overnight. The value of the *Mary R. Koch* plunged, and Koch was obligated to money-losing shipping leases.

The mid-1970s were a period of economic crisis for both Koch Industries and the United States. The years of inflation, recession, and energy shocks transformed America's political and economic landscapes. This period also shaped Koch Industries. In response to the crisis, Charles Koch began to transform the company into an institution that was built for the new era of volatility. The changes made during this time laid foundations for Koch Industries that remained in place for decades. Charles Koch aimed to build a corporation that would not only survive the brutal swings of the marketplace, but profit from them. He built a company that learned constantly from the world around it and prized information discovery above almost everything. It was a company that embraced change and hated permanence, one where every division would be up for sale all the time. He built a structure with centralized control—which emanated from his boardroom—but that also gave managers and employees a remarkable level of freedom. He fused the sophisticated management techniques he learned as a consultant in Boston with the folk wisdom of his mentor Sterling Varner and the free-market religion of thinkers like Hayek and von Mises. Also during this time, Charles Koch built a political action network that he operated in tandem with Koch Industries' business, creating a public influence operation that was arguably unique in the history of corporate America.

Even in the face of a downturn, Charles Koch invested heavily in Pine Bend to ensure its long-term profitability. But investing money alone wasn't at the heart of Koch's efforts to transform Pine Bend. The effort would not be built on cash—it would be built on information. In the face of unprecedented market volatility, Charles Koch and his team adopted a strategy that would inform Koch Industries for decades. It relied on deep analysis and information gathering. Charles Koch couldn't control the market's violent ups and downs, but by understanding them better, he could beat his competitors.

Once again, Charles Koch turned to Bernard Paulson to help carry out the new plan.

Bernard Paulson moved to Wichita shortly after he ended the OCAW strike at Pine Bend. He was promoted to vice president over all of Koch's refinery operations, a role that let him work closely with Charles Koch and Sterling Varner.

Paulson, like other Koch executives, found himself studying information systems just as much as he studied the oil business itself. Accordingly, the first step that Paulson took to revolutionize the Pine Bend refinery was to learn more about the refinery itself.

Paulson began running tests on each unit at the refinery. Every unit served a particular purpose. One unit, for example, was a giant tower that processed crude oil into gasoline. By-products from that unit might get sent through a pipe to another unit that would process those by-products into different fuels. One unit turned some of the most unusable by-products into asphalt. Paulson tested each one by running them under different conditions—running them eight hours a day instead of sixteen, for example. Or he tested them by burning different types of feedstock in them. Then he closely measured the results.

By doing this, Paulson built a new database—a roadmap that let him know exactly how each unit operated while it processed different types of oil or when run for different lengths of time at various levels of intensity. This taught Paulson more about the inner workings of Pine Bend than anyone had known before. He knew when the machines would operate at their most efficient and when they would lag. He became familiar with the inevitable trade-offs that resulted from running one unit longer than another or choosing a different feedstock.

Then Paulson started learning more about the raw fuels that were flowing into Pine Bend to be refined. He began running tests, called assays, on the oil that Pine Bend was buying. Paulson wasn't satisfied with the assays that the unionized workers were running on the oil, so he formed a team in Wichita and moved the testing there. Inside the Wichita laboratories, engineers ran Pine Bend's feedstocks through a battery of assays that peeled away the component parts of each fuel for examination. With this information, Paulson developed a microscopic understanding of each fuel that flowed into Pine Bend's units.

Paulson turned to Koch's sales and marketing team. He told them to learn everything they could about the markets where Pine Bend sold its products. They learned the prices of different fuels at different depots during different times of the year. The marketing team learned the prices of asphalt, which Pine Bend produced, and the prices of Canadian crude oil, which Pine Bend purchased. All of these numbers were compiled into a new and massive data set that showed the complex financial environment that surrounded Pine Bend, the chaotic push and pull of supply and demand for the variety of products that the refinery could make.

This information allowed Paulson to abandon the hunches and guesswork that were often used to run an oil refinery. Now he had a team that could predict with remarkable reliability just how profitable the Pine Bend refinery would be when it processed any given combination of feedstocks and sold them to any given combination of customers.

There was one major obstacle to using this information: the tests and surveys produced far more data than could be processed by any person, or even a team of people. To solve that problem, Paulson used an unlikely tool: he used a computer. This was far more innovative than it might sound decades later. In 1974, computers were still the stuff of myth. NASA was known during the 1960s to have used a supercomputing machine to send astronauts into space. Photos of the high-tech equipment were awe inspiring. Computers were enormous installations that filled many rooms; the machines stood in rows like giant refrigerators with glass doors, holding reels of tape inside of them that processed information at unimaginable speeds. Some computers still used punch cards to make their tabulations.

Paulson had used some of these machines back in Texas, when he worked for the Coastal refinery. He had been experimenting then with the idea of using the computers to produce marketing models and forecasts to help operate the plant. But those models had only been done on a month-by-month basis. Paulson wanted the models to be much larger. He wanted to feed information in and come up with models for each quarter of the year: data sets that would let Paulson know exactly what fuels he should be producing and exactly where he should be selling them.

Varner, an oil-field man more familiar with the world of roughnecks and drilling rigs than with NASA scientists, wasn't impressed with Paulson's plan. "Sterling says, 'Oh, we don't need that,'" Paulson recalled. "I didn't listen. I kept doing it."

Charles Koch quickly grasped the potential that computers held. The company installed several IBM computers in Wichita. Paulson perfected his models and before long he was using them to manage operations at Pine Bend at a granular level of detail. As the computer models improved operations, Charles Koch invested more money in the plant, expanding its capacity, and Koch's share of the market increased steadily.

The management of Pine Bend was smart, even innovative beyond its time, but the biggest source of profits at the refinery did not have to do with computer models or marketing teams. Pine Bend became a gold mine mostly because of geography, and because of a bottleneck in oil markets. Because of its location in northern Minnesota, virtually all of the oil processed at Pine Bend was imported from Canada. Canadian oil was very different from most of the oil refined in the United States. Canadian crude was "sour," meaning it contained very high amounts of sulfur. Sulfur is a contaminant that has to be processed out of the oil to make gasoline—a process that is both difficult and expensive. The sulfur is stripped out in a giant tower called a coker, and the process leaves behind a thick residue that cakes up on the walls and must be scraped out. The residue is used to make asphalt and other products.

Oil that was drilled in Texas or Saudi Arabia, by contrast, was known as "sweet" crude because it had very low sulfur content. This made it a lot cheaper and easier to process—you didn't need coker towers to take the sulfur out. So many of America's oil refineries sprang up around the Gulf Coast because that's where sweet crude was imported and processed.

Very few firms wanted to install the kind of expensive equipment that ran at Pine Bend, but Great Northern had done so. When Paulson took over, Pine Bend was one of very fewer buyers in the upper Midwest that offered to buy Canadian crude. Because there were so few buyers, the Canadian crude piled up—there was an excess of supply. This meant that prices dropped. Koch could buy the sour oil at a price that was significantly lower than oil prices elsewhere in the United States.

But the cheap Canadian crude was only half of the equation. When Koch turned around to sell the gasoline it made at Pine Bend, it sold that gasoline into a midwestern region where there were very few other refineries, causing supplies to be relatively tight and prices high. This made the economics of Pine Bend almost too good to be true. The refinery bought cheap oil that few people wanted, refined it, and then sold the gasoline into scarce markets where demand and prices were high.

Paulson surveyed the market and saw one large competitor. There was a pipeline company called Williams Brothers, which shipped about a hundred thousand barrels of gasoline into the Minnesota area each day. Paulson knew that it cost about 6 cents per gallon to ship the gas from the Gulf Coast, where most American refineries were located. This meant that Koch had a 6-cent advantage over Williams Brothers that it could exploit. "I said, 'We can expand. And we can dry up Williams Brothers,'" Paulson recalled.

The strategy worked. Smaller refineries throughout the upper Midwest went out of business, and Koch Refining Company steadily swallowed their market share. Williams Brothers eventually reversed its pipeline flow, moving new supplies of oil from the upper Midwest into other markets.

In just less than a decade, Charles Koch had transformed the Pine Bend refinery into a perpetual profit machine. Virtually nobody outside

Minnesota even knew that there were major oil refineries in the state, a fact that was true even decades later when Koch Industries became a well-known firm. But the refinery played a pivotal role in making Koch Industries one of the largest and most profitable companies in the world. Pine Bend was "the cash cow, really, that provided the early money for Charles to expand in other areas," Paulson said.

Koch Industries' own confidential financial documents show just how important Pine Bend was for the company's fortunes. In 1981, Koch Industries had at least thirty-two major divisions, and the Pine Bend refinery was by far the most profitable. It netted $60.9 million in pure profit after taxes. That was 22 percent of all Koch's profits that year. (The company earned $273.6 million after taxes.)

The second-most profitable division was Koch Oil: the network of pipelines, barges, and trucks that Koch used to gather and ship oil across the country; the network that relied on the Koch method of measurement to ensure that the company was rarely if ever under when it came to gathering oil. Koch Oil reported $30.98 million in profits for the year—roughly half of what was earned on a single refining facility, covering just seven hundred acres, in Rosemount, Minnesota.

By 1982, the numbers from Pine Bend were even better. Koch Industries cleared $107.8 million in profits. That was more than one-third of Koch's entire profits for the year, of $309.2 million.

Of course, it wasn't the Koch Industries way to brag about such accomplishments. When it came to making money, secrecy was prized above all else. Bernard Paulson was often contacted by outside business consultants who offered to help him run Koch's refineries. These were reputable men whom Paulson knew well, and he knew that there was good reason to hire them and borrow their expertise. But hiring them would have required Paulson to show them how Koch operated. Paulson would have to show them around the banks of computers inside the Wichita headquarters. He would have to share the computer models and explain how they were created. For this reason, Paulson always turned the consultants away. "I didn't want people to know what we were doing," he explained. "Because we did have a method that was, I thought, unique."

Information analysis was only part of the strategy that helped Koch Industries thrive in a volatile world. Charles Koch also redesigned his company's management practices and financial systems. He wanted a management team that wasn't resistant to change, and could act as a shock absorber for future market upheavals. One witness to this transformation was a new hire at Koch, a finance expert named F. Lynn Markel. He would eventually reach the highest levels of leadership at Koch Industries. But back in the mid-1970s, Markel was working for a smaller company in Wichita that ran a chain of television stations. One of his friends from church, named Bill Hanna, asked Markel if he'd be interested in working for Koch. Markel agreed to meet him for lunch at the Wichita Country Club.

When Markel arrived at the club, Hanna wasn't alone. He was seated at a table with a very tall man. When Markel approached, Hanna introduced his companion: it was Sterling Varner, the president of Koch Industries. Markel did his best not to act flustered. It seemed that a casual lunch to talk about a potential job offer had just turned into a job interview with the president of the company. But within a few moments of sitting down, Markel discovered that he didn't need to be flustered at all. Varner naturally put him at ease. Varner must have recognized quickly that Markel was exactly the kind of person that Charles Koch was searching for to fill the corporate ranks. If there is a single example of the prototypical Koch employee, it was Lynn Markel. He was born and raised on a farm outside of Dodge City, Kansas, so he was accustomed to a seven-day workweek. He attended Kansas State University and had no illusions that a college degree conferred on him anything more than the right to work hard for a living. After graduating, he became an officer in the US Air Force, where he served for four years, so he learned to think of himself as part of a larger organization and put the needs of his teammates before his own. Markel had moved to Wichita right after his stint in the air force to work as a financial controller with the Cessna Aircraft Company. Working for a large, publicly traded firm hadn't agreed with Markel. There was a lot of bureaucracy to contend with; he wanted to be more entrepreneurial. He left Cessna and joined a large real estate firm that was expanding rapidly. But that firm went bust, and Markel landed in his current job as chief financial officer for the chain of television stations.

After their lunch, Varner invited Markel to Koch Industries headquarters for more interviews. Markel was sitting in his first interview with one of Koch's top accountants when a slim man with blue eyes opened the door and leaned into the room. The man apologized for the interruption and introduced himself: he was Charles Koch, the company's CEO.

Charles Koch told Markel that he was sorry that he wouldn't be able to interview him in person that day because he was caught up in other business. Markel was stunned. He didn't expect to meet the CEO during a job interview, much less have the CEO apologizing to him. That just wasn't how big companies worked. There were supposed to be several layers of bureaucracy between the CEO and most employees. The CEO was the figurehead you saw at Christmas parties. He wasn't the guy who interviewed you for the job.

The next day, Markel returned to Koch headquarters and was escorted to the second floor, where he was shown into Charles Koch's office.

Koch was wearing a coat and tie, which Markel would soon learn was the official dress code of Koch's senior management. Markel sat down for the interview, and he very quickly discovered that Charles Koch did not have Sterling Varner's warmth and charisma. Koch was more somber, more analytical in the way he asked questions. But this wasn't to say that Koch was cold—he didn't talk down to Markel or interrogate him. Koch's demeanor was friendly, but the questions were unrelenting. Koch zeroed in on Markel's job at the real estate firm. The company had failed, and Koch wanted to know why. Markel explained that the company had expanded rapidly, fueled by debt. But then it was ruined by the very forces that were slamming against Koch Industries every day: an unexpected spike in interest rates hit the firm at a terrible time, making its debt more expensive just when sales were falling.

Koch cut to the heart of the matter.

"He asked me, 'So, if you had so much responsibility over finances at the company, why did you go broke?'" Markel recalled.

Koch's intellect left little room for evasion. His questions made it clear that he could not easily be fooled by accounting jargon, and he wasn't interested in excuses. Markel gave the most honest answer that he could: the firm had been taken down by overheated ambition and a lack of foresight. The ambition led to the huge debt, and the lack of foresight made that debt fatal when the interest rates jumped.

The interview was long, and some of the questions were very sharp. When Markel left the Koch Industries campus that day, he was certain of one fact: he wanted to work for Charles Koch.

Markel was hired as the assistant controller over Koch's oil division. Just over a year later, he was promoted to be controller over the entire corporation. It was a job that gave him a bird's-eye view of all financial transactions at the company and how Charles Koch handled them.

Like many other people at the company, Markel was struck by just how fluid, how adaptable, things were at Koch. There were about two hundred people in the company headquarters, and more were being added every day. It was a big company by Wichita standards, but it didn't feel like a big company. It felt like an ongoing experiment. Roles changed quickly. New hires were brought in. There wasn't a bureaucracy to stifle people or hold back new ideas.

One of the thorniest problems that Markel dealt with was the issue of budgets. It was common practice for each division in a company to set a budget for the year (and sometimes for each quarter) and then to measure how it did against that budget. That was simply the way things were done in corporate America, but the outside world was refusing to cooperate with standard operating procedure. For the first time in history, the price of oil was liable to drop by half in a period of a few months or to unexpectedly double in the same period.

"Frequently, within the first quarter, the budget for the rest of the year was almost worthless," Markel recalled. In spite of this reality, Koch managers still spent a large portion of their time between July and December tabulating and writing up budgets, and the managers expected that their performance would be measured against those budgets.

Many of these employees, like Markel, came from publicly traded firms where the quarterly budget was considered a holy document. Publicly traded firms must report their profits to Wall Street every three months, and a bad report could send shares of the company stock falling. Writing budgets gives companies a way to predict what their quarterly performance might be, and they can telegraph the expectations to investors. In this way, everything inside the business starts to revolve around the budget. Managers figure out how much they are going to spend and how much they are going to earn, and they share the information publicly. Then they would spend the year trying to hit the budget targets.

Because Koch Industries was not publicly traded, it didn't have to transmit its profit expectations to anybody.

Markel sat in on many meetings in the small cluster of offices surrounding Charles Koch's office on the second floor, an area that was the hub for executive decision-making. Markel and others were trying to puzzle out how they could get more precise budget figures when the market veered so wildly from one month to the next. One of the executives in those meetings was a young man named Paul Brooks. He was a former Exxon employee with an engineer's grasp of complicated problems. But Brooks also had a creative streak that hadn't been fully utilized in Exxon's rigid culture, and he quickly became a close confidant of Charles Koch's. During one meeting on budgets, Markel was surprised when Brooks made a simple proposal: "Why not do away with them?"

Charles Koch loved the idea, and so did Markel. Getting rid of budgets would instantly dispose of hours' worth of drudgery that defined a financial controller's life. Koch invented a new set of metrics to replace budgets. And the numbers that the company focused upon were telling. Charles Koch didn't care much about sales or costs—he cared about profits. He wanted to know how profitable any line of business was and how profitable it could be under the right management. He steered all of his managers to think this way. The key thing they needed to focus on was the return on investment, or ROI—what was the best use of Koch Industries' money?

Soon each division was writing a profit *goal* for the quarter, rather than a budget. Sales, costs, and prices could veer wildly, but what mattered was whether a division hit its profit goal for the year. And Charles Koch was thinking in terms of years, not quarters. This was critical for a company in a highly volatile business. A graph showing Koch's sales and costs and the price of oil might spike and dip violently from week to week. But Charles Koch was only interested in whether the return on investment climbed steadily over the years. "You didn't know what the exact trajectory was going to be. But you knew it was up, and to the right," Markel recalled.

To keep things moving up and to the right, Charles Koch had an unwavering philosophy about debt. He was rigid in his belief that debt should be kept as low as possible so that interest payments didn't eat up Koch's cash. The reasons for this were strategic. Every downturn brought opportunities for companies that were prepared. Downturns weakened competitors and made them ripe for takeover. Downturns made assets cheaper to buy. For this reason, Markel and his team were discouraged from borrowing large sums even if banks were more than willing to lend it.

"It was really based upon kind of looking forward to opportunities," Markel recalled. "The reason you like to build up cash and not have a lot of debt is so that you can capture opportunities that you couldn't capture if you were fully loaded in debt and had no cash."

The economic ups and downs would begin to play to Koch's advantage. "When the value of assets out there in the economy hit a low point, that's the best time to buy. It's pretty simple economics," Markel said.

Koch made full use of this strategy. It began to profit from market downturns by snapping up its competitors. This was most evident in Koch's giant oil gathering and pipelines division. Roger Williams, the vice president over pipelines, oversaw an expansion funded by the cash that Charles Koch was pouring back into the company. Koch's pipeline network grew from six thousand miles of pipe when Williams joined in 1969 to roughly fourteen thousand miles by 1976. The company purchased some of the pipe from other firms, and it built between seven thousand and eight thousand miles of new pipeline on its own. This expansion helped make Koch the single largest purchaser of crude oil in the United States by the 1980s.

Even as Charles Koch streamlined his own organization and reduced debt, he operated in a political and economic world that was moving in the opposite direction. Every industry in which Koch operated was becoming subject to new and onerous regulations, price caps, and government controls emanating from Washington, DC. Charles Koch had always been something of a political dissident, espousing views that were outside mainstream politics. But during the early 1970s, his views hardened and prompted him to take action.

During this time, Koch came to embrace a concept that was embedded in the philosophy of thinkers like Hayek and von Mises, but that was rare in the thinking of corporate CEOs. He realized that there were not two separate spheres of American life: the public sphere of government action and the private sphere of business enterprise. Instead, there was only one tangled web of a nation's political economy, the deeply inter-

laced workings of government policy and corporate structures. One intimately affected the other.

This reality was painfully apparent in the oil business. Government
intervention affected every aspect of the industry. And the intervention
reached its peak as Charles Koch was building his company.

On November 7, 1973, shortly after the Arab oil embargo, President Richard Nixon proposed a sweeping government response. The government
would cut the "allocations" of heating oil for homes and businesses by
15 percent, essentially rationing the vital fuel. Nixon said utility companies would be banned from switching from coal to oil as a fuel source.
He would ask Americans to turn down their thermostats by about six
degrees. He would ask Congress to pass a bill that would lower the
national speed limit to fifty miles per hour, curtail the hours that shopping malls could be open, and impose other rationing measures.

"It will be essential for all of us to live and work in lower temperatures," Nixon said during a televised speech. "Incidentally, my doctor
tells me that in a temperature of sixty-six to sixty-eight degrees, you're
really more healthy than when it's seventy-five to seventy-eight, if that's
any comfort."

It might seem odd that a conservative Republican president would
impose price controls and energy rationing, but Nixon's actions reflected
the settled beliefs of American political life in the early 1970s. There was
a broad consensus in America that could be called "the New Deal Consensus," tracing back to the 1930s, when Franklin Roosevelt created a new
regulatory regime. The New Deal reshaped everything in America's business world. It replaced unfettered markets with price controls in some
cases. It gave unions very strong protections that helped workers organize. And, maybe most important, the New Deal convinced Americans
that the federal government should play a large and interventionist role
in the economy. It was loathsome to acolytes of Hayek and von Mises.

FDR's actions were a response to decades of economic stagnation,
when the government largely refrained from regulating markets and
large corporations; an era that was defined by the laissez-faire, or hands-
off, approach to regulation. During that time, the economy was dominated by a new breed of large corporations whose operations crossed

state lines and transcended the control of state-based regulators. The federal government, the only entity powerful enough to constrain the companies, declined to do so on the theory that it would harm economic growth. The government was also constrained by a conservative US Supreme Court, which struck down regulatory efforts after a seminal decision known as the Lochner ruling. In 1905, the court ruled against New York state regulators who tried to penalize a bakery owner named Joseph Lochner. The state wanted Lochner's employees to work no more than ten hours a day. He argued that the regulation violated the Fourteenth Amendment of the US Constitution, which was passed to protect the rights of newly freed slaves. Lochner said that the Fourteenth Amendment also protected his right, and his employees' right, to enter into whatever kind of labor contract they wanted to. The Lochner ruling hobbled lawmakers and ushered in an era of business-friendly legal decisions. During the Lochner era, the court would strike down minimum-wage laws, federal child labor laws, banking and insurance regulations, and transportation laws. The Lochner era was a time of great prosperity in America, but the prosperity wasn't widely shared. There was a tremendous concentration of economic power. A handful of robber barons, like John D. Rockefeller and Cornelius Vanderbilt, amassed huge fortunes, while the people who worked to produce those fortunes—the farmers, weavers, oil rig workers, and others—lived in poverty.

When FDR was elected in 1932, in the depths of the Great Depression, the hands-off era came to an end. Roosevelt, and the Democratic-controlled Congress that worked closely with him, created large-scale assistance and work programs to help employees who'd lost their jobs. They created regulatory agencies to oversee the stock market and prohibited banks from speculating with depositors' money. They established Social Security, or "old age insurance," the precursor of Medicare. They passed the Wagner Act, which empowered labor unions, passed a minimum-wage law, and established the forty-hour workweek. The role of activist government was cemented in American life and would only deepen over the next thirty years.

Even Republicans like Richard Nixon were compelled to intervene. Nixon signed bills to create the Environmental Protection Agency, founded in 1970, and the Occupational Safety and Health Administration, or OSHA, founded in 1971. He signed the Clean Air Act and the

Clean Water Act into law, two pieces of sweeping legislation that would regulate huge portions of the US economy.

Government intervention affected the oil industry as much or more than any other. A complex web of price caps and regulations were put on Koch Industries, and they seemed to confirm every belief that Charles Koch had adopted from Hayek. A new task force in Washington, called the Cost of Living Council, tried to set the price of oil and control markets from a central office. The result was a byzantine mess that hindered companies like Koch Industries and did little to solve the underlying crisis. The Cost of Living Council created an intricate pricing system that split the oil supply into three classes: "old" oil, "new" oil, and "stripper" oil.* The old oil was oil already in production when the price caps hit, and most of it was controlled by oil majors like Exxon. New oil was any oil drilled after the price caps were put into place.

The council put a hard cap on old oil of $5.25 per barrel but let the price of new oil float in an open market, where supply and demand played a role. Predictably, new oil was generally a lot more expensive. This put a major squeeze on independent oil refineries like Koch Industries, which bought oil on the open market rather than drilling it themselves. Big companies like Exxon drilled their own oil and refused to sell it because of the price cap, suffocating markets.

To solve *that* problem, the Federal Energy Administration passed a law that effectively banned the oil majors from holding on to their old crude. The FEA ordered the sale of fifty-six million barrels of oil. And this was all just one program, meant to control oil prices. Other complex schemes controlled natural gas prices and the pipeline industry.

This incensed Charles Koch. He called the Republican Party "bankrupt" for its unwillingness to challenge the New Deal philosophy and its inability to dismantle its political structures. Koch wrote a fund-raising letter for the tiny Libertarian Party in 1975, saying that Republican efforts to regulate markets caused him to have "abandoned them in disgust." Republicans were "no better allies in the fight for free enterprise than the Democratic Party," Koch wrote.

With the Republicans on the sidelines, Charles Koch set out to dismantle the system himself. For years, he had been dabbling in political

---

* "Stripper" oil is drawn from a well nearing the end of its productive life.

philosophy. He owned a small bookstore in Wichita that sold conservative literature. He attended and gave money to the Freedom School in Colorado Springs, which taught courses in Austrian economic philosophy. In the 1970s, Charles Koch took his efforts a step further. He unveiled a plan in 1974 that didn't become widely known for decades, after he had been executing it with remarkable discipline from the CEO's suite at Koch Industries.

In April of 1974, Charles Koch gave a speech at a gathering in Dallas held by a conservative think tank that he'd cofounded, called the Institute for Humane Studies. When Charles Koch addressed the group, his tone was belligerent, even caustic.

"Anticapitalist feelings in the United States are probably more virulent today than ever before," he began. While many CEOs were grumbling about the burden of regulations, Charles Koch chastised his fellow business leaders as being insufficiently loyal to the principles of capitalism. It was a mistake to even characterize America's economy as capitalistic, he said. Koch chastised the business community for having been seduced by the thinking behind the New Deal.

"To date, business has attempted to defend itself by taking a conciliatory attitude rather than exposing the fallacies in the anti-capitalist arguments. For example, when the oil industry and others are criticized for having 'excess' profits, businessmen should argue that in a free market there is no such thing as excess profit—that without high profits there would be no signal to invest more capital in order to increase production to meet the consumer demand that created the profits," he said.

Koch attacked the entire narrative behind the New Deal, claiming that Roosevelt's legislation was not, in fact, in response to a lack of federal-level regulation. Koch said that when the New Deal was passed, the economy was already "polluted by massive governmental manipulations of the money supply."

He said that businesses needed to fight back, and not on the terms that were laid out for them by their opponents. The business community needed to wage a long-term campaign that would change the way Americans thought about the markets and the role of government. Koch said that the campaign should have four elements:

1) Education
2) Media outreach
3) Litigation
4) Political influence

For education, Charles Koch said that business leaders needed to populate public universities with academics who would advocate for free enterprise and do research to support it.

When it came to the media, Koch said that businesses should "appropriately 'reward' the media when they promote the free market and withdraw support when they attack it."

In terms of litigation, Koch suggested that corporations should "announce publicly and vigorously, both as individual companies and through associations, that they will not cooperate with the government beyond the legally compelled minimum in developing or complying with control programs."

For political action, Koch recommended lobbying and "litigation to affect bureaucratic behavior." But when it came to influencing Washington, he sounded a note of caution. He said that engaging with the government tends to corrupt businesspeople, tempting them to game the system through lobbying that delivers profit by hijacking public policy. He said this temptation ultimately undercuts businesses by making them look hypocritical—their support for free markets must be pure if it was to be followed. Therefore, lobbying should be a "limited program," he said.

Charles Koch would remain remarkably true to this basic game plan over the next forty years. The only part that would change significantly would be the "limited" nature of lobbying and campaign contributions. Koch would eventually build one of the largest lobbying and political influence machines in US history. But the rest of the plan was executed almost exactly as he laid it out in 1974.

But as Koch pointed out in his speech, such a plan took time. Its progress would be measured by decades rather than years. And Charles Koch didn't want to wait decades to see results. There was one arena where he could implement changes; one venue where he had near-total control. There was one institution that he could transform into a laboratory where he could test the theories of von Mises and Hayek. This institution would become Charles Koch's privately controlled free-market utopia.

The institution was called Koch Industries.

By 1975, it was clear that Koch Industries was not going to go under. Income from the oil gathering operations and the Pine Bend refinery helped offset losses in the shipping division. Charles and Liz Koch finished construction on their house and began to raise a family there.

After the crisis passed, Charles Koch focused on cementing the gains he had made during his first eight years as CEO. While most companies paid dividends to shareholders, Charles Koch insisted on plowing profits back into the company to fund its expansion. He also worked hard to cement Koch Industries' growth strategy in the minds of his managers and employees. Every year, Charles Koch held an award ceremony in Wichita to recognize employees who had done an outstanding job. One year, he singled out Bernard Paulson.

Standing before the gathering of his brain trust, Charles Koch recited a long list of Paulson's accomplishments: the expansions, the market analysis, the new investments that steadily won Koch more market share. Paulson later said that it was embarrassing to be lauded before his peers, but there was clearly some part of him that enjoyed it.

Charles Koch seemed to be praising Paulson to convey one lesson: Paulson had treated the Pine Bend refinery like it was his own company. Paulson didn't act like an employee; he acted like a small-business owner. Paulson thought for himself, and he treated Koch Industries' money as if it were his own. And Paulson shared in the glory once it was realized.

"He pointed out, 'This is entrepreneurial,'" Paulson recalled. "He said that's what he wanted the entire company to do. To be entrepreneurs."

To a remarkable extent, this lesson was successfully pushed out into the furthest branches of a rapidly expanding Koch Industries, from senior managers like Lynn Markel in finance, to Bernard Paulson, to the lower-level employees like oil gaugers and refinery workers. Employees at all levels of Koch were made to feel like small-business owners. They never owned actual shares of stock in Koch Industries—ownership was reserved for the Koch family and a few small shareholders. But employees *felt* like they owned a piece of Koch Industries. Charles Koch gave them performance-based bonuses and issued them "shadow stock" contracts that paid out as the company's value increased, but that didn't confer actual ownership. The real shares of Koch Industires were tighly held by Charles and David Koch, and a small group of relatives and associates.

The vast majority of employees embraced this culture. They were inspired by Charles Koch's vision.

But there was one exception. And that exception was arguably the most consequential employee that was ever hired under Charles Koch.

The exception was Charles's younger brother, Bill.

CHAPTER 5

The War for Koch Industries

(1980–1983)

Bill Koch became a full-time Koch Industries employee in 1975, at the age of thirty-five. He spent his early years in one of the company's murkiest but most important divisions: Bill Koch came up through the trading business.

Koch's trading division was enmeshed in an industry that managed to touch virtually every American while managing to remain almost entirely invisible. The operations had their roots in Koch's shipping and oil gathering business, where the company became a broker and middleman for crude oil and gasoline products. During the 1970s, Koch expanded its operations, buying and selling oil as a go-between for companies like Exxon and Chevron. These were specialized markets where only a few companies could operate; a trader needed lots of cash, expertise, and access to oil tankers and pipelines. As Koch's traders developed expertise, they branched out and traded commodities that were never priced on an open exchange. A single transaction might yield $1 million or more in profits without ever being recorded with a paper contract. One of these markets was for industrial chemicals that most people couldn't pronounce but that they used every day. Polyvinyl chloride, for example, is used in food packaging and bottles. But the markets to buy PVC were just as confusing and opaque as its chemical formula. The deals were too specialized for open exchanges, and they were often done one-on-one, confidentially, over the phone. Bill Koch was largely responsible for getting Koch Industries into the chemical trading business. It was a business that would become an integral part of the company.

Bill came across chemical trading shortly after he graduated from MIT. He was living in Boston and looking for new companies that Koch Industries could buy with the massive amounts of cash the company was generating. In his search for new investments, Bill Koch stumbled across a chemical trader named Herbert Roskind, who ran what was basically a one-man chemical trading firm called Monocel.

As a trader, Roskind was one of the few middlemen in the global market for industrial chemicals. He sold barges full of sulfur made in Louisiana to factories in Asia that needed it as an ingredient in their manufacturing plants. Roskind spent much of his day in an office in suburban Boston, working the phones to call contacts in Europe or Singapore or Houston, finding people who wanted to buy and sell giant quantities of things like chlorine, caustic soda, polyethylene, and polyvinyl chloride.

Roskind's business was a murky one, built on a network of personal relationships and deep knowledge that only he held. People like Herbert Roskind were vital to the market: rather than having a transparent market exchange, the buyers and sellers had Roskind's brain. He knew who was in the market at any given time; he knew what the demand was for polyvinyl chloride; and he knew what a fair price would be. (Of course, whether a trader like Roskind actually *quoted* the fair price to a customer depended on just how informed that customer happened to be about the market himself.) He had a Rolodex that spanned the globe and a body of knowledge that was integral to success in trading. He knew the habits of customs agents in different countries and knew which shippers could be trusted and which couldn't. He had an almost encyclopedic knowledge of global shipping rates. He knew the negotiation customs of different cultures and different nations, and he was adept at navigating dark markets—where prices were never posted publicly, where prices always came down to one-on-one negotiations.

Bill Koch was fascinated with the possibilities offered by the chemical trading business. Its prospects seemed a lot better than the oil business during the 1970s. The oil markets were jumping up and down, but chemical prices were rising steadily as nations like China opened their doors to global trade, causing demand for industrial chemicals to climb dramatically. Bill Koch arranged a meeting with Roskind, and soon he proposed to buy Roskind's company outright.

Roskind didn't know what to make of Bill Koch the first time he met him. Bill Koch was dressed like a college kid. He looked, in fact, like he was still attending classes at MIT. Everything about him reflected the

MIT style, which might be called Privileged Chic. Koch wore slacks and a button-down shirt, but no jacket or tie. He wore leather loafers with no socks. He drove an old Toyota that had a hole in the floor of the front passenger seat.

Bill Koch's pitch was simple. Koch Industries would buy out Roskind's company and create a new chemical trading company inside Koch Industries, with Roskind as its head. He would get a 20 percent ownership stake in the trading company, and Koch would invest money to make the firm much larger. Roskind would be able to open a new office, hire more traders, and do more business than he'd ever done before.

Roskind went to Wichita to iron out the details, and that's where he met Bill Koch's older brother, Charles. Charles Koch ate with Roskind at the Koch Industries cafeteria and discussed the deal. The differences between Charles and Bill were stark. Charles wore a coat and tie. There was not even a hint of carefree campus life about him. He had an engineer's mind and an engineer's demeanor. Charles drove an older car, too, but there wasn't a hole in the floor. Charles was low-key, but his ambitions were apparent. Roskind asked Charles Koch how his company was doing, and he remembers Koch saying: "Well, we're the second-largest privately held company in America. . . . We'll be going to the first largest if we can do it," Roskind recalled.

"I thought that was a pretty good answer," Roskind said. He agreed to become part of Koch Industries.

Roskind quickly opened an office, hired traders, and installed a telex machine that could send written messages instantly to almost anywhere in the world. His new division was called Koch International Trading Company, and it did not operate a single production facility. It didn't make a pound of sulfur or chlorine, but instead it arranged deals for the transfer of countless tons of commodities.

Bill Koch called Roskind and told him that he wanted a job. He wanted to be a chemical trader. Roskind had his doubts.

"I said, 'Well, Bill, I'll be honest with you,'" Roskind recalled. "I know you have a PhD in chemistry, but we need a PhD in chemical *trading*. And they don't offer those. You'd be welcome to work with us, but I'm going to have to treat you like I treat almost everybody else. And that is, I have to pay you a modest salary and see how well you do."

Roskind pointed out that in the trading business, volatility had its upside. Bill Koch's salary might be low, but just one or two good trades might easily double or triple his pay. A trader's income swung wildly, but the payoffs could be enormous.

Bill Koch's answer was immediate. "I'll take it."

Roskind's office opened at eight thirty in the morning, and the trading began almost immediately. Roskind often arrived early, but the other employees drifted into work, and most of them were not seated and ready to go until around nine. One morning, Roskind was alone in the office at eighty thirty when the phones began ringing. He went from desk to desk, answering the calls because he didn't want to miss a potential deal or give his customers the idea that nobody was home. In the chemical trading business, where written contracts were rare, reputation meant everything. A phone ringing with no answer sent the wrong message.

Later that morning, Roskind called all his employees into the office, including Bill Koch. He tore into them.

"I said, 'I want to tell you something: this office opens at eight thirty. That doesn't mean you walk in at eight thirty. That means you're ready to do business at eight thirty. You're at your desks and you're doing business at eight thirty! Don't be late again.'"

The employees filed out of his office and got back to work. About an hour later, Roskind's phone rang. The call was from Wichita. It was Charles Koch.

Roskind's first thought was that his short career at Koch Industries was now finished. He had just chewed out his boss's little brother. Charles Koch's first words affirmed his fears.

"He says, 'I understand you publicly humiliated my brother,'" Roskind said.

"I said, 'Well, I didn't mean to. I had a meeting of the entire staff, and I laid down the law about how this company was going to be run. And your brother was part of the staff.'"

Charles Koch's response was chilling: "You know, no one's ever talked like that to a Koch."

"I said, 'Well, Charles, I'm really sorry that that's upset you.'"

Then Charles told him: "It's about time someone did that."

Bill Koch was a very fast learner. He sought out Roskind's advice, and once he heard the advice, he followed it. Bill Koch also had one of the most important skills a trader needed: he was very good at dealing with people. Bill Koch was not warm or charming, but he was an expert at listening. He quickly absorbed what the client wanted—and what the client was willing to give up to get it.

Roskind taught Bill Koch that trading was about one thing. "The idea of trading is to take what we have and get what we want," he said. Roskind's metaphor was that the trader begins his day with pennies, and he ends his day with a sirloin steak. Bill Koch was able to turn pennies into sirloin not just because he listened closely to his clients, but because he had the keen mind of an engineer. He saw commodities markets as a complex game board with several dimensions, and he was able to triangulate between the needs of people scattered around the globe, making them meet in a way that produced a profit.

Chemical trading wasn't a simple matter of buying low and selling high. One of Bill Koch's more successful trades shows just how complicated the business could be. Roskind and Bill Koch heard from clients that there was very strong demand in East Asia for a chemical called acetic acid, which was in tight supply. The companies that made acetic acid were aware of the supply crunch, and they were not about to let go of their product easily. This made it almost impossible to buy acetic acid at a price that would make it profitable to turn around and sell it in Asia. But a good trader knows what is happening simultaneously in different markets. Bill Koch knew that the companies that made acetic acid often used corn as a feedstock for the product. Bill Koch also knew how to get corn at a cheap price on the futures market in Chicago. So Koch Trading bought corn on the futures market and bartered it with acetic acid manufacturers for large quantities of their product. Then they sold the acetic acid at a much higher price in Asia.

Roskind said he made $1 million off that single trade. Charles Koch called him personally to express surprise that a single deal could be worth so much.

"I said. 'I'm sorry we couldn't make more,'" Roskind told him.

Like all senior executives at Koch Industries, Bill Koch and Herbert Roskind often traveled to Wichita to provide updates on their business division to Charles Koch. These quarterly meetings were also attended by
a small coterie of executives like Sterling Varner and Bernard Paulson.
Roskind enjoyed being around Charles Koch—it was impressive to see
this tremendously wealthy man eating in the company cafeteria with the
rest of the employees.

Yet Roskind noticed that his traveling companion wasn't enjoying
himself nearly so much. Bill Koch resisted going to Wichita.

When Bill was at company headquarters, he was tense. And it was easy
to spot the source of his irritation: there was something about Charles that
put Bill Koch on edge. Just being in the same room with Charles seemed to
darken his mood. Roskind didn't understand why Charles Koch irritated
his little brother so much. Charles wasn't domineering. His demeanor
was placid; his tone was always cordial. Charles Koch didn't insult people
and didn't pound his fist on the desk. But even Charles's smallest comments caused an oversized reaction in Bill.

"I didn't fully understand what the tensions were," Roskind said. "It
never was over money, I don't believe."

After his successes in the chemical trading division, Bill Koch got a promotion. Or, because of how things worked at Koch Industries, it's more
appropriate to say that Bill Koch was promoted by his older brother,
Charles.

Bill Koch was made vice president of a new division called Koch Carbon, which was typical of the kinds of businesses that Charles Koch and
Sterling Varner liked to pursue: it pushed the company into new territory and new markets by building on what Koch already knew. Koch
Carbon was branching out into the coal mining and processing industries, which built on Koch's knowledge of the fossil fuel business. As head
of the division, Bill Koch would have been encouraged to act like Bernard Paulson or Roger Williams: as an entrepreneur in charge of his own
business.

Bill Koch did this, but in his own way. He built a staff in Wichita,
many of them originally hired by Charles. One of Bill's staffers was a
young finance guy named Brad Hall, who was a prototypical Koch man,

cut from the same mold as Lynn Markel. Brad Hall had been an athlete in college, played baseball at Wichita State University, and knew how to be part of a team. He had the kind of humility that was so deeply baked into his character that he didn't even know he was humble. He was one of those middle-class kids from Wichita who intuitively knew that the world didn't owe them a thing. Hall was also startlingly intelligent—he had the neural processing ability of a skilled engineer and a methodical approach to problem solving. He was a natural acolyte of Charles Koch's, in other words. But shortly after he was hired, Hall was informed he would not be working for Charles. He would report directly to Bill and would help him build up the carbon division.

Bill Koch became enamored of the kind of data-driven analysis that Bernard Paulson relied on to run the Pine Bend refinery. But Bill's version of data analysis borrowed more from the erudite traditions of MIT and the Ivy League than it did from the oil fields of the Midwest. Shortly after they started working together, Bill Koch sent Brad Hall an article that he'd read in the *Harvard Business Review*. The article outlined a computer technique that ran a probability analysis on the internal rate of return for potential deals. The model used something called a Monte Carlo simulation to figure out what the rate of return might be in light of a number of variable factors, like different overhead costs. Bill Koch asked Hall to do a Monte Carlo simulation on a major coal industry deal they were exploring.

Brad Hall's task was overwhelming. He borrowed time on the mainframe computer that took up a large room in the basement of Koch Industries headquarters. The computer used punch cards that had to be individually tailored to each specific model run in each simulation. Initially, Koch's computer engineers punched the cards, but the simulation required so many cards that they just let Hall start punching the cards himself. His small office became overcrowded with punch cards. Hall pushed himself hard to meet Bill Koch's deadline, running simulation after simulation. He came into the office one Sunday morning, skipping church and leaving his family at home so he could work away at the punch cards. Hall knew it wasn't unusual for Charles Koch to work on Sundays and call in other employees to join him. But Bill Koch wasn't at the office when Hall arrived and Bill Koch didn't show up while Hall worked through the day, punching cards and running simulations.

Early in the afternoon, Bill Koch called the office to check in on Hall's progress. Hall began explaining to him how the simulations were going, but Bill kept interrupting him, shouting, "*Ah! . . . Ah!*" Hall couldn't figure out what was going on, and he asked Bill if something was wrong.

Bill replied, "I'm watching this Patriots football game," Hall recalled. After they hung up, Hall returned to the basement to keep running simulations while Bill Koch enjoyed the game.

Hall finished the Monte Carlo simulations and prepared a presentation on the findings for Charles Koch and Sterling Varner. Bill Koch made it clear that he wanted to impress Sterling and Charles, so Hall rushed to a special store in downtown Wichita that rendered his findings onto color slides that could be shown from an overhead projector during the presentation. In the 1970s, this was high technology.

Hall meticulously arranged the presentation and the overhead projector in the boardroom at Koch headquarters. He was still a new hire, and it was thrilling for him to be in the same room as Charles Koch. He was proud of the work he'd done. The computer simulations were extremely complex, and he'd spent hours memorizing his findings so he'd be ready for any questions.

When the meeting started, Sterling Varner and Charles Koch sat down and Bill Koch began the presentation with a brief overview. Then Brad Hall went through the slides, laying out the extensive analysis he'd done on Koch's mainframe computers.

Hall was only a few minutes into the presentation when Sterling Varner interrupted him.

Varner said, "Billy, I know that you and Brad understand all this fancy stuff and everything. I know Brad's done all these calculations. And that's great. But I just want to know: Is this a good deal?" Hall recalled.

Hall was frozen in place.

Is this a good deal? That statement would reverberate in his head many decades later. "It's like somebody hit me with a sledgehammer," he said. He called the statement "classic Sterling." It cut to the quick and exposed how flawed Hall's presentation really was. Brad Hall realized in an instant that he'd gotten lost in the minutiae of his analysis without thinking about the broader strategy that should have been behind it.

He had a thousand computer runs to tell him what the internal rate of return might be under various conditions. But he couldn't present any critical analysis about why the deal might be a good idea over the next decade, or why Koch Industries more than any other company was the right company to do the deal.

"I had no idea what I was doing. I was all tied up in these details and everything. And there's this whole other spectrum of strategy" that Varner employed when considering a deal, Hall said.

Almost right away, Charles Koch began asking questions about other competitors in the business and the marginal suppliers in the industry. They were strategic questions, and they cut to the bone.

For Brad Hall, these questions cemented one realization. Hall knew whom he wanted to work for, and that person was not Bill Koch.

The message could not have been lost on Bill Koch himself.

Like all vice presidents at Koch Industries, Bill Koch had to periodically answer a battery of probing questions from Charles that evaluated how well he was doing. But Bill was different from other executives in one vital way: he owned a big chunk of stock in the company.

Charles, Bill, and David had very large numbers of shares, each son with roughly a 20 percent share of the company that had been left to them by their father. Their older brother, Frederick, also had shares, even though he wasn't involved in operations. J. Howard Marshall II, the former co-owner of the Pine Bend refinery, owned another large piece of the company. Marshall gave some of these shares to his son, J. Howard Marshall III. There was a smattering of other small shareholders, including cousins from Fred Koch's side of the family who were simply referred to as the "other Kochs."

Being a major stockowner complicated Bill Koch's standing with Charles.

As a vice president, Bill reported to Charles. But as a major shareholder, he was, in many ways, Charles's equal. As Bill Koch spent more time at the company, he started to focus more on his role as a shareholder—the one role in which he could contend with Charles on equal footing.

Bill's stock gave him a seat on a special executive committee of the board of directors, a committee that included only himself, Charles, and David, with Sterling Varner as an alternate. Starting in the late 1970s, Bill began to pursue his role on the executive committee aggressively. He peppered Charles Koch with questions about his decision-making and about the company's operations. Charles complied with Bill's questions and sent him reams of documents, only to find new requests were waiting behind them.

Bill's requests started to focus on one issue, and they started to take an accusatory tone. Why, Bill wondered, wasn't Charles reporting certain developments to the entire board of directors?

There was a problem at a Koch Industries office in Denver, for example. Employees there had been indicted for rigging a government lottery system used to disburse energy leases. Why hadn't Charles Koch told the board about this problem earlier, before the indictments were issued? Bill also asked about a pending US Department of Energy inquiry. The department was investigating several companies for possibly violating federal energy price controls. The alleged violations went back many years. The parameters of the investigation were unclear, but someone in Koch finance who studied the issue said that, theoretically, the government might demand as much as $1 billion to compensate for overcharges. Bill Koch asked Charles why he had not reported this fact to the board of directors. Wasn't a potential $1 billion fine worth reporting?

Charles said the $1 billion figure wasn't significant; it was just a theoretical data point. Nobody in the company seriously believed that a fine that large would be imposed. It simply wasn't worth reporting to the board.

Bill Koch was doing more than asking questions. Soon he was using his questions to tell a story to the company's board of directors. He painted a picture of his older brother as an autocrat, a "dictator" who ruled the family company with no tolerance for dissent and a penchant for secrecy. Bill even coined a nickname for his brother, "Prince Charles," and he began dropping it in conversations with coworkers. Charles became aware of the nickname, and did not seem amused.

Bill did more than subtly accuse Charles of wrongdoing. He began to openly challenge him. The biggest challenge that he pursued was against one of Charles Koch's most important business strategies: the use of dividends. Bill pointed out that dividends at Koch Industries were exceptionally low when compared with those of other companies. He argued that this punished Koch's shareholders, what few of them there were. The Koch brothers were tremendously wealthy, but that wealth existed mostly on paper; their access to their wealth was extremely limited. Bill wanted higher dividend payments—he wanted cash up front from his father's inheritance. He complained that he was "one of the wealthiest men in America," but still he had to borrow money to buy a house.

Charles Koch resisted Bill's challenges on every front. He dismissed the idea that Koch should pay higher dividends—he had already explained to the board of directors how dividend money could be put to better use by reinvesting it in the company. He also dismissed the idea that he was secretive and kept important information hidden from the board. He gave directors all the information they needed, he said, and didn't need to give them more.

On April 27, 1980, Charles Koch sent his youngest brother a handwritten note:

> *Dear Bill,*
>
> *What is the purpose of these attacks on me? I hear from all over the country that you're constantly criticizing me. Each of your recent reports to the board includes a slam at me. Even your memos to me are acerbic and accusatory. It seems to me that none of this serves any useful purpose; that, in fact, it is destructive, destructive to you and to the company. Whatever I've done to make you so bitter toward me is in the past. The best course for us both to follow now is to attempt to work together, if not in friendship, at least civilly and in mutual respect without the past suspicion and ill feeling. I, for my part, will do my best to accomplish this.*
>
> *Your brother,*
> *Charles*

Bill did not stop.

On June 12, 1980, he sent a memo to Charles that carried the title: "The Right of Directors to Be Informed on Substantive Issues That Could Affect the Company." It was a broadside against Charles and his leadership, implicitly accusing him of deception and abuse of power. But most importantly, the memo stabbed at the most sensitive nerve that the Koch brothers possessed. It suggested that their father, Fred, would be ashamed of Charles.

"The corporation's good name is dragged through the mud by one set of indictments [in the Denver case]. . . . The corporation's good name is threatened by more such actions," Bill Koch wrote in the memo. The corporation's good name, of course, was their father's good name. Bill implied that Charles was tarnishing it.

During the month of June, Charles recalled getting between six and ten similar memos from Bill. The younger brother was asking for more staff and more money that he could control for a new investment fund. He wanted more responsibility and a stronger voice.

When Bill recalled this period later in media interviews, his explanations for his behavior always quickly devolved into a bitter thicket of childhood resentments and tensions. In a lengthy interview with *Vanity Fair* magazine, Bill recalled a mother who was distant, a father who was severe and parsimonious with his affection, and an older brother, Charles, who was relentlessly manipulative, controlling, and a bully. All of it seemed to come gushing out of Bill in those memos during the summer of 1980. Charles appears to have seen it the same way: "Whatever I've done to make you so bitter toward me is in the past." He saw Bill's complaints over the business as a means for complaining about things that were deep-seated, personal, and largely irrational.

While Charles dismissed Bill's concerns, he also kept trying to sue for peace. Charles called Bill at the end of June and asked him again to stop the "emotional attacks." Bill told Charles that he wanted to have more access to him, more time to ask him questions and have his concerns addressed. Charles agreed to that, and remembers Bill saying that the attacks would stop.

If the attacks did stop, it was only for a few days. On July 3, Bill sent Charles a memo that ended their relationship forever and nearly split the company apart.

The memo was ten pages long, single-spaced. But one paragraph stood out.

"I'm not interested in a battle and would like to settle the problems between us," he wrote. "Since I'm not alone in these concerns, the failure to solve them, which can be done quite easily, will be destructive to everyone concerned. Indeed, if they are not solved, the company will probably have to be sold or taken public."

The company will probably have to be sold or taken public, Bill had written.

There was no going back after that.

In early July, Koch Industries held an emergency meeting of the board. Both Charles and Bill attended. Charles confronted each of Bill's accusations and defended himself. Bill told the board that shareholders, himself included, needed to get more cash out of the company than they were getting. The board agreed to take actions that might address Bill's concerns. Charles agreed to form a "liquidity committee" that would look at paying out more dividends. He also agreed to explore the idea of taking Koch public. Going public would not only entail selling ownership of the company to ordinary investors through Wall Street brokers— it almost certainly would mean that the Koch family would lose control of the firm. But by losing control, the Koch family and other shareholders would get a onetime windfall of at least hundreds of millions of dollars. Bill Koch would be a very rich man, and not just on paper. He would never need to borrow money to buy a house again.

Bill seemed satisfied with the deal. But he had seemed satisfied before. During the board meeting, Charles Koch told the directors that if the attacks from Bill did not stop, he would seek the authority to fire his younger brother.

For a while, the attacks did stop. During this time, Charles called Bill and made a proposition. He asked Bill if he would be the co-executor and trustee of Charles's two children if Charles and his wife, Liz, were both to die. If that happened, Bill and David would split authority for the kids. It was the ultimate expression of trust in Bill, and the kind of agreement that would seem to cement their tie as brothers again. Bill told Charles he "would be delighted."

What Bill did not know at the time was that Charles was working on a memo of his own. It was a long memo that Charles would deliver to the board of directors, and one that would bring about the end of Bill Koch's tenure at the family company.

This memo would not be sent immediately, in part because Bill's twin brother drew everybody's attention elsewhere.

Bill Koch never found a comfortable place for himself in Charles's shadow, but his twin, David, did. David Koch discovered that he had one crucial skill his older brother Charles lacked: he could tolerate being in the public eye.

Charles lived in Wichita, and he spent most of his days either at home or inside Koch Industries' secluded headquarters building. David made his home in New York City, where he attended galas and charity balls and developed the reputation as a rakish bachelor, dating one beautiful debutante after another. He became the public face of the company—to the degree that such a secretive company could have a public face.

Starting in 1980, David also became the public face of Koch Industries' political activity. He joined the US presidential campaign, running as the vice presidential candidate on the Libertarian Party ticket. In doing so, David became the public face of a battle that Charles Koch had long been fighting behind the scenes. In the preceding years, Charles had become a major financial backer and advisor to the Libertarian Party, exchanging letters with successive party chairmen who sought out his advice and support. Charles gave at least tens of thousands of dollars in donations to the party, using his own money and coordinating contributions from his mother and brother Bill. The Libertarian Party's national director, Chris Hocker, wrote Charles Koch a thank-you letter in 1978, saying, "Right now, of course, we'd be in terrible shape without your support." Charles Koch advised and even chastised Libertarian leaders over the years, telling Hocker that he didn't want his large campaign donations to create "false economics" for direct mail solicitation within the party. Perhaps for that reason, Charles Koch often specified how the money should be used.

The Libertarians were a relatively new and profoundly unpopular political party at this time. They made Republicans look like liberals, which is what drew Charles Koch to the cause. He wrote a Libertarian campaign letter in 1975 in which he said that he once supported Republicans but had "abandoned them with disgust." Only the Libertarians, Koch wrote, would fight the "rapidly increasing government control over all aspects of our lives." The campaign document was printed on Koch Industries letterhead, which seemed fitting. It was through his company that Charles Koch was most antagonized by the government. Richard Nixon's newly created EPA enforced a host of complicated new rules that were cleaning the nation's water and air supply. Another agency, OSHA, enforced an array of codes for workplace safety, a category that covered almost every kind of activity inside an oil refinery. The Department of Energy, meanwhile, continued to impose a complicated system of price controls while levying enormous fines on companies that violated the limits.

While this burden grew on Koch Industries, there were some signs of hope that the Libertarian Party might be able to do something about it. Public opinion was turning against government. Vietnam, Watergate, inflation, and economic recession had corroded public faith in the government's ability to solve big problems. Support for deregulation was growing, making it seem like the moment for America to try a more conservative approach to governance.

While Charles Koch continued his political work in the background, David Koch contacted the Libertarian Party and pitched himself to be their candidate for vice president in 1980. The Libertarian presidential candidate was Ed Clark, a popular Californian who won 5 percent of the vote for governor of that state in 1978, which was a remarkably high result for the party. David Koch suggested that he should be Clark's running mate. It appears that one of his chief qualifications for the job was his ability to bankroll it. David Koch's memo stated as much:

"So my proposal is basically as simple as this: as the vice presidential nominee of the Libertarian Party, I will contribute several hundred thousand dollars to the presidential campaign committee in order to ensure that our ideas and our presidential nominee receive as much media exposure as possible."

David Koch was given the vice presidential spot on the ticket. He had warned in the memo that he wouldn't be able to do much campaigning, but it appears that he enjoyed being in the spotlight once he was there. David Koch ended up visiting twenty-seven states, meeting with college students, voters, and activists who were interested in the Libertarian platform.

The Libertarian Party sought to abolish a vast set of government agencies and programs, including Medicare, Medicaid, Social Security (which would be made voluntary), the Department of Transportation (and "all government agencies concerned with transportation," including the Federal Aviation Administration, which oversees airplane safety), the Environmental Protection Agency, the Department of Energy, the Food and Drug Administration, and the Consumer Product Safety Commission. And this is just a partial list. The party also sought to privatize all roads and highways, to privatize all schools, to privatize all mail delivery. It sought to abolish personal and corporate income taxes and, eventually, the "repeal of all taxation."

While David Koch had promised to spend several hundred thousand dollars on the campaign, he ended up spending $2.1 million. The Libertarian Party received just over 1 percent of the vote in an election that put Ronald Reagan in the White House with a landslide.

It must have been disappointing for David Koch to spend so much of his own money, to travel to more than half the states in the country, and to have very little to show for it the morning after the election. But he didn't have time to reflect on this defeat or to step away from work and heal his wounds over his election loss.

Back in Wichita, the familial contest for power was about to explode.

While things appeared peaceful between Charles and Bill Koch during the final months before the 1980 presidential election, Charles Koch had been working on his long memo. Bill was still not aware of the memo, and Charles was planning to give it to the board of directors.

Charles wanted to share his thoughts on two issues that the board was considering: the idea that Koch Industries should pay higher dividends to its shareholders, and the complaints about how the company was being managed overall. Charles Koch's memo was a distillation of his corporate philosophy. As such, it was unyielding. To begin with, the CEO must have far-reaching authority:

"Being an opportunity-seeking company, it's imperative that our management structure be such that prompt decisions can be made," he wrote. "We simply can't function effectively if every business opportunity needs to have months of research and clearance through several tiers of committees. . . . [A]s long as I'm CEO, I'll resist any effort to impede our efficiency by the imposition of any such bureaucratic committee or board structures."

The memo made it clear that the best approach to dividends was Charles Koch's approach: to keep plowing profits and cash back into the company, where it could multiply faster than if it were pulled out. "Our short-term returns aren't going to be as high under this policy, but I believe that if we continue to have this kind of success, that long term, everyone's going to be better off," he wrote. If shareholders disagreed with this approach, Charles Koch offered to buy out their shares and send them on their way.

Charles Koch sent the memo to the directors on November 18. A week later, Charles met with Bill in his office to discuss the matter. Bill ambushed him with an idea: he wanted to call an emergency meeting of the board to immediately consider a "liquidity plan" for the company.

"I said, 'Bill, what? Why are you doing this?'" Charles recalled later during court testimony. Bill replied that "he needed to be a man; he needed to take charge." Charles told him, "If this is what you're determined to do, then we need a divorce. Because this—this isn't going to work."

By "divorce," Charles Koch meant a division of their assets and a separation as business partners. He wanted Bill to figure out what parts of the company he could take with him, and Charles and David would take the rest. Their differences were irreconcilable, and it was time to split up.

The meeting lasted only ten minutes. Bill left the office, and Charles left soon after. It was the end of the day, and as Charles was leaving the building, he noticed that Bill was inside Sterling Varner's office, talking over something in private.

The next day was the Wednesday before Thanksgiving. People were planning their holiday trips, including the company's top lawyer, Don Cordes, who was heading out to visit family in western Kansas for the long weekend.

Charles and Sterling Varner met to talk about Bill. Varner said that during their conversation the day before, Bill had given him three conditions that would entice him to drop his request for an emergency board meeting. Bill wanted to reestablish the executive board committee that included himself, Charles, and David; he wanted to run a large program to invest in new deals; and he wanted roughly $25 million out of the company.

Before he left town for vacation, Don Cordes got a call from Bill's lawyer. The attorney said that Bill was calling for an emergency meeting of the board after all, but he didn't plan to ask for anything drastic. Bill would use the meeting to request that two new directors be elected to the board, a move that would not change the balance of power. Neither Cordes nor Charles Koch was worried about it. Cordes decided to leave for Thanksgiving break.

The day after Thanksgiving, Charles got a call from David Koch. David had gone into the office that day and found a notice delivered to him about Bill's emergency board meeting. The meeting was not nearly as innocuous as had been described to Don Cordes. The purpose wasn't to elect two new directors—it was to fire the entire board and replace it with a new one. And the notice said something even more alarming: it was being sent not just on behalf of Bill Koch but also on behalf of the eldest brother, Frederick Koch, along with J. Howard Marshall III, who had inherited shares in the company from his father.

David and Charles immediately knew what was happening. These three shareholders, when acting together, would gain a slim majority of voting power on the board of directors if Bill had his way. If they replaced the entire board, they would win control of the company. The obvious goal would be to fire Charles Koch as CEO and find a replacement. Bill Koch would be a natural choice. It was clear that Bill had been working hard behind the scenes to arrange this surprise coup. But Bill made a critical mistake: he had given Charles time to respond.

Charles Koch boarded a private jet Thanksgiving weekend and flew to Houston. There he picked up his father's old business partner, J. Howard Marshall II, and Marshall's wife, Bettye. On Sunday night, they all boarded another private jet that took them to California.

Howard Marshall had been unaware of what his son was planning. He only learned of the plot on Saturday, when Charles had called him. Marshall hung up afterward and called his son. When he called Charles back, the elder Marshall confirmed Charles's worst suspicions: "Howard [the younger] is going to vote against me," Marshall said.

Charles asked Marshall what they should do. "He said, 'Well, there's one thing that Howard III understands, and that's money. And I'll go buy my stock back,'" Charles Koch recalled.

Howard III lived in Los Angeles. His father wanted to go there and meet with him personally to close a deal to buy back his son's stock. Charles agreed to fly to Houston and take the seventy-five-year-old Marshall to California himself.

Charles Koch and the Marshalls arrived in California on Sunday night. The next morning, Howard Marshall met with his son and agreed to buy back his stock for $8 million. The deal would move the voting shares back to the elder Marshall and back into the column supporting Charles Koch. It would effectively end Bill Koch's coup. Bill caught wind of the deal and offered $16 million for the shares, according to Howard Marshall II, but the son refused. He didn't want to break the deal he'd made with his father.

The next day, Charles and Howard Marshall went to the son's house to sign the paperwork on the stock sale. As they talked with Marshall III, the phone rang. It was one of Bill Koch's lawyers, calling for Charles.

Charles went into another room and took the call. The lawyer, Jim Linn, said that Bill Koch had called off his special meeting. Linn asked Charles Koch not to make a deal with "that foolish Marshall" kid. They should have a meeting instead to solve their differences.

Charles said he could not agree to that. He hung up and went back into the other room to close the deal. Eventually Marshall's son signed over his shares for $8 million. The coup attempt ended there, and so did Bill Koch's future with the family company.

When they were children, Bill Koch hit his twin brother David in the head with a polo mallet, leaving a permanent scar just behind David's eye. Later, Bill stabbed David Koch in the back with an African sword from their father's collection at the family compound, leaving another scar. David forgave his twin brother for both attacks. David Koch affectionately called his twin brother Billy, and when young Billy flew into rages as a child, David would act as a peacemaker between Billy and Charles. Now, David was put in a position where he would have to choose between them.

There was a board meeting on December 5, at which Bill Koch's failed coup attempt would be dealt with. Sterling Varner asked Bill Koch to resign from the company, and Bill Koch refused.

During the meeting, a motion was put forward to fire Bill Koch. When the votes were counted, the motion carried. Bill Koch's career at the family company was finished. David Koch abstained from the vote.

Although Bill Koch was terminated as an employee, he was still a major shareholder. He continued to use that leverage over Charles, agitating for the company to go public or be sold. During 1981 and 1982, Charles Koch was challenged on multiple fronts to choose one of the two options.

But going public would destroy the machine that Charles Koch had built. It would also mean that Charles Koch would lose control. Shareholders would have a vote. A new board of directors might have the power to fire him. Koch's business strategy revolved around rapid decision-making: managers brought a plan to Charles Koch and Sterling Varner, and they had the authority to approve it on the spot. Publicly traded firms had to take their shareholders into account, leading to the proliferation of the kinds of committees and review groups that Charles despised.

Charles pressed his case to the board and to the small group of share-holders, and his case was a convincing one. When Charles joined his father's company in 1961, the company had three hundred employees. It earned a profit of $3.5 million a year, and paid annual dividends of roughly $150,000. Twenty years later, Koch Industries earned $300 million in profits and had seven thousand employees. Even though dividends were a small share of profits, Koch still paid out $27.5 million in annual dividends because the profits were so high. That was a ninety-one-fold increase over the level paid when Fred Koch died. The company overall was worth $1.5 billion in 1982. It had been worth just 3 percent of that amount in 1967.

Charles Koch made the case to his directors and shareholders that if they stayed at his side, if they believed in his vision, the future would be just as strong.

Bill and Freddie Koch finally came to a resolution with Charles and David. Koch Industries would buy out Bill's and Fred's ownership stakes for more than $1 billion. This would finally sever the business ties between the bothers. Koch Industries borrowed $1.1 billion to finance the buyout. The massive loan cut against Charles Koch's distaste for debt, but it was an emergency measure necessary to expel Bill and regain control.

When it came time to close the deal, Charles Koch turned for help to Brad Hall, the young finance whiz who had helped Bill Koch manage the Koch Carbon division. Hall had since made it clear whom he'd rather be working for, and he was just beginning a career under Charles Koch that would last more than twenty years.

In 1983, Hall accompanied a Koch Industries lawyer on a flight to New York, where they met Bill Koch and his team of lawyers to close the settlement deal to buy out Bill's ownership. There was a festive atmosphere as the papers were signed. Bill Koch, after all, had just earned something in the neighborhood of $470 million. "They were having a big party and everything, and [Bill] wanted to have his picture taken with me," Hall recalled with a sad grin, shaking his head at the memory. "He told me to tell his brother that he still loved him."

About one year earlier, Bill had been fighting Charles for a deal that would have paid out $25 million if he stayed at the company. Now he had several times that amount. Bill was about to embark on a spending spree, describing himself as feeling like a child again. He bought opulent houses in the most exclusive beachfront communities. He bought a helicopter, fine art, and the world's finest wines.

Like his younger brother, Charles Koch had big plans for what he wanted to do with the family fortune.

CHAPTER 6

Koch University

(1983–1989)

In the early 1980s, after he was unfettered from his dissident brothers, Charles Koch began to reveal just what his management dreams would look like.

There was an auditorium at Koch Industries headquarters, and Charles Koch began to hold events there, filling the seats with between four hundred and five hundred of his most senior managers. Lynn Markel, Brad Hall, Bernard Paulson, and others would file into the room and take their seats. The events were not the typical corporate presentation; Charles didn't use the forum to talk about business operations or to hold some kind of pep rally. Instead, Charles Koch often sat in the audience himself, taking notes. The executives sitting near Charles Koch saw that this wasn't a business meeting—class was in session. In fact, they were attending the first seminars in a decades-long curriculum that would become the central work of Charles Koch's life. The curriculum outlined a specific and codified philosophy; an operator's manual that defined an immutable set of rules for creating prosperity. He would ultimately call this philosophy Market-Based Management. But in the beginning, the philosophy had no name. In the beginning, there were only the seminars in the company auditorium.

In the earliest sessions, Charles Koch invited outside speakers to address the crowd. He ran workshops on the Dale Carnegie theory of management that built on Carnegie's famous book *How to Win Friends and Influence People*. These classes focused on the art of management and productivity, and required managers to give short speeches to help them learn to communicate effectively.

The classes got more technical, and more strategic, over time.

Charles Koch invited one of the brightest young business consultants in the nation to speak in Wichita, a Harvard professor named Michael Porter. Porter published a book in 1980 called *Competitive Strategy* that offered a new framework for how to run a business. The book provided a detailed plan for companies to analyze the market in which they operated. Porter visited Koch Industries multiple times, accompanied by a team of consultants. The team helped Koch's managers look into their own business lines and apply Porter's ideas, using good data to figure out the best path toward boosting profits and growing. Porter helped Koch executives learn how to analyze their competitive advantage, analyze their competitors, and come up with the best plan to capitalize on the company's market position.

Then Charles Koch began to teach the classes himself. He led sessions with smaller class sizes, maybe a dozen or so senior managers. This intimate setting helped Charles Koch give more attention to each manager. But he wasn't content for his teachings to reach only the senior leaders. Charles Koch wanted to multiply his efforts. After they attended Charles Koch's lectures, executives like Markel were expected to return to their offices and repeat the lectures to their own employees—executives were even given pamphlets and slideshows to help them. In this way, Charles Koch's lectures were passed down through the chain of command, from his senior managers at headquarters out to the most remote branch offices. The managers who attended Charles Koch's seminars began to call them "Koch University."

Charles Koch wanted to ensure that every new employee learned how things were done at Koch Industries. He also wanted to ensure that the company culture could endure over time. Sterling Varner, for instance, was the father figure who guided Charles Koch after Fred Koch's death. Varner was the company's living library. But Varner was getting older and wouldn't be at the company forever. Charles Koch wanted to codify Varner's teachings before he left.

These teachings—the "classic Sterling" guidelines—were some of the key elements of Charles Koch's new philosophy. Opportunism was one: every employee needed to keep their eyes open for new deals on the horizon. Humility was another: "knowing what you know and what you don't know," as Brad Hall recalls it. Humility dictated that while it was important for Koch to expand, the company needed to expand into fields where it already had expertise. Strength would be built upon strength.

But in the early 1980s, Charles Koch's philosophy was just beginning to be incubated. He didn't have a fully formed set of guidelines to pass on to his managers. Instead, Charles Koch focused on the fully formed set of guidelines shaped by another man, a consultant named W. Edwards Deming. Charles Koch became fixated on Deming, and he set out to apply Deming's methods across Koch Industries.

W. Edwards Deming was not simply a business consultant. He was more like a guru. For many years, he remained an obscure thinker within the United States, but he had become a major figure in Japan, where Deming helped Japanese automakers improve their factory production and build some of the strongest manufacturing companies in the world. Like Charles Koch, Deming stood apart from the mainstream thinking of America's business community, and he wasn't afraid to speak his mind about it.

"Deming's passion was for making better products, or, more accurately, for creating a system that could make better products," the journalist David Halberstam wrote. Deming wanted to overhaul American management using mathematics. He was a quality control engineer at heart, and he thought that the manufacturing process could be improved only by using hard statistics. Deming taught companies to measure what they were doing, to analyze it, and then to improve it.

Deming's concept of continuous improvement was applied throughout Koch Industries, and the results were dramatic. One of the most successful students of continuous improvement was Phil Dubose, the oil gauger in Louisiana who had already mastered the Koch method of measuring oil. Dubose would eagerly absorb the lessons of Koch University. In doing so, he would see firsthand why Koch Industries became one of the largest companies in America even when most people had never heard of it.

After rising through the company ranks over the years, Dubose was promoted in 1982 to oversee Koch's marine operations around the Gulf of Mexico. This put Dubose in charge of a fleet of barges that went from terminal to terminal, collecting crude oil and then shipping it to refineries in Texas. Some of his barges even traveled north on the Mississippi River to Koch's refinery in Pine Bend, Minnesota.

Dubose was terrified by the promotion. There had been two previous managers of the marine unit, and both of them had failed to turn a profit. "If it failed again, I was going to go down with it," he recalled. Dubose was determined to make the shipping barges turn a profit. He knew he had one tool to help him do this: the charts of W. Edwards Deming.

The fleet Dubose oversaw initially consisted of five large barges. They each carried about 8,500 barrels of oil. Each barge had a skipper and crew who lived on the craft while it traveled from port to port. The first matter of business that Dubose focused on was keeping costs down. Fuel was the largest cost the barges incurred. Rather than let the skippers fuel up the ships when they wanted to, Dubose required them to call his office when they were running low on gas. Then he would call the local ports and find the best price for gas, sending the skipper to the best location. This helped cut costs right away.

The tools from Deming helped Dubose go even further. Of all the charts he learned to make, he found that by far the most useful was called a run chart. Even decades later, he'd talk about run charts as if he were discussing a cherished family pet. "The best chart out of all of them . . . is that old-fashioned run chart. It'll tell you where you've been and where you're going," he said.

A run chart broke down all the costs that a barge would incur. It had a separate category for each cost: groceries, fuel, maintenance, ship damage, and supplies. The run chart allowed you to track these costs as they shifted from month to month, letting you see "where you've been and where you're going." Dubose was taught to look for cost spikes. The reason was simple: you figured out what caused costs to spike, and you avoided it. Then you figured out what caused costs to fall, and you replicated it.

The critical part came next. Dubose printed run charts for each vessel and posted them in the skippers' cabins. Each skipper could then see for themselves where they were running up costs and where they were saving money. Dubose turned each skipper into his own manager. Skippers were free to make their own decisions based on the run chart. Then Dubose went further. He started tracking the profits and losses for each barge. This made each skipper a small-business owner and each barge a small business. The skipper had all the information he needed to boost profits and the freedom to act on that information. And Dubose had total visibility into his fleet; he knew which ships were losing money and which were making it.

"It got to the point where the boats were competing against each other. I was just sitting back like a big old Cheshire cat in a tree," Dubose said. Using data to drive changes at the level of each barge, Dubose boosted profits in the marine unit overall. His profit margin reached 33 percent. The trucking division, by contrast, was lucky to see a profit margin of 8 percent or 9 percent. As he boosted profits, Dubose was given more freedom and more resources. He added more ships, buying larger barges that could ship forty thousand barrels of oil at a time.

All the while, he was in contact with managers from Wichita. They helped him prepare his run charts, and they taught him other tricks from Deming. As he talked with more managers, Dubose learned that not everyone embraced the Deming formula. A lot of managers were accustomed to making decisions based on gut instinct. They thought the charts were just a gimmick. But as many Koch Industries employees would learn over the years, Charles Koch did not consider his guidance to be a gimmick. And following his guidance was not optional.

"Some of these poor rascals just couldn't embrace [Deming's] thing. They couldn't get their arms around it. . . . They'd just zigzag a line across with a bunch of numbers. The people who couldn't support that, well, most of them were let go," Dubose recalled.

The Koch University seminars were just the most visible aspect of his efforts to encode his company with a very specific culture. There were other elements of the culture that were being institutionalized behind closed doors.

One of the most important elements of Charles Koch's philosophy was the need to expand, the need to be opportunistic. Some of this was drawn from Sterling Varner, but there was also a part of it that came from Charles and from his view of the world. One of the key lessons that Charles Koch took from the Austrian economists von Mises and Hayek was that markets never stood still. The status quo never survived. Markets always build up and then tear down. It was an evolutionary process that never ended, and companies that tried to fight the process would only be devoured by the forces of change in the end. Charles Koch wanted his company to change and grow with the markets. He wanted Koch Industries to internalize the forces of change and exploit them rather than trying to fight them.

This desire was institutionalized in a small office down the hall from Charles Koch's suite. That's where he started the company's first development group. To lead the new group, Charles Koch turned to one of his brightest young lieutenants, Paul W. Brooks, the employee who had suggested simply jettisoning annual budgets. While Brooks's ideas might have seemed brash or even radical, he was no corporate swashbuckler. Brooks didn't come across as someone trying to impress people around him by parading his shining intellect. He was low-key and analytical and very much like Charles Koch in his deliberate approach to problems. Brooks was part of a small cadre of employees who came to Koch Industries from Exxon in the mid-1980s. Exxon approached the market with a certain hierarchical rigor; it was a company that believed in protocols and an engineer's approach to problems, disciplined and linear. During the 1980s, this approach failed to master the violent ups and downs of the oil business, and Exxon had to let a lot of its talent go, including Brooks. At Koch, Brooks found that he could still think like an engineer but inside an institution that was more flexible, adaptable, and entrepreneurial.

When he was put in charge of Koch's development group, Brooks was given one of the most important jobs at the company. The development group would be an acquisition machine. It would work full-time to identify new companies for Koch to buy and new deals in which to invest. The group would formalize Sterling Varner's instinct to scan the market for new opportunities. The development group was a central hub to which all Koch employees could send potential deals that they'd spotted. Senior managers in every division at Koch were taught to act like scouts in the marketplace, and when they found a deal that was large enough and promising enough, they passed it up the chain of command to the development group for approval. The development group then studied the idea from every angle before deciding how to proceed. The development group also came up with ideas of its own. Over time, executives in the group would undertake blue-sky studies that looked out ten or even twenty years on the horizon and identified new markets in which Koch might want to invest.

Koch's development group would become one of the largest, most effective deal-making machines in the United States. The group would come to embody modern American capitalism in the early twenty-first century, an era when private equity and hedge funds scoured the landscape in search of acquisitions. Charles Koch quietly built a private equity firm inside his offices in Wichita that would rival anything created on Wall Street. In the earliest days, in the 1980s, virtually nobody outside Koch Industries headquarters knew that the development group existed.

The development group made its first major deal in 1981. It came along thanks to Bernard Paulson, the head of oil refining. He had spotted an opportunity in part because of the computer models that he had perfected to help him run the Pine Bend refinery. The data helped Paulson determine exactly which units he should run, what products he should produce, and which markets he should sell into. The computer models gave Paulson a kind of X-ray vision into oil markets. Now, Paulson turned that vision outward, toward his competitors.

Koch Industries sold a lot of crude oil to a refinery owned by Sun Oil in Corpus Christi. But Koch didn't just collect money when it sold crude to Sun Oil. It also collected intelligence.

Bernard Paulson's team knew how much oil Sun was purchasing, and what kind of oil. Then he learned who Sun's customers were, and what those customers paid for Sun's product. Paulson began using his computer models to study the market that surrounded Sun Oil's refinery. He studied what equipment was inside the refinery and at what volume that equipment could process oil. He learned what products Sun was making and at what volumes. He learned where Sun was selling its products and at what price.

The Sun Oil refinery in Corpus Christi processed the same kind of "light crude" that most other refineries used.* Sun Oil did not have the type of coker towers that processed the heavy, sulfur-rich crudes refined at Pine Bend. This made the Corpus Christi refinery somewhat ordinary—it was doing the same thing that many refineries were doing along

---

* Light crude oil has a low viscosity and flows easily at room temperature. Heavy crude is more dense and doesn't flow as easily.

the Gulf Coast. It didn't have the same kind of competitive niche that Koch enjoyed in Pine Bend.

But Paulson saw something in Corpus Christi that even the refinery's owner did not seem to appreciate: he saw that a market opportunity was being wasted. The Sun Oil refinery had equipment that could process oil and turn it into a petrochemical called paraxylene (pronounced pair-uh-ZIE-lene). Paraxylene was one of those products that Koch Industries excelled at making and selling: it was obscure, difficult to produce, and used in one form or another by virtually everyone. Paraxylene was the raw material for synthetic fibers and materials like dimethyl-terephthalate acid and purified terephthalic acid. These chemicals, in turn, were used to make things like polyethylene terephthalate and saturated polyester polymers. Most people have never heard of these chemicals, but they are the building blocks for plastic containers, bottles, drapes, upholstery, clothing like polyester suits, electrical insulation, and photographic film. Paraxylene was something that everybody bought without knowing it. And demand for paraxylene was growing. There were ever-more types of synthetic clothing and an ever-increasing demand for plastic containers to hold drinks or household chemicals.

If Koch bought the Corpus Christi plant, Paulson realized, the acquisition would open up an entirely new market for the company: the market for paraxylene and other petrochemicals. And, true to Koch's philosophy, the market would be new but not entirely foreign. Koch knew the petrochemical business already. It could apply the expertise developed at Pine Bend to manufacturing paraxylene in Texas. On top of all of this, it appeared to Paulson and others that Sun Oil wasn't aware of the opportunity it was missing in Corpus Christi. Sun was making and selling paraxylene but not at nearly the levels that it could.

In September of 1981 Koch Industries paid $265 million in cash for the refinery, and Paulson immediately started expanding it. He more than doubled its paraxylene output. He bought a used hydrocracking tower from a refinery in Europe and had it shipped to Texas, bragging to Charles Koch that he bought the tower for 40 percent of what it would cost "off the shelf." Koch Industries became one of the largest paraxylene producers in the United States.

———

In 1987, Phil Dubose got the promotion of a lifetime. He went from running Koch's marine division and barges to overseeing a vast piece of Koch's pipeline and trucking infrastructure. Dubose's job title was transportation manager for the southeast division (division 5). He was responsible for all of Koch's transportation infrastructure in the southeast quadrant of the nation, a territory that stretched from Louisiana in the west to the Florida coast in the east, and all the way up to New York in the north. Inside this region, Dubose was responsible for the trucking operations, pipelines, and the marine tankers in the Gulf of Mexico. Several branch offices reported directly to him, each with its own superintendent. He spent a lot of time traveling to each office and consulting with the local teams.

"I lived in airports—God almighty! To this day, I still get an uncomfortable feeling about airports. I just lived in those things," Dubose said. "The thing I could never get over was eating by yourself. That was tough."

The machinery and supply chains that Dubose oversaw were exceedingly complicated. But the economic rules that he lived by remained relatively simple. The rules had not changed for him since he had been an oil gauger roving the backwaters of the bayou on a skiff back in the early 1970s. Dubose knew that his career still hinged on whether he was over or short. When he was an oil gauger, Dubose made sure he was over when he drained small oil tanks. Now he had to make sure he was over on a shipping network that covered many states.

The reasons for this had to do with the nature of the pipeline business. Koch made its money in the transportation business by moving oil, not just by selling it. The actual value of the oil in its pipeline was of secondary importance to Koch Industries. What really mattered was ensuring that the oil was moving. When the oil was moving, Koch was paid to collect it and to deliver it. This means that Koch was som what protected from the volatility in prices that continued to roil markets during the 1980s. During the mideighties, for example, a market crash sent many oil drillers out of business and depressed the economy of oil-rich places like Houston. But this volatility did not matter so much to Dubose. What mattered far more to him was being over. He wanted to make sure that his region was selling more oil than it collected, keeping a "comfortable margin" of overages across operations. Of course, it was impossible for Koch to consistently sell more oil than it collected, which is why oil gaugers used the Koch method to under-report how much oil they took.

Every month, Dubose received a packet of information mailed from Wichita. It was the statistical report compiled by the computer whizzes at headquarters. This was Dubose's report card, in effect. And the most important number on the report card, the number that he focused on more than any other, was the overage that he reported. Dubose knew that if his region came in over, he would be praised, promoted, and well paid. If his region came up short, then he would be questioned, side-lined, and ultimately fired. "I lived and died by that" monthly report, he said. "They put it on your desk, and you just stared at it for a couple of hours before you even opened the sucker. . . . That's how you kept your job with Koch. By coming out over. You could not come out short at all."

Some producers complained to Dubose about the company's mea-surement practices—they thought Koch was cheating them by tak-ing more of their oil than it paid for. But the measurement margins in dispute were small, and it was still profitable for oil producers to sell through Koch. Most of the producers were more interested in getting the oil moved quickly and on time, and they didn't want to quibble over Koch's gauging techniques. Dubose ensured that his region was over month after month, and, in doing so, he was favored by the managers in Wichita.

Dubose was not some sort of anomaly. Koch's pipeline and trucking managers across the country, from Florida to Oklahoma to California, took great pains to make certain they were over. Some of these managers, like Dubose, might have thought that they were stealing. Others simply considered the measurement practices to be "aggressive" but fair overall. After all, measuring oil was an imprecise art. Koch executives simply saw themselves as ensuring that the imprecision did not hurt Koch's bottom line. Dubose had learned this himself as early as 1968: *They saw where they could manipulate this because it's such a gray area. And they took advantage of it.* From this point of view, Koch was just playing hardball.

From an outsider's point of view, things looked quite different. For someone who was new to the oil business, Koch's conduct might have looked an awful lot like stealing. This point of view was about to come spilling out into the public realm. And it would do so in ways that endan-gered everything that Charles Koch had built.

CHAPTER 7

The Enemies Circle

(1985–1992)

During the late 1980s, Koch Industries faced two external threats that changed the company's future. The threats were separate—one came from the US government; the other came from Bill Koch—but Charles Koch and his leadership team saw the threats as intertwined. It seemed to them that Bill Koch was still bitter at being forced out of the company and was using the government as his proxy to attack Charles. In fact, the government was pursuing its own criminal investigation into Charles Koch and Koch Industries, an investigation that arose from the years of aggressive mismeasurement inside Koch's oil gathering divisions.

The government threat intensified in May of 1989, when the Senate Select Committee on Indian Affairs held a series of daylong public hearings in Washington, DC. The hearings presented the evidence of oil theft collected by the Senate investigator Ken Ballen and FBI special agent James Elroy, who had surveilled Koch employees.

The issue of oil theft was the subject of one hearing, and that hearing focused exclusively on Koch Industries. The reasons for this were simple. Evidence in the case pointed to Koch Industries as the primary culprit in the oil theft. No other company had such dramatically high overage levels, according to data obtained by the committee. Senate investigators believed that Koch had been caught red-handed, and the other companies had not.* The committee asked Charles Koch to testify at the hearing, but he refused. When the Senate released its final report, it stated declaratively: "Koch Oil ('Koch'), a subsidiary of Koch Industries and

---

* Ballen said that a few other instances of oil theft were discovered, but they were isolated incidents perpetrated by very small companies. It was not the "systematic" theft indicated by evidence collected from Koch Industries.

the largest purchaser of Indian oil in the country, is the most dramatic example of an oil company stealing by deliberate mismeasurement and fraudulent reporting."

When the Senate hearings were complete, Ken Ballen and his team boxed up their evidence and sent it to federal prosecutors with the US Attorney's office in Oklahoma City. The US Attorney launched a criminal investigation that was aimed squarely at Charles Koch. Agent Jim Elroy stayed on the case and intensified his surveillance.

This legal threat coincided with another attack from Bill Koch. Bill had become suspicious of Charles Koch in 1985, when he learned that Koch Industries had repaid almost all of the $1.1 billion in debt that was taken on to buy out Bill and his brother Fred. Koch Industries paid the debt about three times faster than it had expected to. "I was stunned," Bill Koch later told a journalist with *Fortune* magazine. "How could they have so much cash?"

Bill became convinced that his brother Charles had lied to him back in 1983 by dramatically understating the company's value. To Bill, there was simply no other way to explain Koch's meteoric profitability since his departure. On June 7, 1985, Bill filed a federal lawsuit against Charles Koch, Sterling Varner, and Koch Industries, alleging that they defrauded him.

The suit was the first volley in a sprawling battle that would last more than twenty years. The conflict spilled outside of the courtroom and spread to every corner of Koch Industries' business, and into David and Charles Koch's personal lives. Bill sent spies into the company as fake employees. He used wiretaps and hired private detectives to pose as journalists. His public relations team tried to plant damaging stories about Charles Koch in the media.

When Bill Koch heard the allegations of oil mismeasurement and theft, he incorporated them into his strategy. He tried, on his own, to collect damning evidence about the Koch method.

Inside Koch Industries, Bill's attack and the government's investigation were mistakenly seen as one and the same. This created a paranoid mind-set that seeped through the ranks of Koch's leadership. The federal government was seen as illegitimate, as a pawn that could be manipulated by billionaires. A universe of varied institutions—from newspapers, magazines, and government agencies, to law firms and competing companies—was divided into two opposing camps: there were those who worked for Charles Koch, and those who worked for Bill. No institution was seen as being neutral.

For Charles Koch, the twin attacks would sharpen and deepen his feelings toward government. He had always been a staunch foe of regulation, but the events of the 1980s would harden his opposition into a kind of loathing. Before this time, Koch Industries had been pestered and harassed by inspectors from the EPA, and by cumbersome rules imposed by the Department of Energy. But now his company was under surveillance from the FBI, whose agents were interrogating Koch employees in their homes. The threat was immediate, and it was personal. The threat would change the course of Koch Industries—and American politics along with it.

In 1989, the federal investigation into oil theft was transferred to a federal prosecutor named Nancy S. Jones. She was a tough-minded woman from Independence, Missouri, with many years of experience investigating fraud: first for the New York State Attorney General's Office and then for the US Attorney's Office in the Northern District of New York.

Jones took over the case after getting a call from Jim Elroy. She didn't know the FBI agent very well but was receptive when he told her that he had one hell of a case involving theft and corporate fraud.

Jones was skeptical, at first, when Elroy walked her through the evidence he had amassed against Koch Industries. Elroy had obtained compelling material, to be sure, but Jones didn't think it was strong enough to file criminal charges. She had a high bar for filing charges, and didn't like to lose in front of a jury. Perhaps more importantly, Jones didn't like charging low-level employees. To her mind, Elroy's photos and statements from oil gaugers, which proved theft, were not enough. She wanted to know just how high up the chain of command at Koch Industries the culpability went.

Jones empaneled a federal grand jury, which operated in secret to obtain evidence of any high-level conspiracy at Koch to steal oil. The grand jury investigated Koch Industries for many months.

By 1990, Jones was convinced that criminal wrongdoing was underway at Koch. And she believed the theft might have been ordered from high levels in the company. Even at this early stage, Jones felt she had enough evidence to safely charge multiple Koch Oil gaugers with theft. She believed there was also enough evidence to charge a group of higher-level managers with directing the criminal behavior. Jones and Elroy continued their investigation, however, because they wanted to push even higher up the chain of command at Koch, maybe all the way to the executive suite. Their evidence suggested that they hadn't yet reached the primary actors. "There was too much at stake in the case, to settle for the underlings," Jones recalled.

As Jones pressed her case from the US Attorney's office, executives at Koch Industries saw the hand of Bill Koch at play. In September or October of 1988, Koch's top attorney, Don Cordes, heard a "cocktail rumor" that Bill Koch was "trying to get the Senate interested in investigating Koch's measurement practices," according to court testimony later given by Cordes. That same month, Koch Industries received its first subpoena from the Select Committee on Indian Affairs, asking for a huge cache of documents related to its oil gathering practices in Oklahoma. It must have seemed to Cordes that the two efforts were combined, even though that was not true. The Senate investigation was prompted by the investigative reporting series in the *Arizona Republic*. According to Mike Masterson, a lead reporter who cowrote the series and was involved in it from the beginning, Bill Koch did not tip off reporters to the story. They came upon it while reporting on persistent problems on Indian reservations and heard claims about rampant oil theft. Bill Koch had heard about the inquiry and adopted it as a weapon to use against his brother.

Koch Industries responded by circling the wagons against investigators and closing down access to vital records at the heart of its oil gathering operation. Almost immediately when the US Senate began its investigation, Koch Industries issued a new set of "Standards of Corporate Conduct" to employees throughout the company. The standards also included a provision that would likely conceal evidence of oil theft that would have occurred through mismeasurement.

The standards of conduct said that no Koch employee should defraud anyone by making false entries into Koch's books. This would effectively ban the Koch Method of oil measurement, which required oil gaugers to record fraudulent numbers on run tickets and receipts they left behind at oil wells.

The standards imposed a sweeping blanket of secrecy over Koch's operations, stating that "all financial data, business records, technology and information on corporate strategy, objectives or on modeling and other analytical and/or management techniques" were to be considered secret and proprietary information that belonged to the company. In other words, virtually every piece of information at Koch Industries was confidential. This would include any training documents for oil gaugers or any tally sheets that showed overages or shortages in the oil gathering division. The standards barred any employee from sharing any of this information with an outside party without prior approval from a Koch Industries manager. The flow of information about Koch's measurement practices was being bottled up.

On July 11, 1988, Koch's president, Bill Hanna, sent a company-wide memo informing employees how to handle company records. He reminded employees about the code of secrecy for Koch's records that had been distributed before. Then he ordered that "written materials which would be useful to our competitors should be destroyed by shredding, burning, or some equally effective method."

Hanna's memo was a license to destroy evidence. And it was issued at a time when top executives at Koch were aware that the US Senate was investigating Koch's oil measurement practices. Under such circumstances, corporate lawyers and executives often order their employees to take special care to retain records that might be relevant to a lawsuit or investigation. Koch Industries did the opposite. It is unknown how many documents were destroyed because of that memo.

Don Cordes eventually reversed course and told Koch employees to retain evidence that might pertain to oil theft, but he didn't do so until November of 1988, months after Hanna's memo went out. The only reason that Cordes changed the policy was because a Koch employee in Texas complained to Cordes that he had been told to destroy all written evaluations he had made of Koch's truck drivers and oil gaugers.

Bill Koch only fed into the company's sense of embattlement. He launched a privately funded investigation into Koch's measurement practices. He paid private investigators to interview Koch gaugers, and he paid Koch gaugers to speak with his investigators. He submitted some of this evidence to the Senate, even as the Senate was doing interviews of its own. An internal FBI report, which wasn't made public until 2018, indicates that Bill Koch helped submit fifty statements from former Koch employees to US Senate investigators, claiming that the gaugers were stealing oil. The Senate ignored the statements because Bill Koch's involvement made them "suspect," according to an FBI memo. Rather than rely on Bill Koch's help, the Senate and the FBI relied on Agent Jim Elroy's investigation.

Charles Koch did more than circle the wagons. He helped coordinate a broad counterattack aimed not just at his brother but also at the US Attorney's office. This marked a turning point in Koch's history and in its efforts to influence US politics and public policy. His intentions were reflected in a lengthy written response that the company submitted to the Senate after Charles Koch refused to testify at the hearing. The most revealing part of the response was the headline of its first section: "The fact that the hearings were devoted almost exclusively to Koch Industries, Inc., is the result of the activities of William I. Koch and his vendetta against Koch Industries, Inc."

"Koch presented an easy target," the statement said. "It was politically unimportant, and because it would not have an opportunity to present its case or cross-examine witnesses, a one-sided presentation was possible."

At the time, it might still have been accurate to call Koch Industries "politically unimportant." The company didn't have a major lobbying operation in Washington and kept away from the spotlight. Charles Koch spent most of his time funding think tanks, university professors, and litigation in an effort to quietly shift American political culture.

But when faced with the threat of criminal charges, Charles Koch redirected his political efforts. Rather than simply hire lawyers and lobbyists, Koch used a network of front groups, training centers, and political operatives to combat the threat. This time the network wasn't focused on changing political culture; it was focused on the targeted, tactical goal of derailing legal efforts against Koch's oil gathering operations.

A former Koch Industries employee named Ron Howell was at the center of the effort. Howell was the ideal employee to spearhead Koch's political reformation effort in Oklahoma. During his tenure at Koch, Howell had specialized in commodity trading, the same kind of complex and opaque deals that Bill Koch had specialized in back in his days in Boston. Howell knew how to work in murky networks and connect the needs of several parties in ways that could ultimately benefit Koch. He was well suited for operating in the world of politics.

Koch's first tactical goal was to change the political landscape around the issue of oil theft. In its final report, the US Senate had categorically accused Koch Industries of systematic theft. Koch needed to undermine that claim if it wanted to forestall future investigations and litigation.

Howell was well connected in Oklahoma, and was a true believer in Koch Industries. Howell was appalled when he heard that Koch was accused of stealing oil from Indians. He was convinced the allegations were entirely false.

"I'd been in the boardroom many, many, many times for many, many years," Howell said. "It's just a very, very honorable company. . . . So I got angry as much as anything else."

Howell's first job was to reshape the political narrative about Koch Industries in Oklahoma. His strategy was to reach the "producers" themselves, meaning the oil drillers who sold to Koch Industries. The Native American tribes who owned the oil well leases were the most important target. The tribes were the most visible victims of the theft, and they were also the most sympathetic. If the Indian tribes could be brought on board with Koch Industries, it would undermine the entire rationale for a criminal inquiry into Koch's measuring tactics. If there were no victims, then how could there be a crime?

One of the primary victims of Koch's theft was the Osage tribe in Oklahoma. Charles O. Tillman, chief of the Osage tribe, said that a team of employees from Koch Industries came to talk to him about the oil theft allegations after the US Senate released its report.

Koch sent a team of auditors to review receipts from oil leases owned by the Osage tribe. These receipts were compared against Koch's internal figures to determine if Koch had indeed been underpaying the Osage, as alleged by the US Senate. Tillman said the tribe had little capacity to double-check Koch's work. The tribe didn't have an army of accountants at its disposal. The tribal members simply got checks in the mail for their oil leases and trusted the numbers.

"Koch was such a gigantic company," Tillman said. "To me, they were doing good accounting. They were doing good business with the Osage. . . . We didn't have anybody to rely on to refute Koch Industries."

When Koch Industries completed its audit, the company came back to Tillman with surprising news: Koch Industries had not been under-paying for oil. The company told him that it had, in fact, been over-paying the tribe. The audit showed that the tribe actually owed Koch Industries about $22,000. Koch's interpretation was backed up by federal authorities at the Bureau of Indian Affairs, Tillman said. He didn't feel like the tribe could question it.

Tillman and other Osage leaders went public with their belief that Koch Industries had not stolen oil from them. In March of 1990 the local Osage newspaper, the *Osage Nation News*, published a story in which the Osage chiefs said Koch was innocent. The story was quoted in the main-stream *Daily Oklahoman* newspaper, and Koch made maximum use of the chiefs' statements. Don Cordes, Koch's attorney, told the *Daily Oklahoman* that the Osage statement "completely undermines the false alle-gations of the Senate subcommittee."

Charles Tillman would later regret his role in tamping down con-cerns over Koch's practices. His mind was changed after learning of tes-timony unearthed years later in federal lawsuits. He became convinced that Koch had, in fact, stolen oil from Indian wells. "We were wrong," Tillman said. "We were badly informed."

Dudley Whitehorn, another Osage chief who worked with Tillman, also became disillusioned. Several years after the *Daily Oklahoman* arti-cle appeared, Whitehorn was sitting in a local auto shop waiting for his car to be repaired. A former Koch Industries oil gauger sat down next to him and struck up a conversation. Whitehorn said the gauger eventually told him: "We did steal from you." The man seemed contrite. Whitehorn didn't dwell on it. He didn't want to carry a grudge against Koch.

The Osage chiefs might have felt duped later on, but their public com-ments in the early 1990s achieved an important goal. The government suddenly looked overzealous and unfair. This fed into Koch's broader efforts. While Howell was reshaping the story in Oklahoma, Koch was working to do the same thing in Washington, DC.

Charles Koch understood now that he needed a political operation in Washington. Up until that point, he operated as if he could stay out of the miasma of the nation's capital, staying true to his libertarian beliefs and focusing his efforts on the business in Wichita. This left Koch vul-nerable. When Ken Ballen was conducting his investigation, he was con-tacted frequently by high-paid attorneys and experts who worked for companies like Exxon and Chevron. They defended their clients and even helped focus attention on Koch Industries. Koch had no such presence. This would change in the early 1990s.

Koch Industries deepened its relationship with Kansas senator Bob Dole. The Kochs already contributed to his campaigns and political causes, giving $245,000 between 1979 to 1994. David Koch would abandon the Libertarian Party to become the vice chairman of Dole's presidential campaign against incumbent Bill Clinton in 1996. By that time, the family would become Dole's third-largest financial supporter, according to an investigation later published in *Businessweek* magazine.

Dole helped Koch delegitimize the issue of oil theft. Dole submitted the story from the *Daily Oklahoman* into the Senate record, and said that he was concerned that the Senate had rushed to judgment to condemn Koch. Koch amplified his concerns by helping to draw other senators into the fight, including Nancy Kassebaum of Kansas and David Boren and Don Nickles from Oklahoma.

During a speech on the Senate floor in 1990, Dole criticized the committee's work, saying: "Several senators, including myself, Senator Kassebaum, Senator Boren, and Senator Nickles, had very real concerns about some of the evidence on which the special committee was basing its findings, concerns we raised with the committee in successive letters before the report was issued. It now looks like those concerns were well founded."*

As senators fought against the findings of their own committee, Koch put another piece of its plan into place. The biggest threat wasn't emanating from the Senate but from the courts and the US Attorney's office, two institutions that could not be influenced by campaign donations or lobbyists. In response, Koch initiated a long-term plan to reshape America's judiciary system.

---

* During an interview in 2016, Senator Dole had a hard time recalling details about his relationship with Koch Industries. Dole was ninety-two years old at the time, but even at that advanced age, he regularly went to work at his law office in downtown Washington, dressed in a neat suit and crisp red necktie. Dole recalled working with David and Charles Koch, and remembered attending a fund-raiser at Charles Koch's home in Wichita. However, the senator did not recall any events regarding Koch's oil measurement practices or the Senate investigation into them. The topic did not seem to spark a hint of recollection from Dole's long and storied political career.

Ron Howell founded an obscure nonprofit group called Oklahomans for Judicial Excellence. It did something unheard of: it started grading local judges based on their fealty to free-market economic theory. The group created scorecards for state judges, measuring how well their verdicts conformed with the teachings of Hayek and von Mises. The group publicized these rankings with public opinion articles published in places like the *Daily Oklahoman*. The grading system created a way to embarrass judges in the local press by publicizing their low scores. Koch Industries also offered them a way to escape this embarrassment: the company sponsored a series of free seminars that judges could attend if they received poor grades from Koch's rating system. The seminars were not held in stuffy classrooms. Koch Industries paid for judges to travel to a ski resort in Utah or a beachfront condominium, among other locations, relaxing places where the judges might be more open to Koch's message. The company held lectures that emphasized the importance of market forces in society, and warned against the consideration of things like "junk science" that plaintiffs often used to prove corporate malfeasance. The seminars were well attended, sometimes by more than sixty judges at a time. A Kansas state district court judge named Michael Corrigan attended a Koch-sponsored seminar at the Sundial Beach Resort in Sanibel, Florida, and another at the University of Kansas; in between these seminars he handled two cases involving Koch Industries without disclosing the potential conflict of interest, according to an account later published in the *Wall Street Journal*.

The junkets that it organized might have been disclosed or even regulated if they were enjoyed by other public officials, such as members of Congress. But there were no such restraints on treating judges to all-paid vacations, perhaps because no one had thought to organize such events on such a large scale before. Koch's efforts to sway judges evolved over many years. By 2016, it had transformed into a new program that offered free seminars to judges called the Law & Economics Center, which was housed at George Mason University in Fairfax, Virginia, along with Koch's free-market think tank, the Mercatus Center. The Law & Economics Center claimed to have hosted more than four thousand state and federal judges from all fifty states at its seminars. It offered up to a dozen events a year.

This long-term effort would do little to solve Koch's immediate prob-

lem, which emanated from the office of Nancy Jones. She and Jim Elroy
were making strides in the case. They believed they were close to proving
that Koch's oil theft was directed from the highest levels.

Then they hit a wall.

Jones and Elroy had zeroed in on one particular set of Koch's internal
documents they felt would show how the oil theft was directed from
Koch's senior leadership. They had subpoenaed those documents, and
were waiting for Koch Industries to supply them to the grand jury. Then
Nancy Jones got a letter from Koch's lawyer. The company could not
provide the documents Jones had requested. Those documents had been
accidentally destroyed, the letter said.

This was puzzling to Jim Elroy. He knew that Koch Industries kept
backup copies of its corporate documents in an underground storage area; the kind of place where company papers were treated carefully. Elroy said the documents in question were kept under lock and key
in the storage area. Elroy later discovered that the documents had been
checked out of the storage unit, in the same way books are checked out
of the library. The man who took custody of the documents was named
David Nicastro.

Nicastro was no ordinary document courier. He was head of Koch
Industries' security operations and had been deeply involved in the company's response to allegations of oil theft. He had also been dogged by
accusations of document destruction. Back in 1988, Nicastro traveled to
Koch's far-flung oil gauging offices and collected documents that might
have described the Koch method of oil measurement. Nicastro later told
investigators that he'd simply collected the documents and copied them.
But a Koch employee named Stephen Marshall testified in an unrelated
court case that Nicastro ordered employees to destroy documents. Nicastro strenuously denied the allegation in court, and the judge ruled there
was not enough evidence to prove the claim. The judge also pointed out
that Marshall had asked to be paid for his testimony and that he found
Marshall's testimony "not credible."

When the Oklahoma grand jury requested documents from Koch,
Nicastro apparently made a special trip to the underground storage unit
to retrieve them. He then reported that the papers had been accidentally

destroyed. Koch Industries informed Nancy Jones that the documents in question had not been converted into digital files, as had many other corporate documents.

"There was no reason why those records shouldn't still exist. But when the grand jury wanted them, then they were not available," Jones recalled.

The investigation had led them all the way to this batch of documents, and without those documents they didn't feel they could go any further. But that didn't mean that they were going to give up. Jones and Elroy began discussing other ways they could move forward with the case, other investigation tactics they might use, such as wiretapping and gaining informants inside Koch Industries. They would keep pressing, whether important documents were destroyed or not.

Then something happened that punctured a hole in the case—something that would derail the investigation, arguably killing it. Jim Elroy quit. He left Oklahoma for personal reasons. The FBI had offered him a transfer to the Miami office. As a California boy, Elroy had a strong desire to get back to the ocean. He wanted to spend time on a boat and travel on the sea. He had been in Oklahoma for many years and was ready for a change.

Jones wasn't too happy about it. She told him, "You are leaving me now?! And you said you would help me do this case!" Elroy recalled. Elroy was a driving force behind the investigation, and there was no guarantee that the FBI agent replacing him would be as passionate or as skilled. But he was determined to go.

Decades later, Elroy would regret the decision. "It was really selfish. I should have stayed and finished this job," he said. He was pursuing the two brothers who had control over Koch Industries and was confident he would have gotten them. "I know if I had stayed, that Charles and David would be in jail now," Elroy said.

In Elroy's absence, however, the investigation took a sharp turn in Koch's favor. There was a growing body of evidence that Koch Industries might be innocent. Now, in the summer of 1990, the FBI interviewed dozens of Koch gaugers throughout Oklahoma and Texas, and the gaugers all said essentially the same thing: Koch had never instructed them to steal, they had never heard of the "Koch method," and they never falsified their measurements. The gaugers said this even when they were

alone with their FBI interrogators—one gauger was interviewed in a
Dairy Queen parking lot. Other gaugers would contradict this testimony
under oath in later court cases, but the litany of interviews undermined
the case dramatically. The FBI was searching for corroboration, but just
as the interviews started to cloud the picture, there was a management
shakeup at the US Attorney's office. Nancy Jones's boss, US Attorney Bill
Price, quit his job to run for higher office. Price's replacement would be
selected by Oklahoma senator Don Nickles, a close ally of Koch's. Nickles
had previously spoken about the case with Koch's lobbyist Ron Howell,
who remembered pulling Nickles aside at a luncheon to discuss the case.
Nickles would later leave office and open a lobbying shop in Washington, DC, where Koch Industries was one of his clients.

In 1989, Nickles chose a politician and lawyer named Timothy Leonard to fill the US Attorney's job.* This shocked Jones, who had expected
one of Price's deputies, a longtime prosecutor name Bob Mydans, to
be selected. Mydans had years of experience in the office, while one of
Leonard's primary qualifications seemed to be his tenure as a Republican state senator, where he had briefly served with Don Nickles.

Jones quickly developed her own opinion about Leonard. She considered him to be a "political hack." Leonard was aware of her opinion,
and the two of them never had an easy relationship. Leonard thought
that Jones was an intelligent lawyer, but he became concerned about her
work when a judge ruled against her in a high-profile case. Jones was
particularly offended by Leonard's reaction. He assigned Jones's boss,
Arlene Joplin, to be the "second chair" on one of Jones's major fraud
cases. Being second chair essentially meant that that Joplin would oversee Jones's work. Jones pressed ahead. Eventually, Joplin approached
Nancy Jones to talk about the Koch Industries investigation. Joplin's
comments were not encouraging. She said there was lukewarm enthusiasm over at the FBI for the Koch case. The FBI wasn't sure it would dedi-
cate more resources to the Koch investigation.

Jones ended up quitting her job. She was tired of working for a boss
she didn't like and was tired of feeling that she was being micromanaged.
She was also tired of the lack of cultural life in Oklahoma City. She and
her husband wanted to live in a more cosmopolitan city. She said that

---

* Leonard is not related to the author.

the Koch Industries investigation was not a major factor in her decision. It wasn't unusual for an assistant US Attorney to move on to another job and leave a case behind. Jones organized her material and left the case in good shape to be pursued by another attorney.

It would be up to Timothy Leonard to determine how to pursue it.

In April of 1991, as the Koch case was still moving forward, Don Nickles nominated Timothy Leonard to become a federal judge. It was a prestigious distinction for Leonard. He'd been born and raised in the small town of Beaver, Oklahoma, and now he was offered a lifetime appointment to the federal bench.

In November, President George H. W. Bush confirmed Leonard's appointment. Less than four months later, while he was still US Attorney, Leonard dropped the case against Koch Industries and his office sent a letter to the company saying that it would not be indicted. Leonard did not explain publicly why the case was dropped, even though Jones said that the grand jury had obtained evidence showing criminal conduct of Koch Industries employees and managers. Whatever evidence Jones obtained could never be made public because of secrecy rules that govern grand juries.

For years afterward, Leonard's decision raised suspicion that Koch used its political influence to kill the investigation. Koch had obviously deployed its lobbyists and think tanks to influence public figures in Oklahoma, and the trail of influence between Koch, Nickles, and Judge Leonard seemed straightforward: Koch's political ally Nickles appointed Leonard to the US Attorney's office, then Nickles nominated Leonard to the federal bench, and Leonard decided to drop the charges. It seemed like Leonard might have been rewarded for dropping the charges.

There is no evidence, however, to support this claim and there is strong evidence to refute it. The FBI's case file in Oklahoma, released in 2018, shows that there was plenty of reason not to file charges. Dozens of FBI interviews with gaugers failed to corroborate the accusations against Koch. Internal FBI memos also show that it was Assistant US Attorney H. Lee Schmidt, not Leonard, who recommended that the case be dropped.*

---

* Schmidt declined to comment on the case.

It seems that the dozens of FBI interviews convinced Schmidt there simply wasn't enough evidence to file charges. A handful of interviews pointed to wrongdoing, but they seemed outweighed by dozens that undermined the case. The FBI files did not show what evidence Jones obtained from the secret grand jury proceedings, but Leonard later said that Jones never told him or anyone in his office that there was enough evidence to file charges against Koch managers before she left.

There is also evidence to suggest that Leonard actually fought to protect the investigation from political interference. Leonard said that shortly after he arrived, the FBI briefed him about the US Senate investigation into Koch and the political controversies it had ignited. In late 1989, Leonard sent a letter to the FBI in response, chastising the agency for sending him statements about the Koch case made by US senators in Kansas and Oklahoma. "Your presentation of this letter to this office both puzzles and concerns me," Leonard wrote. He went on to say that the investigation was independent, and that the "view of any elected official" regarding the Senate investigation of Koch would "have no bearing on the course of the grand jury investigation."

During an interview in his home, Leonard said that politics played no role in the decision to drop the charges. Leonard said that Nickles did not handpick him for either the US Attorney's job or the federal bench. Instead, it was Leonard who approached Nickles for the jobs. Leonard decided to apply for the US Attorney's job in 1989 after he realized that he would never run for governor. US Attorney was the next best thing. Years later, when there was an opening on the federal bench, Leonard once again approached Nickles and applied for that job. In an interview later, Nickles said he selected Leonard for the US Attorney position because they knew each other from the State Senate. Nickles respected Leonard and knew him better than Bob Mydans, the assistant US attorney.

Both Leonard and Nickles said that they never discussed the Koch case, either during Leonard's job interviews or later. Leonard said he would have remembered if Nickles brought up the case because doing so would have been a major ethical breach. Nickles confirmed this account, also pointing out that it would be inappropriate to do so. "I wouldn't talk about a case," he said.

When pressed on the issue during the interview, Leonard walked into another room and retrieved a weathered copy of the Bible that he said belonged to his grandfather, a Presbyterian minister. Placing his hand on the book, Leonard said: "I never had any contact with Senator Nickles, or any other political person, and there was no political thought or influence that ever entered the US Attorney's decision" on the Koch Oil case or any case.

While there is no evidence that Leonard dropped the charges inappropriately, new evidence would emerge that Koch employees had indeed stolen oil, even if FBI agents in Oklahoma and Texas failed to prove it. This new evidence was revealed thanks to the efforts of Bill Koch.

After Leonard dropped the case in 1992, Bill Koch bankrolled a massive civil suit against Koch Industries, filed in federal court, using an obscure law that lets citizens file lawsuits on behalf of the US government. Bill Koch was essentially acting as a whistle-blower. He happily told journalists that the suit was just another weapon in his arsenal to attack his older brother Charles, and Bill spared no expense in making that weapon as dangerous as possible. He had tracked down Jim Elroy and hired him to investigate Koch's oil gathering business around the country. Elroy spent months combing small towns in rural America, visiting oil gaugers in their homes and collecting their stories. Bill Koch's interviews were more successful than the FBI's in digging up damning testimony.

The case went to trial in Tulsa in late 1999. The testimony was devastating for Koch Industries. During the trial, Koch officials admitted that they earned roughly $10 million in profits each year by taking oil without paying for it. Witness after witness described the Koch method of stealing oil. Jack Crossen, a district gauger for Koch in Oklahoma, described under oath how the company trained him to intentionally mismeasure oil. Phil Dubose also testified and said categorically that Koch's business strategy relied on theft. Tales of theft were told by Koch's own employees from Kansas, Texas, Oklahoma, North Dakota, and New Mexico. A gauger named Ricky Fisher said he rationalized stealing oil just so he could keep his job.

"You're programmed to think and believe you take a little from this man, and it won't hurt him," Fisher said from the witness stand.

The jury found Koch Industries guilty of stealing oil between 1981 and 1985 from federal land and Indian reservations, and of falsifying roughly twenty-five thousand documents in order to underreport how much oil the company was taking.

The fines for Koch could have been enormous. The judge could have levied a $214 million fine just for falsifying the oil sale receipts. But Koch's lawyers were able to settle the case before it went to the penalty phase, paying an undisclosed amount.

In 1989, Koch Industries had complained that it was "politically unimportant." In a few short years, Charles Koch eliminated that problem. Charles Koch's high-minded political network of libertarian thinkers had transformed into an effective, diffuse, and highly specialized lobbying operation. It included front groups like Oklahomans for Judicial Excellence, a campaign finance network, and traditional corporate lobbyists.

Koch's political operations continued to grow even after the legal threats ended in Oklahoma. The operations weren't just effective; they were perfectly designed to exploit the structure of American politics in the 1990s. By that time, the US political and economic system had become one that supported big companies over small. A central feature of the political system was massive complexity, and mastering complex systems was Koch Industries' core specialty.

The deep changes in America's political system began during the Reagan presidency, which was widely seen as an era of deregulation. But that was only half of the story. Reagan did succeed in cutting taxes and stripping away some government rules. Over eight years, he cut the EPA's budget by 28 percent. He cut funding for transportation by 12 percent, siphoning money away from the federal highway system. He also reduced antitrust enforcement, allowing big companies to get even bigger through mergers and acquisitions. Reagan did this, in part, by naming attorney William F. Baxter the new chief of antitrust enforcement at the Department of Justice. Antitrust laws were an economic foundation of the New Deal; a critical counterbalance to the power of monopolistic corporations like Standard Oil. Baxter issued a memo to his legal staff telling them not to worry so much about the concentration of corporate power but to focus instead on efficiency and prices. This subtle change ushered in a wave of consolidation that swept across virtually every sector in the economy.

But in spite of these actions, Reagan soon discovered that he could not dismantle the stubborn machinery at the heart of the New Deal. He sought to dismantle Social Security, but his plan died in the Senate, with a vote of 96 to 0. Medicare could not be touched, either. Together those two programs accounted for almost half the federal budget. The entitlement programs were joined by an increase in military spending. During Reagan's first term, the Department of Defense budget swelled 54 percent to $551.9 billion in 1985. This led to a toxic collision. Reagan cut taxes, but he could not cut spending to a similar degree. The idea behind "Reaganomics" had been that tax cuts would stimulate growth and boost tax revenue. But the federal debt ballooned from $1 trillion when he took office to $2.8 trillion when he left.

The Reagan era created a paradox in the world of governing: key rules were repealed, the free market was praised, but the size and scope of government continued to grow unabated.

The trend continued under Bill Clinton. One of Clinton's first acts was to pass the North American Free Trade Agreement, a pact that opened markets in Mexico and Canada. NAFTA dramatically weakened America's labor unions. Companies once avoided unions by moving to southern, right-to-work states; in the 1990s, they began moving to Mexico. At the end of Clinton's presidency, he signed a law bestowing permanent normal trade relations on China, opening the gates yet wider for companies to shift jobs overseas. Clinton also repealed key banking regulations from the New Deal, like the 1933 Glass-Steagall Act, which created a division between commercial banks that took deposits and investment banks that gambled through speculation. He eliminated decades' worth of rules to restrict risky financial trading in commodities and derivatives contracts. Banks grew larger than ever before.

All the while, the overall size and burden of the federal government continued to grow for most Americans and small businesses. A libertarian group called the Competitive Enterprise Institute marked the increase by tallying the number of pages in the *Federal Register*, which records rules and regulations. In 1986, there were just more than forty-seven thousand pages. By 1995, there were more than sixty-seven thousand. The burden of these rules fell disproportionally on smaller companies, the CEI found.

There was no longer any clear consensus about the balance of power between government and private enterprise. The New Deal era was over, but it hadn't been replaced by a new laissez-faire system. It was replaced, instead, by a theory with an appropriately vague and misleading name: neoliberalism. Neoliberal policies sought free-market reforms like NAFTA but retained federal entitlement programs and heavy defense spending. Its hallmarks were massively complex laws and programs that tried to thread the needle of unshackling markets while preserving a role for the state.

Companies that could exploit this complexity thrived. Koch Industries did it as well as anyone. There was no better example of this than Koch's manipulation of the Clean Air Act, a sprawling set of rules that imposed a perpetual regulatory burden on oil refineries. Oil refineries were a prime target of the Clean Air Act when it was passed because they are a major source of toxic pollution like benzene and smog-producing gases. In 1970, the Clean Air Act put a strict limit on how much pollution the refineries could release.

But a loophole in the act dictated that the regulations would only apply to new oil refineries, not the existing ones. Any refinery already doing business in 1970 was "grandfathered" in to the era of clean air enforcement. This was seen as a way to avoid penalizing existing oil refineries that were built before the era of pollution controls. Congress appears to have thought that the grandfathering clause would be temporary: it was believed at the time that most oil refineries would last about forty years before their equipment wore out. Koch's Pine Bend refinery, for example, was built in the mid-1950s. It might have been retired as early as 1995.

The old refineries were not phased out, however. The opposite happened. Companies like Koch exploited an obscure bureaucratic program called New Source Review that allowed them to expand their existing refineries. The rule stated that any major new equipment added to an old refinery must comply with the newest clean air standards. But compliance was in the eye of the beholder. Oil refineries and their teams of attorneys fought over the definition of critical terms like "new" and "significant."

The refiners took advantage of another loophole. The Clean Air Act exempted new sources of pollution from regulation if companies could prove that curbing the pollution would be unreasonably expensive. This was easy to exploit. The oil refiners all cited the best available technology as the current technology they were already using. Any advances beyond that were arguably too expensive. This created a downward spiral: new pollution control technologies never became cheaper because there was no market for them.

Oil companies expanded their existing refineries during the 1980s and 1990s, gaming the New Source Review program and prohibiting any new refiners from entering the game. The EPA, which enforced the Clean Air Act, pushed for the New Source Review process to be updated, but the update didn't happen. As a result, Koch Industries rapidly expanded its refineries in Minnesota and Texas during the 1990s without obtaining permits that would have limited pollution from the plants, according to data compiled by attorneys at the EPA and the Department of Justice.

DOJ attorney Dianne Shawley later prosecuted Koch and other refineries for illegal expansion. The company was able to exploit the New Source Review in part by overwhelming state regulators who enforced the Clean Air Act on behalf of the EPA. The local regulators were simply not equipped to analyze the reams of data and legal documents heaped upon them when Koch was expanding. The same tactics were used by virtually all major US oil refiners, Shawley said.

The grandfathering clause built a protective wall around a group of companies that were lucky enough to be doing business in 1970. The clause froze the oil industry in midplay, leaving the existing players to have the game board to themselves by making it prohibitively expensive for new players to enter the market and compete. The last large-capacity US oil refinery was built in 1977.

Koch Industries didn't just benefit from political dysfunction. The company used its newly expanded political operations to shape the government in new and innovative ways, using many of the same techniques it honed in Oklahoma.

After the Watergate scandal of the early 1970s, Congress enacted a strict and complicated set of rules around campaign donations. Individuals and companies were capped in how much they could give to any candidate in an election cycle. Donations had to be disclosed publicly, potentially embarrassing both the donor and the politician. Koch Industries circumvented this system in ways that would become widely imitated.

In 1996, Koch Industries created a nonprofit group called the Economic Education Trust. The group did not need to disclose its donors because it was not ostensibly a lobbying or campaign finance organization. Koch funneled money through the Economic Education Trust to state and federal campaigns in Kansas and other states where it did business. In October of 1996, the Economic Education Trust gave $1.79 million to a company in suburban Washington, DC, called Triad Management Services Inc. Triad was supposedly a political consulting firm, but it had a strange business model: it offered its services for free, to Republican candidates. A US Senate report in 1998 concluded that Triad was "a corporate shell funded by a few wealthy conservative Republican activists."

Triad laundered political contributions in a way that was extremely difficult to discern from the outside. The Senate report laid out a basic picture of the money trail: (1) Koch Industries supported the Economic Education Trust; (2) that trust gave cash to Triad; (3) Triad gave the cash to campaign groups like Citizens for Reform, which, in turn, (4) pumped money into elections to defeat Koch Industries' opponents. (Koch Industries also gave at least $2,000 directly to Triad.)

Triad was a new kind of campaign finance machine. It acted as a third party that didn't directly donate money to politicians. Triad hired consultants who created attack ads for Republicans in tight races. Triad was careful in its language. It never used words like "vote for," "support," or "defeat" that might have triggered oversight from campaign regulators like the Federal Election Commission.

Triad was particularly active in Koch's home state of Kansas. The company spent money on four of six federal races in Kansas in 1996, supporting candidates such as Congressmen Sam Brownback and Todd Tiahrt. Republicans won all four of the races in which Triad intervened. One of Triad's consultants, Dick Dresner, said that the campaign company was designed specifically to shield the wealthy donors who supported it. "They use three or four or five or six different ways so they aren't discovered," he said. "Even if their names came up once or twice, the extent of their activities is underestimated."

The Senate report about Triad's activities was a document of frustration. It conceded that the financial shell game behind Triad was so complex that investigators could not make sense of it even two years after the election. The report was clear in its condemnation of Triad's activities, however, and it sent a public warning:

"Most disturbing, Triad is poised to become a model for future elections."

Koch Industries' political operations only continued to expand, but Charles Koch focused most of his efforts inside the company. In 1992, Koch Industries built the largest office tower in Wichita. The structure was located on the north side of Koch's campus and was constructed with dark granite and black windows. The building was the perfect symbol of Koch Industries. The stone gleamed in an enticing way but was dark and inscrutable. People soon referred to the new building simply as "the Tower."

The Tower was a testament to Koch's growth and an expression of its desire to grow even faster. Koch Industries moved two thousand employees into the building. That was more than triple the number of employees who'd been there when Charles Koch took over the company, and it represented just a fraction of the thirteen thousand employees who worked for the company worldwide. But even 2,000 employees couldn't fill the Tower. Almost half the building was empty. The table was set for expansion.

Charles Koch's office was located on the third floor of the Tower, on the north side of the building. His large desk was covered with neat stacks of papers and a telephone placed near the left corner. There was an oil painting of Fred Koch on the wall above Charles Koch's chair. Directly across from the desk, there was an open area with a conference table for small meetings and a small sitting area with a couch surrounded by chairs. The northern wall of the office was all windows, offering a panoramic view of the Kansas prairie and tall grass. The rest of the walls were lined with built-in bookshelves. These books seemed to be Charles Koch's prized possessions. There was a multi-volume edition of the

Oxford English Dictionary. There were works by his favorite philosophers, economists, and historians.

Charles Koch liked to tell people that "true knowledge results in
effective action." True knowledge was the important part of the equation. Charles Koch aimed to discover the truths undergirding society
and business by reading all the books in his library. He wasn't satisfied
anymore to borrow the thinking and methods of people like W. Edwards
Deming. Charles Koch wanted to codify his own understanding of the
truth. In 1990, he put a name to this effort. His set of rules would be
called Market-Based Management.

One of the first things Charles Koch did in his new office was to get
the rules written down. He hired two academics to help him: Jerry Ellig
and Wayne Gable. They were both employees of think tanks that Charles
Koch funded. The men had meetings and hashed out lessons from Hayek
and von Mises and all insights gleaned from decades of running Koch
Industries. They began to distill all of this into a framework that could
guide Koch Industries in its next phase of growth.

In 1993, the team produced a glossy booklet, sixty-three pages long,
called *Introduction to Market-Based Management.* The booklet was an
operator's manual; the rulebook for working at Koch Industries. Charles
Koch taught Market-Based Management with the same rigor that he
had instituted the teachings of Deming. He held seminars for managers, and then those managers held seminars for their employees. Copies
of the booklet were printed and shipped to Koch facilities everywhere.
The unionized workers at Pine Bend sat through lectures about it. Managers looked at charts describing it and broke into small groups to learn
it. A new vocabulary was disseminated throughout the company ranks.
Employees didn't have responsibilities, they had "decision rights." They
weren't managers anymore, but "process owners." The vocabulary was
drilled into everybody.

The words of Market-Based Management were not simple slogans.
They were a code of conduct that would guide life inside Koch Industries
during the 1990s. This was a decade of explosive growth for Koch; a time
when it would take full advantage of economic conditions that favored
complexity and bigness.

But it was also a time of dysfunction and challenge. Charles Koch
liked to say that growing was a lot like the process of scientific inquiry:

You came up with a hypothesis, and then you tested the hypothesis against the hard rocks of reality. You did this again and again until you found out what was true.

The 1990s were a time that tested Charles Koch's deepest hypotheses. He believed that he had discovered the "true knowledge." He believed he had cracked the code for building a prosperous and enduring company, but the hard rocks of reality would not be kind to this hypothesis. As Market-Based Management was rolled out through the company, it would wreak its own kind of havoc. There would be accidents and spectacular business failures. There would be public humiliation and, worst of all, a host of criminal charges brought against the company.

One of the worst debacles happened right inside the company's crown jewel: the Pine Bend oil refinery. And all of it started with the best of intentions.

CHAPTER 8

The Secret Brotherhood of Process Owners

(1995–1999)

A business firm is not just a piece of society, but a mini-society in its own right.

—*Introduction to Market-Based Management*, 1993

Heather Faragher arrived for her new job at Koch Industries' Pine Bend refinery in the winter of 1995. During those long, cold months, the refinery landscape was frozen and bone white. The empty fields surrounding the facility were covered in snow, and the sky was often slate gray. The gloom was broken only by the twinkling lights of the refinery towers in the late afternoon when darkness started to fall.

In spite of this barren landscape, the refinery itself was a vital place, full of life and excitement. Faragher joined the company as an environmental engineer, specializing in wastewater treatment. The refinery produced millions of gallons of water each day tainted with toxic chemicals, and it was Faragher's job to make sure that the water was purified—as much as it could be—before it was flushed into the Mississippi River. This was Faragher's third job as a wastewater engineer. She was only twenty-eight years old but had already done two stints at large paper mills in New York and Alabama.

Faragher's new boss was a kind and energetic young woman named Karen Hall. Hall seemed like a former hippie, a positive woman who was fluent in the language of environmental protection. Soon after Faragher arrived, she got a tour of the environmental engineering office at Pine Bend. It was located in the main refinery office complex in a U-shaped complex of cubicles and offices. Everything was wide open and bright.

The offices had big glass windows—the employees called them fish-bowls—which made the whole floor seem like one big collective space. And everyone inside it was so young. There must have been thirty environmental engineers, and most of them seemed to be in their twenties. There was energy everywhere, and it was more than just youthful exuberance. The employees had a sense that they were part of something big. They belonged to an enterprise that really mattered.

Faragher quickly discovered why this was. During her orientation as a new employee, Koch Industries flew her to Wichita. She joined a group of other new recruits from around the country, and they were shepherded into the opaque glass edifice of the Tower. Just entering the Tower felt like gaining admittance to a secret society. It was obvious that not just anyone could get past the security guards in the hushed lobby. Faragher and the other recruits were ushered deep inside the building and delivered to a large auditorium.

It would be inaccurate to describe what happened next as corporate training. Corporate training can often be little more than a gimmick, one that usually involves a captive audience of employees sitting in a meeting room while bosses recite a script of vaguely inspiring catch-phrases—like "living with integrity," "thinking outside the box," and "a sum being greater than its parts"—which are promptly forgotten once employees get back to their desks and actually start working.

This is not what happened in Wichita. Faragher and her new colleagues were told that they were being let in on a secret. They were about to learn the Koch way of doing business. And Charles Koch, the CEO himself, would arrive to reveal the secrets in person.

Even decades later, Faragher would vividly remember seeing Charles Koch walk out onto the stage to address the crowd. He had bone-deep confidence, the kind that expresses itself in the weird way of making a man simultaneously humble and also completely certain of his beliefs.

During such meetings, Charles Koch explained that there were fundamental laws guiding the natural world: the law of inertia, the law of gravity. These were immutable forces that dictated events. And there were also immutable laws that governed human affairs. History showed, inarguably, that the laws protecting individual liberty and free-market capitalism were the only principles that could form the bedrock of a healthy society. The same held true for creating a healthy company. Individual liberty and free-market capitalism were the cornerstones. These principles would guide every action of every employee inside the company. Commitment to these laws was a precondition to employment at Koch Industries. It was also the surest path to a virtuous and prosperous life.

This wasn't a pep rally. This wasn't corporate training. As Heather Faragher would soon discover, this was her introduction to a new society. She joined this secret society eagerly. But after a year or so at Koch Industries, Faragher was exposed to the dark side of this society, too.

She watched while her bosses and coworkers broke the law and flagrantly poisoned the environment. She stood up and tried to stop them, and that's when the secret society turned against her. Faragher saw firsthand how toxic a workplace could become when everyone spoke the same language and thought the same way, and how dangerous this could be to those who challenged the culture from the inside. She would lose her job, face the risk of doing time in jail, and have her career permanently damaged. All because she tried to do the right thing.

Faragher's experience was not unique. The conduct she witnessed was emblematic of problems at Koch Industries during the 1990s. Throughout the company—from the pipeline division to the Corpus Christi refinery and elsewhere—a common problem emerged from the teachings of Market-Based Management. All too often, an emphasis on boosting profits took precedence over the need to operate safely or to obey the law. A belief in the power of markets created a disdain for the government agencies tasked with regulating Koch. And the people who didn't agree with the principles of Market-Based Management were all but labeled apostates. Understanding what happened to Heather Faragher is the key to understanding why Koch Industries racked up a shocking number of criminal charges and civil complaints throughout the 1990s, branding the company as a kind of corporate outlaw.

When Heather Faragher joined the company in 1995, she only saw the promise of it—the potential. This was years before the sleepless nights, and the federal agents with guns on their hips showing up at her doorstep, and the pressure from her bosses to lie to authorities. All of that came later. In the beginning, there was only the thrill, the thrill of being part of something much larger than herself.

Heather Faragher had grown up about thirty-five miles north of the Pine Bend refinery, in the small town of Bayport, Minnesota. About three thousand people lived in Bayport back in 1990. It was a sleepy community carved into the western bank of the St. Croix River. This was the kind of town where conformity was the norm and where neighbors quickly learned each other's business. But even from a very early age, Faragher knew what it was like to stand apart from the crowd. She learned this from one of the people she idolized most in the world: her father, Ted Lawrence.

Ted Lawrence described Bayport as a "redneck town," and he made it abundantly clear that he did not consider himself a redneck. Lawrence commuted every day to his job in the city of Saint Paul. He worked for the county's child protection services, counseling abused children and their families. He and his wife, Henri, had two kids. The oldest was Heather, and four years later came her little brother, Steven.

The Lawrence household was filled with politics. Ted Lawrence made sure of that. He wasn't just a state social worker; he was also president of his local union. Lawrence spent hours of his free time working on union business and stumping for local politicians. He lived and breathed by the progress of the liberal wing of the Democratic Party, of which he considered himself a lifelong member. In September of 1966, the month Heather was born, Lawrence joined a march with Dr. Martin Luther King Jr. from Chicago to the town of Cicero, Illinois, the site of race riots in the 1950s. Lawrence told the story for many years to come; a story that showed how common people could take action to change a public wrong.

The Lawrence family often accepted foster children into their home on a temporary basis, giving them a place to stay before the state could find them something permanent. The foster kids were often minorities from urban Saint Paul, setting them apart from their neighbors in overwhelmingly white Bayport. The Lawrence home was different.

Ted Lawrence didn't just encourage his kids to be Democrats. He encouraged them to do the right thing. Even more important, he encouraged them to argue. "It was always all right for [Heather] to argue with her mother and father if there was something she disagreed about," Lawrence recalled. "There was lots of humor in our house. There was a lot of yelling in our house."

Heather was a bright kid who always seemed to have a book in her hand. Like many first children, she was a rule follower who was a high achiever in school. She skipped the fourth grade and excelled in the fifth grade. She read far more books than were required. Also, like many first-borns, Heather made a point to walk in her parents' footsteps. During her time off, she helped her dad walk door to door and stuff political pamphlets in mailboxes and hammer campaign signs into the ground. As a union president, Ted Lawrence was on the phone constantly with his union peers, discussing disputes or arranging campaigns. Lawrence was amused when he'd later hear Heather repeat the things he said over the phone. Heather and her little brother, Steven, had been absorbing it all. "That's what amazed me the most, was how much they heard of my phone conversations," Lawrence said. When little Steven was in grade school, he could name every major politician in Minnesota—he had helped campaign for many of them.

Argument was a form of art at the Lawrence dinner table. Ted Lawrence encouraged it. Family dinners became political debates, and Heather was expected to join in. Sometimes this rankled her.

Ted Lawrence remembers an exasperated Heather asking him, "Can't we just talk about the weather?"

"I said, 'No we can't! That's not how it works in this house,'" Lawrence said. Over the years, Heather Lawrence learned how to hold her own. "She got good at arguing."

In spite of all this, Heather's interests took her away from politics. She attended a summer camp for engineering students during high school, and she loved it. It catered to her aptitude in math and science. She got her college degree in engineering and left Minnesota for New York, where she took her first job as a wastewater engineer. After working in New York, Faragher moved to Alabama and worked at paper mills. She married Greg Faragher and took his name. That's when a recruiter called and told her about the job at Koch Refining.

Faragher wanted to move back home to Minnesota. She knew that when she and Greg had kids, she wanted to raise her family in her home state, near her parents and friends. The job at Pine Bend was the perfect opportunity.

During her first year at Koch, Heather discovered the kind of "work family" that people yearn for. Employees at Pine Bend tended to stay there for their entire careers—it wasn't rare to bump into employees who'd been there twenty years or more. The collegiality between engineers made it a joy to go to work every day. There was also a sense of great purpose. Everybody knew that Pine Bend was the crown jewel of Koch Industries.

In fact, the Pine Bend refinery was at the center of Koch Industries' business during the 1990s. It was the primary fountain of cash that allowed Charles Koch to plow money back into the company and realize his dreams of expansion. That reality was made clear on the ground every day—it was hard to miss the fact that Koch was betting its future on its operation in Minnesota.

In 1992, Koch launched a $220 million project to install new refining towers and other equipment that would make cleaner fuels like low-sulfur diesel fuels to meet new standards being set under the Clean Air Act. The project turned a large quadrant of the refinery into a busy construction zone, with armies of contractors coming in and out every day with heavy equipment. A year later, Koch partnered with Williams Companies, which operated pipelines, to build a new gasoline terminal about thirty miles from Pine Bend to serve Koch's customers. In 1995, Koch was considering a new $300 million project to build a mini power plant inside the refinery that would power its operations and sell electricity to the surrounding area.

The production capacity at Pine Bend rose dramatically during this time. In 1985, the refinery was able to process about 137,000 barrels of oil a day. In just one year, Koch boosted that capacity 13 percent to 155,000 barrels a day. Plant supervisors were encouraged to operate machinery in ways that increased production as much as possible even as new units were being added. By 1995, when Heather Faragher was hired, the refinery could process 245,000 barrels a day. Just a year later, it was processing 286,000 barrels a day—more than double the amount from a decade earlier.

The rapid expansion created strains on the system.

Refining oil creates a lot of pollution. The refinery towers and stacks release streams of poisonous gas, while cracking units produce a steady flow of toxic water runoff. Every new barrel refined at Pine Bend only created more pollution. But the limits on these pollutants were not as flexible as Koch's marketing plans. There were strict pollution controls set by both state and federal authorities. The pollution limits were clearly spelled out in state-issued permits that allowed Koch to operate the refineries. These permits were enforced by a web of state and federal agencies. On the state level, Koch was overseen by the Minnesota Pollution Control Agency. On the federal level, it was overseen by the Environmental Protection Agency.

Karen Hall oversaw the division that ensured Koch didn't violate limits on hazardous waste and water pollution. She also oversaw the wastewater "group," which was composed of one person: Heather Faragher.

Faragher's glass-walled office was located next to Hall's. So it was easy for Faragher to pop her head in and touch base with Hall or ask her questions. But it quickly became apparent that there were very few questions that Hall could actually answer. Hall had virtually no experience in the wastewater business and deferred to Faragher when it came to making technical decisions.

This meant that Faragher was largely on her own. One of her first jobs was to get familiar with Pine Bend's complex water treatment center. The plant didn't just have its own sewer system; it had two. One sewer system handled wastewater, and the second sewer system handled "oily" wastewater that was more heavily polluted. These two flows of water were kept in separate piping systems, as the oily water was the more dangerous.

Wastewater from the refinery was treated in a large sewage plant, which cleaned out pollutants. After that, the water was piped into a set of large ponds on the eastern side of the refinery, called "polishing ponds," where the water was allowed to sit so that any sediment it carried could settle to the bottom of the ponds. Sitting in the polishing ponds also allowed the hot wastewater to cool and allowed microorganisms to break down pollutants that weren't caught by the treatment plant.

After sitting in the polishing ponds, the water was sent into a series of small pipes that injected it straight into the Mississippi River. The refinery pumped about 3.5 million gallons of water into the waterway every day. It was critical, then, to test the water in the polishing ponds and make sure that the pollution levels there were not too high. Faragher oversaw these tests.

One of the biggest pollutants that Faragher worried about was ammonia, which was a major by-product of the refining process and damaged the environment in two ways. It was a nutrient that caused algae to bloom in overwhelming quantities, which choked waterways like the Mississippi. In high enough concentrations, ammonia also posed a danger to aquatic life, killing fish by damaging the tissue in their gills. Ammonia was also toxic to humans and other organisms. Breathing ammonia vapors—even when diluted—destroys body tissue and can be fatal in high doses.

The treatment plant cleaned ammonia out of the wastewater in an old-fashioned way: it let microbes eat the substance. This process, called nitrification, cut down drastically on ammonia levels, but it took time. You had to give the microbes plenty of time to eat, and they could only eat so much.

Faragher liked to cut the ammonia level to zero before she pumped it into the Mississippi. But that wasn't always achievable. Instead, Koch aimed to release water that was about forty parts ammonia for every million parts of water—or "forty parts per million," as the environmental engineers say. Running at this level allowed Koch to stay within its permitted pollution limits.

During Faragher's first year on the job, the water treatment plant ran smoothly. She walked from her office down to the treatment plant frequently—sometimes multiple times a day—to make sure the operations met her standards. She became friendly with the blue-collar OCAW workers who ran the plant. Faragher also became close with other engineers in her department. She and her husband, Greg, joined the Koch softball team. After the games, everyone went to a local bar to dance and drink beer. She was part of a team, and she loved it.

Faragher soon discovered, however, that Koch's employees were all on one team, but not all teammates were created equal. There was, in fact, a stark division of power. The differences were not just the obvious ones that defined so many companies, such as the breach between the unionized workers and their managers. At Koch, even the white-collar workers belonged in two camps. In one camp, there were the operations people. These were workers who ran the machines. In the other camp, there were the engineers, like Faragher. They were not considered part of operations. They were more like support staff.

Karen Hall explained that the engineers on her team were like "consultants" to the operations people. The engineers were there to offer their advice and their expertise. But the engineers were not in charge. At the end of the day, the operations people decided what would be done. "They pay attention to us, but we don't run the place," Hall said.

Heather Faragher, then, didn't have any real authority over how the wastewater plant was run. She could just advise and consult with the operations people, who were the ones with the real power.

The operations team that Faragher reported to was run by a twenty-seven-year-old man named Brian Roos. He was a quintessential Koch man. He joined the company in 1990, shortly after graduating from the University of Minnesota with a degree in mechanical engineering. Like so many Koch employees, his real education happened after college, once he joined the company. Roos started as an engineer in the maintenance department and then was moved to the new clean-fuels area. He became a supervisor and eventually was promoted to a senior management position.

Except, at Koch Industries, there was no such thing as a senior manager. Within the confines of Market-Based Management, Roos was known as a process owner, or someone who acted like they had an ownership stake in the company.

The refinery at Pine Bend was divided into five groups, which were known as "profit centers." Each profit center was like a separate piece of property owned by a boss who was responsible for everything that happened within their domain. Koch measured the financial results in each profit center, which, in turn, determined how much money would be steered toward that profit center in the future.

Brian Roos was the process owner over the Utilities Profit Center, a division that included the refinery's wastewater treatment plant, boiler house, cooling system, and other equipment that kept the cracking units running efficiently. Roos spent a lot of time with Heather Faragher, explaining to her how things worked at Koch. She sometimes sat with him in the company cafeteria, where Roos spent long lunches outlining free-market principles that undergirded Koch Industries' philosophy. Roos had an earnestness, a sincerity, that was similar to Charles Koch's. He was a true believer. But under the dictates of Market-Based Management, there was an important divide between his role and Faragher's. Faragher was not part of a profit center. Environmental engineers like Faragher were lumped into a category of nonprofit groups.* The nonprofit groups were like a second-tier workforce supporting the "core" profit centers. This distinction helps explain a lot that went wrong at Koch during the 1990s.

When process owners like Roos read *Introduction to Market-Based Management,* they were warned against using the nonprofit support services too much. Because services like accounting and environmental engineering were essentially "free" to people like Roos, there was a danger that those services would be overused. The pamphlet likened the nonprofit groups to government agencies that handed out free services: there was a danger that the nonprofit groups might become bloated and overly expensive. The nonprofits might therefore drag down the performance of the very profit centers that they were supposed to serve. As they grew in size and cost, the nonprofit service centers would suck resources away from the parts of the company that actually made money.

"The predictable result was often a corporate overhead cost spiral," the pamphlet said.

To counter this cost spiral, Charles Koch created an internal market system: divisions such as Roos's had to essentially pay to use the nonprofit groups. That way, the process owners would have to think twice about sucking up support resources. Of course, in some cases, these "nonprofit" resources were all that stood between successful business and criminal conduct.

Heather Faragher spent a lot of time walking around the refinery. She thought the equipment inside the control room was primitive: most of the screens displayed only a digital readout of numbers—much of the data wasn't even displayed but instead was printed out on a scroll of paper.

---

* Other nonprofit groups included accountants, the human resources team, lobbyists, and lawyers.

The control room wasn't the only place that could use improvement. There were other problems at the refinery—much more dangerous problems—that had been left to fester for years. One of these problems was the refinery's sewer system, which had been decaying without repair. One of the operators who worked at the wastewater plant, named Todd Aalto, had seen firsthand how the infrastructure was falling apart. When inspecting the sewer system, Aalto noticed that the concrete floor of one section had eroded away completely, leaving nothing but wire mesh along the bottom. Shift workers routinely disposed of various chemicals into the "oily water" sewer, dumping large drums of things like naphtha and xylene down into the pipes. It was impossible to measure how much might be leaking out into the outside environment through the cracks and fissures below.

Giant investments were being made at Pine Bend during the 1990s, and Faragher wanted some of that money to go into the utilities infrastructure, like the sewers and water treatment plants. But the engineers couldn't make such decisions; only the process owners. In this case, the decision would have gone up to Karen Hall's boss, a man named Steven David, whom everybody called Steve. He was the boss of all the environmental engineers, but this still didn't give him the same status as a real process owner. The engineers were a nonprofit center, after all. David was forty-two years old and more experienced than Brian Roos. But David was still at a lower rank than Roos in the refinery pecking order.

Faragher proposed new investments and upgrades that could be made at the wastewater plant, but those investments were delayed or rejected time and time again. All investments at the refinery were evaluated with one goal in mind: return on investment. The process owners would put their money where it generated the most profit within the plant. Investing in pollution control technology or sewer pipes just couldn't compete with investing in a new cracking unit that could increase oil production. New equipment was just too profitable. A big investment in new refining equipment might be able to pay for itself within one year. An investment in sewer pipes, on the other hand, might not be earned back for several years.

Still, Faragher pleaded for new investments to Steve David and Karen Hall. She believed that such investments would benefit the company for many years to come. At first, Faragher thought that this argument might win the day. One of the great things about Koch Industries was how quickly projects were approved; there wasn't a lot of bureaucratic decision-making. But Faragher learned that only certain kinds of projects got approval from on high.

"If the payback of the investment was going to be less than a year, they'd basically give you permission and you could run with it," she recalled. "If I needed money for wastewater treatment, it was like pulling teeth. It was like, 'Why do you need that? That's not going to make me any money.'"

At the Pine Bend refinery, Koch was allowed to expel an average of 8.3 kilograms of chromium every day and 714 kilograms of ammonia. That was the letter of the law. But Faragher also wanted to abide by the intent of clean-water laws. Obviously, the intent of the law was to keep large levels of ammonia out of the nation's waterways. That's why the limit of 714 kilograms was set. But setting the limit at 714 kilograms did not mean that regulators wanted Koch to pump 714 kilograms per day into the Mississippi River. The state had set a maximum level of pollution, but the goal was to be under that level. The intent of the law was to encourage Koch to pollute as little as possible.

With that in mind, Faragher designed a water treatment plan that kept ammonia and other toxins at very low levels. When it came to measuring pollution, everyone in her business used the terminology of "parts per million" to figure out how much pollution was leaving the pipes with each gallon of water and how close the company was to hitting its limits.

If the mandatory limit was forty parts per million, Faragher liked to keep the flow at about twenty parts per million. This was a habit that she'd learned at the paper mills. Doing so gave the company a large buffer. Treating water was an inexact science, and there was bound to be unexpected spikes in the level of pollution. Keeping the normal pollution rate low helped the company avoid busting its permit levels in case of an emergency. But maybe more importantly, running at a low rate of pollution helped the company meet the intent of the law. The point was to keep waterways and air as clean as possible.

One day Steve David came to Faragher's office for a talk about the Koch method of wastewater treatment. He drew a large graph on a white board in her office. There was a straight line that ran across the graph from left to right: that was the permit level. Ammonia levels could not exceed that level. Below this line, David drew a squiggly line to represent Koch's actual ammonia emissions (the line was squiggly to represent the natural variation in daily ammonia levels). There was a big gap between the squiggly line and the straight line. This represented that Faragher was emitting far less ammonia than the permit allowed.

David pointed to the line representing low levels of ammonia emissions and said, "You don't have to run here," Faragher later recalled.

Instead, David drew a new squiggly line that ran just below the permit level. David told Faragher that she could run pollution levels there, just below the maximum level. The goal was to keep the ammonia output levels stable. If they avoided big spikes in ammonia output, they could operate just below the level permitted under the law.

Faragher listened intently. She understood what he was saying. Running pollution levels just below the permitted level might seem good for the plant—it was a way to avoid expensive treatment procedures. It was also a way to make sure that the plant was able to run continuously at high volumes. In theory, this plan would work perfectly. There was nothing about Koch's approach that was illegal. Koch could keep its pollution levels just below the legal limit and still operate within full compliance of the law. And the Koch engineers prided themselves on being smart and running efficiently. They were just the kind of people who could keep pollution levels right within the narrow band that they aimed for.

But Faragher was uneasy with this method. It counted on things going just right inside the oil refinery. That wasn't how life really worked.

Things started going wrong around June 1, 1996.

The problem started inside a machine called the sour water stripper, which played a critical role in cutting down on the ammonia emissions that were pumped into the wastewater treatment plant. For some reason, one of the sour water strippers started to malfunction. Only later would it be discovered that a series of trays inside the stripper had built up a layer of residue called "scaling" that made the trays far less efficient. Unfortunately, no one at the plant was aware that this had happened. The trays were buried deep inside the machine, and they could not be seen unless the machine was turned off and disassembled. Doing so would require a partial outage at the refinery. Production would be interrupted. Output would fall. Sales would be hurt. The sour water strippers were allowed to keep running.

Large levels of ammonia started flowing into the wastewater plant. Only so much of the ammonia could be removed by the nitrification process. The ammonia loads were overtaking the microorganisms that were supposed to eat them. As a result, heavy doses of ammonia were sent from the wastewater plant out to the polishing ponds and, ultimately, into the river. Doing this for too long would violate Koch's operating permit. The fine for doing so would have only been about $30,000—pocket change for Koch. But it wasn't the fine that was important. If the high ammonia levels still continued, then the legal troubles would escalate. The entire operation could be endangered.

Brian Roos discussed this problem with the other people in operations, like Todd Aalto in the wastewater treatment plant. Roos also talked with Aalto's boss, a woman named Ruth Estes. These discussions often occurred when Heather Faragher was not around. The operations people had to figure out how to handle the high ammonia levels. Eventually they settled on a rather elegant solution. It wouldn't bust the permit levels. But it wouldn't require the refinery to shut down, either.

From the control room, Todd Alato could pull back on the amount of water that was flushed into the polishing ponds and divert it into a series of large detention ponds on the far end of the refinery. These ponds were enormous: one held twenty-two million gallons of water, and another held twelve million. The ponds were a kind of catchall basin for runoff from the plant, and it was not entirely clear just what was inside of them. The ponds took runoff from the oily water sewer and other pipes within the refinery—the cracked and leaky system where employees dumped naphtha, xylene, and other chemicals. A test by state regulators would later show that soil near one of these detention ponds was contaminated with mercury, chromium, zinc, and other pollutants.

In June of 1996, operators like Aalto started sending millions of gallons of water that was heavily polluted with ammonia into these detention ponds. The technique was known as "stacking" the water, and it had the immediate effect of helping Koch Industries. Because the ammonia-laden water was being stored in these detention ponds, it was not being sent out to the river, where it would count against Koch's permit levels. Engineers like Faragher were testing for pollution in the polishing ponds, not the detention ponds.

Unfortunately, over the ensuing months, stacking the water began to present its own problems. Water levels at the detention ponds rose steadily. Soon, the water was creeping dangerously close to the tops of levees that surrounded the ponds. If there was a heavy rainstorm, it could potentially cause the detention ponds to overflow, sending a stream of pollution into nearby farmland and wetlands.

Roos assigned engineers to figure out just what was causing the high ammonia levels, but they failed to do so. For a number of technical reasons, the engineers did not suspect that the problem was the trays inside the sour water stripper—usually those trays were effective for many years, and the trays in place then were not very old. The sour water strippers were not shut down and disassembled for rigorous inspection.

Roos and his team settled on yet another rather elegant solution to the ammonia problem. Once again, this solution wouldn't bust the permit levels and wouldn't require the refinery to shut down. The large detention ponds at the refinery were not connected only to the sewage system—they were also connected to a vast network of pipes and hydrants used for fighting fires. In case of emergency, water from the detention ponds would power hoses that could douse flames inside the plant.

Fires are a perpetual threat hanging over oil refineries. After all, a refinery is little more than a giant collection of pipes and tanks full of flammable material under very high pressure. Everybody knows that one small flame, within minutes, could give birth to a conflagration that might kills hundreds of people and destroy the facility. To protect against this eventuality, every priority is given to firefighting. At the Koch refinery, a set of hydrants located throughout the facility could be activated rapidly, making use of more than thirty million gallons of water in the detention ponds. Everybody knew that the water in the detention ponds was polluted, and nobody relished the thought of spraying it all over the refinery. But extinguishing a fire took precedence over everything else.

To keep it in peak condition, the firefighting system was flushed out about once a year. This task was overseen by the safety department. Safety employees would drive down to the detention ponds and open a group of special hydrants that drained the entire network of pipes used to fight fires. Doing so would draw water from the detention ponds, flush it through the firefighting system, and then spray it out of the hydrants and onto open ground near the refinery. This ground consisted of open crop fields and wooded land about one mile from the river and its surrounding wetlands. When the safety team flushed the system, they only kept the hydrants open for about an hour or so. It didn't draw down much water from the detention ponds.

As water kept stacking up in the ponds during the summer of 1996, Roos and Estes discussed a novel idea. They could open the fire safety hydrants connected to the detention ponds and flush the water out onto the ground. They decided it would be a better idea to flush the water onto open ground rather than send it to the river, where it would violate Koch's permit level. Roos downplayed the risk of pouring ammonia on the ground. He reminded Estes that ammonia was often used as a fertilizer. "I grew up on a farm. Ammonia is a fertilizer, and that quantity is not harmful. We had a discussion like that, you know," Roos said.

Roos and Estes never determined a clear policy about whether or not it was legally acceptable to drain the detention ponds out onto surrounding land. But in the absence of a clear policy on the matter, the desire to keep ammonia out of the river won out over concerns about polluting the land. On June 18, 1996, the fire safety hydrants were opened and water from the detention ponds was flushed out onto the land. The next day, the hydrants were opened again, flushing more water out of the ponds.

Nobody told Heather Faragher.

Every weekday morning at seven o'clock, there was an operations meeting inside a large conference room at the refinery. This was a chance for supervisors throughout the operation to share information and pass around news from their scattered outposts. Process owners like Roos attended along with shift supervisors like Estes. Environmental engineers like Faragher also attended. During the fall of 1996, ammonia pollution became a topic of discussion. Very high loads of ammonia were still being delivered to the wastewater plant. Shift workers in the safety department were complaining about high water levels in the ponds.

During one meeting, Estes brought up the idea that she'd discussed with Brian Roos: maybe they could just open the hydrants and flush the pond water out onto the land. Faragher's reaction to this idea was immediate and unequivocal: No. That was not possible. With that declarative statement, Faragher gained the undivided attention of her bosses. She explained to them that dumping water on the ground violated their state permit in many ways. To begin with, opening the hydrants would be considered a trick—called a "bypass" in regulatory circles. The state monitored Koch's pollution at an agreed-upon location: the pipes that went into the Mississippi River. Flushing the water out a back door and onto open land was bypassing this monitoring point, a practice that was specifically outlawed in the permit.

But there was more than that: if Koch released chemicals into the environment, it needed to measure how much it was releasing and report those releases to the state if the pollution levels were high enough.* Because Koch didn't measure pollution in its detention ponds, the company might be pouring reportable quantities of pollution out into the environment without telling the state.

And, more to the point, it was the wrong thing to do. Faragher didn't need to consult any manuals or state regulations to make her judgment. It was an easy decision for her, and an instant one. It seemed to her that no wastewater engineer would have to think very long about it to come to the same conclusion. But Steve David, Faragher's boss's boss, did not agree with her. After Faragher had made her point, David told the group that he wasn't so sure about her opinion. There might be more of a gray area there than Faragher was letting on. With that, the meeting broke up.

Faragher left the meeting thinking she had clearly just prohibited the idea of opening the hydrants and flushing out polluted water from the detention ponds. Steve David might have said he wanted to look into it, but that didn't change the fact that she had opposed it. Maybe he could come up with some good reason why Koch could pour out ammonia

---

* In regulatory parlance, releases with enough pollution are called a reportable quantity, or an RQ.

onto the ground, but that didn't seem likely. And the language Faragher used was not ambiguous: this would violate the permit, she said. In other words, it was illegal.

On October 24, 1996, Heather Faragher sent a memo to the environmental team and the plant operators. She told them that Koch would conduct routine pollution testing on November 4, which was a Monday. These were the tests that Koch would then give to the state to prove that it was operating within its pollution limits. Koch would test water at the polishing ponds and at other points within the plant. This was a routine memo—Faragher liked to give everyone a heads-up about the testing.

On Saturday, November 2, days before this test, the wastewater plant cut back its flow of water into the river. More water was sent to the detention ponds, which were already brimming.

The next morning was relatively quiet at the refinery. On weekends the place ran with a leaner staff. Heather Faragher was not at work, and most of the engineers' offices were dark.

Todd Aalto was the operator on shift that day at the wastewater plant. He read the latest lab work on the water being sent to the river, and the ammonia numbers shocked him. A typical target for ammonia might be 40 parts per million. The lab results showed ammonia was dumping in at 110 parts per million. There were other problems. The tests also looked for pollution called "total suspended solids," which measured particulate matter in the water. Koch aimed for 35 parts per million. The tests were showing 72 parts per million.

"I thought, *This is not good*," Aalto later recalled. He knew that if water was sent to the polishing ponds, it could break the ammonia permit levels. So he diverted it. The operators cut the flow of water to the river from about four million gallons to one million gallons. Millions of gallons were sent to the detention ponds.

Koch managers were aware that testing for the state regulators would occur Monday. Shifting the water flow would help them beat the test. During that weekend, an operator in the wastewater plant named David Gardner wrote in a logbook: "I hope these moves prove sufficient in light of tomorrow's annual toxicity testing."

Estes was the shift supervisor on duty that weekend. She had many problems to take care of, but, by Sunday afternoon, it became very clear that she also had a crisis on her hands. There was simply too much water flowing to the detention ponds and a very real risk of overflows.

The hydrants were sitting there, capable of being opened, siphoning off the water. She had a tool at her disposal to easily solve the problem. Estes remembered that Faragher had opposed opening the hydrants. But their boss, Steve David, had undercut Faragher in front of everybody. There did not seem to be a clear answer. And regardless, environmental engineers were merely consultants. As Hall had put it: *We don't run the place. They do.*

Estes had a clear choice on her hands that afternoon: "It would have been basically, 'Our [pond] levels are high, we're about to go over, what the hell are you going to do about it?'" she said.

At seven o'clock Sunday evening, safety department employees went down to the hydrants and began the detailed process of opening them up. Soon enough, fountains of water began pouring out, flowing over open fields and into the woods and low-lying wetland areas.

The operators went home for the night. And they left the hydrants open. When workers arrived around seven for their Monday-morning shift, the hydrants were still spewing water. Employees from the safety team then closed the hydrants, just as the morning operations meeting was beginning in the conference room inside the plant. The state of Minnesota later estimated that roughly six million gallons of water were flushed onto the ground overnight.

On the morning of November 4, Heather Faragher was informed that the safety team had flushed out the detention ponds. She was furious. She had made it perfectly clear that flushing the hydrants was prohibited, that it was illegal. And yet Ruth Estes had gone ahead and opened the spigots—for twelve hours. It was only on that Monday morning, after the damage had been done, that Estes checked with Faragher and Brian Roos to make sure that flushing the water was "kosher."

Estes later told state investigators "I talked to the environmental [team] and Brian about it, and essentially they also viewed it as a gray area, you know."

But there was no gray area as far as Faragher was concerned. "Heather was against it; unequivocally against it," Estes remembered. The group eventually decided to call Koch's legal team.

They reached Jim Voyles, a senior attorney at Koch's headquarters in Wichita. Hopefully he would be a voice of reason who could help cut through the dispute. But Voyles told them during the call that he needed to do more research into the legality of flushing the hydrants. He refused to side with Faragher.

Faragher went back to her office, and she was alone in trying to figure out what to do next. She did some quick calculations, trying to estimate how much water had been released and how heavy the ammonia concentrations in that water had been. This was essentially a guessing game because nobody had measured pollution levels in the detention pond. Ultimately, Faragher decided that the release was not a reportable event—there probably had not been enough ammonia released. But there was still a problem. Faragher felt that she was also required under law to report any pollution bypass releases. During the conference call with Voyles, Faragher brought up the need to report the bypass. "That was discussed in the meeting, and the decision was made that that wasn't [reportable]—that I was wrong," Faragher later told investigators.

On November 16 and November 17, the hydrants were opened again, and water was flushed out onto the ground. This time, nobody told Heather Faragher.

Heather Faragher reported directly to the Minnesota Pollution Control Agency—or the MPCA, as it was called—which was the state-level agency that enforced federal environmental laws. Behind the MPCA stood the US Environmental Protection Agency—the feds. And the feds were not to be tampered with. The feds had the best attorneys in the field, and the feds did not hesitate to pursue anyone who violated the law.

During November and December, there weren't any more heated meetings about dumping ammonia. The issue had been left to lie as an enduring "gray area," something that Jim Voyles in Wichita was looking into. There was no clear policy, and the ammonia continued to flow into the wastewater plant at dangerously high levels. A log notation in early November, for example, indicated that ammonia was flowing toward the polishing ponds at about 170 parts per million, more than four times the level that could keep Koch inside its legal limits. The operations team kept diverting the water into the detention ponds, which crept ever higher.

During this time, something changed in Heather Faragher—something that might have escaped the notice of her bosses. It was around this time that Faragher began to worry that working at Koch Industries might land her in prison.

Ruth Estes was the shift supervisor on Saturday, January 4, 1997. When she arrived at work, she faced a familiar crisis: once again the water levels were dangerously high down at the detention ponds. An employee with the safety department complained to Estes that the ponds were about to overflow—one more rush of water into the ponds might send water spilling onto the nearby roads. Estes simply couldn't send any more water into the detention ponds.

Estes called Todd Aalto at the wastewater plant. She asked him if he could divert the water back into the polishing ponds and the river beyond them. Aalto said that he could not. Estes did not press him on the point, but she also didn't know why Aalto couldn't just send the water to the polishing ponds, where it normally went. Maybe the polishing ponds were full, or their ammonia levels were already too high. Regardless, sending water to the river did not seem like an option to her.

The other tool available to Estes was the fire safety hydrants. With one order, she could drain the detention ponds onto surrounding land. But was it illegal to do so? Estes didn't know.

Koch's lawyer, Jim Voyles, and Estes's managers had intentionally left the matter vague. For all Estes knew, Voyles was still examining the legal issue and might decide that it was completely acceptable. The only thing that Estes was certain of was that nobody had specifically prohibited her from opening the hydrants. It was still an option on the table. So she started discussing it with the operators.

Faragher was on vacation and out of town, so Estes could not call her. Instead, Estes called down to the environmental engineering department, where an engineer was pulling a weekend shift. Estes told him that she was thinking of flushing the hydrants, but the engineer balked. He didn't think it was the proper thing to do. Estes soothed him with a convincing, but untrue, argument. She told the engineer on duty that Faragher had given the tactic the green light. The reluctant engineer said he would defer to Faragher's judgment on the matter.

At that point, "poor Karen Hall walked in," as Estes remembered it. Hall wasn't even supposed to be working that weekend. She just happened to pop into the office to handle some unrelated business. As luck would have it, Hall walked into the control room just as Estes was debating whether or not to flush the water from the detention ponds.

As a lead engineering supervisor, Hall should have been the resident expert on whether flushing the hydrants was illegal or not. But Hall had been studious in her efforts to avoid expertise on the matter. Ever since she became Faragher's boss, Hall made it clear that it was Faragher who had the background and the knowledge to handle wastewater issues. Even when debates arose, such as whether or not to dump ammonia water on the ground, Hall avoided getting involved. When the issue was thrust on her that Saturday, Hall was not ready to deal with it. She vacillated, and Estes pressed her point. Estes said that they were in a crisis— there was no time to debate the legal fine points of what they were doing. The detention ponds might overflow if they did.

"I said, 'Well, do you have a better option? If somebody has a better option, I will by all means be happy to do it,'" Estes later recalled to state investigators. "Our options now: [wastewater] runs to the road, erodes the road, and ends up on the ground anyway, or I direct it somewhere where there's minimal impact. As far as I was concerned, that was the two options."

Estes told Hall that flushing the hydrants was routine—they did it all the time.

When faced with the choice, Hall deferred to Estes. Estes was the one who worked in operations, after all. Hall was just a consultant. The process owners were in charge. "I just bowed to [Estes's] expertise, basically . . . so I figured she knew what she was talking about," Hall said.

Estes decided to drain the detention ponds into a low-lying wetlands area near the refinery. "We figured since there was already a pond down there and there wasn't any, you know, wires or anything building up ice on and falling, that essentially would have the least impact of any area. It was already a wetlands area," she said.*

This time, roughly 2.88 million gallons of polluted water were released.

When Todd Aalto was told that Estes had just drained water from the detention ponds and flushed it into nearby low-lying wetlands, it made him curious. He had never heard of anyone flushing water down to that area.

He decided to go take a look. Aalto walked along a tree line that bordered an empty field beside the oil refinery. As he did so, he witnessed a surreal work of sculpture. The fountains of water spewing from the hydrants had been expelled at such force that the water had splintered small trees and snapped their branches off. A cloud of water and mist had showered the treetops, which now sparkled with crowns of icicles. The raw power of the water was breathtaking.

Heather Faragher returned from her vacation and went into her glass-walled office. She learned that, once again, Estes and her team had opened the hydrants and sprayed ammonia-laden water out into the fields and wetlands.

The first time Faragher had heard about this, she'd been furious. But things were different now. Faragher had already spoken up. She had already told Estes, Roos, and David that flushing waters from the hydrants was possibly illegal and certainly unacceptable. Faragher had even made the case to Jim Voyles, a top lawyer in Wichita. Voyles had undercut her. What was she supposed to do now?

In early 1997, something happened in Faragher's life that made it even more difficult to wage this fight. She became pregnant with her first child. This removed the easiest solution to her problem, which would have been to quit her job. But how could she quit now? How would she and Greg support their child?

---

* While the area in question was referred to as a "wetland" and was near the Mississippi River, the area was not on a list of state-designated wetlands.

Still, there was one thing that kept Faragher from going along with her superiors. She knew that the flushing was illegal. And by keeping her job, she was essentially participating in an illegal act.

She saw only one way to move forward. She had to report Koch's activities to the state.

Shortly after the January 4 flushing, Heather Faragher met with Don Kriens, an official with the Minnesota Pollution Control Agency. She unburdened to him everything that happened.

Kriens was shocked at what he was hearing. He agreed with Faragher that the flushing was not permitted under state law. It was an illegal bypass and might have resulted in unreported pollution. Kriens gave Faragher unambiguous direction. He told her that Koch Industries must cease flushing the hydrants. And if Koch insisted on doing it again, the company must first notify the state.

This was simplicity. This was a solution. Heather had gone to the authorities and gotten an answer. One could have forgiven Heather Faragher for feeling relieved when she left Don Kriens's office. It seemed that she had finally found a way out of her dilemma. The authorities had spoken, and Koch Industries would have no choice but to obey the law. Faragher had no way of knowing how wrong she was. Her problems with Koch had just begun.

When Faragher returned to the refinery, she immediately spread the message: using the hydrants to flush polluted water must cease immediately. And even if Koch was considering flushing the hydrants again, there was no question that the company must first notify the state.

Faragher sent memos to this effect to supervisors, and she personally told the news to Brian Roos, Steven David, and Karen Hall. On January 17, Faragher sent a lengthy e-mail memo detailing the issue to dozens of employees, including Karen Hall, Roos, and wastewater plant operators like Todd Aalto. She even sent the memo to the safety department employees who actually opened the hydrant nozzles.

The memo noted that Koch's lawyers were still exploring whether they could find a way to dump water from the hydrants legally. But the memo made clear that no hydrants could be opened without prior approval from the state. The memo also acknowledged that plant employees had been approaching Faragher with ethical concerns about opening the hydrants.

This wasn't all that Faragher did. She sent another memo laying out clear and strict guidelines for when water could be drained out of the detention ponds and sprayed on the ground. This memo stated that if more than twenty thousand gallons of water—a relatively minuscule amount—was flushed out from the hydrants, then it had to be tested first for pollutants.

The matter seemed to be settled. Heather Faragher had gotten Koch Industries back into compliance.

Now that she had informed Koch Industries' managers about their obligations, Faragher composed a memo to send to Minnesota state regulators. She wanted to report back to Don Kriens at the MPCA to let him know that she had complied with his orders.

Faragher completed this memo, and she ended it with a clear statement that Koch would comply with the state regulators going forward.

Before she sent the letter to the state, however, she was told to send it to Jim Voyles in Wichita. He needed to edit it. When Voyles returned Faragher's memo to her, it was almost unrecognizable. Perhaps the most salient change was at the end of the memo, the paragraph that Faragher had written to ensure that Koch would comply with state law.

Faragher had originally written:

> In the future, we will contact the MPCA if we need to put water on the ground for containment or high levels of permit pollutants. We plan to formalize a policy concerning this issue after we hear back from the MPCA and review all other pertinent regulations.

Voyles deleted that entire paragraph. He had replaced it with the following:

> Koch is unaware of any statutory or regulatory duty to seek approval of or to report this type of discharge unless it is to

*surface water, it results in the release of a contaminant in an
amount exceeding a reportable quantity, or could otherwise
cause pollution of the waters of the state. Nevertheless,
Koch wishes to ensure that it fully complies with applicable laws, regulations, and permits, and would welcome
further dialogue with the MPCA on this issue to avoid any
misunderstandings.*

The difference between these two statements was stark. Faragher had written that Koch would comply with MPCA's wishes. Voyles had written the company wasn't aware of any legal reason to do so. And now this memo was about to be sent to the state under Faragher's name.

That's when Faragher decided to go above her bosses' heads.

Koch Industries had installed a hotline that employees could use to report an ethics complaint. After reading Voyles's edits to her memo, Faragher called it. The first man she reached seemed nonchalant about Faragher's story. He took her name and phone number and said someone would call her back.

Eventually someone did. Years later, Faragher could not remember the name of the man who called her back. (At that time, the head of ethical compliance at Koch Industries was a lawyer named Ben Burgess.)* Faragher spilled her story to the man on the other end of the line. She told him everything: how her legal opinion was being marginalized, how Koch was taking a legal risk by doing so, and about the troubling edits that Voyles had made on her memo to the state. Faragher even talked about the personal toll that all of this was taking on her. She was pregnant, and she was worried that the stress of all this might be hurting her baby. Faragher was having trouble sleeping—the stress was wearing on her mind and body.

After hearing her out, the man in Wichita tried to sooth Faragher. He told her that the situation would be handled. And he insinuated that her concerns might be a bit overblown. He told her, then, to focus on her own health and personal life. "He told me that I needed to be taking

---

* Burgess left Koch after these events, and in 2002 he won an election to become a state district court judge in Sedgwick County, Kansas, where Wichita is located. He remained a state judge in 2015.

care of myself and my baby. 'You're kind of just emotional because you're pregnant,'" she later recalled. "I never heard from him again."

When the phone call ended, Faragher realized that she was on her own.

On February 18, Brian Roos sent a memo to Faragher, Steve David, and an operations manager named Jim Jacobson. The memo was labeled: "In reference to the water policy."

The water policy in question was the one Faragher had laid out in the memo she had previously shared, based on her meeting with the MPCA. Roos informed the team that he wished he had been consulted before that policy was announced. He thought the policy was wrongheaded.

Roos was particularly bothered by the idea that Koch would need to conduct pollution tests anytime it flushed more than twenty thousand gallons of water from the hydrants. He said that these and other constraints were unreasonable.

"I believe there is more red tape here than necessary. For routine use of the fire water for cleaning and flushing, we should not be required to go through this procedure," Roos wrote. Heather Faragher, once again, was contradicted by senior management at the refinery.

There was urgency to this issue. The ammonia loads continued to arrive at the wastewater plant in alarmingly high levels. Once again, the water was being diverted to the detention ponds, and once again the detention ponds were getting dangerously full. The outcome seemed inevitable.

Koch Industries opened the fire hydrants and spewed ammonia-laden water onto open ground on February 25, 26, and 27, and again on March 26, without seeking prior approval from the state. Two men who worked with the wastewater plant—named Charlie Chadwell and Terry Stormoen—did not understand why Koch was dumping polluted water onto open fields around the plant. They were being asked to cooperate with the practice even after they'd gotten the memo from Faragher saying that it was unethical and possibly illegal.

This was just one of many grievances among the OCAW workers at the refinery during the 1990s. It was an unusually tense time between management and the union. It wasn't all-out war like 1972, but wounds from that period lingered. The union men felt disrespected, and the work rules seemed to give them no job security at all anymore. The Market-Based Management teachings emanating from Wichita struck them as a tidal wave of corporate lingo. In many cases, it seemed like little more than a smokescreen used to justify firing any workers that Koch didn't want around. The OCAW employees felt like they knew plenty about running a refinery—they didn't need to learn about property rights and process ownership. There was a brief strike in 1993, and it concluded without much of a sense that anything was accomplished.

Longtime employees like Charlie Chadwell wanted out of the company. In April of 1997, it seemed like Chadwell's desire to quit merged neatly with a need for him to relieve his conscience about the ammonia pollution. Maybe he could do the right thing, and win a generous severance package at the same time. On April 4, Chadwell and Stormoen paid a visit to the Minnesota Pollution Control Agency. When they arrived, they told a story that was even more damning than Faragher's. The two plant workers alleged that Koch Industries made a habit of violating state pollution laws. To prove their point, the two brought along reams of documents: operating logs and internal communication that spelled out the violations in inarguable detail. It was all there: the logs of hydrants being opened for twelve hours, the notations of workers dumping xylene and naphtha down a leaky sewer system meant to process only water with some oil in it, and other complaints about leaky tanks and pollution.

Chadwell returned to the refinery and immediately told his bosses what he had done. He wondered if they might not want to negotiate his exit from the company.

The state regulators were not very far behind Chadwell. They arrived a few days later.

On April 8, 1997, Steve David, Faragher's boss, told her that the MPCA was going to send agents to the refinery the following day for a surprise inspection. He had been tipped off by a source at the agency.

David gave Faragher clear instructions: She could meet with the MPCA investigators when they arrived, but she could not volunteer any information to them. She was to answer their questions with as little information as possible. "Yes" or "no" answers were preferable.

The next day, the regulators showed up unannounced, just as expected.

When the state inspectors arrived, Faragher saw that Don Kriens was with them. He was the official with whom she'd met months before, the one who'd told her Koch needed to stop flushing ammonia onto the ground, or at least give the state prior notification if it did so. Koch had already violated Kriens's command several times.

Kriens and his team of MPCA agents gathered up a small group of Koch employees, including Faragher and David. Kriens asked the Koch employees to take him on a walking tour of the refinery. He wanted to see the detention ponds and other sights.

The state inspectors noticed that Faragher was nervous. She seemed to be having a silent argument in her mind. Every time they asked her a question, even a simple question, Faragher paused. She looked as if she might be comparing different versions of scripts in her head before responding.

Kriens and his team asked Faragher if Koch had flushed ammonia onto the ground at any time besides the incident that Faragher had already reported.

Faragher said that she didn't know. She said Koch's safety department controlled the hydrants, not the environmental engineers. This was not true, and Kriens's team suspected as much. The state now had evidence of several other flushing incidents.

Kriens would later ask Faragher why she'd misled him, and Faragher would not have a good answer. "I was instructed not to give you any information you didn't ask for," she said. She seemed almost surprised by what she had done.

The state inspectors walked down to the detention ponds to inspect them. They walked near the wooded area that had been blasted sideways by the hydrant streams. Two of Koch's safety department employees, Gary Ista and Chris Rapp, met Kriens at the detention ponds and told him what Faragher would not: that the ponds had been drained onto land several times after the incident.

Kriens and his team turned to Steve David. They asked him if he had known about these flushing episodes. Had Koch's environmental team been aware that this was happening?

David told them that the environmental team didn't know about the flushing until January, when Faragher reported the flushing to the state. This was not true. David also left out the fact that he and other senior managers at Koch not only knew about the flushing but had held multiple meetings discussing the issue. One of those meetings had been all the way back in November, when David and Faragher debated the issue with Koch's senior attorney Jim Voyles.

David would later say that he hid the fact of the meetings because Voyles told him the discussions were top secret and protected by attorney-client privilege. Voyles gave David the impression that even acknowledging the meeting would violate the attorney-client privilege, which David was not authorized to do. This was not true, as David would later learn.

Kriens and his delegation walked over to an area called the coker pond, a detention pool often filled with highly polluted water. Kriens had reason to believe that the coker pond had been overflowing its banks, and he asked David if a sewer mechanism at the pond called a "sump" had recently caused the pond to overflow.

David told him no.

Faragher was visibly nervous at this point. The pond had, in fact, overflowed the previous Monday. Faragher was part of a team that was now lying to the state.

Without Steve David's cooperation, it was extremely difficult for state investigators to figure out how much Koch Industries managers knew about the ammonia pollution. The state had piles of work logs showing that the dumping occurred. But those logs told only part of the story. It wasn't at all clear who had ordered the pollution—who had told the safety department to open the valves. It was even unclear how often the dumping happened.

The investigation might have foundered after Koch's team left the state offices on May 8. If nobody inside the refinery told the truth to investigators, it was all but impossible for the MPCA to figure out what was happening inside the refinery. This was how Koch Industries wanted it. Ernie Tromberg, the longtime Pine Bend operator and manager who retired in the early 1990s, said Koch's management team felt that the state had no right to know what happened inside the fence line of Koch's property. Managers obeyed a code of silence to maintain this wall around Koch's operations. They didn't talk about the company's business to outsiders. This was an unspoken rule among Koch's tightly knit team of leaders.

On May 12, Faragher called Kriens. She told him that Steve David had lied during their meeting. She was ready to help the state.

On May 27, Kriens and his team met again with Koch's managers. This time David, Faragher, and Hall were joined by Roos. Once again, Kriens asked if Koch's environmental team had been aware of the ammonia dumping prior to January, when Faragher had reported it to the state. Once again, he was told "No." But this time, Kriens knew the truth. During back-channel meetings, Faragher was helping him understand it.

The state's investigation grinded on through the spring and summer months of 1997. Koch built a legal wall around its refinery, hiring criminal defense lawyers to represent the employees involved in the ammonia dumping. Jim Voyles traveled to Pine Bend from Wichita and helped coach the employees, preparing them for an intense investigation by the MPCA.

Faragher kept going in to work every day, as if everything were normal. She had very little choice. Her pregnancy was progressing, and she was always aware that soon she'd have a child to support. The happy days of her early career at Koch were finished. The sense of community, the softball games, the drinking sessions—all of it had disappeared. Faragher had gained a reputation. She was known to be the complainer, the employee who'd fought her bosses on the ammonia issue.

Faragher kept her mouth shut at work during the long summer months. It was obvious what happened to those who did otherwise. Life had become instantly and thoroughly miserable for Charlie Chadwell and Terry Stormoen, the shift workers who took evidence of Koch's criminal conduct to state officials and then told their bosses about it. Chadwell was reprimanded after cigarette ashes were found in a work vehicle he used—he said he'd been smoking during his shift but not on refinery property. He was suspended. His managers held disciplinary meetings with him. A Koch attorney interrogated Chadwell about his views on Koch's environmental policy. Chadwell didn't cooperate and claimed that he couldn't answer some of the questions because he had short-term memory loss.

Chadwell called in sick after that meeting, and, in response, Koch required him to go see a company doctor who could evaluate his health. Koch's doctor referred Chadwell to a neurologist, who was hired by Koch, and the neurologist, in turn, referred Chadwell to a psychologist, also hired by Koch. The psychologist said that Chadwell did not, in fact, suffer from a memory disorder that would cause short-term memory loss.

Chadwell became even more confrontational. He took a briefcase full of documents from the refinery and gave them to the state, informing his bosses about it after the fact. Koch suspended Chadwell, saying he would not be reinstated on the job until he returned that evidence. Chadwell started telling people that Koch Industries was trying to kill him. He said someone had detonated an explosive device in his mailbox, an act he thought was orchestrated by the company. On December 9, Chadwell met again with Koch supervisors. This time he said he had been lying about the mailbox explosion and that he simply wanted to be fired.

Koch granted Chadwell's wish on December 17. He was terminated.

News traveled fast around the Pine Bend refinery. Chadwell's story was well known. Employees like Faragher saw what happened to employees who worked with state regulators.

On October 27, Faragher gave birth to her first child, a healthy girl. She stayed home and began a maternity leave that would last more than two months. The leave gave her time to think. She focused on her daughter. She trained her mind to avoid thoughts of Koch Industries. She thought the stress would only hurt her health, and therefore the health of her new baby. During the holidays of 1997 and the frigid new year, Faragher kept her eyes and her thoughts on her little girl.

But the problems at Koch came to her doorstep. On March 18, 1998, Faragher was home with her husband and infant daughter when the doorbell rang. She answered it and found a well-dressed man and woman on her front porch.

It was the woman who would lodge herself in Faragher's memory. Actually, it was the pistol on the woman's hip that was memorable. The couple introduced themselves to Faragher as she held the door open. The man was John Bonhage, a special agent with the FBI. The woman was Maureen O'Mara, an agent with the US Environmental Protection Agency. They asked if they could come in and talk, and Faragher said they could. It didn't appear that she had much choice.

O'Mara walked through Faragher's house with the heavy pistol holstered at her side. The pistol said everything that the two agents did not need to say. The full force of the federal government was now investigating the pollution at Pine Bend. Faragher was apparently at the center of the investigation.

Faragher sat down with the agents and her husband, Greg. They asked her about her history at Koch and the issues surrounding the ammonia dumping. They told her that they wanted her to cooperate with them and become a state's witness. They also wanted her to keep her involvement secret from Koch Industries. In short, the investigators wanted her to follow the path that Charlie Chadwell and Terry Stormoen had followed; they wanted her to provide evidence that could lead to criminal charges against Koch Industries.

Faragher said she would cooperate. They gave her their business cards and let it be known that they would be in touch.

As the agents were leaving her home, Faragher asked them if they needed her phone number. She recalled her husband saying, "Heather, they found our house. I think they have our phone number."

In this moment of fear, Faragher called her father, Ted Lawrence. She told him everything that had happened.

"He told me: 'I raised you to do the right thing. So tell the truth. You can sleep on my couch if you need to.'"

On March 31, 1998, Heather drove to an office building where she met with the FBI and the EPA. She talked to them for twelve hours.

———

Inside the refinery, Koch's defense attorneys were meeting extensively with employees, coaching them and questioning them as the federal regulators pursued their criminal probe.

Faragher sat down with a Koch attorney named Susan Wiens to go over the details of the case. Wiens began the interview by asking a series of perfunctory questions, collecting basic information. Wiens didn't seem to be paying much attention as she rolled through this series of stock questions. Then she asked Faragher if Faragher had been speaking with federal regulators.

Faragher answered: "Yes."

"The look on [Wiens's] face was priceless," Faragher recalled. "She said, 'Okay. You've got to excuse me.' She left the room immediately to go talk to someone."

In 1998, the Minnesota Pollution Control Agency fined Koch Industries $6.9 million for the company's pollution at Pine Bend. It was the largest fine of its type in the history of the state.

Federal criminal charges quickly followed after that. In 1999, Koch Industries pled guilty in federal court to criminal violations of environmental laws, both for dumping ammonia and for allowing leaks at the refinery to pollute the surrounding area with oil for several years. The company's plea spared it from fighting the charges in a drawn-out jury trial. No individuals at the company were charged with crimes. The deal allowed Koch to get off easier than it might have. As part of the plea deal, Koch agreed to pay a criminal fine of $6 million while also paying $2 million to Minnesota's Dakota County Park System. It was the largest federal fine ever imposed in Minnesota. Koch Industries also reached an agreement to pay a $3.5 million fine to the EPA.

The guilty plea permanently damaged Koch's reputation in Minnesota, but Koch's attorneys could reasonably be credited with getting the company off lightly. The fines, while historic, would not dent Pine Bend's profitability or cash flow.

Koch did not retaliate against Faragher by firing her. But she was ignored and felt shunned by management. She contacted the criminal lawyer Koch had hired to defend her and asked if he might be able to get her a severance package from the company. He negotiated a deal on her behalf. Faragher quit and got the severance. She never found another job in Minnesota, where she had so desperately wanted to raise her daughter. The Minnesota Pollution Control Agency offered her a job, but with a significant pay cut. She ended up getting a job in another state.

After he was fired, Charlie Chadwell sued Koch, claiming the company violated whistle-blower laws by retaliating against him. Chadwell lost the case when a jury decided that Koch had sufficient reason to fire him for his erratic behavior on the job. Terry Stormoen, the other shift worker who reported Koch's criminal activity, said that he simply quit his job without getting any kind of severance package or settlement from Koch.

Not everyone did so poorly. Brian Roos, the process owner over at Pine Bend's wastewater plant, was promoted to Wichita. By 2010, he had become a manager of strategic planning at Koch's petroleum division. Timothy Rusch, the refinery manager at Pine Bend, became Koch's vice president of construction and refinery services, overseeing projects at both the Pine Bend and Corpus Christi refineries. Jim Voyles, Koch's attorney, went on to have a successful career in environmental law, leaving Koch to join the fertilizer company Mosaic. In 2013, he spoke at a national conference on corporate sustainability held by the National Association for Environmental Management. In 2016, he was a senior attorney for Chevron in Bakersfield, California.

The illegal activity at Pine Bend was not an isolated incident. There were incidents of lawbreaking across Koch Industries, caused in part by a cultural bias toward maximizing profits and abetted by a general disdain for government.

At the refinery in Corpus Christi, for example, Koch managers delayed equipment improvements in much the same way that Brian Roos and others hesitated to shut down the Pine Bend refinery to inspect the sour water strippers. In April of 1996, an environmental technician named Sally Barnes-Soliz went to state environmental regulators and told them that Koch Industries had been lying about illegal emissions of the chemical benzene, which causes cancer. Barnes-Soliz worked at the Corpus Christi refinery. The state had ordered Koch Industries to cut benzene emissions from the refinery. Koch had told the state it complied with the order. But Barnes-Soliz said this was a lie. "The refinery was just hemorrhaging benzene into the atmosphere," she later told *Bloomberg Markets* magazine.

Barnes-Soliz reported the high emissions levels to her bosses. But like Faragher, she said, she was sidelined. Koch reported much lower levels to the state, filing false reports that undercounted how much benzene it was emitting. Thanks in part to assistance from Barnes-Soliz, federal prosecutors filed a ninety-seven-count criminal indictment against Koch. The company disputed that Barnes-Soliz was a whistle-blower, pointing out that Koch managers themselves reported wrong-doing to authorities when they discovered that a manager had falsified pollution reports. Most of the ninety-seven counts against Koch were later dropped, a sign, Koch's attorney said, that prosecutors had been overzealous. A federal judge ended up fining the company $10 million for the violations and ordering it to pay another $10 million to Texas authorities to fund environmental work. Barnes-Soliz said Koch retaliated against her whistle-blowing: "They were pressuring me to quit," she told *Bloomberg Markets*. She did so in 1996. Koch insisted that Barnes-Soliz had a poor performance record and her departure was unrelated to the benzene pollution.

In Koch's pipeline division, managers delayed needed repairs to boost profits. Phil Dubose, the onetime oil gauger who rose to senior levels in the transportation department, said he was shocked at the sorry state of Koch's pipelines. They were leaky and poorly cared for. Koch often didn't even trim foliage that grew over and around the pipes as it was supposed to do to keep a clean right-of-way. The EPA sued Koch in 1995 for negligence of the pipeline system. The agency alleged that Koch spilled roughly twelve million gallons of oil between 1988 and 1996 and caused 312 spills in six states. The company was eventually fined $30 million for the pipeline leaks, which was the largest fine of its kind in US history.

The most tragic case happened in Texas. One of Koch's neglected pipelines began to leak butane vapors into the air in the summer of 1996. Two teenagers named Danielle Smalley and Jason Stone were driving near the pipeline leak when it ignited and caused an explosion. The two kids were burned alive. Smalley's family sued Koch and won a judgment of $296 million, another record-breaking amount. The family later settled for an undisclosed amount. These fines and charges, combined with those for the ammonia dumping at Pine Bend, marked Koch Industries as one of the largest, most flagrant violators of environmental laws in the United States during the 1990s.

But the judgments and indictments did not slow Koch down. This was a period when Charles Koch was focused more than ever on expanding, and expanding rapidly. The problems exposed at Pine Bend and elsewhere were not being isolated and contained. They were being exported.

CHAPTER 9

Off the Rails

(1995–2000)

Koch Industries executives gathered for a secret meeting at an offsite corporate conference room in Wichita. They were gathered to be told about a new strategic initiative. It is safe to say that this meeting is where the problems started.

The business leaders heard a presentation from a young Koch employee named John C. Pittenger. He was a new breed of Koch employee. He didn't graduate from Kansas State University or the University of Oklahoma; he went to Princeton University for his undergrad and to Harvard for his master's degree in business. Koch hired him from a consulting firm called Monitor Group, which was run by Michael Porter, the Harvard management guru who'd given some of the earliest seminars on competition strategy at Koch Industries in the 1980s.

Pittenger moved easily in the world of East Coast money. He knew the latest management theories, consulting trends, and buzzwords being handed down by the Ivy League. He could have easily worked for any firm on Wall Street, but he decided to leave that world and work for Koch. He did this after seeing firsthand how the company operated when Koch had hired him as a contract consultant.

Lots of other business school graduates were following in Pittenger's footsteps. Koch was hiring more Ivy Leaguers and MBAs than ever before. The educated business class was finally catching on to what was happening inside the Tower in Wichita.

During the offsite meeting with Koch's top executives, Pittenger helped explain how they'd be running their business over the next decade. They learned that growth would be more important than ever. It was time to expand. Time to take advantage of the economic conditions encouraging bigness in corporate America. In typical Koch fashion, the company developed a specific strategy to grow, one that came complete with its own vocabulary. The framework was called the Value Creation Strategy, or VCS.

Every Koch business leader was expected to create their own Value Creation Strategy. They needed to look for new companies to buy, new plants to build, and expansion projects for existing plants. This wasn't exactly new—growth was ingrained in Koch's DNA from the beginning, when Sterling Varner encouraged his employees to keep their eyes peeled for investment opportunities. But the VCS regimen was different. Business leaders knew that Charles Koch would cut or increase their bonus pay based on the Value Creation Strategies they delivered. Expansion was once applauded; now it would be required.

This change rippled out through the ranks. Deals were proposed and sent to Wichita—everybody wanted a big acquisition under their belt. Charles Koch had historically been merciless when it came to assessing these deals, but a certain bias toward acquisitions crept into Koch Industries' decision-making by 1995. Koch's own track record fostered this bias. Koch Industries' sales were roughly $24 billion a year, more than 135 times what they had been when Charles Koch assumed control in 1967. The profits and the cash flowing in the door seemed to be proof that Koch's philosophies worked. The company knew how to grow—the market itself had delivered its verdict. Charles Koch listened to that verdict. He pushed the company forward even more aggressively.

"There's a tremendous focus on growth, okay, from Charles. . . . The whole thing is growth," recalled Brad Hall, the Wichita State graduate who joined the company in 1975. Hall rose through the ranks to become a business leader by 1995, allowing him to work closely with Charles Koch as more and more acquisitions were being made.

As it turned out, Hall would spend many years of his life helping clean up the wreckage from those deals. It was wreckage that might have been avoided. "I think Charles got cavalier," Hall said.

What resulted was a kind of perpetual motion machine: a company that grew and then cited that growth as justification to grow even faster. One employee, a rising star, would take this philosophy to heart. He was ambitious, smart, and determined to prove his worth to Charles Koch. His name was Dean Watson.

Dean Watson joined Koch Industries in the early 1980s when he was just twenty-two years old, freshly graduated from Kansas State University. He was intense and physically imposing, standing six foot one, or "six foot two in cowboy boots," as he likes to say. He had sandy red hair and a competitive streak that seemed woven into his muscle fiber. He'd been a star on his high school football team, but an injury kept him from playing in college. When he was sidelined from the football field, Watson found another realm in which he could compete. He discovered that he had a mind for finance and complex systems. He took business and accounting classes, and he excelled.

After he joined Koch Industries, Watson approached the world of business in the same way he had played sports—with the intensity of a coiled spring. He was a natural leader with a deep and commanding voice and a way of stating his judgments with supreme confidence. Watson could talk for hours about marginal profits and competitive industry dynamics and expansion opportunities. He shifted easily between abstract management concepts and microscopic operating details of anhydrous ammonia pipelines in the Gulf of Mexico. He didn't tell people that they needed to follow a business plan. He said, "We need to execute violently against what we've been asked to go do." Watson threw himself into his career. Koch was his life. He didn't know his neighbors because he worked all waking hours at the Tower. And it made him very happy. He was part of something big.

Watson was fearless, and this might be part of what endeared him to Charles Koch. Watson's colleagues and peers couldn't help but notice his particularly close relationship with Charles Koch. Watson dropped into Koch's office to share ideas and seek his mentor's advice. If he was walking past Charles Koch's office, Watson even felt comfortable popping his head in and interrupting the chief executive. On one occasion, Watson did so to talk over some arcane mechanics of oil prices.

"His door was open, and I knocked on the door and said, 'Hey, Charles, I've been thinking about this,'" Watson recalled. "And so we were talking about internal price transferring and the distortion of pricing in the markets . . . and I bet he spent forty minutes with me, [writing] on the back of a sheet of paper, and we were drawing graphs and pictures and philosophizing. I mean, he was very, very open and very kind to me."

Watson wasn't shy about challenging the people around him, but there was something almost disarming about it. It didn't seem like he was trying to exert his status but was just possessed by an idea. This alone isn't what propelled Dean Watson to the center of Koch Industries' growth in the 1990s. What propelled Watson was his track record in the business. He was named president of a relatively obscure division called Koch Fertilizer. In this capacity, he oversaw a fertilizer plant in Louisiana that Koch purchased when another company wanted to unload it cheap. The division also included a pipeline that shipped fertilizer north to farming states like Iowa and Nebraska.

Running the fertilizer division might have seemed like an insignificant job to people outside of Koch. But Watson knew better. The fertilizer plant was an example of Koch's strategy for "rapid prototyping," a phrase that Watson used to describe Koch's business experiments. Rapid prototyping was the process of trying new ventures on a small scale to see how they worked. It was the method that Koch used to branch out into different industries. Failure would be part of the process, so Koch kept its initial ventures small. Divisions like the fertilizer business were all learning laboratories.

Koch Industries learned a lot with its fertilizer business. Among other things, the company learned that American agriculture had slowly and quietly turned into a fossil fuel business. This strange fact would launch the largest expansion effort in Koch's history. It was nothing less than a play to take over a vast portion of America's food system.

Koch's fertilizer plant was basically an oil refinery, but instead of transforming crude oil into gasoline, it transformed natural gas into nitrogen-based fertilizer. It might seem odd that crop fertilizers were produced from fossil fuel. The reasons for this were diverse, but they had a lot to do with the industrialization of the American farm.

During the 1990s, American farmers were producing more food than ever. Barn-sized combines and tractors tilled farms that stretched for thousands of acres. This system was entirely dependent on artificial fertilizers, because even the best, deepest topsoil in the Midwest couldn't support such massive yields of corn and soybeans year after year. To achieve the megaharvests, farmers applied a mixture of three chemicals to supercharge the soil: potassium, phosphorus, and nitrogen.

The first two chemicals are mined from the earth, just like coal. But nitrogen is different: there aren't large deposits of nitrogen underground. Before World War II, farmers had to plant special legume crops to "fix" nitrogen in the soil through special nodules in their roots. This was time consuming and complicated. But in the early 1940s, a pair of German chemists figured out how to produce nitrogen artificially. They invented something called the Haber-Bosch process, which fixed nitrogen inside a refinery using natural gas as the primary input. This was revolutionary. Nitrogen fertilizer became the lifeblood of modern farming.

Koch's facility in Louisiana used natural gas to create a nitrogen-rich chemical called anhydrous ammonia. It used the pipelines to ship ammonia north, where farmers applied it to the soil. The fertilizer plant looked very much like an oil refinery; it was a knotted landscape of inter-weaving pipes and tanks studded with giant cracking towers. And the facility was operated a lot like an oil refinery—Koch Industries was able to apply what it had learned at Pine Bend and Corpus Christi. Dean Watson employed a team of natural gas traders to get him the cheapest possible sources of feedstock, and he used computer models to run the plant at peak efficiency, just as Koch's refinery managers did.

The fertilizer business itself was a platform for growth. It was a listening post to learn about all the businesses that the fertilizer business touched. Dean Watson "executed violently" against this task. He met the players in the food industry, and he studied the markets for food and crops. Soon enough, he and others started to see how Koch Industries might compete in the food business.

The entire food system appeared to be one immense machine that laundered energy from fossil fuels into food calorie energy that humans could eat. At the beginning of the supply chain was the fossil fuel—gasoline used by tractors and natural gas used to make nitrogen fertilizer. The next link of the chain were farmers raising crops and animals, using the fossil fuels as they went. After that came the food processing industry, like the grain mills and slaughterhouses. Finally, there were the grocery stores and restaurants that distributed the final food products. Koch Industries planned to insert itself into every link of this chain. Charles

Koch had made his company the single largest purchaser of American crude oil in the span of a decade. Now his company might be able to do the same thing with food.

Dean Watson was promoted from overseeing Koch's fertilizer production to overseeing a new division called Koch Agriculture. This division would be the cornerstone of a business plan that was so large in its ambition, so vast in its scope, that nobody outside the company would have believed the plan was real.

Koch Agriculture first branched out into the beef business, and it did so in a way that gave it control from the ranch to the butcher's counter.

Koch bought cattle feedlots. Then it developed its own retail brand of beef called Spring Creek Ranch. Dean Watson oversaw a team that worked to develop a system of "identity preservation" that would allow the company to track each cow during its lifespan, allowing it over time to select which cattle had the best-tasting meat. Koch held blind taste tests of the beef it raised. Watson claimed to win nine out of ten times.

Then Koch studied the grain and feed industries that supplied its feedlots. Watson worked with experts to study European farming methods because wheat farmers in Ukraine were far better at raising more grain on each acre of land than American farmers were. The Europeans had less acreage to work with, forcing them to be more efficient, and Koch learned how to replicate their methods. Koch bought a stake in a genetic engineering company to breed superyielding corn. Koch Agriculture extended into the milling and flour businesses as well. It experimented with building "micro" mills that would be nimbler than the giant mills operated by Archer Daniels Midland and Cargill. Koch worked with a start-up company that developed a "pixie dust" spray preservative that could be applied to pizza crusts, making crusts that did not need to be refrigerated. It experimented with making ethanol gasoline and corn oil.

There were more abstract initiatives. Koch launched an effort to sell rain insurance to farmers who had no way to offset the risk of heavy rains. To do that, Koch hired a team of PhD statisticians to write formulas that correlated corn harvests with rain events, figuring out what a rain insurance policy should cost. At the same time, Koch's commodity traders were buying contracts for corn and soybeans, learning more every day about those markets.

Koch Agriculture was growing rapidly, but Charles Koch was distracted by a different matter. He was busy talking with lawyers in Topeka, where his brother Bill was waging a full-scale legal war against him.

The lawsuit Bill filed in 1985—alleging that Charles Koch underpaid him for his share of the company—had grown into a sprawling legal sinkhole, sucking in dozens of lawyers, judges, clerks, and investigators. The reasons for Bill Koch's crusade were becoming increasingly hard to decipher. Was it over money? Brotherly competition? The simple desire to avenge his firing?

If the motivations for this fight were shadowy, then the tactics Bill employed were even darker. The *New York Times* later uncovered documents showing that Bill Koch hired investigators to pose as journalists and dig up incriminating information on Charles Koch.* One investigator was offered a $25,000 bounty if he could persuade a national newspaper to publish damaging information about Koch Industries. Bill hired detectives to collect trash outside the homes of Koch Industries lawyers and he later bragged to *Vanity Fair* that he'd hired "an Israeli-trained former marine" named Marc Nezer to run security operations and use surveillance devices like bugs and cameras. Bill Koch's lengthy interview with *Vanity Fair* included the kind of excruciatingly personal information Charles Koch did not share with close friends. Bill Koch detailed his therapy sessions and the scars of his childhood. The *Wall Street Journal* published a front-page story under the headline "Blood Feud." The first paragraph of the article began, "To hear William Koch tell it, his brother Charles is a liar, a cheater, and a racketeer."

During the late 1990s, Charles Koch found himself consumed by the battle against Bill. His company was under attack, his reputation was under attack, and he faced the prospect of paying millions of dollars or more to his brother if he lost the federal lawsuit in Topeka. As these dis-

* The investigators were hired by a firm called Decision Strategies International, which was under retainer, according to documents uncovered by the *Times*.

tractions swallowed Charles Koch's attention, his company was growing faster than ever.

There was a secret group inside Koch Industries dedicated to expanding the company. In the late 1990s, Brad Hall was put in charge of it. This was the small team with the anodyne name of "the corporate development group," or simply "the development group" as most people called it. It was essentially a small brain trust located inside the executive suite. Very few people outside the company knew it existed. The development group was modeled on a new kind of investment machine that was springing up on Wall Street, called a private equity firm. These firms institutionalized a trend that had started in the 1980s, when investors realized there was more money to be made in buying existing companies than in creating new ones. The eighties and nineties were the era of mergers and acquisitions and so-called leveraged buyouts. Private equity firms borrowed large sums of money to buy companies, sometimes stripping them for parts and selling off their assets. Other times, the companies became a playground for business turnaround artists who swept in, cut jobs, cut pensions, closed money-losing divisions, and then sold the resulting company.

The development group that Brad Hall oversaw resembled these private equity firms in some ways. But there was a fundamental difference. Koch's development group had patience. It thought on a timeline of ten or twenty years, not twelve to eighteen months. And, unlike virtually any other private equity firm, Koch's group had only two shareholders to answer to: Charles and David Koch.

For these reasons, Koch made acquisitions like nobody else. It tended to rush into markets when others were leaving. It tended to buy companies only when they were distressed and no one else wanted them. Koch was accustomed to the wild volatility of energy markets, so the company knew that most downturns were temporary.

The development group was the central hub of many spokes. Each major division at Koch Industries had its own development team, looking for acquisitions. Sometimes these teams made the deals on their own; other times they passed them on to Hall's central group for clearance. Being head of the corporate development group might have seemed like a plum assignment for someone like Hall. It was unfortunate, then, when he discovered that the group was a dysfunctional mess. The development group was bloated. There were too many people across the company looking at too many deals. And these people were not the right kind of people. Koch had begun to stock its ranks with MBA students from the best business schools around the country. Brad Hall spent a lot of his time trying to unteach these kids what they learned at Northwestern University or Harvard. And there was the cultural element as well. Many executives inside Koch Industries saw that a type of freelance culture was growing among the young guns. They were looking out for themselves, not the company.

Charles Koch was not there to school these new employees. The company had grown too large for that, and he was spending much of his time in closed-door meetings with lawyers to fend off Bill Koch's latest attacks. The culture inside Koch Industries was beginning to drift. It borrowed some of the worst impulses from Wall Street—a hunger for high-profile deals, a desire for giant personal paydays, short-term thinking—and combined them with Koch Industries' mandate for growth.

The Value Creation Strategies were piling up. Brad Hall and his team were trying hard to evaluate them. But the corporate development group could not control the growth. A lot of the decision-making had been pushed out to the smaller development groups in each company division. They were out making acquisitions on their own.

Koch Agriculture was about the make the biggest, and most disastrous, of them all.

The largest animal feed maker in America was called Purina Mills Inc. In 1997, the company was up for sale. A group of bankers brought the deal to Dean Watson's attention. With just one acquisition, he could make Koch Agriculture a colossus.

Purina Mills was based in St. Louis and had been around for more than a century. It was well known for making pet food. Almost everyone with a dog knew about Purina's products and its famous red-and-white checkered logo. But there was a giant part of Purina that was largely hidden from public view. Over many decades, Purina Mills had become the largest maker of livestock feed in the United States. This was a particularly vibrant business during the 1990s, thanks to a revolution in the way animals were raised for meat.

The pig industry was emblematic of this shift. Even up until the 1970s, most pigs were raised in an environment that people would recognize as a farm. Pigs lived in hutches and could walk around outside. Pigs were fed grain that was often grown right on the farm where they lived. When it was time to slaughter the animals, they were loaded onto a truck and driven to a nearby sales barn where slaughterhouses bought the animals based on a competitive market price.

All of this changed with the advent of the industrial pig farm. The hutches were replaced with vast warehouses that could hold thousands of animals at a time. The warehouses were fitted with automatic feeding and ventilation systems. The local sales barns closed down and were replaced by large-scale farms where farmers raised ten thousand pigs at a time under contract for a company like Tyson Foods. This transformation had an odd side effect: it neatly split American agriculture into two spheres. There were farmers who raised animals in factory barns, and then there were farmers who raised grain to feed them. Purina Mills stepped into this breach as the feed provider of choice, and it made a fortune. The company operated fifty-eight giant feed mills across twenty-four states. In 1996 it sold 5 million tons of grain for $1.2 billion. It was earning gross profits of about $176 million a year.

But 1996 was a down year for Purina Mills, a time when commodity markets were roiling. Grain prices shot up to record highs and then crashed again. The company lost sales because it had to raise prices sharply. Margins were squeezed. The firm lost $10 million that year. It was the perfect takeover target for Koch Industries. Koch looked at a struggling Purina and saw tremendous potential in the long term. Purina's national network of feed mills was unmatched. The underlying market structure that Purina served wasn't going to change at all. When markets rebounded, which they would, Purina could generate huge profits.

This didn't mean that the executives who led Purina Mills were excited about selling it. The company had a storied history in St. Louis and a legacy of independent leadership. Senior executives at the firm weren't instantly seduced by the idea of being owned by an energy company out of Wichita. Purina's chief operating officer, Arnie Sumner, counted himself among the skeptical. He had been with the company

more than twenty years. He was a New Englander, a transplant to suburban St. Louis who still had a slight trace of a longshoreman's accent.
Sumner wasn't a flashy guy, and he wasn't too impressed when Koch first
approached the company.

Koch's ambitions for Purina were vast. The company would transfer
all of Purina's grain purchasers to a central desk in Wichita, where they
would become a trading desk to buy and sell commodities. These traders
would be able to supply all the grain that Purina needed, while also sup-
plying other major customers like Tyson Foods and Cargill.

"I think they thought they were going to buy commodities for the
world . . . because they could do it better than anybody else," Sumner
recalled. Koch also planned to build a new network of specialized "wet"
feed mills that could process food waste into animal feed. Those mills
would create whole new sources of feedstock for Purina—wet potato
peels instead of soybeans, for instance. Purina could sell the feed through
its unrivaled network of dealers.

Because of these ambitious plans, Koch was able to offer a surprisingly giant sum of money for Purina. Dean Watson and others offered
a price for Purina Mills that included the value Koch thought it would
produce after its improvements had taken hold. Purina itself was worth
about $109 million. Koch would pay $670 million to buy it.

Such a rich price was impossible for Purina's management to deny.
"Koch came along, and they made a huge offer for the stock," Sumner
recalled. "That's the whole reason it was sold. People wanted to cash out.
We were all led to believe that this was going to be a great thing."

Koch made one pivotal decision when it bought Purina: it financed
almost the entire deal through debt. This was a stark departure from earlier deals, when Koch had used its own cash reserves to buy new businesses. It was extremely difficult to borrow hundreds of millions of
dollars from one place, so Koch Industries went on a road show of sorts,
convincing different groups of bankers to lend it money for the Purina
deal.

Koch ended up borrowing the money with two massive sources of
debt. The first was a $200 million loan (called a term loan) that was pro-
vided by a network of banks. The second source was a group of corporate bonds (called notes) worth $350 million. Koch also set up a line of
revolving credit in case it needed extra cash. Koch made up the rest of

the purchase price with roughly $100 million of its own money in the form of equity that it handed over to the new Purina Mills. The deal was closed in March of 1998.

Koch wasted no time in making good on its investment. Koch employees began to infiltrate Purina's offices in suburban St. Louis. Koch had more than $550 million in debt hanging over its head, but the Koch people didn't seem worried about it. "I think everyone within Koch thought they knew more than anybody else," Sumner said. "It kind of got crazy."

One of Dean Watson's first and most important jobs was to integrate Purina Mill's operations into the broader machinery of Koch Industries. There was more to this than figuring out how to process Purina's payroll out of Wichita or how to train Koch's traders to buy and sell grain for Purina's mills. That was the easy part. The more difficult element was psychological. Watson had to figure out how to subsume Purina's corporate culture into Koch's. Watson referred to the entire acquisition, in fact, as a "long-term culture-shift play."

The process began with a seminar in Market-Based Management. Watson needed to teach the philosophy to Purina's top leadership, just as Charles Koch had first taught it to his own senior managers. The parameters of MBM demanded total conversion on the part of new employees. But Purina Mills already had a corporate culture of its own.

You could call it the Danforth culture, named after Purina's founding family. The Danforth name carried a mythical reverberation that could only be heard by Missouri ears. The Danforth family was the state's equivalent of royalty, having mastered all three important realms of midwestern civic life: business, church, and politics. The patriarch, William H. Danforth, founded the Ralston-Purina Company more than a hundred years before Dean Watson showed up. Danforth's son, Donald, took over the company and became a fixture of the St. Louis business community. Danforth's grandson, John Danforth, was an ordained Episcopal priest who went into politics and became a US senator.

The Danforths had their own way of doing business at Purina, generation after generation. Even the company's logo—a famous checkered logo with nine squares, four white and five red—were a symbol of the founder's philosophy. The four corner squares in the logo represented the four necessary elements of human well-being, according to William Danforth: physical, social, mental, and religious. These four elements blended together to make a corporate culture that executives would describe as being like family. As such, employees were not discarded. If an employee's job was eliminated after he'd been with the company for forty years, he could rely on Purina to find a place for him. He could totter into work until he no longer cared to—his joints would give out far earlier than his job security. Such an arrangement was considered perverse under the philosophy of Market-Based Management. Letting someone work past their prime only robbed precious resources from potential new employees.

Shortly after Koch Industries took control of Purina, Purina's senior management team was called into a meeting. The executives arrived at a hotel in the western St. Louis suburbs, where the wide windows look out over rolling green hillsides and the rooftops of suburban cul-de-sacs. Roughly two dozen Purina executives sat down in the conference room. These were men who'd been with their company for decades, many of them with the white hair to prove it. They were not a class of eager college graduates attending a Market-Based Management training session in Wichita.

Dean Watson stood before them and explained that the first step toward being an employee of Koch Industries was learning MBM. Learning the philosophy wasn't a benefit of being at Koch—it was a precondition to working there. Purina's executives would need to understand the five dimensions to MBM. They would need to internalize Koch's Ten Guiding Principles—not memorize them, but internalize them. These principles included integrity, compliance, and value creation.

Arnie Sumner, Purina's chief operating officer, listened to the presentation and thought it sounded like management consultant sloganeering. The nature of a good merger, in his mind, was when two companies meshed their corporate cultures. But Koch wasn't trying to mesh with Purina's culture; it was trying to eradicate it. The Purina executives didn't swallow it. They didn't think it was necessary to erase their neural pathways and start anew under Charles Koch's tutelage.

Dean Watson became agitated in the face of this resistance. "He got up on the stage and started screaming and yelling," Sumner said. He remembered Watson shouting: "Who the hell do you think owns this damn thing? You guys are going to do what the hell we tell you to do. If you don't like it, get your ass out!"*

If this was a sales pitch, it was less than inspiring. Senior executives began quitting the company soon after the meeting. They took retirement packages or moved on to new jobs. Watson seemed to realize his mistake immediately.

"Afterward, he said to me, 'I really screwed up, didn't I?'" Sumner said.

Things started to go south for Purina Mills because of a change in government policy. It wasn't an OPEC-style embargo that unleashed an era of volatility in food production. It was Congress. For the preceding half century, the world of agriculture had been remarkably stable. Prices for crops like corn and soybeans moved around, but they moved within a narrow band. The food industry was a lot like the oil industry during the 1960s. It was predictable.

This changed in 1996, shortly after Republicans took control of Congress. Newt Gringrich, the Speaker of the House, led the Republican Revolution, and farm programs were one of the conservatives' first targets. Farm programs were the cornerstone of the New Deal. Back in 1933, farming was a pillar of America's middle class, but the business was whipsawed by violent booms and busts. The Great Depression had been the biggest bust of all. In response, President Franklin Roosevelt created an intricate system of price supports and crop quotas using pages stolen from the books of Soviet-style central planning but burnished with a patina of capitalistic freedom. Farmers had production limits, but the limits were voluntary. The guidelines were encouraged by subsidies. Many farmers got checks in the mail to ensure they let part of their land lay fallow—they got money for nothing. In 1996, Congress passed a bill called "Freedom to Farm" that largely abolished the New Deal farm programs. Subsidies did not disappear, however. They were simply replaced with a complex system of insurance payments and "disaster" relief. (It

---

* Dean Watson did not remember this encounter. He said it was rare for him to lose his temper at work, and if he did lose his temper, it would have run counter to the teachings of MBM, which does not seek to coerce or control employees.

turns out that virtually every year is a disaster of one kind or another for farmers. The so-called disaster payments turned into a dependable flood of cash to large-scale farmers.) What did get abolished were the production controls. Farmers were encouraged to grow as much food as they could, market prices be damned.

This caused a wave of volatility to flood through every nook and corner of the farm economy in 1997 and 1998. Purina Mills was sitting right in the center of it. Purina bought grain from farmers and sold feed to livestock producers. Both of those businesses rose and fell in wild and unpredictable swings, each one hurting Purina Mills in a different way.

The brain trust of Koch employees around Dean Watson had to figure out how to respond, and they were utterly unprepared to do so. A lot of his team members were the "freelancers"—the MBAs from business schools on the East Coast or in Chicago. "We had no depth when it came to local knowledge, which was our ability to understand the nuance of the businesses we were in," Watson said. "Most of what we relied on was from the free agent markets. . . . You had no idea how these guys and gals would react when the shit started hitting the fan."

The heaviest damage started to emerge from an unlikely place: Purina's business selling pig feed.

Before the deal to buy Purina closed, Watson had been warned about Purina's pig business. It turned out that Purina owned some pigs, which was odd. Purina sold feed; it didn't raise animals. Watson was told that Purina had signed some contracts to buy baby pigs and then turn around and sell those baby pigs to farmers. The idea seemed to be that Purina would lock in the business to sell those farmers feed as the pigs matured. Watson asked one of his lieutenants, a former Cargill employee, about the pig contracts. He told Watson that the exposure was limited. Purina didn't own the pigs for very long; it was basically acting as a middleman.

As it turned out, Purina's exposure to the hog business was not limited at all. The volatile markets exposed that fact. In 1998, the US hog market experienced a shock comparable to the stock market crash of 1929—a market convulsion that obliterated all the rules everyone thought applied to the business. The root of the problem could be traced to the very industrialization that created Purina Mills' feed business in the first place. Now that hogs were raised on factory farms, the supply of animals was enormous and inflexible. Farmers were raising herds of tens or even hundreds of thousands of pigs. When prices started to fall, these industrial farms couldn't adapt quickly. They had mortgage payments to meet on the big pig houses, and they needed to keep production high. Factory farms were a machine that wasn't easily turned off. The flow of pigs continued into the slaughterhouses, and prices fell even further. Then everything spun out of control. Hog prices plummeted, sucking the entire business into the ground almost instantly. The price of hogs fell from about 53 cents per pound to 10 cents per pound in a matter of months. When adjusted for inflation, this was the lowest price for pigs in US history. It cost far more to raise a pig than the animal was worth.

Purina Mills should have been insulated against this crisis. It only sold feed, not the hogs themselves. But with its decision in 1997 to start buying baby hogs, Purina had exposed itself to the risk of falling pork prices. Dean Watson began to discover just how large that exposure was. As one farm economist put it at the time, the rational number of hogs to own in 1998 was zero. Purina discovered this fact quickly. It bought baby hogs, and turned around to sell them to the farmers. But there were no buyers. The farmers refused to take them.

"The people who we were supposed to be selling the pigs to were basically saying: 'Sue me.' The people we had bought the pigs from were saying: 'You're not getting out of my contract or I am suing you,'" Watson said. "All of this ownership risk that I was assured didn't exist started to just come out of the woodwork."

There was no central repository in which all these hog contracts were kept. That meant there was no easy way to figure out how much money Purina stood to lose. The company was discovering its contractual obligations with each new angry phone call that came into its pig division. One giant pig contract was sent into the company via fax from a large pig company in Pennsylvania. No one on Watson's team had been aware of the contract before it arrived.

"I remember asking the question 'How in the *hell* can this show up in a fax without us knowing about it?'" Watson said. "You kind of get these deer-in-the-headlight looks."

In December of 1998, Watson was named CEO of Purina Mills. His job was to stanch the bleeding. At the time, he was still working at Koch's headquarters in Wichita, but Koch chartered him a private jet to St. Louis that departed each Monday morning at five thirty. He spent his weeks at Purina headquarters and flew home on the weekends to see his family.

The hog market crisis raced forward faster than Purina Mills' leaders could respond. And Purina could not respond quickly to the market convulsions because it was shackled with debt. In mid-1998 it owed about $557 million. The company had to post periodic payments of several million dollars just to pay interest.

Watson tried to mollify crowds of angry bankers. One group of lenders, who had about $200 million on the line, traveled to St. Louis to hear Watson tell them how he planned to pay their money back. His ideas were less than convincing. In early March of 1999, just three months after Watson became CEO, the ratings agency Moody's downgraded Purina's debt. The likelihood of anyone getting their money back started to look slim.

Watson struggled to keep his troops in line. The freelancers with MBAs knew very well that the ship might be going down. Loyalty was not at a premium. At one point, Dean gathered employees around him as he stood on a desk in one of Koch's trading rooms. He exhorted the crowd, saying, "Look, I've got to have everybody. All hands on deck. You're grabbing an oar [to help paddle], or you get your ass off the boat, because I can't wait anymore."

Brad Hall was dispatched from Wichita to St. Louis to start digging through Purina Mills' files and figure out just how big its losses might be. The picture that emerged was terrifying. Starting sometime in 1997, before Koch Industries bought the company, Purina Mills had hatched a plan to boost hog feed sales by purchasing baby pigs and then providing them to farmers to raise. The farmers agreed to feed the pigs Purina products. The company had locked in guaranteed sales, and it was easy money for a while. So Purina expanded the program. It provided more pigs under contract to big companies like Tyson Foods, selling more feed and then buying even more pigs. By the end of 1997, Purina effectively owned six million pigs, making it one of the largest hog producers in the nation. When Koch purchased the company, it missed this fact because it hadn't looked closely enough. The deal was too hurried; growth had taken precedence over diligence.

By 1998, Purina Mills was on the hook to purchase about $240 million worth of hogs that had literally zero financial value. Brad Hall went back to Wichita to inform Charles Koch about what he'd found.

Charles Koch was just returning his full attention to the business. His months of distractions from Bill Koch's litigation were finally coming to an end. The federal jury in Wichita ruled in Charles Koch's favor in June of 1998, finding that he had not deceived his brother Bill when he sold the company. It was a complete and unambiguous victory for Charles Koch—he owed Bill nothing. Bill appealed the verdict and called Charles a "crook" in the resulting newspaper stories, but this was to be expected. The appeals went forward, and Bill Koch lost them all. Charles Koch wasn't given time to celebrate. The disaster at Purina Mills was awaiting his attention.

Most people who have worked with Charles Koch have never seen him get angry. Charles Koch doesn't yell, or even raise his voice. During one meeting of senior executives, a manager said there was no "fucking way" he would comply with an order from Charles Koch. In response, Charles Koch simply closed his meeting folder, stood up, and left the room.

When Brad Hall explained what was happening inside Koch Agriculture, Charles Koch became as angry as Hall had ever seen him. Hall stood in front of Koch and walked him through the pig contracting scheme at Purina. It was hard to guess just how much money Koch Agriculture would lose from its stake in Purina Mills. Koch was able to escape some of the contractual commitments to buy hogs. It might be able to hedge some of its other contracts. The losses might approach $80 million—or they could be higher, Hall said.

It wasn't just the financial losses that seemed to enrage Charles Koch. It was the fact that Koch executives missed the lethal liability hiding within Purina's business. Charles Koch snapped.

"How'd this happen?" he demanded of Hall. Charles Koch was incensed with Dean Watson and some of the MBAs who'd worked on the Purina acquisition, Hall remembered. Charles Koch was staring at a catastrophe, and one that appeared to have been entirely avoidable.

Dean Watson's life was a rapid rotation of flights between Wichita and St. Louis, and conference calls with angry bankers and furious customers who demanded that Purina Mills live up to its contract obligations. "Every assumption we had made had just been blown out of the water. We're in just an awful, awful spot," Watson said. "We knew what we wanted to do, we just didn't have the time to do it. . . . Honestly we were just like, 'Holy shit.'"

During one meeting, Watson was interrupted by one of his attorneys bursting into the room. The attorney had just tried to call one of his counterparts in Wichita and was told that nobody in Wichita could speak to him.

"What do you mean they can't talk to you?" Watson remembers asking. The attorney said there had been an order given from on high in Wichita: all communication between Wichita and Purina Mills must cease.

Another executive came into the office with a worried look on his face. He told Watson that he too had been cut off from talking with a counterpart at Koch Industries. Four or five senior people gathered in Watson's office, wondering how to move forward.

Watson did the only thing he knew to do. He called Charles Koch to ask what was going on.

"He said, 'Well, we're doing this for the protection of Koch Industries. We need to narrow the scope of the interface. You will be given a person that you can talk to—so all your communication will go through that person,'" Watson recalled.

Watson felt that Charles Koch made the right decision for Koch Industries. It was important to protect Koch from the burning building that was Purina. But Watson still argued against the move. He didn't think it would help Purina survive.

Charles Koch tried to calm his young protégé. "He chuckled, in that laugh of his, and he goes, 'Dean, don't worry. Everything will be all right,'" Watson remembered.

"That was the last thing I ever heard from Charles Koch."

Watson was in Wisconsin, attending one of the countless "pig meetings," when he got a phone call. His attendance was requested at the Crestview Country Club in Wichita. He needed to meet with the three men who comprised Purina Mills' board of directors. The men had been appointed by Koch Industries, and they were not friendly toward Watson. They were the only people who could fire him.

Watson arrived early at the country club. The parking lot was nearly empty. Watson spotted a car there that he knew belonged to one of Koch's directors. He peered inside the car windows and saw three suitcases in the back. That meant the directors would be catching a flight to St. Louis directly after the meeting. It was likely to be a short encounter.

Watson had no illusions about what was underway. "I've been in business a long time. I've seen what happens at Koch," he said.

Watson walked into the spacious clubhouse and proceeded up a flight of stairs to a meeting room often used by Koch. The room had big windows looking out over a putting green. The three directors were waiting for him.

"I said, 'Okay, boys. Let's get this over with.'"

Watson was fired from Purina Mills at that meeting. But he still worked for Koch Industries. He was told at the country club that he needed to go to Koch headquarters to speak with Bill Hanna, the president of the company.

Hanna ran the company while Charles Koch was preoccupied with his legal troubles in Wichita. Hanna also sat in on the key meetings about Koch Agriculture and oversaw many of the vital decisions for the business. He had been a mentor to Watson and told Watson that he was an example of what a Koch employee should be, an example who should be emulated by other business leaders.

The meeting with Hanna was also short. "He told me, 'I never believed in what you were doing. You and Charles were so far out there, I kind of let you go,'" Watson remembered. "The second thing he said is that 'I've talked to everybody else, and nobody else wants you.'"

None of the other business divisions at Koch would hire Watson. After breaking this news, Hanna complained about a knee problem he was having and made other small talk. Then Watson was shown out.

"The meeting lasted about five minutes. Twenty-year career. Just, boom. Just like that." Watson returned to negotiate his severance package, doing so across the table from an old drinking buddy. Both times Watson was in the office, Charles Koch's door was closed.

The day he was fired, Watson returned home. His wife was having a garage sale. He told her the news. That morning, he had been CEO of one of Koch's largest and fastest-growing divisions. He joked with his wife that he'd gone from CEO to head of floor sales on their driveway.

Even fifteen years later, the pain of this was still raw for Watson. He hashed over the details of the Purina collapse in his mind, trying to figure out exactly how he could have stopped it. In a fundamental way, Koch Industries was still his life, even though he was no longer there.

"I swear to you, it still haunts me to this day," he said.

Watson never lost respect for Charles Koch and always spoke fondly of his old mentor. He never lost respect for Charles Koch's philosophy. Watson had been one of Market-Based Management's brightest pupils, and he always believed in its principles. The markets levied their verdict, and their verdict was sometimes harsh. It was never forgiving. He abided by the laws of the markets.

"Oh, it's ruthless. It'll absolutely rip your heart out."

There was only one way that Purina Mills might survive without declaring bankruptcy and defaulting on loans that Koch had taken to fund its purchase: an influx of money from Koch Industries. Purina's leaders made a compelling case to Koch: If Koch would just invest more money, Purina could weather the downturn. In just a year or two, Purina might be able to emerge stronger than ever. Koch had owned the firm for barely a year and had invested more than $100 million of its own money. Surely Charles Koch didn't want to lose that entire investment by sending Purina into bankruptcy.

"True knowledge results in effective action," as Charles Koch liked to say. Pouring money into a failing business venture like Purina Mills would not change the market's verdict. Doing so would only steer that money away from other ventures where it could be more profitably invested. It was better to let the thing die, no matter the short-term pain that might be inflicted. This was one of the principles of Market-Based Management. What good were principles if you abandoned them when tested?

In late August of 1999, Koch Industries informed Purina that it would get no extra money from Wichita. Koch owed Purina nothing. Soon after, Purina failed to pay $15.75 million in interest expenses that were due. Two weeks later, it failed to pay $2.1 million in principal payments. When Purina blew through its payment dates and became delinquent, it set off a cataclysmic chain of events. The banks accelerated their payment demands rather than giving Purina more breathing room. The lenders were desperate to get whatever money they could while the firm was still solvent. The frenzy only ended on October 28, when Purina filed for bankruptcy.

With Purina in Chapter 11, Koch Industries stood to lose its $100 million investment. The bankers stood to lose much more. And they did not accept this fact easily, in part because they knew how much money Charles Koch had. Charles Koch's wealth was well known in spite of his penchant for secrecy. *Forbes* magazine publicized Charles Koch's status as a billionaire and Bill Koch's extensive litigation that dragged the family's finances into a public courtroom. Press reports from the *Wichita Eagle* to the *Wall Street Journal* showed that Koch Industries enjoyed billions of dollars in revenue each year. This was one of the reasons bankers had been willing to risk more than $500 million to finance the Purina Mills acquisition. Now Charles Koch was telling them they would have to kiss that money good-bye. He wouldn't pay them back.

Koch appeared to have structured the deal in a way that protected it from the bankers' claims. Koch used debt that was called "non-recourse" debt, meaning that lenders could not collect the debt from Koch Industries itself—they had no recourse against the parent company. They could only collect debt against the assets of Purina Mills.

But there was a way around this clause. It was called "piercing the corporate veil." Piercing the corporate veil is one of those arcane strategies known only to a small subset of deal makers and lawyers whose careers took off during the merger boom of the 1980s and 1990s. A banker can pierce the veil by showing that nonrecourse debt was actually a sham used by a borrower to escape liability. For nonrecourse debt to be justified, the parent company needed to be truly independent from the entity borrowing the money.

Lawyers pored over the details of the Purina acquisition with the goal of proving one argument: that Purina was essentially a division of Koch Industries, not an independent company. If they could show that Koch was responsible for what happened at Purina, then Koch would be on the hook for Purina's bad debt.

This was not a particularly hard case to prove. Dean Watson, for example, had been Purina's CEO. But had he ever truly been independent from Koch Industries? When Watson was in trouble, he called Wichita. Purina's payroll was processed in Wichita, along with other administrative functions. One of Purina's most vital business activities—buying the grain to make its feed—had been shifted to Koch Industries' trading floor. It was impossible to make the argument that Koch was not fundamentally involved in Purina's daily operations.

The banks would sue Koch in order to pierce the veil, and going to court was a risky proposition for Koch Industries. Piercing the veil was a "binary" proposition: either the bankers pierced the veil, or they did not. With a single verdict, a bankruptcy judge could expose Koch to enormous liabilities.

If Koch lost the court battle, it could also affect the entire system that Charles Koch built over thirty years. By the late 1990s, the company was an impossibly dense interlocking set of supposedly independent subsidiaries and joint ventures. This arrangement allowed Koch to become enormous by swallowing up dozens of smaller companies while shielding it from the full liability of owning each of those companies. If a Koch subsidiary went bankrupt, then Koch would only lose its investment in that subsidiary; it wouldn't be on the hook for all the debt and outstanding obligations of that subsidiary. But if banks in the Purina bankruptcy pierced the veil, it could call into question the walls between all of Koch's divisions. "Imagine all the Koch subsidiaries," said the financier who worked on the Purina bankruptcy. "The last thing Koch wants to do is guarantee all the obligations of these entities."

Lawyers working for the banks determined that their case was strong enough to make it past the first hurdles of a lawsuit. This meant that Koch faced the real risk of trial, and the bankers' negotiating team highlighted this risk to Koch's attorneys. The negotiators dropped the word "litigation" a lot. They made it clear what kind of dirty laundry would be dragged into open court. They emphasized just how eager they were to file a complaint. In short, they leveraged the legal threat into a bargaining chip.

Koch finally agreed to pay $60 million to help Purina emerge from bankruptcy in a stronger position. This was a coup for the banks. A worst-case scenario for Koch was losing its entire investment in Purina of $100 million. By the end of its negotiations with the creditors, Koch lost all that money and paid an extra $60 million on top of it.

This failure would reshape Koch Industries going forward. The company fortified its corporate veil, creating a corporate structure that was even more complex and opaque than before. Koch called its divisions "companies" and treated them like independent entities to make sure the veil was strong. Koch might publicly claim that its various business units had so much autonomy only due to the tenets of Market-Based Management. But the real reason was to avoid liability.

After the banks were paid off, Charles Koch began to dismantle Koch Agriculture. It was a very public failure. For the first time in memory, Koch Industries made sweeping staff cuts in Wichita. Roughly five hundred employees and three hundred contractors lost their jobs. Many of those jobs were at the highest reaches of the company. Brad Hall gutted Koch's development group, for example, firing most of its employees. The group had grown bloated, unwieldy, and ineffective. So had many other parts of the company.

"I told Charles, we ought to be in the *Harvard Business Review* as an example of piss-poor management," Hall recalled.

CHAPTER 10

The Failure

(2000)

Charles Koch drove himself to work every day. He was a billionaire, but he still drove a sensible sedan to the office. He arrived at the Tower early and often walked up the back stairwell to his office on the third floor. Charles was the most powerful person in the company. During the course of his day, he seldom encountered people who were not directly answerable to his authority. But as he climbed the stairs to work, and as he sat at his desk and looked out over the flat grasses north of Wichita, it could be said that Charles was, in many important ways, a failure.

The previous decade had been a public embarrassment. To the degree that Koch Industries was written about in the popular press, the stories tended to focus on Koch's lawbreaking and litigation. To the degree that Charles Koch himself was written about, he was described as a character in a pathetic family feud that showed just how crazy billionaires could be. To the degree that Charles Koch's tenure as CEO was written about, it was hard not to question how effective his leadership had been. He had spent years honing a management philosophy that had sown problems throughout the company. Oil gaugers interpreted Koch's push for "continuous improvement" as a reason to steal from Koch's customers. The refinery managers had interpreted Koch's push for "profit centers" as a reason to dump pollution into wetlands and delay investments that would have reduced pollution. The common teachings of MBM had too often turned into a language of groupthink, prompting managers to persecute whistle-blowers rather than heed their important warnings. MBM's focus on growth had encouraged irresponsible acquisitions that piled up losses and public failures like the collapse of Purina Mills. Koch Industries was flush with cash, thanks to the heavily subsidized and regulated oil markets that were its core business, but the failure of Koch

Agriculture seemed to prove that MBM was not, in fact, a blueprint for running successful ventures in other business sectors.

This mattered to Charles Koch. He believed that the CEO was ultimately responsible for a company's conduct. If a company was dysfunctional, the leadership was to blame. As he said when he was being deposed by Senate investigators, "Ninety percent of the problems in industry are caused by management, not by the worker. The main management is the one that should be fired" if there's a problem. According to this logic, there was a reasonable argument to be made that Charles Koch should be fired. Charles Koch said that the late 1990s were one of the most difficult times of his life.

"The worst was when we had that, that trial, where we were being sued by a family and stockholders and all this stuff," he recalled. "And I'm thinking, 'God. Look—all the money we've made them, and this is what we get?' So it was depressing. . . . It just . . . it took me a while to adjust to that."

Still, every day, Charles Koch drove himself into work. He parked his sensible sedan in the employee lot, and ascended the back stairwell and stationed himself at his desk very early. He left very late in the evening and he often took a briefcase home to review papers during his off hours. And during the long days of his workweek, as he sat at his desk, Charles Koch saw something that nobody else could see. He could see Koch Industries for what it really was. The company was intentionally opaque and secretive, and its complex network of divisions and subsidiaries was so diffuse that even some senior people at the company were not aware of the full organizational structure. But there was one focal point from which the whole machine could be observed—and that point was Charles Koch's desk. He was the only one who could see the entire machine for what it was. And he believed in it.

Charles Koch was in a position to see the seeds of strength in Koch Industries; seeds that might have been overlooked by other people during the turmoil of the 1990s. He saw all the elements that would later make Koch Industries one of the largest, most powerful corporations in America. Market-Based Management might have fostered business failures, but it had achieved one thing: It gave all of Koch's employees a common language. It gave them a common mission, and this is more important than it might sound. By the year 2000, Koch Industries was a sprawling confederation of divisions spread across different segments of the economy. As many companies have discovered, this can be a recipe for disaster: it can foster fragmentation, miscommunication, and managerial fiefdoms that compete against one another. But Charles Koch had drilled into each employee the value—the necessity—of MBM. Years of doing this created a unified workforce, a workforce where employees could shift from one division to the next and understand each other perfectly.

The fact that Koch employees thought with a long-term view was another strength. It was a strength that Charles Koch fought dearly to earn. He spent years battling to keep his company private, fighting his brother and dissident shareholders for years in court. He fought against conventional wisdom to make this happen, not just by remaining privately held, but by refusing to take large dividend payments out of his company. The reward for this struggle was the ability to think in terms of years and decades rather than in quarterly earnings or monthly reports.

Another strength was knowledge. Charles Koch had built an organization that learned, and learned constantly. Every transaction was a data point, every relationship was a conduit for information, every business unit a listening post. At Charles Koch's direction, the company had filled whole rooms of its basement with computers and processing power, the ability to churn and analyze mountains of information. Koch built a company around learning.

Charles believed there were quantifiable laws that drove the world, unbreakable laws that were true whether a person believed in them or not. These laws were the principles by which he tried to live and run his business. He never doubted these principles, even in the darkest days of the late 1990s. The principles had been correct. He had simply made mistakes in carrying them out.

So he would do better. His solution was simple:

"I just work harder."

PART 2

THE BLACK BOX ECONOMY

CHAPTER 11

Rise of the Texans

(2000)

Over the course of one short year, Charles Koch and a small team of trusted executives reinvented Koch Industries. The company was redrawn in a series of urgent and sometimes tense private meetings, an effort that was kept secret from the outside world and even employees. The Koch Industries that emerged on the other side of this transformation was radically different from the faltering machine that Charles Koch oversaw in 1999. The firm was reshaped from its boardroom all the way down to the refinery floor.

The revolution began with a purge. Charles Koch needed a new leadership team to take him where he wanted to go. Bill Hanna, the company's long-serving president and chief operating officer, was replaced. F. Lynn Markel, the true-blue Koch employee who joined the company in 1975 and rose to become its chief financial officer, was replaced. Corliss "Corky" Nelson, a vice president and head of Koch Capital Services, who had been with the firm since 1978, was replaced. The chief technology officer, replaced. The vice president and head of structured finance, replaced. The purge reached down into Koch's business units as well. The head of Koch Petroleum, replaced. The CEO of Koch's polyester division, replaced. The head of trading across Koch's divisions, replaced.

After the purge was complete, Charles Koch didn't replace his leaders with fresh employees who were hired from the best business schools or other companies. Instead, he promoted loyalists who knew the Koch way. The new CFO, Sam Soliman, graduated from Texas A&M University and had worked most of his career at Koch. The new head of Koch Petroleum, David Robertson, spent his entire career at Koch, having joined just after he graduated from Emporia State University in Kansas. The new president and COO, Joe Moeller, was a Koch lifer and a gradu-

ate of the University of Tulsa. The new team was composed entirely of
men who were steeped in Charles Koch's values and who were imbued
with the lessons of Koch University. These were people who spoke the
language of Market-Based Management. Charles Koch promoted players from his own farm team into the big leagues.

The change in personnel was only the beginning. Between 1999 and
2001, Charles Koch and his team overhauled the company's strategy and
its corporate structure. The new strategy emerged from a set of private
debates after Charles Koch pulled his new management team into meetings and pushed them to think of a way forward. It seemed that every
idea was put on the table and considered. There was discussion of moving Koch's headquarters out of Wichita so the company might have a
better chance of recruiting top talent—it had always been a tough sell
to convince people to move to an isolated city in south central Kansas. Houston and Scottsdale, Arizona, were proposed as new homes for
the company. There was even talk of breaking apart the company and
of David Koch potentially selling off his ownership stock. Charles Koch
drove his team forward, pushing them to consider every possibility. His
message to the new leaders seemed simple: "I don't like losing," as one of
them recalled. Their new mission in life was "Stopping stupid," ending
the follies of the 1990s.

The evidence of past mistakes was still everywhere in 2000. Koch
Industries was still carrying the accumulated litter that was left behind
by countless Value Creation Strategies, years of acquisitions, and rapid
growth. As Koch reviewed its holdings, one executive described the corporate structure as representing a table piled high at a rummage sale, full
of odds and ends that had no apparent rationale for belonging together.
Koch began to unload these properties, selling off pipeline holdings like
the Chase Transportation Company. It sold a chemical firm called Koch
Microelectronic Service Company and closed down a new $30 million
chemical plant in Bryan, Texas. Over a period of years, Koch would sell
off thousands of miles of pipelines. The corporate odds and ends were
discarded.

The remaining businesses at Koch were restructured and streamlined.
The most important division, Koch Petroleum, was renamed Flint Hills
Resources and given new leaders. Other businesses were consolidated
under a new, simplified structure that put them under the umbrella of

a few new companies like Koch Minerals, Koch Supply & Trading, and Koch Chemical Technology Group.

This change in Koch's corporate structure and strategy ushered in a decade of unprecedented growth. Over the following decade, Koch Industries became perfectly suited to thrive in the strange political economy of the 2000s. It was an era that favored big corporations that could master complex systems—in both markets and in the political system—two characteristics that already defined Koch Industries. It was also an era that favored debt-fueled expansion and buyouts, a skill that Koch Industries came to embrace and dominate. The biggest profits of the decade were gained by financial companies and trading firms, a shadow economy into which Koch Industries expanded dramatically. By the end of the decade, Koch Industries came to reflect the broader American economy, where tremendous wealth was generated for a few, wages stagnated for most, and the biggest US companies grew larger than ever.

During this decade, one of the most important features of the new Koch Industries was the impervious strength of its corporate veil—the legal barrier that separated Koch's various divisions. Under the new structure, Koch Industries became little more than a holding company, a big investment firm that owned a lot of smaller, nominally independent firms. And those companies would be strictly segregated from one another, and from Koch central, by a thick wall designed to be legally impenetrable. The corporate veil became reflected in the vocabulary of Koch employees. They didn't refer to the company's subsidiaries as units or divisions, but as "companies," reinforcing the notion that each unit was fully independent. Many of these "companies" developed their own internal systems for human resources, information technology, and other services, creating just the kind of big, redundant systems that most US corporations were striving to eliminate. These redundancies might have cost Koch money, but their value far outstripped the cost. Koch could now argue persuasively that each company division was a stand-alone company, one that could assume its own liabilities. Never again would angry creditors be able to threaten the cash reserves of Koch Industries' central treasury, as the lawyers from Purina Mills had done. Now liability would only travel to the top of each company that Koch held. This new structure would allow Koch Industries to amass billions of dollars in debt over the next decade, heaped onto divisions that were nominally independent companies.

The strategy of dividing Koch Industries' various holdings into independent companies was often discussed in terms of free-market principles—animated by the principle that the company would survive or fail on its own merits in a market system. In fact, the strategy was a way to expand while limiting the downside risk. Shielding Koch's liability increased the company's appetite for new acquisitions because the risk of failure was contained. During the 2000s, Koch would make deals that dwarfed anything Charles Koch had even considered during the 1990s.

Koch Industries, the central holding company, institutionalized this drive to expand. The company created a new team of top executives called the business development board, whose sole job was to look for other companies to buy. This group was essentially a reincarnation of the central development group that Brad Hall had overseen in the late 1990s, but it was restructured in a way that made it larger, more influential, and capable of closing deals that were larger by an order of magnitude than anything Koch had done before. The new development group rivaled any deal-making entity on Wall Street. The team had a steady river of cash to work with thanks to the steady flow of money generated at Pine Bend and other assets. The team also made use of Koch Industries' nearly pristine credit rating,* which made it cheap and easy to get big loans.

Even this new strategy—to push for growth and limit risk with a corporate veil—rested on a deeper, more important idea. This idea was the centerpiece of Koch's new game plan, which relied on one competitive advantage more than any other: Koch's superior information.

Koch was seen by outsiders as an energy company, but, within the firm, it was seen quite differently. Charles Koch and his lieutenants considered Koch to be an information-gathering machine that built up stores of knowledge that were deeper and sharper than its competitors'. This strategy traced back to Koch Industries' earliest days, but with the

---

* While the Purina Mills fiasco hurt Koch, it did not permanently damage the company's credit rating, which was based on Koch's long-term financial track record. By 2016, Koch still had an AA- credit rating from Standard & Poor's, close to the highest rating reserved for ultrasafe investments like Treasury bills.

new business development board in place, it reached the level of a fine art. Koch's newly designed companies, like Koch Minerals, each had their own mini development teams that became like searchlights, trained on the various industries in which they operated. Whatever they saw and learned was transmitted to the central development board, which synthesized the information with knowledge that was flowing in from Koch's other companies. The development board also undertook studies of its own, looking for new opportunities beyond the existing Koch universe. The development board ran blue-sky studies in which it teased out economic trends going out ten to twenty years, considering how Koch could make bets that would yield big returns in the future. When the development board saw a deal it liked, it moved with stunning speed. There were no layers of bureaucracy between the board and Charles Koch—there was only a short walk down the hallway. There were no public shareholders to consult, only Charles and David Koch. Again and again, Koch exploited these advantages. The development board recommended acquisitions, and Koch Industries acted before its competitors even seemed aware of what was happening.

Charles Koch made significant changes to how the company operated new facilities once it purchased them. He imposed a new compliance regime that helped avoid the sort of legal troubles that ensnared almost every significant part of Koch's business up until the 1990s. Like everything Charles Koch did, this new effort carried its own slogan: "10,000 percent compliance," meaning that employees obeyed 100 percent of all laws 100 percent of the time.* This slogan might have seemed banal, even empty, to Koch Industries employees in the beginning. There isn't a company in America that doesn't profess to obey the law. But the glib nature of the slogan was deceiving: it represented an entirely new way of operating. Koch Industries expanded its legal team and embedded them into the firm's far-flung operations. Now if process owners like the managers at Pine Bend decided to release ammonia-laden water into nearby waterways, they often had to first consult with teams of Koch's lawyers. Koch's commodity traders consulted the legal team when devising new trading strategies. Teams of inspectors from the legal department descended on factories and threatened to shut them down if

---

* 100 multiplied by 100 equals 10,000; hence 10,000 percent compliance.

managers couldn't prove that a valve had been properly inspected. The mandate to comply with the law was very real, and it served a strategic purpose. Koch would keep state and federal regulators off its property.

Taken together, this was the most important restructuring since Koch Industries was first unified and reorganized after Fred Koch's death. At most publicly traded firms, such overhauls are announced through press releases and explained at length in interviews with the business press. At Koch Industries, a premium was put on secrecy. Part of this was cultural: Charles Koch always believed that his business dealings were a private matter that journalists had no business in scrutinizing. But a larger reason for the secrecy was strategic. In a company that set itself up to exploit its superior knowledge, it became imperative that no one—not the public and certainly not competitors—could know what was happening inside the black box of Koch's corporate tower. The restructuring "was done in a way that it wasn't very obvious to the market or to the employees, even," said a former senior executive who was intimately familiar with the process. "You don't necessarily want to attract attention."

During the year 2000, it was easy for Koch to avoid this kind of attention. This was due in large part to the fact that the United States was undergoing its own change in management, and the process was anything but smooth.

In Washington, DC, people lined the sidewalks of Pennsylvania Avenue on the morning of January 20, 2001, Inauguration Day, in spite of the bitter rain and gray skies. The motorcade of George W. Bush rolled past the crowds, and the newly elected president couldn't help but notice the signs held high behind the police barricades and cordons. The hand-painted placards said: "Hail to the Thief," "BUSH LOST," and "Restore Democracy and Count All Votes." They were just the most visible expressions of a deep conflict that had simmered since the presidential campaign of 2000. The campaign itself had been a display of American confusion. Amid all the heat and noise, there didn't seem to be any kind of debate about the central issue of what role the federal government should play in terms of regulating private enterprise. The broad, national political consensus behind the New Deal had effectively died during the 1970s, but it seemed to have been replaced by no new consensus at all. Ronald

Reagan's deregulatory revolution had failed. The entitlement programs of the New Deal and the later Great Society programs under President Lyndon Johnson (like Medicare and Social Security) remained in place. But now these entitlement programs were coupled with the belief that government should keep its hands off the market. The Clinton administration had only solidified this paradoxical view of government. It cut regulations on banks and boosted government programs.

If the new era was defined by any term, it was still the soupy and ambiguous term of "neoliberalism," which combined the machinery of a welfare state with deregulatory efforts for the select few special interest groups that had the money and lobbying power to make their case heard in Washington, DC. There wasn't a concrete ideology behind this approach and no public political consensus to support it. The political campaign of 2000 reflected this reality. It seemed as if George W. Bush and his Democratic opponent, Vice President Al Gore, spent the entire campaign working as hard as they could to become indistinguishable from each other.

Bush ran as a left-leaning "compassionate conservative"; Gore ran as a right-leaning liberal. The electorate rewarded the candidates with a vote that was split down the middle. In the state of Florida, the margin of victory for Bush was an infinitesimal 537 votes, a difference that was statistically nonexistent. Lawsuits broke out over a recount effort, and the election was decided by litigation rather than by democratic participation. The government hardly seemed capable of orderly continuity.

Bush's first months in office were unfocused, desultory, and involved clearing brush at his ranch in Texas. He pushed for tax and educational reforms. Then the terrorist attacks of September 11, 2001, drew the world's eyes to the smoking towers of the World Trade Center and the ruined face of the Pentagon. For the ensuing eight years, the nation's attention was almost entirely focused on the issues of war and terrorism—issues that seemed to pose an existential threat to the nation.

Beneath the smoke and noise of international conflict, the wheels of the economy continued to grind, and the structure of the economy was remade under the Bush administration. Bush and his vice president, Dick Cheney, both moved to Washington from Texas, where they had deep roots in the fossil fuel industry. They brought with them more than just an affinity for the big energy companies of their home state, such as Exxon and Enron. They also brought a governing philosophy that reflected the antiregulatory sentiment of the Lone Star State.

The Bush era would be regarded as a time of deregulation, when rules were stripped away from the private marketplace, and the reach of the federal government over corporations was curtailed. In reality, the Bush presidency only accelerated the trends begun under Reagan and continued under Clinton—and it pushed these trends to an obscene extreme by the end of the 2000s. The government grew larger, more complex, and more intrusive than at any point in history, giving rise to a hyperregulatory state. At the same time, rules were dissolved and enforcement was dropped at key pressure points in the economy, where only a handful of giant companies could operate. The paradoxes of neoliberalism were in full bloom.

Bush cut taxes in a way that primarily benefited the richest taxpayers and financial firms that earned money from capital gains. This caused federal revenue to crash, particularly during times of economic downturn. While the government was cut in some ways, it was enlarged in others. Bush pushed for, and received, a new Medicare program that paid for the costs of prescription drugs, costing tax payers tens of billions of dollars each year. In the wake of 9/11, Bush dramatically expanded national security spending while spending trillions of dollars on wars in Afghanistan and Iraq, which would later be referred to as "credit card wars" for their effect on the federal debt.

In this environment, corporations that could manage complexity, in both the markets and in regulatory affairs, were the economic winners. And among these companies, a certain kind did better than all the others. There was one sector of the economy that grew far faster than the rest: the financial sector. The decade of the 2000s was defined by the financialization of everything. The financial deregulation acts passed by Bill Clinton launched an industry of trading and speculation activities that dwarfed anything even during the Reagan era, when Wall Street gained the reputation as a greed machine that produced multimillion-dollar paydays for a handful of financiers. Banks started trading exotic instruments based on the value of homes, crops, metals, stocks, and energy. The smartest college graduates went straight from top-tier schools like MIT and Harvard to the trading floors of Wall Street.

Koch Industries, an industrial conglomerate based in Kansas, seemed particularly unsuited to thrive in this environment. The company seemed confined to the business of making things and processing raw materials in complex, expensive facilities. A Koch engineer in Texas didn't seem to have anything in common with a banker in New York.

In fact, while the world was looking elsewhere, Koch Industries built a financial trading desk that rivaled anything operated by Goldman Sachs or Lehman Brothers. Koch Industries, known for crude oil and natural gas, became a world leader in making and trading some of the most complex financial instruments in the world.

Koch's trading business was a strategic centerpiece of the company's growth strategy over the next decade. It was also the most striking example of Koch's ability to amass and exploit information asymmetries, learning more than everyone else and turning huge profits from this advantage. There were no markets more complex and more opaque than the trading markets born during the Bush administration, and Koch Industries mastered them. To understand how Koch Industries more than tripled in size in ten short years, it is critical to understand Koch's trading operations.

When the era of financialization began, Koch Industries was already poised to exploit it. Koch had been building expertise in the field for decades. Unsurprisingly, Koch Industries first entered the world of exotic financial instruments when it started trading in the one commodity Koch knew best: crude oil.

Koch began trading crude oil in the earliest days of the modern market, back in the 1970s. To understand the world of derivatives and futures markets that Koch later came to dominate, it is helpful to go back to that moment when the markets were newly born, and Koch was just starting to build its beachhead in the financial world.

Koch's earliest trading desk was based in Houston. And it was run by a young man who started as a clerk for the company. His name was Ron Howell.

In the late 1970s, Ron Howell made one of the most significant investments in the history of Koch Industries. He went to an office supply store and bought a big oak conference table. It had a leaf in it, so that it could expand and make room to seat about six people. This table was a major advancement in Koch's trading operations. Howell bought it because he could see that the world of oil trading was transforming, and Koch Industries was poised to dominate the new markets.

Back then, Ron Howell's job might have seemed easy enough: he sold the gasoline and other fuels that Koch Industries produced at its refineries. As the senior vice president of supply and trading at Koch, Howell made sure that Koch's fuel went straight from the refineries to the highest-paying customer. Gasoline was the kind of product that seemed to sell itself—there was always demand for fuel. People at Koch referred to Howell's job as the "dispossession of molecules," meaning that he simply had to find a home for the various fuels that Koch produced. This seemed straightforward. But Howell's job was the kind of job that produced insomnia and ulcers. It forced him to retire when he was in his thirties before the job killed him.

When he talked about oil trading, even decades later, Howell often used words like *whippin'* and *savage*. The savagery of Howell's average workday began when he walked into the office in Houston every morning and picked up the phone to sell the first barrel of gasoline or diesel fuel. The stomach acids started to boil the instant Howell tried to establish what might seem like a basic, simple fact: the price of oil that day.

Determining the price of oil at any given minute was an arcane art practiced by a network of traders around the world. They spent their days on the phone with one another, arguing, cajoling, bluffing, and bullying. The fact is that nobody really knew the price of a barrel of oil, or gasoline, or diesel fuel. Everybody had to guess, and the person who could guess with the most precision walked away with profits that were almost limitless. The person who guessed wrong faced instant, brutal downsides in the market.

There was a common misperception that the price of oil floats up and down on a global market. Every day, business commentators and journalists talked about the "price of oil" as if it were like the price of General Electric stock—a price that was determined by millions of buyers and sellers who traded on large, open exchanges.

In fact, there was no global market for oil. Oil was bought and sold inside a constellation of thousands of tiny nodes where transactions and prices were totally hidden to outsiders. One of these nodes, for example, was the big complex of oil tanks that Koch Industries owned in St. James, Louisiana. Another node might be an oil terminal off the coast of Scotland, where oil drilled in the North Sea is stored. These were the kinds of places where oil refineries bought crude oil or Amoco bought gasoline. Prices from the sales were never posted on any exchange. The real price of oil, back when Ron Howell was selling it in the 1970s, was negotiated between two people over the phone.

When he sat at his desk in the small Koch trading office, Howell made phone call after phone call, trying to figure out how the price of oil might be changing at all these different nodes. Everyone on the phone line was trying to learn from him, bluff him, oversell him, and undercut him. He had to triangulate between truth and lies to figure out the real value of oil before it changed again. "I can't even tell you how dynamic it all is," he said. "You almost have to be in it for a period of time to understand the complexity."

While this was ulcer-inducing, Howell did have one advantage. Koch Industries was one of the bigger members of a very small club of companies that could even dream of trading crude oil. The market wasn't open to the masses for a simple reason: a trader needed to be able to ship and deliver huge quantities of actual, real oil. This required barges, pipelines, and refineries to be at the trader's disposal. Howell was one of those traders. He could buy ten thousand barrels of crude in the North Atlantic and sell it in the US Gulf Coast because Koch could charter the barges to take it there.

There were, of course, a handful of "speculators" in the early days of the oil markets. These were people who bought oil without ever expecting to actually handle it or deliver it. They were making a bet that they could sell their contract at a higher price before the time came to load a barge. This was a dangerous game. A trader like Howell might be able to sniff out a speculator and simply refuse to buy the oil contract off his hands, putting the speculator in a desperate position because he knew he couldn't actually take delivery of all that oil. A trader like Howell could hold out until the speculator was forced to give away the oil for pennies on the dollar when it came time to accept delivery. This was a well-known trading maneuver called "the squeeze," and it was a pitiless tactic that could financially ruin a person in a matter of hours. Traders like Howell (and his counterparts at Chevron and Exxon) were more or less immune to the squeeze. Howell could accept delivery of the barrels of oil, maybe at a loss, but not at a catastrophic loss.

In the beginning, before he bought the big table, Howell began his trading career in Wichita. But as Koch's operation grew, he moved the office to Houston because that's where the talent was. Houston was a hub for the energy industry, home to some of the nation's biggest producers and pipeline companies. By the late 1970s, it was also home to the most talented oil traders. Howell decided to open shop where these traders were willing to work.

Koch's trading office resembled a small, boutique law firm. There was a row of offices that ran down a hallway, and inside each office was a trader, with his door closed, frantically working the phone. Each trader focused on a particular niche in the market: selling natural gas supplies in the Gulf Coast, for example, or buying crude oil in the upper Midwest. When one trader learned something significant, he had to leave his office, run down the hall, and tell other traders who might be able to profit from the news. "I would watch our guys, and they'd nearly run into each other, running from office to office," Howell recalled. All of these traders were trying to piece together the movement of energy prices, based on the pieces of information they gleaned from each sale.

As he watched his traders run from office to office, Howell had a pivotal realization. Every time a trader sold a barrel of oil, the transaction produced an ultravaluable by-product: information. Each sale was a price signal. And as Koch bought and sold hundreds of thousands of barrels of fuel around the world, it began to accumulate this ultravaluable information in one place.

This information could then be paired with yet more ultravaluable information that only Koch Industries had access to: the huge output of price signals that were generated by Koch's oil refineries and pipelines. These physical plants gave Koch's traders a window into the future. Koch knew, for example, when it was about to shut down the Pine Bend refinery for repairs, or when it might be shutting down a pipeline. When this happened, Howell's traders could start gaming the downstream effects on local energy markets—all those opaque nodes that would be affected. And they could do this before any other traders even knew it was happening. There is no way to overstate the value of this kind of inside information. If Pine Bend closed one unit, it could create cascading effects throughout the US oil markets. Other refiners and merchants would substitute one kind of fuel for another when they learned that Pine Bend was closing, which, in turn, caused yet other merchants to make substitutions and changes. When a Koch trader knew what was coming, they could buy and sell before anyone else priced in the coming changes. It was like seeing into the future, while at the same time creating it.

Koch's stores of information became a growing and vital advantage in the market. And that's why Howe decided to stop the hectic traffic in the hallways. He wanted the traders to sit together. They should share everything they learned, as they learned it.

On his lunch break one day, Howell went to the office supply store and bought the big oak table with a credit card. He didn't remember how much it cost, but it seems possible that the return on investment for that table was the among the highest of any acquisition in Koch's history.

Howell moved the big table into a meeting room at the trading office and informed a handful of traders that this would now be their workspace. They weren't happy about this—they saw their private offices as a sign of prestige. But Howell insisted. First, he seated four traders around the table, equipping them with telephones and trading books. Everybody shared everything they learned as soon as they learned it. These were traders working in different markets and selling different products. But that made them like the proverbial blind men who approached an elephant, each feeling and describing a different part of it. When they pooled their impressions together, a picture of the giant beast began to emerge. Koch was developing a view, in real time, of highly complex and interrelated markets for crude oil, diesel fuel, and natural gas liquids.

Other traders began dropping into the room, asking about the latest news. Howell installed the leaf in the table to expand it so six traders could sit there. Then he bought a second table and put it in the room. "Before long . . . everybody wanted to be in the office, because that's where the information was," Howell said.

This arrangement would become the foundation from which Koch's trading floor was launched. Over the next twenty years, the trading infrastructure would expand dramatically, but the underlying strategy would remain the same: the traders working in a cluster, gathering information, sharing it, and using their insights to prosper in complex markets where only a handful of firms dared to do business.

In 1983, the expansion of Koch's trading efforts really began. That's when Howell brought another piece of large furniture into the trading room. This was a heavy, bulbous television screen that was hung on the wall. If the screen had fallen from its anchor, it might have killed somebody. But its presence was vital. The wide screen was filled with simple rows of numbers, in black and white, that blinked periodically. The traders referred to it as the Merc screen, and it changed everything about their job. It also ushered in an era of derivatives trading and financial engineering that would define the economy of the 2000s.

Merc referred to the New York Mercantile Exchange, which was also called the NYMEX for short. It was a Wall Street exchange that celebrated its hundred-year anniversary in 1982. Even though it had been around for a long time, the NYMEX was a backwater of the financial industry. The big shows on Wall Street were the exchanges where stocks and bonds were sold. On the NYMEX, people were trading products like butter, eggs, and cheese. Or, to be precise, it's where people traded paper contracts that were based on the value of butter, eggs, and cheese. It was something called a "futures" exchange.

The futures market was very different from the oil market where Koch Industries was doing business in the late 1970s. In the oil markets, people bought and sold physical shipments of crude. In the futures markets, they bought and sold paper contracts. Futures contracts had been around for more than a century and were an integral part of the food system. Corn, pork, and soybean futures were traded on the Chicago Board of Trade. The NYMEX specialized in eggs and butter. The futures market wasn't big—traders in the market tended to be farmers and big grain millers. They used futures contracts to limit their risk.

The owners of the NYMEX weren't content with their sleepy corner of the financial world, and they decided to expand their business and sell contracts for new kinds of products. The NYMEX introduced the first futures contract for crude oil in 1983.

At first, the birth of oil futures contracts looked like a threat to Koch's business model. Howell and his team spent years figuring out how to be the smartest blind men in the dark cave of the physical oil business and making the best guess as to the real price of oil. Koch Industries had gained an expertise in exploiting the opacity of oil markets and wringing the best price out of its counterparties. The new oil futures contract created something that was anathema to this business model: transparency.

When the NYMEX debuted its oil futures contract, it created a very visible price for crude oil that changed by the minute on a public exchange. Again, this wasn't the price of real crude; it was the price for a futures contract on crude, reflecting the best guess of all market participants as to what a barrel of oil would be worth in the future. Even though the futures price wasn't the real price, it provided everybody with a common reference point. Now, when Koch called up someone to buy oil from Koch's tank farm in St. James, that customer could look at a screen and start haggling based on what the markets in New York were saying the price of oil was worth.

"It was the first time that there was a common, visible market signal," Howell said. "It just kind of sucked the oxygen out of the room for that physical trading."

Some of the older traders wanted to avoid using the futures contract for this reason; it undermined their advantage in the physical market. But there was no fighting the rise of futures. The contracts became indispensable for big companies looking to limit their risk. Airlines, for example, bought oil futures contracts to lock in future jet fuel prices. Big oil refiners bought futures contracts to lock in the price of crude in future months. The number of oil futures contracts proliferated. There were contracts to buy crude oil going out three months, six months, even a year.

Howell embraced the new market. He hung the Merc screen in his newly built trading room and urged his traders to pay attention to it. Like other oil refiners, Koch started buying and selling futures contracts on the NYMEX, in part to hedge its own risk. It wasn't long before executives at Koch Industries realized that the birth of oil futures contracts presented them with more than just a way to cushion themselves from risk. Trading oil futures presented Koch with a chance to make money, independent of its refineries. Speculating in the futures market would become a line of business unto itself.

Koch Industries had almost inadvertently developed an expertise in trading over the years. Traders like Howell got into the business for the simple goal of "dispossession of molecules"—moving Koch's product. In doing so, Koch Industries had become one of the world's best traders in the physical markets for oil—the markets where real oil was bought and sold. Howell and his team realized that those skills could carry over into the newly born paper markets. And the market for paper oil futures appeared to be much larger and more profitable than the market for physical oil. Koch had been able to apply that inside information before, but now it could apply it to a massive market. Oil futures greatly magnified the power of the information that Howell and his traders were sharing around the oak table.

In the stock market, it is illegal to trade on inside information. If a CEO knows that her firm is about to buy a smaller competitor, she cannot go buy shares of that smaller firm before the news is publicly announced and the shares jump in value. The idea behind the ban on insider trading is that it makes the markets an even playing field for ordinary investors.

Futures markets are different. When regulators built the modern futures markets during the 1930s, in fact, they *wanted* traders to use inside information when they bought and sold futures. This way, the thinking went, the markets would quickly reflect the most accurate price possible. When traders used inside information to buy or sell contracts, their actions would quickly send price signals to everyone else.

While it was legal to use inside information in the futures markets, the power to do so was concentrating into fewer and fewer hands during the 1980s. Koch Industries was one of relatively few firms in the world that was able to ship oil by the barge load while simultaneously making bets in the futures market about what would happen when that barge load of oil arrived on shore. Koch exploited this advantage to the fullest extent. The company expanded its trading office in Houston, hiring traders who did nothing but buy and sell in the futures markets. Koch's trading strategy was built around the high-value information that was gleaned from Koch's refineries, pipelines, and storage tanks.

By 1985, Koch Industries had built a trading operation that was proficient in playing both the physical and futures markets for energy. Howell, however, wasn't willing to stick around and enjoy the fruits of his efforts. His daily life as a trader was still savage and still punctuated by whippin's. He was burned out. He retired from the trading business in 1985 and moved back home to Oklahoma, where he took up a career in politics. He would later help Koch Industries fend off legal challenges in the state related to Koch's intentional mismeasurements.

Howell never traded oil again. But the trading system he helped build in Houston only continued to grow. The oak table was replaced by rows of cubicles, where traders sat side by side. The small trading office was traded for a larger—and then larger—office.

The age of trading was just getting underway.

Koch Industries wasn't the only company that understood how much money could be made in energy futures markets. Goldman Sachs, Lehman Brothers, J.P. Morgan & Co., and other Wall Street banks started trading oil futures in the early 1980s. These banks already had big trading floors for stocks and bonds, so they applied their knowledge to the commodities markets.

But even the biggest Wall Street banks were at a disadvantage when they went up against the traders at Koch Industries, British Petroleum, or Amoco. The Wall Street banks didn't have access to inside information. Goldman Sachs didn't own refineries or pipelines and couldn't get a sneak peek into where markets were headed. The banks had to resort to second-rate information that was publicly available, like government reports on monthly energy supplies. It was a losing proposition.

In the mid-1990s, the Wall Street banks came to Koch Industries, asking for help. "We kept getting approached by banks, who say, 'Hey, Koch. You guys are so good at this physical stuff, we'd like to partner with you,'" recalled a former senior Koch executive who was heavily involved in trading operations. The banks came to Koch with the same pitch: the banks would handle "all this financial stuff," while Koch handled the physical end of trading and shared information from its operations.

If Koch executives were flattered by the attention from Wall Street, they didn't show it for long. "We kind of got curious—or, suspicious is the better term," the executive recalled. Rather than help the banks out, Koch set up a team to study why the banks were so interested in their business.

Koch hired the outside consulting firm McKinsey & Company to study what was happening in commodities markets during the 1990s. McKinsey reported that the world of trading had grown even larger and more profitable than Koch Industries had suspected. As it happened, the futures contracts that Koch was trading had become the "plain vanilla" products in a rapidly booming market. Now there were more exotic, more opaque, and far more profitable financial products on the market. These products were called "derivatives." That's where the real money was.

A derivatives contract is one more step removed from reality than a futures contract. A futures contract was at least notionally based on the real delivery of a real commodity at some point in the future. But now the banks were creating derivatives that were based on the value of underlying commodities like oil and natural gas, but that never required the delivery of the actual commodity itself. These new products had arcane names like "swaps" and "OTC contracts."*

When McKinsey gave its report to Koch, trading derivatives was almost entirely the domain of Wall Street banks, which had cornered the market for products that were both complex and financially dangerous. A derivatives contract carried the potential to make huge profits but also the potential to deliver losses that redefined the savagery of a down market. This was due in part to the sheer scale of a derivatives contract. In the physical market, Koch could speculate on a large storage tank of oil. In the derivatives market, it could speculate on the value of ten thousand tanks of oil without ever having to lease an actual tank of fuel in the real world.

Throughout the 1990s, the federal government did all that it could to stoke the size and scope of derivatives trading. The Clinton administration ensured that federal regulators took a hands-off approach to derivatives contracts and did not regulate them in the way that futures contracts were regulated. A typical futures contract was undergirded by a set of rules that made markets more stable—a futures contract required traders, for example, to set aside a certain amount of money in reserve to cover losses or required the trades to be posted on transpar-

---

* OTC stands for "over-the-counter," which basically meant it was a contract that wasn't defined by the rules of an exchange. It was just a contract between two parties, tailored specifically to their needs. A futures contract, by contrast, had to meet certain criteria set by the exchanges like the Chicago Board of Trade.

ent exchanges. When the Clinton administration passed the Commodity Futures Modernization Act of 2000, the law mandated that derivatives would not be treated the same way. The market for derivatives would remain dark, and it would explode in size.

When the Bush administration came into office, the rise of derivatives markets accelerated. Energy derivatives were particularly hot. The Houston-based energy company Enron made derivatives a central part of its business, replacing the boring world of actual energy production with the enticing world of swaps and OTCs.

After analyzing the McKinsey report, Koch Industries decided to put itself in the center of the booming derivatives market, focusing on the field of energy trading. Charles Koch consolidated all of the company's trading operations under one corporate umbrella that was named Koch Supply & Trading. When managers at the oil refinery in Pine Bend wanted to buy a new shipment of crude oil to process, they did not use their own traders; they simply called Koch Supply & Trading, which did the ordering for them.

Putting all of the trading capacity under one roof would do more than simplify Koch's operations—it would amplify them as well. That's because all of the traders would benefit from the information sharing effect that Ron Howell helped engender around the oak table. When a trader at Koch Supply & Trading bought a large shipment of crude oil for Pine Bend, he or she could then place bets in the futures market to hedge the risk of buying so much physical crude at one time. Then a trader sitting nearby could sell a derivatives contract related to the crude product that was just purchased.

Even as the markets changed, Koch's unifying strategy remained the same. It would enter the new markets using the advantages of its past: the inside information that it gleaned from its operations.

"If you have a physical capability, you have a lot more options. It provides you this physical presence, building up all this knowledge that you can trade around," said Brad Hall, the executive who ran Koch's development group and helped clean up the mess at Purina Mills. After the Purina fiasco, Hall became deeply involved in Koch's trading operations. The success of Koch's trading desks relied heavily on the flow of information from its refineries and pipelines, according to Hall and others.

Naturally, the consolidated office of Koch Supply & Trading was based in Houston, which had slowly evolved into the Wall Street of energy trading. Koch purchased a building in the southwest part of town, not too far from Rice University, and converted it into a bank of trading offices. The building bore a remarkable resemblance to the Tower in Wichita— it was a cube of dark glass that was inscrutable from the outside. This opacity was fitting because Koch Industries' trading operation was the one division of the company that Koch was least willing to discuss publicly. Even back in 1981, Charles Koch had insisted on a veil of secrecy around it. When a group of bankers tried to convince Charles Koch to take Koch Industries public, he told them he was worried that doing so might let the world learn just how much money Koch's commodities traders earned. Koch's trading profits were so high that Charles Koch worried that counterparties might stop doing business with the company (presumably out of fear that Koch traders made so much money that it must come at the expense of anyone on the other side of a trade).

Charles Koch voiced those concerns at the dawn of modern commodities trading. By the year 2000, the traders' profits had grown by an order of magnitude, and Koch Industries was even less willing to discuss what happened on its trading floors.

CHAPTER 12

Information Asymmetries

(2000–2004)

It was still dark when Brenden O'Neill drove his car through the tree-lined streets of suburban Houston, making the short commute from his home to the Koch Supply & Trading office. He usually arrived for work around seven in the morning. Or, to be specific, he arrived for work around seven a.m. in the *Houston* morning, as opposed to the London morning or the Singapore morning. There was no single morning for a commodities trader like O'Neill. Instead, there was a rolling series of mornings, each one representing a signal point at various places along the globe, marking the passage of global markets that circled the world and never slept. London, Singapore, Moscow, Geneva. Activity in these markets advanced with the horizon of dawn, passing one major trading hub after the next. O'Neill liked to be stationed at his desk when the markets hit the all-important New York morning, and trading began with a frenzy on Wall Street. By that time, O'Neill was ready to execute transactions worth several hundred million dollars.

O'Neill was thirty-one-years old. He seemed like an unlikely candidate to work in the world of high finance. He had never worked on Wall Street and didn't have a degree in finance or economics. But O'Neill was exactly the kind of person whom Koch Industries hired to staff its trading floors. The company preferred engineers to financiers and preferred graduates of midwestern state schools to the Ivy Leagues. O'Neill had graduated from the University of Kansas with an engineering degree and spent most of his career working at Koch Industries' oil refinery in Corpus Christi. He still dressed like a refinery worker. The standard uniform for a Koch derivatives trader wasn't a pin-striped suit with cufflinks, but khaki pants with a short-sleeved golf shirt. He lived in a modest one-story home in the western suburbs of Houston with his wife, Heather. It was a snug fit for their family, but it worked well enough. The house was only a ten-minute drive from the Koch Supply & Trading office, a building with black windows that looked like an obsidian cube, tucked away in a quiet, commercial neighborhood near the Houston Zoo.

The headlights of O'Neill's car cut across the garage entrance to the tower as he approached. It was early in the winter of 2000, and the temperature was in the lower fifties—a freezing spell by Houston's standards. The morning temperature was a salient fact for a derivatives trader. The weather meant everything. The weather determined how the markets might buck and heave throughout the day as commodities traders tried to figure out how much heating gas, electricity, and crude oil might be consumed across the United States. Unexpected temperature changes could change these calculations in an instant. One of the first things O'Neill did every day was read through a series of proprietary secret weather reports produced by Koch analysts. He needed to gain an edge over the New York morning. He parked his car in the company garage, and headed toward his trading desk.

The interior lobby of 20 Greenway Plaza was colorful and visually dazzling, like a geode hidden inside a black stone. The spacious atrium rose up several stories, and the open space was crisscrossed by a series of silver escalators that slanted upward at interlocking angles, like something out of an M. C. Escher lithograph. The walls were covered with grids of lighted squares glowing yellow and with metallic circles that looked like jumbled points on a graph. A security guard was stationed at a circular wooden desk in the center of the space.

O'Neill rode the elevator up to Koch's trading floor.

Koch's trading floor was a cavernous room that sprawled for several thousand square feet, taking up an entire floor of the office building. O'Neill walked through a maze of trading desks as he made his way to his work station. The traders sat side by side in long rows, each trader facing one or more bulky computer screens. The desks were covered in piles of papers and files and telephones that were used at a punishing level of intensity throughout the day. By seven o'clock, many of the desks were already filled. Not too far from O'Neill's desk, for example, Koch's in-house meteorologist was hard at work developing reports that he would soon e-mail out to the teams of traders. Even though the office was crowded, the trading floor wasn't a loud or unruly place. It wasn't a commodities pit where red-faced men in loosened ties yelled orders across the room. It felt more like the headquarters of an insurance brokerage or an investment research firm. The day was filled by the ambient clatter of keyboard typing and the background murmur of salespeople working the phones.

O'Neill settled into his desk and turned on his computer. His face seemed weathered in a way that was particular to the place he grew up— Wichita. His features were drawn and narrow, his cheekbones high and sharp. He was lanky and had sky-blue eyes. Both of his parents were raised on small farms, and he never knew a life of wealth, let alone entitlement. Now, after joining Koch Supply & Trading, O'Neill had a chance to become something different. He had a chance to get rich. He spent his days working in the epicenter of an unprecedented wealth machine called the derivatives market. This was the supercharged engine of America's economic growth during the 2000s. The profits from derivatives were larger, in fact, than the profits for the real, underlying economic activity that derivatives were based on—you could make more money from selling natural gas derivatives than selling natural gas. O'Neill managed to become one of the insiders who knew how things worked inside the black box, and this knowledge gave him a once-in-a-lifetime opportunity. He had the chance to make so much money, off a single giant trade, that he might be able to elevate himself out of the American middle class forever.

It was almost an accident of circumstance that O'Neill found himself in the position to make a fortune almost overnight. His path to Koch's trading floor began in a humble working-class neighborhood in Wichita. O'Neill's dad worked as an engineer at the Boeing aircraft factory, earning a decent middle-class living. O'Neill's mom stayed home and took care of the kids, which entailed the workload of an executive-level position—O'Neill was the youngest of nine children. He shared his childhood bedroom with three of his brothers, all of them sleeping in a matching set of bunk beds. The family had enough money to get by; a typical family vacation was a weekend trip to Kansas City to watch a Royals baseball game. Ever since he was young, O'Neill wanted a richer life than his parents had. He wanted to be a doctor because doctors made a lot of money and lived in the big houses near the Wichita Country Club. He would take his kids on real vacations and maybe give each kid their own bedroom.

O'Neill never considered working for Koch Industries until he was well into college. He was attending KU when a recruiter from Koch came to campus and pitched O'Neill on the idea of taking a summer internship. O'Neill paid a visit to Koch headquarters. He couldn't believe what he saw. The place was crawling with all these guys who were so young. O'Neill was interviewed by a former Exxon employee named Kyle Vann, a senior manager in the company's oil group, who couldn't have been any older than his midthirties. And these guys weren't just young—they had money. They didn't even have to brag about having money; it was obvious in the way they carried themselves. The guys at Koch had that same air of confidence as the members of a winning football team. O'Neill wanted to be part of this. He took the summer internship and was paid $3,000 a month, a staggering sum. It was more than many kids in Wichita made in a whole summer.

After he graduated, O'Neill took a job in 1991 with Koch Industries as a process engineer at the Corpus Christi refinery. He was paid $40,000 a year. He got married in 1995 and started a family. The O'Neills would have four children.

O'Neill loved his job and was promoted up through the ranks to be a lead engineer at Corpus Christi. By 1995, he was making about $60,000 a year and sometimes received bonuses of $10,000 or so.

But somehow, O'Neill's paychecks never seemed to provide enough money to keep pace with America's middle-class expectations. The O'Neills didn't vacation extravagantly, but they did try to get away with the kids when they could. It turned out to be more expensive than they expected. They didn't hire a nanny or drive expensive cars, but O'Neill's income never seemed to quite cover expenses. Over time, they put a few thousand dollars on a credit card here and a few thousand there. They counted on O'Neill's bonuses to help pay off the debt. But the debt seemed to grow with a life of its own. It seemed like one day they turned around and here was this horrible truth: they owed about $60,000 in credit card debt.

O'Neill knew that he needed to make some sort of change in his life—he needed a way to make more money. In 1996, the opportunity arrived when he heard that there was an opening in Koch's commodities trading division in Houston. He had zero trading experience outside of some amateur forays into the stock market; he belonged to an investment club with some friends who made stock picks to see if they could outperform the market. But he decided to apply anyway. He discovered that Koch didn't care all that much about prior trading experience. For example, Kyle Vann, the former Exxon engineer, had risen to a senior position over Koch's trading operations. The company wasn't looking for Wall Street swagger; it was looking for analytical engineers who approached the market in the same way they approached complex problems inside Koch's pipeline and refinery divisions. O'Neill was hired and moved his family to Houston, first renting a home and then buying a four-bedroom house in the suburbs.

Trading wasn't a path to instant riches. Koch hired former engineers, and it paid them like engineers—O'Neill started his new job at the same pay grade as before, about $60,000 a year. The bonuses got a little bigger, however, and the O'Neills were able to start digging themselves out of debt.

That morning, as O'Neill sat at his desk in early 2000, upper-middle-class comfort seemed like it might be within his reach. Or maybe even something greater than that. O'Neill's computer was now fully alive. He opened his e-mail program and began to scroll through messages and reports that came in overnight and in the early morning hours. This information was starting to coalesce into a picture in O'Neill's mind. He was beginning to see a trade taking shape, and a very large trade at that. He saw a strategy, in fact, that might very well lift him out of the financial strain that had defined his life up until that moment. He looked over the numbers as they scrolled and blinked on his screen, and as the Houston morning progressed, he began making phone calls.

Over the next year, O'Neill would execute a trade that was larger than any he'd ever done before. And it was a trade that was only possible, in all of its massive scope, because of the strange way that America's financial markets had evolved over the previous decade, creating a small node within the economy that minted millionaires and billionaires.

If O'Neill could pull off his trade as he imagined it, he could become one of them. If he had confidence that he could do it, it was because he had been trained by the best in the business.

Koch's trading office in Houston was overseen by a man named Sam Soliman. Like O'Neill, Soliman had cut his teeth in Koch's Corpus

Christi refinery. He was a graduate of Texas A&M and an engineer by training. Before working for Koch, Soliman was an officer on a US Navy nuclear submarine, and even years later, when overseeing Koch's trading floor, Soliman carried with him the bearing and ethos of someone in a military chain of command. It seems that spending extended periods of time submerged in the ocean, confined next to a nuclear reactor, had impressed upon Soliman certain habits of discipline and risk assessment. He was tall and thin, with a head of thick, dark hair, and spoke with exacting precision. Soliman was considered a "talent sifter," meaning that he hired young and bright employees, put them in profoundly challenging positions, and fired the traders who couldn't handle the challenge. This talent sifting was a vital part of Koch's strategy to build a trading floor from scratch during the late 1990s and early 2000s. Engineers like O'Neill were given a crash course in trading and graded every day by their profits or losses.

When describing the trading culture under Sam Soliman, trader Cris Franklin replied, simply: "No mistakes." And Franklin was one of the traders on Soliman's good side. "At any moment, you could get tapped on your shoulder and you're leaving. It was extreme stress for most people," Franklin said. "There are people I know today who say that when they drive by the building, their heart races. And they haven't worked there in a decade."

On any given afternoon, the dozens of traders sitting in long rows outside of Soliman's office were trafficking in wildly diverse classes of commodities and financial products. Koch operated desks that traded crude, natural gas, and derivatives contracts based on crude oil and natural gas. Other traders handled futures contracts in metals, soybeans, corn, and wheat. After mastering the markets in these products, Koch branched out into more obscure territory. Cris Franklin, for example, worked on a desk that traded short-term commercial bonds—the same products made famous in the 1980s by notoriously voracious traders at Wall Street firms like Salomon Brothers. Franklin's team then started trading financial products like swaps and derivatives based on interest rates and currency values. Koch even created its own financial products to trade. It pioneered a class of futures contracts for obscure petrochemicals like propylene and ethylene, selling them to big companies that bought plastics in bulk and wanted to hedge their risk.

Deep analysis was at the heart of Koch's trading strategy. Franklin, for example, was hired into the trading unit after working in Koch's pipeline division. He had impressed his bosses there by developing a software program that could help Koch run its hypercomplex network of pipelines and natural gas processing plants. Franklin's program synthesized enormous amounts of data about pipeline flows and gauge pressures to simulate how the system could ship the most gas. When he started trading interest rate swaps, he used the same approach. Every trade began with research, which undergirded the trader's view of how things worked in a certain market. Traders never executed a strategy based on hunches. Koch hired teams of analysts who worked alongside each trader to provide reams of data and analysis. The importance of this analysis was reflected in Koch's pay structure—the company changed its payment structure so that profits were split between the trader and her supporting team of analysts. This put the analysts on equal footing with the traders. Melissa Beckett, who worked on several of Koch's trading desks as both an analyst and trader, said Koch was unique in this regard. Other trading shops might consider analyst reports to be an afterthought; at Koch, those reports were the bedrock where a trade began.

Traders on Koch's floor considered the rest of the world to be a herd, and not a particularly smart herd at that. There was an overwhelming amount of activity in the markets, but seemingly very little insight. When Koch cautiously branched into a new market, the traders were often surprised at how easy it was to make money there with just a little bit of forethought. "We couldn't believe how the incumbent counterparties couldn't see the enormous profits that existed in those markets. Even though these were very established markets . . . dominated by the large banks, or large incumbent parties, like insurance companies, et cetera. But they just looked at it fundamentally very different," one trader said.

It turned out that most of the counterparties in the market were obsessed with the near-term horizon. On Wall Street, entire teams of traders were focused entirely on what was about to happen in the next three months. The investment culture had become trained to trade around the next set of corporate quarterly earnings; public reports that could cause major bounces for stocks or commodity prices. This near horizon was bombarded by millions of hours of attention and human brainpower, with investors jockeying to position themselves to benefit from a quick shift in the market. This left entire continents of the marketplace unexplored; terrain that Koch was quick to enter and dominate.

For example, traders at Koch would never "short" the oil market, making a bet that oil prices would drop. Making a short bet was sloppy, and the kind of thing that anybody could do. Rather than make such simple bets, Koch relied on its mastery of the world's complicated, opaque energy markets. Koch traders tended to make "basis trades" or "spread trades" that were based on complicated price relationships between different products at different locations around the world. Koch didn't bet that the price of gas was going up, but that the price of gas in the Midwest was going to rise relative to the price along the Gulf Coast. To make these trades, Koch used a set of tools that few other companies could use. If Koch thought there was going to be an oversupply of oil in the Gulf Coast region, for example, it might snap up leases on giant oil barges, knowing that when the oversupply hit, companies would be scrambling for extra storage space and willing to pay a premium for the leases that Koch bought on the cheap. This was a much safer way to execute the trade than simply shorting the price of oil—even if Koch was wrong about the supply glut, the downside was limited because Koch could still sell or use the barge leases and almost certainly break even.

Koch maximized the advantage of having "inside" information gleaned from its refineries and other assets. Inside information helped traders like Melissa Beckett sharpen their trading strategies as she bought and sold futures contracts for oil at her desk in Houston. When Koch's traders made assumptions about the oil market, they could test those assumptions against the real data that was emanating from Koch's refineries. But Koch Supply & Trading did not rely exclusively on inside information. It aggressively gathered and analyzed huge amounts of data from outside sources. It used the publicly available data that all traders used—like the federal reports that tracked the volume of crude oil being stored in the United States. This data was good, but often stale, published weekly or monthly, and rarely drilled down into specifics. So Koch found other ways to learn about the market. The Customs Service, for example, kept databases of the manifests submitted by oil tankers entering US waters, data that revealed what kind of oil the tankers carried and for whom they were carrying it. By collecting and analyzing reams of this data, Koch could reverse engineer a picture of oil shipments and flows that was granular in its specificity. Koch could learn exactly what its competitors were refining, how much they were refining, and on what day they refined it.

Koch also discovered that the National Parks Service published data showing the snow pack in the California mountains, data that Koch could analyze to determine how much water would be flowing in future months to generate power at California's hydroelectric plants. This helped Koch predict with great accuracy the future supply of electricity and the resulting demand for natural gas.

Because weather conditions had such a big impact on electricity and natural gas demand, Koch raided the newsrooms of places like the Weather Channel to hire their best meteorologists. The weather scientists were all too happy to leave their television gigs and multiply their earning power. The meteorologists arrived at work around four thirty or five o'clock in the morning and started running their computer models that analyzed several sources of weather data around the country. If they could deliver a forecast that was one or two degrees sharper than the forecast everyone else was using, it could give Koch's traders an edge. The company's proprietary weather report was circulated early in the morning and updated throughout the day. The Koch meteorologists watched the local weathercasters and scoffed. The B-team players had been left behind in the television studio to forecast for the public. "I can outforecast any of those guys on TV," one former Koch meteorologist recalled.

All of these information streams were centralized, analyzed, and then shared widely within Koch's trading group. The purpose of gathering all of this information was to find "the gap," as Koch's traders called it: the gap between reality and what the market believed was reality. Koch gathered enough information to get a sharper picture of reality than its competitors. Then it placed bets that would make money when the market corrected itself, closing the gap, and came closer to the real-world conditions. When O'Neill was promoted from the oil refinery to the trading floor in late 1996, his job was to find gaps in the natural gas market. He was stunned to see how much money a person could make in this hidden niche of America's energy industry.

———

On the first day he reported to work at 20 Greenway Plaza, O'Neill held the obscure job title of analyst on the Gulf Coast Basis desk. The moment he sat down at his desk, Sam Soliman's talent sifter began to shake back and forth, testing O'Neill's instincts. O'Neill was perpetually aware that at any moment the tap on the shoulder might come, and he'd be escorted out of a job.

O'Neill did okay at first. He seemed to have an aptitude for the business. He was trading abstract natural gas financial contracts, but he quickly learned that even this abstract business was conducted according to the Koch way. The foundation of Koch's natural gas trading business was a 9,600-mile-long collection of pipelines that ran along the Gulf Coast and snaked through several states in the Southeast. Koch purchased these pipelines and the company that owned them, United Gas Pipe Line Company, in 1992 in a deal worth at least $100 million. The timing of the deal was no coincidence. It occurred just one year after the George H. W. Bush administration revolutionized the gas business. The deregulation of America's natural gas business was one of those historical episodes that garnered little attention but that created sweeping changes throughout the economy. These changes gave a handful of companies the chance to make a once-in-a-generation windfall of profits.

Prior to the first Bush administration, the history of the natural gas industry wasn't too different from the crude oil business—the government intervened in deep and distortive ways to encourage production while protecting consumers from high prices. Back in the New Deal era, Franklin Roosevelt created a legal regime, headed by the Federal Power Commission, that regulated the business from the wellhead to the kitchen gas burner. The federal government capped the price that gas drillers could charge for gas, which kept natural gas prices low for consumers. But there were toxic side effects from these price caps: by the 1970s, the price was so low that producers didn't even bother to drill new gas wells. Predictably, new supplies dried up and gas shortages ensued. Customers turned the gas valve, and nothing came out. Even a New Deal–era government monolith like the Federal Power Commission couldn't force producers to drill for gas if they didn't want to.

In 1978, President Jimmy Carter stripped away the price controls to unleash market forces that might encourage new supplies. But Carter's "deregulation" was hardly a libertarian dream. It created a wildly complex set of rules and price controls that sought to let the wholesale price rise and fall while protecting consumers from the highest price spikes. This was a Faustian bargain that would play out repeatedly in US policy making from the 1980s on. Lawmakers repeatedly passed deregulation measures that only went halfway, stripping away some controls while trying to shield average people from the true volatility of the market. The ensuing market structures were usually defined by complexity and dysfunction, and the natural gas industry was no different.

The Federal Power Commission was replaced by the Federal Energy Regulatory Commission, which held hours of hearings and collected reams of public comment to parse out the minutiae of when companies could raise prices and when they could not. The regulatory state could never get the porridge just right. High prices in the late 1970s were replaced by supply gluts and falling demand in the 1980s.

George H. W. Bush tried to tear the system up and start over in 1991. The FERC issued a regulation, called Order No. 636, that broke apart the existing natural gas companies. This single order redrew one of the nation's largest industries, and an energy system on which millions of people relied for heat and electricity.

Under the new regulatory scheme, the natural gas industry was divided into three components:

1) Gas drillers who sold natural gas
2) Pipeline companies that transmitted the gas
3) Consumers who bought the gas

The pipeline companies that transmitted the gas became like railroads—they didn't own gas like they did in the old days, they just shipped it. Anyone could book space in a pipeline to have gas shipped. This created a new market. Now there was feverish buying and selling of gas at every node of a pipeline. A new class of merchants arose to traffic in this market, chief among them being Koch Industries and its neighbor in Houston, the energy giant Enron.

Senior managers at Koch Supply & Trading saw the potential profits to be made in the growing natural gas marketplace and rushed in to capture it. Koch followed the lead of Enron in cutting deals to manage the nation's natural gas infrastructure on behalf of the gas consumers.

The infrastructure had originally been built with a focus on reliability, ensuring that there was enough gas to meet demand. The big pipeline companies built underground domes in which to store gas—surplus supplies that they could then dole out in times of scarcity. In the age of deregulation, this infrastructure was used like a casino gaming table, every niche explored for ways in which it could turn a profit.

In the old days, an underground gas dome might be filled up and emptied about once a year. Under Koch's management, the domes were filled or emptied eight or nine times a year. Customers who bought the gas were promised that they would have supplies when they needed it, and Koch's traders were free to buy and sell supplies from the underground domes in the meantime. Deals like this were called "origination" deals because they essentially originated new markets for gas. As was often the case at Koch, the company wasn't just interested in the revenue from deals like this. It was more interested in the real-time window that origination deals could provide into the natural gas markets. Just as in the early days of the crude oil markets, information about prices was both scarce and incredibly valuable. There were not yet electronic exchanges that showed a visible price of natural gas, and government data on sales were irregular and relatively slow to come. Every origination deal provided fresh and precise information about prices, supply, and demand.

Koch went so far as to fold its origination group into its trading group, to encourage information sharing: "Now it's all one company. There's one trading book," a former senior executive recalled. "There's no more origination profit and trading group profit. There's one profit."

This profit flowed from inside information. "The most important thing you can have as a trading company is deal flow. The more flow you see, the more knowledge you have," according to the former senior executive. "And sometimes you don't mind even if the [deal] flow just breaks even for a while. That's okay. Because that gives you new knowledge on price direction and all that. You'll ultimately make much more money long term."

This gave traders like O'Neill an advantage in the trading markets—Koch's pipelines and origination teams were an information-generating machine. The United Gas Pipe Line system, which was renamed Koch Gateway, included 120 connections with other pipeline systems, each one a node that could yield information about natural gas prices.

O'Neill spent his day on the phone, calling around to brokers and other traders and customers, feeling out where they might be on price. He also called other Koch traders to find out what they were hearing. One of his favorite colleagues to call was Jeff Stephens, who traded at Koch Gateway's connection to the "Henry Hub," a Louisiana pipeline distribution complex that became a major market for gas sales. The Henry Hub was one of the industry's price setting markets, and in the late 1990s Stephens seemed to be single-handedly brokering most deals on the hub. "He *was* the Henry Hub cash market," O'Neill recalled. Stephens berated and cajoled other brokers and customers. When they said they didn't want to place an order because the low market might "bounce," Stephens would scold them by saying "Eggs don't bounce!" Before the era of the electronic exchange, Stephens was a living, breathing market ticker, and O'Neill made full use of his services.

At the end of his first year of trading, O'Neill produced promising results. His trading book yielded $7 million in profits. Of course, that was back in the quaint and early days of the gas market, before things really picked up steam.

Koch's traders often got off work early, between four thirty and five o'clock in the afternoon, after US market trading ceased. The traders were mostly in their late twenties or early thirties, and they enjoyed going out for drinks after work. They didn't party hard, in the way that later became synonymous with the hard-charging world of Wall Street traders. The Koch people didn't snort cocaine and visit strip clubs. In fact, their drinking sessions might have seemed disappointingly dull to outsiders: a bunch of engineers sitting around in golf shirts sipping craft beers.

One of their favorite gathering places was a pub called the Ginger Man, located near Rice University, not too far from 20 Greenway Plaza. The pub was located on a quiet side street, set back behind a grassy patio area. It was a small, wood-framed bungalow that was obscured from view during summer months by leafy trees that sheltered picnic tables and a large front porch. Customers walked past a small picket fence to enter the patio and then up a set of rickety wooden steps. A small placard by the front door announced drink specials on a hand-written menu scribbled in brightly colored chalk.

Inside, the bar was pleasingly dim and cave-like. Although the Koch traders were unaware of the fact, the bar was a near replica of the Coates Bar in Minnesota, where the union workers used to gather in the 1970s after their shifts at the Pine Bend refinery. The layout of the two establishments was virtually identical, with a long bar extending along the left side of the room and wooden tables clustered along the right side. The ceiling was low in both places, and the wood-paneled walls seemed to be stained the same honey-blond color. But the Ginger Man was more refined—it was like the Coates Bar reimagined by an interior designer who kept the charming elements and jettisoned the unseemly parts. While the Coates Bar served Miller Lite or its equivalent, the Ginger Man had a menu of dozens of craft beers that were arrayed along the bar with their own custom taps. The Koch Industries traders didn't drink like their blue-collar counterparts up in Minnesota—they didn't line up shots of hard liquor to be pounded one after another, as the OCAW president Joseph Hammerschmidt had done.

But the Koch traders were just like their unionized predecessors in one way. When they got together and drank at the Ginger Man, they bitched about how underpaid they were.

Koch had hired engineers to staff its trading desk, and it continued to pay them like engineers once they learned the job. O'Neill, for example, was still making $60,000 a year. There was a creeping awareness spreading throughout the trading floor that things didn't have to be this way. There were rumors that traders over at Enron were making multiples of $60,000. And Wall Street banks started calling with job offers that were far richer than what Koch offered.

O'Neill was not a disloyal person. He had worked for Koch his entire career. But financial pressures were beginning to press down on him. His credit card debt, in particular, was problematic. In this, he wasn't alone. America's middle class stopped seeing significant pay increases after the 1990s, but they did enjoy a new source of spending power: an easy availability of credit. The loosening of laws around banking during the eighties and nineties paved the way for a flood of consumer debt. At places like nearby Rice University, credit card companies set up booths to greet incoming students, promising easy access to large lines of credit. It had never been easier for Americans to borrow, and they used the privilege to supplement the lag in their paychecks. The tide that lifted all boats during the 1990s was fueled by credit cards that carried 14 percent interest rates or higher. The monthly payments could eat a person alive. O'Neill and his wife were happily married, but that didn't mean it was easy. They lived within a constricting web of household spending budget. It was hard not to argue when money was tight.

It might have been disappointing, then, to discover that Koch's trading floor wasn't an easy path to riches in the mid-1990s. When O'Neill earned $7 million for the company that first year, he might have reasonably expected a large bonus. At the end of the year, he discussed his performance with Sam Soliman and was told that his incentive reward would be $25,000. That was about 0.004 percent of what O'Neill had just earned for the company. Soliman seemed sympathetic to the idea that traders should earn a bigger cut of the profits. But Charles Koch seemed intent on paying the traders like engineers. And O'Neill's bosses knew that his best annual bonus at the refinery was $10,000 a year.

"Sam's like, 'It's a lot better than the refinery, right?'" O'Neill recalled with a laugh. "And I'm like, 'Yep. Yep. You're right. It is.'"

Not all traders were as compliant. Some of them quietly slipped away to join Enron or big banks. They did so with the knowledge that there were fortunes to be earned. Just seven months after he joined the Gulf Coast Basis desk, Brenden O'Neill got his chance to see this world for himself. He was promoted to trading natural gas derivatives, and ushered into the world of real money.

Sam Soliman stretched his top traders. When a trader did well at one thing, Soliman tended to promote them into a new role with which they had zero experience. If they performed well in this spot, they could be promoted once again. If not, tap on the shoulder. Good-bye.

Brenden O'Neill was promoted to the natural gas options desk. A natural gas option is a derivatives contract, and O'Neill knew virtually nothing about derivatives before joining Koch's trading team. He would now be trading millions of dollars a day in contracts. He figured that he'd better learn what he was doing, and fast.

A person couldn't just enroll in college and take a class in trading natural gas options. O'Neill didn't take time off and attend Harvard Business School. He didn't have a mentor, and he didn't have an industry group that he could turn to for training. So he bought a textbook off the shelf, called *Option Volatility and Pricing Strategies: Advanced Trading Strategies and Techniques,* by Sheldon Natenberg. It was basically a high-end version of *Options Trading for Dummies.* He read the book on his own time and started to learn the mechanics of how things worked inside the black box of the derivatives market.

Here is a brief description of a derivatives contract, in one paragraph, that is still torture to read. Pretty much all derivatives traded by people like O'Neill were either "calls" or "puts." A call is a contract that lets somebody buy something at a certain price. O'Neill could sell you a call that would allow you to buy a tank of natural gas for $5 in March, even if the real price for gas at that time was $10 a tank. It was like an insurance contract against rising prices. He could also sell you a put that would allow you to sell a tank of natural gas in March for $5, even if the real price at that time was $2 a tank. It was like an insurance contract against falling prices.

Again, these derivatives contracts didn't even deal with real gas. They dealt with gas futures contracts. So, O'Neill was buying and selling insurance contracts on futures contracts. He spent his days examining these futures contracts, and watching their price rise and fall. This was complicated. For natural gas, there were several different futures contracts: there were contracts for delivery of gas in March, then April, then May, then June, and so on. In the eyes of a trader like O'Neill, each month's contract was like a different commodity in and of itself. The May contract might be doing one thing, while the March contract was doing something different. He examined the behavior of all the different contracts and sold people insurance products—derivatives—for every different month.

O'Neill started experimenting with these new markets. He bought and sold puts and calls options, and then started to figure out more complex maneuvers. He could buy a put on a May futures contract, and then turn around and start buying and selling volumes of that futures contract as a way to hedge the option in a complex interplay that is called trading the "underlier." It didn't take long before he realized that these machinations could generate tens of millions of dollars.

Where did all this money come from? Why were the profits so enormous? The best way to understand it is to know that O'Neill was sitting in the middle of a giant game of tug-of-war. On one side of the rope, pulling hard, was every company that drilled natural gas and sold it. This side of the rope wanted gas prices to be as high as possible, because they were selling it. On the other side of the rope, also pulling hard, was everyone who bought natural gas and burned it. These parties wanted gas prices to be as cheap as possible, since they were buying it.

Back and forth these opposing interests tugged, and the bright red line in the middle of the rope was the going price for gas. Sometimes the gas producers were winning the game and pulled the red line way over toward their side, making the price very high. At other times, the consumers won the game and pulled the red line way over to their side, making the price very low. The stakes of this game were almost incomprehensible—the total national market in natural gas was worth several hundred billion dollars a year. When the red line of price went one way or the other, it was the financial equivalent of a tectonic plate shifting in the earth. The rumbling and shaking shook loose billions of dollars in one moment, money that flowed from the pockets of consumers to producers as the price moved positions. And when that money was disgorged, it passed through the hands of traders like O'Neill, who kept a portion of it for themselves. In the final analysis, the people who were buying his derivatives contracts might be a big utility company in Ohio that burns natural gas, or a big company in Oklahoma that drills and sells natural gas. These entities would pay real money for insurance contracts that protected them from shifts in the price. If the price was moving, O'Neill and Koch Industries stood to make millions. Volatility was the trader's best friend.

O'Neill honed his trading strategies over the year. And he began to make one bet more than any other. He didn't bet that gas prices were going to rise, and he didn't bet that they were starting to fall. He just started betting that they would be volatile. He did this by snapping up options and then snapping up their underliers in the futures markets, buying them and selling them in a way that stripped out the price component of the bet. He didn't want to bet on price. He wanted to bet that the price was going to change and change more than people expected it to. One reason he kept betting this way was because it kept making money. After the natural gas markets were deregulated, volatility started to become the norm. The sleepy days of price controls were over, and now the price could shoot up or down in minutes.

That's why, when he came into work in the early winter months of 2000, O'Neill started to get excited. He was starting to see a very large play unfolding, one that would dwarf anything he'd attempted at Koch before. All of the data that he'd amassed was pointing in one direction as the weather got colder in January and February. All of the signs were pointing toward unprecedented volatility.

When O'Neill turned his computer on in the morning, he would find numerous reports available to him that were produced by Koch's teams of analysts and traders. He was on an e-mail list for an internal report called *WinterSkinny*, for example, which was sent to a long list of Koch employees both inside and outside the trading unit. The *WinterSkinny* report had a commentary section that summarized the state of the market in simple language—one e-mail read: "To sum up the commentary section in fewer words, 'I don't know where it's going, and nobody cares anyway.'"

Other internal reports, such as the *Daily Analysis*, were not written in English—or in any language that most people would understand. It was composed of complicated graphs and spreadsheets that showed electricity usage, as well as weather pattern analysis for cities like Denver, Las Vegas, and Eugene, Oregon, that compared "Temps vs. Normal." One graph even showed detailed water levels for a reservoir above the Grand Coulee Dam in Washington State, which provided hydroelectric power.

These reports were coupled with flash alerts from throughout Koch Industries. Plant managers, refinery operators, and others were encouraged to share any information they learned that might affect markets. The trading unit built an internal instant messaging system called Koch Global Alerts that sent the news to traders in real time—an innovative technology in the late 1990s and early 2000s.

Traders sitting shoulder to shoulder in O'Neill's office read through these reports and news flashes all morning, synthesizing what they learned into trading strategies. The traders created PowerPoint slideshows outlining their strategies and presented them in conference rooms to their colleagues. The presentations were shared across trading groups—Cris Franklin, who traded interest rate swaps, might find himself sharing a strategy with natural gas and crude oil traders, and vice versa. The traders were encouraged to pick apart each other's plans, criticizing the strategies and, ideally, making them stronger.

In 2000, two Koch analysts and a reservoir engineer produced a slide-show entitled "Natural Gas Point of View 2000–2001." In this report, they accurately predicted a coming disaster that would contribute to blackouts along the West Coast, the bankruptcy of major utilities, and skyrocketing costs for many consumers.* The seventh slide of the presentation concluded that in the case of a cold winter, "storage inventories will be depleted." This blunt conclusion was the only sentence on the slide that was underlined and written in bold type.

The assessment matched what O'Neill was seeing in the markets. During the 1990s, cheap and abundant natural gas had been taken as a given in the American economy. Large new wells had been discovered, and supplies were plentiful. More power plants were built to burn the fuel, which was used as an alternative to coal and nuclear power. In the late 1980s, the price of gas spiked to $2.27,† and it hovered around that level for the decade and was trading for $2.22 in late 1999. The long years of price stagnation seemed to have convinced many consumers and producers that low volatility and cheap gas were the normal state of affairs.

In early 2000, O'Neill and his team realized that this was a deeply mistaken assumption. Koch was in a privileged position to see the coming shortage. The company didn't just operate a huge pipeline; it also owned a huge but obscure company called IMDST,‡ which arranged gas storage leases for about one billion cubic feet of gas. Managing storage was a critical part of the business. As O'Neill liked to say, there wasn't a lot you could do with gas once it was pumped out of the ground: "You either burn it, or you store it. You can't do anything else with it." Companies stored it by injecting it into underground storage units, and Koch

---

* Readers will learn more about this disaster in chapter 13, "Attack of the Killer Electrons!"

† Specifically, the price was $2.27 per million British thermal units, or MMBTU in market lingo. This is the basic unit of measurement for natural gas used by traders, and all figures in this chapter are MMBTU. A British thermal unit is a measure of energy put out by a given volume of gas. A million BTUs can be about one thousand cubic feet of gas.

‡ The full name was IMD Storage, Transportation and Asset Management Company LLC, and the company was based in Texas.

saw that the inject rates were historically low. The industry was behind its historical storage levels, according to the "Natural Gas Point of View" slideshow, which stated that "More prolific injection path seems impossible with current fundamentals."

The squirrels were not burying enough acorns, in other words, and the winter was about to hit. At the same time, there were more hungry squirrels than ever. US energy consumption was on the rise as people plugged more and more devices into their walls, from extra television sets to home computers. A historic shortage of gas appeared to be in the making. Koch Industries wasn't the only company to see the coming storm. Traders gossiped over beer and shared tips over the phone, so it was well known in certain circles that firms like Enron were starting to put on trades betting that gas prices would rise.

While traders might have seen what was coming, it appeared that the general public did not. O'Neill saw a gap in the market in early 2000. A giant gap. The price of gas options was cheap—too cheap to account for what was apparently coming down the road. In other words, the insurance policies against a sudden price spike were not as expensive as they ought to have been. So O'Neill started snapping up the options and holding on to them, knowing that they would become more valuable.

As usual, he wasn't just making a bet that prices were going to go up. He was primarily betting that markets were about to become more volatile. He built up a large position with his natural gas options and underliers that was "long volatility," meaning that he bet volatility would increase. He assumed that the positions would provide a good return for Koch Industries. He was wrong. He grossly underestimated the riches that the coming volatility was about to deliver.

Senior executives in Koch Supply & Trading realized that they could no longer pay their traders like engineers. There was a competition for talent, and too many well-trained people were bleeding off the Koch trading floor. There was one person who seemed to resist big paydays for the traders: Charles Koch.

The business failures of the 1990s impressed on Charles Koch the need for humility among his workforce. The thinking went that it was the high-flying ambition and loose planning that led to many of the business losses at Purina Mills. Charles Koch put a premium on culture among his employees. Among the most important attributes was valuing the team over the player, and the company over the individual. There was something unseemly about the grousing of commodities traders who clamored for ever-larger bonuses. If traders got giant bonuses, it might incentivize them to act like lone wolves, seeing a personal payday instead of the long-term well-being of the company. In the risky business of derivatives trading, Charles Koch knew that a lone trader could cause immeasurable damage.

This viewpoint held sway for many years, but the defections began to change things. So did a shift of personnel at the top. Sam Soliman, the previous head of trading, stepped aside to become the chief financial officer of Koch Industries when Charles Koch began overhauling the firm in the early 2000s.

A newer hire in the trading division started to change the trading culture in Soliman's absence. His name was David Sobotka, and Koch hired him directly from Wall Street. Sobotka worked for Lehman Brothers before joining Koch in 1997. He was somewhat of an odd bird within Koch. He had matriculated from Yale, not Texas A&M, and he looked every bit the part of a Wall Street dandy. He had a boyishly handsome face with tousled, wavy hair, and clearly knew how to handle himself in a five-star world. But unlike other Ivy League grads, he managed to embed himself successfully into Koch's management machinery, learning to talk the language of Market-Based Management. While he might have used the catchphrases of MBM, Sobotka also imported vital pieces of the Wall Street trading culture into Koch's operations. Sobotka imposed a bonus and compensation structure that matched the norm at other trading firms. There would be no more bonuses of $25,000 for traders like O'Neill. Instead, they would get a cut of the profits they earned for the company. This was a novel thing at Koch Industries—it does not appear that Charles Koch allowed for a true profit-sharing bonus pool to exist anywhere else at the company. But the potential profits of derivatives trading demanded a change in course. Under Sobotka, the trading floor would take 14 percent of the total profit they earned. That 14 percent take would be split up among the managers, traders, and analysts, in a split that Sobotka and his leadership determined was fair.

Charles Koch never seemed comfortable with this model. But it had a dramatic effect on the traders.

It was a cold winter in 2000. Demand for electricity was strong. There wasn't enough natural gas injected into underground storage units. Utilities were burning gas and demanding more. Suddenly, everybody in the world wanted to buy insurance against volatility. During the three short months between March and May in 2000, the price of natural gas shot up 57 percent, from $2.88 to $4.52. The markets roiled, with billions of dollars being hauled from consumers to producers in a matter of weeks. O'Neill was in the middle of it, collecting millions. Traders who had sold him options earlier in the year were calling him up seeking to buy them back. He sold when the price was right.

"We got lucky to a certain degree because it got cold early," he recalled. "We made much more money than we probably thought we would."

It wasn't a straight path to riches. In July the natural gas market pulled back sharply, and prices fell. It seemed that the market was correcting itself—the run-up in March had been an aberration, an overreaction. It looked like there was a chance that O'Neill had simply gotten lucky and gotten a short-term payday. The gas price dropped 14 percent to $3.75.

Other traders in O'Neill's group had made naked long bets, positions that counted on natural gas to keep rising. They started to unwind these positions in July out of fear that they would lose all the gains they'd achieved that year. It seemed possible that the market might sink back into a steady equilibrium. O'Neill, however, remained firm in his position. He thought of the words from his mentor, Sam Soliman, who had overseen him when O'Neill was first learning how to trade. O'Neill had often grown nervous when it appeared that the market was moving against him. But Soliman counseled patience. The Koch way wasn't to react in the moment. It was to hold a long-term view. Soliman called this "managing to expiration," meaning playing out a position until it expired. Short-term thinking was the death of a good trader—there were just too many wild variables that might cause a market to fall from one month to another. These variables often didn't have any relation to the underlying reality of the market. People have a terrible habit of making bets that things will revert to a "norm." This is the same impulse that delays the bursting of a stock market bubble: many investors convince themselves that undesirable outcomes must be unlikely because their consequences will be so painful to bear. It's human nature.

O'Neill was not betting on a return to the norm. He was betting on volatility and sticking with his position. And almost immediately after markets dropped in July, the upheaval returned. In one month, the price of gas shot up 27 percent. Orders were piling up, and supplies were tight; customers who needed natural gas in the spot market started paying dearly to get it. During the 1970s, gas shortages caused an interruption of delivery—pipeline companies simply closed their spigots when price controls made it infeasible to deliver gas. This caused factories to shut down and lights to go out.

After the deregulation of the 1990s, it was the market that would enforce such rationing, and the main tool at the market's disposal was the punishing power of high prices. This made perfect sense economically, but caused problems socially. Natural gas wasn't a product that people could easily stop using when it got pricey. It was embedded in the electric and industrial base of America, so consumption remained strong and prices kept rising.

The run-up in gas prices continued for the rest of the year. In the fall, the price of gas jumped to the highest levels in years, hitting $6.31 in November, almost double the price just months before. Across the country, this volatility played out with terrible effect. It contributed to months of rolling blackouts in California, where factories ceased production, stores closed down, and auto accidents occurred when the traffic lights blinked out. In December, the price of gas hit $10.48. O'Neill cashed out of his position. He tallied the profits from his trading book. He'd earned roughly $70 million for Koch through his plays in the options market.

By contrast, the entire pipeline company of Koch Gateway, all 9,600 miles of pipe with 120 connection points to other customers, earned only $15.3 million, according to government filings. The black box economy of derivatives, once a shadow market, had far surpassed the real economy in its earnings. O'Neill said his entire trading team earned as much as $400 million of profit in one year. And that was just a single team.

———

After the books were closed on the year 2000, it was time for O'Neill to get his bonus. It would be his first payout under the Sobotka bonus pool regime. It would be his first taste of what other traders in the business were making, from Enron to Lehman Brothers. He knew that 14 percent of the profits would go to the floor, which would have equaled nearly $10 million. But that amount was split up among himself and others like Sobotka and Jeff Searle, a trading manager who reported to Sobotka.

One trader after another was called into Searle's office to learn what their bonus for the year was. O'Neill's turn came. He sat down to hear the news. He would be paid $4 million.

"We talked about how it was a life-changing number," O'Neill said. "I was very appreciative."

With a single paycheck, O'Neill was propelled up through the ranks of American economic life. He broke through the upper atmosphere of the middle class. He would no longer worry about making mortgage payments. He would no longer argue with his wife about cutting back to meet the monthly budget. He would no longer fret about the quality of public schools in his neighborhood. All the financial worries that had encompassed his life since he bunked in the basement with his brothers were gone.

The O'Neills sold their single-story, 2,428-square-foot home. Just before Christmas 2002, they bought a newly constructed, 4,820-square-foot house that sat far back on a wide grassy lawn in a tree-lined neighborhood in town. It had a pool in the backyard with a diving board. The O'Neills were able to hire a nanny to help with the kids, and began taking skiing vacations. They joined a country club and enrolled all of their children in private school.

If there was a downside to being a millionaire, O'Neill was hard-pressed to describe it. The new money ends up going faster than a person might think—private school might cost between $80,000 and $100,000 a year for all the kids. Nannies aren't cheap. A ski trip might cost $20,000. It turned out that before long, you were spending all that money without even doing anything extravagant like buying rare art. But still. This wasn't the same thing as worrying about paying off the credit card each month, or worrying if you had enough money to pay for all the activities the kids had signed up for.

O'Neill worked for Koch Energy Trading until 2004, when he left to trade on his own. He got tired of working at a big company and enjoyed being independent. He formed a hedge fund that specialized in energy trading, dabbled in the oil well business, and continued to live in Houston.

For all the money he made, O'Neill retained a great deal of humility. He realized that other people in his business were making far more money than he did. A $4 million annual compensation was somewhat prosaic among the top derivatives traders in America. At Koch Industries, he personally knew many other millionaires. O'Neill was also able to recognize the difference between himself and the people he worked for. He knew that he kept only a fraction of the profit he earned, even in the best years. There were other people, not too far from his orbit, who earned hundreds of millions of dollars. That kind of money created a completely different kind of life, which he couldn't fathom.

"I made enough money . . . to where I was comfortable. But I wasn't powerful. It didn't bring power with it. It just brought comfort." O'Neill said. He wasn't rich enough, as he put it: "Where you have enough money where you can influence things."

That kind of money was accruing to his bosses at Koch, and to the bosses above them.

CHAPTER 13

Attack of the Killer Electrons!

(2000–2002)

*The problem, therefore, lies as much in the national political cul-
ture as in the specifics of California's ill-fated experiment.*

— *Yale Journal on Regulation,* 2002

*Who would have thought? All we wanted was a bigger, healthier
tomato.*

—Government bureaucrat, *Attack of the Killer Tomatoes!,* 1978

Koch's trading division was always expanding into new territory. Koch's
traders sought out new, opaque markets where the economics were complex, the rewards were enormous, and Koch could press its advantages
of deep analysis and inside information. One of the richest horizons for
new trading in 2000 was an emerging market for something that had
never been traded before: electricity.

The new commodity in this market was called a megawatt-hour.
This was a basic unit of power that could be bought and sold like an
oil futures contract.* The size of this new market was breathtaking. The
national electricity market was worth roughly $215 billion a year, mak-
ing it more than twice the size of the airline or telephone industries. The
natural gas market, by contrast, which had earned Koch Industries such
rich profits during the 1990s, was worth a mere $90 billion. The market
was even more enticing because only a handful of firms were prepared
to trade megawatt-hours in 2000.

Koch Industries was one of them.

---

* A megawatt-hour is the amount of electricity needed to power roughly 330 homes for
an hour.

Koch formed a division that traded electricity futures called Koch Energy Trading. The company selected a young man named Darrell Antrich to pioneer its venture into the megawatt markets. Antrich was only twenty-eight years old. He looked even younger than his age, with a lean physique and closely cropped light-brown hair. When he arrived for work at Koch's trading floor in Houston, Antrich wore a button-down oxford shirt and khaki pants, and could have easily passed for a young conservative college student. His youth was a good match for the ambition and novelty of the new team that he would lead for Koch.

Antrich helped build a team of traders who would focus on trading nothing but megawatts. Their cluster of desks was located near the natural gas trading floor where O'Neill had made his fortune, and the new electricity traders would benefit from the same infrastructure that helped O'Neill. They had access to Koch's internal weather reports and flash alerts from the pipelines and refineries. They built a complex software system to help predict demand for electricity around the country, along with detailed flow charts of power grids and transmission pathways.

The trading infrastructure was up and running, ready to do business, but there was one significant problem: the electricity markets in which it would trade were still being built. There was an important truth embedded in this situation: Koch's trading floor was only one half of the coin of the marketplace. The other half of the coin was the public policy and politics that would create the trading market itself. It was common for Koch's traders and other libertarians to talk about markets as if they were organic systems that lived, grew, and evolved on their own if only left alone by the government. In fact, markets are always a system of exchange created by rules, and those rules are almost always created by the government.

This was certainly the case for the new electricity markets in which Koch was hoping to trade. A new market for electricity was being created in the United States, piece by piece, during the 1990s. One state after another was changing the rules of the power business in a process that was called deregulation—but that was a lot more complicated than simply repealing rules. The deregulation effort was really more of a reregulation effort, a political movement to shift the rules in favor of independent traders and away from a state-regulated utility system that was born in the New Deal era. It wasn't clear until years later what an important role Koch Industries played in helping shape the effort.

As Darrell Antrich was helping set up Koch's trading desk, another arm of Koch Industries was actively shaping the markets in which Antrich would trade. Koch was uniquely prepared to execute on this double-edged strategy. The company's ability to influence politics had expanded dramatically since the early 1990s, when Koch was investigated by the US Senate. Over the next decade, Koch expanded its political lobbying office, increased its political contributions, and funded libertarian think tanks. Perhaps most significantly, Koch Industries became a vital supporter of a little-known national policy network called the American Legislative Exchange Council, or ALEC, which pushed efforts to deregulate electricity trading around the nation. ALEC promoted these policies in state legislatures where policy making was often ignored by national media outlets and where political influence came cheap.

The economic rewards of this approach proved to be enormous, but they also came at a cost. This cost was paid most dearly in the state of California, where electricity deregulation ushered in a statewide economic disaster.

Darrell Antrich would end up getting engulfed by this disaster. Years later, he found himself being deposed by federal investigators and accused of orchestrating illegal market manipulation from Koch's trading floor. This would have been surprising to the people who worked with Antrich every day. Everything about Antrich was straight-arrow. He graduated from Texas A&M in 1992, and he embodied the midwestern work ethic so prized at Koch. He was known as a conservative family man, a guy who might go out socially but wouldn't close down the bar. He was quiet, reserved, and had the analytical mind of a well-trained accountant. He worked for the accounting firm Ernst & Young for a year before being hired by Koch in a midoffice support job helping traders, and was later promoted through the ranks.

To understand what went wrong, it is important to understand the political process, which Koch heavily influenced, to deregulate the energy markets of California. The giant state was a gold rush for electricity traders, and the ensuing calamity there was a microcosm of America's political economy of the 2000s. The policy process to set the rules, while open to the public, was largely ignored and driven by lobbyists and special interest groups like ALEC. The mind-numbingly complex system that resulted was then gamed and manipulated by a tiny group of traders who understood the rules of the game better than anyone else. When the bottom fell out, these traders and the general public blamed the state of California, which scrambled to stanch the bleeding with taxpayer money and bailouts. All the lessons of the 2000s were there in California, early in the decade, and they were ignored.

One man who couldn't ignore the lessons, because they destroyed his career, was the public official who was later credited with being the author of California's deregulation plan. Oddly enough, he was a liberal Democrat, and a moviemaker, no less. His name was J. Stephen Peace, and he worked in the state capital of Sacramento.

It is significant that the disaster began in Sacramento. One reason the chaos originated there is that almost nobody paid attention to what happened in Sacramento. The world's attention was focused on other parts of California—Hollywood, the world's entertainment capital, and Silicon Valley, the world's technology capital. Sacramento, by contrast, wasn't the capital of anything, other than California's state government.

While the power outages and economic crisis in late 2000 would draw worldwide attention when they unfolded, very little attention was being paid in 1996, when the state dismantled and rebuilt its electricity industry.

That isn't to say that Stephen Peace didn't try. He did his best to draw a crowd, and had the flair of a natural showman. He was tall and slender and looked a lot like the actor Jack Nicholson, with a wide forehead and thick, sharp eyebrows that amplified his facial expressions. His parents were both schoolteachers, and Peace said his family's motto was "It's better to be a smartass than a dumbass," a piece of wisdom that he employed in public hearings. When he disagreed with someone's opinion, he was quick to call it out as "happy horseshit."

Peace was put in charge of the effort because he was head of the State Senate's energy committee. He was an unlikely champion of deregulation, being both a Democrat and a skeptic of free markets. But the momentum to deregulate California's markets was unstoppable, and Peace thought he could shape the effort for the better. He was known in

Sacramento as a lawmaker who relished in the challenge of dealing with profoundly complicated issues.

Steve Peace had the storyteller's gift. Like a lot of kids who grew up in Southern California, Peace had fallen in love at a young age with the business of moviemaking. When he was in his twenties, Peace and two of his high school buddies came up with an idea for a campy humor film called *Attack of the Killer Tomatoes!* Peace produced the movie, cowrote it, and starred in it. He was only twenty-five years old when the film was released in 1978. It became a cult sensation and made him moderately wealthy. The success of *Killer Tomatoes!* was puzzling to almost everybody. The movie didn't even have many killer tomatoes in it. But everything about it—from the clumsy jokes to the wooden acting—was painfully low-budget. Many people might have enjoyed it simply because it was so bad.

It only became apparent years later that *Attack of the Killer Tomatoes!* was prophetic in important ways. The movie captured the spirit of the age, and it documented the kind of political struggles that would eventually ruin Peace's political career. At its core, the movie is about government incompetence and institutional decay. The tomatoes make only a few cameo appearances as they attack Californians enjoying the fruits of American middle-class life. What's more important is the fact that the tomatoes were unleashed by incompetent government scientists working at a top-secret USDA test plot, who accidentally create a strain of lethal fruit.*

The tomatoes kill civilians and attack cities across the nation. But the president just sits at his desk and signs blank pieces of paper. The Senate holds hearings but does nothing. The army sends in soldiers, and they end up sitting in offices, arguing, and looking at maps on the wall as the country is destroyed state by state ("There goes Arkansas!" one soldier declares). The only effective institution in the movie was the public relations industry, which bombarded Americans with the idea that the tomato attack was a blessing.

Peace had a feature role in the film. He played a mentally unbalanced commando who doesn't seem to realize that World War II is over. He runs around most of the time dragging a deployed parachute on the

---

* At least, this is what the viewer is left to gather. The screenwriting isn't exactly airtight.

ground behind him. If Peace was cynical about American politics, he wasn't without hope. His stepfather was heavily involved with local Democratic politics, and Peace became intrigued with the political process. He got a job as a legislative staffer and saw the process of lawmaking up close. When he was twenty-nine years old, he decided that he would run for a seat in the California State Assembly. He won the seat, and over the next decade, he won the confidence of his fellow legislators. One of the first things that anybody seemed to mention about Steve Peace was that he'd starred in the tomato movie. It was an invitation not to take him seriously. But his coworkers soon discovered that Peace had a real interest and aptitude in taking on the most intractable issues. There were whole continents of public policy where even the most hardened lawmakers didn't dare to tread, areas that were so tedious and so complicated and so lacking in public exposure that they promised to swallow public-service careers whole. Regulating public utilities was one of these areas. Just the phrase "regulating public utilities" was enough to make a citizen change the channel or skip to the next news article. It was one of those ironic facts of America life: very few issues affected people more deeply than providing them with electricity, but very few issues drew less public interest.

For whatever reason, Steve Peace was profoundly interested in the topic. He learned the issue from top to bottom and from inside to out. If caught in the hallways of the state capitol, Peace could immediately be drawn into a heated and hours-long conversation about California's utilities companies and regulatory structure. Because of this knowledge and interest, Peace was given more committee assignments and more responsibilities. He won a race to become a state senator, and became a leading authority on electricity and utilities.

This is how, in 1996, Steve Peace came to lead the state's efforts to break apart the existing electricity industry and replace it with something new. Over a matter of months in 1996, he oversaw a grueling process—it would earn the nickname "the Peace Death March"—to produce a bill that was described as being as thick as a telephone book, which created the new markets for trading megawatt-hours.

When Peace held public hearings on the issue, he realized the audience for public policy debates was minuscule. But the hearings revealed a long and complicated history that reflected the changing nature of

America's economy. Back in the "hands-off" days of laissez-faire economics, in the late 1800s and early 1900s, California's electricity was a free-market dream. Companies set up shop wherever they wanted and built big power plants and transmission lines to carry power. They charged a market price for electricity. But this turned out to be problematic. Electrical utility companies tended to be monopolies—there was really only room for one big company to operate in any given area, and it was expensive to build power plants and grids. The monopolies charged exorbitant prices for their power, because they could. They also refused to build transmission lines to rural areas or other neighborhoods where they didn't feel like they could make a profit.

Electricity—and therefore modernity itself—was something of a luxury good. This was unpopular. People wanted the luxury of electricity, and the government responded to their wishes. This gave rise to a model that prevailed during the era of the New Deal consensus: the utilities remained monopolies with private owners, but they were tightly regulated and overseen by the government. Agencies like the California Public Utilities Commission were created to make sure that the utilities didn't price gouge customers and that they offered reliable service.

This system worked so well that everybody forgot it existed. Rates remained reasonable, and the public commissions worked in the background to ensure it. Electrical power was extended into virtually every corner of American life and became something akin to a basic human right.

Then the age of volatility hit in the 1970s. Electricity prices rose along with those for oil during the era of the OPEC embargo. The bureaucrats who oversaw the electricity business didn't know how to respond effectively. It seemed like they could never get the porridge just right; prices rose, and the utilities stumbled from one year to another without clear direction. The bureaucrats bickered. What price was "reasonable"? When was a rate increase "justified"? Public faith in the system diminished. At the same time, environmental laws made it harder to build new power plants. The American public put a premium on not living in the haze of a nearby coal plant and dying of respiratory illness at an early age while their children suffered from asthma. This slowed the construction of new facilities. Real scarcity of power emerged at times in California even as regulators managed to cut down electricity usage by encouraging conservation.

This stoked an effort to deregulate the industry in the 1990s. The idea was to replace highly regulated monopolies with competitive markets where people could buy and sell electricity freely. The power of the invisible hand would make electricity cheaper every day, and would give utilities incentives to become more efficient and increase production.

Again, this is an excruciatingly dull story that nobody wanted to hear about back then.* When Steve Peace began to hold public hearings in the summer of 1996, the events garnered virtually no media attention. While there would be plenty of national media coverage later, when the catastrophe unfolded, there appears to have been zero national coverage when the deregulation bill was being written.

This is not to say that the auditorium was empty on the warm summer evenings when Peace and his colleagues would convene to begin debating about megawatt-hours and reasonable rates. In fact, the room was often full. The seats were filled by a class of people who got paid a lot of money to watch the proceedings: lawyers, lobbyists, and consultants who represented large utility companies, natural gas companies, and trading firms like Koch Industries and its fellow energy conglomerate in Texas, Enron.

The well-dressed lobbyists who filled the seats in Peace's hearing room were just the most visible piece of a much larger political influence operation. Peace would come to understand this better when he got invited to speak at industry events about deregulation. The invitation came from a strange and little-known organization called the American Legislative Exchange Council. He was as surprised as anyone to find himself, a Democrat, speaking to the group.

ALEC was an umbrella group that coordinated efforts among conservative state legislators around the nation. ALEC's mission, and its organization, was a novel innovation. State legislatures were often seen as policy backwaters. ALEC stepped into the breach by giving much-needed resources to overworked and underpaid state lawmakers. This innovation was born of necessity in 1973, when liberal politics dominated Washington. ALEC's founder, a religious conservative activist named Paul Weyrich, felt it would be far more effective to push policy ideas on the state level. He was right.

---

* Or today, for the most part.

By the time Peace arrived to address the group, ALEC was deeply committed to promoting electricity deregulation, even though the business community was torn on the issue. The reason for ALEC's support was straightforward: the group's policy positions were effectively bought by the highest bidder among its corporate members, including big companies like Koch Industries and Enron. This structure came about because ALEC had been only marginally successful in its early years, with few resources and an anemic membership list. Then ALEC's leaders struck on a novel idea: they would seek corporate sponsorship. This idea played well with business conservatives who believed that government agencies should act more like private corporations, promoting ideas with the highest market value. ALEC offered corporations the chance to become dues-paying members of the organization. Over the years, a pay-to-play structure emerged at ALEC. The dues-paying corporations didn't just determine which policies would be promoted; they actually coauthored the bills that ALEC's legislative members took back home and tried to pass.

ALEC created a set of "task forces" that addressed issues of concern to the corporate members. The task forces were directed by a team composed of corporate representatives and state legislators. This partnership appears to be unique in American history, giving companies an unprecedented chance to craft public policy.

Brand-name companies like Procter & Gamble and Coors Brewing joined ALEC. But Koch Industries was one of the most active participants. Koch almost always sent a representative to ALEC's task force meetings, recalled Bonnie Sue Cooper, who was chairman of ALEC in 1997. A Koch lobbyist named Mike Morgan was on ALEC's board of directors with Cooper. In the late 1990s, when ALEC was struggling financially, Koch's political network loaned the group $500,000 to keep it afloat.*

Koch Industries also gained a reputation as an important leader within ALEC because the company was particularly willing to give money to lawmakers' campaigns. At the time, the return on investment

---

* ALEC's board meeting documents make multiple references to the loan. The most specific source for the loan is given as "the Koch Foundation," presumably referring to the Charles G. Koch Charitable Foundation or the Charles Koch Foundation.

was relatively high when it came to funding a state legislator in his or her race. Even a few thousand dollars could still make a difference.

During the 1990s, Koch Industries and Enron were key members of the ALEC task force that pushed for electricity deregulation across the nation. Their reasons for doing so were obvious—deregulation would open huge new trading markets that they were ready to enter—but it wasn't at all clear in the beginning that they would win their case. ALEC's utility company members opposed the deregulation plan. Deregulation would break apart the existing utility model, forcing companies to buy their power from traders rather than produce it at their own plants.

Koch and Enron won the battle in part because they could afford ALEC's premium membership fees. The utility companies got outbid in ALEC's lawmaking auction. "It's a situation where you buy a seat at the table, and then you have the opportunity to vote and drive policy," an exasperated utility lobbyist named Tim Kichline later told the *Austin American-Statesman*. "We don't have enough votes. . . . If they are going to do something we like, they don't need our votes; and if they are going to do something we do not like, we can't stop them."

After Koch and Enron won the fight, ALEC crafted "model bills" for electricity deregulation. In states like Mississippi and South Carolina, ALEC's model bills were introduced almost verbatim. In California, the Republican state senator and ALEC member Jim Brulte was on hand to help guide the legislative efforts alongside Steve Peace. Without pressure from groups like ALEC, it's not at all clear that deregulation would have happened at all. The general voting public certainly wasn't pushing for it—people weren't taking to the streets with placards and banners demanding electricity trading. Even under the best circumstances, the benefit of deregulation to consumers was likely to be minimal. Consumers would have to shop between electricity providers only to gain a savings of a few dollars, or even a few cents, on their electricity bills.

Even though he drove the legislative effort to deregulate, Peace remained uneasy. He remained skeptical of the free-market advocates. He knew markets might be more efficient in the long run, but they also created a lot of volatility. The market didn't care if an average family in San Diego could afford to keep their lights on, or if customers wanted a predictable cost of electricity from month to month. The industry lobbyists and trade groups didn't seem to fully appreciate this. But Peace saw that there was no stopping the train.

"I realized that this all was in motion and was many years in the works," Peace said.

Peace and Brulte passed the bill in August of 1998. The law was radical in nature. It instantly broke apart the state's big utility companies. The utilities became glorified middlemen, buying energy on an open market from traders at Koch and Enron and then selling it to the utility's customers. The utilities had to sell their power plants to outside companies—many of them in Texas—that operated the plants as independent companies. The utilities also lost their transmission lines, which were taken away and turned into something that resembled a railroad or a pipeline. Anybody could now schedule power to run across the transmission lines, making them the common carrier of power. The world of electricity trading, in other words, was starting to look a lot like the world of natural gas trading that made Brenden O'Neill's team so rich.

It would take two years for the bill to take full effect. But by 2000, the markets were open, and the gold rush had begun. Koch Industries was one of the few companies ready to capture the opportunity.

Koch Industries had constructed its own intelligence network, from the ground up, to support its new team of traders as they bought and sold electrons.

Traders on the electricity desk analyzed the new marketplace with an internally developed tool called the West Power Clearing Model. It used a software program that sucked in and synthesized huge amounts of data to determine the supply and demand for electricity in places like California. The model considered how high electricity reserves were at key nodes in Southern California, the "Desert Southwest," and Northern California. It also considered the cost of electricity transmission along power lines and the different price of power at several locations. This helped traders start to make "basis plays," as they did in the oil markets, exploiting the changing prices within fractured markets. The model also integrated published information about upcoming power plant outages, expected gas prices, and anticipated demand for energy.

Darrell Antrich helped lead the small team of traders who started using the West Power Clearing Model when California markets were open for business. One of the star traders on his team was a young woman named Melissa Beckett, a graduate of Fort Hays State University in Kansas. She was a small-town girl with the work ethic to prove it. The trading floor was dominated by young white men, but Beckett managed to hold her own among them. She gained respect for her trading acumen and had a no-frills air about her, wearing her hair in a shoulder-length bob cut and dressing in low-key attire like white blouses with dark slacks. She arrived at work early and worked the phones relentlessly, calling around to brokers and other traders and utility companies to get a feel for the going price of electricity. During her career at Koch, Beckett had worked on the crude oil desk, so she was privy to the vast stream of data that Koch used for trading. She used the data to calculate the marginal cost of electricity. Then they could compare it to prices in the market and get to work trying to outsmart everyone else who was selling power.

Figuring out the cost of electricity was only part of the equation. The Koch traders also had to figure out the legal parameters of the California market in the bill passed by Stephen Peace.

The bill created a new market on which Koch's traders could buy and sell megawatt-hours: a market called the California Power Exchange. It was basically a wholesale market where utilities bought power, thousands of megawatt-hours at a time, to meet their customers' needs.

There was a wrinkle in this exchange that would later cause calamity. The prices on the Power Exchange could float with market conditions. But the prices that utilities could charge their customers for the power they bought on the exchange were frozen. The utility companies had pressed to freeze customer rates at high levels as a way to recoup the $20 billion to $30 billion in power plant upgrades the utilities made before the new law forced them to sell those same power plants. The state agreed to freeze electricity rates—at a price that was higher than wholesale power—so the utilities would be guaranteed a comfortable profit margin for the first few years of deregulation.

When everything went south later, trading companies like Enron, who were actually breaking the law, would scapegoat the rate freeze and call it a "price cap," using it as evidence that California had created a distorted marketplace that was simply begging to be exploited. In fact, the rate freeze was not a cap at all but a *floor*—a guarantee that prices would be high enough for the utilities to recoup their sunk costs. It appears that virtually no one in 1998 believed that wholesale electricity prices might actually go higher in the age of deregulation. The law did not contain a clause that would unfreeze rates and allow them to rise if wholesale prices spiked.

There was one more vital piece to the California law that would cause problems later. This was the emergency system put into place to make sure that the utility companies wouldn't lose power if nobody was selling megawatts on the Power Exchange. To make sure the system was reliable, California created a new nonprofit authority called the California Independent System Operator, which was based just outside Sacramento. This agency was like an air-traffic control tower—it was staffed with engineers and operators who made sure that the electrons were flowing on time and in proper volume. The Independent System Operator, or ISO, only came into play once trading was finished on the open Power Exchange.

The Power Exchange was a "day ahead" market, meaning that utility companies shopped there for electricity they planned to use the following day. After trading closed on the exchange, the traffic controllers at the ISO made sure there was ample supply for the following morning. If things started to look haywire for the next days, the ISO operators could buy the emergency supplies it needed to keep the lights on. These operators also had a special authority that didn't get much attention in 1998—they could buy electricity at the last minute, at high prices, to shore up the grid if it looked like there was going to be a shortage. This was designed to be a safety net, and one that would be rarely used. The market was set up in a way to ensure that the Independent System Operator barely purchased any electricity.

Steve Peace, for one, believed that only a tiny fraction of electricity would be bought in emergency markets by the Independent System Operator. As it turned out, the higher prices on the emergency ISO market turned out to be too strong of a lure for the new traders at Enron and Koch to ignore.

When Melissa Beckett started her day on Koch's trading floors, she bought and sold electricity contracts in the same way other Koch traders bought and sold crude oil futures. But this time, her customers were the large utilities in California that had been stripped of their power plants and forced to buy megawatts on the open market. Beckett and her team of megawatt traders were one of the most important players in California's new market.

Her trading desk wasn't glamorous. It looked like the desk of a telemarketer. The traders sat shoulder to shoulder in their stations, speaking into black microphones, checking their computer monitors, occasionally glancing up at the large television screen suspended from the ceiling that gave them minute-to-minute headlines. Their desks were covered in drifts of papers and file folders, littered with empty coffee cups and boxes of Kleenex tissue perched on top of files.

Through the course of an average morning, Beckett called traders, brokers, and customers west of the Rocky Mountains. She greeted them by name—"What's going on, Billy?"—and began to haggle with them over the cost of a megawatt-hour. She sounded casual, but Beckett was trading based on information, analytics, and the projections produced by Koch's elaborate West Power Clearing Model.

California's new electricity markets were ambling along peacefully during their first years of operation. Prices were relatively low, as legislators like Steve Peace had expected them to be, and the market was relatively stable. Most of the power was bought and sold in the day-ahead Power Exchange and very little power was traded in the emergency hourly markets, where prices were much higher.

But then, during the first days of January in 2000, the West Power Clearing Model began to produce some very strange numbers. It seemed that there was a supply crunch looming in California. The state had not built a new power plant in about a decade, and demand had been rising steadily. Water reservoirs were getting low, thanks to a dry year with little rainfall. A hot summer seemed to be on the way. Demand was high and supplies were tight, which meant that prices would soon be rising. This was essentially the same analysis that Brenden O'Neill was seeing on the natural gas desk. There would be a spike in both gas and electricity prices, which were closely connected.

There was a small problem, however. California's day-ahead market on the Power Exchange had a price cap on it. This created a potential distortion in the market: the real price of power might float higher than the capped price, which would force producers to trade at a loss. There seemed to be some gaming going on in this market in response to the price caps—it looked like some utility companies were intentionally underscheduling their loads in the day-ahead market to try and evade the price caps. The traders believed that California's new system was imperfectly deregulated because of the price caps, and they also seemed to believe that the state's political leaders were too dumb to recognize the fact or change it. The traders weren't sympathetic to the idea that they should abide by the price caps if the market dictated otherwise.

The thinking of Enron traders was captured in recorded phone calls, later obtained by investigators, which included gems such as: "Grandma Millie, man . . . now she wants her fucking money back for all the power you've charged . . . jammed right up her ass for fucking two hundred fifty dollars a megawatt-hour."

It would be up to the traders, then, to figure out how to make the markets work in spite of California's jerry-rigged system. In the spring of 2000, these traders were looking to do one thing—they were looking to "gain length," as Beckett put it. They were looking to own mega-watts and sell them at a price higher than the state-imposed price caps on the California Power Exchange. The only way to get a higher price for the megawatt-hours was to sell them in the small emergency market on the day that power was needed: the ISO market. But Koch was prohibited from doing this—only companies that owned a power plant and could promise to deliver the power on a given hour could sell into the ISO market. Koch needed to find a way to break into the hourly markets, regardless of what the rules said. Or, as Darrell Antrich would later put it when questioned by federal investigators: "We thus concluded that we were more likely to be profitable on our positions if we had the flexibility to carry our long positions into the real-time power market."

Antrich discovered a pathway into the pricier ISO market almost by accident. He was meeting with a salesman for a power plant company named Tom Nesmith, who pitched Antrich a novel idea. It was called "parking." It would deliver Koch the profits it desired in California. Federal regulators later determined that the trading technique violated the law.

———

Antrich wasn't looking for a new trading technique when he first met with Tom Nesmith. He just wanted information. There was one critical piece missing in Koch Energy Trading's intelligence network. Koch Industries didn't own any power plants, so it didn't have access to the kind of inside information that made its energy trading desks so successful. Antrich was on a quest for such information, and he tried to get it by forming information-sharing systems with utility companies that owned the plants.

Antrich approached one such utility outside California: Public Service Company of New Mexico, or PNM, as most people called it. The company owned a power plant in Arizona that sold electricity into California. This meant that PNM could sell into the coveted ISO market. Antrich wanted PNM to sign a deal that would give Koch's traders access to PNM's inside information, such as information on plant outages, its own weather forecasts, and other data that could give Koch a head start on responding to changes in the market. In return, PNM would get access to Koch's trading analysis, its secret in-house weather projections, and its forecasts on natural gas markets, among other things.

Antrich and his team drew up a consulting agreement for PNM that spelled out the information-sharing agreement, and he pitched it to Tom Nesmith. The salesman was interested in this arrangement. But he wanted to pitch Koch on a special opportunity: the parking trading strategy that Koch could execute in partnership with PNM. The strategy was apparently dreamed up by traders at Enron, and it was later judged to be illegal.

Enron traders seem to have invented the parking scheme sometime in the late 1990s. To execute a parking trade, a trader at Koch or Enron sold electricity from a power plant in California to a customer outside the state, like PNM in Arizona. This sale was made in the day-ahead market, where prices were capped. But the sale was bogus. The next day, when power was supposed to be delivered from California to PNM, the utility would suddenly sell the exact same amount of power from Arizona into California, and into the much pricier ISO hourly market. The two sales would be orchestrated to cancel each other out: 100 megawatts out of the state to PNM, and 100 megawatts into the state from PNM.

Here's why the scheme was fraudulent: the electricity never made the round-trip journey that the paper trail would indicate. Instead, the power was generated at the original point inside California, and then sold to a customer in California the next day without ever leaving the state. It was only a paper game between PNM and Koch that made it *look* as if Koch had moved electricity from California to Arizona, and then back into California again. In reality, the power had just gone from point A to point B inside California. The reason this is so important is that, under the arcane rules of California's system, the power from Arizona was allowed into the pricey ISO market, while the power from California was not.

Once PNM learned how to park power, it started pitching the service to trading companies. One trader was hesitant to sign up because he was worried he might get stuck having to actually deliver electricity across state lines. But Nesmith assured this trader by saying: "[L]uckily, you're the guy with the hand on the throttle in this case." Federal experts would later interpret that remark as showing that PNM always considered the parking transactions to be little more than a ploy on paper.

Nesmith understood that a company like Koch could make huge profits by parking power. Accordingly, PNM charged a high price for the service: according to Koch's agreement with PNM, Koch paid an upfront fee of $345,600 to participate in the parking strategy. Koch also paid an additional fee of $1 for every megawatt-hour it traded through the parking deal.

On February 28, 2000, Koch Energy Trading signed a contract with PNM to park power in the coming months. The deal essentially allowed PNM to rent out its status as an out-of-state utility company, and allowed Koch to buy its way into the pricey hourly market in California.

Koch's agreement with PNM allowed Koch's traders to start parking power in July. But they began much earlier than that. Electricity prices spiked in May, thanks in part to the supply crunch that Koch saw coming through its supply-and-demand models. When prices spiked, parking allowed Koch to capture the opportunity. "I am excited about practicing in the next few weeks, as well as the opportunities the parking gives us for this summer," Antrich wrote.

On May 22, 2000, Koch Industries executed one of its first parking transactions. On that Monday, Koch sold 950 megawatt-hours of power into

California's Power Exchange. The price on that day-ahead market was high: Koch was paid $108.99 per megawatt-hour—average prices that month were about quadruple what they had been one year before. An unusual heat wave had driven up power prices sharply as businesses and residents cranked up their air-conditioning.

The state was facing a shortage of electricity and the Independent System Operator declared a stage 2 power emergency because reserves were below 5 percent. This meant that the agency could start initiating blackouts if demand stayed high, and the administrators were desperate to find backup sources of power to keep the lights on.

Koch's parking arrangement allowed it to take advantage of this desperation. On the same day that it sold electricity into the Power Exchange, Koch's traders "parked" 650 megawatts of power with the Public Service Company of New Mexico. This meant that Koch informed the state of California that it was planning to export the 650 megawatts to PNM the following day, even though Koch had no intention of doing so, according to federal investigators. The reported export was essentially a sham—Koch knew that when it came time to export the power, Public Service Company of New Mexico would report to the state it was sending the same amount of power *into* the state. This paper game allowed Koch's traders to sell electricity in emergency markets that were otherwise off-limits to traders like Koch.

Of the 650 megawatt-hours that Koch parked with PNM, Koch was able to sell 50 megawatt-hours directly to the Independent System Operator at a price of $336.40 per megawatt-hour. Then it sold 450 megawatt-hours to the Power Exchange's "day of" market for $539.95. Koch sold another 125 megawatt-hours of parked power to a utility company for $625. It sold the rest to Enron for $320.

The transaction yielded $315,788 in profit. Investigators would later say that this kind of deal came at a dear cost to the state. By parking power, electricity traders were diverting power from the day-ahead Power Exchange and forcing the Independent System Operator to pay exorbitantly high prices for the power, a cost that was passed on to the utility companies.

Gaming the system was creating dire, real-world effects. Power was cut at the Orange County government building, forcing employees to go home early. In the Santa Clarita Valley, north of Los Angeles, the school district paid emergency prices to keep students in session, including penalty payments of up to $10,000 an hour. On June 14, Koch's traders executed another remarkably profitable and complex parking transaction that yielded $874,523 in profits.

On June 15, Darrell Antrich e-mailed an old friend named Brian Arriaga, who had previously worked for Koch's trading office. Arriaga had since moved on to a new job, but the friends bantered back and forth during the workday.

Arriaga e-mailed Antrich at two in the afternoon to comment on the remarkably warm weather in California, which had pushed electricity prices to record highs.

"Isn't it a little too early in the summer for the Santa Anna [sic] winds?" Arriaga wrote. "I hope you guys were long!!"

Antrich, who was presumably busy that afternoon, did not reply until 5:19 that evening, long after the markets had closed.

"I can't even begin to tell you how well things have been going," he wrote. "We have been doing parking with PNM and have made over 2 million in the last 2 weeks. WHEE!!"

On June 14 and 15, temperatures rose above 100 degrees in many parts of California. It was 103 in San Francisco and 109 in San Jose. Air conditioners kicked on in millions of homes and businesses throughout the state. The heavy load bogged down transmission lines and sapped power plants. Prices skyrocketed.

Lights blinked on the wall-sized electronic maps and screens inside the cavernous control room of the California Independent System Operator, just outside Sacramento. Traders there looked at spreadsheets on their computer monitors and desperately called from broker to broker, looking to buy supplies to keep power running. These traders were frantic with good reason: the technology of the modern power grid dictated that demand had to be met exactly at all times. If the supply was not met, even for a matter of moments, it could cause a system of cascading and uncontrolled blackouts that could leave millions without power.

By the afternoon of the fourteenth, it became clear that the ISO might fall short on its power supplies. Power reserves fell below 7 percent, so the state declared a phase 1 emergency, giving it the authority to begin rolling blackouts. At 1:22 in the afternoon, San Francisco's utility company, Pacific Gas and Electric, started cutting power to blocks of thirty-five thousand customers at a time, leaving them in the dark for between sixty and ninety minutes and then shifting the blackout to other neighborhoods. The lights went out at a microbrewery on Haight Street. People who worked from home got in their cars and took their PowerBook laptops to coffee shops in nearby cities where the lights were still on.

The worst was yet to come.

Throughout the autumn, electricity traders continued to game the system, using incomprehensibly complex schemes to shift megawatt-hours away from the day-ahead power exchange and into the hourly ISO markets. As winter approached, outside events conspired to help these traders, as if invisible gremlins had been released into the state to wreak havoc. A natural gas pipeline ruptured in Southern California, interrupting key fuel supplies. A storm hit the coast and clogged intake valves for a nuclear plant with seaweed, forcing the facility to go off-line and taking its megawatt capacity with it.

This created a destructive feedback loop—every time power prices rose, it gave traders more reason to manipulate the markets, which caused prices to rise yet further. By the time January rolled around again, the state found itself in a summer-like environment of high demand, limited supply, and exorbitant prices.

The market dysfunction began to take its toll on the state's three big utilities. The state had forced them to sell their own power plants, so they had no choice but to buy all of their power on wholesale markets. The rate caps prohibited the utilities from passing the higher costs on to consumers. The frozen rates were designed to be a floor price, but now that wholesale market prices had skyrocketed, the frozen rates were suddenly a price cap. No one had expected this. Losses were approaching $10 billion for two of the three big utilities: San Francisco's PG&E and the Los Angeles area's Southern California Edison Co. There was simply no way that the utilities could keep passing on power to their customers at such a deep cost without declaring bankruptcy.

Steve Peace found himself in the odd position of knowing more than anybody about California's dysfunctional markets but being able to do little or nothing at all about it. Because he was no longer on the Energy Committee of the state senate, Peace wasn't in a position to intervene.

And even if he was, there was very little that the senate could do. He was left to watch as state legislators and electricity regulators scrambled to keep the system afloat. The scene might have looked familiar to him. It wasn't completely dissimilar to a vignette about halfway through *Attack of the Killer Tomatoes!*, when the US Army was scrambling to destroy the marauding tomatoes. The camera panned across the army command center, which was a scene of chaos. Papers were spread everywhere; soldiers were working at makeshift tables and shouting back and forth at one another. They bickered and scrambled around, powerless against the tomato menace.

There was a similar fatalism playing out at the ISO offices near Sacramento. The traders looked shell-shocked, walking around with their cheap Styrofoam coffee cups while lights blinked on a wall map of the state transmission routes. There was nothing the traders at ISO could do: they were price takers who had to pay whatever it took to avoid a blackout.

It was only then, as ISO was being gouged, that Steve Peace could have seen one of the biggest mistakes he had made while negotiating California's deregulation laws. During all the marathon hours of debate and negotiation, the lawmakers had not paid enough attention to one vital issue: the issue of market power. Market power was a concept that animated lawmakers who crafted the New Deal, and it referred to the ability of companies to demand higher prices even when the laws of supply and demand did not justify them. Monopolies had market power. Utilities had market power. The traders at Koch and Enron now had market power. What the lawmakers didn't take into account back then was the peculiar nature of commercial electrons and electrical power. Unlike other commodities such as corn and oil, electrons cannot be stored. They must be transmitted and used in real time as they are created. This made the electrical grid particularly vulnerable to market power. The grid had to be expertly orchestrated to match supply and demand almost perfectly: if enough electrons weren't forced down the wires to meet demand, then the system could shudder, and blackouts could result. In other words, system reliability dictated that demand must be met in real time—buying that last megawatt of power to meet demand was a necessity rather than a luxury. The market for that last mega-watt hour was a seller's market, and the savvy trader could exact a ransom price.

The only entity with the authority to correct the dysfunctions of market power was the state. And that's what forced the state of California to finally intervene in the electricity crisis. As it happened, the Republican governor who pushed for deregulation in the 1990s, Pete Wilson, had left office. He was replaced by a Democrat named Gray Davis. It would be up to Davis and the state legislature to solve the mess that deregulation left behind. Gray Davis was a popular, if somewhat bland, governor. He was a career politician, elected with 58 percent of the vote. Electricity deregulation wasn't his specialty, but a few months into his term, it was clear that Davis wouldn't be dealing with anything else.

The weekend of January 12, 2001, was a long holiday weekend. It was also the last three days before the state's electric grid might fail. The big utility companies had major debt payments due the week after the Martin Luther King Day holiday, and it was becoming apparent that they didn't have the money to pay. The consequences of a default for the big utilities were difficult to predict but would almost certainly be catastrophic. Mandatory blackouts would cut power to hospitals, airports, shopping malls, and homes.

Gray Davis formed a war room in the state capitol and worked there through the weekend. He set up a live satellite link between California and the Federal Energy Regulatory Commission offices in Washington. California's state lawmakers were on hand through the weekend to write emergency legislation that Davis could sign when markets opened up Tuesday morning.

Davis quickly discovered that energy traders were not willing to compromise. Market prices were nonnegotiable. They would get their money. A Texas-based trading firm called Dynergy made clear that it would rather see one of the state's biggest utility companies, Southern California Edison, go into bankruptcy than forgive the utility for its debt. The state needed to craft a bailout bill that was friendly to Dynergy's terms. "If we can't get this bill through in the next two days, this will start to unravel," Dynergy president, Stephen W. Bergstrom, told the *Los Angeles Times*. "When and if they . . . default on Thursday, it puts us in a position where we have to take them into bankruptcy, and I'm sure others will be right beside us."

FERC also refused to compromise in important ways. The agency was in limbo between the Clinton and Bush administrations and wasn't inclined to intervene. This left Davis and the state legislature with one option. The state would use its credit rating and money to step in and keep the broken market system afloat. The legislators found a clever way to do this: they could use a relatively obscure agency to buy electricity supplies and pass them on to the utilities.

Over the weekend, Davis and his team spent hours negotiating over what price the state would pay for the electricity. Davis tried to negotiate for a discount. He wanted to pay 5.5 cents per kilowatt-hour over three years. The traders and their industry group said they wanted at least 8.5 cents per a kilowatt-hour over three years. Davis had no leverage, and the traders knew it.

Negotiations carried on through Monday and then into Tuesday. The debate was largely over how much the state would have to pay. The figure would clearly reach into the billions. Throughout Tuesday afternoon, the state legislature debated an emergency bailout bill in the same room where Stephen Peace helped write the original deregulation measure so many years before, when almost nobody could be bothered to attend his hours-long hearings. Now the situation was suitably disastrous enough to draw the attention of the national press. By late Tuesday evening, it appeared that the legislators had come to a rough understanding of what the final emergency legislation might look like. State assembly leaders started whipping votes into line. They fashioned a bailout before the utilities went under.

Around this time, a truck driver named Mike Bowers steered his semitruck off the freeway and onto the side streets of Sacramento. He had a record of mental illness and a long criminal history. For reasons that were never entirely clear, Bowers accelerated his rig to seventy miles an hour and drove it into the side of the capitol building. The truck hit the capitol building like a missile. When the cab slammed into the white stone walls, the fuel tanks exploded, sending a ball of flame climbing over the face of the building. Somewhat miraculously, Bowers was the only person who died that evening.

The next morning, as the blackened face of the capitol building continued to smolder, Gray Davis declared a state of emergency. At that point, he was simply stating the obvious. Amid the smoke and carnage, the lawmakers were able to pass the bailout plan.

During the spring of 2001, a story line emerged about the electricity crisis that eventually hardened into conventional wisdom. It was a story about legislative stupidity and incompetence. This narrative was cemented by Gray Davis's bailout plan. The state was obligated to buy electricity for the utilities but prohibited from changing any of the underlying market dysfunction. Wholesale prices continued to soar. The traders continued to profit, and the state opened its treasury to pay for it all. Between January and June, the state bought about 30.8 million megawatt-hours at the price the market demanded. The price to taxpayers was roughly $9 billion.

And even with this, the grid remained unstable. Utilities ordered rolling blackouts, cutting power to neighborhoods and shopping districts and leaving traffic signals dark. Taxpayers were heavily subsidizing a Third World electricity grid. The state had created the deregulation scheme, so many citizens blamed the state. The politicians hadn't listened closely enough to the free-market evangelists at Enron. Now the overcomplicated mousetrap was destroying itself.

This narrative was misleading. The biggest misconception was that the state had deregulated the wholesale market for power while imposing "price caps" on electricity rates for consumers. It sounded like an absurdly designed system, and it reeked of pandering to voters—in this case electricity customers—who wanted a free ride. It also helped explain why the big utility companies were going bankrupt, because they couldn't pass on their high costs. Of course, it was the utility companies that had pushed for the rate freeze, and they had done so with the expectation that the frozen rates would deliver them outsized profits over several years. In San Diego, the rate freeze had been lifted, and it didn't change much beyond shifting the exorbitant prices directly onto the broader populace.

Another misconception was that the deregulation law's complexity was somehow to blame for the high prices. News stories mentioned that there was a Power Exchange market and an ISO market and there were price caps and different rules for imported and exported power. It made the system handbook sound like a plate of spaghetti that distorted the market and made high prices almost inevitable. In fact, it was the traders and power generators who decided to game the system using the complex rules as a way to hide their behavior.

Finally, there was little discussion of the fact that federal regulators had the authority to combat the crisis but chose not to use it. California's deregulation law called for FERC to police any market manipulation, and it was FERC that decided not to penalize traders and generators in late 2000 when it discovered that prices were unjustly high. FERC refused to intervene for months as the crisis worsened.

Another part of the narrative remained entirely absent. In all the stories and headlines that were generated about the California power crisis, one name remained notably absent: Koch Industries. This wasn't accidental.

On November 20, 2000, Koch Industries was given the chance to expand on its parking strategy in California. PNM offered Koch a new contract to park power over the summer of 2001, a time when prices were expected to be high. The offer must have been enticing.

PNM's signature was on the contract but Koch's was not. Koch walked away from the parking scheme, just when the strategy was arguably the most promising.

Other firms ramped up their market-gaming schemes as electricity got more expensive. But Koch appears to have cut back. It seems that Koch imposed a sense of discipline, and a long-term point of view, that eluded its competitors. Enron, for example, feasted on manipulative trades—not only parking, but also gratuitously manipulative trades with names like "Fat Boy" and "Death Star"—in part to help it meet company-wide quarterly earnings targets. Koch Industries had no such concerns.

Back in 1968, when the oil gauger Phil Dubose joined Koch Industries, he joined a company that thrived on exploiting gray areas. But skirting the law had drawn the attention of the FBI and the US Senate, and Charles Koch had learned a lesson from that. His trading team would not aggressively push into legal gray areas. They didn't need to. Koch had enough advantage using its inside information to trade in the

dark, lightly regulated derivatives markets. Getting caught up with bla-
tant market manipulation would only serve as a distraction.

This was certainly the case in California. There were plenty of politicians complaining about market manipulation, even if FERC had
stepped aside. It wasn't hard to imagine that, down the road, there might
be more investigations, maybe even a US Senate hearing or two.

Koch's priorities in the winter of 2000 were telling. PNM's trading
team was persistently trying to convince Darrell Antrich and his team
to park more power with the firm. But Koch wanted something else
entirely—Koch just wanted PNM's information. Darrell Antrich and his
team turned the table on PNM. Amid the golf outings and meals, Antrich tried to convince PNM that the real gold mine lay in sharing inside
information about outages, transmission, and weather forecasts. In the
end, Koch won. PNM signed an information-sharing agreement in late
January of 2001. This strategy helped Koch avoid the attention that soon
settled on Enron, which became the public face of market manipulation
when it was exposed. Koch had engaged in market manipulation on a
far smaller scale, but it had done it nonetheless. Because it was willing to
remain anonymous, virtually no one knew about Koch's role in the crisis.

The California crisis ended in April, when FERC decided to intervene.
FERC issued an order on April 26 that addressed one thing: the issue of
"market power," or the ability of power traders and merchants to manipulate markets. It imposed a firm price cap in the hourly ISO market.

FERC also ordered that refunds be paid to consumers if it found that
prices had been artificially inflated, reversing its decision in November.
FERC ordered all power generators within the California system to offer
electricity in the real-time markets if they had it, rather than exporting
it or holding it off the market. In June, FERC issued a follow-on order
that intensified the crackdown. It greatly expanded the pool of trades
that were subject to price caps, including "bilateral" trades that happened outside the ISO market (these were one-on-one swaps that were
like derivatives contracts).

After these orders were issued, the crisis abated. Market prices fell
gradually at first, then dropped dramatically in June, even as the warm
summer months hit the state. The conditions that traders blamed for the

crisis had not changed. There were no new power plants built, there was no significant change in demand for power or a change in the weather. But the crisis ended. The prices fell again.

Enron declared bankruptcy in December of 2001. Koch, Shell Oil Company, and other traders who also manipulated markets fought the charges in court. The battle dragged on for years. Thousands of pages of documents and court testimony were generated as the companies and regulators fought over complex and arcane maneuvers like parking power.

Koch claimed it was innocent of manipulation. The company accurately pointed out that it was accused of far less manipulation than many of its competitors. In one court filing, Koch was found to have illegally exported 175 megawatt-hours of power during the summer of 2000. Shell, by contrast, illegally exported 1,657 megawatt-hours. While Koch's parking trades were small, there was overwhelming evidence that Koch had manipulated markets, evidence based on Koch's own internal documents. A panel of FERC commissioners ruled in 2014 that Koch's parking transactions, while proven, were so small compared to its competitors that the FERC could not prove there was a "pattern" to its behavior, sparing Koch the harsher penalties imposed on Shell and other companies. Koch settled the charges over the manipulation in late 2015 with a payment of $4.1 million to California. Koch Energy Trading was later sold to Merrill Lynch. Darrell Antrich continued to work on the trading floor in Houston, after Merrill Lynch took over.

In California, cynicism toward the state of California became a near-permanent posture of the electorate. Governor Gray Davis was the first casualty. In 2003, Davis was thrown out of office after a statewide petition forced a recall election. He lost the special election to a man with no government experience: the movie star Arnold Schwarzenegger.

Steve Peace's life in politics was also ended by the crisis. He was forever known as the coauthor of the disaster. Peace had accurately diagnosed the problem as events unfolded. During the crisis, he made an odd habit of approaching the lectern in the state capitol and simply saying: "FERC. Enron." It was a statement of desperation; he was trying to say that the system was being gamed by traders and abetted by weak regulators. Ultimately, it just made him sound unhinged. His statements were vindicated by the evidence, but only years after the fact. By that time, he was living back in San Diego. He is CEO of Killer Tomatoes Entertainment, which manages a franchise of movies based on the original (including *Return of the Killer Tomatoes!* and *Killer Tomatoes Eat France!*).

After the electricity markets cooled in California, the business was never quite so white-hot again. Melissa Beckett ended up transferring to another trading desk, this time in fertilizer markets. But this isn't to say that profits quit flowing from Koch's trading desks in Houston. When one market cooled, several others began to heat up. Over the next decade, Koch traded derivatives based on housing mortgages, interest rates, and other exotic financial instruments. Koch even opened a special unit that traded stock in public companies, buying and selling several million shares of different firms and developing algorithms to find the best value.

The trading desks, however, were far more important to Koch Industries' business than as simple profit centers. The money from trading was important. But, as always, the lifeblood of the trading group was information. The desks sucked in giant stores of data from about every corner of the American economy and used their superior knowledge to trade on it. This trove of information and analysis was put to use throughout the corporation. The trading desks became a source not just of cash, but of market intelligence. The traders were like scouts in the marketplace, identifying places where Koch could invest.

Charles Koch took the techniques learned in abstract markets and applied them to the real-world industries he knew so well. He talked repeatedly not about trading but about a trading mind-set. The world was filled with assets and filled with opportunities to buy and sell. Superior information would allow Koch to make superior acquisitions. The massive amounts of cash that Koch generated across its operations would be put to use buying and selling assets in the real world.

In 2003, the wave of acquisitions would begin.

CHAPTER 14

Trading the Real World

(2002–2005)

Back in the early 1970s, when Charles Koch took over the Pine Bend refinery, Koch Industries' habit of buying and selling other companies was still something of a rarity in corporate America. Koch was an outlier, a quirky family-owned firm willing to spend huge sums of cash to buy out other companies and take them private. By 2003, however, the rest of corporate America had followed suit. There was a growing wave of so-called private equity firms that were on the march across the American economic landscape, searching for companies to buy and take private.

To the private equity world, America's entire business community was a game board, a financial market where companies could be bought and sold like oil futures. Private equity deals became a defining feature of American economic life during the 2000s. There were $91 billion in private deals at the dawn of the century. The deal flow rose to $133 billion in 2003, and to $197 billion in 2004. Thousands of companies were taken private each year. Dozens of new private equity funds sprang up in New York, Chicago, and San Francisco. Some of these private equity firms were run by nameplate financial firms like Lehman Brothers and Barclays Capital. Others were little-known start-ups with names like Oaktree Capital Management. One of the better-known private equity firms, Cerberus Capital Management, named itself after the mythical three-headed dog that guarded the gates of hell, for reasons that were not entirely clear.

Koch Industries, although it had almost zero name recognition, put itself aggressively into the hunt, competing directly with the largest firms on Wall Street. Koch had an edge over the competition. The company was flush with cash, had only two shareholders to answer to, and was willing to close deals that scared away other companies. In a matter of just a few years, Koch Industries would execute some of the largest private equity deals in America, with acquisitions worth nearly $30 billion.

Charles Koch made it abundantly clear to his team that they would work toward one goal: to maximize Koch's long-term return on investment. The firm wasn't looking for quick returns. Koch would press the advantage of Charles Koch's patience, looking for deals that other investors might avoid because the payouts wouldn't come for years. Charles Koch institutionalized the company's "trading mentality" by embedding it in a new, secretive group that was formed on the third floor of the Tower, near Charles Koch's office. This group rivaled any private equity firm in the nation. It was called the Corporate Development Board.

Charles Koch sat on the Corporate Development Board, and directed it. He was joined by a small cadre of his top leaders. This small group of men would direct a series of acquisitions between 2002 and 2006 that would fundamentally transform Koch Industries, while also more than doubling its size. In 2001, Koch's annual sales were about $40.7 billion. By 2006, they would be $90 billion.

The Corporate Development Board was essentially a reincarnation of the development group that Brad Hall had led in the late 1990s. Hall was replaced as head of the group in 2002 by Ron Vaupel, who had been president of the Koch Hydrocarbon Division. But Vaupel was not working alone. In its new incarnation, the Corporate Development Board was closely controlled by the company's most senior executives. The board included Joe Moeller, the president of Koch Industries, and Steven Feilmeier, who had recently been named as Koch's chief financial officer. Sam Soliman, the previous CFO, who now led a massive trading operation at Koch's Houston office, also sat on the development board. The final board member was John Pittenger, the Harvard MBA graduate who helped drive Koch's Value Creation Strategies back in the 1990s.

The board didn't tend to meet in a formal manner. It didn't gather every month in Koch's boardroom and hold a meeting where minutes were kept, as did Koch's formal board of directors. Sometimes the board met in a smaller conference room on the third floor, near Charles Koch's office, with some members calling in and participating over speakerphone. The timing was improvisational and reactive to conditions in the market. There was a time sensitivity to the meetings; the board often considered acquisition deals that were the subject of intense competitive bidding. There wasn't time to pay heed to formality and scheduling.

By 2002, the board had access to multiple, ultra-high-value flows of information that fed into it from every arm of the company. The board sat at the center of Koch's black box. Charles Koch, for example, was privy to detailed updates from every major division in Koch Industries because the division leaders came to Wichita quarterly to report their results. He had the chance, at those meetings, to quiz them on whatever topic he wished. The board could also draw on the vast pools of data and analysis being generated every minute on the company's trading floors in Houston.

The development board drew on other important sources of information. It was constructed as the center hub that had spokes reaching out to smaller development groups that were embedded in Koch's various divisions. For example, divisions like Koch Minerals and Flint Hills Resources had development groups analyzing potential deals in their respective industries at a ground level. They fed important information and bid ideas back to the Corporate Development Board.

When employees in one of Koch's various development groups saw a potential acquisition that was large enough, they were called in front of the board to present it. This was not pleasant. Everyone knew that there was a profound asymmetry between what the development board knew and what anyone else at the company knew. An ambitious Koch employee who thought they had a good idea never knew how it might be received by the board.

If going before the board was intimidating to business leaders at Koch, it might have been doubly intimidating to Steve Packebush. He was a thirty-eight-year-old marketing guy who grew up on a Kansas farm. He attended K-State and joined Koch Industries straight out of college, in 1987. He had never worked anywhere else. In 2003, Packebush was a marketing guy with Koch's small fertilizer division, called Koch Nitrogen.

If all of Koch Industries' business units were a professional sports league, then the Koch Nitrogen team would be in last place. The division was small, losing money and cutting production at its primary fertilizer plant in Louisiana, where it had laid off about half its workforce.

Koch Nitrogen had sold off its ammonia pipeline network and seemed to be a caretaking unit whose main job was to babysit a handful of assets that were left behind after the now-legendary collapse of Koch Agriculture back in 1999. If an up-and-comer at Koch Industries was looking to make a name for himself, he would have stayed away from Koch Nitrogen.

But in 2003, Steve Packebush and a team from Koch Nitrogen made an appointment to appear before Charles Koch and senior executives at the Corporate Development Board. The nitrogen team wanted to convince Charles Koch to give them hundreds of millions of dollars to buy a group of money-losing fertilizer plants.

As it turned out, this would be one of the first deals considered under Koch's new acquisition regime. It would also be a test. It would determine how well Koch could export its trading mentality into the real world.

The Koch Nitrogen team filed into the boardroom in Wichita and took their places. The team included Steve Packebush and his boss, Jeff Walker. They had prepared their case, and this was their moment to pitch it directly to Charles Koch.

During such meetings, Charles Koch sat and listened to the presentations, statue-like. He let the presenters talk, often without interjecting. When it came time for him to ask questions, Koch was, almost invariably, soft-spoken and utterly unsentimental. He looked for weak spots. He tried to smoke out any executives who were inflating the prospects of a deal, or, conversely, those who might be too timid to realize the upside of taking a bigger risk.

Packebush's investment thesis might have seemed ripe for puncturing. The thesis was first developed around the year 2000, when natural gas prices spiked. This volatile surge had exposed the terrible weakness of many high-cost fertilizer producers in the fertilizer business. Natural gas was the primary ingredient of nitrogen fertilizer, accounting for roughly 80 percent of its production cost. One of the fertilizer plants that was punished by the spike in gas prices was Koch's plant, in Louisiana. All of the US fertilizer plants, in fact, were exposed as being the weakest animals of the global herd. Natural gas wells were relatively scarce and unproductive in the United States. Other countries, with more plentiful gas supplies, could make fertilizer much cheaper. Imported fertilizer had an edge that seemed like it would be permanent.

Packebush and his colleagues responded to the crisis in a very Koch way—rather than panic, they launched an in-depth study of their situation. When they studied the fertilizer markets, Packebush's team confirmed that Koch's Louisiana plant was a permanent loser. But that didn't mean that *all* fertilizer factories were permanent losers. His team believed that the bloodletting would only go so far, and then the market would stabilize. When that happened, a small island of winners would be left behind. These winners would be supported by strong local demand for their product. Modern US farmers were a lot like modern motorists: they had become utterly dependent on fossil fuels. Without nitrogen-based fertilizers, US food production would decrease substantially, maybe as much as 40 percent. There was no plausible future wherein nitrogen fertilizer demand would drop to zero, or anywhere near zero.

Packebush and his team began mapping out what the postapocalyptic fertilizer industry might look like. They figured that after half the US fertilizer production was wiped out, then the remaining plants would be in the best competitive position. The Koch Nitrogen team believed it would be smart to buy any fertilizer plants in the United States that went up for sale, but only if Koch could pay the price of replacement value—meaning the amount of money that it would take to rebuild the plant if it were destroyed. In other words, it would be smart to buy the plants for the cost of their physical equipment and not much more. At that price, the plants could stay in business for years, even if they didn't exactly thrive.

The Koch Nitrogen team had to figure out which plants to buy. They settled on an unlikely target: one of the largest fertilizer producers in the United States and a powerhouse of modern agriculture, a gigantic, farmer-owned co-op based in Kansas City called Farmland Industries.

Koch Industries had been closely scrutinizing Farmland Industries since at least the 1990s. This was only natural for Koch—Farmland was a big competitor in fertilizer, grain, and other markets. Koch didn't just want to compete against Farmland—it wanted to understand Farmland better than Farmland understood itself. Koch put together a small team that X-rayed Farmland's business. A team at Koch studied every piece of publicly available data about Farmland and then reverse engineered the data to figure out what was happening inside the giant cooperative. Koch used the data to figure out Farmland's cost structure, profit margins, and cash flows.

It didn't take long for Koch to grasp a truth that was well known to Farmland executives, which was that nitrogen fertilizer sales were pivotal to the company's business model in 1995. Koch also detected a weakness in Farmland's business model. Farmland was a co-op, meaning that it was owned by thousands of members who also sold their products through the firm. It was a uniquely midwestern form of capitalism that blended community control with industrial scale. In this way, Farmland was the opposite of Koch Industries, which was tightly held by Charles and David Koch. Farmland was owned by thousands of farm families and small business owners who shared in Farmland's annual profits and voted on its actions. But it also hindered Farmland—decisions were influenced by its member-owners, who considered factors beyond the simple return on investment.

"It was Socialism," as Koch Agriculture president Dean Watson put it. And Koch's traders believed that Socialism was always destined to fail.

Farmland would, in fact, collapse. And the company's fertilizer plants were the catalyst that destroyed it. During the 1990s, Farmland's fertilizer plants were immensely profitable, dispensing waves of cash. Farmland's member-owners used this money to expand, buying pork processing plants, grain elevators, and even an oil refinery. Free cash flow from nitrogen fertilizer helped fund it all. This was possible because natural gas was cheap. By the end of the 1990s, Farmland was one of the largest purchasers of natural gas in the United States; it was buying all the supplies it could get to stoke the fertilizer money machine. In doing so, Farmland had become an energy company without even realizing it. Farmland had gotten deeply entrenched with a commodities business during an upcycle, without thinking too hard about what life might look like during the inevitable down cycle.

When the crash came, it decimated the profits in Farmland's nitrogen division. This sapped the cash flow to every other division. The whole co-op machine began to falter. Farmland couldn't pay its debt obligations, which increased its debt obligations as creditors demanded repayment. In 2002, Farmland was trying to raise as much capital as possible by selling off its businesses. Bankruptcy looked imminent.

Packebush and his team studied Farmland's network of fertilizer plants, and they identified something that no one else saw. Farmland owned a constellation of plants that zigzagged through the Corn Belt in a crooked line that looked a little bit like the Big Dipper turned on its side. The long handle of the Dipper started up in Fort Dodge, Iowa, and ran in a long slope down through some of the most fertile cropland on earth, down through the town of Beatrice, Nebraska, where there was a large nitrogen plant, and then bending to meet Dodge City, Kansas. At the edge of the Dipper's cup was Farmland's crown jewel—the company's massive fertilizer plant in Enid, Oklahoma.

Farmland's plants had a key advantage: they were located right next door to their customers—the farmers. This gave them an edge on transportation costs. If these plants closed, there would be a dramatic fertilizer shortage. It would be simply impossible to import all the fertilizer that midwestern farmers needed.

The Farmland plants were similar to Koch's oil refinery in Pine Bend. They were perched on exclusive real estate, giving them an advantage over their competitors. Demand wasn't going to disappear, and it wasn't feasible for new competitors to set up shop nearby.

Perhaps most important, nobody else in the marketplace attributed this value to the Farmland plants. When Farmland put the plants up for sale, the co-op got very little interest. There were two big, publicly traded fertilizer companies that seemed like natural buyers, called Agrium and CF Industries. But these companies were also embroiled in the natural gas crisis and seemed obsessed with their quarterly losses and the near-term economics of the fertilizer business. These companies had to explain themselves to investors every quarter and focused on the losses that were likely to occur this year and next.

The Koch Nitrogen team made its pitch to Charles Koch and the development board. The team wanted Koch to spend somewhere in the neighborhood of $270 million for a group of fertilizer plants—that could produce about 1.8 million metric tons of fertilizer a year—at the very moment when those plants were delivering absolutely gruesome quarterly reports to their current owner.

The plan seemed preposterous in many ways, and Charles Koch

wasn't convinced at first. As he and the development board considered the plan, they applied a set of rules that would help usher in years of future growth:

1. The Target Company Had to Be Distressed

Koch was only interested in buying companies or assets that had fallen on hard times. Part of the logic behind this was simple: distressed companies were cheaper. They could be purchased at a discount. But the company had to be distressed in the right kind of way. Ideally, the firm should to be distressed because of managerial negligence or poor decision-making. That way, Koch could reverse the poor strategies when it was the owner. The goal was to improve operations and profits at the distressed firm to boost its value. When that happened, Koch could hold on to its new profit-making machine or sell it.

2. The Deal Had to Be a Long-Term Play

Koch wasn't looking to buy and flip companies. The deal needed to make sense over the five-, ten-, or even twenty-year time frame. This played to Koch's advantage as a private firm. It could hold an asset through the stormy weather of commodities cycles, improving the underlying investments along the way until they were worth much more. This long-term strategy would open the door to a raft of acquisitions that other firms would not consider. Publicly traded firms, and even private hedge funds, looked for deals that showed a return within one to two years. Koch would face far less competition for the deals that paid off over many years later.

3. The Target Company Had to Fit with Koch's Core Capabilities

In the new era, Koch would stick to its knitting. It would expand into new industries only if the new line of business closely resembled something Koch already did. If Koch didn't know how to do a certain business process better than its competitors, then it would stay out of that business. New acquisitions had to build on Koch's expertise and had to branch out from the company's current strength.

The development board eventually decided that the Koch Nitrogen plan fit all three of these criteria. Packebush and his team were given author-

ity to spend hundreds of millions of dollars to execute it, and they did
so before their competitors were prepared to act. The timing was perfect. Farmland's CEO, Bob Terry, was frantically working to dismantle
the co-op and put its biggest assets up for sale. He was hoping to get as
much money as possible from the fertilizer plants. He was puzzled when
he was contacted by a little-known energy company in Wichita.

The delegation from Koch Industries arrived at Farmland's headquarters
building on a mild spring day, March 27, 2003. Farmland's headquarters
were located in a new office tower just north of Kansas City, another relic
of the co-op's recent profits. The Koch team arrived at the appointed
time, walking through the glass doors and into the spacious lobby. Koch
Industries employees, around this time, wore a uniform of button-down
shirts and blazers. They were soft spoken, unfailingly polite, and single-
mindedly focused on the task at hand.

Steve Packebush was with the team, and as he walked through the
lobby, he passed by an enormous mural that Farmland had installed on
the wall. The mural was itself a piece of history, and a testament to Farmland's former greatness. It was painted by a student of artist Thomas
Hart Benton and was a symbolic history of Farmland's rise to greatness. The mural also told a story about what was happening in corporate
America, and the broader meaning of Farmland's collapse.

The mural depicted how Farmland came to be, back in the 1920s. It
showed a group of men and women, dressed in Depression-era clothing,
sitting next to a tree and a bale of hay. They are watching a pitchman, who
waves his arms out to a horizon of fertile fields and a skyline of grain elevators. He is selling them on the promise of a co-op and the prosperity
that could be realized by banding together. Just behind him, two men are
slouched below a tree, one of them idly chewing a stalk of wheat. These
two men are the "skeptics," doubtful that the co-op structure would work.
Over the next seventy-four years, Farmland proved the skeptics wrong.
In 2003, the co-op was owned by roughly five hundred thousand farmers.
They shared the profits that Farmland generated from more than $12 bil-
lion in annual revenue a year. These farmers had a real say in how Farmland conducted business and they shared in its success.

It would not be entirely fair to consider Packebush one of the "skeptics." His father, in fact, had been a Farmland owner and member. He wasn't quick to criticize the co-op model. But he wasn't going to be sentimental about it, either. The model had failed, at least in Farmland's case. The American economy in 2003 was a private equity economy. Even up until the 1960s, US companies operated under something that could be called the "managerial theory" of capitalism, meaning that the interests of shareholders took a backseat to the decisions of managers. Even CEOs at big, publicly traded companies did what they thought was best for the long-term health of the firm. The wealth of shareholders was only one factor among many in their decision-making. A typical CEO thought about rewarding employees, supporting the community that their company called home, and reinvesting profits to invent future products. This arrangement fell apart during the 1970s, when price shocks, inflation, and recession meant that public shareholders got a terrible deal for their money. The rate of return on capital was 12 percent in 1965, but only a meager 6 percent by 1979. This malaise laid the groundwork for a revolution in corporate management.

A group of academics devised a new way to think about corporations, called the "agency theory." Under this new way of thinking, a company's CEO wasn't in the driver's seat—he or she would simply be the "agent" of the shareholders. The balance of power was flipped. Now the shareholders would have the upper hand, and they would essentially tell the CEO what to do. Within this framework, the CEO's only real job was maximizing the return for shareholders. Everything else, from employee pay to civic commitments, even long-term company value, took a backseat to maximizing return to the owners.

The rise of private equity firms intensified this transformation. Private equity firms bought existing companies and ran them in the best interests of the new owners. Between 2000 and 2012, private equity firms would invest a total of $3.4 trillion as they took companies private. More than eighteen thousand companies were thrust into an extreme form of agency-theory management. Labor costs were slashed, headquarters were moved, and expenses were cut across the board.

Koch Industries had been operating under the agency theory for years—the primary interest of managers was to increase the return on investment for the primary shareholders, Charles and David Koch. Packebush and his team were agents for Koch's shareholders. They were hoping to buy the most valuable pieces from the wreckage of Farmland and reshape them to deliver the highest profit.

There was a large table inside the conference room at Farmland head-quarters. Next to the table, a series of tripods were arranged, each hold-ing a large, poster-sized photo of Farmland's fertilizer plants. The glossy photos were designed as an enticement, showing off the plants' big tanks and tall towers. If the Farmland executives believed that the posters might excite more bidding at the auction, they had reason to be disap-pointed. Only two companies showed up that day: Koch Industries and the Canadian fertilizer company Agrium.

The delegation from Koch took their seats along one side of the table. The representatives from Agrium sat down on the opposite side of the table, facing Packebush. The teams from Agrium and Koch were joined by Farmland's lawyers and bankers, who led the auction.

Agrium was the largest publicly traded nitrogen fertilizer producer in the United States, with about $2.1 billion in annual sales. Agrium was worth billions, so it had the money to spend on Farmland's plants. But more importantly, buying the plants would have been a good strategic fit for Agrium—it was already the industry leader. Koch was a nobody in the nitrogen business, having been forced to close down its plant in Lou-isiana when gas prices spiked.

But Agrium had reason to be a hesitant bidder that day. The glossy photos couldn't hide the fact that Farmland's fertilizer plants were los-ing about $50 million a year. It seemed possible that Agrium was at the table only because Koch Industries had arrived. Koch and Farmland had already announced a preemptive agreement for Koch to buy the facili-ties. Agrium might very well have showed up just to nip a competitor in the bud.

Koch had a key advantage over Agrium. Koch's shareholders could fit around a small kitchen table. The Agrium team had to answer to a multitudinous crowd of shareholders on Wall Street. If they made the wrong decision, Agrium's stock price could fall within minutes. Farm-land's plants would likely drag down Agrium's profits for years to come. Charles Koch had come to peace with this fact. Agrium's shareholders had not.

Before the auction, Koch had offered Farmland around $270 million. Agrium forced Koch to sweeten its bid to just more than $290 million. But Agrium wouldn't go further than that. After a relatively short and desultory auction, Packebush and his team stood up from the table as victors. The glossy photos of the fertilizer plants were taken down and tossed in a dumpster. Eventually the mural in Farmland's lobby was disassembled and shipped off to the National Agricultural Center and Hall of Fame, a tourist attraction in Bonner Springs, Kansas. The mural sat behind a velvet rope and was scrutinized as a relic of the long-forgotten past.

After it acquired Farmland's fertilizer plants, Koch Nitrogen was renamed Koch Fertilizer and moved to a huge office on the fourth floor of Koch's headquarters tower, just above Charles Koch's office. Koch instantly started pouring money into the plants. Over the next ten years, it spent roughly $500 million to outfit the plants with new technology while streamlining production. Koch Fertilizer abandoned the co-op sales model and began trading supplies to the highest bidder (rather than giving preference to the farmer-owners) throughout the Corn Belt.

Koch installed a team of fertilizer traders in the office, including Melissa Beckett, the star trader who'd once specialized in trading megawatt-hours. The traders bought and sold supplies around the globe, learning more about fertilizer markets each day. Within a few years, Koch Fertilizer built a global distribution network. Koch founded a new company, called Koch Energy Services, which bought and sold natural gas supplies to keep the fertilizer plants stocked. The energy traders sat on the fourth floor, just next to their counterparts trading fertilizer.

Steve Packebush was named CEO of Koch Fertilizer in 2003. Being part of the Koch Nitrogen team had paid off nicely. He lived in a very large house, by Wichita standards, and ran a division that would become one of Koch's largest and most profitable. It wasn't bad for a Kansas farm kid with a degree from K-State.

Shortly after the bankruptcy auction, a former Farmland employee approached Packebush. He said he had something that Packebush might want. It was one of the glossy poster boards that Farmland printed up for the auction. The Farmland employee had fished it out of the dumpster.

Many years later, that poster hung on the wall in Packebush's office. He could gaze at it while the traders outside his door haggled for natural gas supplies and bargained over the price of nitrogen in China. As it turned out, the poster, and the fertilizer plants, would be one of the smaller trophies Koch Industries acquired.

CHAPTER 15

Seizing Georgia-Pacific

(2003–2006)

This time the delegation from Koch Industries was dispatched to Atlanta. They arrived at Georgia-Pacific headquarters, one of the largest, most opulent buildings downtown. The Georgia-Pacific tower, at 133 Peachtree Street, rises knifelike into the sky, its sides encased in gleaming red granite that shines in the morning sun. The building projects an image of authority, ego, and power. It would have seemed preposterous, at that moment, that the small team of executives from Wichita would soon take command of the entire building.

One of the Koch executives on the team was Jim Hannan. Within a few years, he would become Georgia-Pacific's CEO. On that hot summer morning in 2003, however, Hannan was just a guest. Georgia-Pacific invited the Koch team to its headquarters that day because they hoped Koch Industries might buy a small part of the timber company's business: a set of struggling pulp mills. It was hardly the kind of deal that would make the newspapers.

What wasn't visible to anyone outside Koch at the time was that Jim Hannan and his team were only a very small piece of a much larger machine inside Koch Industries. They were the landing team for Koch's Corporate Development Board, which was about to execute a series of corporate takeovers worth more than $25 billion. The board was targeting dysfunctions in the market, places where the public was undervaluing assets that Koch could step in and seize. Georgia-Pacific was one of those undervalued assets. The Delaware corporation DuPont was another one. The distorted, short-term thinking on Wall Street had depressed the value of both companies. Koch had the cash on hand to exploit those mistakes. That's what Jim Hannan and his team were in Atlanta to do that day.

Hannan, like Steve Packebush, was a prototypical Koch man. He was lean and athletic, with a square jaw and a manner of speech that was utterly earnest, sincere, and laced with unbendable self-confidence. Hannan was educated at a small school, earning a business degree from California State University, East Bay, in Hayward, and worked as an accountant before joining Koch. Then his real education began. He was hired as a finance guy and promoted from division to division, and from job to job. His real training wasn't in finance per se but in the Koch method of doing business. By 2003, he was a fluent speaker of Market-Based Management. By the time he arrived in Atlanta that day, Hannan had become the chief financial officer of the Koch Minerals division.

Hannan's presence in the lobby of Georgia-Pacific's headquarters was even more bizarre than Koch's presence at the auction of Farmland's fertilizer plants a few months earlier. Koch's interest in Farmland could at least be explained by Koch's ownership of a fertilizer plant and a few ammonia pipelines. There was absolutely no conceivable reason for Hannan and his team to buy the assets of a timber company that would cost several hundred million dollars. Koch Minerals specialized in trading and shipping petroleum, coal, sulfur, and other dry goods. Koch Industries, as a whole, had zero experience in the wood and paper business. Yet here was a team from Koch, having requested an appointment, and having made it abundantly clear that they were ready and able to spend very serious money if Georgia-Pacific was willing to part with a few of its assets.

The team from Koch walked into the spacious lobby at the foot of the Georgia-Pacific tower. The lobby was like a spacious, public mall, with a small coffee shop, a convenience store, and hundreds of well-dressed professionals walking in every direction. Georgia-Pacific was one of the world's largest wood and paper products companies in the world, with about fifty-five thousand employees spread across the country. The firm owned dozens of giant wood, pulp, and paper mills, and reported $20.3 billion in sales in 2003.

Georgia-Pacific treated the delegation like visiting royalty. The Koch team was scheduled to receive a private investor's presentation, to be given on the fifty-first floor of the tower, which employees had taken to calling the "Pink Palace" because of its red granite facing.

The fifty-first floor held an almost mythical status within Georgia-

Pacific. The top floor was home to the company's executive suites and the executive dining room. It was easier to get invited to an exclusive cotillion ball in the old-money neighborhoods of Atlanta than it was to get an invitation to the fifty-first floor. Hannan and his team stepped into a special bank of elevators and were ushered upstairs.

When they arrived at the top of the tower, the elevator doors opened onto a wide corridor that was a hushed cocoon of luxury. The hallways were lined with lush rugs, and the walls were appointed with oil paintings that evoked America's frontiersman past. Hannan and his team walked past china cabinets in the hallways, filled with antiques, and then passed through a set of open doors made from thick, richly colored hardwood with large brass knobs embedded in the center, surrounded by brass etchings that looked like oak leaves, radiating outward. The doorway took the Koch team into Georgia-Pacific's executive dining room, a large solarium with floor-to-ceiling glass walls that looked out over downtown Atlanta. It felt like the dining room of an elite country club, elevated to Olympian heights. The coffee and food were served on fine china.

Hannan was making mental notes as he looked around at the paintings and china cabinets and other works of art.

These are too lavish, Hannan thought. He would eventually change all that.

After some small talk, the Koch team was given a private investor's presentation about the pulp mills that Georgia-Pacific had put up for sale. The sale, and Koch's interest in it, stemmed from deep financial problems that were plaguing Georgia-Pacific. The company had been limping along for years, burdened by debt and a motley collection of different business lines it had purchased during a years-long acquisition spree.

Georgia-Pacific was founded in 1927 and, in its earliest days, was basically just a big lumber yard. The company expanded rapidly over the decades, at one point owning more than six million acres of trees. As American timber companies wiped out the nation's supply of old-growth timber, Georgia-Pacific was a pioneer in finding replacement products. It figured out how to replace hardwood oak with cheaper material by using special glues to turn soft pine trees into composite products like plywood.

Over time, Georgia-Pacific became a chemical company and started to resemble an oil refining company. It owned big processing plants and bought raw materials (timber instead of crude oil) that it processed into commodity products (plywood rather than gasoline). The company used its profits to buy out competitors during the 1990s. The company's ambitions turned out to be its undoing. In 2000, Georgia-Pacific bought a tissue-paper company called Fort James, which itself was the creation of a recent merger between two giant tissue-making companies. At the time of the purchase, Georgia-Pacific was already carrying $6.5 billion in debt. It borrowed another $10 billion to buy Fort James. The theory was that the new Georgia-Pacific would control both the timber business and the paper business, controlling the entire supply chain, from forests to paper plates. But the purchase was so lavish and so surprising that even the buyout enthusiasts on Wall Street were put off. Georgia-Pacific's stock fell after the deal was announced.

Three years later, Georgia-Pacific's stock price was still struggling. Wall Street analysts just couldn't figure out how to value a firm that was halfway in the wood products business and halfway in the consumer paper business, two industries that were very different in their particulars and also in their business cycles. Shares of the company bounced around unimpressively, and it was never quite clear how the Fort James purchase was going to deliver strong growth.

Georgia-Pacific was looking for a way out of this morass, and executives on the fifty-first floor of the Pink Palace believed that one way forward was to sell off some assets, like its pulp mills. Koch's Corporate Development Board had become a national hub for the private equity firms that trafficked in such deals, so Koch's team quickly became aware that Georgia-Pacific was looking to unload some of its properties.

On the day that Koch visited Atlanta, Georgia-Pacific's presentation on its pulp mills was given by a long-time G-P employee named Wesley Jones. He gave them an overview of the pulp business, the cornerstone of which was a massive mill located in Brunswick, Georgia. The mill produced something called "fluff pulp" and was the largest such mill in the world. The term fluff pulp was a little misleading. The factory actually produced giant rolls of compressed wood fiber that looked like paper towel rolls about the size of a car. The rolls were sent to factories around the world that processed the pulp into soft, absorbent material used in diapers and feminine hygiene products. Georgia-Pacific built the Brunswick mill to feed growing demand for fluff pulp in Asia, as a burgeoning middle class in China and India had more money to spend on disposable diapers. But the bet hadn't paid off yet—exports remained more sluggish than the company would have liked.

After Jones finished his presentation, Hannan began to dissect everything he had just heard with question after question. Hannan asked about Brunswick's raw material markets. How did the mill procure its trees? What was the market for timber like? Was it volatile? Did the mill buy its wood under long-term contracts or at a spot price? Jones answered the questions gamely, even if it was a little unclear to him why an oil and gas outfit out of Kansas was interested in any of it.

When the questions were finished, the delegation from Koch Industries got up from their seats, exchanged pleasantries, and headed back to Wichita. The biggest expansion in Koch's history was about to get underway.

After their trip to the Pink Palace, Hannan and his team agreed to buy Georgia-Pacific's two major pulp mills. Koch Industries formed a new shell company, called Koch Cellulose LLC, which took possession of the two major pulp mills for $610 million.*

This acquisition would have been among Koch's biggest in the 1990s, but in 2003 it was just a down payment. Charles Koch favored a trading strategy that he called "experimental discovery." It entailed making a small bet in a new market and seeing if the bet paid off. Even if a Koch trader lost money on the trade, they gained insight. If they made a profit, the bet could be expanded.

The pulp mill purchase was just one of many experimental discoveries. Almost as soon as the pulp mill deal was closed, Jim Hannan was switched onto a new team. This one examined the assets of a different company, the old-school chemical conglomerate DuPont.

In 2003, DuPont was like Georgia-Pacific in one key way—investors didn't quite know what to make of DuPont's unwieldy collection of business divisions. DuPont had a highly profitable biotechnology division, but its earnings were dragged down by some of its old-line chemical

---

* About $73 million of this price was Georgia-Pacific's debt that Koch assumed with the purchase.

plants. DuPont's management thought it could boost its stock price if it sold some the company's legacy plants. One division DuPont was keen to unload was one of its oldest and best known: the synthetic materials unit that made products like Lycra and Stainmaster carpet. The synthetic fibers helped make DuPont a household name, but global competition turned Lycra into a commodity, and, like most commodities, it was suffering from booms and busts in the market. Naturally, all of this was attractive to Charles Koch and the Corporate Development Board.

Koch could secure natural gas and oil supplies better than almost anyone in the world, which would shield it from some of the price risks that were hurting DuPont. There was another attractive feature to DuPont that was similar to the Georgia-Pacific deal. Koch had gotten good at running refineries, and many of the skills it learned in that field could be applied equally well to making fluff pulp, Lycra, and Stainmaster carpet. The business involved paying people to sit in large control rooms and monitor machines that process raw, sometimes dangerous materials. At the Brunswick mill, the people in control rooms oversaw towers that dissolved wood pulp and spinning wheels that turned it into rolls of pulp. At the DuPont plants, the people in control rooms oversaw towers that mixed petrochemicals into compounds that could make clothing. Charles Koch believed that the company could do these jobs equally well, while using each new company as a way to branch into new industries.

In November of 2003, Koch agreed to buy DuPont's synthetic fiber plants for $4.4 billion.* Just as it had done with the Georgia-Pacific pulp mills, Koch Industries installed layers of corporate veil around the project to protect Koch's investment. It purchased the assets from DuPont by using two shell companies, called KED Fiber Ltd. and KED Fiber LLC. The chemical plants themselves would be housed under a new company, called Invista, that had its own board of directors and nominal independence from Koch Industries. The deal more than doubled the size of Koch Industries' workforce, adding eighteen thousand employees to Koch's fifteen thousand.

---

* It is unclear how much of this sales price was financed by debt and how much in cash, because Koch Industries was not obligated to report that figure. However, in 2009, almost five years after the acquisition, Koch reported that Invista was carrying roughly $2.6 billion in debt. That year, Koch paid down $1.6 billion of that debt.

Hannan was named president of the intermediates business at Invista ("intermediates" in this case meaning chemical products that were used to make synthetic material). This was the first time that Hannan, a finance guy, was put in charge of operations. He oversaw complicated, sometimes dangerous, chemical processing machinery and was responsible for the safety and competence of employees who worked around that machinery. It was a steep learning curve. And the learning curve had to do with a lot more than just overseeing operations.

Over the next two years, Hannan got a front row seat for Koch's actions as a private equity firm. He would play an instrumental role in "Kochifying" both Invista and Georgia-Pacific, absorbing both firms into the Koch Industries system. Koch managed these new divisions in ways that were both typical of private equity firms, but also iconoclastic. It used common tools of the private equity boom—heavy debt, a strong corporate veil, and deep financial analysis—but it also imposed a vision that was particular to Charles Koch. While Koch pushed down costs in some areas, it also spent billions on its new holdings rather than stripping them for parts, as some firms did.

Invista became a laboratory to impose another key feature of Koch's operating philosophy: its new, unbending insistence that all Koch operations obey every law and regulation that was applied to them. This strategy emerged from the painful lessons of the 1990s, when Koch Industries had developed a regulatory rap sheet that gave the company a reputation for borderline criminality. And this strategy was particularly vital to the Invista purchase, with which Koch instantly inherited a network of large factories full of dangerous equipment and chemicals. Each factory was a collection of potential federal violations, and Koch was relying on a workforce of strangers to comply with these rules. The Invista workforce was larger than Charles Koch's entire company, and now he would have to make sure that each and every one of them had his very best interests at heart. It was Hannan's job, in part, to make sure that this was the case, at least for the division that he oversaw.

After Koch took over Invista, it placed help-wanted ads in the business press, advertising open positions for compliance attorneys. This is how

Koch came to hire a liberal environmental lawyer named David Hoffmann, who lived in Cleveland.

Hoffmann had never even heard of Koch Industries before, and he was intrigued when he saw the want ad. He wanted to leave the world of billable hours and go in-house at a corporation. The job posting at Koch seemed like the perfect chance. But first, Hoffmann had to sell his wife on the idea of moving to Wichita. She was involved in the theater scene in Cleveland, loved urban culture, was an outspoken liberal, and didn't like the idea of living in central Kansas. Her father was a medical professor and an environmental activist. He didn't respond well when he found out where his son-in-law wanted to work.

"When he found out I was working for Koch Industries, he was like: 'I gotta sit down and talk to you,'" Hoffmann recalled. "We had this really bad dinner conversation. I almost got disowned."

With the disapproval of his father-in-law and the grudging acceptance of his wife, Hoffmann moved to Wichita in 2005. He spent more than two days sitting in an auditorium, learning about Market-Based Management. He and his wife found the one coffee shop in town where the liberals hung out. They bought a house in the historic district. Hoffmann still didn't know if he would be helping Invista comply with environmental laws, as the job posting had promised, or if he would be aiding and abetting a corporate conspiracy to pollute the environment, as his father-in-law had feared.

When Hoffmann arrived at work, he discovered something that would have surprised outsiders who considered Koch Industries to be little more than a rogue corporation. Hoffmann became part of a corporate compliance SWAT team. Its dedication to obeying the law wasn't just genuine, it was fanatical. They were about to fundamentally transform Invista.

Hoffmann worked in the new Invista headquarters, a low-slung annex of offices that were connected to the east side of the Koch Tower in Wichita. He joined a team of so-called subject matter experts, or SMEs, in Koch parlance. The team had fewer than a dozen people, and each one was an expert in a different area of regulation, like health and safety rules or industrial waste management. It was significant that this team was based in Wichita rather than in the facilities that they would oversee. The compliance team would no longer be broken up among the various facilities, occupying second-rate offices and vying for the attention of the plant managers. Back in the 1990s, Koch's legal compliance team followed the lead of the operations managers. At the Pine Bend refinery, Heather Faragher and her team had been subordinate to the process owners. Now, the power dynamic would be transformed. The operations managers had to listen closely to the compliance team. The environmental lawyers had power.

The centralized compliance team was located a short walk from Charles Koch's office. The team was sent out into Koch's new factories to meet with plant managers and make site visits. The occasions were similar to an army general visiting a forward operating base for inspection. The managers knew that Hoffmann's team was carrying the full weight of Koch Industries' leadership team. The visits were often a surprise. They were not always pleasant.

Hoffmann worked with Jim Mahoney, a large man with bright blue eyes and a blunt manner of speaking. Mahoney could be affable and friendly, but any trace of collegiality seemed to disappear when he set foot onto Invista property. He and Hoffmann were led through the facility to inspect its compliance program, and Mahoney didn't so much ask questions of his tour guides as he demanded answers from them. In one facility, Mahoney grilled a manager about a set of pressure relief valves— Mahoney wanted to know about the safety inspections of the valves. It wasn't that the valves were malfunctioning, broken, or posed any kind of danger. Mahoney simply wanted more information about how the valves were being inspected, and the manager was not providing satisfactory answers.

Mahoney snapped.

"He said at one point, 'I'll close this plant right now if you can't tell me the answer to this question,'" Hoffmann recalled. "It scared the shit out of people." To strengthen their enforcement, Hoffmann's team hired local attorneys near the plants to act as eyes and ears on the ground, monitoring compliance when the subject matter experts from Wichita weren't visiting. Hoffmann and Mahoney were spreading Charles Koch's new doctrine, called the 10,000 percent compliance rule. The mantra described a simple idea: Koch's operations would be in 100 percent compliance with the law, 100 percent of the time.

Koch Industries backed up the philosophy with drastic actions. In

Victoria, Texas, Koch discovered that a benzene treatment system wasn't operating according to code. The system was immediately shut down. In Camden, South Carolina, Koch discovered that DuPont had expanded its processing equipment without getting proper permits beforehand and was running the machines out of compliance. Similarly, DuPont had expanded a boiler in Seaford, Delaware, without getting the proper permits and was running the boiler without the proper pollution control technology. In the past, Koch had tried to solve such problems on its own, before regulators discovered what was happening. This time Koch reported everything to the EPA, disclosing nearly seven hundred violations to the agency just months after Koch took ownership of the new factories. Koch entered into an agreement with the EPA that gave the agency power to audit Koch every quarter to ensure that it was complying with a schedule of improvements. Koch spent about $140 million to get everything up to code. Then it sued DuPont for $800 million in damages.

This 10,000 percent compliance regimen was applied across Koch's operations, from Invista to Georgia-Pacific, to the refineries at Flint Hills Resources. There was more behind it than the good-hearted desire to be a solid corporate citizen. The strategy was a pragmatic tool to maximize profits. When Koch bought new factories and companies, it simply needed them to run smoothly and efficiently. It needed to keep them out of legal trouble and keep federal inspectors off company property. Violating the rules cost money and created distractions. Ten thousand percent compliance eliminated them. With those distractions gone, Koch could execute the more important elements of its growth plan. Those elements could be observed at Georgia-Pacific's pulp mills, where things changed immediately after Koch became the new owner.

The Brunswick pulp mill plant was a surreal landscape that mixed pastoral southern charm with a futuristic, mechanized world scaled up to the size of giants. The wooded hills around the plant were traversed by two-lane country roads. Confederate battle flags hung from the beams of old wooden porches where small groups of people sat and sipped cold drinks in the afternoon, waving to motorists as they passed by. As the road descended down toward the mill, the idyllic landscape gave way to the industrial. The narrow road outside the plant was often crowded by long rows of trailer trucks loaded with recently cut pine trees. Just inside the gates, truck after truck deposited its load onto an impossibly tall pile of tree trunks. The pile was arranged in a semicircle at the foot of a giant mechanical claw that towered several stories in the air. The claw pivoted and grabbed a bunch of limbs like a drunken giant, feeding them to a chipping machine the size of a small apartment building. The fountain of golden wood chips was funneled inside the plant, where they were liquefied and pressed into the paper-like rolls of fluff pulp.

Wesley Jones, who had given the investor presentation to Hannan and his team, was the head of Georgia-Pacific's pulp division in 2004. He saw firsthand how Koch Industries revitalized the operation. Jones had watched the pulping operation decline during a long era of deprivation and underinvestment. The problem traced back to Georgia-Pacific's corporate culture. When he first joined the company, there had been a scrappiness to it. Georgia-Pacific managers liked to employ the word "maverick" to describe their corporate culture. Then Georgia-Pacific went on its corporate buying spree in the 1990s, and the company started focusing on administrative function and cost reduction. Experimentation and failure were not quite so prized, while paperwork and superior process were. Decisions had to be approved by committees, investments were slowed, and autonomy was shifted from the ground level to the ranks of middle managers or above. The problem grew worse after the deal to buy Fort James in 2000. After that, the executives slowed down capital investment plans as they steered more money into paying off debt. The neglect was causing wear and tear on the plant's equipment. Jones was worried that the machinery would start to break down, in large and noticeable ways.

Then Koch bought the company. Soon after that, Jones wanted to buy a complicated new processing tower that would help speed up production. The tower would cost somewhere between $35 million and $40 million. At Georgia-Pacific, Jones would have gotten together a formal proposal for the investment and then pushed the proposal uphill through a dense thicket of bureaucratic channels where any vice president could veto it and any two vice presidents could debate its merits indefinitely. In 2004, he mentioned the investment idea, almost offhandedly, to someone from Koch. Then he found himself on the phone with someone in Wichita who asked him about the tower and what it could do.

Jones was given approval to spend about $40 million. Over the phone.

"It was like a month or two after the acquisition. I was kind of floored," Jones recalled. "I remember putting the phone down and thinking, *Damn . . .*"

Koch carried out other changes at Georgia-Pacific that exploited Koch's private ownership. Koch jettisoned the use of budgets, for example, just as it had done back in the 1980s. Because it was a publicly traded firm, Georgia-Pacific's employees invested countless hours of their time to write quarterly and annual budgets, setting out targets to be met to please shareholders. This created a circular logic—invent a budget, then work to meet it—that caused strange distortions to the work flow and wasted effort inside Georgia-Pacific.

Karen Marx, a logistics manager at Georgia-Pacific's tissue paper mill outside Savannah, said that managers at the mill used to rush to meet targets at the end of each quarter, speeding up shipments leaving the plant, whether it was necessary or not. "It was always like 'Let's get more shipments out the door,'" Marx recalled. This ended when Koch took over. Budgets were replaced by "goals," which were drawn up in an almost hasty manner, taking perhaps one-tenth of the time to produce. The only purpose of the goal was to give Koch executives a rough idea of their cash expenditures for the year. Managers were not pressured to meet the goals. They spent much less time trying to predict the future—and zero time trying to impress stock analysts or outside shareholders.

Charles Koch gained confidence from the pulp mill experiment. He was so confident that just a year after buying the pulp mills, Charles Koch was considering a plan to buy all of Georgia-Pacific outright and take the company private. Koch Industries could apply the same techniques to the entire company: 10,000 percent compliance, targeted investment, and flexible management that didn't focus on quarterly results.

But Georgia-Pacific wouldn't come cheap. The company would cost at least three times the $4 billion Koch paid for Invista, and it would require multiple billions of dollars in debt. Charles Koch hated debt. He strove for years to maximize his company's cash flow, boost its savings, and keep borrowing at a minimum. This is what gave Koch the flexibility to seize opportunities quickly; the company wasn't hampered by high debt payments.

The private equity business, however, turned this theory on its head.

Debt was the lifeblood of the private equity industry and the broader American economy during the 2000s. The theory behind debt-heavy deals was simple, ingenious, and immensely profitable for the very small number of companies that had the ability to exploit it.

To make a debt-fueled deal work, private equity firms hunted for companies that were struggling, but produced a lot of cash. The equity firms then borrowed huge sums of money to take the target company private and then used the cash flow to pay down the debt. The plan was brilliant in its simplicity—the private equity firm borrowed other people's money, then used other people's companies to pay that money down. Once the debt was paid down, the private equity firm still owned the company itself. The company had paid down the debt, and the private equity firm got to keep the wealth that remained afterward. Once that happened, the private equity firm could sell off the target company or keep it and reap its annual profits. It was like borrowing money to buy a house, if the house could somehow generate the money to pay off the mortgage. The only way to lose money was a calamitous decline in the value of the business itself, which did occasionally happen. But the odds were stacked in favor of the private equity owners.

A key part of making the whole strategy work, of course, was the creation of a very deep and strong corporate veil. It shielded the private equity firm from catastrophic losses. The debt was loaded onto the target company, and if the company failed, the equity firm only stood to lose the money it had invested—often just a tiny fraction of the purchase price. The losses were contained, shifted, and kept off the balance sheet of investors like Koch Industries.

Koch Industries put this plan into play to make the largest acquisition in its history. First Koch formed a shell company called Koch Forest Products, making an audacious bid to purchase all of Georgia-Pacific for the sum of $21 billion. The purchase would be financed by debt, which would be loaded squarely onto the shoulders of the newly created, privately held Georgia-Pacific company, called Georgia-Pacific Holdings. This new firm was nominally independent. Charles Koch sat on its board of directors, of course, but the board's very existence fostered the appearance that Georgia-Pacific was a stand-alone company. If things went terribly wrong, the repercussions would go no further than the legal seawall that Koch was building around its new investment.

Georgia-Pacific was already limping along under roughly $8 billion in debt, delaying capital investments so that it could pay off interest payments. Koch Industries loaded an additional $7.5 billion in new debt onto the company. Within the private equity world, this wasn't irresponsible, but virtuous. "To acquire Georgia-Pacific, we took it deep into debt—to the point where unless performance improved, Georgia-Pacific would be in violation of its loan covenants," Charles Koch later wrote. Now debt became a virtue rather than a burden, a force that established motivation and self-sacrifice among those who carried it.

Koch Industries announced its plan to take Georgia-Pacific private in mid-November of 2005. The deal made Koch the largest privately held company in the nation.* Koch would be adding fifty-five thousand new employees to its workforce of thirty-three thousand, more than doubling the company in size once again. Jim Hannan was quickly informed that his services were no longer needed at Invista. He would move to Atlanta and help Koch absorb the largest acquisition in its history.

Koch had learned a lot about corporate takeovers since the disastrous purchase of Purina Mills in the 1990s. Back then, Dean Watson gathered the Purina executives together and informed them that they would subscribe to a new business philosophy. The result was a shouting match and a wave of defections. When Koch bought Georgia-Pacific, it sent an initial landing team of just seventeen employees to Atlanta to take control of the company, Jim Hannan among them. The delegation from Koch Industries represented about 0.001 percent of the total Georgia-Pacific workforce. It was obvious that Koch did not plan to make this a hostile, rapid takeover.

Hannan was joined by a senior member of the Corporate Development Board, Joe Moeller, who had been president of Koch Industries. Moeller assumed the job of chairman and CEO of Georgia-Pacific. His

---

* Koch perpetually competed with the food-and-grain-processing giant Cargill for this distinction. Cargill would later overtake Koch in the rankings and remained number one. Koch executives privately said that outside analysts almost always failed to capture Koch Industries' full size, and erroneously counted Cargill as being larger—which suited Charles Koch just fine.

small cadre of Koch employees would set about steering the ship of Georgia-Pacific, and they would do it with a light hand. Most of the senior leaders at Georgia-Pacific were allowed to stay. Wesley Jones, from the Brunswick mill, was promoted from running the pulp division to overseeing operations across the entire company. The Georgia-Pacific team was allowed to remain the Georgia-Pacific team and allowed to retain the bulk of what they considered to be their corporate culture. They did not dress in the Koch uniform of button-down shirts with no tie and possibly a blazer. Koch Industries had never taken such a soft touch with another corporate culture. There was a looseness to the process that was new.

But drastic change came quickly, and it was driven by the force of debt. The executive suites on the fifty-first floor of the Georgia-Pacific tower, which Hannan thought were "too lavish," were dismantled almost right away. The executives were kicked out of their offices and sent down to the fiftieth floor. The corner office of the previous Georgia-Pacific CEO, A. D. "Pete" Correll, was cleared out and turned into a meeting room. The desk, the furniture, and the art on the walls were replaced with a meeting table surrounded by unremarkable black office chairs. It looked no nicer than any meeting room in any suburban office park in Kansas, although with a nicer view. The executive dining room was emptied out and turned into a meeting space where managers could book events with clients.

Hannan moved to Atlanta and bought a house. Within a year, he was promoted to replace Moeller as the CEO of Georgia-Pacific, directly overseeing the biggest investment that Charles Koch had ever made. He was forty-one years old.

Hannan's office on the fiftieth floor of the Georgia-Pacific tower was modest but well appointed, with a big desk and a small conference table surrounded by tasteful wooden chairs. He would spend more than a decade as CEO of the company, finding ways to manage Georgia-Pacific in a fashion that spun off enough cash to pay off its debt while also giving his two most important shareholders a satisfactory return on their investment.

In 2016, there was one item in Hannan's office that told an important story. On the polished wood credenza directly across from Hannan's desk, he had prominently displayed a paper Dunkin' Donuts coffee cup.

It's an odd piece of décor. It was cheap, and it was a constant reminder of one of Hannan's biggest business failures. Early in his tenure, Hannan led a $200 million acquisition of a paper company in California called Insulair, which made the Dunkin' Donuts cup. The cups had special insulation, and Georgia-Pacific planned to sell them to big chains like 7-Eleven. The deal was a flop. It turned out the cups were too expensive for convenience stores, and Insulair was sold off.

Hannan liked to keep that failure at the front of his mind. He could look over and see the cup at any moment when he was on the phone or writing a memo. He cherished the uneasy feeling it created. It kept him on edge, and this was the key to thriving in the private equity economy. The heavy debt required ever-better performance and leaner operations. The pressure to achieve this never stopped. It was transmitted from Charles Koch, to Jim Hannan, to the cadre of executives who worked around him.

Then, perhaps most importantly, it was transmitted down the chains of command to the ground level of Georgia-Pacific. This is where middle-class Americans were making a living during the 2000s. The pressure affected everyone there, on the ground level, even if they didn't fully understand where it was coming from.

CHAPTER 16

The Dawn of the Labor Management System

(2006–2009)

When Koch Industries bought Georgia-Pacific, it inherited a network of giant paper mills and timber operations scattered throughout the mountains and valleys of the Pacific Northwest. The mills in Oregon and Washington were connected by an economic circulatory system of rivers that carried barges full of timber, wood chips, and finished paper products from one location to another. The beating heart of this circulatory system was Georgia-Pacific's massive warehouse complex in Portland, Oregon. It was here, inside the giant warehouses, that a bitter battle played out over many decades, virtually unnoticed by the outside world. This battle was a microcosm of a larger fight that intensified during the age of private equity in the 2000s. It was a fight waged by the hourly warehouse workers, whose jobs and wages were under relentless attack over decades. The attacks came from successive waves of owners, each one buying the company and then trying to squeeze ever more profits from the region's mills and warehouses. The battle would culminate after 2006, when Koch Industries bought the warehouses.

A Georgia-Pacific warehouse worker named Steve Hammond was embroiled in this battle for many years. He would leave it broken and defeated, but he didn't start out that way. In the beginning, back in the late 1970s, Georgia-Pacific's warehouse was the doorway to a middle-class life for Hammond and hundreds of his coworkers. Over the ensuing decades, the warehouse became something like an economic island: one of the last employers in the region to offer solid work and solid pay for people who didn't have a college degree. Hammond watched as this island began to sink, slowly and steadily, as workers' pay, benefits, and job security were stripped away further, year after year. This was the story of America's low-skilled middle-class workers during the age of private equity.

The Georgia-Pacific warehouse in Portland is cavernous and filled with the echoes of squealing tires and humming motors from the busy traffic of forklift trucks driving around inside it. The forklifts navigate within mazelike rows of paper products, stacked high into the shadows of the ceiling rafters. The stacks hold crates of paper towels, pallets of napkins, and other products, all of it wrapped in clear plastic to keep it clean in transit. Hammond worked for more than thirty years in the warehouse and came to know almost every inch of the place. The facility was vital to Georgia-Pacific's operations on the West Coast. Paper products from mills in small towns like Camas and Wauna, Washington, were ferried by barge down the Willamette River to a dock on one side of the warehouse, where the cargo was unloaded and stored. Trucks pulled into large bay doors on the other side of the warehouse, where they were loaded with product to be shipped to spots in Oregon, to California, to Colorado. The busy crews of forklift drivers, who accounted for the vast majority of the warehouse workers, hauled the cargo from the stacks to the waiting trucks. The big warehouse where Hammond worked was operated in tandem with two other Georgia-Pacific warehouses near the river. The three warehouses, along with the mills, had been bought and sold by several corporate owners during Hammond's tenure. They were eventually purchased by Georgia-Pacific and then by Koch Industries in 2006.

Hammond was hired at the warehouse in 1972, the very same year that Koch's militant labor union at the Pine Bend refinery fought its losing battle against the company. He was just nineteen years old at the time. Hammond's parents had just gotten a divorce, and he was kicking around his childhood neighborhood in southeast Portland. It was a neighborhood of modest ranch houses with small yards bordered by sagging chain-link fences. It is fair to say that Hammond didn't seem destined for greatness at the time. He was hanging out with his friends, smoking dope, drinking beer, and earning about $2.40 an hour working at a small factory that made fence posts. He got a call from the warehouse, then owned by a company called Crown Zellerbach, that changed his life. A woman on the phone was looking for Hammond's older brother. Hammond said that he wasn't around, and the woman sounded frustrated. She needed someone to work a shift at a local warehouse that day. "She said, 'Well, how would you like to start at this place, four o'clock today?'" Hammond recalled. He said, "Okay."

Hammond drove down to Front Avenue, a street that passed through warehouses, oil terminals, and factories along the river. When he arrived at the factory for the first time, he was put to work right away. He learned how to drive a forklift and started working the night shift. He made $5.05 an hour.* This was more money than Hammond's dad made as a public school teacher with decades of experience. The money was simply amazing, and the jobs were plentiful. Hammond kept coming back.

He and the other warehouse workers were organized under a particularly fierce, energized union with a funny name: the Inlandboatmen's Union, named after the river barge workers who plied the Columbia and Willamette Rivers. Everyone called it the IBU for short. Hammond had never seen anything like the IBU. On Sundays, the union held an open meeting for its members at the union hall in downtown Portland. About two or three hundred members showed up, and those who hadn't already been drinking began drinking immediately. The meetings were long and spirited and social, and the sense of solidarity was electric. "You could always count on a good fistfight or something for entertainment, you know," Hammond recalled.

The union guys tended to give each other nicknames—there was Dodger and Magneto and Gary the Anarchist—and Hammond later earned his own nickname, the Hammer. He wore this nickname uneasily. It must have been a little bit ironic, like calling a very skinny man "Fatty." Hammond might have been many things, but he didn't seem like a hammer. He was a quiet guy, with wide brown eyes and delicate features that could only be described as regular. When Hammond imitated someone screaming in anger, he still managed to do it with a whisper. Hammond was congenial and got along with the people he worked with, including the managers and supervisors. He repeatedly described

---

* That's equal to about $30.93 an hour in 2019 dollars.

the warehouse as being like a family, and it was clear that he aimed to get along with his relatives as best he could.

Hammond wasn't militant. He didn't have to be. The union took care of that part for him. The union negotiated relentlessly on behalf of its members. It boasted about its past labor disputes during the 1930s, which were characterized by strikes, violence, and intimidation. Using this history as a lever, the union won remarkably generous terms for its workers: a pension plan for their retirement; a health insurance plan with no employee premium payments; generous sick leave and absenteeism policies; great starting pay; and seemingly permanent job security.

"Once you got in there and working—I was working right alongside guys that were schoolteachers and things. It just paid so much better—they'd gotten like a job in the summer, when there was no school, and it paid so good they just stayed," Hammond recalled. "So we had quite a few guys that were college educated and working in there." Hammond didn't want to drive a forklift his entire life. He left the job briefly, tried other things, but then returned in 1981 because of the good pay and benefits. He didn't leave for another thirty-five years.

In the mid-1980s, Hammond started hanging around with a pretty girl named Carla Hogue. They drank a lot and partied with friends. Then, Carla Hogue got pregnant. In 1985, she and Steve Hammond had a daughter named Sarah. Steve and Carla later got married and had a second child, Stephanie, in 1989. The Hammonds bought a small home in Vancouver, Washington, just north of Portland. They settled there in part because the property was cheaper than in downtown Portland, although it made for a long commute. Their house payment was about $650 a month, a burden that was easy to meet because he and Carla both worked: he at the warehouse and she as a medical assistant.

Life wasn't easy for the Hammonds. While work was steady at the warehouse, it was also organized along strict lines of hierarchy and seniority put in place by the union. Hammond started at the bottom of this hierarchy when he returned to work in 1981, which meant that he got stuck with night shifts. He worked for twenty years before he earned the seniority to work days. When his daughters were young, Hammond left for work in the afternoon. He got off his shift around one in the morning and drove home, passing the baton to Carla, who left for her job around four thirty. Steve got to bed around two thirty, slept until the girls woke up at six or so, and then took care of them in the mornings. Hammond usually worked seven days a week, volunteering for overtime shifts to earn the extra pay.

The schedule began to grind away on Steve and Carla's relationship. The bars and partying receded, although the drinking continued. The fun drained out of things. Hammond felt like he was being pushed by Carla to achieve the milestones of middle-class life. They bought a bigger house, and their monthly payment jumped to $1,300 a month. Now the bills were hard to meet.

The tension culminated, and their marriage dissolved during a trip to one of the most stressful places on earth: Disneyland. Carla bought a package trip to the theme park using the family credit card. Steve felt like they didn't have the money to take a vacation, let alone a trip to California. To help cover these costs, Steve went down to the union hall and cashed out a special emergency account that he kept there—it was common back then for workers to set aside cash to cover costs if they went on strike or suffered an injury that kept them off the job. His account had accrued about $1,200 over the years, and he spent it at Disneyland. It was quite possibly the worst trip of his life, although he and Carla tried to give the girls the full Disney experience.

"It was a miserable time. Her and I didn't speak hardly for the whole time down there—just kind of keeping it away from the kids," Hammond said. "I was so pissed off. We didn't have any money."

Steve and Carla divorced not too long after that. They sold the big house, and he moved in with his mother. They juggled responsibility for the girls. He continued to work odd hours at the warehouse, and the girls figured out how to get themselves to the school bus in the mornings.

The one thing Steve Hammond didn't have to worry about during all of this turmoil was losing his job, his health insurance, or his retirement pension. It is unclear, exactly, what Hammond would have had to do to get fired from the warehouse. The culture there would have been familiar to the unionized OCAW workers at Koch's Pine Bend refinery in the 1970s. Workers weren't afraid of their bosses. It wasn't uncommon for a forklift driver to share a slug of whiskey with a manager on the warehouse floor. Everyone laughed when a driver named Kerry Alt accelerated his truck too quickly, and an oversized bottle of beer came careening off the back, where it had been stowed for safekeeping. Alt jumped out and scrambled after the bottle as it rolled across the concrete floor. The bosses looked the other way. If a supervisor had chosen to discipline Alt, he would have had to do so through the union's grievance procedure. It wasn't worth the trouble. In this environment, Hammond was a straight arrow, and he was promoted up the ranks through the years.

One of Hammond's close friends was promoted even faster and left the union ranks to become a manager. He was Dennis Trimm, an imposing man standing six foot six. Trimm became foreman in the 1990s and was then promoted to supervisor, putting him in the ranks of management and cutting his ties with the Inlandboatmen's Union. Even then, when Trimm "went company," as the union members called it, he and Hammond remained friends. They still drank together on their time off, still joked on the warehouse floor, and still visited each other's families. There might have been a bright line between the union workers and their supervisors, but there wasn't animosity between them.

This began to change during the 2000s, however, and it changed dramatically in late 2005 when Koch Industries bought Georgia-Pacific and its warehouses that lined the Willamette River.

As the warehouses and their timber mills were sold over and over again, Dennis Trimm came to know the chain of CEOs who ran the company in succession: from Crown Zellerbach, to James Goldsmith, to Fort James, and then to Georgia-Pacific. Out of all of the leadership teams, he was most impressed with Georgia-Pacific's. The CEO, Pete Correll, often visited the warehouse to look the place over and talk with the management team. Correll was a lanky, personable man worth at least several million dollars, but also willing to talk with the local supervisors as if they were valued members of his team. Georgia-Pacific installed a special satellite system in all its facilities so they could receive quarterly broadcasts in which Correll talked about the company's goals and strategy. Trimm and his colleagues gathered in a conference room in the warehouse in 2005 to watch one final broadcast from Correll. Their CEO informed them that they would soon have new owners.

After Koch Industries bought the warehouse, Charles Koch never visited—at least, not as far as Trimm was aware. Instead, Koch Industries began to flood the supervisors with online training seminars and worksheets. Trimm usually spent his day out on the warehouse floor, driving among the stacks in a small cart to make sure that everything was running smoothly. But now he found himself in his office for long periods of time, watching training videos that were uploaded from Wichita. This is when Trimm began to hear for the first time about Market-Based Management. He learned about the five dimensions and the Ten Guiding Principles. About roles and responsibilities and mental models. And this is how he came to know Charles Koch.

In one video, produced by Koch Industries, Charles Koch can be seen sitting in front of a black screen. He wasn't speaking into the camera but was looking past it, sideways, as if at an interviewer. Charles Koch's thick hair was neatly combed and parted, but it still possessed its unruly waves, once blond, now thoroughly white. Koch wore thin-framed glasses and a blue button-down shirt with no tie or jacket. He looked like a kindly professor, or the dean of an economics school, perhaps. In the video, he didn't just talk about business goals and strategy. He talked about philosophy, the laws of the market, and the nature of humankind. He also talked about his father.

"My father considered work ethic—attitude toward work—as critically important for developing yourself, and, in fact, being healthy and happy through your life," Koch said. "The values that were most important to him, I would say, were integrity, humility, work ethic, experimentation, entrepreneurship, thirst for knowledge." Charles Koch continued: "I would say those are all key elements in Market-Based Management and all parts of our guiding principles."

Koch's voice was rich and deep but also understated, slowed by a midwestern drawl that never seemed to be in a rush to get to the next sentence. It was clear to Trimm that Charles Koch wasn't just explaining some kind of training manual. This was an all-encompassing philosophy. Managers like Trimm, then, were either all in or all out.

Trimm learned that watching Koch's online videos, and completing the related worksheets, was mandatory. If he didn't keep up with his scheduled viewing, someone from the human resources department e-mailed him with a reminder to stay on track. About a year after Koch took over the warehouses, Trimm was informed that he would attend a three-day seminar to further his education in Market-Based Management. The event was held in a hotel near the Georgia-Pacific mill in Camas, Washington.

On the day the seminar began, Trimm sat down at a table with a large group of other supervisors, and even one or two unionized workers.* Almost from the beginning, Trimm realized that the three-day session was not going to be a relaxing corporate retreat. The seminar began with an address from an MBM trainer named Benjamin Pratt, who had flown in from Atlanta. Pratt presented himself as someone who carried secret knowledge, directly from inside Koch's Tower in Kansas. The attendees were expected to pay close attention to his lessons.

"It was like watching a German war movie," Trimm recalled. "He was very direct. He told us: 'You *will* have homework. You *will* complete it before the next morning.'"

The crowd was shown more videos of Charles Koch, who talked about the guiding principles and his family's history. They were given a copy of Charles Koch's 2007 book, *The Science of Success*, which was something like an owner's manual for anyone practicing MBM. They were given worksheets and pamphlets that broke out specific elements of the philosophy. They were told that it would be smart to keep a copy of Charles Koch's book near their desk to consult periodically.

During a question-and-answer session, some of the employees expressed their concerns about recent management decisions. Over the previous years and months, Georgia-Pacific left many job positions open as people left the company, slowly trimming the workforce through attrition. This accelerated once Koch took over the company. "They went through like a hot knife through butter and started getting rid of people right and left," Trimm said. The remaining managers had more work on their plates. Some people found that they were staying at the office ten, twelve, or even eighteen hours a day just to complete their assignments. Many of them had assumed that the workload was temporary. Surely, they thought, there was a hiring binge waiting just around the corner. But the new hiring never seemed to materialize. Some of them started to worry that it never would.

Toward the end of the three-day seminar, an employee raised his hand and asked Pratt: Would Koch be hiring to beef up the workforce?

---

* Some foreman jobs at Georgia-Pacific were held by union members, even though a lot of the functions they performed were managerial. These positions would become fewer over time.

The employee complained that people were working punishingly long hours just to finish their basic job requirements.

Pratt replied that if they didn't like the hours, they could look for employment elsewhere.

"That silenced the room," Trimm recalled.

Increasing the bottom line became Trimm's prime directive. Supervisors were told to maximize efficiency across the warehouses (or the "assets," as they were called in the parlance of private equity). Several billion dollars in debt were hanging over Georgia-Pacific's operations, and that debt could only be serviced by squeezing every possible new dollar in profits out of the mills and warehouses. It fell to supervisors like Trimm to figure out how to do it.

Trimm adapted to the Koch Industries ecosystem. He began to understand the meaning of his new "role and responsibility." He was a property owner, and he needed to make his piece of land more profitable. He drew up a plan to rearrange parts of the product stacks in a way to speed up forklift routes from the dock to the loading bay. The plan was rejected, but he kept trying to act like an entrepreneur, coming up with money-saving techniques and plans. Trimm quickly discovered that the best way to cut costs was the simplest: he had to find ways to get more work out of each forklift driver while they were on the clock. In 2006, Trimm had a new tool that would let him do that in ways that were previously unthinkable.

Just when Koch bought Georgia-Pacific, the company was using a newly installed software system in its warehouses that was designed to boost the productivity of its workers. It was called the Labor Management System. The groundwork for the system had been laid before Koch arrived, with a series of odd time trials that Trimm and his associates ran on the workers. The strange tests had been conducted with little fanfare. They seemed like a curious experiment at the time, and there is little indication that anyone in the warehouse paid much attention to what was happening. Dennis Trimm joined a group of supervisors on the warehouse floor and assembled a team of lift drivers. They told the drivers to run a series of routes through the warehouse without picking up or dropping off any cargo. They were simply to drive from point A to point B—say, from the loading bay back to bay B-1. Then, the drivers were asked to go from point A to point B again, dozens of times. Trimm and the other managers recorded the time it took to drive between locations and entered the numbers into a database. The drivers went on circuitous routes all throughout the warehouse, tracing the time it took to go down different lanes and around different corners, creating a rich map of how long it took to drive just about anywhere in the facility.

These tests were part of a broader effort to digitize operations at the warehouse. Back when Steve Hammond had started, the lift drivers gathered their orders on paper sheets and found the different locations in the warehouse in a directory that looked something like a phone book. Some of the inventory was simply recorded in the memory of a supervisor who happened to remember which brand of grocery bags was stowed in which stack. Then, during the 1980s, the company built its own digital catalog of the inventory, which could be recorded and managed from a computer. It took a lot of trial and error, but eventually the system, called the OIS, helped cut down on the paperwork necessary to track shipments through the warehouse.

Georgia-Pacific wanted to improve upon the OIS, and it did so by hiring an outside data firm called RedPrairie. RedPrairie specialized in supply chain management systems, which had been revolutionized during the software boom of the 1990s. Georgia-Pacific's use of the system was common. Companies across corporate America, from Amazon to Walmart, perfected the art of digital management programs to make their distribution systems as efficient as possible. By 2004, the technology was remarkable. A label with a bar code on it could be affixed to any pallet of products made in a Georgia-Pacific mill, such as the Wauna, Washington paper mill, for example. When the pallet arrived at the warehouse in Portland, that bar code was scanned and its information recorded in a database. The computer in Portland recorded that the pallet was from Wauna, and also which machine inside the Wauna mill made the product and at what time. If there was a defect in the product, Georgia-Pacific could track the mistake back to the machine and the minute at which it occurred.

This was the inventory management aspect of RedPrairie's system, which was called the Warehouse Management System, or WMS. It was a big improvement over the OIS. RedPrairie also created a different suite of software tools that went alongside the inventory management system. This suite didn't help control the inventory; it helped control the workers. This was the Labor Management System, or LMS.

The LMS tracked workers with the same level of detail used to track the pallets. Each worker was assigned what was essentially their own bar code. The LMS system tracked them throughout their workday, their workweek, and eventually their entire career. Every minute was recorded. Every minute was analyzed. Nothing was lost on the LMS.

Koch Industries inherited the LMS when it bought Georgia-Pacific. But Trimm and others said that Koch used the system in new ways that reflected Koch's particular philosophy. "When G-P had [the LMS], we didn't use it that much. We were a little bit more lax," Trimm recalled. "Once Koch had it, the policies got a lot stiffer."

When the LMS went operational, the forklift drivers arrived for work at the warehouse to find that their day-to-day operations were no longer just dictated by foremen and supervisors. They were run, instead, with the help of an algorithm inside a set of black boxes that no one could see. The algorithms never slept, churning around the clock as they subsumed and analyzed enormous volumes of data from every point along Georgia-Pacific's vast supply chain. Everywhere that a bar code was scanned, the information was fed into the LMS. The computers simultaneously analyzed incoming orders from customers that were hundreds of miles away. They tracked the location of every parcel and crate of toilet paper as it rolled off the factory line at the plant in Wauna and as it was loaded onto a barge, shipped downriver, and then hoisted dockside at the warehouse. They tracked every parcel as it was brought into the warehouse and was stacked and then as it was loaded into the back of semitrucks and sent to Target or Costco. The LMS paid attention to all of this activity, everywhere, at once, in a way that no human ever could. And then it synthesized the information near instantaneously and generated the list of tasks that employees would perform once they arrived for work.

The LMS redefined what it meant to be on the clock. An employee was either on the grid or off the grid. If they were on the grid, they were working. If they were off the grid, they were not. When they were off the grid, they essentially ceased to exist in the eyes of the LMS and Georgia-

Pacific, and they were off the clock. Over time, the drivers yearned for the minutes when they were off the grid.

The older guys, in particular, had trouble adapting to the new system for understandable reasons—they had spent twenty years or more working with paper order sheets and verbal commands from humans. The LMS disposed of all of that.

But even younger employees, who didn't know a workplace without the LMS, found themselves ground down under the daily pressure. One of these young employees was named Travis McKinney, and his career working under the LMS illuminated just how much things had changed since Steve Hammond started working at the warehouse.

McKinney was hired in 2004, shortly before the LMS went live. He seemed like someone who might quickly adapt to life under the LMS—he was a computer nerd with a blog and an affinity for technology. McKinney earned the nickname Magneto when the other guys realized that he was a comic book fanatic who often traveled to sci-fi conventions. Someone found a picture of him online, dressed in full costume as the *X-Men* villain Magneto. His nickname was assigned to him instantly and permanently. McKinney didn't seem quite at home with some of his tattooed, hard-drinking coworkers. But his affable nature and outgoing manner helped him fit in. Magneto was a hard guy not to like.

McKinney had every reason to be grateful that he had a job at the warehouse. Some of the older guys, like Steve Hammond, fell into the job. McKinney had to fight very hard just to get in the door. Full-time jobs with good benefits were hard to find in 2004. When Georgia-Pacific posted the warehouse job, McKinney visited an office to submit his application. When he arrived, there were dozens of other people already lined up for the job. He heard that more than two hundred people applied for the position.

People were clamoring to be a forklift driver because job security at most companies had all but disappeared over the previous thirty years. Up until the 1990s, American workers lost jobs in a "cyclical" way, meaning that they got laid off when the economy went into a down cycle but got rehired when demand returned and the company needed them again. During the 2000s, job loss became "structural," meaning that companies cut jobs permanently in a strategic effort to cut costs. As unions fell away, so did contracts that limited job cuts. As recently as the 1990s, 69 percent of US companies had "no layoff" rules that would cushion workers from volatility and ensure that more jobs were retained through the down cycle of a recession, but that security had been quietly traded away. By the mid-2000s, only 3 percent of companies had such rules.

Companies cut jobs even as the economy grew and profits rose. In 2004, about 13 percent of workers were forced out of a job. This was roughly the same percentage that was fired or laid off during the recession of 1981, which had been the worst downturn since the Great Depression. In this regard, American workers faced a level of insecurity that was akin to being in a state of permanent, deep recession. The workers hurt most by this volatility were those with only a high school education or less; the kinds of employees that once filled the ranks of the unionized workforce.

McKinney knew that demand was fierce for the Georgia-Pacific warehouse jobs, but he was surprised at just how rigorous the hiring process was. He took several hours' worth of exams testing his math and reasoning skills. He sat through interviews and filled out lengthy questionnaires. But he was willing to do it, and do it in his cheerful way. After sitting through all the tests, he was hired.

McKinney's workdays at the warehouse were monotonous. When he arrived, McKinney got into the forklift truck he would drive for the shift. Each truck was outfitted with a large digital display screen and keyboard. McKinney logged on to the system, typing in his unique username and password. When his login was complete, McKinney was on the grid.

The LMS dispatched McKinney on his first assignment, telling him where to pick up his first load of cargo. He drove to the assigned spot, then pulled out a bar code scanner and aimed it at a tag near the cargo, pulling the trigger and logging his current location into the LMS. Then, his next prompt appeared on the screen. He was told to drive to bay B-1, for example, where further instructions awaited. He was also informed how long it should take him to drive to bay B-1—a time that was based on the averages determined by those driving tests so long ago. A clock began ticking down immediately as McKinney drove to the rendezvous point. Once there, he pulled out his scanner, pulled the trigger, and logged his arrival. The LMS recorded how long it took him to make the trip. His performance was recorded. In this way, he proceeded from prompt to prompt for hours at a time.

Trimm, their supervisor, monitored the drivers from his office. The LMS showed Trimm a bird's-eye view of all the warehouse activity. He could see how the LMS automatically scheduled drivers to move cargo from the bays to the waiting semitrucks in a never-ending migration of game pieces across a complex board. The drivers were unaware of the larger tapestry and simply performed their piece of it. Trimm was told not to interfere with the LMS assignments. Doing so would interrupt the complicated and interlocking set of assignments that the LMS designed. Humans were encouraged to stay out of it.

But Trimm was encouraged to make sure that drivers weren't failing the LMS's goals. At any point in the day, Trimm could pull up the work log of any driver. The log showed, minute by minute, what each driver had been doing during the day. Trimm was told to look at two important metrics. The first metric was a driver's performance against the time standards.

The second metric Trimm looked for was any gap in time. These were the moments when the driver was not on the grid. Any loss of a few minutes or more was recorded. The drivers were told to keep a written log of their lost minutes, called "indirect time," to account for the moments when they were off the grid. Indirect time might include the time to take a bathroom break, drink water, or stop to ask someone a question. Only a small number of activities could justify taking indirect time off the grid. Chatting with coworkers, for example, was not accepted. When Trimm saw gaps, he questioned drivers and made sure they could provide an explanation for their lost time. If they made an emergency phone call home, or defecated, or stopped to eat, they needed to have it recorded in their indirect log. Employees were reprimanded if they could not explain the purpose of their indirect time.

It was a relief, then, when Travis McKinney scanned into his last location of the day and logged out for the night. It was the first moment of his day when he could enjoy indirect time, direct his own movements, and not have to explain his actions to anyone.

On payday, McKinney and the other warehouse workers sometimes drove a few blocks away from the warehouse to have a beer at a local strip club called the Nicolai Street Clubhouse. To get there, McKinney drove west from the warehouse, across a set of railroad tracks, and past rundown factories and industrial warehouses. The club was located in a one-story redbrick building on a corner. A white sign facing the street advertised "Crazy Beer Specials" and "!DANCERS!!"

These beer-drinking sessions were the closest thing the warehouse workers had to the raucous union hall gatherings that Steve Hammond knew from his youth. Since that time, the union hall had been moved to a new building closer to the warehouses, but almost no one went to the meetings anymore. The meetings were usually only attended by the IBU's small leadership council, who gathered in a small conference room. They talked over pension finances or issues with the health care plan. One or two forklift drivers might show up for the meetings, and they were depressingly sober.

When McKinney arrived at the Nicolai Street Clubhouse, he could easily find his coworkers in the dim and tiny bar. Most of the tables were just inside the front door. The guys sat there and drank cheap beer from plastic pitchers. The patrons stared over toward the small wooden stage, right next to an open door that led into the kitchen. The stage was horseshoe-shaped and surrounded by a row of cheap, metal-framed seats. When it came time for their shift, the women mounted the stage by way of a small staircase and danced beneath a fluorescent-tube sign advertising Playboy Energy Drink. A cheap plastic fan mounted on the wall behind them cooled the stage. The narrow wooden ledge around the stage was known as "the rack," and the men gathered in the seats around it, looking up at the stage and placing their newly earned dollars along the ledge. At a certain point in the routine, the nude women approached the men and swept up the dollar bills in their hands before leaning forward and performing acts of astounding physical intimacy and athleticism.

Some guys sat in the back of the bar, at a row of video lottery machines, slouched there amid the beeping and buzzing. McKinney said it was something of a sport to "watch the guys gamble away their paychecks" in front of the video screens. The forklift drivers could swap stories and complaints and gripe about the LMS over their beers. They could talk about their weekend plans and fishing trips and their kids. They shared a kinship that closely approximated solidarity.

But even this pale form of solidarity began to fade. Over time, fewer people stopped by the Nicolai after work. They were fried after working under the Labor Management System. But there was more than fatigue to blame. The LMS wasn't just tiring them out. It was turning them against each other.

The LMS accrued huge volumes of data on each employee. Koch Industries used this data to further motivate its workers to become more productive. Warehouse managers collated the log reports and printed sheets that ranked all the warehouse workers on their performances. The sheets were divided into three colored subcategories: the green zone, the yellow zone, and the red zone.

Employees in the green zone performed at or above the 100 rating, meaning they matched or beat the LMS's average recorded times for their driving. Those in the yellow zone typically scored an 80 rating. They didn't match the LMS goals, but they were B students. Those in the red zone received ratings of 70 or 60, lagging far behind the LMS benchmarks.

Employees who ranked in the red zone were reprimanded after the results were tallied. They were also exposed to their peers. Koch printed the LMS rankings and posted them on a bulletin board in a public area of the warehouse, where the drivers could see it when they arrived for work. Predictably, the green players had a little extra spring in their step. The red players slouched. The greens and yellows made sport of teasing the reds—jokes were made about poor eyesight and physical impairments.

With each new posting, the drivers shifted spots within the race. They paid close attention to their rankings, because the losers were culled from the herd. Drivers who lagged too long in the yellow and red zones could be reprimanded, then "put on notice." Then they could be put on "last chance" status, with a final warning to improve. Then they could be terminated.

This system seemed harsh to the old-timers at the warehouse, but they might have understood the ranking system better if they'd read Charles Koch's book, *The Science of Success*. Right there, on page 89, Charles Koch explains the ABC process of employee retention at Koch Industries. The A performers are a company's competitive advantage, he explained, while the B performers are the necessary workers who keep the enterprise running. The C performers, on the other hand, do not meet expectations, and can drag the business enterprise down with them. "Focused strategies should be put in place for C-level employees to improve performance through training, development, mentoring, or role change," Charles Koch wrote. "Employees who do not quickly respond to these efforts and continue to perform at a C level should not be retained."

Life at the warehouse, then, became a scramble to stay out of the bottom third of the LMS rankings. The most prominent victim of the ABC process was the forklift driver Kerry Alt, the driver who'd lost his oversized beer bottle many years before when it fell out of his truck. Alt seemed to be incurably slow. It wasn't that he was lazy. It was that he was pathologically deliberate. Alt looked at the LMS screen, looked up the bay where he had been directed, and then looked back down at the LMS screen to double-check that he was in the right place. Then he picked up the cargo, double-checked where he was supposed to take it, and drove in a deliberate manner to the appointed spot.

Alt lived in the red zone, ranking after ranking. Everybody saw it. Trimm had known Alt for years and felt a friend's pity toward his situation. Trimm tried to find jobs that would keep Alt out of the center of the action, or keep him off the grid altogether. But there just weren't that many tasks available. Koch didn't need someone to sweep the floors. It needed its employees to be on the grid, moving product. Alt was kept in the game and never seemed to break into the yellow or green zones.

This was a hellishly stressful time for Alt. He complained to his bosses that he was just trying be safe and deliberate. He pointed out that Koch valued safety, and he was trying to be safe rather than drive in a hurry. But his coworkers managed to drive faster without having accidents, and the LMS rankings publicly rebuked Alt's argument.

"They forced him out," Trimm said. "Everybody knew that Kerry was a hard worker. Or tried to be hard. He just couldn't do it. I felt sorry for him."

Kerry Alt and his wife bore hard feelings toward Koch Industries after he left the warehouse. But he could have taken solace from page 90 of *The Science of Success*, in which Charles Koch explains that C players at one company need not be C players elsewhere.

"Inability to create value at one company does not mean the same will be true elsewhere. Employees may be much more successful in another organization that has needs or a culture better suited to their talents and values," Koch wrote.

After he was forced out from his warehouse job, Alt had a hard time finding an enterprise where his talents were valued. He had worked at the warehouse for more than twenty years and made the mistake of attaching his identity to his job. When he lost it, he didn't quite know where to pick up.

"He kind of went into a depression and started drinking more," recalled Alt's wife, Shirley. He eventually applied for disability insurance from Social Security and collected his union pension. The couple sold their house and moved to a cheaper neighborhood. Shirley picked up work as a housecleaner to help pay the bills. Years later, Alt had difficulty speaking and could not recall much of the ordeal at Georgia-Pacific. "I was getting sick of it," Alt recalled. "I felt pretty bad. I programmed it out of my mind."

The drivers weren't the only employees who were ranked. Every month, Trimm and his fellow supervisors received a report card. It quantified the performance of the three warehouses in Portland, and compared their performance against every other Georgia-Pacific warehouse in the country.

Trimm's operation was ranked according to a few key metrics, including the number of safety accidents (which he said were few) and the proportion of cargo that was damaged during shipment. The most important metric, however, was called "cost-per-case," meaning the cost that Koch had to pay to move each case of material through the warehouse. The lower the cost, the thicker Koch's profit margins. Cost-per-case became a constant focus of conversation when supervisors met with the drivers. It was the metric that everything was pushing toward: fewer people moving more product ever more efficiently.

The Portland warehouses did well on their report cards, but their competition was fierce. The managers and drivers were reminded constantly that the three warehouses in Portland were the only three warehouses that Georgia-Pacific owned outright. The other distribution centers were run by third-party contractors, and Georgia-Pacific had enough clout to push these contractors to keep their prices low. Most of the contract warehouses used nonunion labor, Trimm understood, and some of them were located in rural areas where labor was cheaper. Trimm was fighting an uphill battle to keep his operation in the A or B class, and, for many years, he was successful. But he always knew that if he slipped, he would be replaced. If the warehouse as a whole fell behind, it also might be replaced by an outside contractor.

The other pressures on Trimm had to do with safety compliance. It was drilled into his mind, day in and day out, that Koch subscribed to the 10,000 percent compliance rule. In the eyes of Trimm and his fellow supervisors, this didn't just mean being safe; it meant being safe in exactly the way that Koch prescribed. If a manager or driver didn't follow each rule to the letter, they could be disciplined. Managers were taught to be ever vigilant about any safety violations and to report them immediately.

It was exhausting, and at times the exhaustion seemed to be created by design. The drivers were pitted against one another in the rankings. The supervisors were pitted against every other facility in the country. And all the while, more product was moved through the warehouses at a cheaper rate. All of these forces pushed toward a place that would do more work, with fewer people, for less money. "I even said to a couple of guys I worked with, I said: 'Man, this is just an exercise in getting rid of people,'" Trimm said.

The warehouse could not get rid of Travis McKinney. He stuck to the job. He was often forced to work overtime, arriving before dawn on the weekend mornings, logging into the LMS, watching his screen populate with commands, running the circuits as quickly as he could to beat the time expectations. McKinney did this because he knew exactly what waited outside the warehouse doors if he lost his job.

McKinney and his wife both worked long hours to meet their mortgage payment—modest as it was by Portland standards—to pay their health care bills, and to keep the refrigerator stocked. But life never stood still, of course. At one point, McKinney's wife was demoted at the grocery store, which cut her pay dramatically. The couple also had their first child, a little girl, who was diagnosed with autism. They paid large medical bills. McKinney had to buy gas for his long commutes. Property taxes increased.

Like most middle-class Americans, they often turned to credit cards to cover the gap between their monthly expenses and their income. It was remarkable how quickly small purchases added up on a credit card statement. The McKinneys carried credit card balances of $15,000, even $20,000, whittling away each month at the interest payments. In this regard, they were not unusual. The average credit card debt for indebted American households climbed steadily through the 2000s, rising from $14,185 in 2002 to $16,911 in 2008. The average interest rate on this debt was nearly 19 percent, meaning that households spent about $1,300 just to keep up with interest payments each year.

McKinney knew that his unionized job was a rare treasure in this economic landscape, with its health care benefits and a pension. So he reported to the warehouse each day, he worked the overtime when they told him to, and he endured the maze race of the LMS. The other drivers did the same.

Steve Hammond often felt sick when he arrived for work. He had watched the life drain out of the warehouse floor since Koch Industries took over. The work had never been great—no one dreamed of growing up to drive a forklift. But the work used to be tolerable. The camaraderie, the pranks, the sense of belonging that was conferred by membership in the IBU, all these things together made it possible to come to the warehouse every day. And now all those things had been eliminated. The drivers were robots, focused with laser-like intent on the task of pushing down the cost-per-crate and hitting the 110 rating in the LMS system to remain safely in the green zone. People didn't talk to each other anymore. From the moment Hammond arrived at work, he looked forward to going back home.

In 2008, Hammond decided to do something about it. He announced that he would run for election to become a full-time employee of the Inlandboatmen's Union. He would take up the cause of his coworkers, and he would fight to remake the job into something like it had been before.

Hammond had very good reason to believe that he could change things as an IBU labor negotiator. During the 1990s, the IBU had folded itself into a very large and very militant union called the International

Longshore and Warehouse Union, or the ILWU. Everyone knew the ILWU simply as the "Longshoremen," and they were arguably the strongest union left in the United States. The IBU office was now located in the Longshoremen's union near the Georgia-Pacific warehouse. Outside the union hall, a stone obelisk was etched with the Longshoremen's insignia: a fist enclosed around a cargo hook that looked like a medieval weapon. And above the hook, etched in stone, was the Longshoremen motto: "An Injury to One Is an Injury to All."

Hammond ran for election to become the IBU's "patrolman," meaning second in command to the union's regional director. To his shock, Hammond won the election narrowly. It would be up to him, now, to take on Koch Industries and turn back some of the changes that had been so punishing to the warehouse workers. "I think people just hated themselves for working there," Hammond said. "I felt like . . . I was gonna try and help. I just kind of wanted to see if there was something I could do, to where people didn't feel sick coming to work all the time."

While Steve Hammond prepared to do battle with Koch in late 2008, the battlefield around him changed. A convulsion tore across the economic landscape and shattered the structures that had stood there before. Everything would be different in its wake. It was the worst downturn to hit the economy, and Koch Industries, since the Great Depression. And there was every indication that Charles Koch was not ready for it.

CHAPTER 17

The Crash

(2008–2010)

During the summer of 2008, David H. Koch was in a charitable mood. He had good reason to feel optimistic and generous. David and Charles Koch split their shares of Koch Industries down the middle, with each brother owning a little more than 40 percent of the company. During the preceding decade, their fortune had swelled. In 2002, David's half of the family fortune was worth roughly $4 billion. By 2008, it was worth roughly $19 billion. The size of this sum was difficult to comprehend. If a person earned $300 an hour and worked full-time, with no vacation, he or she would need to work 30,449 years to earn $19 billion. David Koch had come by the amount in one short lifetime.

And unlike his brother Charles, who stayed back home in Wichita and worked long hours in the Koch Tower, David Koch was inclined to enjoy his fortune. He moved to New York City and became a luminary in the rarified social scene of the very wealthy and the very famous. He attended the opera and gallery openings. He supported the ballet and lived in one of the most expensive apartments in the city. When he sold one apartment and bought another, it made the newspapers. In a city that was home to almost incalculable wealth, David Koch was likely its richest resident. And he was inclined to share his good fortune.

In October of 2007, David Koch gave $100 million to the Massachusetts Institute of Technology, his alma mater and that of his brothers and father. The money founded a cancer research center, a cause that was dear to David Koch's heart after his own successful struggle with prostate cancer. David Koch gave $20 million to the American Museum of Natural History for a new wing to display dinosaur bones. He gave $20 million to the Johns Hopkins School of Medicine, in Baltimore, also to study cancer.

Then, in July, David Koch made a donation that grabbed national attention. He gave $100 million to the New York State Theater, a grandiose building in Manhattan that was a social hub of the city's high society. The theater hosted some of the prime events of elite social calendars, nights when David Koch and his wife, Julia, joined the other prominent couples, attired in tuxedos and gowns, to laugh and share small talk in the lobby before they were seated to enjoy the New York City Ballet or the New York City Opera at Lincoln Center. Now, the theater would be called the David H. Koch Theater.

David Koch had plenty of latitude to make such charitable gifts. The *New York Times* reported that the gift to the State Theater amounted to roughly one-half of 1 percent of David Koch's wealth, but even this overstated the size of the donation. The gift would be made over a period of ten years, which meant that it really represented a small fraction of the money that David Koch earned from the interest on his fortune—something akin to a microtithe. He could make such gifts without concern that it would substantially diminish his wealth.

During the summer of 2008, there was good reason to believe that David Koch's wealth was poised to grow even more. In the preceding eight years, Koch Industries had transformed from a midsized natural resources company into a diversified industrial conglomerate and private equity house. Charles Koch had believed during the 1990s that his company could become a giant. During the 2000s, he proved that he was correct. It is true that the foundation of Koch Industries' profits still rested on the fossil fuel business. The refinery in Pine Bend remained a reliable fountain of cash that kept the rest of the system flush with money to invest. The fuel pipelines and the Corpus Christi refinery also contributed a steady stream of profits. But Koch also owned Georgia-Pacific, Invista, and one of the largest and most profitable nitrogen fertilizer companies in the United States. Its trading desks in Houston, New York, and London rivaled those of any investment bank. Koch's growth was not slow and steady—it was seismic, with periods of steady advancement that were punctuated by great lurches forward. Charles Koch had claimed to crack the code of creating prosperity, and the wealth machine he built now seemed unstoppable.

David Koch gave interviews to the media, and he was effusive and benevolent in his remarks. It seemed that he was ready to give even more. He told the *Times* how he was inspired by one of his neighbors, the billionaire private equity titan Stephen Schwarzman, who had recently given a gift of $100 million to the New York Public Library. "I admire people like that immensely, who have great wealth but are generous in terms of supporting worthy causes," Koch said.

This era of goodwill, this summer of giving and plenty, turned out to be the high point of American economic life. This was the crest of the wave after a decade of growth. Nobody knew this at the time, but the wave was about to crash. There were signals of trouble even in July of 2008. Oil prices were high, the housing market was slowing down, and a big investment bank had just failed. But only in retrospect would people realize just how good things were at that time. Things would not be that good again in America for at least another decade.

The first signs of trouble were detected by traders in Houston, on Koch's trading floor. It was difficult, however, to piece together the bigger picture from these early signals. First came the unmistakable signs of weakness in the housing market. Orders started to slow at Georgia-Pacific, which churned out plywood, insulation, and gypsum building panels that were installed in new homes and buildings around the country. Even as early as 2006, the market was slowing. By 2008, it seemed as if new home construction was grinding to a halt. Gasoline prices were rising too high, too quickly, and the market was growing white-hot as speculators pushed up prices because of demand from China and other developing nations. In 2007, crude oil was trading for less than $60 a barrel; by July of 2008, it was trading for a record $145 per barrel. The extraordinarily high prices forced consumers to ration their use, pushing down demand and cutting into Koch Industries' sales of gasoline. As consumers cut back their spending, it hurt retailers and restaurants.

More lights started flashing red on the trading screens during the late summer weeks. By then, many people were predicting a recession. But very few predicted the true extent of what was about to happen.

Cris Franklin, the young trader in Houston, watched it unfold. By 2008, he was working on a trading desk called the FXIR, or Foreign Exchange and Interest Rates. As such, he spent his days in the vortex of international finance and had a front-row seat as those markets seized up. While Franklin did not work with Koch's large stock-purchasing desk—the entity that bought and sold millions of shares of stock in companies around the country—he was later able to review data from that operation. It was almost sad, in retrospect, to see what unfolded in those numbers.

"There were warning signs, in hindsight," Franklin recalled. "Afterwards, being able to look at the price action of their trading strategy . . . that's a clear sign that the market was unwinding its risk over a period of time before the crash took place."

The risk, as it turned out, was everywhere.

The risk extended all the way into the foundation of the economic system—the households occupied by working people like Steve Hammond and Travis McKinney at the Georgia-Pacific warehouse in Portland. These households had not seen a significant pay increase for many years, but they continued to increase their standard of living in line with what they expected it should be. The gap between what they earned and what they spent was met with debt. The amount of US household debt exploded between 2000 and 2008. At the beginning of the decade, the total household debt was equal to about 100 percent of the entire nation's annual gross domestic product, meaning the value of everything created in the economy that year. By 2008, household debt was about 140 percent of the GDP. It was difficult to find any comparable debt increase in the nation's history.

Most of this debt was carried in the form of home mortgages. The mortgage had once been the cornerstone of a household's wealth. Home prices were once thought to obey a simple law, rising incrementally and permanently. But during the 2000s, home prices pulled away from the course of incremental growth and ballooned. This was driven, in large part, by the Federal Reserve, which kept interest rates at a historically low level for a historically long period of time. The cheap interest rates made it much easier to borrow money for a home, and a whole industry sprung up to feed the new demand. Companies like Countrywide Financial sent agents out into every corner of the country to find any customer who might be willing to sign mortgage papers. The loans became exotic and loosely governed. People signed on the line without thinking through what the complex financing terms might mean down the road. This was the era of teaser rates and balloon payments and interest-only adjustable-rate mortgages. The deluge of cheap money and easy loans inflated a circus tent above the once-sleepy real estate industry and turned everybody into a speculator.

This alone might not have destroyed the economy. But it was coupled with the shift of financial trading into the black box of a shadow banking system. When people borrowed mortgages, for example, those loans were instantly sold off to a financial trader somewhere, rather than being left to sit on the balance sheet of a bank. Then the loans were packaged into complicated debt structures, such as collateralized debt obligations, or CDOs, that were bought and sold. The CDOs, in turn, became a fertile resource to make yet more money as traders bought and sold a type of insurance on CDOs called a credit default swap. All of these financial instruments were essentially just varied forms of the derivatives contracts that Brenden O'Neill learned how to trade when he joined Koch Energy Trading in Houston. O'Neill made millions buying calls and puts, but in the world of shadow banking, his trades were considered conservative. Across the globe, countless options contracts and derivatives agreements were traded, based on the underlying value of home mortgages, consumer credit card debt, and even the debt of corporations like General Electric.

All of these derivatives bets were opaque. They were often made during a phone call between two people, and the nature and size of the derivatives bet were recorded in secret, only by the two parties. This did not happen by accident. The derivatives market was built in very much the same way that Steve Peace helped build California's electricity trading market back in the 1990s. It was built by overworked legislators, working in bland hearing rooms, writing complex legislation that was bird-dogged at every step by well-paid lobbyists.

In the late 1990s, a Clinton administration regulator named Brooksley Born, who was head of the Commodities Futures and Trading Commission, argued that derivatives should be regulated by the CFTC and traded on transparent exchanges. She was effectively shouted down by Clinton's Treasury secretary, Robert Rubin, who was a former trader with Goldman Sachs, along with Rubin's deputy Larry Summers and Fed chairman Alan Greenspan. Born was painted as an unsophisticated Washington insider who didn't quite understand the benefits of modern finance, in much the same way that early critics of California's power trading system were criticized for not understanding the benefits of allowing Enron and Koch to trade electricity by the megawatt-hour.

The financiers and their advocates won out in both cases. The Clinton administration ensured that the derivatives market would remain dark, outside the view of regulators and exchanges, when it passed the Commodity Futures Modernization Act of 2000, which exempted derivatives from CFTC oversight. The functioning of the derivatives market was left to the best judgment of whoever made the bets. The black box financial system swelled during the 2000s. In 1992, there was roughly $11 trillion worth of derivatives contracts, according to the estimate of one industry trade group. By 2001, there was $69 trillion worth of derivatives. By 2007, there was $445 trillion.

In late 2008, nobody knew what liabilities had been accrued by anybody else. People were making derivatives bets over the phone and being left to guess what other bets their counterparty might also be making. A derivatives bet removed a certain kind of risk called price risk—it gave you a kind of insurance against wild price swings in the market. But it introduced a deeper kind of risk that people overlooked, called counterparty risk, meaning the risk that whoever took your derivatives bet might go broke before they could pay their obligation.

This is what led to the panic. Counterparty risk became an unquantifiable and lethal force that detonated randomly across the globe. The most spectacular detonation happened inside the opaque trading structure of the Wall Street firm Lehman Brothers. That company had amassed enormous holdings in CDOs and other mortgage debt. But that wasn't even the worst of it.

Lehman was using the CDOs and other mortgage products as collateral to borrow huge amounts of money. This debt was in the form of overnight loans, called repurchasing agreements, or repo loans. Wall Street firms like Lehman counted on repo loans to stay in business; they used the borrowed money to keep the lights on. Companies felt comfortable making these overnight loans because there was collateral to back it up. But panic set in when people realized the collateral might be worthless. The overnight loan market froze up, and Wall Street investment banks didn't have money to stay open.

Lehman Brothers declared bankruptcy on September 15, 2008. And then the true panic began. The overnight repo loan market froze. The value of CDOs plummeted, which triggered billions in credit default swap payments that companies didn't have the cash to meet.

The losses on Cris Franklin's trading desk were enormous. But they weren't the kind of losses that might drag Koch Industries down with Lehman Brothers. Charles Koch had built a large trading operation, but he had built it according to his conservative philosophy. A framework of strict limits was placed on the size of bets that traders were allowed to make. Cris Franklin and other traders frequently met with risk control officers, who made the traders walk through the nature of their positions, analyzing how deeply things could go bad in the worst-case scenarios. The traders were only allowed to bet up to a threshold called the "value at risk" limit, or VAR. The traders knew their VAR, and they knew that there was no surpassing it. It was a red line that could not be crossed. The VARs limited Koch's upside when the market was rising, but now they protected the firm during the crash. Koch had built moats around the trading desks, and now those moats protected it from a wildfire.

But even with the VARs in place, Franklin's team lost money. There was no way to unwind the trades quickly enough to avoid losses. In a short period of time, Franklin's team had hit their "drawdown limit," meaning that they had lost all the money they were authorized to lose. Franklin was informed that Charles Koch would personally decide whether to shut the team down or to authorize it to keep trading. To keep the trading team intact, Koch Industries needed to invest more money. Before he put the money down, Charles Koch wanted to talk to the team members in person. Franklin was told that the team would be going to Wichita.

Franklin and his coworkers worked feverishly to prepare their presentation for Charles Koch. They flew to Wichita and were escorted into the black Tower. The mood inside was somber. It was remarkable how quickly things were moving during late September of 2008. Several years of economic growth were unraveling in a matter of days. Hundreds of thousands of jobs were disappearing. Hundreds of billions of dollars in wealth were being immolated. Days after Lehman Brothers collapsed, the last two investment banks on Wall Street disappeared when Goldman Sachs and Morgan Stanley were transformed into bank holding companies.

Franklin's entourage was led to the boardroom. They took their seats around the big wood table in the windowless chamber. Charles Koch sat at the head of the table and invited the trading team to explain why it should continue to exist. Franklin didn't expect to do much talking, but shortly into the meeting, Charles Koch started directing questions down the table toward him. Franklin is soft-spoken and straightforward in his manner. He was tense during the meeting, but tried his best to answer each question thoroughly and succinctly. He was shocked that Charles Koch was speaking to him at all—the CEO billionaire seemed like he might have bigger things to worry about. Franklin had only met him a few times, once before during a meeting in Wichita under much happier circumstances. Franklin didn't think he had spoken one word during that first meeting, and so he was shocked afterward when he ran into Charles Koch, who looked at him and quickly said: "Hi, Cris!" Franklin hadn't remembered even telling Koch his name.

Now Charles Koch was boring into him with question after question, and Franklin realized that the CEO wasn't just necessarily concerned about the market forces at play behind Franklin's losses. Charles Koch was trying to determine Franklin's character. He seemed interested in making sure, above all, that he could trust Franklin to carry on trading. Were Franklin's losses the result of hubris or short-term greed? Was Franklin trying to dodge responsibility or shade the truth? Franklin explained his reasoning behind the trades he made, his understanding of interest rates and currency markets, and why he believed that Koch should stay in the business of trading there.

The one thing that Franklin did not observe in Charles Koch was panic. There was nothing desperate in the way Charles Koch was questioning the team from Houston. He was questioning what Koch's future trading strategies should be, and didn't seem flustered by the amount of money they'd already lost. At one moment, Charles Koch simply went silent. "I do remember Charles Koch at one point, at the end of the meeting, kind of just sitting there and thinking . . . you know, processing if he was going to allow us to go on," Franklin recalled. "He was essentially weighing what was he willing to invest, based on his confidence."

During the weeks of the crisis, others who worked with Charles Koch saw him behave in the same way. He seemed calm and analytical. He wasn't shaken, as he had been after the collapse of Purina Mills. He wasn't despondent, as he was back in the early 1970s, when he worried that the OPEC embargo might sink his company. He was steady now, during the greatest economic crisis since the Great Depression. Charles Koch seemed to view the unfolding calamity as if it were a massive trade. He was weighing what he was willing to invest, weighing what he needed to cut.

A senior employee named Jeremy Jones came into frequent contact with Charles Koch during this period. Jones was an engineer and financier from Boston who was running a venture capital group inside Koch Industries, called Koch Genesis. The small venture was the kind of thing that was near and dear to Charles Koch's heart. Jones and his team found new technologies for Koch Industries to invest in, such as biofuels and nanomaterials, that could provide the company with years of growth. Now that the horizon was on fire, it was time to retrench rather than expand. Charles Koch seemed to make that shift effortlessly.

"He goes back to his core thinking of: What's our point of view around what's going to happen? How long is this downturn going to take? How is that going to affect people's buying patterns?" Jones recalled. "And how long is it going to take—given this housing crisis—to get through this deleveraging?"

If Charles Koch was more confident in his company's future, he had reason to be. The company he oversaw in 2008 was larger, more diverse, and more adaptable than it had ever been before. It was built to withstand market shocks. Some divisions were hit hard, such as Koch's building products divisions and its carpet fiber factories. But other divisions fared much better, such as its oil refineries and trading desks. The financial pain was very real, but there never seemed to be any doubt that Koch Industries would come out the other side as a healthy and profitable enterprise.

The company's survival, of course, did not ensure the survival of any given job at Koch Industries. The employees in Wichita felt this fact in their bones. Dread permeated the hallways at Koch Industries, and in offices across the country, fed by the knowledge that every job was now considered expendable. It was not a happy occasion, then, when employees were told that there would be a companywide meeting held in a large auditorium in Koch headquarters just before Christmas.

Such annual meetings were usually a time to celebrate the upcoming holidays and reflect on the good fortune of the year that had passed.

They were a time for Charles Koch to wear a goofy Christmas sweater or perform a skit involving Georgia-Pacific products. This year, as Jeremy Jones and his coworkers filed into the auditorium, they knew that they might be hearing the worst.

Charles Koch took the stage, and his mood was somber. As he stood in front of the crowd, he described the severity of the economic downturn. He didn't try to varnish the ugly truth or avoid stating directly what many of them knew was coming. Charles Koch walked through each division of the company and explained the damage that was being done. There was less demand for construction materials at Georgia-Pacific. There was less demand for carpeting and clothing at Invista. There was less demand for fertilizer, less demand for gasoline from the refineries. Not everyone at the company would come back from the holidays to a job.

"He was standing up there in front of probably two thousand people, saying, 'Look, we're obviously going to get through this. But I'm going to be very honest with you folks. We're going to have to make some very serious adjustments to get through it," Jones recalled.

One of the adjustments hit Jones. His venture fund, Koch Genesis, was shut down. Other adjustments had already begun to ripple quickly through Koch's operations across the country. In early October, Koch closed a Georgia-Pacific plywood mill in Whiteville, North Carolina, eliminating 400 jobs. Two weeks later, Koch cut 400 jobs at an Invista plant in Seaford, Delaware. Then 395 jobs were cut with the closure of a petrochemical plant in Odessa, Texas. Three hundred more jobs were cut at a Georgia-Pacific plant in Alabama. In early December, 575 jobs were cut at Invista in Virginia. Another 70 Georgia-Pacific jobs were cut in New York. In January of 2009, 150 jobs were cut at Koch Industries headquarters in Wichita. Within a few months of Lehman Brothers' bankruptcy, Koch cut at least 2,000 jobs.

The bloodletting at Koch, while rapid and unprecedented in size, was mild compared with what happened in the rest of the economy. In September of 2008, US employers cut 159,000 jobs, the worst monthly purge in five years. But even those cuts were shallow and didn't reflect the depth of the downturn. In October, 240,000 jobs were cut. Then 524,000 in December. Then 598,000 the next month. Then 651,000. Then 663,000.

Many of the jobs lost in 2008 never came back. Between 1948 and 2007, only about 13 percent of people who lost their jobs could not find a new job within six months. By 2010, that number would soar to 45 percent. Unemployment became a way of life rather than a temporary setback. The desperation that these workers felt would transform the next decade of American political life.

But the desperation was not felt evenly. Things looked very different from Charles Koch's office. The downturn was painful—David Koch estimated publicly that Koch Industries' profit in 2009 was half of what it was the previous year. But even in light of these diminished profits, the downturn presented opportunity for Koch Industries. After forty years of living and working in the volatile world of commodities markets, Charles Koch had finally built a machine that was poised to thrive, even profit, in the midst of violent market corrections. This capability derived, in part, from something that Charles Koch called "the trading mentality." This mentality held that it didn't matter so much if markets were going up or down; what mattered was that the traders could see ways to exploit large shifts in the markets. During volatile times, companies and governments and competing traders were thrown off balance. Prices diverged. Supplies were interrupted. Gaps emerged between market prices and underlying values. Koch became nimble, even expert, at exploiting those gaps for its gain.

"When the market is constant, traders don't make money," explained Melissa Beckett, the star trader who'd once traded electricity futures. "Traders make money on change."

Because of its trading mentality and capabilities, Koch Industries could seize opportunities during the crash that were unattainable to most companies, and certainly to most households. This opportunity was most evident in the oil markets, where Koch's traders spotted a trading opportunity that would be worth millions of dollars in pure profit.

They seized it.

For the first time since World War II, the economies of Japan, Europe, and the United States entered into a recession simultaneously. The impact on global oil markets was immediate and catastrophic. Oil fell from nearly $145 a barrel to roughly $35 a barrel in a matter of months. The reason was oversupply. When prices were high, oil companies ran at full throttle to produce as much crude as possible. When demand collapsed, all that oil was stranded, with no one to buy it. This oversupply created an obscure follow-on effect that was only visible to people like Koch's oil traders in Houston. The markets entered a rare period that the traders called "contango." Koch looked for gaps in the market, and this was one of the biggest in years.

It's difficult for outsiders to even understand the nature of a contango market. In essence, the price of oil in spot markets, which reflect the price of oil today, tends to be lower than the price of oil to be delivered in the future. This is attributable to a host of complex reasons.* In the relatively rare scenario when oil today is cheaper than oil in the future, the markets are said to be in contango, and it doesn't tend to last very long. Usually the market reverts to its normal state of cheaper oil in the future.

When the market goes into contango, it presents a whole host of ways for Koch's traders to profit. In late 2008, the potential profits were extraordinary. The size of the contango became enormous—the gap between oil sold today and oil sold for delivery a few months out became roughly $8 a barrel. A more common level of contango would be in the range of $2 or $4 a barrel. And the gap wasn't just wide, it was long-lasting. The markets remained in contango for several months.

Koch Industries, and a handful of other giant oil producers, were able to exploit this gap in a special way. Because Koch Industries traded in both the futures markets and the physical markets, it could execute something called the "contango storage play." One former senior trader within Koch Supply & Trading called the contango storage play a "bread-and-butter" strategy for Koch's crude oil department.

The mechanics of the contango storage play seem deceptively simple. A trader at Koch Industries buys oil in the spot markets, where it is cheap. Then, the trader sells oil for delivery in the futures markets, where oil is more expensive. When the contango gap is $8, it is easy to picture how quickly the profits pile up. The trader can buy oil for $35 and sell it for $43, almost instantly.

---

* One reason for this is that people selling oil in the futures markets are willing to take a somewhat lower price, just to lock in the sale. And people buying oil today are willing to pay a higher price because oil tends to be scarce. When oil prices in the future are lower, the market is in "backwardation," as the traders call it.

There is a catch, however. To execute the contango storage play, the trader must be able to do something that most traders can't do—they must be able to deliver the actual, physical oil in that future month. If a typical oil speculator—who did not own an oil refinery, storage tanks, or an oil tanker ship—tried to execute the contango storage trade, they could find themselves shut out. Executing the contango storage trade didn't just require deep knowledge of arcane shipping markets and transportation law; it also required deep relationships in the private world of oil production. "You have to have a lot of support systems to take advantage of it," Beckett said. Koch had that support system. Koch could deliver the oil.

Outsiders who tried to get in on the trade during 2009 were denied. A commodities trader in St. Louis, named S. A. Johnson, complained to the *Kansas City Star* that he couldn't execute a contango storage play. Johnson said the math behind the trade was blindingly obvious. But making the trade required signing deals with supertanker companies, large oil producers, and even pipeline owners. Johnson could not get these parties to return his calls. "They don't want me to play," he said.

During the early months of 2009, Koch's traders piled into the contango storage play. Koch bought the cheap oil and sold the more expensive futures. It stored the oil for future delivery in tanks that Koch already leased. The trade was so profitable that Koch began to lease supertankers filled with oil, using them as temporary, floating storage units. The tankers floated in the Gulf of Mexico, waiting for their moment to deliver, allowing Koch to increase its trade without fear of a squeeze. The handful of other companies that could execute this trade, such as BP and ConocoPhillips, also leased supertankers and kept them floating on the sea, waiting to deliver their cargo. BP told its investors that the contango storage play earned the company roughly $500 million in the first quarter of 2009 alone.

As news of this trading tactic became public in mid-2009, it prompted allegations that Koch and other traders were manipulating oil markets by keeping supplies off the market and raising prices at the pump. This was true, but only to an extent. It was the global recession that caused demand to disappear, which in turn caused near-term oil prices to collapse. Without that oil glut, the contango storage trade would have been impossible. Traders in Koch's oil department saw themselves as reacting to market conditions, not manipulating them. By holding oil for later delivery, Koch Industries was helping correct a gap in the market, even if it was profiting by doing so.

"The market's really wanting you to do it," Beckett said. "The market is oversupplied in the front, today, which is why the price is low. So, they're wanting some supply to disappear. The market is communicating there is too much of something." Koch was listening to the market, buying up oil today and holding off delivery of oil until tomorrow when demand was higher.

The contango storage trade helped Koch cover its losses through the darkest period of 2009, as the firm cut jobs and idled its factories.

During the winter of 2008, even David Koch was forced to adjust his behavior and his outlook. He was getting more requests for big donations after his previous gifts had been publicized. But David Koch didn't think this was the time to make new donations. There were other concerns that weighed on his and Charles's minds. Koch Industries would weather the economic downturn. But another crash was taking place that could be far more dangerous. It was the crash of American conservatism and Koch's political agenda. Even as he held meetings to address the economic crisis, Charles Koch was contemplating this political crisis as well.

One evening in Houston, Cris Franklin and his wife prepared for an exclusive social event. They were invited to the home of Koch Supply & Trading president Steve Mawer for a dinner party, along with other senior managers and traders. There was a special guest that evening. Charles Koch was in town, and he wanted to address the group.

It wasn't unusual for Charles Koch to come to Houston and meet with traders. Charles Koch didn't get involved in the minutiae of day-to-day trading, but he liked to meet with supervisors like Franklin and talk through their strategies. Tonight's dinner seemed to be different. It seemed unlikely that Charles Koch would talk about trading strategies at a dinner party. He apparently had something else he wanted to discuss.

Franklin had reason to be in good spirits when he and his wife arrived at the party. After his visit to Wichita, Franklin learned that Charles Koch had approved Franklin's request for more money. The currency and interest rate trading group would stay in business. This was, as it turned out, a wise decision. Franklin and his team plunged into the wreckage of the currency markets and found new opportunities for trading on the volatility, just as Koch's oil traders managed to do with the contango storage trade. Franklin's team became profitable again. Within a matter of a few years, their profits would hit record highs.

Franklin and his wife walked inside Mawer's home to join the guests who were standing in clusters, enjoying a social hour before dinner. The house was filled with conversation among traders and their spouses. Franklin spotted Charles Koch in the crowd.

Charles Koch stood and smiled, chatting with guests as if he were a visiting dignitary. There was something about Charles Koch that made him approachable at this stage in his life. He resembled a professor of economic philosophy as much as a hard-charging CEO. His youthful competitiveness, which once had a hard edge to it, seemed to have softened. Franklin told his wife that he wanted to say hello to the CEO and introduce her. They walked across the room and waited to shake the hand of one of the richest men in the world.

As he waited to meet Charles Koch, Franklin decided to make a joke. His wife's maiden name also happened to be Koch, although he knew she was of no relation to Charles Koch's family. Not only was his wife unrelated to the Koch family, she pronounced her last name as "cook," rather than "coke." Franklin decided he'd make sport of the difference when he introduced her to Charles.

"I said, 'You know, Charles, my wife, her maiden name's spelled K-o-c-h, and she says that you're aren't pronouncing it correctly,'" Franklin said. "He looks at me, and he's like, 'Oh, really?' He's totally lighthearted and fun about it."

Charles Koch told the young couple a story that had become family lore in the Koch household. He said that his father, Fred, had grown up pronouncing his last name in the Dutch manner, with a guttural *ch* sound at the end. But once, when sitting in a train station, Fred Koch was paged over the loudspeaker and the announcer mispronounced his name as "coke." Fred decided he liked that version much better, and it became the family name going forward.

Koch never managed to fully adopt the easy familiarity with people that he'd so admired in Sterling Varner. But he had managed to build his own way of bonding with people. The self-deprecating humor, the avuncular manner, the low-key button-down shirt and jacket with no tie—all of it helped. The crowd of traders around Charles Koch were willing to follow him, and they were keen to hear what he wanted to say.

After dinner, the guests retired to a large living room, where chairs were circled around a spot where Charles Koch stood to address them. The meeting was more like a talk at a literary salon than a business presentation. Charles Koch didn't want to talk about Market-Based Management, the state of oil markets, or even Koch's business strategy. There were larger, more pressing issues on his mind. He wanted to talk about the state of the country, the state of political parties, and "the current of America," as Franklin recalled it.

Charles Koch addressed a question that had worried him since the 1970s: "Where is free capitalism at risk?"

After the crash, it seemed as if capitalism was at risk across the United States. The dominant public narrative blamed the crash on a failure of the free market and private enterprise: greedy bankers had been given free rein and taken down the economy. When it looked for a solution to the problem, the American public turned to the federal government, not the free enterprise system.

First came a giant federal bailout plan, designed and orchestrated by the Bush administration. The price tag for this bailout was placed at $700 billion. The US Treasury used taxpayers' money to buy bad loans and rotten assets from the very banks that created them. Treasury Secretary Henry Paulson, a former Goldman Sachs executive, promoted the plan on national television, saying it was vital to stopping another Great Depression. A Republican, in other words, was made a passionate argument for government intervention on the scale of the New Deal. Surprisingly, the strongest resistance to this plan came from Paulson's own party. Republicans in Congress voted against the bailout in September of 2008. The stock market crashed more than 700 points when they did so. The plan was eventually passed. It was seen as a last stand for the theory of laissez-faire.

Even worse, from Charles Koch's point of view, was the election of Barack Obama to the presidency in November. Now, Democrats controlled all three branches of government. The mood of America was decidedly running against Charles Koch's beliefs. The mood was deeply

"illiberal," as he would call it. There was clamoring for more government intervention, more regulation, and more money for entitlement
programs.

What was unspoken, but what Charles Koch understood, was that
all of this would also mean more taxes. In January of 2008, even before
the Democratic takeover, Charles Koch warned that too many Americans were putting too much faith in government programs to solve their
problems. The result was inevitable: "To support that spending, taxes
will escalate," Charles Koch had written in the company newsletter. Who
was always the primary target of higher taxes in American history? The
richest Americans and the largest corporations. Charles Koch happened
to be sitting atop one of the largest fortunes in the world, and one of the
largest private corporations in the country. The Democratic Party had
been explicit in its promise to tackle concentrated wealth.

This moment was dangerous, in Charles Koch's view. Free enterprise
had not seen such a direct threat since Franklin Delano Roosevelt's election. Roosevelt's New Deal had hemmed in corporate America for the
following thirty years. Barack Obama's presidency promised to do the
same. The comparisons were neither subtle nor hidden. On November
24, 2008, the cover of *Time* magazine featured a photo illustration with
Barack Obama's face superimposed onto FDR's body, sitting in a car,
smiling, complete with a long-stemmed cigarette holder. The headline
read: "The New New Deal."

The new New Deal already seemed to be in the works. Just over a
month after he became president, Barack Obama passed a government
stimulus package aimed at boosting economic growth. The package was
valued at $787 billion and included new spending programs on infra-
structure and renewable-energy programs. There was intense political energy behind these interventions. The public narrative held that a
political savior had come along to tame the worst instincts of a private
market run amok.

But the story that Charles Koch told his employees that night at the
dinner party was very different. As he spoke to groups of employees,
Charles Koch spun a story about government malfeasance, public igno-
rance, and increasing harm to free enterprise and prosperity. Charles
Koch did not believe that markets needed to be tamed. The very fact
that so many people subscribed to this belief seemed to prove that most

American voters were profoundly misinformed. Even the nation's CEOs and business leaders were delusional on this point. They refused to accept the most important, most overriding fact: the American economy was not a free enterprise system in the first place. It was not a free enterprise system when FDR was elected, and it certainly was not one now. Government control and intervention were so deeply embedded in the American way of life that people didn't even see it anymore. People failed to understand that it wasn't the free market that caused the collapse of 2008, it was overweening government control and interference that caused the crash of 2008, and the crash of 1929, for that matter.

This is what Charles Koch had said back in 1974 when he addressed his think tank, the Institute for Humane Studies. Back then, he told the crowd before him that "we ourselves have abetted the destruction of the free enterprise system."

He continued: "[W]e have allowed the free market to be blamed for fostering economic crises, when, in fact, a free market did not even exist at the time the crises occurred. A comment on the Great Depression will illustrate this point. Those who believe that the pre-1929 economy, polluted by government manipulations of the money supply, was a free market are defenseless against the charge that the Depression occurred because of unregulated market activity."

After these crashes, in the most bitter of ironies, the American people blamed capitalism for the problem, and heaped yet more government intervention onto the problem in the hope of solving it. This is what Charles Koch believed happened under FDR, who misdirected the people from the real cause of the crisis and made the problem worse by pushing the New Deal. Charles Koch noted, in a 2009 company newsletter, that the economy was sluggish and dipped into recession during the 1930s after the New Deal was passed. What Charles Koch failed to mention in the newsletter was that the country enjoyed three decades of economic growth where prosperity was widely shared during the ensuing era of the New Deal consensus, which didn't truly end until the mid- to late 1970s.

In 2009, Charles Koch believed that America was making the same mistakes again. The crash of 2008 was caused by "misguided government policies" rather than the shortcomings of free enterprise, he believed. These policies included the Federal Reserve Bank's continued intervention in the money supply. The Fed kept interest rates extraordinarily low for an extraordinarily long time during the 2000s, in hopes of boosting economic growth. Charles Koch blamed that intervention for leading to the housing bubble, a point of view that was almost inarguably supported by all available data.

The true threat to prosperity, Charles Koch said, was not untrammeled capitalism. It was the risk of a centralized, command-and-control system imposed by Barack Obama and the Democrats of Congress. It was the risk that people would be fooled by the public narrative that only big government could deliver an equitable society and economic growth. At Koch Industries, they would be doing all they could do to fight this looming threat. The efforts would begin with each employee, as they did their job each day. Koch Industries itself had become a microcosm of free enterprise, a system that sought daily to obey the true laws of prosperity. The citizens of this microcosm were expected to hold true to its values and to spread those values to others to the degree that they could.

This kind of message found a receptive audience in Steve Mawer's living room. Employees like Cris Franklin instinctively understood Charles Koch's message. As the event broke up and everyone went home, Charles Koch's words echoed in Franklin's head. He saw the germ of truth in them. "You can measure the morality of a society by the number of laws they have. Well, we have a lot of laws. That's unfortunate," Franklin said.

Charles Koch left Houston that night and made his way back to Wichita. Once there, he resumed the routine that had occupied him since the 1970s. He woke up very early in his family estate, on the wooded property where he was raised, got ready for work, and was often in his car and on the way to the office before seven-thirty. He pulled into the employee lot as it was just starting to fill up. He sometimes preferred to take the stairwell to the third floor, rather than the elevator, walking up the extra-wide staircase that was bordered with well-marked hand railings. At the dawn of 2010, the Koch Industries Tower was a monument to Charles Koch's success. He had set out to show the world that he had discovered the laws of creating prosperity, and his company seemed to be living proof that he'd done so.

As Charles Koch reached the third floor and walked down the hallway, he passed the boardroom and executive suites that were the command center for a corporate empire. Tens of thousands of employees. Billions of dollars in revenue and profit. Offices and trading desks that spanned the globe. The company's operations touched the daily lives of virtually everyone who used gasoline, wore spandex, lived in a home with gypsum-paneled walls, swaddled their children in diapers, and counted on the heat to come on when they adjusted their thermostat. Koch Industries had a hand in all of it. The company had just survived the greatest economic shock since the Great Depression; it had adapted, trimmed back, and even found ways to profit during the chaos. And now, as it emerged, it was in a stronger position than ever before.

Charles Koch entered his spacious office, walked past the sitting area with its tasteful couch and reading table, past the walls lined with bookcases. He sat down at his desk, where just to his left he could look out the windows at the expanse of green prairie grass. In quiet moments, he could turn and gaze out at this horizon when he needed a quiet moment to think. But this bucolic view is not what Charles Koch faced, most of the time.

On the wall opposite Charles Koch's desk, he had hung a painting that was quite unpleasant. His daughter, Elizabeth, had painted it. It was a picture of dark hues, heavy on the red, showing the face of what appeared to be a Chinese peasant. The man's face was bruised and beaten. His expression was one of suffering. The painting seemed to be a reminder, and a warning. It was a totem of life under repressive regimes; the face of Communism, Socialism, and state control. It seems telling that Charles Koch gave it a place of such prominent display, hanging it where it was never far from his view. Charles Koch seemed to believe that the United States was slipping toward tyranny. When he looked out on the horizon, he saw a threat. The power of the state was rising, and Koch Industries was directly in its crosshairs.

But Charles Koch, in all his years, had never backed down from a fight. And the world was about to learn this fact for itself.

PART 3

GOLIATH

CHAPTER 18

Solidarity

(2010–2011)

In the early morning hours, small traffic jams appeared around Koch Industries headquarters campus, as thousands of employees made their way to the company parking lot. The lines of cars edged slowly into the parking lot, nose to tail, as early as seven thirty. Everyone knew that Charles Koch was probably already at the office, his modest station wagon parked just a few spots down the sidewalk from an entrance into the Tower.

Most employees parked in a large lot just north of the headquarters complex. After getting out of their cars, they flashed their company-issued ID badges to a security guard and then walked down a staircase to the subterranean tunnel that led into the headquarters building. The tunnel walls were decorated with photomontages of Koch Industries' history, black-and-white pictures of the first trading desks, the Pine Bend refinery, and a smiling Fred Koch. The history of the place, and its story, was reinforced to every employee by the time they arrived at the elevator bank to take them to their offices.

It was impossible, now, for Charles Koch to meet all of his employees. It was even impossible for him to teach his management techniques through the Koch University model of the 1980s, when he taught his managers in large seminar settings and had them, in turn, teach their own employees. The company was too large and too sprawling. Just between 2004 and 2007, the company had grown roughly six times larger, adding seventy-three thousand men and women to the payroll. Charles Koch believed, however, that every new employee needed to subscribe to Koch Industries' philosophy, to learn its vocabulary and embrace its mission. This was most important for the employees who worked in the Tower, and who walked through the pedestrian tunnel each morning.

These employees were the elite corps of the workforce, the overseers of Koch's holdings around the world. They were like the managing partners at a large holding company, overseeing Koch Industries' far-flung investments. While the job was more difficult than before, Charles Koch found new ways to integrate each employee into the fabric of his company, to teach them the philosophy that he called Market-Based Management.

The training began with a stringent hiring process that selected only a certain kind of employee. Koch Industries developed a four-part interview process that revolved around Charles Koch's Ten Guiding Principles. Job candidates, many of them fresh out of college, were led through lengthy lists of questions that sought to determine if they would adhere to Koch's principles. Only the select few were chosen.

"You need diversity in certain ways," explained Randy Pohlman, who directed Koch's human resources division until the mid-1990s. "But if you're Koch Industries, you don't want people who don't believe in free markets. They're not going to be successful there. That's not the kind of diversity you want. . . . If you're going to start hiring every other person as a Socialist to have nice diversity—it's not going to work," Pohlman said.

Once the free-market adherents were hired, Koch began training them immediately. The new hires were collected in groups and led down a long hallway in the basement of the Tower, to a large conference room where round tables were set up to accommodate them. Their training session began with a video address from Charles Koch, projected on a large screen. He laid out the central tenants of MBM, and emphasized the importance of learning the code. And after the video was finished, employees learned the specific codes and rules of this new way of thinking. They broke into small groups and ran through simulations where they put the principles into practice. The training sessions lasted roughly two days. Once employees were on the job, the culture and the vocabulary were reinforced daily in every meeting and conversation, to create a kind of deep muscle memory of the culture.

The unity among Koch Industries' employees was hard to overstate, or even articulate, to outsiders. This was a cadre of people who worked for a secretive company that made the world work. They operated the mind-numbingly complex machinery that lay just beneath the surface of modern society: the pipelines, refineries, fertilizer plants, clothing factories, and trading desks. The stupendous profits that they realized from doing so only seemed to reinforce their sense of superiority over the outside world. When it came time to fight the outside world, it wasn't done with malice or disregard. It was done with a sense of pity. People outside the Koch campus seemed misguided, uneducated, somewhat oblivious to what it took to keep the lights on. Koch Industries would patiently work to correct these problems and make the world a better place.

One of the true believers inside Koch Industries was a young academic named Abel Winn. He had finished his graduate studies at George Mason University, home to the Mercatus Center that Charles Koch founded, and was fluent in the work of Hayek and von Mises. Winn didn't know it at the time, but when he was invited for a job interview in Wichita, he was given a remarkable privilege. He got to interview with Charles Koch himself.

The two of them met in Koch's employee cafeteria, a large and pleasant facility that was voted by one local paper as the best restaurant in Wichita. Because it was a job interview, Charles Koch took Winn to a private dining room. Almost from the moment they sat down, Charles Koch put Winn at ease. Koch was self-effacing and more eager to hear about Winn's experiences than to talk about his own. Koch began quizzing Winn right away. He wanted to learn more about Winn's specific field of experimental economics. Winn had studied the discipline at George Mason, under the Nobel-winning economist Vernon Smith. Experimental economics was a system to test economic theories in a laboratory setting. This idea seemed to appeal to Charles Koch—experimental economics might provide a way to prove or disprove the underlying principles of Market-Based Management.

Charles Koch asked Winn about the limitations of the experiments. Could an experimental economist run studies that revealed the best way to teach people? Could a study show whether public schools were effective?

Winn said it wasn't as simple as that; experiments couldn't effectively measure such large issues. But the experiments could break down smaller components of a school system and test their effectiveness. "You couldn't do an entire educational system, but maybe features of the system," Winn recalled saying.

Charles Koch seemed impressed. He hired Winn to become director of a new joint venture between Koch Industries and Wichita State University, an academic center that would test the veracity of MBM's claims and pioneer new discoveries about markets and human behavior. The new partnership would be called the MBM Center at WSU. The Wichita State administration renovated several classrooms in the basement of a historic building called Clinton Hall to make room for the center back in September of 2006.

After he was hired, Winn helped design a large laboratory in the center where he could carry out his experiments. He installed a warren of computer stations, each one walled off from the other by partitions. The computers were networked together and linked to a device that Winn controlled, called the master box. His test subjects were students, many of them from the business school's accounting and finance departments. They would be the economic guinea pigs. When an experiment got under way, the students sat at the computer stations, unable to see what their neighbors were up to because of the tall partitions. The students played complex computer games that were designed to simulate real-world economic problems, like buying a home or bargaining over a contract. The simulations were run from the master box, which tabulated the students' responses and created databases for Winn to analyze in search of patterns.

One of Winn's most important experiments was designed to figure out how Koch Industries could defeat its opponents. Specifically, the experiment sought the best way to overcome an economic dilemma called the "holdout problem."

The holdout problem was commonly encountered by Koch's pipeline division. Any given pipeline might travel hundreds or even thousands of miles in length, passing through land owned by hundreds of property owners. A pipeline company had to convince each of these property owners to sell their land (or at least grant a right-of-way through it) along the pipeline route. This was no easy thing. Landowners are inclined to make companies pay dearly for the privilege of crossing their property. The cost of assembling the property rights and leases for a new pipeline route can quickly balloon.* The real problem arose when a pipeline's

---

* It's true that pipeline companies can use eminent domain authority to force property owners to hand over rights to their land, but that option is reserved as a last resort. Even then, it is not free, as, under the law, the property owners must be offered "just compensation." With eminent domain, the cost and time involved in pipeline construction increase dramatically if property owners hold out for higher prices.

path ran across the property of a holdout, meaning that ornery breed of property owner who stubbornly refuses to sell. A single holdout had extraordinary power to slow down a pipeline project and raise costs. The most intransigent holdouts simply refused to sell at all. Winn's experiment was designed to find a way to outmaneuver them.

The master box, in this experiment, became the pipeline company. The students, in their warren of cubicles, became the property owners. The master box was preprogrammed with buying simulations. It sent price signals to the students, who chose to accept or deny the bids. The chief aim of the experiment, as Winn and a coauthor later wrote, was to "discourage hard bargaining among the sellers."

As the experiment got under way, the master box bombarded the students with different strategies. Roughly 140 students sat alone in their cubicles, unable to see their neighbors, watching the computers as slides flashed across the screens with various offers for their land. They clicked when the price was right. The master box ran its scenarios again and again, collecting data every time. Eventually, it gathered more than seven thousand observations about the students' behavior.

As a result, Koch Industries developed a very rich data set that would help the company understand the holdouts and how to beat them.

Steve Hammond, a holdout, worked in a crummy little office on the second floor of the Longshoremen's union hall in Portland, just down the street from Georgia-Pacific's warehouse. Hammond was as surprised as anyone when he won the election to become a union official in 2008. He was also the first to admit that he had no idea how he was going to fight Koch Industries. "I was in over my head," he recalled.

Hammond wasn't alone. He was elected as the second in command of the local IBU chapter, a position that was known as the business agent. His new boss, the IBU regional director, was a guy named Gary Bucknum. Unfortunately, Bucknum had also just been elected to his position. He was a rookie who was also surprised to find himself as a union boss. Bucknum had run for office on a whim. He didn't work for Georgia-Pacific but for an oil terminal company that was also represented by the IBU. When he won the election, Bucknum's reaction was simple: "Oh, crap."

Bucknum ran for election because he'd grown disillusioned with the union leadership. The union seemed weak. Grievance filings went nowhere. Pay and benefits were lagging. Bucknum had a stubborn streak—he complained so much to his union leadership that he'd earned the nickname "Gary the Anarchist" among the IBU workers. In spite of his militant nickname, Bucknum didn't look like a union thug. He was thin and had large, round eyes and thick glasses. He would not look out of place at a comic book convention. His union militancy seemed almost fussy—like the stubborn refusal of an accountant to accept a spreadsheet where the numbers didn't add up. Fair was fair. The rules were the rules. When the IBU didn't back the rules aggressively enough for Bucknum, he made a choice. "Rather than sit there and complain about it, you put yourself out there to try and do something."

By 2009, Hammond and Bucknum were working side by side. The IBU, while technically independent, rented the office space from the Longshoremen after the two unions became affiliated. A bright-blue IBU flag hung on the wall outside the office door. Just inside that door, there was a small meeting room with a table and chairs, some filing cabinets, and a coffee urn. On the other side of that was the cramped office where Bucknum and Hammond sat at a broad table with two computers. The big window behind them offered a sweeping view of Portland's industrial underside: an electrical substation, a gravel parking lot pitted with large puddles, and a view of passing freight trains. This would be the IBU's command post for a prolonged battle with Koch Industries.

The battle began in 2010, when it was time to renegotiate the labor contract for Koch Industries' two largest distribution centers on the Willamette River, the so-called Front Avenue warehouse and the Rivergate warehouse farther downriver. These were the locations where Hammond had worked since the 1980s. This was the place that he wanted so much to change. The contract negotiation would give him the chance to finally do it.

The size of the task was monumental. The decline of working conditions for IBU employees was even more severe than many of them understood. This degradation was illustrated by an analysis of labor contracts at the warehouse complexes going back to the 1970s. The analysis shows that the warehouse workers became more productive every year, moving more containers with less labor. But even as they did so, they were growing poorer. In 1975, for example, warehouse workers like Hammond earned $6.90 an hour. By 2005, they were making $19.74 an hour, which sounded like a large increase. But when adjusted for inflation, the warehouse workers were actually earning $25.77 an hour back in 1975. Over three decades, in other words, Hammond and his coworkers had taken a 23 percent pay cut. And while they were earning less, their work became more onerous. The LMS didn't give them time to talk or blow off steam. They logged the minutes they spent in the bathroom, had to explain the minutes they spent telling a joke.

This economic stagnation wasn't unique to the Georgia-Pacific warehouse workers. Between 1948 and 1973, American workers' productivity rose steadily, and their wages rose with it. But in the early 1970s, as the age of volatility shook apart the New Deal policy infrastructure, the rise in productivity broke free from the wages that were paid for it. Productivity rose 74.4 percent from 1973 until 2013. Wages rose only 9.2 percent.

Hammond and Bucknum were elected to somehow reverse the downward slide of the IBU workers. Their work began a few months before the labor contract officially expired in March of 2010. They had a matter of weeks to prepare before the official negotiations began. They didn't know what to expect from Koch, but they knew that the IBU rank and file was prepared to hold out for a new and better deal.

Abel Winn closely scrutinized the data he developed at the MBM Center at Wichita State. Some clear patterns emerged early on in the experiment. In some ways, the data was discouraging—it seemed at first as if there was no easy way to overcome the holdout. The master box computer ran its various simulations, and, in case after case, it revealed that holdouts were hard to beat. One stubborn landowner could get a lot of money for their property—if they chose to stand firm.

Over time, however, one promising strategy emerged from the tests. One simulation showed that a pipeline company might beat down the holdouts if it negotiated with all of the property owners at once, rather than buying one plot of land and then moving on to the next. This buying strategy seemed to inject a level of uncertainty into the sellers' minds—each seller didn't know if his or her neighbors would sell or not, which increased the pressure on them to do so.

This strategy worked even better if the sellers were walled off from one another and didn't know what price their neighbors were being offered. If the sellers couldn't compare notes—in other words, they didn't know how much the master box was willing to pay—they could be bargained down to a lower price.

Winn realized that it was tough to pull off this kind of bargaining in the real world. Neighbors were always liable to talk. A company couldn't manage to act in total secrecy. But it was best to keep the sellers in the dark as much as possible.

Or, as Winn and a coauthor would later summarize it in an academic paper based on the experiment: "In the field, truly simultaneously bargaining may be difficult or impossible to implement, but it may be approximated by limiting the flow of information between sellers."

In this way, bargaining against the holdout was not all that different from trading in commodities markets. The advantage went to the party that had the most knowledge and could best exploit any asymmetries of information.

It was best to keep the holdouts guessing, and on the defensive.

When Hammond and Bucknum negotiated a labor contract, they usually sat down with the senior managers or owners of small, privately held firms. They typically hammered out a new labor contract in one or two months. Things would be different with Koch Industries.

When it came time to negotiate, Hammond and Bucknum faced a team of trained labor negotiators whose full-time job was to travel around the country forging labor agreements at Georgia-Pacific facilities. Corporate labor negotiators learned their craft at some of the nation's leading law firms and corporate consultancies. They trained to beat back unions for a living, a skill that was in high demand and well-compensated. The online job networking site LinkedIn, for example, listed "union avoidance" as a job skill that could be added to profiles and endorsed by colleagues. The industry of well-trained people who were paid to undermine union strength was booming, and the IBU leadership knew it.

The IBU negotiating team, in contrast, consisted of rank-and-file warehouse workers. They were elected by their peers to sit on a bargaining committee of six members who would help Hammond and Bucknum. Some of the committee members had never negotiated a contract before. The lead negotiator on the 2010 committee was David Franzen, a longtime coworker of Hammond's who had a hot temper and a reputation as a brawler.

The IBU team had to learn the art of labor bargaining in a matter of weeks. They didn't have the money to hire consultants, and it would have been a waste of time to search LinkedIn for people with skills like "labor organizing" or "solidarity." Still, the IBU team did the best it could. They got help from two college professors at the University of Oregon, who offered training to local unions through a program called the Labor Education & Research Center, or LERC.

When the IBU asked for help, the university dispatched Lynn Feekin, a soft-spoken woman with thick, gray hair who still had the midwestern accent from her many years of living in Wisconsin. Feekin had worked with unions in the Midwest before moving to Oregon to teach. She was joined by a fellow professor named Ron Teninty, a fast-talking expert on labor contracts who seemed to take glee in spending long hours poring over the minutiae of labor agreements.

Feekin and Teninty arrived at the Longshoremen union hall and held a crash-course session for the IBU team in a large meeting room, just down the hallway from the IBU office. The team gathered around a large, collapsible table with rolling office chairs set around it. Behind the head of the table, the wall was adorned with black-and-white photos documenting the Longshoremen's glory days of the past: portraits of past union presidents staring gloomily down, shots of the shipping yards and union hall meetings. Far down at the other end of the table, a big window looked out onto a wall of pine trees planted outside the union hall. The IBU had rented out the meeting room for the day, and it was going to be a long one.

During the hours-long series of lectures, Feekin walked the IBU team through the formulaic legal process of contract negotiation. There was a set of prescribed steps for the negotiations, and a set of legal pitfalls that the negotiating committee should avoid. But Feekin's primary goal was to teach the IBU negotiators a larger lesson. She wanted to teach them how to get the best contract possible when they found themselves up against trained negotiators. Her main message to them was not to count on their silver tongues. The back-and-forth in the bargaining room was not, in fact, as important as what happened outside the room. It was the power dynamic—the balance or the imbalance of leverage between employer and employee—that ultimately determined who would win or lose in the contract negotiations.

The IBU team knew, intuitively, that these dynamics were not in their favor. Union membership in America declined virtually every year between 1975 and 2010. By the time the IBU was ready to take on Koch, only about 10 percent of wage and salary workers belonged to a union. This decline reversed the force of gravity in the labor market—now non-unionized workers were the most powerful force, stripping away pay and benefits from organized labor. When most of the workforce didn't have job security or pay raises, the job security and pay raises won by unions seemed like an unfair privilege.

Other cultural changes pushed unions into retreat. Back in the 1970s, it was difficult for a company to lock out workers and replace them during a strike. This was in part due to the strength of picket lines, but also because it was seen as unethical to replace workers who were on strike. This changed in 1981 when Ronald Reagan fired federal air traffic controllers who were on strike and replaced them. Reagan didn't change any laws; he simply set an example. Afterward, the risks of a strike were far higher for workers.

But Teninty and Feekin gave the IBU team hope. Teninty pointed out that no company wanted to face a protracted labor dispute. Teninty explained that the IBU must show Koch Industries that the union was strong and that its workers stood in solidarity.

"Your job is to convince the employer that it's better to settle with you than to fight with you," Teninty remembers saying. "That's, frankly, the name of the game. That's how unions have worked forever." This was inspiring talk for guys like David Franzen. He had been a forklift driver his entire adult life (outside of a three-year stint in the US Navy). His bosses and the LMS directed his every move at work. Now he was in a position to speak back to them. This sense of hope and inspiration would be hard for Franzen to recall, after everything that happened next. "That was a lot of beers ago," he said. "A lot of bad memories."

The first negotiating meeting was held at a Georgia-Pacific warehouse, inside a conference room upstairs. Bucknum was joined by Hammond and the six negotiators from the warehouse. The Koch team included a trio of managers from the warehouses, but they didn't do much talking. The Koch effort was led by Don Barnard, a professional labor negotiator whom Georgia-Pacific had flown in from Atlanta. Barnard was polite and inscrutable. He said his hellos and got straight to work.

Bucknum watched as Barnard set a thick three-ring binder on the negotiating table. If the IBU team had shown up ready for a fight, what they got instead was a bureaucratic process, one that was administered by the unsmiling—but utterly amiable and inoffensive—Don Barnard. He listened pleasantly as the IBU laid out its desires: The annual pay raises. The increases in health care. The IBU had even hired an outside expert to come up with new rules around the LMS software system that might make the workday a little less grinding on employees.

Barnard took it all in and consulted the three-ring binder. Then he informed the IBU team what would be possible. For starters, he said, the IBU needed to drop the health care plan that it administered for employees and put the workers into Koch Industries' health insurance plan. It would be necessary to do this before Barnard could even think about negotiating wage increases. The union pension plan was a problem as well. Koch Industries preferred that employees entered a 401(k) plan run by the company.

Barnard agreed that changes should be made to the workplace rules: they needed to become far stricter. The absentee policy, in particular, needed adjustment. The warehouse workers were afforded far too many chances to miss work without being disciplined. Koch Industries proposed an absenteeism policy that would allow them to miss less than 1 percent of their total scheduled time.

Neither Hammond, nor Bucknum, nor anyone else on the IBU team had experienced anything like this. Typically, the union asked for a 6 percent raise, and the company countered with 3 percent. Now the union was asking for 5 percent and being offered an overhaul to the entire labor agreement in return.

The proposal that the IBU abandon its existing health care plan was particularly offensive. Since the 1960s, the warehouse workers' health care plan had been owned and operated by the IBU and administered through a health care trust. The union owned it, controlled it, and set the rules. When Koch Industries revealed the rules of its own health plan, it was apparent that they violated almost everything that the union stood for. Koch's health plan used a so-called "cafeteria-style" membership, whereby members could pick and choose their levels of health care coverage. This meant that a young employee who was single and had no children might pay a monthly premium of $150. An older employee who had four children, on the other hand, might pay a monthly premium of $500. In the IBU trust plan, every member paid the same premium. The single employee paid $300. The father of four paid $300. It was an economic embodiment of the union's solidarity. The Koch health plan would institutionalize division between the workers. The drivers were already competing against each other in the LMS rankings. Now it would be each worker for themselves in the health care plan.

The Koch negotiating team insisted that their proposals were not simply a way to save money, but reflected Koch's principles. Employees needed to act like owners and entrepreneurs. That was why, for example, Koch Industries didn't just want the workers to join a cafeteria-style health care plan; the company also wanted workers to pay more money out of pocket for their premiums. Previous versions of the IBU plan had covered the entire monthly premium. Now Koch Industries insisted that it would only pay 80 percent of the cost, with employees picking up the rest of the tab. The logic behind this proposal traced back to the earliest days of Market-Based Management. Charles Koch believed that if a service was free to an employee, then the employee would overuse it. Employees needed to have "skin in the game" when it came to receiving health insurance.

Koch's principles made labor negotiations difficult. It was hard to meet in the middle when Koch believed that the union's approach was destructively misguided. Still, the IBU tried to argue. That's when they discovered an infuriating pattern to Koch's bargaining method. David Franzen or Steve Hammond would propose something to Barnard. Barnard would nod his head, look at his binder, write some notes, and then say that he needed to contact Atlanta to share the new idea. The IBU team came to believe that Barnard wasn't in charge of the process and needed to get clearance from headquarters. After the IBU made a proposal, the Koch team would gather its things, get up, and leave the negotiating room, promising to return soon with an answer.

Hours passed. Afternoons passed. Bucknum took the negotiating committee out for lunch. Guys paced on the sidewalks outside and smoked cigarettes and talked on their cell phones. Finally, the Koch team returned.

"They'd say, 'Well, we've looked at your proposal,'" Bucknum said. "They wouldn't say 'No' directly. They'd just go: 'This is our counterproposal to what you said.' Or: 'We're sticking with our prior proposal on line eleven,' or whatever. It was like watching paint dry, talking to these people."

Koch dragged out the bargaining in another way: Barnard only agreed to meet three days a week. Monday was a travel day, as Barnard flew to Oregon from Atlanta. Friday was also a travel day, when he flew home. The meetings sometimes ended at two in the afternoon, because it was five o'clock in Atlanta, when people started to go home from work.

Negotiations took on a predictable tempo. The teams sat down in the morning. The IBU proposed something. The Koch people left for hours, returned, conceded nothing, and then indicated it was time to go home for the day. After negotiations wrapped up on Thursday, the Koch team returned to Atlanta. Sometimes it was weeks before they could find another opening on their calendar. Nine months into the negotiations, it seemed like they'd made no progress. Yet the IBU team held tight.

Finally, a small victory. Don Barnard agreed to let the IBU retain its health plan rather than moving into the Koch plan, as long as the IBU employees were willing to pay out of pocket, for the first time, to keep the privilege. In the beginning, they would pay 20 percent out of pocket, and then 25 percent in forward years. After so many grinding hours of negotiation, the IBU took the offer.

Almost immediately after this development, however, the IBU was informed that Don Barnard no longer worked for Koch Industries. They would be getting a new negotiator to deal with. There was something disconcerting about this abrupt departure, like watching a diplomat of some hostile government get executed right in front of you for disobeying his rulers. The IBU team was convinced that Barnard was fired for letting the IBU keep its health care plan, although Barnard's former boss insisted that this was not the case.

Regardless, Barnard's departure sent a chill through the team. Back in his cramped office at the Longshoremen hall, Bucknum tried to figure out who Barnard's replacement would be. Bucknum was told through back channels to the Koch negotiators that the IBU team would "sorely miss Mr. Barnard." Bucknum said this warning turned out to be true.

When Don Barnard reported back to Atlanta, he reported to a man named Ken Harrison. Harrison was vice president of labor relations for Georgia-Pacific, overseeing the company's negotiations with labor unions at various plants.

Harrison was a trim man in his early sixties, nearing the end of a decades-long career. His hair, once bright red, had faded to a thin and silvery gray. He wore a tightly trimmed goatee, also gray, that highlighted the severity of his high cheekbones and slender face. His face could convey a lot of feeling with even a small grimace or a half smile. Harrison measured his words with extreme care and dispatched them with a surgeon's precision. Harrison began traveling frequently to Portland to negotiate directly with the IBU.

"You could tell that he thought this little group of a hundred people in Portland, Oregon, was beneath his pay grade. He didn't really like to be bothered by us," Bucknum remembered. "He didn't look kindly at us—or the people on his side of the table."

With Harrison in charge, the negotiations took a harder turn. Barnard had been infuriating, in his placid way, but Harrison was simply unmovable.

"I remember Ken Harrison looking across the table once and going 'What part of "no" don't you guys get?'" Hammond recalled. Hammond shook his head and widened his eyes at the recollection. The IBU team subscribed to the naïve notion that the bargaining session would be a series of compromises. Harrison disabused them of this notion.

"It just floored us all, you know?" Hammond said. "Because we just never heard anything like that. Now, bear in mind that we're just a bunch of forklift drivers and stuff. We're deckhands on boats, and things like that, negotiating against lawyers. The working man really didn't have too much of a chance against those guys anyway."

When he wasn't at the negotiating table, Harrison had a surprisingly easy air about him. When asked how he came to be one of Georgia-Pacific's top officials over labor unions, Harrison cracked a half smile and replied, "A drunk sailor charted my course through life."

Harrison earned degrees in both business and law before spending his career at Georgia-Pacific. One reason Harrison was so stern at the negotiating table, so measured in his words, was that he knew loose language could create a chaotic process. If the other side didn't believe what you said, it could upset expectations and create uncertainty and delays. That could undermine the company's leverage.

"Full faith and credit; your word's your bond," Harrison said. "If it's not, you're going to be paying more than anybody else."

Harrison, then, did not improvise. Like Koch's commodity traders, Harrison based his actions on deep analysis. During every negotiating session, Harrison and his team set up a private "caucus room" where they could strategize. It was possible to do this because the negotiations had been moved from the Georgia-Pacific offices to a nearby hotel called the Red Lion, which was seen as neutral territory. The parties rented one room for their meeting, and Koch rented a second room for its team. Inside the caucus room, the Koch negotiators drank hot coffee and sat at a table with their laptops as they conferred.

The caucus room was essentially a makeshift trading floor. Harrison and his team developed a point of view on the large, multiyear trade to which they were committing Koch Industries. They evaluated the multiyear price that Koch should pay for the IBU workers' labor, and they treated this trade exactly as Koch treated a multiyear hedge on oil prices. They sucked in data from diverse sources like federal labor statistics, private financial services, and even other labor unions. Backed by a team of analysts with spreadsheets, they analyzed the market and figured out their view on what the true price of the labor should be. This was a technique that Koch Industries had used since at least the 1990s. Randy Pohlman, the former Koch human resources executive, said Koch's team in the caucus room used spreadsheets to tweak and tailor the numbers even as negotiators worked next door.

When Harrison and the team settled on their price for IBU's labor, they were encouraged not to pay a penny more. While Koch didn't introduce any radical new negotiating tactics to Harrison's team at Georgia-Pacific, the new owners did provide a new emphasis: "Run it more efficiently at a lower cost." Because of the billions in debt that Koch loaded onto Georgia-Pacific, Harrison was told to help cut costs and lower overhead wherever he could. (Koch later said that Harrison's superiors don't remember giving him this directive. But the company did embrace the strategy of making Georgia-Pacific more efficient.) This explained the deep gulf between what the IBU wanted and what Koch was willing to offer.

After the process dragged on for months, the IBU implemented lessons they learned from Lynn Feekin. They decided to fight outside the negotiating room.

The IBU set up a large stage in Pioneer Courthouse Square, a public plaza in downtown Portland. The plaza was shaped like a shallow bowl, bordered by a gently ascending slope of stairs where curious onlookers sat and watched the show. Bucknum and David Franzen arrived for the rally, carrying placards stapled to wooden sticks, with the IBU insignia and the message "WE ARE ONE—RESPECT OUR RIGHTS." Another protestor carried a sign that said: "CORPORATE GREED MAKES ME SICK."

This was the modern-day equivalent of a union picket line—meaning that it was no picket line at all. The IBU rally was held in partnership with a local progressive political group called Portland Rising and a national group called Jobs with Justice. It was a circus-like event designed to garner publicity and to shame Koch Industries into agreeing to a better deal. The IBU didn't have the clout to actually go on strike, and the members knew it. The rally was a publicity tool, not an economic weapon.

Before the march, several speeches were made from the stage. Fists were raised. A bullhorn was used, in spite of the presence of a nearby microphone and podium. Corporate greed was denounced. Workers were extolled. Bucknum sat nearby the stage, smiling sardonically when someone snapped a photo of him. The look on his face was almost pained. There was something about the rally, something about the protest in general, that felt out of step with mainstream American politics. Even in the Obama era, the American way of life had become centered on individual achievement. It was a nation that worshipped its entrepreneurs, its star athletes, and its self-made celebrities. There was something almost . . . *unbecoming* about a group of people assembling publicly to demand a bigger paycheck. The shouts and cries rose up from the square, echoed off the nearby skyscrapers, and then seemed to fade away. The media coverage was anemic; the attention paid to the rally, minimal.

Perhaps most importantly, the event was held several miles from the warehouse. The marchers paraded down the middle of the streets downtown, but their goal was to attract attention, not to slow production. Ken Harrison heard about the rally from local contacts in Portland. "I live in Atlanta," he said. "It didn't do anything to me."

The rally didn't hurt Koch's bottom line, but it stoked energy among the IBU members. Hammond and Bucknum decided to harness the energy. They scheduled a vote on the contract terms that Ken Harrison was proposing. If the union members voted against it, it might increase the IBU's leverage by garnering headlines and laying the groundwork for a strike.

The contract vote was held in the big auditorium on the ground floor of the Longshoremen hall. The room was an architectural embodiment of union militancy. Along one wall, a big white banner displayed an old prose poem, "The Scab," by the novelist and journalist Jack London. It began: "After God had finished the rattlesnake, the toad, and the vampire, he had some awful substance left with which he made a scab." The poem went on from there, and became even less kind toward workers who might cross a picket line. Along another wall, a sentimental mural depicted the Longshoremen's glory days, with stoic workers standing strong among the cranes and cargo ships. It was impossible, in that auditorium, not to feel enveloped in the proud history of labor unions. It seems that the Georgia-Pacific workers were intoxicated by the environment when they arrived to vote on the contract.

Still, the vote results surprised everyone. All of the warehouse workers voted on the contract, and all of them voted it down. "The Longshoremen . . . were just blown away by it. They'd never had anything like that," Hammond recalled. The union workers left the hall exultant. They had shown their resolve to beat the Koch brothers.

The IBU informed Harrison's team about the news. It planned to return to the negotiating table with new leverage, a new wind at their back. "They were all pretty dang tickled pink, you know," Franzen recalled. The members were saying, "We're gonna show them, we're gonna take it to them. We're going to *do* this."

Then something unexpected happened. Ken Harrison quit meeting with them. As time dragged on and Harrison refused to show up, the union's fighting spirit began to curdle into something else. Franzen and his colleagues were given the one thing that they needed the least. They were given time to start thinking things over. And Koch Industries knew just how to get them thinking.

During 2010, Abel Winn put the final touches on his study exploring ways to defeat the holdout. In September he submitted his findings to a peer-reviewed publication called the *Journal of Economic Behavior & Organization*. Winn had reason to be optimistic that his paper would be selected for publication. His data showed something quite striking.

Early data from the experiment suggested that it might be impossible to beat a holdout. Different strategies could undermine the holdout's leverage, but the holdout couldn't be eliminated. There was, however, one strategy that nearly decimated the holdout problem. The data was just astonishing on this point. The best way to destroy a holdout's position was to make them expendable.

Winn discovered this fact when his experiments divided the virtual landowners into groups and then made it clear that some of them might be cut loose if they bargained too hard. In this scenario, the pipeline company was looking to buy up land on which to build a route, but it could take alternative paths. It wasn't necessary in this case to get *all* of the landowners to sell in order to build the pipeline. The company could assemble a path while excluding some landowners.

This strategy created a beautiful dynamic, from the pipeline company's point of view. It embedded competition between landowners. It made each neighbor's bargaining power the deepest liability to his or her neighbor's. Everybody started looking over their shoulders and worrying that they might be undercut if they held out too long for a higher price. "When there's competition, that completely blew the problem away," Winn said. "Everybody behaved much better."

As it turned out, the IBU workers faced outside competition, and their managers at the warehouse made sure they were constantly reminded of it.

While the labor union waited to meet again with Harrison, the warehouse employees reported to work every day. They also continued to attend regular team meetings with their managers. During these meetings, the managers discussed day-to-day operations, but they also focused on something else: the relentless competition that the facility faced every day. Dennis Trimm, the warehouse manager who helped implement the LMS, said the main message delivered during many of these meetings was simple: "They can replace you tomorrow."

The employees were shown slideshows illustrating the report cards that Trimm reviewed at least once a month, data showing how the Portland warehouses stacked up against other distribution centers in the Georgia-Pacific network. The Portland warehouses usually ranked near the top, but they had to fight to stay there every day. The other facilities, not coincidentally, were nonunion shops, staffed by outside contractors. The third-party contractors competed against one another to provide cheaper labor to Georgia-Pacific, and they also competed against the IBU. Koch was evaluating, every day, whether or not to replace the IBU team with outsiders.

The fervor from the contract "no vote" began to dissipate. It began to seem like a liability, in fact. The no vote was left to hang in the air as a permanent reminder of the union's militancy, as evidence that the union was in reality an obstacle to Koch's efficient operation of the warehouse.

David Franzen's coworkers began to call his cell phone. The bravery was gone from their voices. They implored him—begged him, almost—to find some sort of settlement with Koch. They wanted the contract to be closed, the deal-making finished. Even if the contract was less than they'd hoped for, they needed to know that a contract was in place. "They were calling me, literally crying on the phone. Guys with families and stuff: 'We can't go on strike. We'll never come back. We'll never have another job. They warned us,'" Franzen said.

The pressure on the IBU intensified dramatically. Hammond and Bucknum were notified that the IBU's pension fund had been deeply wounded by the financial crisis. The fund had lost about one-third of its value, they were told, and might be considered insolvent. This meant that the federal government might take over the plan and cut retirement benefits dramatically. There was a near panic at this prospect. The retirement payments might be cut in half.

Bucknum stayed awake until the early morning hours, sitting at a computer in his home, trying to figure out the legal complexities of pensions. He never did get a clear picture of where his union members stood. The IBU asked Koch Industries if it would participate in a plan to shore up the pension, as all other employers who worked with the IBU had agreed to do. Koch said it would participate only if employees also paid into the pension relief fund out of their paychecks, a hard line position no other company took, Bucknum said.

It had been nearly a year and a half since the contract negotiations began. The workers had no new contract. They were afraid of being replaced. They appeared to be making no headway. And now they feared losing their pension. The Atlanta negotiating team contacted Hammond and Bucknum, and informed them that they had found a time to meet.

This is what the IBU would get.

They could keep their health care, as Barnard had agreed to. But they would pay 25 percent of the premium costs, not 20 percent. Beyond making the plan more expensive, this also exposed the workers to more risk. If the price of health insurance rose sharply during the life of the contract, the employees were on the hook to pay 25 percent of the premiums, no matter the cost. The IBU would accept Koch's new attendance policy, unaltered. If a worker had an absence rate of more than 1.9 percent of their total work time, they could face discipline and termination.

There would be no changes to the LMS system. Any notion of transforming the system was discarded by the IBU negotiators as they fought to protect the health care and pension plans. Pay increases would be minimal. The IBU would get a 2 percent raise the first year, a 1 percent raise the second year, 2 percent the following year, and 1 percent the next. The pay raises were the equivalent of treading water. The employees would remain in the IBU pension plan, but they would pay out of pocket to rehabilitate it.

Another clause limited the IBU's ability to honor picket lines—a crucial provision that was increasingly common in labor contracts around the country. This provision broke the solidarity between unions, making it a fireable offense to refuse to cross each other's picket lines. The strike at Koch's Pine Bend refinery in 1972 lasted as long as the Teamsters refused to cross the OCAW's picket line. Now unions couldn't honor a picket line beginning from day one without being terminated.

This was the contract that Koch offered in the winter of 2011. Hammond tried to push back. Hammond remembered the Koch team telling him: "We gave you last, best, and final. What don't you understand about those words? That's your last offer, the best you're going to get out of us. If you turn it down, it's going to get worse."

The IBU scheduled a new vote on the contract.

David Franzen entered the union hall that night ready to encourage his coworkers to go on strike. He thought the company was bluffing and that it wouldn't dare to lock out the workers or replace them. Even if it came to that, he seemed willing to take the risk. But before Franzen could take the stage and address his coworkers, Gary Bucknum stopped him.

"I had to get him off to the side," Bucknum said. Bucknum told Franzen: "I recommend that you take it. Because it's all downhill from here."

When Steve Hammond took the stage to address his fellow union members, he said essentially the same thing. Hammond had a defeated air about him. He became a union official buoyed by hope, determined to make a change. In December of 2011, the best he could achieve was an unhappy compromise and partial surrender. He told the IBU members to vote in favor of the contract because they had no better options.

There was rage among the members. They had fought for months. They attended rallies. They hadn't had a pay raise in a year and a half as the bargaining dragged on. Most poisonous of all was the feeling of dashed expectations. The union was supposed to make life better for its members, and the union had failed. The members had voted down the previous contract, unanimously, and now they seemed to have nothing to show for it.

Alan Cote, the IBU president from Seattle, stood in front of the crowd and explained to them the hard realities of bargaining against Koch. People didn't want to hear it. "One guy stands up and challenges the president of the union, like, 'What the hell do *you* know? You're just a cook from a towboat, and you ain't shit to me!'" Bucknum recalled. The badgering continued. For all their work, Hammond, Franzen, and Bucknum were rewarded with the contempt of their peers.

But even this contempt could not be translated into concrete action. The notion of striking was inconceivable. There were mortgages to pay. Health insurance to keep. Credit card bills. Tuition checks. The members of the IBU had no choice but to stay on the job. They voted to accept the contract.

Gary Bucknum decided not to run for reelection. The sleepless nights, the working weekends, and the disappointment were too much. Hammond, however, did run for reelection, and won. He had been whipped at the bargaining table, and he knew it. The sense of hope that led him to become a union leader now became a sense of resignation. He became a man who was playing a defensive game and who was quick to admit that he was losing it.

But there was evidence that the IBU's struggle was not for nothing. Hammond and his team did win victories for their members, even if those victories seemed small. Ron Teninty, the University of Oregon professor, translated into a spreadsheet all the available IBU contracts for Georgia-Pacific's Front Avenue and Rivergate warehouses between 1975 and 2016. (Some contracts during the 1980s and 1990s were missing and not included in the analysis.) Teninty found that the IBU had won modest gains for the warehouse workers between 2010 and 2016. He included wages, health insurance, and pension benefits into an estimate of warehouse worker earnings, and found that their total hourly compensation rose from $25.37 an hour in 2010 to $34.50 in 2016.

When adjusted for inflation, the workers' hourly pay rose, but only by 8 percent over six years, or roughly 1.3 percent a year. In later years, a larger share of those pay gains went into the cost of maintaining health insurance. It hardly felt like spending money in the workers' pockets. Looked at from a longer time frame, their compensation had only risen 9.5 percent since 2000—a gain of just 1.7 percent a year, on average. These gains were marginal, to be sure, but many nonunion workers suffered worse.

Still, the warehouse workers were losing ground over the long run, and they knew it. When adjusted for inflation, the workers were earning 21.5 percent less in 2016 than they'd earned in the contract that expired in 1981. For employees like David Franzen, this wasn't an abstract concept.

He worked at the warehouse in the eighties. Thirty years and countless hours of labor later, he was given a significant pay cut for the effort.

When the negotiations were finished, Franzen went back to driving a forklift. During the year and a half of negotiations, Franzen said he began to be cited for violating the LMS rules. He'd always ranked high in posted delivery times, but now he began to get dinged for smaller infractions, such as being outside his work area at inappropriate times. He argued against these citations and claimed they were inaccurate. But his temper eventually boiled over. He cornered a manager one day and berated him for what Franzen perceived to be unfair treatment of fellow employees. Later, Franzen saw this manager at a bar and invitations were exchanged to go outside. No one went outside and no fists were swung, but the damage was done.

Franzen was put on a "last chance agreement," meaning that one more work violation could get him fired. He said he remained on that agreement for six years. He had little doubt as to why he was getting in more trouble at work. "As far as being the lead negotiator—they had it out for me." Koch Industries disputed that Franzen was disciplined for LMS violations and said he was only put on "last chance" status for losing his temper with a coworker. The company fired Franzen in early 2018 when he failed to return to work after taking leave for a worker's compensation claim.

Ken Harrison retired in 2012 and opened a labor negotiating consulting firm. When asked about the workers at the IBU, Harrison seemed genuinely sympathetic. But Koch Industries had determined a market price for their labor, and that's what it paid. "People always want more," Harrison said.

It is unclear if Charles Koch was even aware of Georgia-Pacific's battle to tame the IBU. It was just one contract negotiation among many. But even though the fight with the IBU was a small part of Koch's overall operations, it was a microcosm of the bigger battles that Charles Koch and his company were just beginning to fight.

Charles Koch had been disturbed by the election of Barack Obama, and the ascendancy of progressive politics in America. Since the 2008 election, Charles Koch's deepest concerns had been confirmed, and then heightened. The stimulus plan passed in early 2009 was worrisome enough. It helped entrench the notion that the federal government had a large role to play in solving economic problems, while simultaneously adding significantly to the nation's debt. Charles Koch believed that each dollar in extra debt only increased the likelihood of further tax increases.

And the stimulus was just the beginning. Obama initiated a national fight over health care that was not dissimilar to the fight between Ken Harrison and Steve Hammond over the IBU health plan. Obama pushed for a national health care system built on the same ideological foundations as the IBU plan—Obama's Affordable Care Act was built on the premise of solidarity. While there would be sliding scales of cost for the plan, it was designed to provide every American with health insurance, regardless of their income. To pay for this system, the Affordable Care Act levied more taxes on the richest of Americans, such as Charles and David Koch. The entire framework of the Affordable Care Act went against everything Charles Koch had been fighting for. Rather than having people pay for health care out of pocket, giving them "skin in the game," the health care plan entrenched and increased a publicly subsidized insurance system that distorted prices and ruined proper economic incentives. The Affordable Care Act was passed in March of 2010.

And even this was not the end. The Obama agenda continued to roll on, backed by Democratic majorities in Congress. The administration targeted the banks next, imposing new regulations to cut back on speculation and derivatives trading. Regulators at the Commodities Futures Trading Commission started contacting Koch Industries, asking the company about its oil trading strategies. The tendrils of creeping government appeared in almost every industry where Koch operated.

But all of these things were insignificant compared to the biggest threat, the largest battle that loomed in front of Charles Koch in 2010. The Obama administration planned to attack the very core of Koch Industries' business. The next item on the Obama agenda was to slow carbon emissions from the United States and around the globe. If this effort was successful, it was not at all clear how Koch Industries could continue to exist in its present form. At the very least, any hard cap on carbon emissions could cost Koch Industries hundreds of billions of dollars, if not more.

The Obama agenda put Charles Koch in the unfamiliar position of being "the holdout." Now it was Obama, and his supporters, who sought to assemble a political pathway, paved with votes in Congress, to take America toward a future that Obama envisioned. This future relied less on fossil fuels. Charles Koch intended to deny Obama this path.

Barack Obama had seemingly unstoppable momentum behind him. But there was no indication that this intimidated Charles Koch. Perhaps that was because he'd been preparing for such a fight for at least twenty years, building a political influence operation in Washington, DC, that was without parallel in modern America. When it came time for Charles Koch to play the holdout, he was supremely prepared.

CHAPTER 19

Warming

(2008–2009)

Every year, in December, Charles Koch hosted a private party at his home. It was a gathering for the elite group of Koch Industries employees who donated the maximum legal amount of money to Koch Industries' political action committee. As the evening got underway, a parade of cars drove through the gates into the wooded compound of Charles Koch's childhood home. The attendees parked their cars in neat rows on the spacious lawn and walked up the driveway through the winter wind and into the warm, brightly lit entryway.

There was a cheerful cacophony inside, with about two hundred people milling around in large rooms and hallways. The attendees were employees, executives, and their spouses, dressed in their holiday best, eating heavy hors d'oeuvres from the trays carried by uniformed waiters. Charles and David Koch held court in the living room, sometimes standing side by side, as guests filed past to pay their respects. Charles was courteous and smiling. But he also had a habit of managing the party like a company meeting. When David Koch and a guest began talking at length about David's art collection, Charles Koch interrupted to remind the pair that there were guests waiting behind them in the line. "Charles says, 'David, you've got to move it along,'" one guest recalled. "That's kind of Charles. It's kind of like 'This is the process. We're greeting everybody. We're having pleasantries.' And then they move."

There was a sense of exclusivity, of special belonging, that animated the people in the room. The holiday party was held around the time of the annual board meeting, so many board members and senior executives found time to attend. To receive an invite, an employee needed to donate $5,000 during the year to Koch's PAC. The money was bundled and donated en masse to political candidates who were favored by Koch's

PAC officials. It was understood that the PAC always needed donations and that Charles Koch paid close attention to its performance. Having one's name listed in federal campaign disclosures was something akin to being listed in a country club directory. It looked good. There was another, unspoken perk to donating: it indicated that the employee in question had just finished a profitable year and had a big bonus to show for it. When employees didn't show up from one year to the next, it created suspicion that maybe their bonuses hadn't been so fat.

While the gathering was always festive, there was an air of tension hanging over the party in 2009. The attendees had put lots of money into the PAC during the previous election—a total of $2.6 million in 2008—and yet Barack Obama still won and Democrats held large majorities in Congress. Virtually every political cause that Koch Industries cherished was in retreat. The Republican Party seemed in danger of becoming a permanent minority. The Libertarian Party didn't even rate as a political afterthought.

In the corner of Charles Koch's living room, there was an elevated area that held a bookcase, filled with collector's editions of Charles Koch's favorite thinkers, like Hayek and von Mises. The collection seemed like a museum piece now, a collection of antiques that were being left behind by the march of history. The guests stood in clusters near the books, commiserating about the state of politics, the free-falling markets, and waiting to hear what Charles Koch might say about it all.

Every year, Charles Koch made a short speech at the party. Sometimes he was joined by Richard Fink, the top executive over Koch's political operations. Charles Koch's speeches tended to be anodyne and courteous. He thanked the gathered employees for their support and reminded them how vital it was to maintain economic freedom in the United States, both for the long-term health of Koch Industries and for the populace. In 2009, however, Charles Koch's speech was urgent. He felt that the future of America was imperiled. He thanked his guests for their contributions, but the guests understood that the political fight was just beginning.

One threat from the Obama administration seemed more dangerous than the rest. It was the threat of a massive new regulatory regime to limit greenhouse gas emissions that trapped heat in the Earth's atmosphere. The threat of such had been slowly building for decades, under both Republican and Democratic administrations. Charles Koch fought against it the entire time. Now the threat appeared to be imminent. While both Obama and his Republican opponent, Senator John McCain, campaigned on a promise to limit uncontrolled carbon emissions, Obama made carbon control a pillar of his platform. Since the very month Democrats took control of Congress in 2006, they started working on a carbon-control regime. That effort was well under way, with a proposed law working its way through Congress that was more than a thousand pages long. With their wide majorities in the House and Senate, Democrats were ready to hand the bill to a president who was eager to sign it.

There was a belief, within Koch Industries, that the carbon-control regime could put the company out of business. It was impossible to overstate the stakes of the coming fight. The bill in Congress sought to wholly reorganize America's energy system. If this happened, there was reason to believe that the world would follow America's lead. There were already two global treaties seeking to impose carbon limits worldwide— one signed in Rio de Janeiro in 1992 and the other in Kyoto in 1997—and the American regulatory regime could be quickly incorporated into this global framework.

A carbon-control regime would expose Koch to a brand-new regulatory structure, but it could also choke off decades of future profits as the world shifted away from burning fossil fuels. Koch's sunk investment in the fossil fuel business was measured in billions of dollars, reflected in the value of its two oil refineries, pipelines, and other assets. The future revenue to be derived from these assets arguably numbered in the trillions of dollars in future decades.

In 1989, Charles Koch was caught unprepared when the US Senate investigated oil theft on Indian reservations in Oklahoma. Charles Koch learned from the experience. Things were very different in 2009. As recently as 1998, Koch Industries spent as little as $200,000 a year on lobbyists in Washington, DC. By 2005, Koch was spending $2.19 million. When the Democrats took over Congress in 2006, the spending exploded, reaching $3.97 million in 2006, then $5.1 million in 2007. The prospect of an Obama presidency intensified the effort. Koch Industries spent $20 million on lobbying in 2008. Koch augmented these lobbying expenditures with campaign donations. In 1998, the Koch Industries PAC spent just over $800,000. In 2006 it spent $2 million. In 2008 it spent $2.6 million.

Even these expenditures didn't come close to capturing the size of Charles Koch's political machine. Since at least 1974, Charles Koch had envisioned a political influence machine that was multifaceted, including think tanks, university research institutes, industry trade associations, and a parade of philanthropic institutions to support it financially. The machine was a reality now.

The think tanks and academic programs were funded through nonprofit foundations such as the Charles G. Koch Charitable Foundation and the Claude R. Lambe Charitable Foundation. In 2008 alone, the Charles Koch Foundation gave out $8.39 million in grants and gifts, while the Lambe Foundation gave $2.56 million. These grants supported conservative scholars and paid for supposedly independent policy reports released by Washington think tanks. The libertarian Cato Institute think tank, which Charles Koch cofounded and continued to support, operated with annual revenue of $23.7 million in 2008, up from $17.6 million in 2001.

In later years, this political operation became known as the "Kochtopus," a name that evoked a many-tentacled entity that seemed to grasp every lever of policy making. This nickname gave the Koch political apparatus an air of invincibility, as if it were an unbeatable juggernaut with which Charles and David Koch could buy off politicians, write policies, and tame the federal government to their wishes. This caricature failed to recognize a central truth about the market for influence in Washington, DC: there is no straight line between spending money and getting what you want. The market for influence and policy outcomes was a murkier and more complex market than any other in which Koch operated.

That night, at his home in Wichita, Charles Koch made it clear that he was determined to win in this market, just as Koch Industries had won in so many others. The survival of the company seemed at stake.

At that very moment, the biggest source of trouble for Koch Industries was a small group of dedicated liberal congressional staffers working long hours in an obscure basement office in Washington. This team had been laboring for years to write the thousand-page law controlling greenhouse gas emissions. The team was composed of underpaid, overworked idealists. One of them was a workaholic named Jonathan Phillips. Phillips didn't know much about Charles Koch at that time.

Which helps explain why Phillips was still optimistic that history was on his side.

In a different world, Jonathan Phillips could have ended up as a Koch Industries employee. He fit the Koch mold. He was entrepreneurial, idealistic, and thoroughly midwestern. The first time he was old enough to vote for president, in 2000, he voted for George W. Bush. Like so many Koch employees, he was trim and athletic. Phillips had short blond hair, and his blue eyes projected an air of absolute sincerity when he spoke.

Phillips might have become a perfectly respectable conservative if he hadn't served in the Peace Corps, which took him from the cozy confines of suburban Chicago to a tent in Mongolia. He gained a broader view of the world and America's role in it. He lived amid extreme poverty and developed nuanced views about capitalism. He watched from overseas as George Bush launched an invasion of Iraq that was strategically disastrous and morally troubled. Phillips returned home from the Peace Corps and tried to figure out how he could help make the world a better place. He enrolled in the John F. Kennedy School of Government at Harvard and, after graduation, got a job on Capitol Hill as a congressional staffer in the House of Representatives. This is how Phillips found himself in the center of an effort to redraw America's energy system.

In the winter months of 2009, Phillips worked in the Longworth House Office Building, a towering stone complex near the US Capitol. The hallways inside the Longworth Building were austere and cold, lined with marble and capped with vaulted ceilings. Every morning, Phillips walked past these grand corridors to a stairwell that took him to the basement. Down there, the floors were made of varnished cement and the ceiling was covered in exposed ducts, pipes, and vents. Phillips walked to a set of doors that looked like they might conceal a utility closet. This was the headquarters for the Select Committee on Energy Independence and Global Warming.

The Committee on Global Warming was formed in 2007, one of Nancy Pelosi's first official acts after she became the Speaker of the House. Creating a select committee sounds mundane, but it was actually a radical act of rebellion, at least in congressional terms. To understand why, it's important to understand the structure of Congress.

It's common to think of the US House of Representatives as a single organization with 435 members who propose laws and then vote on them. In fact, the House is a collection of smaller governing bodies, each with its own authority, called committees. There's a committee to write tax law and another to write environmental law, for example. Each committee has a chairperson, who acts as the committee's CEO. Bills in the House are written by committees, then passed by a vote of the committee members. This structure gives tremendous power to committee chairs, and it explains why any bill to limit greenhouse gas emissions never had a chance of passing.

The committee that oversaw climate change was the House Committee on Energy and Commerce, which in 2007 was led by the Michigan Democrat John Dingell Jr. Dingell had been chair of the committee, or the ranking Democrat on the committee, since 1981, and he wasn't friendly to any bills that might limit carbon emissions. Dingell wasn't just close to the Detroit automakers in his home state, he *was* the Detroit automakers, owning more than $500,000 worth of stock in the auto industry.

Rather than push Dingell to pass a climate change bill, Pelosi just went around him and created the new House Committee on Global Warming and Climate Change out of thin air and stowed it in the basement of the Longworth Building. Dingell was less than enthusiastic. "These kinds of committees are as useful and relevant as feathers on a fish," he told a reporter. So Pelosi put the Massachusetts congressman Ed Markey in charge of her new subcommittee. Markey was a passionate advocate for environmental regulation, and from the very beginning, Markey seemed dedicated to getting real results. He hired in the most talented staffers he could find and he immediately set to work to break down the barriers that had prevented climate change regulation for years.

Ed Markey built a team that resembled one of those motley groups of experts who are drawn together to pull off a bank heist. There was Jon Phillips, an expert in renewable-energy legislation. There was Joel Beauvais, a well-paid attorney and Clean Air Act expert who took a horrific pay cut to help the committee write its carbon control bill. There was Ana Unruh Cohen, a onetime congressional staffer who later studied climate change policy for the Center for American Progress, a liberal think tank. There was Michael Goo, a congressional staffer who seemed to know everyone in the House. And there was Jeff Sharp, a onetime lobbyist and campaign worker who specialized in communications. Everyone on the team knew that they were overworked and underpaid. But they felt like they were part of something big. Lots of people came to Washington to change the world. This committee was on the precipice of actually doing it.

Almost immediately, the Committee on Global Warming started to agitate and provoke virtually everyone in Congress. The committee didn't have the authority to pass bills, but it had the authority to hold hearings, which it began to do at a militant pace. Phillips spent a great deal of his time booking hearing rooms and bringing in experts to testify. Sharp, the communications guy, helped calibrate the hearings to generate as much media attention as possible. Along with experts and politicians, the committee began inviting celebrities to testify. Phillips met the actor Rob Lowe and ushered him around the Capitol before Lowe testified at a hearing on electric cars.

"We were always looking for celebrities. We're always looking for, like, tearful stories," Phillips recalled. "We're always looking for ways to connect emotionally with people to raise the profile of the issue. It's as much a communications apparatus as it is a fact-finding mission."

Jonathan Phillips and his teammates weren't driven by the hunger for attention. They were driven by a cause. They truly believed that the future existence of human life on Earth was hanging in the balance. To understand their dedication to this cause, it is useful to consider the story that the committee was trying to communicate through its marathon series of hearings.

This was a story of an unprecedented geological event that was initiated by humankind. It could be described as the detonation of a gigantic carbon bomb. The essence of this story would become a contested battlefield in itself, with groups like Koch Industries spending millions of dollars to sow doubt about the basic facts of the matter and the broader meaning of those facts.

The fuse of the carbon bomb began to smolder sometime around the year 1800, when industrialized cities started burning coal to heat homes and power primitive engines. In 1850, about 198 million tons of carbon were released into the atmosphere.

Carbon is a curiously durable element. It can float in the sky for thousands of years without breaking down. Carbon has another important characteristic—it is translucent. That means that it blocks sunlight, just slightly, like a veil of smoke. This translucence is vitally important to life on Earth. A thin layer of compounds like carbon dioxide and water vapor in the atmosphere act like a shield, retaining some of the sun's warmth on the surface of the planet. The mechanics of how this works are simple and well understood. About two-thirds of the sun's heat hits the Earth, but then bounces off into space. The remaining third of the heat is kept on Earth because the thin layer of translucent elements trap it there. For about the past four hundred thousand years, carbon levels in the atmosphere bounced around in a very narrow band, between roughly 200 and 400 parts per million. This period of relative climate stability coincided with the rise of agriculture and the development of civilization.

The fuse of the carbon bomb was truly lit in 1859, when Edwin Drake hit his gusher of an oil well in Pennsylvania and began the age of oil in America. When a barrel of crude oil was burned, it released about 317 kilograms of invisible carbon dioxide into the air. In 1890, 1.3 billion tons of carbon were released into the sky. Some of it went back into the trees, some of it went into the oceans, but some of it stayed in the atmosphere. In 1930, 3.86 billion tons of carbon were released into the atmosphere. In 1970, 14.53 billion tons of carbon were released into the atmosphere. It was joined by other industrial gases that wafted up from factories, refineries, feedlots, and fertilizer plants, gases like methane and nitrous oxide that were also invisible and seemingly harmless. Some of these gases blocked far more light than carbon, on the order of thirty to fifty times more. As more of these gases were released into the atmosphere, more heat would be trapped. This is incontrovertible.

In the 1950s, a chemist and oceanographer named Charles David Keeling installed an air monitor on top of Mauna Loa volcano in Hawaii. Its measurements showed that carbon was accumulating in the atmosphere. In 1959, carbon composed 316 parts per million in the atmosphere. In 1970, it composed 325 parts per million. In 1990, it was 354 parts per million. Concurrent with this discovery, scientists tested air samples that were trapped in tiny bubbles in the glaciers of Antarctica. This proved that during the early millennia of human existence, carbon levels remained in the narrow band between roughly 200 and 300 parts per million. Now that carbon levels exceeded that threshold, it raised troubling questions: What would the world's climate be like at 360 parts per million? Or at 380? Or at 400? There was no certain answer.

In 1988, a group of scientists working with the United Nations formed a consortium called the Intergovernmental Panel on Climate Change, or IPCC, which set out to synthesize the research on global climate change occurring around the world. Initially, the IPCC was very cautious and even seemed to downplay the potential risks from higher carbon concentrations. The panel said that more study was needed, and that no rash actions should be taken that might dampen the prosperity that came from burning fossil fuels. Each ensuing IPCC report, however, became more certain than the last. Carbon concentrations were increasing, which inevitably trapped more heat in the atmosphere. Humans were responsible for the increase. The future implications were unpredictable, but could be severe. The world could expect more dramatic rainfall events and bigger storms in part because warmer air held more moisture. Areas that were parched would become drier. Weather data showed that the world was already getting warmer, as would be predicted when greenhouse gases increased.

While the scientific community was in agreement on these facts, the American public was in doubt. This wasn't accidental. As early as 1991, Charles Koch and other executives in the fossil fuel industry helped foster skepticism about the evidence of climate change. When George H. W. Bush announced that he would support a treaty to limit carbon emissions, the Cato Institute held a seminar in Washington called "Global Environmental Crises: Science or Politics?"

The seminar featured scientists who questioned the prevailing view that humankind's carbon emissions caused the Earth to warm, including Richard S. Lindzen, a professor of meteorology at MIT, Charles Koch's alma mater. A brochure for the seminar featured a large-print quote from Lindzen in which he said: "The notion that global warming is a fact and will be catastrophic is drilled into people to the point where it seems surprising that anyone would question it, and yet, underlying it is very little evidence at all."

The seminar was not a fringe event. Lindzen and other speakers at the conference were invited to join White House staffers in the Roosevelt Room while they were in town for the conference, according to an internal White House memo from Nancy G. Maynard, who worked for the president's Office of Science and Technology Policy. Maynard's boss forwarded the invitation to Bush's chief of staff, John H. Sununu, under the subject line "Alternative Perspectives on Global Warming."

Koch Industries, ExxonMobil, and other firms spent millions of dollars to support the idea that there was an "alternative" view about climate change between 1991 and 2009. These groups had a distinct advantage in the debate. It took many decades for firm scientific consensus to take shape. Scientists are, by nature, cautious and self-doubting. They were hesitant to push the narrative further than the data would support. And the mechanisms of climate change were impossibly complex and hard to quantify. It was difficult to estimate, for example, just how much carbon the world's oceans might be able to absorb over time, or exactly how many degrees the earth might warm over a hundred years if the atmospheric levels of carbon reached 400 parts per million. Even as the global scientific community slowly cohered around the understanding that human activity caused climate change, this cottage industry thrived— a cottage industry built to highlight all the points of uncertainty in the scientific debate.

ExxonMobil eventually abandoned this strategy, but Koch Industries persevered. In 2014, Koch Industries' top lobbyist, Philip Ellender, said that the evidence was in doubt. "I'm not a, you know, climatologist or whatever," Ellender said. "Over the past, I think, hundred years, the earth is warmer. Over the past roughly eighteen, it's cooler.* . . . Whether or not the increases and fluctuations are anthropologic or not is still a question."

In private, Koch Industries officials were even more dismissive of the science around climate change. One former senior Koch Industries executive, a trained scientist who only made business decisions after first analyzing reams of data, explained that he believed global warming was a hoax invented by liberal politicians who sought to use the fiction as a way to unite the populace against an invented enemy. After the fall of the Soviet Empire in 1991, this executive explained, American elites needed a new, all-encompassing enemy with which to frighten the masses, and

---

* This statement is provably untrue. NASA data shows that eighteen of the nineteen hottest years on record occurred since 2001.

so they invented one with global warming. All the data on atmospheric carbon levels and rising temperatures were part of this conspiracy, the executive said.

This is what lent the sense of desperation to Phillips and his team, as they conducted their series of hearings on climate change. Phillips and his colleagues were painfully aware of the data underpinning climate change. They spent their days reading the scientific research about global climate change, and they felt like they had a window into a terrible truth that most people needed to see. This was the reason behind the parade of hearings and the celebrity appearances that they held on Capitol Hill. Their desperation derived from the fact that no one seemed to be listening.

When Markey's committee realized that hearings alone weren't changing the political dynamic, they took a more provocative step. They wrote a bill of their own. The Select Committee couldn't pass the bill or even introduce it for a vote. But the team knew that the mere existence of a bill would make the issue all the harder to ignore.

The shape of the bill reflected the politics of the time. There were many ways that the government could stanch greenhouse gas emissions. Congress could tax carbon emissions, incentivizing companies to use lower-carbon sources of energy. Or Congress could regulate carbon like a pollutant, setting strict limits on its release. Rather than take these straightforward approaches, the committee settled on a complicated, far-reaching regulatory structure that embodied the internal paradoxes of the neoliberal philosophy that dominated policy making from the Clinton administration onward. The bill sought to dramatically expand the reach of government, while harnessing the power of private markets. In this case, the approach was called cap and trade.

There was surprisingly little dissent within the committee against this approach. "Very early on, people got the sense that this is going to be a cap-and-trade bill," Phillips recalled. "The think tanks in town and everyone in the talking head community—no one was talking about a carbon tax. Everyone was talking about cap and trade as being the vehicle. At that time, there was sort of this consensus that it was the moderate, most economically efficient way of dealing with pollution."

Phillips said it was also attractive because it had the advantage of enjoying bipartisan support. "It was a Republican idea," he said.

The cap-and-trade policy was made famous under President George H. W. Bush, who used it as a way to combat acid rain. The concept was simple. The government capped the total amount of a certain pollutant that could be released. But then it gave companies a license to release that pollution. A company could pollute as much as it desired, but it paid the price to do so by purchasing pollution "credits." If a company cut the amount of pollution it released, it could earn credits for doing so and turn around and sell them. This created a "market" for pollution. Polluters paid to pollute, companies earned money by cutting pollution. All the while, government determined how much total pollution was allowed by setting the cap. The government could turn the screws and push the caps downward, making a stronger and stronger incentive to cut emissions.

Cap-and-trade gained support after Bush imposed it on power plants that released sulfur dioxide, which created acid rain. By 2008, emissions were 60 percent lower than they had been in 1980. More importantly, the cuts were made at much lower costs than people had predicted. The cap and trade system on sulfur dioxide was imposed in 1990.

With their bill, the Markey committee aimed to create the largest cap-and-trade system in history. The limit on greenhouse emissions affected virtually every corner of the modern economy, from automobiles, to power plants, to factories. The policy mechanisms to do so, laid out in the bill's thousand pages, were almost impossibly complex.

Ed Markey unveiled the bill in May of 2008, giving it the consumer-friendly name of "iCAP." After Obama became president, Nancy Pelosi became emboldened. She helped initiate a coup in the Energy and Commerce Committee. A usually perfunctory vote on the chairmanship went against Dingell. He was replaced by the California liberal Henry Waxman, who vowed to pass a law to control carbon emissions. Ed Markey and his committee, after years of agitating from their basement office, were now in a position to do more than agitate. They were in a position to govern. They had opened a pathway to push their bill through Waxman's committee.

The iCAP bill was put on the legislative operating table in 2009 and opened back up. It would become known as the Waxman-Markey bill, an ambitious cap-and-trade system that quickly became a centerpiece of Obama's legislative agenda. The bill had been in the works for years and had been the subject of hundreds of hours of congressional hearings. In the early days of the Obama era, even more hearings were held. The select committee worked even harder as it drafted new language and met with members of Congress and lobbyists from the energy companies and environmental groups.

The long days of grinding work in the basement office were thrilling, in a way, for Phillips. He had the sense that he was a part of history. And he wasn't the only one. At night, Phillips and his friends went out to drink at cheap bars. They must have felt something like the young staffers back in the 1930s, when the mighty legislative pillars of the New Deal were being put into place. They were laying the governing framework of future generations.

They were part of the strongest governing coalition in years, or perhaps decades. An acquaintance of Phillips's, a young speechwriter named Dylan Loewe, wrote a book during that time entitled *Permanently Blue: How Democrats Can End the Republican Party and Rule the Next Generation.* Galley copies were passed around Washington. People read Loewe's prediction that the Democratic Party was in a position to hold the White House and Congress for the next quarter century, and this prediction seemed entirely believable. The Republicans had been reduced to a factional minority with no clear path back to power. The Democratic Party had the force of history at its back, pushing it forward.

Koch Industries' lobbying office was located on the eighth floor of a majestic stone building two blocks from the White House. In early 2009, David Hoffmann—the environmental attorney who'd helped impose Koch's "10,000 percent compliance" doctrine at Invista's factories—was still relatively new to Washington, DC. After working for several years in Wichita, he requested a transfer to Washington in 2007 so that he and his wife could enjoy more big-city culture. He moved into an office at Koch's lobbying shop, even though he was still a compliance attorney. If Hoffmann sympathized with certain elements of the Obama revolution, he also saw the ugly side of the federal government—the complex bureaucracy, and the overbearing paperwork to comply with environmental laws. The Clean Air Act, he said, was a prime example. To comply with the law, there are "literally thousands of items that you need to go over to determine compliance. It takes a full-time staff, working around the clock, to get some of these compliance reviews completed."

Even though he wasn't a lobbyist, Hoffmann helped his peers in Koch's public affairs division by lending his expertise on compliance matters. That's why he got dragged into the largest lobbying fight Koch had ever waged, against the cap-and-trade bill that Phillips and his team were then constructing.

Before 2008, Koch's lobbying efforts had been fragmented. There was a team of lobbyists working for Invista, one for Georgia-Pacific, and another for the oil refining division, Flint Hills Resources. This fragmentation reflected Koch's commitment to maintain its corporate veil, organizing its various divisions under a legal structure that categorized each division as an independent business. This structure helped Koch contain its legal liabilities, but it also hobbled its corporate lobbying efforts. Because Invista and Flint Hills didn't coordinate closely, they might be duplicating their efforts or sending mixed messages to lawmakers. In 2008, Koch Industries consolidated its lobbying operations into a single, newly formed company called Koch Companies Public Sector. Now all of Koch's lobbyists worked side by side, sharing information and strategies as they worked toward common goals.

Hoffmann led an internal committee at Koch, studying how the company might not only adapt to a cap-and-trade regulatory scheme but how it might prosper from it. He came to this role almost accidentally. The newspapers were full of stories about the Waxman-Markey bill. Hoffmann knew that if the law passed, it would instantly become the most significant law that he and his compliance team at Invista would need to contend with. He formed the committee to study the issue. He thought that Invista might find novel ways to comply with the law that could be copied by other divisions at Koch Industries. He was steeped in the ways of Market-Based Management and believed that adapting to a cap-and-trade regime fit perfectly within the MBM framework. "Charles Koch wants to empower his employees to project where industry is going," Hoffmann said. "We felt like we were doing exactly what the Koch philosophy meant to us. Which is: hope for the best but prepare for the worst."

Hoffmann enlisted a handful of fellow Invista employees to help him. He consulted with Koch's lobbyists. And he quickly realized that there was reason to be optimistic about Koch's future in a cap-and-trade world—or at least there was reason to be optimistic about Invista's. Invista was already making investments that cut its carbon output. The company was refitting older factories with new furnaces, for example, fired by natural gas rather than coal. Such efforts saved money and increased efficiency, but they could also be transformed into carbon credits that Invista could sell. Koch Industries also operated smaller divisions that made pollution-control equipment. If cap and trade passed, those divisions could see a boost in business.

Hoffmann labored under the assumption that some sort of cap-and-trade bill was inevitable. What he didn't know then was that he held the minority opinion within Koch's lobbying office.

Every Monday morning, Koch's team of lobbyists gathered in a large meeting room just down the hallway from the office's main reception area. As the lobbyists filed in for their weekly meeting, they took their seats around a large wooden table in the center of the room. The table was set with thick leather coasters with the Koch Industries logo embossed on them. Other than that, the decorations were spartan. A pad of white paper stood on a tripod near the window, on which to write ideas and sketch out strategies. The only artistic adornment in the room was a small metal sculpture on the shelf of a lumberjack, an apparent homage to Georgia-Pacific and its past workforce.

The weekly meeting was led by Koch's top lobbyist, Philip Ellender. He didn't share the habits of a typical lobbyist. He lived in Atlanta, working out of Koch's offices there, and commuted to DC by airplane. While most lobbyists arrived for work around nine thirty or ten in the morning after spending late nights at dinner parties, Ellender operated on Wichita time. He arrived early and spoke frequently on the phone with colleagues in Kansas. He was also a true believer in Charles Koch's philosophy. "We're a bit philosophically more pure," Ellender explained, "in that we recognize that we are unabashedly free traders, that we believe in profiting by the economic, not political, means. We're against cronyism. We're against subsidies. We're against mandates." He peppered his speech with the vocabulary of Market-Based Management.

As Koch Industries became more politically influential, it became increasingly insistent that its lobbyists were pursuing a purely ideological mission. Koch's lobbyists and public relations teams said their goal wasn't to boost Koch Industries' profits, but to champion the ideas of freedom and prosperity. Ellender and others were quick to highlight the times when Koch lobbied against subsidies or tax breaks that might benefit the company. Still, Ellender and his team focused overwhelmingly on the issues that did matter to Koch's business, such as arcane rules about chemical safety, rate billing, and taxes on oil companies. Koch Industries also accepted the subsidies and tax breaks that were in place for it—Ellender said that refusing to do so would put Koch at an unacceptable disadvantage to its competitors.

For all the talk about ideological purity, Ellender's operation reflected a more complicated reality. The lobbying business didn't operate along clean partisan lines. There was a cartoonish image of a Washington lobbyist that most Americans held in their mind—the image of a well-dressed influence peddler who took politicians out to expensive dinners and cocktail cruises on the Potomac River. With enough steak dinners, enough cruises, and enough campaign contributions, the thinking went, any politician eventually succumbed to the lobbyist's wishes. If this view of lobbying was ever accurate, it was certainly irrelevant by 2009. The reason for this was structural: the number of corporate lobbyists had exploded over the previous thirty years. Thousands of lobbyists were trying to push their message, but the messages could only be received by a very narrow audience. There were only 435 members of the House of Representatives and 100 members of the Senate, a total of 535 channels into which all of America's special interests were forced to funnel their message.

The competition for those channels was more intense with each election cycle. In 1983, groups seeking to influence Washington policy spent about $200 million. By 2002, these groups—including corporations, labor unions, and advocacy groups representing retirees or environmental activists—spent $1.82 billion on lobbying, a sevenfold increase. By 2010, spending on lobbying had nearly doubled again to $3.55 billion. And this figure captured only a share of all lobbying expenditures—

the share that was reported under public disclosure laws, which didn't account for campaign contributions or issue-related advertising.

The rise in lobbying spending was not spread evenly across interest groups. Corporations and business groups far outspent other interests, like labor unions and consumer advocates. By 2012, corporations, trade associations, and businesswide associations were responsible for 78 percent of all lobbying expenditures, according to an analysis by the political scientist Lee Drutman. Business interests outspent other interest groups by a ratio of 22 to 1 in 1998, and 35 to 1 in 2008, Drutman found.

Even within these ranks of big corporate spenders, Koch Industries stood apart. The biggest corporations far outspent everyone else. About 90 percent of all US corporations did not even have one full-time lobbyist, and were only represented through trade associations. The biggest companies, like Koch, had a significant advantage.

In this environment, the primary job of Koch's lobbyists was to gather and analyze information. Inside information was perhaps even more important in the market for influence than it was in the market for crude oil. Congress was an impossibly opaque system, a complex pipeline network of policy ideas that flowed between 535 offices in the House and Senate. Minute-by-minute updates on the inner workings of Congress were extraordinarily valuable, and out of reach for most companies. Koch's lobbyists, like most other corporate lobbyists, spent their time gathering detailed intelligence. They determined which bills were originating from which offices, which bills had momentum and which didn't, which politician needed help with a campaign and where that politician stood on issues that were important to Koch. This need for inside information explains why so many lobbyists are former congressional staffers. The former staffers have personal relationships with lawmakers and their staffers. They know which bills will be debated and moved forward through the system. A lobbyist's value comes just as much from knowing about this process as it does from being able to influence it.

Ellender's team was small, considering the size of their job. Koch Companies Public Sector had only five full-time registered lobbyists in 2009. The defense contractor Lockheed Martin, by contrast, had an in-house team of thirty lobbyists that year.

Ellender's permanent team of lobbyists knew a great deal about Republicans in the House and Senate. Koch Industries had given gener-

ously to Republican candidates and conservative causes over the years—
in the 2008 election cycle, Koch Industries gave $1 million to Republicans
and just $186,500 to Democrats.

When Ellender and his team met in 2009, they needed to figure out a
way to learn more about the newly empowered Democrats. This might
seem like an impossible task for Koch's small cadre of lobbyists—the
entire Koch team could fit around the conference table, with chairs to
spare. But their lobbying power was bigger than their numbers might
suggest. Each Koch lobbyist was like the regional manager of a franchise.
They built expertise on certain policy issues, like climate change legislation or derivatives trading, and they had the ability to hire contractors
from outside firms if they needed to beef up staff. This allowed Koch
to build up or reduce its expertise on different topics as they arose in
Congress. Sometimes, the outside contractors joined Koch's team for its
Monday meetings.

One of the lobbyists at Ellender's meeting table was a woman named
Kelly Bingel, a contractor with Mehlman Vogel Castagnetti, a bipartisan lobbying shop. Firms like Mehlman Vogel were a shock absorber
that protected corporations from populist passion. When conservatives
took over Congress, Mehlman Vogel hired out its Republican lobbyists
to help negotiate the new environment. When liberals took over, Mehlman Vogel hired out its Democrats.

Koch Industries first retained Mehlman Vogel in 2007, when Democrats gained control of Congress, paying the firm $10,000 a month
through 2008. By the end of 2009, Koch was paying the firm $20,000 a
month and retaining thirteen of its lobbyists, including Bingel. She was a
former staffer for Senator Blanche Lincoln, the Arkansas Democrat, and
was on a first-name basis with many Democratic senators and staffers.

Bingel was part of a hidden political movement in 2009 that could be
called "Democrats for Koch Industries." She spent time hanging around
the cheap congressional cafeterias, like the one in the basement near Jonathan Phillips's office. When Bingel saw a staffer she knew, she sat down
and traded gossip. She spent time on the phone, collecting tips. When
her staffer friends wanted to get out of the office, Bingel took them out
to lunch. Bingel became a liaison between Koch Industries and the liberal politicians whom the company had spurned for so many years. "My
job was to introduce them to Democrats," she said.

There were two ways for a lobbyist like Bingel to get the attention of a politician. The first was to work for that politician and remain close to their staffers after leaving, as Bingel had done. The second way was to raise money for the politician. This is why lobbyists frequently host fund-raising lunches, banquet dinners, and other events. The issue of fund-raising had to be treated delicately. Bribery is illegal in the United States. If a lobbyist offered money to a legislator in return for a vote, then both people could end up in prison.

To compensate for this fact, an elaborate system of etiquette had taken root in Washington. A lobbyist showed up, made an impassioned pitch to a legislator, and then left. Later, the lobbyist called the legislator's office to say how thrilled the lobbyist would be to hold a fund-raising dinner for the legislator. If the lobbyists mentioned fund-raising in the middle of a pitch meeting, it would be akin to going shirtless to a formal dinner. Everyone in the room would be shocked.

When Bingel brought her colleagues from Koch Industries to meet Democratic politicians, they followed the well-honed lobbyist playbook. They focused on three factors that could sway the legislator's thinking. The factors were:

1. The Preferences of a Legislator's Voters. This was the most important factor to a lawmaker. A legislator cares, more than anything, about winning the next election. They seek to stay safely within the zone of voter approval.

2. The Broader Political Impact of the Vote. Because every legislator belongs to a political party, they also obsess about their standing within the party and their political future. A good lobbyist points out how any given vote fits into the party's goals.

3. The Personal Convictions and Idiosyncrasies of the Legislator. This was the most frustrating and most ambiguous factor. Legislators are only people, at the end of the day. Most of them ran for office for deeply personal, and sometimes irrational, reasons. It could not be overestimated how profoundly these personal motivations play into a legislator's votes. Good lobbyists were intimately familiar with a lawmaker's personal quirks and convictions.

During a typical meeting with a lawmaker, a Koch Industries lobbyist pulled all these levers of influence. To pull the first lever, the lobbyist
highlighted the deep ties that Koch Industries held with the legislator's
voters by listing the jobs that Koch provided in the state or congressional district in question. To pull the second lever, the lobbyist might
talk about legislative issues that were important to the lawmaker's party.
What was left unsaid, but understood among everyone in the room, was
the sizable volume of Koch's political donations, which could help any
politician's standing in their party. Finally, the good lobbyist catered to a
lawmaker's personal quirks, talking about a given issue in terms of keeping taxes fair in one office, and talking about the same issue in terms of
infrastructure investment in another.

Bingel and the other Democrats for Koch helped the company understand the intricate power dynamics within the Democratic majority in
Congress. It was clear that most Democrats in the House felt empowered
to push the Obama agenda. But talking with staffers in the cafeterias
yielded important insights about it. Obama's chief of staff, the former
congressman Rahm Emanuel, wanted Obama to push his agenda in
three phases, with three major bills that would pass through the House
and Senate like train cars in a row. First would be health care reform,
second would be financial industry reform, and third would be climate
change legislation. This was useful to Koch Industries, ExxonMobil, and
other fossil fuel companies that wanted to derail the carbon control
efforts. If the climate change bill was the caboose of the legislative train,
then the opponents had more time to mount a fight against it.

As they worked through their long Monday morning meetings and
sketched ideas on the white notepad, Koch Industries' lobbyists crafted
a plan to do just that.

David Hoffmann worked for months on his study that explored how
Koch Industries might adapt its business to a cap-and-trade bill. He was
excited by his findings. Hoffmann's committee discovered opportunities for Koch to make money in a market for carbon emissions. Invista
released huge amounts of nitrous oxide into the air, a chemical that
trapped heat at a magnitude of 290 times greater than carbon dioxide. If
Invista cut its nitrous oxide emissions, it could reap extremely valuable

carbon emission credits. The future under cap-and-trade might not be entirely bleak.

In spite of these findings, Hoffmann wasn't sure that anyone at Koch was interested in his committee's work. It seemed like his reports and updates were being ignored. Hoffmann realized why after he was invited to attend a senior-level meeting of Koch's lobbying operation. The topics of the meeting were EPA enforcement of the Clean Air Act and the Waxman-Markey cap-and-trade bill.

The meeting convened in the same conference room where Koch's lobbyists held their Monday-morning strategy sessions. Hoffmann didn't usually attend such meetings, but was apparently invited to this one because of his role as an environmental compliance attorney. The first part of the meeting dealt largely with a new push by the EPA to strengthen air emission rules. Philip Ellender led the meeting, but the session was attended by some of the most senior people in Koch's political operation.

This included Richard Fink, who was second only to Charles Koch in the political shop. Fink had a hand in virtually all the facets of Koch's political influence operations, from the Cato Institute think tank, to the academic studies at George Mason University, to the registered lobbyists. Only a handful of people knew about the inner workings of all these groups, and Fink was one of them.

Also at the meeting was Laurie Sahatjian,* one of Koch's most senior attorneys, who specialized in environmental compliance. She was joined by Don Clay, a former EPA official who had worked for Koch's lobbying office since the 1990s.

Before he sat down in the conference room, Hoffmann believed that Koch's approach to the Waxman-Markey bill might be to mitigate its effects on the company, as he was trying to do. As the discussion got under way, he realized his opinion was in the minority.

When the meeting turned to the cap-and-trade bill, the discussion began with some banter and small talk. Most of the attendees let it be known that they thought climate change was "a hoax," Hoffmann recalled. This was difficult for him to absorb. The people in the room were very intelligent. Many of them had an almost encyclopedic knowledge of the emissions released from Koch's factories and refineries and

---

* Laurie Sahatjian married and changed her name to Laurie McCausland.

how those emissions interacted with the Earth's atmosphere. The science of global warming was not fundamentally complex: carbon trapped heat in the atmosphere, more carbon trapped more heat, and humans were releasing unprecedented amounts of carbon into the sky.

But Hoffmann realized that most of the people in the meeting doubted the underlying problem that Waxman-Markey sought to address. If global warming wasn't real, then there was no justification for the law to exist. The feeling in the room was that the Waxman-Markey bill posed an existential threat to Koch Industries. Koch's lobbying team was particularly aggrieved by the bill because it seemed as if the law was specifically targeting oil refineries in an effort to replace them with wind farms and solar panels.

Koch's lobbyists circulated a pie chart that seemed to prove their case. It highlighted a complicated provision of the cap-and-trade law that was seemingly being weaponized against Koch. The provision in question was the so-called carbon allotment. In essence, when the cap-and-trade law took effect, the government would instantly distribute allotments to the private sector that allowed companies to release a certain amount of greenhouse gases into the atmosphere. These allotments were the starting point of the carbon trading market; after a company used all its allotments, it would be forced to pay money for all the additional carbon it released.

Under the proposed law, roughly $1 trillion worth of carbon allotments would be allocated in the beginning. The biggest share of the allotments, totaling about 37 percent, would be handed out to electrical utility companies. The theory behind giving so many allotments to utilities was that it would ultimately ease the regulatory burden on most consumers, who didn't have a choice but to use electricity. The oil refineries, by contrast, would receive just 1.7 percent of the allotments. This tiny sliver of allotments was barely visible in the pie chart that Koch's lobbyists were circulating. Even Hoffmann was swayed by this graphic presentation.

"It was pretty clear that Congress was targeting the refinery industry," he said. "It did seem starkly unfair."

There was even more for Koch to worry about. The government could ratchet down the allotments over time, squeezing the refineries even harder. It looked like a plan to make oil refining a thing of the past.

As it happened, the carbon allotment provision of the Waxman-Markey law was written by Jonathan Phillips, the twenty-nine-year-old congressional aide who was toiling away in the basement of the Longworth Building. Phillips had no idea that he had just become Koch Industries' chief antagonist. He was too busy working.

During the spring of 2009, the long-held liberal dream of passing a cap-and-trade bill was starting to look like a reality. Henry Waxman was in charge of the House Energy Committee, Ed Markey was lobbying his fellow Congress members, and President Obama was speaking in favor of its passage. The Committee on Global Warming spent years provoking Congress into action, and now that action was here. Phillips and his coworkers knew that they had one chance to get it right.

Phillips was asked to write a significant portion of the bill that would create a mandate to spur energy production from renewable sources like wind turbines and solar panels. Creating an economically transformational law wasn't nearly so hard in 2009 as it had been in the early 1930s, when Franklin Roosevelt's administration laid the groundwork for the New Deal. The basic policy machinery of the New Deal was still in place, which created a self-propelling momentum to increasing federal power. As Phillips and his colleagues sought to construct a cap-and-trade system, all they had to do was tweak the massive legislative structure that was already in place. The entire Waxman-Markey law, in fact, was really just an amendment of the Clean Air Act, the Federal Power Act, and other existing laws. It wasn't even necessary to create a new federal agency to implement the law. The carbon cap could be imposed and policed by the EPA, and the renewable-energy mandate could be imposed by the Federal Energy Regulatory Commission, for example.

This was, in short, Charles Koch's worst nightmare. As the government became more powerful, it became easier to expand those powers.

The technical aspects of the bill were mostly settled by early 2009. Phillips and his colleagues were now working on another aspect of the bill: its politics. They needed to win support from a majority of Democrats, which was problematic. One inarguable fact about the cap-and-trade bill is that it would put a price on carbon and thereby increase energy prices, at least in the near term. Oil prices would go up. Coal prices would go up. Electricity bills would go up. Congress members knew that supporting the bill would draw relentless political attacks when higher energy costs were realized. It was true that stemming carbon emissions might mitigate an eventual climate disaster, but this wouldn't help a congressman get reelected in two years' time.

Phillips and his colleagues needed something more than an argument to persuade hesitant Democrats. Luckily, they did have something: an immense pot of money called carbon emission allotments. When a cap was put on carbon, the right to pollute with greenhouse gases would instantly be worth at least billions of dollars. And the government would possess a newly invented piggy bank from which it could disburse the money.

Based in part on observations of carbon trading markets in Europe, most experts estimated that the price of carbon would float around $13 to $15 a ton in the first years of the market. The Waxman-Markey bill allowed for roughly $1 trillion in allotments during the first thirteen years of the law's enactment. The initial allotments might become even more valuable over time because the bill called for total greenhouse gas emissions to fall 17 percent from their levels in 2005 by the year 2020.

"We created a commodity out of nothing," Phillips said.

The committee invited conservative Democrats to negotiate how the allotments would be allocated, creating a windfall available to early adopters of the cap-and-trade system. Phillips and his colleagues held closed-door meetings with staffers for congressmen like Gene Green of Texas and Virginia's Rick Boucher, whose home districts were rich in fossil fuel jobs. The political horse trading gained intensity through April and May as Waxman-Markey gained support in the House. Phillips said that the energy-backed Democrats bargained hard for a big share of allotments. The committee couldn't help but comply. "The last thing we wanted to do was be responsible for shutting down US industry," Phillips said. "So they had a captive audience."

The biggest share of allotments—about $378 billion worth—was given to the electrical utility companies. Just 6 percent of the allotments would be paid to support renewable-energy sources and energy efficiency plans at the state level. That was less than the 6.5 percent offered to natural-gas-fired utilities.

Phillips said that the oil refiners pushed hard for more allotments, mostly through the office of Gene Green, who had multiple oil refineries in his home district in Texas. Ultimately, they agreed to a price. The bill would pay out $17.8 billion to the oil refiners. Phillips and his colleagues made this concession over the protests of environmental groups, who already claimed that the cap-and-trade system favored polluters. Even with that pressure coming from liberal Democrats, the subsidy to oil refineries seemed necessary to get the bill passed.

"They got a great deal," Phillips said.

His view was not shared by Koch Industries' lobbyists. While Phillips was using carbon allotments to target conservative lawmakers who were hesitant to support the bill, Koch's lobbying shop was employing different tactics.

David Hoffmann heard the strategy laid out during the meeting of Koch lobbyists. Koch decided to target moderate Republican politicians who might be tempted to support the measure. There were not enough Republican votes in Congress to kill the bill, but Republican resistance could help slow its passage and make conservative Democrats think twice about supporting it. These were the very same votes that Phillips and his colleagues were trying to secure in the early summer of 2009. If Koch could peel away support from the Republican side, the effort might collapse.

"It was all about identifying those representatives who were on the fence," Hoffmann recalled. "I just remember them talking about individual representatives they needed to reach out to."

There was no better target, in this effort, than a deeply conservative congressman from South Carolina named Bob Inglis. He was a close ally of Koch Industries, who had taken the company's campaign donations and toured its factories. But Inglis would later admit that he was a "heretic" on one issue: global warming. It would make him an example to his peers—and destroy his career.

Bob Inglis was a reliably conservative Republican with a solidly conservative voting record from one of the most conservative congressional districts in the most conservative state in the country. It went without saying that he didn't think global warming was real.

"For six years, I said climate change was nonsense. I didn't know anything about it but that Al Gore was for it," Inglis recalled. "That was the end of the inquiry for me. Al Gore's for it. I'm against it. Next."

Inglis might have remained rooted in this belief if he hadn't been elected to Congress and then become a senior member of the House Committee on Science, Space, and Technology. During his tenure on the committee, Inglis traveled to Antarctica and toured a laboratory that tested ancient air bubbles trapped in ice cores from deep inside ancient glaciers. The evidence from these tests astounded Inglis and seemed simply inarguable. The evidence showed that atmosphere carbon concentrations were increasing dramatically. Al Gore wasn't anywhere nearby to interject his opinion.

The facts just stood alone.

A slow change unfolded in Inglis's thinking. The change was fed by other trips he took as a member of the Science Committee. He visited coral reefs that were dying because of the increased carbon levels in the water, which made oceans more acidic. He studied the heat-trapping effects of carbon and the enormous levels of carbon emissions from industrial activity. He came to believe that carbon emissions were a slow-moving, man-made disaster that might eventually endanger life on Earth.

When he ran for Congress in 2008, Inglis ran on a platform that supported the renewable-energy industry. He saw it as a way to win jobs for his home district. Inglis didn't see any political danger in this position—he had a keen feel for his voters in the Fourth District of South Carolina, a largely rural area that included the small cities of Greenville and Spartanburg. He thought that betting on conservation and renewable energy was betting on the home team. General Electric manufactured wind turbines in his district, and a Michelin factory there manufactured tires designed to increase gas mileage in cars. When he ran for office, one of his slogans was "The road to energy independence starts in South Carolina."

When Inglis talked about controlling carbon emissions, he talked about it using the vocabulary of markets, and capitalism, and innovation. Pollution became a problem if the pollution didn't carry a price, he believed. This was the classic market problem of "externalities," when companies externalized the cost of their production, like pollution. Carbon emissions were arguably the largest externality in the history of humankind. The cost of the emissions would be born heavily for future generations, and companies burning carbon today didn't have to pay a dime for it.

"Coal-fired technology gets away with belching and burning into the trash dump of the sky without paying any tipping fee* for the damage that it's causing there," Inglis said

In spite of this conviction, Inglis couldn't get behind the Waxman-Markey bill. He felt like it was too complex and too sprawling to actually work. But Inglis couldn't let himself simply vote "no" on Waxman-Markey. "I had this rather Boy Scout notion that if you're going to oppose, you better propose," he said.

In late May, Inglis proposed a law called the Raise Wages, Cut Carbon Act of 2009. The bill was similar to many New Deal laws in that it was severe, far reaching, and elegant in its simplicity. It proposed putting a tax on carbon but matching it with a cut to payroll taxes. This meant that any tax increase on consumers could be offset by a tax cut on their earnings. And if people wanted to avoid the tax on carbon, they had the freedom to shift away from carbon-intensive fuels. The tax would feature a "border adjustment," meaning that it would be levied on imported products from China and other countries, ensuring that the cost of carbon wouldn't be unfairly heaped on US manufacturers.

In spite of this, Inglis was closely aligned with Koch Industries for most of his political career. After he was elected in 2004, Koch invited Inglis to tour the company's Invista factory in his district, which provided about a thousand jobs. Inglis remembered Koch's lobbyists flying in from DC to accompany him on the tour. He shook the hands of employees, learned about Invista's product line, and had a delightful time. The affection seemed mutual. Between 2005 and 2006, Koch's PAC donated $7,000 to Inglis's campaign, becoming his fourth-largest contributor. For the 2008 campaign, Koch's PAC donated $10,000 to his campaign, becoming his second-largest contributor.

In 2009, the impending vote on the Waxman-Markey bill put Inglis in a bind. He had long claimed global warming was a danger, but now his convictions would be put to the test.

The pressure intensified in late May, when the Waxman-Markey bill

---

* A tipping fee is the fee a person must pay to dump garbage at a private garbage dump.

was passed by the Energy and Commerce Committee, which had stifled the effort for so many years under John Dingell. Henry Waxman, the new chairman, pushed the bill through committee so quickly that it even surprised the staffers working on it. Phillips had believed that passing the bill through the committee would be harder than passing it through the entire House, because the committee was heavily staffed by conservative Democrats with deep ties to the energy industry.

"I got emotional [during the vote]. I remember looking around on the dais, and my eyes were welling up," Phillips recalled. "That really was the day where it was like, 'Oh, holy shit. This might happen. This is *probably* going to happen.'"

It looked like the bill would be voted on by the entire House in June. This was breathtaking speed in the world of legislation. Within a month of the bill passing committee, every member of the House would have to figure out where they stood on the cap-and-trade bill. Bob Inglis was no exception. As he tried to figure out if he would vote for Waxman-Markey, Inglis kept in close contact with his campaign donors. Like most congressmen, Inglis spent hours, every week, raising cash. He never had the luxury of focusing entirely on the job of policy making; the midterm election of 2010 was just over a year away, and Inglis needed to have plenty of money on hand.

Inglis raised cash in a small office building just a short walk from his office on Capitol Hill. The office was in a nondescript townhouse that was home to the National Republican Congressional Committee, the fund-raising arm of House Republicans. It was illegal for members like Inglis to use their own offices to raise money, so the NRCC provided them with a small call center for the task. Inglis and a staffer showed up at the NRCC and walked down the hall to a small, private office, which Inglis called a "cubby," that had two chairs and two phones. Inglis's staffer worked the phone until she had someone on the line, handed the phone to him so he could ask for money, and start dialing for the next donor.

Koch Industries was a reliable donor, so Inglis made sure to call them early.

Inglis called Koch's lobbying office to see if he could count on the company's support again. Calls like the one to Koch were the easier calls—he was maintaining a relationship rather than trying to build a new one.

The call went poorly from the beginning. The lobbyist whom Inglis usually spoke with wasn't there. He asked if a Koch lobbyist might be able to attend a fund-raising breakfast. He was told that that would not be possible. The call ended quickly.

"I just remember it being a little bit chilly," he recalled. He hung up and thought to himself, *They're not giving me any money this cycle.*

The phone call was just the first of many messages that Koch Industries would send to Inglis.

Jonathan Phillips stood in the gallery of the chamber of the US House of Representatives, looking down on the wide-open floor area with its concentric half circles of seats for the members of Congress. It was Friday, June 26, 2009, the day that the House would vote on the Waxman-Markey bill. Phillips wasn't at all sure that the bill was going to pass. Support was narrow, and any defections from the Democrats could sink it. It appeared that some defections were in the offing. Pelosi seemed to be working the crowd, making deals, quieting concerns. "Pelosi was doing I don't know what sort of horse trading," Phillips recalled. "Those are the type of tough votes where she's making promises, you know?"

Over the next several hours, Republicans and conservative Democrats voiced their opposition to the bill based on a shared foundation. They didn't attack the evidence about climate change or challenge the need to promote renewable sources of energy. Instead, they attacked the Waxman-Markey bill as an economic disaster; an expensive tax on everyone that would raise the prices of electricity, gasoline, and energy. The theory behind the cap-and-trade system, of course, was that market forces would help solve the price problem over time as companies invented new technologies that were carbon free and introduced them to the market.

After nearly eight hours of procedural maneuvers and debate, Ed Markey rose to speak. He didn't seek to rebut many of the attacks one by one, but answered them with a call to take part in history. "This bill has the ambition of the moon landing, the moral imperative of the Civil Rights Act, and the scope of the Clean Air Act all wrapped up in one," he said.

After exhausting their arguments, the Republicans prepared to make their closing statement. They reserved the privilege for a rising star in the House, a former conservative talk-radio host from Indiana who was first elected to the House in 2001, named Mike Pence.

Pence walked to the rostrum and looked down for a moment before beginning his speech. He was a striking figure, a handsome man with a square jaw and stark white hair. His training in show business was apparent the moment he started to speak. While other congressmen stumbled through their speeches, reading awkwardly from a script, Pence was at ease.

"It's hard to know where to start," he said, shaking his head. And then he paused, a long, dramatic pause that ate up much of his allotted speaking time but had great effect.

Everyone was listening. "This economy is hurting. American families are struggling under the weight of the worst recession in a generation," he said, with great sadness and great compassion in his voice. "In the midst of the worst recession in a generation, this administration and this majority in Congress are prepared to pass a national energy tax that will raise the cost of energy on every American family."

And then Pence did something that none of his colleagues seemed to have done during the course of an eight-hour day. He looked directly into the C-Span camera and talked directly to the viewers there, whoever they might be. He pointed his finger at them and exhorted them to get up and make a difference. "If you oppose the national energy tax, call your congressman *right now!*" he bellowed. "Alexander Hamilton said it best: 'Here, sir, the people govern.' We can stop this bill. We can do better. And so we must."

It was an impassioned speech, but Pence's rallying cry seemed oddly out of place. There didn't seem to be some great crowd of voters in the C-Span audience ready to mount a rebellion against the Obama agenda. Pence finished his speech and stepped back in the gallery, looking like a pied piper with no one to follow him.

After several hours, the debate was finished, and the roll call vote began. Phillips and his colleagues watched as the votes were tallied, and their elation grew with every minute. The margin of victory became insurmountable. A one- or two-vote margin turned into a seven-point margin. The bill passed 219 to 212. Gene Green, the conservative Texas Democrat from oil refinery country, voted for the bill, as did Rick

Boucher, from coal country. Remarkably, eight Republicans broke ranks to support the bill, more than Phillips or anyone on his committee might have expected.

When the vote was tallied, Phillips and his colleagues went to the staff office of the Energy and Commerce Committee. These were nice offices, a big space that was far removed from the basement warren where Phillips had worked for years. Bottles of champagne were popped open, glasses were passed around. Both Waxman and Markey were in the room, talking with staffers. Both men gave a speech. There was a tremendous sense of accomplishment in the room. As they drank and laughed and clapped each other on the back, everyone seemed sure that the bill would pass the Senate within months, probably by Christmas.

"We did what we set out to do," Phillips said. "I totally felt like this is what I came to Congress for."

Every quarter, Charles Koch held meetings in the company boardroom to evaluate the progress of each major division in his company. He peppered the business leaders with questions, probing their presentations for weak points and questioning their plans for the future. By the middle of 2009, Charles Koch was getting similar presentations from his political operatives. He sat at the large, polished wood table and listened as top operatives in his political network walked through the events of the past months, shared their analysis of the landscape, and laid out their plans for the future.

In the middle of 2009, the news from the political operation was unrelentingly bad. The Waxman-Markey bill had passed the House and was fast-tracked toward the Senate. To make matters worse, Obama's stimulus bill was doling out billions of dollars to Koch's emerging competitors in the wind, solar, and renewable-energy industries.

As with any business unit, Charles Koch absorbed this information with apparent dispassion. He asked for data and analyzed it closely. One senior political operative recalled sending Charles Koch a spreadsheet with polling data on voter attitudes. The presentation included "top line" figures, showing broad voter attitudes that were accompanied by several "cross tabs" of detailed data that broke down the results by demographic group. As the operative was presenting his findings to Charles

Koch and other directors of the company, Koch interrupted to question them about the data.

Charles Koch asked about figures in the cross tables. He wanted to know why women in one geographic area felt the way they felt. The operative was shocked at the level of granular knowledge behind the question. Charles Koch was paying just as close attention to his political efforts as his corporate endeavors.

It seemed even more surprising that Charles Koch could keep all of these political operations straight in his own head. The contours of Koch's political machine were intentionally obscured and complex. Outside analysts would spend years trying to piece together all of its various pieces. The political machine consisted of at least dozens of shell groups funded by anonymous donors, some of them staffed by current and former employees of Koch Industries. The network included the main lobbying office in Washington, DC; all of the contract lobbyists it hired; a relatively obscure activist group called Americans for Prosperity with chapters in several states; at least several private political consultancies; the Koch Industries corporate PAC; various think tanks; academic programs and fellowships; and a consortium of wealthy donors that Charles and David Koch convened twice a year to pool large donations for Koch's chosen causes. And these elements were just the most visible pieces of the Koch political machine.

The entirety of the political apparatus could only be viewed from the top, by a handful of people with the authority to see the entire operation. These people were Charles Koch, David Koch, and their top political operative, Richard Fink. Of the three of them, Charles Koch unquestionably had the most authority. It was Charles Koch, then, who had the most influence over how this political machine would react to the surprising momentum behind the Waxman-Markey bill. His reaction might have been unsurprising to anyone who knew him well. Charles Koch had been unyielding in his years-long legal battle against his brother Bill. He had been unyielding in his battles with relatives and shareholders who wanted to take the company public. He had been unyielding in his battle against labor unions. He was unyielding now.

Koch's political machine was deployed, in 2009, in ways that it had never been deployed before. Millions of new dollars would flow into a new political network at the state level. Hundreds, possibly thousands, of new activists would be brought on board. New attack campaigns were launched. New political candidates were chosen and supported.

In the fight that Charles Koch was about to wage, there would be no compromise. There would be no effort to amend the Waxman-Markey bill or win subsidies through the emission allotments. There would be no effort to suggest an alternative path to lower carbon emissions, such as a carbon tax. There would not even be an acknowledgment that climate change was real.

The central strategy would remain the same as the one conveyed in Koch's lobbying office earlier in the summer. The primary target of Koch's campaign would be Republicans who supported the Waxman-Markey bill, and any Republicans who stood against Koch on the issue of climate change.

These Republicans were the primary targets for a reason. Koch's long-term plan was to reshape the Republican party, and these members would be made an example of. The strategy wasn't necessarily new, but the means that Koch used to pursue it were unprecedented.

After the Waxman-Markey bill passed, Phillips and the other members of the Global Warming Committee handed off most of their work to their colleagues in the Senate. Congress was called into recess for the Fourth of July break, and members went back to their districts for the annual tradition of constituent meetings and parades.

During the holiday recess, the Global Warming Committee's communications director, Jeff Sharp, kept working, monitoring media reports about the Waxman-Markey bill. The Senate would pick up debate of the measure in the fall, and Sharp wanted to stay on top of the story in the meantime. Over the Fourth of July holiday, Sharp started getting some disturbing phone calls and e-mails. There were protests. And the protests were remarkable. Protestors were standing along parade routes, on Independence Day, waving placards and shouting at the members of Congress as they passed by. Sharp couldn't remember anything like it happening before.

"At each parade, there is a group of four to six people in the parade screaming and yelling: 'No cap and trade! No cap and tax!' Like, viscerally angry on that issue. In the parade. This is a parade, right? Most parades, as you go through the parade, at that time, people were not yelling and screaming about an issue, let alone a very specific issue like cap and trade."

The protestors were also showing up at the congressional members' town hall meetings, those boring civic obligations that never drew more than a half dozen people or so. The town halls were crowded now with angry constituents who hectored the congressional members with shaking anger in their voices. These protestors didn't look like typical protestors. They were middle-aged people. Mostly white. Affluent looking. Not the kind of people that most Congress members were accustomed to seeing protest in public.

Sharp received a video from the town hall meeting held by a Delaware Republican named Mike Castle, who'd voted in favor of the Waxman-Markey bill. Protestors lined the back of his town hall. They hooted and bellowed. They repeatedly brought up the cap-and-trade plan.

"On this energy thing," one protestor said, "CO_2 emissions have nothing to do—and the greenhouse effect has nothing to do—with global warming. It's all a hoax! Personally, for the life of me, I can't understand how you could have been one of the eight Republican traitors."

At the word *traitors*, loud applause broke out. Castle, standing at a podium, dutifully took notes as the protestors made their arguments. After the event, a woman in the crowd pigeonholed Castle and informed him that the Earth was, in fact, cooling. She asked if he knew how much the "cap-and-tax" system was going to harm the poultry industry in Delaware.

Sharp watched these videos over and over. The comments struck him as odd. Cap and trade and global warming had never elicited such visceral anger from the public. People didn't normally show up at parades and yell about one single issue. And he kept hearing the same phrases, the same talking points, again and again. The protestors talked about "cap and tax" and a "hoax" and an "energy tax." It was as if the protestors had been coached or handed a script. This wouldn't have been groundbreaking—Sharp had seen such tactics used up close during his years in the PR and lobbying businesses.

When he saw these protests, Sharp saw a coordinated campaign. "I remember watching that and [thinking]: *Something is Astroturf–smelling about that event,*" he recalled. "It did not feel organic."

Sharp kept watching the video of Mike Castle getting berated at the town hall. And he kept thinking about the protestor in back who called climate change "a hoax."

"I remember watching it, and being like, *Where did that guy get that from?*"

CHAPTER 20

Hotter

(2009–2010)

If sufficiently developed and organized, public sentiment, as manifested in Congress, can prevail over presidential intransigence.

—Jon Meacham, *The Soul of America:*
The Battle for Our Better Angels, 2018.

As hot as it is today, if we keep working this issue, it's going to get even hotter for Barack Obama and Harry Reid! Because I think the American people are fed up! Don't you?

—Tim Phillips, president of Americans for Prosperity,
speaking at a rally outside the US Capitol, August 7, 2010

This was unmanageable. Bob Inglis was standing in an auditorium, in front of a very large crowd, trying to make himself heard. He was hosting a town hall event and had a microphone in his hand, but his words were drowned out by heckling and shouting. He seemed dazed, like he couldn't quite make sense of what he was seeing.

The first thing that didn't make sense to Inglis was the sheer size of the crowd. There were roughly five hundred people in the room, maybe more. This was incomprehensible. Bob Inglis had been holding town hall events for years and was lucky to draw fifteen or twenty people to each event. Americans simply didn't turn out for civic events, even if you provided free food. But one of his meetings that summer drew an estimated seven hundred people. The fire marshals arrived at that one and turned people away.

The second thing that didn't make sense to Inglis was the rage. The crowd, all of them, were boiling with anger. At most political events, it was rare for anyone in attendance to stand up and speak into a microphone; the few people who did were the same handful of gadflies who spoke at every meeting. This crowd was different. They weren't just ready to stand up and speak. They looked ready to charge the stage. They were shouting. Booing. Cupping their hands around their mouths and catcalling.

The crowd was shouting, and Inglis was trying to make his voice heard and to calm things down a little bit. But the acoustics in the auditorium were awful, and the sound system was crummy. His voice was drowned out.

One of Inglis's political aides, a young man named Price Atkinson, was out in the crowd, carrying a microphone to hand to the attendees to let them ask questions. Atkinson was wearing a suit and tie, and his short, dark hair was neatly combed. At one point, Atkinson leaned over and held the microphone for a particularly agitated middle-aged woman with long, dark hair who wore a peach-colored shirt. The woman was waving a ream of papers in her hand. She said they were copies of the Affordable Care Act, the proposed law better known as Obamacare. She had spent hours reading through the entire bill, she said, and was horrified by what she saw there.

"There are things in this health care bill that people don't realize are in there!" she cried out. "They want to put a *chip* in every one of us! It talks about it right here!" she said, flipping through the pages. She claimed that if Obamacare passed, every American would be mandated to have a microchip implanted in their body, allowing the government to monitor the populace.*

This proclamation evoked cross-shouting from the rest of the crowd. People raised their hands for the microphone. More shouting ensued. The woman seemed determined to read pertinent portions of the bill, and crowd members began to shout, "Let her *read* it!" as other crowd members booed and catcalled.

---

* No version of the Affordable Care Act ever proposed to implant a microchip in every American. The theory that such a provision was part of the law appears to be based on early draft versions of the bill that were never passed. The proposal would have allowed the US Department of Health and Human Services to collect data on medical devices like pacemakers. This data collection would have helped speed recall notices of such devices and could also help gauge their efficacy.

Inglis tried, again, to speak. This was how it went all summer. The crowds who attended his public meetings were enraged with Washington, DC, enraged with Barack Obama, and enraged with Inglis himself. They were enraged about government bailouts, the stimulus, Obamacare, and, very often, about the Waxman-Markey cap-and-trade bill that Inglis had voted *against*. Inglis discovered that voting against Waxman-Markey wasn't enough. The crowd was aware of Inglis's views on climate change and his proposed bill to pass a carbon tax. He tried patiently to explain the fifteen-page bill he had proposed and explain how the carbon tax would be balanced by a cut in payroll taxes. But the crowds were not convinced. They called the Waxman-Markey bill, which was just then being debated in the Senate, the "cap-and-tax" bill and the "crap-and-tax" bill.

Amid all the shouting, Inglis saw small things that were deeply puzzling.

During the town hall meeting where the woman waved her pages and warned about being microchipped, Inglis saw something behind her. There, in the back of the room, a person was filming the event. And they were using a nice video camera, set on a tripod. This stuck in Inglis's mind. It seemed to signify something.

"It wouldn't be your average person who comes with a tripod and sets up," he said. Somebody was helping.

When heated protests broke out across the country over the Fourth of July weekend of 2009, one of the larger events was sponsored by a little-known political group called Americans for Prosperity. Strangely enough, this event was held in the deep-blue, liberal state of New Jersey, which had voted overwhelmingly for Barack Obama. The event was hosted by Steve Lonegan, Americans for Prosperity's state director in New Jersey. The protest was held in a large city park, and Lonegan was slated as one of the main speakers.

It was sunny that day, and Lonegan wore a short-sleeved button-down shirt and a red necktie when he walked out on the large stage to address the crowd. He stood near a podium draped with a bright-yellow banner, called the Gadsden flag, that showed a coiled rattlesnake above the motto "Don't Tread on Me." The flag dated from the Revolutionary War, and it became a common sight that summer.

When Lonegan grasped the microphone, he didn't look like a revolutionary. He looked exactly like what he had been for twelve years, which was a small-town mayor. His shirt was tucked into his slacks, and his necktie seemed to be knotted just a little too tight. He was slightly portly and wore glasses. But he was a good speaker and he knew how to rile up a crowd. Lonegan, a Republican, had honed his speaking skills during the decade that he was mayor of the small, liberal town called Bogota (pronounced Buh-GO-dah). He sharpened those skills even further after he left public office, when he became a traveling evangelist for the political vision of Charles Koch.

Lonegan was hired as one of the first state directors for Americans for Prosperity. When he joined AFP, as insiders called it, Lonegan was just one of a handful of state directors. The group was founded in 2003, and within a year, it included state-level chapters in Kansas, Texas, and North Carolina. AFP was small and quirky and a marginal force in American politics back then. Its budget was about $3 million in 2003 and just $1 million in 2004. Still, Lonegan felt a close sense of camaraderie with the early directors and board members of AFP. Lonegan reported directly to the AFP president, an activist named Tim Phillips, whom Koch had hired in from the conservative Christian movement. When he joined AFP, Phillips stopped campaigning against abortion and gay marriage and started campaigning for tax cuts and regulatory rollbacks. This was a message that Lonegan believed in passionately, and he took up the cause with gusto. He started raising money for AFP's New Jersey chapter—in over six years, he claimed to have boosted the annual fund-raising take in his state from $150,000 to $1.6 million.

Lonegan invested countless hours of his own time. He drove from town to town throughout New Jersey and gave speeches at libraries and Rotary club meetings, and even at Democratic Party gatherings. He hosted a local radio show where he preached against the creeping reach of state authority in New Jersey. He often drove for hours to show up at some public library where only four or five people arrived to hear him speak.

Now people were listening. That Saturday on the Fourth of July, Lonegan was looking out over a crowd of hundreds. They were mostly older and almost entirely white. They looked affluent. Someone had brought a large American flag that swayed in the breeze. Dozens of people brought camping chairs that they'd set up in a rough semicircle on the grass in front of the stage.

The crowd was united in their outrage but disparate in their complaints. A man with white hair, sunglasses, and cargo shorts held a placard that simply read: "I WANT MY COUNTRY BACK." A middle-aged woman in a straw sun hat held a yellow, stenciled placard that read: "JUST SAY NO. NO MORE SPENDING. NO MORE TAX INCREASES. NO GOVT RUN BUSINESS." Other signs read: "SAY NO TO SOCIALISM!" And "SILENT NO MORE!"

If the crowd's grievances were diffuse, then it was Lonegan's job to focus them. He united the crowd by giving a stump speech that AFP helped him fashion over many years.

"You know, we've been hearing a lot about global warming, right?" Lonegan said. "The reason that we're redistributing our nation's economy and industry around the world—it's under this *pretense* of global warming. We've heard now how we're destroying the environment, and we're destroying the polar bear population."

At the mention of polar bears, the crowd groaned and booed. Lonegan had them. He stoked their discontent by claiming the EPA was suppressing a report showing that the polar bear population was actually increasing, in spite of Al Gore's hysterical warnings. To underscore his point, Lonegan introduced his guest speaker, a man dressed in a polar bear suit, who had been wandering through the crowd carrying a sign that said, "I am AFP!"

The guy in the polar bear suit, introduced as "Prospero the Polar Bear," stepped up to the microphone as the crowd started to chuckle.

"I don't know—how many of you can hear me?" Prospero asked into the microphone, as it reverberated with feedback. "There's too many polar bears!"

This drew sweeping laughter. "When I grew up, there was plenty of space," Prospero continued. "Now there's fifty thousand of us. And we just keep making more and more. They say it's getting warm and icebergs are melting. Well, I needed more space, so I came down here." The Prospero routine killed. As Prospero stepped back, Lonegan took the microphone and quoted the founding fathers and the US Constitution, driving home the importance of liberty and the constraints that must be placed on government. The rhetoric was elegant and forceful. It equated the cap-and-trade bill with government tyranny, and the fight against the bill with America's primal struggle against oppression.

Lonegan's rhetoric was strategic. By emphasizing the centrality of climate change legislation to popular discontent with American politics in 2009, he was carrying forward the corporate lobbying campaign that Charles Koch had initiated from the boardroom in Wichita. This strategy was central to AFP's role in Koch's political network. From the earliest days of AFP's inception, the group operated as something like a fast-food franchise. AFP was composed of semiautonomous state chapters, but all of them served products from the same menu. The menu was designed with great care and specificity by Charles and David Koch and their lieutenants in Koch's lobbying operations. This meant that state-level directors had a lot of autonomy. Lonegan developed his own pool of local donors and had the freedom to hire his own field directors and to determine where he spoke. But ultimately Lonegan and other state directors were told by AFP headquarters what they should say and how they should say it.

"I had to report to the national office," Lonegan recalled. "They gave guidance on where our issues would lie. . . . So, I would report regularly to my boss on what issues were emerging, and then we'd determine how they'd want to address it. Not every issue that I saw as an issue did they think was an issue."

This blend of local autonomy with centralized control created a political organization that was uniquely powerful and effective. AFP could mobilize the type of popular citizen involvement that most people referred to as grassroots support. But it coupled this popular support with intelligence and guidance developed inside one of the most well-funded corporate lobbying operations in America. This meant that AFP could get people marching in the streets, and it could get them marching in the exact streets and zip codes of congressional districts where their marching would most effectively benefit Koch Industries' strategic interests. The lobbying shop, under Philip Ellender, attained the kind of real-time, granular political intelligence that only the largest corporations had the resources to develop. That information was then shared with a multistate network of ground-level activists of the kind that Lonegan had built over many years in New Jersey.

Koch's lobbyists were unique in their ability to closely coordinate with the network of "third-party" groups that Koch Industries supported and nurtured. Koch's lobbying office held conference calls "daily—multiple times every day" with Koch operatives who coordinated the activities of the third-party groups, according to one person familiar with Koch's political operations.

The coordination could also occur at the highest levels. Richard Fink, Charles Koch's top political lieutenant, sat on AFP's board of directors from the beginning. He also sat in on the lobbying strategy meetings in Washington of the kind that were attended by Ellender and the compliance lawyer David Hoffmann.

The potency of this tight coordination would not be felt during AFP's early years. During the George W. Bush era, AFP wasn't much more than a political sideshow. Even by 2008, the organization was doing the political equivalent of cheap stunt work. The group hired out a hot-air balloon to fly around with a placard claiming that concern over climate change was nothing more than "hot air." It hired cameramen to accost people who showed up for an Al Gore speech on global warming the summer of 2008, asking them why they drove to the event if driving meant that they burned fossil-fuels.

AFP's full power was not mobilized until the Waxman-Markey bill threatened Koch Industries. As the threat of regulations on carbon emissions increased, Charles and David Koch dramatically increased the funding and reach of Americans for Prosperity. In 2007, the group had a budget of $5.7 million. By 2009, that budget was $10.4 million. In 2010, it was $17.5 million.

In 2009, AFP became a central part of the Koch network's political influence operation. The group filed paperwork for chapters in thirty-three states and the District of Columbia. The state chapters opened pages on Facebook and built e-mail lists for volunteers. Lonegan had a hard time keeping up with the increases in funding, staff, and new state chapters.

While the funding increases were important for AFP, something else was happening that was even more significant for the group. Lonegan and AFP finally had an audience. After Barack Obama's election, Lonegan was no longer speaking to crowds of four or five people at public libraries—he was speaking to hundreds. The crowd that showed up for the Independence Day rally was just the beginning. There were people everywhere, even in New Jersey, who were fed up with the direction of American politics and were becoming activists for the first time in their lives. This movement would come to call itself the Tea Party.

As it turned out, Charles Koch had laid out a white tablecloth and fine china for this tea party many years in advance. The causes Charles Koch had been advocating—cutting the national debt and halting the reach of federal government into private markets—were causes that Tea Party activists cared about passionately.

Koch Industries and the leaders of Americans for Prosperity did not create the Tea Party or even orchestrate it. But they were ready for it, and prepared to steer it and shape its concerns. Lonegan and others at AFP helped make climate change regulation a central focus of the Tea Party movement. When Lonegan hosted rallies, he and his team were ready to record the e-mail address of anyone who shared it. They made phone trees and hosted volunteer training sessions. They passed out the phone numbers of local congressmen to activists and coached them on the best time to call. (Late night was sometimes best so that volunteers could leave voicemails, which would be waiting in big batches when the politician showed up for work the next day.) They taught volunteers the fine art of calling talk-radio programs and getting on the air, coaching them to mention the right website address or phone number when they were on the air.

Lonegan and his colleagues did more than just get Tea Party activists to focus on the Waxman-Markey bill. Americans for Prosperity also helped direct the activists' passion toward a very specific group of targets: Republican politicians. Attacking the Republican party was one of AFP's central strategies from the earliest days. In 2006, Lonegan attended a private AFP event hosted by Charles and David Koch, in Aspen, Colorado. The event was an annual symposium attended by wealthy conservative political donors, academics, and activists that Charles Koch began to convene in 2003, just as he helped launch Americans for Prosperity. The seminars were another innovation in Charles Koch's broader political strategy: rather than fund his political causes alone, Charles Koch sought to enlist fellow donors. Twice a year, the donors attended seminars in Aspen, Palm Springs, or other scenic getaways, pledging their money to Koch's causes and hearing speeches from politicians who auditioned for Koch's political support. When Lonegan heard Charles Koch speak at the seminar in 2006, he was inspired by Koch's ambitious vision and strategic intelligence. Lonegan was also impressed by Charles Koch's strategy of using his donor group's resources to attack conservatives rather than liberals. The strategy seemed counterintuitive, but effective.

"I'm a big fan of Charles Koch. I think he's a brilliant guy and very well read, and he gets it," Lonegan recalled. "He said, 'The problem we have is not the Democrat Party. They're doing what Democrats do. Our problem is the Republican Party. We've got to make Republicans act like Republicans.'"

Koch and Americans for Prosperity pressured the Republican party from the right, steering it away from the compromises of neoliberalism and pushing it toward a vision that was espoused by Austrian economists like Friedrich Hayek. It gained more volunteers every day, and it steered them toward one target: Republican politicians like Bob Inglis.

Bob Inglis's congressional district in South Carolina contained the tiny town of Boiling Springs, located just a little bit north of Spartanburg. The town was easy to miss. Its most prominent feature was a strip of stores near Highway 9 and a Walmart Supercenter on the north end of town. But Boiling Springs became an important landmark on the political map in 2009, when a woman named Maria Brady had a vision from God. The vision arrived when she was at work, and it would set her life on a direct collision course with Bob Inglis.

Brady and her husband, Michael, owned a printing company in Boiling Springs that published the local newspaper, *Boiling Springs Today*. Maria was working from home when she had the epiphany, sitting in front of the computer. She heard a voice in her head that said very clearly: "Quit complaining. Quit complaining and do something."

Brady had been complaining a lot during that winter of 2009. Business at the printing shop collapsed after the financial crash. The company printed advertising circulars, and local businesses cut their advertising budgets sharply during the deep recession. Maria and Michael laid off workers, scaled back production, and worried about paying the bills. Yet whenever Maria turned on the television news, she saw that the same Wall Street CEOs who'd caused the crash were getting multibillion-dollar rescue packages from the government. They weren't even losing their bonuses.

After she heard God's voice, Brady fell down on her knees and prayed, asking what He meant and what He wanted from her. When Michael returned from the printing shop later that day, he looked like he'd seen a ghost. He told Maria that God had just spoken to him and told him that he needed to do something to help his country. Maria shared her own vision. It was clear: they were being called to do something.

Maria began to scour the Internet. It was April of 2009. She came across mentions of a new form of revolt by people fed up with the condition of America. She heard about events that people were calling Tea Parties. The notion of throwing a Tea Party was romantic. Patriotic. It conjured images of the earliest American revolutionaries throwing off the yoke of imperial Britain.

Tea Parties first became part of the national conversation in February of that year, during a broadcast on the financial news network CNBC. The anchors were discussing the Obama administration's proposal to modify many consumers' mortgages after the crash made millions of houses worth less than the debt that was owed on them. The anchors cut to a commentator named Rick Santelli, who was reporting live from the trading floor of the CME Group in Chicago. Behind Santelli were rows of traders at desks, buying and selling futures contracts and other derivatives. They did not appear happy. Santelli was highly agitated, and expressed his contempt at the idea that the government might bail out homeowners who found themselves trapped in expensive mortgage agreements.

"The government is promoting bad behavior!" Santelli shouted into the camera. He mocked the Obama administration while the traders around him clapped and cheered him on. Santelli turned and gestured back behind him toward the trading floor and shouted, "This is America!" And then he yelled to the traders: "How many of you people want to pay for your neighbor's mortgage that has an extra bathroom and can't pay their bills?"

The traders booed loudly, and Santelli turned to the camera to ask, "President Obama, are you listening?"

"We're thinking of having a Chicago Tea Party in July," Santelli continued. "All you capitalists that want to show up at Lake Michigan, I'm going to start organizing. I think we'll be dumping in some derivatives securities. What do you think about that?"

The idea of throwing Tea Parties began to spread. The movement was organic and improvised, driven by people like Maria Brady. Ordinary people who had never been politically active reached out to friends and formed e-mail chains to stay in touch. Middle managers, housewives, plumbers, and even commodities traders began to organize.

Maria and Michael Brady assembled an e-mail list of friends and neighbors and helped form the Boiling Springs Tea Party. They planned a Tea Party for Tax Day in mid-April. Maria ordered a costume for Michael, with a tricornered hat and an elegant jacket with golden lapels. When he wore the outfit, he looked like he'd stepped straight out of 1776. Hundreds of people showed up for the protest, even though it had been organized on short notice. Maria was amazed. When she held a placard in public for the first time, she felt more than happy. She felt a sense of belonging.

"It was the hardest thing I've ever done," she recalled. "I loved it. It was a trip. It felt good to realize that 'Hey, I'm not by myself.'"

In the weeks after the protest, members of the newly formed Tea Party chapter of Boiling Springs stayed in close contact. They planned a bigger rally, this one to be held on the Fourth of July.

This time Maria and Michael had help. They connected with the South Carolina chapter of Americans for Prosperity. Tea Party groups around the nation were doing the same thing. Maria and Michael Brady were neither directed by Americans for Prosperity nor even inspired by Americans for Prosperity. But AFP provided its Tea Party groups and others with concrete means of assistance that amplified their message and energy in vitally important ways.

Americans for Prosperity's South Carolina chapter formed a Facebook page and website that became a central clearing hub for Tea Party activists. When people like Maria Brady threw up their arms and went to the Internet, they found the Americans for Prosperity site. It listed ways that they could get involved. It provided a platform to connect with fellow activists.

The site promoted Maria and Michael's upcoming Fourth of July protest, and it included Michael Brady's name and telephone number for anyone interested in attending. The page also included a long list of other activists planning to hold protests on Independence Day. The AFP site also included a nationwide database listing the times and locations of town hall meetings that Congress members planned to host, encouraging the activists to attend. Bob Inglis's town halls were on the list. The website included a form to fill out that automatically sent letters to member of the US Senate informing them to "vote no on cap and trade."

AFP chapters in New Jersey and elsewhere offered free chartered bus rides to protestors to attend a rally in Washington, DC, that summer. Once in Washington, protestors were given free box lunches and glossy protest signs. The protestors were joined by Tim Phillips, AFP's president, who gave rousing rally speeches.

This close coordination masked key points of disagreement between Tea Party activists and the political vision of Charles Koch. One of the very few rigorous studies of the Tea Party found that the political beliefs of the group were far from libertarian. Tea Party activists strongly supported popular entitlement programs such as Medicare and Social Security, for example. They weren't animated by a hatred of big government but by the belief that entitlement benefits were being unfairly diverted to people who didn't work hard and didn't deserve them. Their grievance was the exploitation of the middle class, not the existence of robust New Deal–era safety net programs. The racial tinge to the grievance was unmistakable, but also complicated. Many Tea Party chapters took great pains to avoid any racist language at their protests and welcomed minority members. But it was unmistakable that the unworthy beneficiaries of entitlements, in their eyes, were Hispanic immigrants and African-American residents of the inner city.

Maria Brady, for one, had no idea who Charles Koch was in 2008. She didn't study Hayek or von Mises or read papers from the Cato Institute. Instead, she began her political education on the Internet. The stories she found there were outrageous. She read that Nancy Pelosi had ordered two jumbo jet planes for her own use, and that Congress had approved of the purchase, using taxpayer money. Brady and her husband were paying for Nancy Pelosi's private jet, and *nobody* was talking about it!*

---

* This story was not true. When Pelosi became Speaker of the House, she was afforded the use of a military aircraft to travel to her home district in California. She did request a plane that was larger than that of her predecessor, Republican Dennis Hastert. He had used a smaller plane because his home district was in Illinois, and the smaller plane could not make the trip to California without refueling.

Brady did find one trusted source for news and education that was recommended to her by many friends and fellow patriots. She began to watch the television show of a commentator named Glenn Beck. "I kind of got an education. My start of my education was Glenn Beck, I guess. Because that's the only person that was talking about the issues that I agreed with."

Glenn Beck was the most prominent voice in the American Tea Party movement, and understanding Beck's political philosophy was critical to understanding the Tea Party and the relationship of the Tea Party to Charles Koch's political efforts.

Glenn Beck's television show on Fox News drew close to three million viewers in 2009, beating the combined ratings of all his competitors' shows. Beck spent many years honing his skills as a political entertainer on talk radio, where provocation was the currency of the realm. Debate was better than discussion. Suspense was better than satisfaction. Outrage was better than understanding. Glenn Beck elevated this genre to the level of high art. The narratives he spun on his show were terrifying and purported to reveal the broad contours of chilling global conspiracies. He affected the persona of a high school teacher, wearing a cheap, ill-fitting coat and tie. He stood in front of a chalkboard. During one show, the chalkboard displayed three logos: The United Nations symbol, the Islamic crescent, and the iconic Communist hammer and sickle. Beck explained that these three logos represented the three global movements that were currently hard at work to enslave and control his viewers.

"The world is on fire," Beck said in a remarkably casual and civil tone. "And there are three groups of people that want a new world order."

One of Beck's favorite targets was the Obama administration's efforts to promote alternative fuels, which Beck portrayed as a vast conspiracy to steal wealth from the middle class and transfer it to an elite group of liberal billionaires. The first phase of the conspiracy, Beck explained, was to fool everyone into thinking that human activity and the burning of fossil fuels was changing the world's climate. Climate change was a lie, Beck said, perpetuated by dishonest scientists who cherry-picked and fabricated evidence.

Americans for Prosperity helped promote this point of view. Phil Kerpen, AFP's national director of policy, joined Glenn Beck on his show during the summer of 2009 to help Beck analyze global warming and the clean energy conspiracy. Kerpen sat opposite Beck, near the chalkboard that was covered with a spiderweb of interlocking circles and arrows. The conspiracy outlined there was complex and involved several think tanks, government officials, nongovernmental organizations, and government programs. Beck reminded viewers that the clean energy crusade was meant to steal their liberty.

"This is the head. This is the *head*. This is at least a main player in what is going on in America!" Beck exclaimed. Then he looked directly into the camera and said: "I believe, America, that this is probably the biggest—and correct me if I'm wrong . . . This is the biggest story in history. It is the hijacking of our republic. Yes or no?"

Kerpen nodded his head in agreement. "I think you're right," Kerpen said. "And the shame, the amazing thing to me is, that they're so brazen."

Beck was encouraged by these remarks, and incensed.

"This is gigantic money! And let me tell you something, America. Nobody is doing this stuff on television," Beck said. "It is the hijacking of our country."

Beck's show informed Maria Brady's self-education. She researched the Freemasons, paganism, and the US Senate. "Our government is running everything," she said. "They were taking over everything, and they did a lousy job. Everything they put their little grimy hands on, they messed up. I am one hundred percent sure that what's wrong is that the government controls everything."

This was von Mises on the retail level. Brady, in her way, was coming to the same conclusions that Charles Koch had come to many decades earlier. But she didn't hold the antiseptic free-market views of an Austrian economist. Her Internet research led her to darker places.

"I am totally convinced that probably seventy percent to seventy-five percent of our government is being run by Satan worshippers," Brady said. "That's what's wrong with this country."

Maria Brady's point of view did not lend itself to roomy political debate or to compromise with people of differing beliefs. She became a political activist who was unyielding and religiously dedicated to saving her country from evil forces.

With the guidance and help of Americans for Prosperity, Brady found her first political target. It was the congressman from her district, who was running for reelection, named Bob Inglis.

When Bob Inglis held a town hall meeting in Boiling Springs, Maria Brady and her compatriots were prepared. Brady sent out an e-mail to her list, informing her fellow Tea Partiers about the event. When Brady arrived, she had a wad of small slips with the words "pink slip" written on them. She stood outside the event and passed out the pink slips to her friends. The idea was to throw these toward the stage at some point, signifying the fact that voters were ready to send Bob Inglis packing. Brady found a seat in the front row, so she was ready when Inglis took the stage and started speaking. She estimated that the crowd was between three hundred and four hundred people.

For Brady, the pivotal moment came during the question and answer session. She wanted to know one thing: How could Bob Inglis vote to allow Nancy Pelosi to buy two luxury jets for her own use on the taxpayer's dime? She took the microphone, and she asked this question, and she was horrified by his answer.

"He didn't know anything about it!" Brady recalled. "He looked at me, and he was like, '*What?* What are you talking about? I don't know anything about this.'"

This was the moment when Brady realized that she had to do everything in her power to make sure Inglis lost his seat in Congress. While it was untrue that Nancy Pelosi had purchased two jets, Brady was correct on one point: Inglis seemed utterly incapable of dealing with her question. He stood on the stage in a navy blazer and white button-down shirt, trying to talk in measured tones to a crowd that was shouting.

One woman interrupted Inglis, shouting: "I'm afraid of Obama!" Inglis stopped and asked the woman: "Why are you afraid?" At this, the crowd erupted. A man shouted, "Because he's a Socialist!"

"Let me ask you something. This is very helpful," Inglis said. "Where are you getting that?" He was smiling and waving his hand, acting like he was engaged in a collegial conversation about politics. Someone shouted that they were "getting that" from Glenn Beck.

"Glenn Beck," Inglis said. "Here's what I'd suggest: turn that television off when he comes on." This is when Inglis lost the crowd. They erupted in a wall of boos and shouts. Once again, he could barely be heard over the cacophony. He tried anyway.

"Let me tell you why. He's trading on fear. I think that when you trade on fear . . . you're not leading. You're following fearful people," Inglis said. Brady remembered that moment because that's when her friends started throwing their pink slips at Inglis.

Inglis was not a stupid man or an inept politician. He knew how to work a room. The reason he failed repeatedly to win over the crowds at these town hall meetings was that he would not say what they wanted him to say. His campaign slogan for 2010 was "America's sun is still rising." This was a horrible slogan, and Inglis knew it. Nobody felt like the sun was still rising. He knew that he needed to say, "Okay, I hate Obama as much as you do. Even more than you do." He knew that needed to be seen as "trying to bring back the good old days before the black man went into the White House," as he phrased it. "I just didn't want to be that person. I wanted to be the person who was saying that 'Yeah, this is about the future of fuels. And I know we're in the midst of the Great Recession, but we're Americans and we can overcome this.'"

Inglis kept his slogan and stayed the course.

Koch Industries' activities in South Carolina were just one piece of a broader strategy, and a central focus of this effort was to defeat the Waxman-Markey bill before it could be passed by the US Senate. Steve Lonegan, AFP's director in New Jersey, came to understand the broader strategy during conference calls and meetings with Koch's political operatives. Koch Industries would ramp up its operations outside the Senate to turn up the heat on the politicians who worked there. The effort would employ all of Koch's political assets, from its campaign donations to its lobbyists and even its think tanks.

One immediate target would be the Republican lawmakers who voted for the Waxman-Markey bill in June. They would be made an example of, just like Inglis. There were eight of these Republicans in all, and three of them were from New Jersey: Congressmen Chris Smith, Leonard Lance, and Frank LoBiondo. Lonegan immediately set about making their political lives a living hell.

LoBiondo's office was flooded with phone calls criticizing him for his vote on Waxman-Markey, forcing one of his aides to fax between 100 and 150 summaries of the calls to LoBiondo each day. Many of the calls came from out of state. It was exasperating and exhausting to keep up with. Lonegan's tactics went beyond those typically associated with political campaigns. He and his growing team taught the newly energized Tea Party activists how to inflict the maximum amount of pressure on the "Three Taxateers," as he dubbed the congressmen.

"You do a rally in his backyard. You get lots of people to call his office and say, 'What the hell are you doing?' E-mails, phone calls. You have them confronting him when he goes out to the diner. Again, this is where teaching people how to be good activists comes in. Most people don't know what to do," Lonegan said. "So, I would teach people."

The purpose of Lonegan's effort was not necessarily to drive the Three Taxateers out of office. All three of them kept their seats. The goal was to send a message to the US senators. AFP targeted conservative Democrats such as Senator Max Baucus, who had a significant fossil fuel industry presence in their states. It also targeted wavering Republican senators. By tormenting the New Jersey congressmen, AFP showed that there was a steep price for supporting climate change regulations.

When the bill moved into the Senate, it needed to first pass through one of the powerful Senate committees. This presented a moment when the entire effort to regulate carbon emissions might be killed in the crib. Senate committee hearings did not draw much public attention. The committee hearings were slow and boring and filled with technical arcana. This delay in the process offered Koch the best chance to kill cap and trade. Koch Industries seized it.

The Democratic Senate majority leader, Harry Reid of Nevada, was a master of manipulating the political process. It was telling that he assigned the Waxman-Markey bill to the Senate Committee on Environment and Public Works. The committee was chaired by Barbara Boxer, a friend of environmental protections from California, and a true believer in the cap-and-trade system. The Democrats did not just control the committee, they held an overwhelming majority of its seats, with twelve Democratic votes to the Republicans' seven. Republicans didn't have much of a chance to stop the bill from being passed and sent to the entire Senate for a vote.

Still, the leading Republican on the Environment Committee, James

Inhofe, from Oklahoma, was not deterred. He had one advantage. The Senate was built in a way that maximized the power of the word *no*. The House of Representatives operated under the rules of a simple majority rule. The Senate was designed to thwart the idea of majority rule and prize consensus between the parties. It took sixty votes in the Senate to end debate on a topic. Bipartisanship wasn't a virtue in this arena, it was a necessity.

On the morning of the first Senate hearing, just after the Fourth of July recess, Inhofe took his seat at the center of the horseshoe-shaped committee dais, just next to Boxer. She began the hearing by preemptively criticizing Inhofe as an obstructionist. He didn't hesitate to respond.

"You have stated that we're the party of 'no.' Well—that's true. We say 'no' to higher energy costs. 'No' to subsidizing the East and West Coasts at the expense of the heartland. 'No' to more bureaucracy and red tape. 'No' to the largest tax increase in American history and 'no' to sending our manufacturing jobs to China and India," Inhofe said.

Inhofe's embrace of the word *no* telegraphed to the Senate that Democrats were on their own. The Democratic Party held a supermajority of votes in early 2009, but the supermajority was fragile. Max Baucus, for example, had voted against a cap-and-trade bill in the past. Claire McCaskill of Missouri said in 2009 that she would vote against the measure. In this environment, getting to sixty votes would be difficult.

During July and August, Inhofe and Americans for Prosperity cleared the playing field of any Republican participants. By the fall, all the Republicans on Barbara Boxer's committee were boycotting the proceedings. One afternoon hearing, Boxer sat alone at the center of the dais. Arlen Specter of Pennsylvania, a conservative Republican on the committee who'd switched his affiliation to the Democratic party in April, told the *Pittsburgh Post-Gazette* that the boycott was an act of "really excessive partisanship," which surpassed what he had seen before in the Senate. "I have been a party to some very heated disagreements, but they have been disagreements on the merits, on the substance. . . . But you can't disagree with an empty chair," he said.

The chairs remained empty. Barbara Boxer initially said that her committee would pass a bill and put it before the entire Senate for a vote by September 8. Then, in late August, that date was extended to late September. And then it was delayed into October.

The bill fell under the shadow of larger, more visible legislative fights. The Senate was simultaneously debating the Affordable Care Act, which drew Tea Party protestors out in crowds to town hall meetings and parades. Americans for Prosperity fed these efforts, arranging for bus rides and compiling e-mail lists to inform its members of the time and location of the public meetings they could attend. The fight over Obamacare drained the time, attention, and resources of Harry Reid, the Obama administration, and the rest of the Democratic Party leadership. Everyone knew that there was only so much momentum, so much political energy to be spent in Washington. This was the key advantage that was given to Koch Industries. In the Senate, the advantage always went to the opponent who wanted to stop something rather than build something.

In October, Barbara Boxer and Harry Reid employed something called the nuclear option: putting the bill to a vote in the committee over the objections of Republicans. The bill passed without a single Republican vote. The bill was tainted now, stained as being partisan. Each passing week made it easier for other senators to stand aside and let the bill sink.

When the cap-and-trade bill moved to the Senate floor, it set off a frantic race among senators who sought to shape it, support it, or kill it. During this period, Koch Industries sought to raise the temperature even higher on any senator who considered supporting the bill. To do this, Koch employed a tactic known as the "echo chamber," of which it had become a master. The echo chamber allowed Koch to amplify its message while hiding its hand.

The strategy originated from the network of think tanks and academic programs that Charles Koch had been building for almost forty years. In 1974, when Charles Koch laid out his strategy for launching a libertarian revolution in the United States, he listed education as the first of four pillars in his strategy.* He had pursued this strategy with great success, building the Cato Institute think tank and academic centers like the Mercatus Center at George Mason University. These efforts had a philosophical, almost noble, feel to them. The stated goal was to

---

* The other three pillars were: media outreach, litigation, and political influence (or lobbying).

fund scholars and big ideas that would slowly move society toward an understanding of Charles Koch's political vision. By 2009, the educational enterprise had become a network of shell enterprises and hidden funding streams that gave immediate tactical support to Koch Industries' lobbying goals.

Ideas are the raw material of all legislation. In Washington, DC, there is a surprisingly small congregation of think tanks, policy shops, media outlets, and academic institutions that shape the daily political conversation. Over the decades, Koch Industries became adept at seeding this territory with its own ideas, and its own thinkers, in a way that hid its influence.

The echo chamber tactic began when Koch's lobbyists would commission and pay for an academic study, without claiming credit for it. That study, seemingly independent of Koch, was then fed into a series of think tanks and foundations that Koch controlled. Finally, the work of those think tanks was weaponized into the raw ammunition of political campaigns. Taken together, it had the effect of making the message from Koch Industries' lobbying shop seem far louder, and far more popular, than it really was. This, in turn, had a surprisingly strong effect on senators and other lawmakers, who paid close attention to public sentiment.

In 2007, for example, Koch Industries quietly funded the work of a Democratic-leaning think tank called Third Way. The think tank promoted "New Democrat" policies such as those embraced by Bill Clinton: neoliberal policies that sought to combine New Deal goals with free-market methods. Lobbyists at Koch's office knew that Third Way's economic study program supported free-trade policies such as NAFTA. Such trade policies were under attack in 2007 because they did not deliver the economic benefits that they had promised to huge swaths of the American population. The textile industry of South Carolina, for example, was decimated by trade agreements, such as NAFTA. This was stoking opposition to such trade agreements among both Democratic and Republican politicians.

Koch Industries supported free-trade agreements and wanted to ensure the passage of future trade deals, while blocking any reversal of existing deals. The possibility of any trade war was dangerous for Koch Industries not just because the company had extensive business holdings around the world. To take one specific but very high-stakes example:

Koch's Pine Bend refinery, still a major profit center for the company, was deeply dependent on oil imports from Canada. Any trade disputes ignited by renegotiating NAFTA could dramatically hurt Koch's profitability. Koch's lobbyists knew that they wouldn't get much of a hearing from Democratic politicians. Very few liberals saw an upside in 2007 in carrying water for Koch. That's why Koch used Third Way to make its point: liberals listened to Third Way.

The Koch lobbying office directed money to support a Third Way report that was published in November of 2007, entitled "Why Lou Dobbs Is Winning." Dobbs was a cable television personality who carved out a niche railing against free trade deals that he said harmed the middle class. The Third Way report cast Dobbs as part of a dangerous "neo-populist" movement that threatened to harm America's future by making the country turn inward. The report did not cite the support from Koch Industries, nor does it appear that Third Way acknowledged Koch's support anywhere in its publicity materials. The report's acknowledgments did give thanks to Rob Hall, a lobbyist for Koch's Invista division, thanking him for "his support in helping us conceive of and design Third Way's trade project," without disclosing Koch or Invista's funding. Third Way was not obligated to disclose its support from Koch Industries in its tax filings, and did not. Koch successfully pushed its view on trade while barely leaving a fingerprint.

In 2009, Koch's use of the echo chamber was more targeted and better amplified. The operation began at Koch's lobbying office, where a senior manager directed lobbyists to pay for a third-party economic report that would undermine support for the Senate's cap-and-trade bill, according to a person familiar with Koch's political operations.

To produce the report, Koch's lobbyists selected a reliably conservative economic think tank called the American Council for Capital Formation. The ACCF didn't hide its free-market leanings, and tax filings showed that it was funded by ExxonMobil and other corporate interests. But Koch Industries took pains to hide its involvements in the report it commissioned in 2009. Koch enticed another lobbying group, called the National Association of Manufacturers, to "sponsor" the report, with the understanding that Koch Industries would pay for it.

The Koch network had funded the ACCF for years, although it disguised its contributions by using the Claude R. Lambe Charitable

Foundation, which the Koch family controlled. In 2006, the Lambe
Foundation gave ACCF $40,000. It gave $50,000 in 2007. Koch hired
the ACCF to produce a study looking at the economic damage that
a cap-and-trade bill would cause the US economy. A person familiar
with the arrangement said that a study of this kind would cost roughly
$100,000. In both 2008 and 2009, the Claude R. Lambe Charitable
Foundation gave $100,000 to the ACCF. Then its contribution dropped
back to $50,000 in 2010.

The report was released in August of 2009. It carried the kind of dry
academic title that conveyed a sense of credibility and seriousness in
Washington, DC: *Analysis of the Waxman-Markey Bill "The American
Clean Energy and Security Act of 2009."* The report's lead author was a
long-time ACCF economist named Margo Thorning.

The study was announced with a press release from the National
Association of Manufacturers. The announcement made no mention of
Koch Industries' involvement. Instead, the study appeared to have the
backing of a trade group with the interests of a wide range of manufacturing companies at heart.

The study was brutal in its assessment of Waxman-Markey. "Unfortunately, this study confirms that the Waxman-Markey Bill is an 'anti-
jobs, anti-growth' piece of legislation," NAM's executive vice president,
Jay Timmons, said in the press release.

The study's predictions were dire, in part because the ACCF used
a set of economic assumptions underlying its analysis that most other
studies did not use. The group, for example, predicted that renewable
sources of energy would be slower to come online than many analysts
predicted, which would leave the United States in an energy crunch. The
ACCF estimated that the Waxman-Markey bill would destroy 2.4 million
jobs between 2012 and 2030 if it was passed. It estimated that electricity
prices would jump 50 percent by 2030, while $3.1 trillion in economic
activity would be lost.

Once the ACCF's study was published, Koch Industries carried out
the next phase of its echo chamber system. The study was quickly promoted by a think tank called the Institute for Energy Research, which
sent out a press release on August 13 that highlighted the study's findings. The IER was an outgrowth of the Institute for Humane Studies,

the libertarian think tank cofounded by Charles Koch.* By 2009, the IER was funded by Koch Industries and other companies, and a former Koch Industries lobbyist named Wayne Gable sat on IER's board of directors.

After the study was promoted by the IER, it was then recycled by another Koch Industries–affiliated think tank. This one was called the American Energy Alliance, and it was essentially the political action arm of the IER. The AEA was organized under the tax code in a way that it could be directly involved in politics, while the IER was organized as an "education" foundation that could not lobby or get involved in political campaigns. Where the IER was high minded, the AEA was something more of a street brawler. The AEA was headed by a former Koch Industries lobbyist named Thomas Pyle, who remained in close contact with his former colleagues at Koch's lobbying shop.

The AEA produced a series of political radio advertisements that were based on the new ACCF findings, along with other statistics that highlighted the potential economic threat of a cap-and-trade bill. A narrator in one of the radio ads intoned: "This tax will further cripple our already struggling economy—costing more American jobs. . . . Higher taxes and more job losses—what could Congress be thinking?" A corresponding fact sheet for the ad cited the ACCF for this claim. The AEA political ads were targeted in a way that benefited from keen knowledge of how the Waxman-Markey bill was then working its way through the Senate. Lindsey Graham of South Carolina was a particular target. "Why would Senator Lindsey Graham support a new national energy tax, called cap and trade?" one advertisement began. Citing the ACCF study, the advertisement claimed that "cap and trade . . . could significantly increase electricity bills, gas prices, and cost American jobs."

In all of these statements and advertisements, the same set of numbers were used again and again: More than two million jobs lost. Electricity prices would be 50 percent higher by 2030. These facts were also carried into Congress in the form of direct testimony. When the Sen-

---

* The connection between IER and the Institute for Humane Studies was first revealed by the journalist Lee Fang. He reported in 2014 that the IHS temporarily lost its charter, and then reformed as the IER.

ate Finance Committee sought to learn more about the economics of climate change, the committee invited Margo Thorning to testify. The ACCF study was submitted as evidence beforehand.

"It's pretty clear the costs outweigh the benefits," Thorning told the committee. Chairman Max Baucus, the conservative Democrat from Montana, pointed out that the ACCF findings were far more negative than most. "You're a bit of an outlier," Baucus said.

"We tried our best to build in realistic assumptions," Thorning had said earlier.

Inside Koch Industries, the ACCF report was seen as a tremendous victory. Koch's point of view had been carried out into the world in real force—in press releases, Senate testimony, think tank discussions, and political attack ads. And Koch's name wasn't anywhere to be seen.

Koch Industries wasn't the only company to use these tactics. Exxon-Mobil also funded third-party groups that sought to raise doubts about the science behind climate change and to fight the cap-and-trade bill. But Greenpeace, the environmental activist group that fought hard to limit air pollution, found that Koch Industries fought to undermine the scientific consensus around climate change for longer, and more fiercely, than even Exxon. A 2010 Greenpeace analysis of spending on climate-denial groups between 2005 and 2008 found that Koch Industries and its affiliates spent $24.9 million to support such groups, almost triple Exxon's $8.9 million in spending.* And Koch was more uncompromising than Exxon, whose lobbyists made it known that Exxon might support some sort of carbon emissions plan, such as a carbon tax.

The efforts to undermine popular support for a cap-and-trade bill were effective. In late 2009, 57 percent of Americans believed there was strong evidence that global warming was real, according to a poll from the Pew Research Center. While this was a majority, it was a slimmer majority than in 2008, when 71 percent of Americans believed it. In 2006, 77 percent believed it.

---

* Greenpeace's analysis might overstate Koch's support for so-called climate-denial groups. Greenpeace's tally includes the total funding for entities like the Cato Institute, which created doubt about climate-change science but which also engaged in other antigovernment activities. Still, the difference in funding is so dramatic that it seems almost certain that Koch invested more than Exxon did during this period.

As the Senate debated, Koch Industries applied yet more pressure. While punishing Congressmen who voted for Waxman-Markey, then tarnishing the bill through its echo chamber, Koch employed another tactic. This tactic was informed by the insight that Abel Winn had derived from his study of beating holdouts: *When there's competition, that completely blew the problem away. . . . Everybody behaved much better.* Koch Industries would intensify competition among lawmakers by promoting competitors to challenge them.

In 2009 and 2010, Koch Industries' political network created new Republican candidates, seemingly out of nowhere, who rose up and challenged sitting congressmen and senators. Koch's chosen candidates attacked the incumbents from the right, claiming that the Republican Party was insufficiently conservative and too accommodating of the Obama agenda. The overwhelming message was that compromise with Democrats must end.

Bob Inglis was more surprised than anyone to find himself challenged by one of Koch's candidates. Inglis earned an 84 percent rating from the American Conservative Union, which tracked lawmakers' votes. He discovered that voting in line with the union 84 percent of the time was not enough. Inglis was seen as a holdout against Koch's agenda because he stubbornly continued to advocate for controlling greenhouse gas emissions.

Inglis's competition came in May, and it arrived in the form of a prosecuting attorney from Spartanburg named Trey Gowdy. Inglis and Gowdy had been longtime allies and even friends. Inglis heard the news about Gowdy's candidacy one morning when a friend called and told him. He collapsed back into bed. Gowdy was a formidable opponent. Koch Industries gave no money to Inglis during that campaign cycle, but contributed at least $7,500 to Gowdy. Americans for Prosperity promoted Inglis's town hall meetings to Tea Party activists so that they could arrive to protest, but there is no evidence that AFP directed such actions against Gowdy or questioned his conservative credentials. Gowdy, in turn, proved that he would support Koch Industries' most important policy concern in the summer of 2009.

Inglis and Gowdy met at a candidate forum to debate the issues that summer, held under a large tent next to a highway. The moderator was a conservative talk-radio host. There were two other candidates with Inglis and Gowdy, but Inglis considered Gowdy to be his only true competitor.

The moderator asked all the candidates if they believed climate change was man-made and then added: "Would you support a bill that taxes carbon emissions?"

This drew a hearty laugh from the crowd. They knew exactly how painful Inglis's squirming must be. Inglis took the microphone and proceeded to alienate almost the entire audience:

"I do believe that humans contribute to climate change. And, actually, let me strike that. I don't *believe* it. It's not an article of faith for me. My faith tells me to look at the data. The data says that's happening. And that's why I have a proposal that's not cap and trade." He explained the details of a carbon tax bill and how it would be "revenue neutral" by cutting taxes on wages.

When Gowdy rose to speak, he said succinctly, "No on cap and trade, no on carbon tax."

"I've been a prosecutor for sixteen years," Gowdy continued. "I'm used to having things proven to me and proving it to other people. Global warming has not been proven to the satisfaction of the constituents that I seek to serve."

Gowdy was interrupted by loud applause. The crowd kept applauding and hooting while Gowdy took his seat.

Bob Inglis knew he was losing the campaign. What he didn't know was that he wasn't alone. Koch Industries and Americans for Prosperity were replicating the strategy in congressional districts across the country. In Washington, sitting Republican lawmakers started talking nervously about being "primaried" by Koch-funded candidates. One wrong step could expose them to fierce competition. As Winn might have predicted, everyone started behaving much better.

As it pressured Republican lawmakers from the outside, the Koch network built a hard wall of "no" votes around the Waxman-Markey bill in the Senate to contain its support.

Since at least 2008, Americans for Prosperity asked politicians to sign a pledge that they would "oppose any legislation relating to climate change that includes a net increase in government revenue." It was phrased in a way to look like an antitax measure rather than a promise to kill any effort to control greenhouse gas emissions. But it achieved the same goal. Putting a price on carbon—through a cap-and-trade system or a carbon tax—was seen as the most realistic way to control carbon emissions. Only the federal government had the authority to impose that price, so Koch's pledge killed the effort in its tracks.

The "carbon pledge," as it was called, was signed by 223 state and federal politicians in 2009. One of them was the Indiana Congressman Mike Pence. Pence, who had called climate change a "myth," was the only member of the Indiana delegation to sign the pledge. In this sense, Pence was a trailblazer. By September of 2010, four members of Indiana's delegation had signed the pledge and a total of 627 state and federal lawmakers and candidates had done so.

As Koch Industries encircled the Waxman-Markey bill with its carbon pledge, the Democrats put their energy into passing Obamacare, which was approved in the Senate on Christmas Eve 2009 and signed into law in the spring of 2010. Then the Democrats put their energy into the Dodd-Frank financial reform bill, which imposed new regulations on Wall Street banks. It passed the Senate in May of 2010 and was signed into law in July.

The cap-and-trade bill languished during these months in the Senate, as the group of senators led by John Kerry tried fruitlessly to find some sort of bargain that could make the bill palatable to sixty senators. All through the spring and summer of 2010, the political atmosphere grew hotter, stoked by AFP and other conservative groups, and the issue of carbon regulation became more toxic.

This was the period when Bob Inglis was fighting in a primary election against Trey Gowdy, set for June of 2010. Inglis refused to abandon his campaign slogan "America's sun is still rising." Looking back, Bob Inglis said that there was one moment when he should have realized he was going to lose. It happened to be the one moment in his political career when he was most worried about being assassinated. It happened during a town hall meeting in a public school near Inglis's home in Travelers Rest. Because the event was so close to his house, he brought his wife and children. When they arrived, the crowd was so large that the local fire marshal was turning people away. Even before Inglis started speaking, a crowd outside was getting furious.

The atmosphere inside was even worse. The auditorium was stuffy and crowded and full of raw anger. Inglis knew that many of his neighbors around Travelers Rest carried guns on their person. He was certain there were many guns in the room that night. When he took the stage, he began to give his stump speech. Under normal circumstances, he would have pointed out his wife and children in the audience, which was a standard gesture for a congressional candidate. That night, he didn't do it.

"I didn't introduce my wife and kids because I was concerned about their safety. You could just tell, in the pulsating anger in the place, that it wouldn't be good to introduce your wife and kids," Inglis said. "If I was going to get shot, it probably was going to happen there. At that town hall meeting."

At the end of the night, a woman close to the stage yelled at Inglis: "We don't trust you anymore!"

If a congressman lost the trust of his voters, there was no recovering from it. When the primary vote was held on June 22, Inglis attended a watch party with his campaign staff in downtown Greenville. The event turned out to be a chance for Bob Inglis's close friends and family to witness the most public and humiliating defeat of his political life. He lost the race with 29 percent of the vote to Gowdy's 70 percent.

Inglis worried about what this might mean for future politicians. "I was really quite sad about the rise of this populist fire that can only burn things down. It can't build anything up. I continued to be saddened that this fire, which I thought would burn out, has only gotten hotter."

It is difficult to identify the exact moment when the cap-and-trade bill died. There was no vote to declare its final defeat. The measure simply lost momentum and then died quietly. In late April of 2010, Lindsey Graham dropped out of the gang of senators who were pushing the bill. No Republicans were willing to step in and replace him. Harry Reid announced that the Senate would work first to pass comprehensive immigration reform before addressing climate change.

Jonathan Phillips and the other staffers who'd written the bill knew that Reid's decision was a death sentence. The moment of opportunity to pass meaningful greenhouse gas regulations had passed.

Americans for Prosperity emerged from the summer of 2010 in its strongest position ever. Steve Lonegan, in New Jersey, had a hard time keeping up with the organization's growth. There were more people and more resources pouring in than ever before. When Lonegan joined AFP, it was a political upstart, a group of outsiders like a pirate crew, fighting to change government policy from outside the system. This culture was rapidly disappearing, replaced by a streamlined, corporate model.

"In the early days, we were rambunctious. There were less controls," Lonegan recalled. "But as things got bigger and bigger, they had to put in more, like, lawyers and bureaucracy. Though it was still effective, it did become somewhat more bureaucratic. But I think that was out of necessity."

As AFP solidified its position, it also began to entangle itself tightly with the Republican Party and change it from within. AFP went on a hiring spree and poached young and aspiring talent from the Republican Party. Two-thirds of all AFP directors were drawn from it. Perhaps more importantly, roughly one-third of all the AFP state directors who left AFP went directly from that job to positions in Republican Party politics, taking with them their contacts and education from Koch's political operation.

The deep ties between AFP and the Republican Party were only discovered years later, when two Harvard political scientists, Theda Skocpol and Alexander Hertel-Fernandez, conducted one of the only rigorous independent studies of the newly expanded Americans for Prosperity network. "These data show that the AFP federation has been able to penetrate GOP career ladders," Skocpol and Hertel-Fernandez wrote. The employees who went back and forth tended to be "young men in their thirties or forties" who would presumably have long careers in politics ahead of them.

AFP was reshaping the Republican Party and strengthening it at the same time. In 2010, the Koch network shifted its focus from fighting the Waxman-Markey bill to electing as many Republicans as possible in the midterm congressional election.

In November, a wave of votes from Republicans and Tea Party activists destroyed the Democratic majority in the House of Representatives.

Republicans also made strong gains in the Senate, although it didn't win control. The era of the Democratic supermajority of sixty votes was firmly buried. The filibuster would once again become a remarkably powerful tool of opposition. Now, if Harry Reid wanted to pass a bill, he would need Republicans to join a vote to end a filibuster debate. This was a possibility of vanishing likelihood.

The magnitude of this victory was immense for Koch Industries. Of the eighty-five newly elected Republicans who arrived in Washington, seventy-six had signed Americans for Prosperity's carbon pledge, vowing they would never support a federal climate bill that added to the government's tax revenue. Of those seventy-six members of Congress, fifty-seven of the signees had received campaign contributions from Koch Industries' PAC, according to an analysis by the Investigative Reporting Workshop at American University. Koch Industries had terminally stalled the Waxman-Markey bill in the Senate, and now it had salted the earth behind it, ensuring that a new climate change bill would never grow.

One of the earliest acts of the new Republican majority was to halt funding for the Select Committee on Energy Independence and Global Warming. The team began to box up their files and personal belongings and emptied out the basement office of the Longworth Building.

Jonathan Phillips, the young staffer who'd written sections of the bill to promote renewable energy, left Congress and took a job with the US Agency for International Development. He traveled to Africa and helped companies there build new clean energy infrastructure. Two of the legal experts on the team, Michael Goo and Joel Beauvais, moved to the EPA, where they started working on a plan to regulate carbon emissions from coal-powered utility plants. The EPA rule, called the Clean Power Plan, was the closest thing to a carbon control law that officials in the Obama administration felt they could achieve. Americans for Prosperity quickly caught wind of this and immediately began recruiting opposition to it through its website.

In the absence of regulation, greenhouse gas emissions continued to soar. In 2011, humans emitted 32.27 billion tons of carbon into the atmosphere, a rate that was more than 150 times what it had been before the industrial revolution. Concentrations of carbon in the atmosphere rose every year after the death of the Waxman-Markey bill. Scientists had warned that humans should strive to keep carbon dioxide levels at 350 parts per million to avoid catastrophic environmental impacts. As the Waxman-Markey bill was debated, carbon levels hovered around 370 parts per million. Within five years of its failure, levels hovered at 400 parts per million, the highest ever recorded during human existence.

After he left politics, Bob Inglis formed a group that promoted free-market solutions to the problem of climate change. His view remained unpopular in Republican circles. And everywhere he went, Inglis had that nagging feeling from 2010, when he had looked at the back of a town hall meeting and seen someone with a video camera, mounted on a tripod, filming him, someone "that maybe had a little bit of help, you know what I mean?"

Someone still seemed to be helping.

Inglis attended a debate over climate change policy in Washington, DC, hosted in part by the Libertarian Reason Foundation. When he arrived, Inglis found something curious. On each empty seat had been placed a campaign-style button. The buttons read simply: "70–29." This was the vote margin by which Inglis had lost to Trey Gowdy, 70 percent to 29 percent.

The buttons stuck in Inglis's mind. Someone had to print them, pay for them, and disperse them over the empty seats. Things like that took money and coordination. A couple of years after he was kicked out of office, Inglis finally had a strong suspicion as to who could do that. When he held the button, one thought crossed his mind:

"It seems to me that it has Koch written all over it."

Charles Koch had reason to be exultant as 2010 came to a close. Koch Industries had faced an unprecedented economic threat in the form of the Waxman-Markey bill and had played a vital role in derailing it. His own political ideals had faced an unprecedented threat in the seemingly permanent Democratic majority in Washington and the popularity of the Obama agenda. He played a vital role in destroying it. Koch's political operations were larger, more influential, and more powerful than ever.

But Charles Koch still felt threatened. He felt that the fight was still in its early stages. There was no time to waste with victory parties. On September 24, he sent a letter to wealthy political donors whom he was hoping to enlist in his cause. "Everyone benefits from the prosperity that emerges from free societies. But that prosperity is under attack by the current administration and many of our elected officials," Charles Koch wrote. "We must stop—and reverse—this internal assault on our founding principles."

The letter was an invitation to Charles Koch's eighth private gathering for wealthy conservative donors and the politicians who sought their help. The conference was in January of 2011 at a resort near Palm Springs, California.

Security around the donor conference was intense. Attendees registered for the event by contacting the Koch Industries lobbying office in Washington, DC, rather than the host hotel. When attendees arrived, they were required to wear an identification badge at all times. They were also warned not to leave materials behind, or to post on social media while they were at the event. No one from the media was allowed inside.

Charles Koch had a pithy piece of wisdom that he liked to share with his political operatives. It was a saying about whales and harpoons. "The whale that comes above sea level gets harpooned," is how one person remembered it.

The allegory was clear. It was safer to remain below the surface. It was better for Koch's political operations to remain anonymous. This helped explain the complexity of Charles Koch's emerging political organization, the endlessly complicated interlocking network of shell organizations and secret donations. It also explained the security and secrecy around the donor meetings that Charles Koch hosted twice a year.

The events had grown larger and more lavish since 2006, when Steve Lonegan attended one of the earliest conferences in Aspen. Since that time, the events had been attended by Supreme Court justices Antonin Scalia and Clarence Thomas; GOP congressmen Mike Pence, Tom Price, and Paul Ryan; Republican governors Bobby Jindal and Haley Barbour; and celebrity speakers like Rush Limbaugh, Charles Krauthammer, and John Stossel. At the summer conference of 2010, one of the keynote speakers was the Tea Party leader Glenn Beck, whose speech was entitled "Is America on the Road to Serfdom?"

But secrecy was becoming difficult to maintain. Americans for Prosperity was one of the most influential political organizations of 2010. A number of investigative reporting outlets began to dig into Charles and David Koch's long history of political involvement, including the Center for Public Integrity and the Investigative Reporting Workshop at American University. Both groups published deep reports that outlined the Koch brothers' extensive political donations. Activist groups took note as well. In March of 2010, Greenpeace released its forty-three-page report entitled *Koch Industries: Secretly Funding the Climate Denial Machine*, which detailed Koch's extensive giving to groups like the Mercatus Center, the Cato Institute, and the Competitive Enterprise Institute.

The publicity culminated in August of 2010 when the *New Yorker* magazine published a detailed report of Koch's political history, with contemporary accounts of Americans for Prosperity's coordination with Tea Party activists. The article, "Covert Operations: The Billionaire Brothers Who Are Waging a War Against Obama," was written by Jane Mayer, one of the most prominent investigative reporters in America. It cemented the Koch brothers' role as public figures who were deeply influencing political affairs. A widespread narrative raced through American politics, a narrative that the Koch brothers hadn't just assisted the Tea Party but had created it. The story line was inflamed by the 2010 Supreme Court decision *Citizens United v. Federal Election Commission*, which lifted restrictions on campaign donations to independent political groups. This opened the gates for unlimited cash to be poured into the third-party groups that Koch became masterful at employing. It appeared that there were no constraints on the political power that billionaires could wield. The Koch brothers were seen as the primary beneficiaries of the new landscape.

The whale had breached. The harpoons began to fly. When Charles Koch arrived in Rancho Mirage for the eighth donor conference, he found that the veil of secrecy had been lifted for good. Roughly a thousand protestors were gathered outside the Omni Rancho Las Palmas Resort & Spa. The resort was a collection of low-slung buildings built in the style of adobe haciendas, encircling a pool and a golf course. The protestors filled the street just outside, standing between the row of palm trees that swayed in the placid breeze. Security officers stood on the hacienda roof, looking down at the crowd, while cordons of local police officers in riot gear squeezed the big crowd inward from the sides. The police justified their militarized presence based on the fact that there were several federal judges inside the resort at Koch's gathering.

The protestors were raucous and wore brightly colored costumes. They carried big banners that read: "Quarantine Koch," alongside neon biohazard symbols. They carried placards that read: "Uncloak the KOCHS!" and "TEA PARTIERS ARE KOCH SUCKERS!" They chanted and sang songs into loudspeakers.

The din could be heard throughout the resort. But inside the conference rooms, the seminar proceeded. Charles Koch made it clear to the attendees that the event was not a junket; not "fun in the sun," as he put it. The gathering was a work trip, a chance to press their strategy. He spoke about the political struggle in nearly apocalyptic terms. At a donor conference in 2011, he told the crowd that America's future could literally be endangered if Barack Obama won reelection. "This is the mother of all wars we've got, over the next eighteen months, for the life or death of this country," Koch said.

Charles was the star of the seminars, but he was a reticent one. He didn't like the business of shaking hands with politicians and getting his photo taken with them. When given the chance, he passed up opportunities to meet even very senior political leaders who asked for one-on-one time with him. If anything, he seemed to look down on them.

"I remember talking to him. I think he viewed the folks in Congress as victims of the system. I know he did," said one person familiar with Koch's political operations. Charles Koch, who prized long-term thinking and who preached about the importance of creating incentive systems and bonus payments to reinforce it, looked at Congress and saw a dysfunctional system that was riven by toxic incentives. Politicians were just caught up in that system. They almost couldn't help but do the wrong thing.

"He understood what the process was. You have members of Congress. They get elected every two years. And it's hard to be independent. It's hard to get things done. It's hard not to spend a lot of time being political and raising money. And he just—I think he saw the system as broken," the person said.

The political machine that Charles Koch built was immensely successful—not at fixing this broken system, but at ensuring that it remained hobbled and incapable of passing the kind of sweeping business regulations that defined the New Deal. He applied long-term thinking to a system defined by short-term election timetables, and he won many of the most important fights he cared about.

After the Palm Springs conference wrapped up, Charles Koch traveled back to Wichita. He reported for work at the Koch Tower and found paperwork waiting for him in his executive suite on the third floor. While he spoke about politics in terms of war and destruction, the state of affairs inside Koch Industries told a different story. One of the surprising truths about life under the Obama presidency was that it was very good, economically speaking, for Charles Koch and Koch Industries.

During the Obama years, Charles Koch's net worth doubled. His fortune would grow larger and faster than during any previous period. One reason for this explosion in wealth was the death of the cap-and-trade bill. There would be no price on carbon to constrain the fossil fuel business. Instead, the new drilling technique called fracking would help enshrine fossil fuels as a central part of American economic life.

Koch Industries stood at center stage during this shift in America's energy industry, and it reaped rewards in ways that people on the outside could not see. When it came to the business side of Charles Koch's life, the whale was still deep underwater, growing larger and more powerful than ever before.

CHAPTER 21

The War for America's BTUs

(2010–2014)

In the winter of 2010, while the cap-and-trade bill was languishing in the US Senate, Koch Industries began to quietly execute a series of business deals. The deals might have looked strange—maybe even irrational—to outsiders. In March of 2010, for example, Koch announced that it was expanding its pipeline capacity in southern Texas by 25 percent. This was akin to building a very large parking garage outside a shopping mall that no one visited anymore. Southern Texas was a sleepy backwater of the oil business, an oasis of barren scrub brush and scattered towns with lonely oil derricks. Oil production in South Texas had stagnated for years. But Koch was spending millions to increase its pipeline network there.

In the following months, Koch's series of deals accelerated. In September, Koch announced a partnership with an obscure company called Arrowhead Pipeline to move 50,000 barrels a day of crude oil out of southern Texas. This was roughly half of the entire region's production at the time. Then, a month later, Koch announced a partnership with another little-known firm, called NuStar Energy, to reopen sixty miles of defunct pipeline, to carry 30,000 barrels of oil a day.

In November, Republicans won control of the US House of Representatives. A month later, Koch announced another deal, this one the largest yet—the company would build a brand-new sixteen-inch pipeline from remote Karnes County, Texas, to Koch's refinery in Corpus Christi, capable of carrying 120,000 barrels of crude oil a day. The new pipeline had the potential to be expanded to carry up to 200,000 barrels a day. In February of 2011, another deal: Koch bought the Ingleside Pier in Corpus Christi, an export terminal through which Koch could ship 200,000 barrels of oil a day on barges. Two months later, Koch announced a new twenty-inch pipe running from Pettus, Texas, to Corpus Christi, capable of carrying 250,000 barrels a day.

These deals garnered very little attention. There were a few corporate press releases and small stories in local media outlets. What outsiders didn't realize was that Koch Industries had just built a superhighway for crude oil, carrying hundreds of thousands of barrels a day from southern Texas to Koch's refinery in Corpus Christi, with an off-ramp at the Ingleside Pier that could carry excess supplies to foreign markets.

The puzzling part about this superhighway was that it was built to carry oil supplies that didn't seem to exist. The highway began in a region of Texas called the Eagle Ford Shale. Production there had been flat. In fact, the one accepted truth about US oil production was that it had peaked in the early 1970s and would never again increase. The Eagle Ford region was no exception. In 2007, there were fifty-one oil-drilling rigs in Eagle Ford, producing about fifty-four thousand barrels of oil a day. By late 2008, there were sixty-two oil rigs in the region, producing fifty-seven thousand barrels a day. In 2010, Eagle Ford's production actually fell to about fifty-five thousand barrels a day.

Nonetheless, Koch was building a system to move hundreds of thousands of barrels of crude from the region. These deals were part of a strategy that Koch had been formulating for over a year. Koch saw something in Eagle Ford. It was something that others also saw, but that Koch was the first to exploit. While production was flat until early 2010, the number of drilling rigs had more than tripled in just over a year, from thirty to 104. This number was a leading indicator. The wells would start pumping, and new oil would start to flow. Koch Industries was poised for the change.

The wells being drilled into southern Texas were the face of an energy revolution that would redefine global oil markets and the American economy. They were part of a once-in-a-generation transformation that crept up quietly and then changed everything. In one short decade— from 2005 to 2015—America went from being the largest importer of refined petroleum products to the largest exporter of refined petroleum products. A country that was once the poster child for peak oil discovered that it was home to oil and natural gas deposits that were likely larger than those found in Saudi Arabia. The entire story about fossil fuels was reversed before many people even realized what was happening. These changes were every bit as cataclysmic for oil markets as the OPEC embargo had been in the 1970s. But this time, the changes accrued to America's benefit. The cost of oil plummeted, OPEC was defanged, and America became essentially self-sufficient as an oil consumer.

The revolution was catalyzed by a suite of oil-drilling technologies that were used together in a drilling process called hydraulic fracturing, or fracking. Fracking had been around for decades, although it was fatally unprofitable. The method was kept on life support only by giant and long-lasting government subsidies and tax breaks. Fracking only became commercially viable thanks to the oil price spikes of 2007 and 2008. When fracking became widely deployed, it opened up massive fossil fuel reserves in the United States that were long considered unattainable.

This revolution, while far reaching, did not change one important element of the energy business. The revolution did not change who benefited most from the energy business (at least during its first decade). The fracking economy was new, but the primary beneficiaries were old. The companies that benefited most were the long-standing legacy players, like Koch Industries.

The fracking boom played to Koch's advantages, and one of these key advantages was Koch's capacity to thrive in volatile markets. The fracking boom unleashed a period of almost unprecedented volatility between 2010 and 2014. Koch Industries was built to respond to volatility, and its expertise was evident in Koch's hidden effort to build the oil superhighway out of the Eagle Ford region.

The effort began when Koch's commodity traders started to receive early signals that something big was about to happen in oil markets.

The first signals emerged on the natural gas trading desks sometime around 2009. This is when the advent of the fracking boom was first detected.

The previous two years had been wildly unstable. In 2007 and 2008, crude oil prices spiked to record highs. Natural gas followed crude oil upward, as it tends to do. Energy prices crashed during the recession due to weak demand, which was predictable. But then something strange happened: oil prices started to climb again, but natural gas prices didn't follow them upward. Instead, gas prices started to slide. Then fall. Then collapse.

The reason for this was startling. Natural gas supplies, long thought to be growing scarcer every year, had suddenly started to increase. In late 2009, the United States produced 1.65 trillion cubic feet of natural gas a month. In two short years, the supply skyrocketed by 23 percent, reaching 2.03 trillion cubic feet a month in 2011. And this wasn't a fluke. By 2015, the supply would reach 2.3 trillion cubic feet.

This was the start of the fracking revolution. Fracking is a shorthand term that refers to a group of three technologies that, when used together, make it possible to extract natural gas deposits that were once unreachable. The first technology is called microseismic imaging, a system used to map underground gas deposits trapped in dense shale rock. Shale gas deposits were previously considered unattainable because of their weird formation: the deposits are composed of broadly diffused gas droplets trapped in rock. The deposits are shaped like a giant dinner plate—wide and shallow. Drilling into them is like punching a nail through the plate, which allows the drill to tap a tiny portion of the gas.

This is where the second technology comes in: horizontal drilling. With horizontal drilling, the nail could penetrate the dinner plate and then make a sharp right turn, traveling through the heart of the entire deposit. The final technology was a group of chemicals, known as proppants, that could be injected into the shale rock along with sand, dislodging gas and allowing it to be sucked to the surface. When gas became expensive in 2007, it finally justified the expensive process of extracting it through fracking.

The earliest waves of the fracking boom came as a surprise to Koch's leadership team. The boom was catastrophic for gas prices, which fell roughly 85 percent between 2008 and 2012, from a peak of $12.69 per million BTUs (or British thermal units, a metric that's widely used as the basic measurement of energy use) to a mere $1.95. As it turned out, this catastrophe played to Koch's advantage because natural gas is the primary ingredient for nitrogen fertilizer. When prices fell, Koch was suddenly able to make its fertilizer for a fraction of the cost. It was a breathtakingly lucky break. Retail prices for fertilizer stayed high because of strong demand from farmers, who needed fertilizer more than ever to keep production high. When gas prices and production costs collapsed, Koch's profit margins swelled. Koch was the fourth-largest fertilizer maker in the United States thanks to its purchase of Farmland's fertilizer plants in 2003, for pennies on the dollar. Now those plants were printing cash.

Still, Koch's senior management was uneasy. They hadn't seen it coming.

"You look back and go, 'Yeah that was obvious! How'd I miss it?'" said Steve Feilmeier, Koch Industries' chief financial officer. "We started reflecting on 'How did we miss that?'"

This reflection occurred largely in the offices of Koch's crude oil and refinery division, Flint Hills Resources. Once they began looking into the fracking business, Koch's managers began to anticipate where it might go next. They missed the advent of new gas supplies, but it helped them see the next step. Brad Razook, who was CEO of Flint Hills, had reason to believe that the fracking revolution wouldn't stop with natural gas deposits.

Brad Razook and other senior executives at Flint Hills worked in windowed offices that ring the top story of the Tower, offering them views of downtown Wichita to the south and flat grasslands and suburban subdivisions to the north. The middle of the top floor is filled by a sprawling maze of cubicles. This is where Flint Hills' traders work.

The trading pit could easily pass for a branch office of any insurance company in central Kansas. No one was shouting orders or waving their hands in the air. There was just the quiet murmur of people on the phone. The beige dividing walls between desks were decorated with drab attempts to individualize each cubicle, like cardboard cutouts of the Wichita State University mascot—a scarecrow-like figure called WuShock—and family photos. The only signs of the global reach of the young traders were the multiple computer monitors at the desks, flashing with numbers and charts. A set of clocks along one wall display the local times at trading hubs around the world.

Koch's young traders observed odd occurrences in oil markets during 2011. The traders who bought oil supplies for Koch's Pine Bend refinery observed chaos in local midwestern markets. New supplies were coming into the market from North Dakota, of all places, causing supply gluts, bottlenecks, and transportation problems. And all of this was happening in a region where the oil industry had been dead for decades. The new oil coming out of North Dakota was similar to the new natural gas supplies: they were drilled by frackers in a region called the Bakken Formation. A fountain of crude oil sprang up in the Northern Plains, and no one knew how to deal with it. "It was almost comical how much crude was coming online," said Tony Sementelli, Flint Hills' chief financial officer. "It was very curious to us because it was almost unthinkable."

Razook and Sementelli started holding meetings to figure out what was going on. The signals from the marketplace were confusing. Fracking had already opened new pools of natural gas. But the big question was whether the process could be repeated with crude oil. The oil glut in North Dakota was an uncontrolled experiment to answer this question. But the results from that experiment raised only more questions. If fracking could work in North Dakota, could it work elsewhere? If it did work, how large were the oil reserves that might be tapped for drilling?

When faced with this uncertainty, Razook responded in a way that reflected twenty years of training. Razook had joined Koch Industries in 1985, after graduating from Kansas State University with an undergraduate degree in business administration. His real education came at Koch University. His education included the lessons of Charles Koch's mentor, Sterling Varner, who told his rank-and-file employees to keep their eyes open for opportunities at all times. By 2010, Sterling Varner's wisdom had been formalized into a routine process. Koch's traders reported what they saw, then Razook and Sementelli shared what they were learning, and Koch Industries moved fast to exploit the opportunity.

Razook reassigned one of his most important employees, Brad Urban, to study fracking full-time. Eventually Urban's team grew to include more than a dozen people. They studied the North Dakota market and explored where the fracking boom might lead next. They wanted to discover the next Bakken Formation before anyone else.

One reason why the fracking boom caught everyone by surprise was that fracking had been around since the 1970s. The technology failed to deliver any meaningful results for forty years. It was simply too expensive to be economically viable. Fracking, in fact, was only kept alive thanks to repeated government intervention. The fracking industry was essentially a ward of the state for decades, kept alive by lavish government subsidies, tax breaks, and government-funded research.

In 1980, a federal law called the Crude Oil Windfall Profits Tax Act included a tax break for natural gas supplies produced in unconventional ways, like fracking. The purpose of the tax break was to nurture new energy sources. The tax break was stupendously generous, providing 50 cents for every thousand cubic feet of gas. The so-called Section 29 tax break remained in place for decades. The National Bureau of Economic Research estimated in 2007 that the tax break would cost the federal government $3.4 billion between 2007 and 2011 alone.

The federal government also stepped in to support the frackers with long-term, expensive, experimental research. It was the kind of research that private companies were reluctant to provide for risky technologies. The government-run Sandia National Laboratories developed the three-dimensional microseismic imaging that made fracking possible. A federal project called the Morgantown Energy Research Center, or MERC, partnered with companies to set up experimental drilling operations to put fracking to the test. It was two engineers with MERC who patented the vital technology to drill horizontally—or directional drilling, as the industry called it. In 1986, a Department of Energy program, partnered with private companies, was the first to demonstrate a multistage, horizontal fracture in the Devonian Shale.

In spite of all this help, fracking never turned a profit. It was a marginal industry populated by dreamers and wildcatters who were promising big returns, kept alive by welfare benefits.

This changed quickly in 2009. Business and government partnerships figured out how to make the fracking process ever cheaper. Then, the price spike of 2008 made fracking competitive. After that, the industry gained steam and a self-reinforcing momentum. Banks started to give loans to frackers, from Pennsylvania to North Dakota, and these frackers turned their eye to new reservoirs of fossil fuel.

Brad Urban and his team canvassed the industry. Koch's traders bought oil supplies and quizzed the drillers. By doing so, they discovered the next horizon for the fracking business. It was something called tight oil. This was crude oil trapped in porous rock. Tight oil tended to be extremely "light" crude, meaning that it had low sulfur content, which differentiated it from heavy-sulfur oil of the kind that was imported from overseas.

As it happened, Koch's refinery in Corpus Christi specialized in refining light crude. It also happened to be that one of the biggest deposits of light, tight oil was in located in southern Texas, near Corpus Christi's backyard. Oil drillers told Koch about an area called the Eagle Ford Shale, a crescent of land that curved from southwest Texas up through the big empty space between San Antonio and Corpus Christi.

Koch started to gather estimates of how much oil might be retrievable through fracking in Eagle Ford. The region produced about fifty-five thousand barrels a day before the frackers arrived. It might produce as much as a hundred thousand barrels a day—maybe two hundred thousand—when new wells were installed. Before long, people were talking about five hundred thousand barrels a day.* Urban's team hired an outside geologist to study the land and try to triangulate the truth between the boasts of various wildcat drillers. The team at Flint Hills came to believe that a flow of at least two hundred thousand barrels a day was realistic.

The Koch team began to formulate a plan. Koch planned to capture and ship as much of the tight oil as it could get from Eagle Ford, and send it to Corpus Christi. It seemed likely that a sudden glut of supplies from Eagle Ford would create a surplus, just the kind of bottleneck that Koch had seen in the Bakken. That meant that the oil would be cheap. If that happened, Koch's Corpus Christi refinery might suddenly turn into a second Pine Bend refinery—a facility that could buy unusually cheap supplies thanks to a local oversupply and then sell gasoline into expensive retail markets.

Koch had an advantage over other refineries in Corpus Christi due to an accident of history. A majority of the refineries around Corpus Christi processed mostly imported oil, which was heavy in sulfur. Over the years, these refineries invested millions to install equipment specialized for refining the heavy, sulfur-rich crude. Koch was an outlier in this respect. The Corpus Christi refinery processed more light oil because that's what it used as a feedstock for its chemical plant that

---

* Even the most optimistic of these forecasts profoundly underestimated how much oil would come gushing from the ground.

made paraxylene. In other words, Koch was perfectly poised to accept a new surge of light oil. Its competitors wouldn't be able to process the new supplies.

There was a risk, however. The frackers were just starting to move into Eagle Ford, and the market was up for grabs. There was a good chance that the frackers would sell their crude to refineries in the Houston area. If Koch Industries wanted the oil to flow to Corpus Christi, the company had to move fast. Razook and Sementelli started talking to engineers to figure out how much it would cost to build a new network of pipelines between Eagle Ford and Koch's refineries. All of the estimates came back at "plus or minus 100 percent," meaning the cost was either going to be the estimated price or about double the estimated price. Koch, and other companies, liked to fund projects with a plus or minus 10 percent risk factor.

After months of study, Razook, Sementelli, and Urban had a plan. They wanted to build pipelines to a region where they didn't know how much oil there might be, for a cost they couldn't estimate. Corporate planners were accustomed to having some variables in their plan. But this was different. "Everything in this project was a variable," Sementelli said. Nonetheless, they were ready to take the project to Charles Koch.

Koch Industries' boardroom was still located across the hall from Charles Koch's office. Visitors walked into a spacious lobby on the third floor of the Tower, passed by a bust of Fred Koch that sat on a pedestal, and turned left to walk into the chamber. The room had no windows and dark wood paneling that created an almost claustrophobic feel, as if the attendees inside were in a diving bell. Recessed lighting in the ceiling shined down on a large, wooden table that dominated the center of the room. The table was shaped like a ring, with a hollow center in the middle, and it was surrounded by wheeled office chairs. This is where Koch's business leaders presented their ideas.

Razook and Sementelli pitched their plan to Charles Koch, David Robertson, and Steve Feilmeier. They explained how the Eagle Ford Shale would likely surge with new tight oil production in the coming years, and how Corpus Christi was poised to refine the cheap supplies. The parallel to Pine Bend—Koch's cash cow for so many decades—

didn't even need to be emphasized. "They certainly understand a feed-stock advantage," as Sementelli put it.

Razook and Sementelli's plan was uncertain, risky, and carried a dangerously vague price tag. The pipelines alone would cost hundreds of millions of dollars. Or maybe double that.

Charles Koch and his team seemed to understand the play instantly. They encouraged it. "We didn't have to sell," Razook recalled.

"They were just wanting to make sure we were thinking big enough," Sementelli remembered.

They went big on the plan. They formed the partnerships, expanded the pipeline network, and they bought the export pier. Then they reached out to the oil drillers they knew in Eagle Ford and started signing contracts to buy all the oil these drillers could provide. Koch's pitch to these drillers was enticing. Koch would provide the pipelines for transport. The company would provide the refinery to process the crude. And if the drillers didn't want to sell the oil to Koch, Koch could provide the export terminal for drillers to sell their crude for export.

By 2011, Koch had invested hundreds of millions in pipelines and signed contracts to ship hundreds of thousands of barrels a day. This investment was entirely a gamble. If Eagle Ford was a failure, the investment would be a total loss. Koch would own miles of worthless pipeline traversing miles of desolate scrub brush.

"It was hundreds of millions [of dollars] in the logistics phase," Sementelli said. "That was all risk. I mean, we didn't really know a lot of the variables."

Then the oil started to flow.

The Eagle Ford region produced 82,000 barrels of oil a day in July of 2010. At the end of the year, it was producing 139,000 barrels a day.

At the end of 2011, Eagle Ford produced 424,000 barrels a day. This turned out to be nothing.

In late 2012, Eagle Ford produced 811,000 barrels a day. This was more than fourteen times what it yielded before the frackers arrived.

At the end of 2013, production hit 1.2 million barrels a day.

At the end of 2014, it hit 1.68 million barrels a day. The oil that flowed out of Eagle Ford each day was equal to almost 20 percent of all the oil produced in the United States, even back at the peak of production in 1970. Eagle Ford's production was equal to roughly one-third of all US production in 2008.

The fracking revolution was shocking, overwhelming, and transformative to oil markets. It created an entirely new energy economy. It wasn't just the size of the new oil reserves that changed everything—it was the structure of the new fracking industry. Since at least the 1960s, the oil business had been controlled by large, centralized cartels, from the group of companies known as the Seven Sisters to the national oil producers in OPEC. Cartels like OPEC could more or less change oil output on command. Saudi Arabia, in particular, had the ability to turn off the spigots or ramp up production, depending on the Saudi monarchy's wishes. But the American reserves were tapped by thousands of independent drillers. Nobody was in control. When it looked like the world was oversupplied with oil, the frackers weren't willing to shut off their wells and wait for prices to climb. Instead, each driller hung on as long as possible and sold whatever they could into the market. A fracking well only shut down when there was no other alternative. This feature of the fracking business would depress oil prices for years. Even when the oil prices fell by half during a crash in 2014, many frackers kept pumping. And those who stopped were only waiting in the wings to get back in business. The world oil markets, once characterized by terrifying scarcity, were now dominated by stubbornly high supplies coming out of the United States.

While this was transformative, not everything in the oil business changed so dramatically. When the tidal wave of new US oil supplies finally arrived, the wave crashed into a refinery system that had not changed in fundamental ways, in more than forty years. The refinery system was a narrow bottleneck that choked off the flow of oil in unpredictable ways, delivering profits for refinery owners that beat the world average by an order of magnitude. This bottleneck was the segment of the energy industry where Koch Industries excelled, and it was critical to Koch's play in Eagle Ford.

Along the Gulf Coast of Texas, the most pristine skylines were the white towers of the oil refineries. The refinery town of Port Arthur, for example, was a humble collection of crumbling stone buildings, bandaged with sheets of plywood over broken windows. The sidewalks were jagged with weeds and cracked cement. Many of the houses needed paint jobs and new roofs. But when one left town and drove along the coast, the vast, white towers of the oil refineries appeared like a mythical city. These self-contained cities behind tall fences and barbed wire were active around the clock, steam pouring from the towers during the day and lights twinkling on their crowns throughout the night. It seemed impossible to imagine how much money was made inside their perimeters.

Nobody had built a major new oil refinery in the United States since 1977. In that year, when Jimmy Carter was president, a new refinery in Garyville, Louisiana, went into production. This marked the last time a major new competitor entered the refining market.

The primary obstacle to building a new refinery was the Clean Air Act, which required new facilities to comply with pollution standards that existing refineries were allowed to avoid. As outlined earlier, the existing refineries exploited a provision of the Clean Air Act called the New Source Review, which allowed them to expand their old refineries in ways that skirted the onerous pollution controls applied to new refineries. The Department of Justice came close to charging the refineries with violating the Clean Air Act but instead allowed them to stay in business with more stringent controls. The legacy refineries, including Koch's, have operated under that consent decree ever since. While the consent decree might have helped curb pollution, it did nothing to foster competition in the refinery business. The Clean Air Act froze the game board of refining competition, leaving only the incumbent players in place. They were left to divvy up the business among themselves.

During the 1980s, ownership of the nation's refineries consolidated into fewer and fewer hands. After the Reagan administration loosened antitrust enforcement, a wave of mergers swept through the industry. The mergers accelerated during the Clinton administration. Between 1991 and 2000, there were 338 mergers among oil refiners. The consolidation continued through the Bush administration.

In 2002, there were 158 refineries in the United States. By 2012, there were only 115 producing fuel.* From administration to administration,

---

* There were an additional thirteen refineries that produced lubricating oils and asphalt in 2012.

Democratic to Republican, it seemed like the federal government did all it could to ensure that no new refineries entered the market. A company called Arizona Clean Fuels attempted to build a multibillion-dollar refinery, starting in 1998, to help ease tight supplies in the Southwest. The project was hindered by years of permit disputes. Even by 2009, the company was still promising to break ground. In 2011, the project seemed dead, but it was revived. By 2018, there was talk that the refinery might be built, but regulatory hurdles still remained.

Fewer and fewer companies refined oil, and they did it at larger and larger facilities. Even without new refineries, US refining capacity increased between 2002 and 2012 from 16.5 million barrels a day to 18 million barrels a day.

While the refiners were processing more oil, however, there was evidence that they increased production just enough to keep up with rising demand, and no more. There was no incentive to increase capacity to the point where it might bring gasoline prices lower.

By 2004, the refining industry was already "imperfectly competitive," according to a report from the US Government Accountability Office. The report found that refiners had tremendous market power and that "refiners essentially control gasoline sales at the wholesale level." The GAO investigation found that the consolidation made gasoline more expensive for consumers. The increased market concentration "generally led to higher prices for conventional gasoline and for boutique fuels," the report concluded.

By the time the Eagle Ford tsunami arrived, US oil refineries were running full tilt, processing just enough oil to keep up with demand for gasoline. By 2016, US refineries ran at an average of 90 percent of their total capacity, compared to the global average of 83 percent. Only India ran its oil refineries at a tighter capacity. There was simply no excess capacity in the system, and no new companies willing to enter the business and pick up the slack.

The bottleneck was severe. By 2015, even ordinary refinery outages caused catastrophic price increases for gasoline. That summer, BP partially shut down its refinery in Whiting, Indiana, to repair a set of leaky pipes. The closure caused gasoline prices in Chicago to spike by 60 cents a gallon, while gasoline prices rose throughout the surrounding region. It was the biggest such price hike since Hurricane Katrina decimated the

Gulf Coast in 2005. Capacity was so tight that even routine repairs had hurricane-like effects.

In this environment, the profitability of US refiners was breathtaking. In 2010, the average profit margin to refine a barrel of crude oil in the United States was roughly $6 a barrel, by far the highest in the world. The next-highest profit margin was in Europe, where it was about $4 a barrel. One year later, US refining profit margins had swelled to over $16 per barrel—nearly triple the next-highest rate of almost $6 a barrel in Europe. These profit margins were partly the gift of fracking, which delivered copious amounts of cheap oil to refine. In a double stroke of good luck, fracking also cut the cost of natural gas, which refiners used to power their plants. US refinery profits pulled far and above those found elsewhere in the world.

If Koch Industries reaped the average level of profit on refining oil at Corpus Christi that year (and the company claims to be above average in this regard), and operated the refinery for 350 days of the year at 280,000 barrels per day (both conservative estimates), then the company would have earned $1.2 billion in profits from that refinery alone.

The profit margins fell sharply after 2011, sinking to around $13 per barrel in 2012 and then $12 in 2014. But the profit margins never fell close to zero, and were always well above margins for refineries around the world.

Koch enhanced the profitability of its Corpus Christi refinery complex* by using its trading desks in Houston. From their vantage point, Koch's traders could see the reality of the US fossil fuel system, which was a fragmented network held together by aging infrastructure. There was no national, let alone global, price for oil and gasoline. There was only the constellation of opaque nodes where real oil and gasoline were bought and sold, and the tanker farms, gasoline terminals, and import piers where barges were loaded and unloaded. It wasn't easy to get fossil fuels from one region of the country to another. Markets in California were hemmed in by the state's clean-fuels standards, locking in high prices

---

* Koch's complex in Corpus Christi includes two refineries. For the sake of simplicity, the complex is referred to here as simply Corpus Christi, or the Corpus Christi refinery.

there. Markets on the East Coast were dependent on a single, aging pipeline called the Colonial Pipeline, which carried gasoline from the Gulf
Coast all the way to New Jersey. (Koch Industries was the majority owner
of the Colonial.) This fractured market provided abundant opportunities for trading, and Koch excelled in executing on them.

Corpus Christi became the hub for a number of trades that were,
in the eyes of traders, simply elegant and beautiful. Koch bought the
cheap oil that was piling up in terminals around the Eagle Ford Shale,
the superlight crude that only a limited number of refineries could process. Then the traders sold refined gasoline products into markets of
thriving metropolitan areas where gasoline supplies were tight, such
as San Antonio and Austin, Texas. Both of those cities were growing,
thanks in part to the fracking boom in Texas, and the growth locked in
strong demand for gasoline. Neither city had a robust public transportation system and both of them were defined by sprawling networks
of highways that conveyed motorists from far-flung suburbs to work
every day.

In this environment, the Corpus Christi refinery became a second
Pine Bend, an asset that was located right in the center of a massive market dysfunction that produced supranormal profits. In the understated
words of Koch's former oil trader Wes Osbourn: "They have an asset
that's advantaged on a lot of their competitors."

Koch traded around Corpus Christi in other ways, maximizing the
advantage that it had earned by being the first to build pipelines deep
into the Eagle Ford. The wave of ultralight oil was too much even for
Koch to handle. It exported what it could. Then it spent hundreds of
millions of dollars to upgrade the Corpus Christi refinery with machines
that processed even higher amounts of sweet crude, raising its capacity
to roughly 305,000 barrels a day. In July of 2014, Koch Industries paid
$2.1 billion to buy a newly built chemical plant in Houston that pro-
cessed light crude oil into a chemical called propylene, used to make
industrial chemicals and plastic products such as films, packages and
caps. The propylene plant was another reservoir to capture the influx
of light crude and provide another market in which Koch Industries
could grow.

The trades that could be built around Corpus Christi and Eagle Ford
Shale seemed impervious to loss, and they returned enormous prof-

its even as oil prices fell and the economy moved sideways from 2011 through 2015.

There was, however, one growing threat to Koch's oil refining operations. Oil industry analysts started to worry about something that seemed incomprehensible in 2008 when oil was scarce. The fracking boom raised the prospect that the era of "peak oil" might be replaced by an era of "peak demand." Even though it was cheap, demand might fall. Consumers, for the first time in memory, had an alternative choice in energy markets: fuels like wind power and solar energy.

The Obama administration failed to pass a carbon regulation bill. But it had been far more successful in stoking the rise of alternative energy sources. The primary vehicle for this effort was the stimulus bill, which provided an unprecedented $90 billion in subsidies for renewable-energy sources. The bill also incentivized an additional $100 billion in private-sector funding. Just as the government nurtured fracking technology for many years, its renewable-energy subsidies helped make wind and solar power more affordable. And the subsidies were once again transforming the energy industry.

In 2007, renewable-energy sources provided only 6.5 percent of all the BTUs consumed in America, while fossil fuels provided 85 percent. By 2013, renewables provided 9.5 percent of the total energy, while fossil fuels provided 81.8 percent. (The biggest loser in the energy sector shift was coal, which was displaced by natural gas as a fuel for power plants.) This might seem like a small shift, but in commodities markets, even small changes can have broad ripple effects.

The Obama administration further compounded this effect by pushing for new fuel efficiency standards for vehicles, pressuring automakers to make a fleet that consumed less gasoline even as electric-powered cars became more affordable.

Even as Koch refined the Eagle Ford crude oil, signs of peak demand for gasoline were emerging across America. The energy industry consulting firm Turner, Mason & Co., which counted Koch Industries as a client, estimated that the rise of renewables would cause demand for finished petroleum products in the United States to fall by 0.1 percent on an average annual basis between 2016 and 2025. This low-growth environment posed a threat to Koch's Eagle Ford play. If demand for gasoline weakened, prices would fall and profit margins would shrink, perhaps permanently.

Koch Industries employees saw this threat plainly. It was evident in Koch's own backyard. Giant windmill farms were erected across the flat and windy state of Kansas, their development spurred along by state lawmakers. In Kansas, the political support for wind energy was bipartisan. Even the Republican governor, Sam Brownback, was enthusiastic about helping the wind industry expand in the state. Building wind farms and a new utility grid created jobs. The wind industry was a rare beacon of future growth in the state. Fracking hadn't taken hold in Kansas, cattle feedlots were struggling, and farming could only support so many families.

Like twenty-nine states across the country, Kansas legislators passed a law requiring state utility companies to buy 10 percent of their power from renewable sources in 2011, increasing that level to 20 percent by 2020. As a result, wind farms were becoming more plentiful, and the cost of building them was steadily falling as the young wind industry improved its techniques. Renewable energy was on track to steadily displace fossil fuels in Charles Koch's home state and elsewhere.

Charles Koch knew that such developments were not inevitable. If government policy was responsible for supporting renewable energy, then government policy could be changed.

One of Charles Koch's primary skills was identifying undervalued commodities. By 2013, it became evident that political power in the state of Kansas was an undervalued commodity.

The state was deeply Republican and still largely rural. This meant that most Kansas state officials—the occupants of the state house and the state senate—were elected during primary contests in their home districts. A state politician in Kansas might be elected by no more than a thousand voters during a primary race. Such elections drew a turnout level near zero and generated almost no media attention. It was common for a campaign to cost $10,000, on the upside.

Many Kansas state lawmakers were like Tom Moxley, a rancher from the tiny town of Council Grove, about a hundred miles northeast of

Wichita. Moxley was in his midsixties when he ran for a seat in the state-house in Kansas's Sixty-Eighth District. He figured it was his time to do some public service after decades of running a small business.

Serving in the Kansas statehouse was a little more serious than join-ing the local volunteer fire department, but not by much. The 125 mem-bers of the Kansas House convened every January for a legislative session that usually ended in May. When they were in session, they met in the state capitol building in Topeka, a sleepy city about an hour west of Kan-sas City.

Moxley joined the legislature in 2007. Over the next few years, he learned how things worked. Then, starting around 2011, he watched Koch Industries transform everything. A central focus of Koch's efforts was beating back the mandates to support renewable energy. Because Moxley sat on the House Energy and Environment Committee, he had the chance to see Koch's strategy play out firsthand. In 2013, a string of experts descended on the capitol in Topeka to testify about renew-able energy. Moxley called these scholars "heavy hitters"—the kind of high-profile people who rarely showed up for a statehouse hearing. The scholars came from think tanks like the Cato Institute in Washington, and they testified about the deeply damaging economic effects of wind power and government mandates.

Renewable-energy mandates were passed in Kansas in 2009 as a bipartisan compromise. The state was about to approve construction of a new coal-fired plant, and the mandates to buy renewable energy were included in the approval. The concerns were economic as much as environmental—Kansas generated the vast majority of its power from coal and was being hurt by high coal prices, even as neighboring states were getting cheaper energy from natural gas. Wind power was getting cheaper by the year, thanks to state mandates across the country and stimulus money from Washington. Kansas wanted an alternative to coal.

In 2013, a Kansas statehouse member from Wichita pushed a bill to remove the renewable-energy mandates. He was Republican Dennis Hedke, the chairman of Moxley's Energy Committee. Hedke was a geo-physicist who did consulting work for regional oil and gas companies, and his fixation on repealing the renewable-energy mandates seemed odd to Moxley, who supported the new coal plant in 2009 but also saw the benefits of wind and solar power. "Wind power has turned out to be less expensive than about any other source for Kansas," Moxley said. "I think the renewable [energy mandates]—that part has been generally good for everybody."

The Kansas statehouse held a number of hearings on global warming. The heavy hitters lined up to testify. Moxley broke these experts into two groups: the "true believers," who thought man-made climate change was an impending environmental crisis, and the "naysayers," who said that the science was in doubt and the problem of climate change was being promoted by hysterical liberals. The true believers were brought in by the wind industry lobbyists, who were just starting to get a foothold in Topeka. The naysayers were brought in by Koch-funded groups, including Americans for Prosperity, the Heartland Institute, the Beacon Hill Institute, the Kansas Policy Institute, and the Kansas Chamber of Commerce.

The hearings transfixed Moxley because he didn't know if he was a naysayer or a true believer. He was a staunch Republican, and therefore inclined to distrust Al Gore and the EPA. But just like Bob Inglis, Moxley got a scientific schooling in carbon emissions, and it changed his thinking. He gradually came to believe that the naysayers did not have a serious case. "I'm open to good science, but those guys were just throwing dust in the air and not making a case," Moxley recalled. He turned against them completely when it was proved that one of the climate skeptics had shown legislators a chart on the Earth's climate that conveniently omitted the last hundred years, when temperatures began to escalate.

While the arguments over global warming were unconvincing to Moxley, Koch Industries was using other tools to help legislators come around to its point of view. Moxley started to hear stories from his colleagues about a changing political landscape.

During primary elections in rural districts, Koch Industries and its various political arms were dropping $50,000 into local primary races. This was a pittance by national political standards, but it amounted to a shock-and-awe campaign in towns like Larned, Kanapolis, and Great Bend. Koch Industries was expert at coordinating with other conservative groups, Moxley said, such as the National Rifle Association, the pro-life group Kansans for Life, the state Chamber of Commerce, and, of course, Americans for Prosperity.

Moxley observed a recurrent strategy. He said that Koch handpicked a candidate in a primary election, told that candidate to stay home, and then scorched the earth beneath their opponent with negative messages in the form of postcard mailings, advertisements, and door-knocking campaigns. Such efforts intensified in 2012 and wiped out incumbents who seemed resistant to Charles Koch's political vision.

"The bottom line is, they flipped the [Kansas] senate from pretty traditional Republican kind of thinking to 'Koch' kind of thinking. And it's pretty dramatic. We're still living with it," Moxley said. He grew disdainful of a new breed of state legislators who showed up in Topeka and seemed more concerned with toeing a line set out by Koch Industries than they did with thinking for themselves.

"They're like numbskulls. All they're going to do is take orders from the Chamber and Koch and so on," Moxley said. "They're not thoughtful. They're not people that read the newspaper or have a history background. They just do what Koch wants done."

Koch's efforts in Kansas were part of a multistate campaign to push back renewable-energy subsidies. Koch's primary targets were so-called renewable energy standards that required states to buy wind and solar power. Koch characterized these mandates as a form of crony capitalism. The Heartland Institute, which Koch funded, helped write a bill to repeal such standards. The bill was then taken up by ALEC, the Koch-funded conference of state legislators, and then introduced in more than a dozen states between 2013 and 2014.

ALEC's efforts bore fruit. Ohio repealed its renewable standard, as did West Virginia. In Kansas, the fight lasted for years. Moxley repeatedly voted against the bill to repeal the renewable-energy mandates, as did a handful of other Republicans and many Democrats. But the financial power behind the bill was too strong to resist. In 2015, a version of the bill finally passed, removing the mandates and making the renewable-energy standards voluntary. This was only a partial victory for Koch. Wind power continued to gain ground in Kansas in part because it was so cheap. The utility companies were already meeting their renewable standards whether they were mandatory or not. Still, Koch had managed to achieve an effect in Kansas and other states that was similar to what it had done in Washington. It politicized the issue of renewable energy. It had stained the efforts to stoke competition in the energy industry as a form of government corruption, and it drew a red line that Republican politicians could not cross.

Moxley ended up leaving the Kansas legislature in 2016, when he decided not to seek reelection. "I kind of aged out," he said. But his time in the conservative Kansas statehouse changed his thinking about human-induced climate change. He was more worried about it than before. He went back to his ranch in Council Grove, installed a large set of solar panels, and now only pays for electricity off the grid for about five months in the winter. About a year after he left politics, Moxley began to recover from the experience.

"I was just walking across the yard, and broke out in a whistle," he said.

By 2014, a sense of mastery infused the corporate culture at Koch Industries. The company was thriving, even during an era of almost unprecedented volatility in the global energy business and weak economic growth in the United States. A geyser of cash flowed from Koch's oil refineries, thanks to the Eagle Ford Shale play and the continued profitability at Pine Bend. Profits were soaring in Koch's massive network of nitrogen fertilizer plants, thanks to the collapse of natural gas prices. Business was strong and profits were rising at Georgia-Pacific, thanks to a recovery in the housing market. The company's success seemed like the proof of concept for Market-Based Management. Koch Industries seemed to have its hand in everything—paper towels, gasoline, clothing, corn, derivatives trading—and somehow it succeeded even as different markets rose and fell.

Charles Koch and his team had also proven that they could master the art of politics. The Obama revolution was crippled. The days of a permanent liberal majority and a new New Deal were in the past. It was true that Obama had been reelected in 2012, but his governing power was hemmed in by a Congress that slid further into Republican control with each election. Koch's chosen congressional candidates gained more seats in the midterms of 2014. Across the states, Koch's political network was more powerful than ever. The greatest legislative threat to Koch's business— greenhouse gas regulation—was relegated to the fringes of American political life. Charles Koch had faced a political movement that he considered to be dangerous to America's future, and he had largely prevailed.

As always, Charles Koch had his eye on the far future. The vast majority of profits that flowed from Koch's operations were recycled right back into the company. Koch Industries initiated an acquisition spree that was only paralleled by the wild growth strategies of the 1990s. During 2013 and 2014, Koch Industries spent billions of dollars to amass new assets and enter new lines of business. It acquired companies in an impossibly diverse array of industries: from steel, to glass, to greeting cards.

In late 2012, Koch bought a stake in the privately held glassmaker Guardian Industries, making Koch the largest shareholder. Koch placed an executive on Guardian's board and monitored the company's performance, eventually purchasing the rest of Guardian's shares. In 2013, Koch paid $7.2 billion to buy the technology company Molex, which made electronic sensors and chips. This acquisition gave Koch its first major presence in the technology sector and it also played to Koch's strength as a commodity company; Molex made its products by using huge quantities of rare earth materials and metals.

Also in 2013, Koch invested $1 billion to help build a high-tech steel mill in Arkansas, anticipating that the specialty steel it produced would be in high demand as America's economy improved and replaced its aging electricity grid. Somewhat strangely, in April of 2013, Koch financed a deal to buy the greeting card company American Greetings and take it private in a deal worth $878 million. Outsiders wondered if that wasn't some sort of add-on to Koch's paper business, but it seems that Charles Koch just thought the card company was a good buy. In August, Koch paid $1.45 billion to purchase Buckeye Technologies, a company that made specialty fabrics and materials out of wood and cotton, which was then tucked into the Georgia-Pacific division.

The sense of mastery within Koch Industries only intensified in 2014 when Charles Koch and his team expanded and renovated company headquarters. The corporate campus had not grown significantly since the Tower was built in the 1990s, and now Koch needed more room to accommodate its growing workforce. The only hindrance to this expansion was Thirty-Seventh Street, the busy two-lane road that ran through the north side of the headquarters campus. Many employees had to park on the north side of Thirty-Seventh Street and use an underground pedestrian tunnel to get safely into the Tower. To alleviate this problem, Koch Industries paid to have Thirty-Seventh Street torn out and rerouted in a large semicircle that arced around the headquarters. The newly laid Thirty-Seventh Street created a giant horseshoe shape. Inside the horseshoe, Koch built a new office building with 210,000 square feet of space and enough room for 745 employees.

The most noticeable renovation, however, was the wall.

Koch Industries erected an earthen wall that encircled the north end of the complex, running in a curve along the newly rerouted Thirty-Seventh Street. The wall was tall and sloped, with trees planted along its length. Before the wall was erected, visitors could turn from Thirty-Seventh and steer directly into Koch's visitors' lot. Uninvited guests could walk directly from the lot into the Tower's lobby. Now the only means of entrance were a series of checkpoints. Two of the checkpoints were located on the north side, where metal gates had been installed into the side of the wall. To gain access, a visitor had to first receive an e-mail from the address DoNotReply-SAFE@kochind.com that included a bar code in the message. A security guard inside a squat building next to the gate scanned the bar code with a red light. If accepted, a yellow guardrail rose up and allowed the visitor to pass inside.

The wall around Koch Industries reflected the cost that came with Charles Koch's political victories. For decades, Charles Koch had fiercely guarded his privacy. In just a few short years, he had become a public figure and a walking political cartoon. The "Koch brothers," meaning Charles and David, had become fodder for countless political ads and exposés. Their image became a shorthand illustration for the influence of big money on politics. Charles Koch began receiving death threats in steady volume. The earthen wall helped keep such threats at bay. Now packages delivered to Koch Industries were received first in a bomb-proof room at the Tower where packages ran through X-ray machines to scan for bombs. When Charles parked in a special lot with indoor access to the building, Koch Industries became more fortresslike and more culturally insular, even as it extended its reach further each day into industries that underpinned modern life.

Charles Koch could spend his long working days surrounded entirely by people who were beholden to him for a paycheck. His office was the epicenter of a corporate empire over which he had almost unchallenged control. But for all this power, there was one thing that Charles Koch could not control, and that was the passage of time. He turned eighty years old in 2015. But it didn't seem that anyone expected him to retire.

"They'll take Charles out of there on a stretcher. And I think he'll be the happiest that way," quipped Leslie Rudd, one of Charles Koch's long-time friends in Wichita.

But even if he never retired, Charles Koch could not lead the company forever. And this raised a troubling question: Could Koch Industries thrive without him? The politically correct answer among Koch employees was that Market-Based Management would be able to carry on without the charismatic CEO who created it. Charles Koch's wisdom had been codified into a machine, this thinking went, and the machine could thrive without his personal intervention. But history was replete with examples of companies that had stagnated once their founders left. Koch Industries seemed like a prime candidate for this fate. Charles Koch insisted on maintaining control over the company since he became CEO in 1967. No one knew how the corporation would operate without him.

Charles Koch had a contingency plan. He had placed a hedge bet against mortality and the passage of time. There was a possibility that Koch Industries might be passed down to an heir, a young man who could carry on the Koch name and the tradition of family ownership.

Charles Koch was raised in a household with four sons, four potential heirs to the family business. Charles, on the other hand, had only one son. He had vested many hopes, and many years of work, in him and by 2015, Charles Koch's son was seen as the heir apparent.

His name was Chase Koch, and everyone who met him thought that he might be CEO of Koch Industries one day. But what people didn't know was if he'd be ready to do it. Or, more importantly, whether he wanted to.

CHAPTER 22

The Education of Chase Koch

(1977–2016)

When he was a young boy, Chase Koch might have seemed unteachable. But that didn't mean that his father didn't try. On Sunday afternoons, Chase Koch and his older sister, Elizabeth, got personal lessons from their father.

It was common for families in Wichita to attend church on Sunday, sending the kids to Sunday school while their parents listened to sermons from the altar. This was not the tradition in Charles Koch's household. Charles Koch developed his own curriculum to teach his children, a curriculum that taught them about his systematic view of human behavior and how best to organize human society. On Sundays, Charles Koch gathered Elizabeth and Chase in the family library.

The library was a large, imposing chamber in the back of the house, with walls that were lined by thousands of books. The books on philosophy, history, and science were the raw material of Charles Koch's worldview, which he had encoded in Market-Based Management. When they sat down for their lessons in the library, Elizabeth and Chase Koch were likely the only people on earth to get such deep, one-on-one lessons in MBM from the creator himself.

Charles Koch played taped lectures from economists like Walter E. Williams and Milton Friedman. As the economists and philosophers droned on, Charles Koch periodically stopped the tape and quizzed his children.

"He'd pause it and then say, 'Okay, well, what did you kids learn from that?'" Chase recalled. Chase was maybe eight years old at the time; certainly "in the single digits," as he remembered it.

Elizabeth, the oldest child who always seemed eager to please, was attentive to the lessons and earnestly answered her father. Chase struggled to stay awake. "Literally half the time, I'd get caught, like, with a baseball hat over my eyes, because I would be sleeping through it," he said. "And my sister, being the good first child . . . she was valedictorian in her class or second in her class. And so she was, at a very early age, just gobbling this stuff up."

Charles Koch tried to teach his son, but it appeared that his son did not want to learn. Chase's obstinance, or apathy, posed an obstacle to Charles Koch and his future plans.

Those plans seemed clear to everyone from the first day Chase Koch was born, in June of 1977. At that time, a group of employees at Koch Industries took it upon themselves to print a banner and hang it up above their desks, where Charles Koch would see it when he returned to the office.

The banner read: "WELCOME CROWN PRINCE."

If the birth of Charles Koch's daughter had not been greeted the same way, it might have had something to do with the conservative culture of Wichita at the time. "In those days, it was logical that your son followed you," said Leslie Rudd. "A lot of people around the area—the kids followed their fathers." This was the Koch family tradition. Charles Koch had followed his father, Fred, who had pushed him, disciplined him, taught him to fight, and then pressured him to return to the family company and run it. It seemed natural that Chase would, in turn, follow Charles. "Charles was preparing Chase for success. But it's damn near impossible to do, to build the drive and all of those things into a person," said Rudd, who went on vacation with Charles Koch and attended many Koch family events.

Charles and his wife, Liz, worked hard to instill a competitive drive in their children. They informed Chase and Elizabeth that the children must find a sport outside of school at which they could excel. When Chase was about ten, his parents enrolled him in a local basketball league, which was sponsored by the Salvation Army. One of the league coaches was Brad Hall, who later became CFO of Koch Supply & Trading. Hall often watched Chase Koch play and saw a gangly, mediocre player. But Hall was impressed with the kid's values. Chase worked hard. He wasn't arrogant. He didn't advertise his last name to anyone. Hall remembered seeing Charles Koch at the games, watching closely.

When it was clear that Chase had no future in basketball, the family focused on a different sport: tennis. Chase showed aptitude here. If Charles Koch was born with a brain for math, Chase Koch was born with a body for tennis. Chase was tall and lean, with powerful legs. He could get to the far corners of the court before his opponent. He had a strong swing. Unfortunately, playing tennis required that Chase Koch spend large amounts of his free time—weekends, nights, and summers—at the Wichita Country Club.

Just like his father, Fred, Charles Koch vowed that he would never raise any "country club bums." But Chase Koch seemed to want very much to be a country club bum. It turned out that he was quite sociable and liked having friends. Eventually, Chase's natural talent for tennis won the day. He was allowed to spend long hours each day, and whole days in the summer, with his friends, as long as he was on the tennis court.

Things weren't as easy for Elizabeth. She never found her equivalent of the tennis court. Outside the confines of sports, social interactions were fraught and complicated for the Koch children. Elizabeth Koch wrote later about the difficulties of growing up as the daughter of the richest man in town. She could go wherever she wanted, but could never escape the family name. "I want people to like me, and as a small child growing up in a small town, I learned that having money makes people sort of hate you on the spot," Elizabeth Koch wrote.

Every year, a portrait of the Koch family was printed and sent out as a Christmas card to Koch Industries' employees. The family posed in that awkward manner all professional photographers seem determined to create: Elizabeth Koch sitting on the floor, with her father kneeling behind her, his arm around her shoulder. Chase and his mother hovering behind them, with frozen smiles. Elizabeth never seems to have escaped the feeling of awkwardly posing as Charles Koch's daughter. As a young adult, she was filled with anger, and it strained her relationship with her parents.

"I am such a terror," Elizabeth Koch wrote in an online essay in 2007. "I'm angry that those girls on the playground in sixth grade called me a rich bitch when they knew nothing about me except my last name. I'm angry that I have everything in the world I could possibly want and yet I'm still angry."

Spending time on the tennis courts removed some of these pressures from Chase Koch's life. Things were uncomplicated and straightforward on a tennis court. There was often very little talking. Everyone focused on the ball. Chase Koch was on a tennis court in the mornings, afternoons, and weekends. He practiced hard and drove himself. Soon, Chase was playing in regional tournaments and winning. He became recognized as one of the best young players in Wichita, and then was recognized as one of the best players in Kansas. He became one of the top players in the Missouri Valley Conference, which covered several states. On the tennis court, Chase Koch's last name didn't matter. And if Chase Koch was winning, his father didn't express dissatisfaction.

By the time he was in middle school, Chase Koch's tennis regimen became difficult to sustain. All of his free time became dominated by tennis. When he spent time with his mother, it was so they could drive to regional tennis tournaments. Chase began to burn out. He started to hate the game. And he rebelled.

"I got exposed to new groups of friends and got to hang out with them, and just enjoyed that part of life instead of tennis," Chase recalled. "In some of these regional matches, I intentionally started throwing matches, and, like, tanking, because I wanted to get home and party with my friends, basically."

Chase's mother, Elizabeth, couldn't understand what was happening. He was losing now in the early rounds, when he used to win easily. It vexed her, and brought her to tears.

"So she reported this back to my father," Chase said.

After hearing about Chase Koch's failure on the court, Charles Koch invited his son to come down to Koch Industries headquarters for a talk. Chase expected that they might have lunch. When he arrived, there was no lunch.

Charles Koch gave his son a choice. Summer was about to begin, and Chase could do one of two things. He could spend his summer working for Koch Industries, or he could reapply himself to tennis and play competitively again.

Chase would be fifteen years old that summer. It was his last summer before high school. He chose to work for the family company. He thought that he would get an office job, learn some things, and have the evenings to spend time with his friends. Plus, he'd earn some money. The decision was easy.

"I said, 'Fine, you get me a job. I'm so sick of this. I'm tired. I'm burned out. I want to do something else,'" Chase said.

The next day, Chase Koch woke up to discover that his father had packed his bags for him. Chase would be leaving for the summer. A driver arrived to give Chase a ride. They would travel four and a half hours due east of Wichita, to a tiny town called Syracuse.

Within thirty minutes of leaving Wichita, the land flattened out and grew desolate. There was very little to interrupt the landscape of open grassland except for the occasional oil derrick. Two hours outside of Wichita, a person can feel totally marooned in the center of a prairie. Two hours after that, Chase Koch arrived at his destination.

Syracuse was home to one of Koch Beef Company's largest cattle feedlots, a centerpiece of the doomed company's effort during the 1990s to reinvent the agribusiness sector. Chase could smell the place from miles away. Roughly fifty thousand cattle milled around in muddy pens beneath a grain silo, which was one of the tallest structures in the Syracuse skyline. Chase Koch was dropped off and shown to his quarters. He would live in the single-wide trailer of a guy named Kelly Fink, the feedlot's manager. Fink told Chase that he'd be sleeping on the couch for the summer. Chase set down his things, and tried to settle in. Fink slept down the hallway, in the trailer's single bed.

Chase suspected that his father had given Kelly Fink specific orders to break Chase's spirit. Chase was assigned to shovel shit and pick weeds. "The first two weeks, I was just bitter, because they handed me a shovel and said, 'Go shovel out that stall and then go pick all these weeds.' And it was just a lot of busywork just to get my head right."

Chase worked at least ten hours a day, seven days a week. He got one day off, the Fourth of July. On that day, his parents called him from Vail, Colorado, where they were vacationing. They told him that it was snowing there. Wasn't that remarkable?

Chase kept working and slowly got to know Fink. Then he started to like him. Then, strangely, he started to like the work. Toward the end of the summer, Chase felt something he'd never really felt before. He felt like he had endured an ordeal, and had really earned something.

When Chase was in sixth grade, his father had helped him write a paper. Chase's assignment was to pick a philosopher and write about the philosopher's ideas. Charles Koch told his son to pick Aristotle, and they read Aristotle's work together. Charles Koch wrote notes on Aristotle in his neat, engineer's script, listing page numbers from Aristotle's significant work for Chase to pursue. When Chase turned in the paper, he summarized what he believed was one of Aristotle's most important ideas.

"Aristotle taught that the goal in life is to be happy and to be happy you need to use your natural ability," Chase Koch had written.

Now, at the end of the summer, before his freshman year of high school, Chase was starting to understand what Aristotle had meant. And what his father had meant. Chase Koch was feeling happy. He was feeling a sense of accomplishment.

Chase enrolled for his freshman year of high school at the Wichita Collegiate School, a private academy located on a spacious, grassy campus less than two blocks from the Koch family compound. To get to school each morning, Chase could leave the front gate of the Koch estate and take a left turn on Thirteenth Street, heading due east, passing the front gates of the Wichita Country Club, and then taking a right turn into the parking lot of his high school. This is the small geographic circuit in which he spent the majority of his adolescence.

The Wichita Collegiate classrooms were located in a group of modest, beige-brick buildings, set back from the street behind a screen of leafy trees. On the east side of campus there was the football field and the track, and then, farther back, a cluster of tennis courts. This is where Chase Koch spent an inordinate amount of his free time as a teenager. The tennis courts were the domain of a tall, imposing man named Dave Hawley, one of the winningest tennis coaches in Kansas history.* On a typical spring afternoon, Hawley walked from court to court in the tennis complex, calling out to his players in a booming voice. Hawley was uncompromising in his discipline and demands. If he felt that students weren't practicing hard enough, he sent them home. If he felt they were

---

* During Hawley's career at Wichita Collegiate, his players won fifty state titles by 2018 and he was inducted into the National High School Tennis Coaches Association Hall of Fame.

falling short of their own ability, he let them know in unvarnished critiques. Still, Hawley could be friendly and gregarious. He gave lessons to little kids when things were quiet. While coaching a small girl, Hawley reminded her that tennis wasn't like bowling; you couldn't take your time to set up a shot. The game was an intimate competition against an opponent who didn't want to give you time to think, and who wanted to be unpredictable. As he lobbed balls toward the little girl, Hawley called out to her, "You never know what's coming! You never know what's coming!"

Chase Koch thrived in this world. Over the course of his high school career, Chase faced more than a hundred competitors, and beat all of them except for one. The one student who beat Chase was Matthew Wright, a classmate and fellow player on Hawley's team.

Chase Koch was one of the best players that Hawley ever worked with during his decades-long career. "If I had a Mount Rushmore of players that I've coached, he'd be on it," he said of Chase. "He'd be one of the four—at the very outside, one of the six—best players I've ever coached on the boys' side."

Chase Koch's style of play reflected his personality. His game relied on two primary strengths: his ability to quiet his mind and react in real time to his opponents, and his willingness to work harder than nearly everyone else in the state. Hawley noticed Chase Koch's quiet demeanor almost immediately. The tennis team spent a lot of time together, and Hawley had hours to observe Chase interact with his classmates. What Hawley saw was a kid who defied expectations. Everyone in Wichita knew who Chase was the moment he walked into a room. The aura of power and wealth around the Koch name was inescapable. Yet somehow Chase Koch made this aura invisible. He didn't act superior. He didn't act like he was better than anyone else. He did drop stories about private jets and the fact that he could attend the US Open in New York every year with his family. Chase seemed happiest on the court, where he competed in silent exertion. "If you had no idea who he was, you never would have known who he was," Hawley said.

Chase approached tennis as if it were a seven-day-a-week job. Hawley never saw Chase take it easy during practice. Chase developed a game that Coach Hawley called an "all-court game." Chase's primary skill was the ability to be anywhere on the court before his opponent could get a ball there. Chase's strategy relied in part on wearing his opponents down, volley after volley, until they made too many mistakes and crumbled. It was a strategy that relied on hard work, long practice, and physical conditioning. There wasn't some secret genius in Chase Koch's serve. He just outworked the competition.

Still, Chase Koch could never beat Matt Wright. If Chase was impressive, Wright was slightly more so. Their close proximity in talent drove a friendly competition between the teammates. During those intense hours of practice, it was often Chase Koch and Matt Wright who fought the hardest against each other.

Chase won more freedom as he excelled in school and tennis. He got a Ford Explorer and, during his sophomore year, he got his driver's license.

On the evening of Saturday, September 18, 1993, Chase took the car out for the evening. He planned to take a group of his friends to a shopping mall. Chase was in the driver's seat, and, like so many teenage boys, he must have luxuriated in the freedom it gave him. He accelerated, and felt the speed and power of the Explorer.

Chase Koch was in charge, and he was going fast.

That evening, a woman named Nola Foulston was out for a walk. She happened to be the prosecuting attorney for Sedgwick County, which encompassed Wichita. As she strolled along, Foulston saw a Ford Explorer driving through the neighborhood. She would later say that the Explorer was going so fast that she took notice of the car and remembered what it looked like. The car was barreling through residential streets. It is unclear if she saw the teenaged boy who was driving.

At that moment, a twelve-year-old boy named Zachary Seibert was out for a jog. Zac, as he was known to his parents and two siblings, ran a three-mile loop from his home, about three times a week. His father, Walter, had helped him trace out the route. Walt himself had been an accomplished runner; he met Zac's mother while he was training in Boulder, Colorado, to run in the Olympics. Zac was the couple's oldest child and, in September of 1993, Zac was almost thirteen years old and becoming an enthusiastic runner. He often woke up before five in the morning to get in a run before school started.

Walt taught his son to be mindful of cars. That evening, while Zac was running south through the neighborhoods near his family's home, he stopped at the intersection on East Douglas Avenue, a four-lane road that was a major thoroughfare for crosstown traffic. He stopped at a pedestrian crosswalk beneath a traffic light, and pressed the button to activate the crossing signal. Zac had his headphones on and was listening to Kris Kross, an upbeat hip-hop group with a driving beat.

The traffic light on Douglas turned yellow, and then red. A big van slowed down and stopped in the lane closest to Zac. The van would have obscured Zac's view when he looked left to scan for traffic heading west on Douglas Avenue. Walt had coached Zac on looking both ways when he entered a crosswalk, so presumably Zac did so. Then he jumped into action, running out into the street.

Chase Koch was driving the Explorer on Douglas with at least one friend in the car. They were going to a shopping mall called Towne East Square, presumably to waste away the hours of a Saturday night in the tradition of teenagers everywhere, hitting the food court, meeting up with other friends, browsing the windows.

Chase was going fast. He was about a block away from the mall, and driving in the left lane. As he approached the crosswalk, the traffic light was red and the big van was stopped in the right-hand lane.

Just as Chase passed the van, Zac lurched out in front of his car. There must have been less than a second for Chase to respond. The front right corner of Chase's car struck Zac, and Chase kept driving. He went about two hundred yards until he came to a parking lot, where he turned his car around. He called 911 to report the accident from his car phone.

Zachary Seibert was still alive when the ambulance arrived and transported him to HCA Wesley Medical Center. Someone called his father, Walt, who rushed to the hospital to be at his son's side. When he arrived, Walt was told that Zac was still alive. Details were sparse, but it appears that everyone involved already knew that the driver of the car was the son of the richest man in town. This created an awkward, painful dynamic. Walt Seibert didn't think much about it because he was desperate for news about his son, but he couldn't ignore the dynamic for long.

"At the hospital, there was a cop . . . from the Wichita Police Department that actually told me not to 'seek a pound of gold.' At that moment, when I don't know if my son is living or not," Seibert recalled. He assumed the police officer was referring to the notion that the Seiberts might sue the Koch family in order to profit from the tragedy. Seibert said such an action was inconceivable to him.

Zac died roughly an hour after arriving at the hospital.

Charles Koch was more than a prominent citizen of Wichita—his company was one of the city's economic engines. On Tuesday, September 21, 1993, subscribers of the *Wichita Eagle* learned that Charles Koch's son, Chase, was driving the car involved in a horrific tragedy.

Charles and Liz Koch took swift action to protect their son. But they also took action, just as swiftly, to expose Chase Koch to the dire consequences of his mistake. They did so in a way that was severe and that ensured Chase could never deny the reality of what he had done.

To protect Chase, the Kochs employed Don Cordes, the bulldog attorney who was general counsel for Koch Industries at the time. Cordes became the Koch family's spokesman, and he conveyed a narrative that minimized Chase Koch's culpability in the accident.

Cordes told the *Wichita Eagle* that Chase Koch thought the traffic light over the crosswalk was yellow as he approached it, an account that Chase had provided to authorities after the accident. Cordes said it seemed unlikely that Chase Koch was speeding, in part because there were no skid marks at the scene of the accident. "We are going on the theory that, when he swerved to the left, if he would have been going at a high rate of speed, he would have spun out of control. This is just one of those tragic things," Cordes told the paper. "There was no drinking, no drugs. This was a straight-arrow kid. Good grades, athlete."

It might have been easy for Charles and Liz Koch to shield Chase behind their company lawyer. It might have even been pragmatic. They didn't know the Seibert family, and didn't know if the family might seek to extract its "pound of gold."

But the Kochs chose a different strategy. Shortly after Zachary Seibert died, Charles and Liz Koch told their son to visit Zac's parents in their home; to be accountable for what he had done. At the time, Walter Seibert was still trying to process what happened. Elizabeth Koch accompanied Chase to the Seiberts' home. Walt Seibert said that he wanted to talk to Chase privately and suggested that he and Chase could sit in the front seats of the Seibert family's van. Chase agreed to it. When they closed the doors, Chase and Walt were encased together in silence. Walt Seibert could see that the sixteen-year-old next to him was distraught, and maybe terrified.

"I just wanted him to tell me his version of what happened. He was extremely, extremely nervous. Maybe I don't blame him, for what he went through," Seibert said. Chase apologized, and his deep remorse seemed utterly sincere. Seibert pressed the boy for details about the accident.

"He basically just said he didn't know what was happening. He thought the light was yellow, and didn't say anything about speeding," Seibert recalled. This fact would gnaw at Seibert later, because he felt like he hadn't gotten the whole story. County prosecutor Nola Foulston later told him that she had seen Chase's vehicle speeding through neighborhoods before the accident. But while Chase might have fumbled his words with Seibert that day, he later admitted in open court to running the red light and accepted blame for what he had done.

Charles, Liz, and Chase Koch attended Zachary Seibert's funeral. A friend of the Seibert family would later tell the *Wichita Eagle* that it was "emotionally wrenching to watch [the Koch family] at the funeral . . . It took a lot of courage to walk in that group of people. And every eye in that church was on them."

Chase Koch must have felt those eyes on him. This was the kind of experience that burns into a person's mind. Chase Koch had been careless and reckless in a way that is common among teenage boys. But in an instant, the carelessness reaped consequences that could never be erased, for anyone involved.

Nola Foulston recused herself as prosecutor because she was a potential witness in the case. A special prosecutor named Stephen Joseph was appointed to the case, and he charged Chase Koch with misdemeanor vehicular homicide. This was a lesser charge than involuntary manslaughter, a felony that could be applied to traffic accidents where drivers acted with conscious knowledge that they were threatening human life, or acted with a total lack of concern for other people's safety. Joseph didn't think that the facts of the case warranted such a serious charge.

Chase Koch plead guilty to vehicular homicide in December. In January, just as he was beginning the second half of his sophomore year in high school, Chase was sentenced to a year and a half of probation, one hundred hours of community service work, and a nightly curfew that would last ten months. He was also required to pay for Zachary Seibert's funeral expenses and to take a defensive driving course.

Walter Seibert said he was satisfied with the sentence and believed that justice had been served. But decades later, Seibert was still bothered by his conversation with Chase Koch in the van. He felt that Chase tried to evade responsibility. "He was with three other teenagers in the car. So they were screwing off. They were fucking around, driving at too high a speed," Seibert said. "He didn't tell me about going through a red light. He didn't tell me about not seeing the light. The thing is, he was so, so obviously nervous. I can't honestly totally blame him. But the bottom line is, he still killed my son. And he didn't own up to anything he did."

Seibert was not aware of it, but Chase Koch would never be able to escape what he had done. As he grew older and rose through the ranks of Koch Industries, Chase Koch rarely mentioned the accident. But he lived with it every day of his life. "I wish I could take it all back," Chase Koch said about the accident. "I can't forgive myself for what I did. And I don't expect anyone else to."

The accident permanently removed an element of innocence from Chase Koch's life. There was before the accident, and there was after. In the time after, the memory of what happened never went away. "I take full responsibility for what happened," Chase said. "And I think the reality is that I'm going to live with this the rest of my life."

During the second half of his high school career, Chase Koch once again found his place on the tennis court. His high school career record was 110 wins and 14 losses. All of those losses were against his teammate Matt Wright.

When Chase Koch was a senior, Coach Hawley suggested that he play doubles with Matthew Wright at the state championship. Hawley believed that Chase richly deserved a state title, and he could get it by playing with Wright. Chase told Hawley he'd think about it over a weekend. When he came back on Monday, Chase said that he didn't want to do it. Winning a state title didn't seem as important as being measured on his own merits.

After Chase Koch's senior year of high school, an emergency meeting was called among managers at Koch Industries' oil refinery in Corpus Christi. A manager had just been informed that Charles Koch's son would be coming to work there for the summer. This set off something close to a panic. One of the employees at the meeting that day was Brenden O'Neill, the engineer who would later earn millions trading derivatives for Koch.

"It was kind of funny," O'Neill recalled of the meeting about Chase's arrival. "It was like. 'What are we going to do?' 'We're going to take care of him and keep him busy and give him some stuff to do.'"

O'Neill didn't find the situation funny for long. He was informed that Chase Koch would work directly under him. This required a painfully tense balancing act. Managers felt that Chase had to be pushed, but also had to be treated well. The job had to be hard, but not grueling. O'Neill was in charge of managing this contradiction day to day. O'Neill was given one key warning from his boss: "Don't let him get hurt."

When Chase arrived, he wasn't what O'Neill had expected. He was tall, quiet, and completely unpretentious. "He wasn't a workaholic at eighteen, I'll put it that way," O'Neill recalled. "He didn't act like, 'Hey, I'm going to take over the company someday.'"

Early in the summer, Chase told a story that put O'Neill at ease. Chase said that before he came to Corpus Christi, his father had called him into his office and then called the plant manager on the phone while Chase was listening: "Charles calls up the plant manager and says, 'If Chase screws up, I want you to fire him on the spot. And if you don't have the balls to do it, I'll do it myself,'" O'Neill said. "Chase told me that. The plant manager didn't tell me that."

O'Neill found Chase Koch to be a surprisingly normal teenager. Chase wanted to make friends and spent a lot of time working on his car, installing a souped-up stereo and speaker system during his free time. O'Neill gave Chase jobs that kept him away from the cracking units and refinery towers, where flammable chemicals flowed at high pressure. Chase analyzed spreadsheets of data from the refinery operations and helped O'Neill and his colleagues analyze the units' performance. It was the Goldilocks job—just educational enough without exposing Chase to too much danger.

O'Neill very rarely saw Chase get agitated, let alone lose his temper. One of the few instances this happened remained vivid in O'Neill's mind decades later. As they were working in the office one day, an employee from the payroll department came in looking for "Charles Koch," probably referring to a directory that listed Chase's full name: Charles Chase Koch.

Chase knew that the payroll employee was referring to him. "I could tell that he was, like, visibly offended that he called him Charles," O'Neill observed. Chase's response was swift and terse. "My name's not Charles. It's *Chase*."

Fred Koch went to MIT. Charles Koch followed in his footsteps and attended MIT for both his undergraduate and multiple graduate degrees. David Koch went to MIT. Bill Koch went to MIT.

Chase Koch went to Texas A&M. Chase majored in marketing. He didn't play tennis, and he lived, for the first time, outside the small circuit of the Koch family compound, the Wichita Country Club, and the Wichita Collegiate School campus. When he moved to College Station, Texas, Chase lived in a place where the Koch name didn't mean anything. For the first time in his life, he could be Chase, rather than Chase Koch.

After graduation, Chase Koch decided not to move home. He wanted to cut his own path and work for a company where his family name wasn't written on the front door. He moved to Austin, Texas, and got hired at a small consulting firm, doing marketing work. During his off hours, Chase started playing music and joined a band that played gigs around Austin. They played covers of Led Zeppelin, Pink Floyd, and Widespread Panic songs, alongside some original material. It was "jam-band stuff," as he called it, played for an audience heavily lubricated with beer.

This was a happy life for a while, but a sense of uneasiness began to creep in. He was living like an ordinary, workaday white-collar guy. But in his world, this life could be considered a failure. The mythology of his father hung over him. His dad earned multiple degrees from MIT and became CEO of Koch Industries in his early thirties. Compared to this, it looked like Chase Koch was stagnating, even failing.

In 2003, Chase Koch traveled to New York to watch the US Open with his family. When the game was rained out, Chase joined his father and their family friend Leslie Rudd for lunch. When they sat down, Rudd started asking Chase how he was enjoying Austin. How was the marketing gig? How was life? Was Chase happy? Charles Koch sat silently and watched. Chase tried to act disinterested and dodge the questions. Things were fine. The job was good. Austin was great.

Rudd did not relent. He pressed Chase—why didn't Chase come back to Wichita and work for the family business? Why was he wasting time down in Texas playing in a band? Then Rudd put on the hard sell. Chase should give a hard look at coming back to the family company.

"What I said to him was: 'Chase, it's a fabulous company. Your dad's a great CEO,'" Rudd said. "'It's fine if you want to turn it down, but you've got to earn the right to turn it down. You've got to go—find out what it's about, work there, and then decide. You can't just say no hypothetically.'"

Chase looked over at his father, who seemed to be acting studiously disinterested in Rudd's line of questioning. Rudd insisted later that Charles Koch didn't put him up to the job of convincing Chase to return. Rudd said he cared about Chase and gave him advice that he would have given to his own son.

The conversation changed Chase Koch's life. He quit his job in Austin, quit the band, and came back home to Wichita. Soon after he returned, Chase Koch attended a meeting with his father and Steve Feilmeier, Koch Industries' chief financial officer. Charles Koch and Feilmeier explained that Chase Koch would take a series of jobs that were something like a training course. He would receive the equivalent of an MBA degree during his first years at the company. But the MBA degree was specifically tailored to Koch's way of doing business. Chase Koch's real education about the family company had begun.

Chase Koch began a rotation of high-level jobs that exposed him to the strategic pillars of Koch Industries' modern business. It was telling what Chase Koch did not learn. He was not sent to the oil refineries, or to a pipeline farm, or to a natural gas processing plant. Charles Koch didn't necessarily want to teach his son about the energy industry. Instead, Charles Koch selected a series of jobs that reflected what Koch Industries had become over the last decade and how it planned to carry on into the future.

The rotation of jobs was set forth, roughly, as follows:

Class 1. Private equity acquisitions and mergers.
Class 2. Accounting and taxes.
Class 3. Market-Based Management training.
Class 4. Trading.

One of Chase's first assignments was to Koch's development group, the internal committee that looked for new companies to acquire. He joined a division called Koch Equity Development, which bought shares of publicly traded firms. Chase worked in this office when Koch's acquisition spree was at its peak, shortly after the Invista and Koch Fertilizer deals and during the $21 billion purchase of Georgia-Pacific.

Chase assembled spreadsheets and did other analysis to figure out the best ways to value a company. This was critical to Koch Industries' overall strategy of developing a sharper, more accurate view of the marketplace than its competitors. Koch was looking for gaps in the market, small dysfunctions that presented opportunities for Koch to seize.

Chase also worked in a group of tax and accounting analysts. This might sound arcane and boring. Nobody grows up dreaming that they'll become a tax analyst. But Chase would have discovered that these skills were just as critical to Koch's success as was the company's expertise in managing complex pipeline and refinery systems. There was virtually no terrain in the American economy that was more complex, more prone to manipulation, and more financially valuable than the American tax code.

Managing Koch Industries' massive tax liability—measured in the billions of dollars each year—created a deep tension between two of Charles Koch's primary philosophical principles.

The first principle was that government taxation was little more than state-sanctioned theft. Murray Rothbard, who cofounded the Cato Institute with Charles Koch and Ed Crane, called taxes "state robbery," to take one of many examples. Taxation forcibly took money from a successful group of people and spent it in ways that those people couldn't control.

It seemed morally justified to avoid paying taxes however possible. But the second principle Charles Koch believed in was that of 10,000 percent compliance. Charles Koch espoused obeying the letter of every law, every day. When the law required a company to pay taxes, it must pay taxes.

These two competing ideas led Koch to approach its tax bill in a way that became standard for large corporations in America, from Apple to General Electric. Koch used the US tax code's own complexity as a tool to avoid paying as much in taxes as possible. The company created numerous companies, limited liability corporations (called LLCs, for short), and subsidiaries around the globe. Many of them seemed to be little more than a name on a post office box. Charles Koch, for example, is listed as an employee or director of such companies as KCM Advisors/ GP, LLC; EKLP, LLC; and FHR Alaska Guarantor, LLC.

It took massive amounts of time and effort to scatter these legal entities in a network around the globe, but the payout for doing so was enormous. By 2016, the US federal government was losing about $128.5 billion a year in tax revenue from corporations due to the use of tax havens like the Cayman Islands or the small European nation of Luxembourg. Such tax havens were only available to bigger companies that could afford to employ teams of tax analysts, attorneys, and traders to carry out the plans.

Koch Industries, like many US companies, had an office on Grand Cayman, the biggest island in the small Caribbean nation. Koch's office was nondescript and easy to miss. It was located at 802 West Bay Road, a palm-tree-lined street that ran down the west side of the narrow island, just a few minutes south of the Ritz-Carlton Golf Club.

Grand Cayman is an island nation with no income tax and a permissive set of corporate laws that have only basic requirements for a company to register there. A company need only have a nameplate on a door, and perhaps an employee or two, to set up shop on Grand Cayman. The tax-free zone of the Cayman Islands drew some of the largest financial firms in the world to Grand Cayman, the largest of the islands. There was a private school system on Grand Cayman that compared in quality to those of the United States, along with high-end shopping, nightclubs, golf courses, and seemingly endless miles of beach on which to spend the weekends.

Koch Industries had a surprisingly diverse array of holdings in the

Caymans, considering that the nation had few natural resources and very little in the way of industrial infrastructure. A liberal activist group called American Bridge combed through business registries in the Caymans and found more than two hundred companies it suspected were tied to Koch, with names like Koch Minerals Cayman, Ltd., Koch NGL Cayman, Ltd., and Koch Nitrogen Shipping, Ltd.

The ways in which Koch could employ such companies to avoid tax payments was revealed in 2014, when a batch of tax documents was leaked to a watchdog group called the International Consortium of Investigative Journalists. The documents, prepared for Koch Industries by the tax consulting firm Ernst & Young, laid a roadmap for shifting money from Koch's operations to tax havens in Europe. The arrangement, called "Project Snow," created a complex web of obscure companies that shuttled hundreds of millions of dollars between them. Koch used its Invista division as a key component of Project Snow. It created an internal bank, called Arteva Europe Sárl, that coordinated cash flows between the various companies. The bank established a Swiss division that seemed designed to benefit from Switzerland's low tax rates. Money was passed back and forth, shares were converted into debt, and companies were dissolved along the way. Some of the strategies seemed like financial alchemy—in one case, a loan for $736 million was shifted between companies until it eventually landed with a US subsidiary that was "both the debtor and the creditor of the same debt," effectively cancelling the loan. The Center for Public Integrity reported that Arteva paid just $6.4 million in taxes on $269 million in profit between 2010 and 2013, and never had an annual tax rate higher than 4.15 percent. When the tax documents were leaked, Koch's public relations team said that the company followed applicable tax laws.

Chase Koch's education as a tax analyst at Koch would have taught him that paying a tax bill was no simple thing. It was an arena of complex strategy and potentially immense profits. In this way, tax analysis was similar to the next set of skills that Chase Koch would acquire. After working in acquisitions and taxes, he wanted to move to the part of Koch Industries that he knew was vitally important. "I said, 'Send me to Houston. I want to be in the pit with the traders,'" Chase recalled.

When Chase Koch was first given the chance to trade commodities, it was akin to the first time he gripped a tennis racket. He discovered an arena in which he could excel and in which he very much enjoyed spending time.

On the tennis court, Chase didn't have to talk or explain himself. He only had to face his opponent. On a trading desk, something similar happened. Here, the market rendered a clear-cut verdict on whether Chase had made a good or a bad decision. The market didn't care about Chase Koch's last name. It only cared about what he did. Chase didn't have to worry if anyone was pulling strings for him. The market numbers were clear and inarguable.

"That was the first time . . . my blood started to move in my body," Chase recalled with a laugh. "You know what I mean? I got really excited about something. Because I liked that feedback of trading—the market feedback—and just the energy on the trading floor."

Chase got a view of the trading operations that even most traders never got to see. He spent weeks shadowing Brad Hall, the CFO of Koch Supply & Trading, who gave Chase Koch a detailed overview of Koch's entire trading group. Hall taught Chase about the intricate accounting and tax systems that supported Koch's trading operations and gave Chase a view into forging large energy deals with Arab princes in the Persian Gulf, executives of Asian oil refineries, and CEOs of American companies like United Airlines.

It was clear to Hall and other leaders that Chase Koch was being groomed for a senior leadership position in the company. Chase worked like he wanted to earn it. "He was just full of questions and wanting to understand. He was the opposite of just going through the motions," Hall recalled.

Chase only sat on the trading desk in Houston for about a year before he was rotated back to Wichita to work on the Koch Equity Development team. Around this time, in 2006, Chase started feeling restless. His rotation through different jobs at Koch gave him a perspective on the company that very few people could attain. But he felt that his education was wide and shallow. He hadn't mastered anything.

The chance to settle down and master one part of Koch's business came when a job opened up in Koch Fertilizer. Steve Packebush was still president of Koch Fertilizer, and he offered Chase a job that put Chase in the middle rungs of the division's hierarchy. Chase became a regional salesman, traveling around the northern central United States and selling fertilizer to farmer co-ops.

Early in his tenure, Chase Koch tagged along with a more senior salesman on a call to a customer in Iowa. The customer was irate about an earlier deal and complained for a long time before he even noticed that Chase was in the room.

"Finally he looks at me, and he's like, 'And who are you?' I was like, 'Well, my name is Chase,'" Chase recalled.

"And he goes, 'You don't know shit about fertilizer!'" Chase said.

Chase replied "You're right, sir. But I'm hoping you can help me with that."

Chase grinded it out as a salesman and learned about the nitrogen fertilizer business in an up-close and granular way. Then he shifted to the part of the business that he loved the most: he joined the small group that traded fertilizer for Koch and was given a small portfolio to trade a nitrogen-based product called UAN fertilizer.* His trading record was successful enough that he was given a larger and larger portfolio. He estimated that he was eventually trading roughly half of the entire trading book.

This was a time when Chase's career accelerated, based solely on the money he was earning in the markets. No one could accuse him of getting ahead on his name alone, and coworkers said that Chase seemed happy.

Wes Osbourn, who traded oil in Koch's Wichita office, arrived at work early. But he never seemed to arrive early enough to beat Chase Koch in the door. No matter how early Osbourn arrived, Chase Koch's car was always already parked in the lot.

One evening, when a group of traders went out to dinner, they invited Chase Koch to come alone. Osbourn thought this was a mistake. He didn't want to hang out with the CEO's son.

"I was like, 'Ugh. I don't want to go to dinner with this guy because he's going to be so arrogant. I'm not going to be able to take it,'" Osbourn said.

---

* UAN stands for urea-ammonium nitrate.

As it happened, Chase Koch arrived at Osbourn's house early, and the two of them sat around talking before dinner. Osbourn was shocked. Chase Koch was actually a nice guy, and he seemed genuine. Over the course of the evening, the façade never cracked. It seemed like he wasn't faking it.

"If I hadn't have known any better, I wouldn't have known who he was," Osbourn said. "I remember at the end of dinner, we're sitting there having a cocktail, and I remember telling him how much I was not looking forward to that night. And I couldn't believe how down to earth he was. And [Chase] was like, 'Well, I appreciate that very much,'" Osbourn recalled.

The compliment was genuine, and Chase Koch must have appreciated it. But the compliment was also a sharp reminder. No matter how he acted or what he accomplished, he was still Chase Koch. The boss's son.

Chase Koch's sister, Elizabeth, followed in the footsteps of her uncle Freddie. She left Wichita, moved to New York, and appears to have had no significant operational role with the family company. Elizabeth became a writer, producing essays, short stories, a book review, and other works of fiction that she published under a pseudonym.

Elizabeth founded a publishing company in Brooklyn, called Catapult Press, that specialized in experimental fiction and other niche books. She retained a seat on the board of the Charles G. Koch Foundation and sometimes attended the foundation's meetings in Washington, DC. One Koch lobbyist recalled Elizabeth's visit to the public affairs office. She arrived hours early, and the lobbyist was given the job of entertaining her. They sat in his office and made small talk. She commented approvingly on the office's feng shui, and the lobbyist found her to be pleasant company.

It seems that Elizabeth's contact with Charles Koch was both limited and strained. In 2008, she wrote an essay for the literary magazine *Guernica* that was a first-person account of a woman having an unpleasant reunion with her father after not seeing him in years.

Elizabeth wrote:

> Last week my father came into town. I hadn't seen him in six years. I got drunk. He watched me eat dinner, his eyes wide,

mouth open. My boyfriend said the chicken bone cracked
between my teeth like a candy cane.
    The next morning, my father said good-bye. He kissed my
cheek. "You have a considerable hunger."
    "You don't say," my boyfriend replied.

As a child, Elizabeth had been an eager pupil of Market-Based Management. As an adult, she left the burden of working at Koch Industries to her brother.

After his successes on the fertilizer trading desk, Chase Koch got a promotion. Steve Packebush moved Chase into a new role in international development. Chase began traveling the world, helping Koch Fertilizer expand its reach. During this time, Koch Fertilizer built a network of terminals in Brazil, Mexico, Australia, the United Kingdom, and France.

Pleased with these results, Packebush promoted Chase Koch again, in 2012, to lead a division that made specialty products, called Koch Agronomic Services. This job put Chase into contact with venture capitalists, inventors, and the heads of start-up companies. They made high-end chemicals that were designed to counteract nitrogen fertilizer's extravagant inefficiency. Most nitrogen fertilizer leached straight into the air and local streams after farmers sprayed it on their soil. Nitrogen runoff from midwestern farms coursed into the Mississippi River and down into the Gulf of Mexico, where the high nitrogen levels stoked algae growth that sucked oxygen out of the water and created enormous "dead zones" that decimated aquatic ecosystems. Koch bought a company called Agrotain that made additives to slow the process and keep nitrogen in the soil.

Chase loved his work at Koch Agronomic Services as much as he loved trading. It was thrilling to meet with inventors and get pitched on their new products. Chase was more than just Charles Koch's son now. He had a track record of his own in the fertilizer business. He had done sales calls in Iowa. He had traded UAN supplies from Wichita. He'd helped build terminals around the world. He knew what he was talking about.

Packebush called Chase Koch into his office one day and offered Chase the biggest break of his career. Koch Fertilizer was going to spin off its energy business, which bought natural gas, and create a stand-alone fertilizer unit. Packebush wanted Chase to become president of the new Koch fertilizer division.

"Packebush said, 'You're ready to take the keys to the beast,'" Chase recalled.

Chase became CEO of his own company with three thousand employees and operations around the world that earned several billion in revenue each year. The business owned multibillion-dollar fertilizer plants that required around-the-clock supervision and vigilance to prevent lethal accidents. It was easily one of the most important divisions of Koch Industries, ranking in size only behind Georgia-Pacific and Flint Hills Resources.

Packebush was offering control over all of this to Chase Koch, if he wanted the job.

"What I was thinking at the time," Chase recalled, "was, *Oh, shit.*"

For the first time, Chase would be the public face of Koch Industries. The occasion was a groundbreaking ceremony in October of 2013 at the company's fertilizer plant in Enid, Oklahoma. The company erected a small tent outside the plant for the event, and Chase arrived in a suit and tie, a level of formality that was rare for senior Koch executives. This was one of the first big public speeches of his career.

Koch Fertilizer was investing $1.3 billion in the Enid plant to expand its footprint and ramp up production. There was a gold rush in the fertilizer business at this time, thanks to the crash in natural gas prices, which boosted profits. Koch was pressing its advantage, expanding its plant before competitors could enter the field and steal its market share. This was the kind of announcement that companies liked to publicize with ribbon cuttings and other ceremonies that drew local civic leaders. Under the small tent, the folding chairs were filled by Enid's civic leaders, plant employees, and local law enforcement officers.

It was an awful day to make a speech. Strong, gusting winds forced everyone to cling to their papers, and Chase's hair was blowing into a mess when he stepped onto the small wooden stage and walked to the podium. He delivered his remarks gamely, however, speaking over the wind, and then turned to watch the earth mover perform its ceremonial role. Chase also delivered remarks to a ballroom filled with more of Enid's business leaders. This time the sound was better. Chase read from a script, which had the oratorical verve of a press release:

"Going forward, we are very, very excited about the future of Koch Fertilizer," Chase said. "We see positive trends in global demand as the population grows from seven billion to nine billion over the next thirty to forty years, driving the need for more efficient products, more services, and more innovation as we keep up with this trend."

Chase Koch didn't come across as trying to impress anybody. He acted like the same guy whom so many people had encountered over the years: quiet, low-key, and humble. As he took over Koch Fertilizer, Chase revealed his leadership style, one that was developed over decades of hard work, often in solitary spaces like the tennis court or trading desks—he was quiet, focused on the matter at hand, and driven. If he came across as subdued, he also seemed like someone who was increasingly comfortable in his own skin. He could never escape the Koch name, but he was starting to wear it with a sense of ease.

Chase Koch's confidence might have come, in part, to changes in his personal life. On November 1, 2010, Chase married a Wichita girl named Annie Breitenbach, a registered nurse who had gone to college at the University of Kansas. Leslie Rudd noticed a change come over Chase after the wedding. Annie Koch clearly had a mind of her own. She made her own decisions. Her independence seemed to give Chase his own foundation as an adult. "I think that [Annie] was an ideal wife for Chase," Rudd said. "She's smart. She's got resolve, and she's got her own opinion; it's not influenced by Charles or Liz. I think Chase feels that. He feels he's got support beyond his family."

Chase and Annie Koch spent $3 million to buy a seventy-acre parcel of land in Wichita for their home. Much of the property remained undeveloped. Chase Koch now had his own family estate. He became a father when he and Annie had their son. A second son followed.

In the small circle of Wichita business leaders, a lot of people were talking about Chase Koch. His rise to the highest levels in Koch Industries seemed assured. Ever since Chase was a kid, the specter had hung over his head—"WELCOME CROWN PRINCE"—and now he was on his way to filling the job. The pathway to Koch's senior executive suite seemed to be short, straightforward, and predictable.

The only thing standing in Chase Koch's way was the fact that he was miserable.

Being Koch Fertilizer's president wasn't what most people might think it would be. The job was an exhausting, never-ending cycle of meetings. Chase Koch often arrived at Koch headquarters around five or five thirty in the morning, well before dawn, and was at his desk at an hour when many fathers had breakfast with their kids. Chase got there early to prepare for the meetings, which started around six thirty and proceeded—"wall to wall"—until six or seven at night. The meetings didn't leave time for Chase to develop much of a strategic vision for Koch Fertilizer. He was too busy on the treadmill of supervising a sprawling, complex, and dangerous industrial system.

Chase wasn't willing to let details slide. He knew that small oversights could cascade into a catastrophe. He didn't let decision-making slip into other people's hands. And this turned out to be a strategic mistake.

"I let it overwhelm me," he said. He began taking his misery and stress home with him. His family life suffered.

Chase paid a visit to David Robertson, a longtime Koch executive who became president of the company in 2005. Robertson was a taciturn executive who spoke forcefully with carefully chosen words. He was a strict adherent of Market-Based Management. He was also seen as a potential future CEO of Koch Industries. If he got the job, Robertson would be the first CEO without the last name Koch. This made him a competitor, in some people's eyes, to Chase Koch. No one knew which way the future might break.

If Chase Koch and David Robertson were both vying for the CEO position, they didn't act like adversaries. Chase turned to Robertson for help when he needed it the most, and Robertson offered him wise advice.

"I walked into Dave's office. I was like, 'I need help. I'm really struggling in this,'" Chase recalled.

Robertson asked Chase to walk him through a typical day. Chase talked about the meetings, the bottomless needs of the organization. The strain it was taking on him. Robertson told Chase that he had fallen prey to a classic mistake of leadership. He was carrying too much on his shoulders.

Robertson said, "*You* control your calendar. You're the only one that can say 'No' to things. . . . Take accountability for your own role and actually work on things where you can add value," Chase recalled.

Chase tried to learn how to delegate. He made sure he had the right people working for him and trusted them to do their jobs. But still, it didn't feel right. Chase realized he was much happier before he'd been promoted, when he ran Koch Agronomic Services. He loved the innovation of the job, meeting with investors and inventors. Chase recalled a piece of advice that David Robertson had given him. Robertson said the most important thing a leader can do is develop a vision. Now Chase had a clear vision. It just wasn't the vision that everyone else in Wichita seemed to have for him.

Chase Koch called a meeting with Steve Packebush and told him the news.

"Steve, I'm not the right guy for this role," Chase said. He wanted to quit.

Packebush tried to talk Chase out of it. "He said, 'Just give it some time. This takes time to really learn the stuff,'" Chase recalled.

Chase wouldn't bend. He wanted Packebush to spin Koch Agronomic Services into an independent company, and Chase wanted to run it. The job was less prestigious, and it would look like a step backward, if not a permanent step away from the path to becoming CEO. But this is exactly what Chase Koch insisted that he do.

"I was like, 'I need to be over here. This is where my passion is,'" Chase said.

In late 2015, Chase Koch demoted himself. He stepped away from the straight, upward path to succeed his father. His reasoning was simple: "Life's too short."

When asked, years later, about his most important strategic decision as head of Koch Fertilizer, Chase Koch thought for a while. Then he mentioned his decision to quit.

"That was a big strategic decision, I think, for the overall business and for me personally," he said. The education of Chase Koch taught him that it was more important to follow his own path, regardless of the expectations of others. It does not appear that he ever regretted it.

———

Chase Koch's decision disrupted what appeared to Koch employees as a clearly laid plan of succession. When Chase stepped aside, an unspoken competition began among senior Koch executives to become the first CEO after Charles Koch left the company. This wasn't the only source of uncertainty for Charles Koch in 2015. Even for someone who embraced volatility, the events of 2015 and 2016 were unsettling.

The American public, it seemed, wanted to go its own way, regardless of the consequences. There were murmurs of rebellion everywhere, which culminated in a crisis of American governance that threatened to upend the political project that Charles Koch had labored over for forty years.

There were rebellions and problems within the company as well. A stubborn, deadly set of problems emerged inside Georgia-Pacific, one of Koch's largest and most important divisions. Perhaps most frustratingly, these problems refused to be tamed by the tenets of Market-Based Management. People were dying, and the best efforts of management didn't seem to be working.

The anger among American workers was bubbling up, burning particularly hot in Georgia-Pacific's warehouse operations in Portland, Oregon. That's where Steve Hammond was about to make his final stand as an official with the IBU labor union.

CHAPTER 23

Make the IBU Great Again

(2015–2017)

Steve Hammond volunteered to become a union official because he wanted to make things better. He wanted to improve life at the Georgia-Pacific warehouse. He wanted to curb the power of the Labor Management System and win pay raises for the employees. He wanted to restore the Inlandboatmen's Union to its former greatness. Instead, he spent a remarkably large portion of his time tangled up in long, complicated disputes with Koch Industries.

The IBU had hundreds of members in Portland, who worked for several companies. But Hammond estimated that he spent 75 percent of his time handling complaints from the hundred or so employees at the Georgia-Pacific warehouse. The Labor Management System was grinding them down. They were forced to work overtime, and were disciplined or fired for small infractions and absences. The employees came into Hammond's office constantly with their complaints, demanding that he help them and file grievances. They begged him to win a better labor contract when negotiations reopened. Every day, when he went into the office, Hammond walked past the big stone plaque outside the union hall with the motto "An injury to one is an injury to all." The motto felt like an open challenge to Hammond. It was an open question whether the motto, and the solidarity that it expressed, was a museum piece, or whether it was an animating force that might be employed for the benefit of workers.

This question was at the heart of Hammond's last battle with Koch Industries in 2016. And this question was at the heart of a troubling trend inside Georgia-Pacific. Confidential data from inside the company showed that the number of worker injuries at Georgia-Pacific was rising steadily each year, as Koch pushed workers to maximize profits and increase production. The rate of both small injuries and serious injuries was on the rise. Burns, amputations, and deaths on the job were increasing year over year, even if the public wasn't aware of it. Hammond did not have access to this data and was unaware of what was happening. But he saw firsthand that the pressure on workers was intensifying. It was his job to put into practice the theory that an injury to one was an injury to all, and to show that workers might still have power to determine the conditions of their workplace.

In 2015, Hammond still worked in the little IBU office on the second floor of the Longshoremen's union hall, but he had a new boss. Gary Bucknum had stepped down as regional director and was replaced by a man named Brian Dodge, who went by the nickname Dodger.

Dodger was short and wiry, but he had the aura of an imposing union boss. He spoke in loud, staccato bursts, and his blue eyes gleamed with intensity. He had striking features, with a square jaw, spiky white hair, and commanding, deep-set eyes. He made it clear in passing conversation that he carried a knife on his person at all times. Shortly after he took the job, Dodge gave Hammond his own nickname, "the Hammer," which didn't fit Hammond's owlish presence but seemed fitting for a union man.

The Dodger and the Hammer sat side by side in the cramped office. Hammond often remained silent while Dodge took phone calls from IBU members up and down the Columbia River. "Hey, brotherman," Dodge said when answering the phone. Then he bellowed: "You just *fucked* me!" before breaking into near-maniacal laughter. He launched into the disputatious patter of a union boss: "Yeah. Ouch. Pay ten more an hour. Tankerman—not a lead tankerman—makes forty dollars and forty cents. Okay—so that's okay. Thirty-four dollars. That gives me something to push at them."

In 2015, the Dodger and the Hammer were going to take on the biggest challenge of their new partnership. It was time to renegotiate the labor contract with Georgia-Pacific. The brutal negotiations of 2010, which lasted eighteen months, had left the union scarred and nearly broken. When that contract was about to expire in 2013, the IBU didn't negotiate but chose to preemptively surrender. With the backing of the union members, the Hammer and the Dodger told Koch that they wanted to "roll over" the 2010 contract, meaning that they would accept all its terms and keep it in place for two years. This cemented the defeats of 2010—including the low annual pay raises—but it allowed the union members to keep their pension and spared them another draining battle.

In 2015, the union members made it clear that they didn't want to roll over again. They wanted the Dodger and the Hammer to fight for something better. It was around this time that Steve Hammond started drinking every day. Drinking had always been a part of life at the warehouse. Guys would share beers in the parking lot after a shift. Hammond used to drink Scotch on special occasions, sipping a glass of expensive Glenlivet now and then. After starting his full-time job at the IBU, he started drinking Scotch weekly, then nightly, then switched to the cheaper stuff, like Dewar's and Johnnie Walker Red.

"Pretty soon I was drinking a half to three-quarters of a bottle a day," Hammond said. "I'd just sit [at home] every night and get blasted. Then I'd fall into bed, wake up, feel like shit, and go in and go to work."

If Hammond's drinking had become toxic, so had life inside the IBU. A weird dynamic had developed between the union officials and the employees. It was sort of like the dynamic between a parent and an angry teenager, an intimate bond that was woven with threads of resentment and dependence. Back in the 1980s, union members considered the IBU officials to be like spokesmen—the union members decided what they wanted, and the union delivered the message. Now the union members seemed to consider the IBU officials to be like a second layer of management. They thought the IBU officials were somehow in charge, somehow capable of bargaining for a better deal with Koch, and somehow in the position to resolve disputes with Koch management at the warehouse. Hammond believed that this modern view was exactly backward. The real strength of a union came from its members, and their willingness to stick together and strike. It didn't come from the union office. And yet, all the union members kept turning to the union office, seeking solutions.

The Dodger got an early lesson in this dynamic after he became regional director and negotiated the contract rollover in 2013. The IBU members agreed to the rollover, but only grudgingly. Dodge felt the rollover was their only choice. After just a few contacts with Koch, Dodge quickly learned the limits of bravado as a negotiating tactic. Koch was unmovable. "Guys in California get thirty dollars an hour. These [IBU] guys get forty! How the fuck can I go in there and try to get them big raises? You tell me—please! I have no idea," Dodge said.

When Hammond had joined the union, the members met every week. Now they met once a month (excluding July and August). The meetings used to draw two hundred people. Now they drew about fourteen. Most members who attended were on the union executive board, meaning that one or two members showed up who weren't required to be there. When large numbers of union members did show up, it was to complain. And when they complained, they wanted Hammond and Dodge to solve their problem.

"You almost feel like you're Mom and Dad in there," Hammond said. Life in the warehouse seemed to get worse by the day, and the union should have made things better. Disengagement and cynicism were contagious.

The discontent throughout Georgia-Pacific went beyond economic concerns. As productivity and profits increased, serious injuries had increased in tandem. There was something broken with the system, and the problem was intractable. Senior leadership at Georgia-Pacific was aware of the problem, from CEO James Hannan down to the managers on the factory floor. But nothing they did seemed to slow the injury rate between 2010 and 2018. In 2014, the number of worker deaths spiked to a level that hadn't been seen since the early 2000s. Concerns were mounting at the highest levels. "What we do is kill people at Georgia-Pacific," said one longtime employee at Georgia-Pacific.

When Koch Industries purchased Georgia-Pacific in 2005, it inherited a new monitoring system at the company, called TRAX, that recorded a wide variety of metrics about the company's operations. This information was collected in a centralized database for analysis, allowing Koch to improve safety and increase productivity throughout the company. Analyzing data in the TRAX played a vital role in helping Koch boost profits and helping Georgia-Pacific pay down the billions of dollars loaded on its balance sheet after the acquisition. A key metric recorded by the TRAX system was workplace injuries and accidents.

Between 2005 and roughly 2009, the TRAX data set was spotty. The company was still engineering the system, figuring out what to record and training employees to enter data into it. By 2010, TRAX was fully operational. That year, the system recorded a total of 579 "OSHA recordable injuries" across Georgia-Pacific, meaning injuries that were significant enough that they must be reported to the US Department of Labor's Occupational Safety and Health Administration. That year, one worker was killed at Georgia-Pacific.

Managers at Koch Industries had reason to be satisfied with these results. They marked a significant improvement over Georgia-Pacific's performance before Koch purchased the company. Throughout the 1960s and 1980s, worker safety standards were abysmal. "It was like 'Welcome to [Georgia-Pacific]. Watch your ass,'" one employee recalled.

Even by the early 1990s, Georgia-Pacific was reporting six worker deaths a year across the country. Things improved that decade but worsened during the early 2000s. This was the period when Wesley Jones, the Georgia-Pacific executive in Georgia, said the company dramatically cut back investment in its factories because it was loaded with debt. In 2000, seven workers were killed at the company. Six were killed each year in both 2001 and 2002. Things improved once again, and in 2004 no employees were killed.

Koch Industries was delivered something of a reprieve beginning in 2008, when the housing market crashed. Orders for building materials slowed dramatically, and during the recession that followed, orders for paper and tissue plummeted as well. During this down cycle, Koch Industries did what it does best: it invested against the economic cycle, pouring billions of dollars into Georgia-Pacific. A lot of this investment went toward improving safety measures.

This was no simple matter. Workplace safety is an engineering problem from hell. It involves an almost limitless number of factors that interact with one another in impossibly complex ways. A plant manager must consider the dangers of each giant machine, and the multiple ways that each machine might take someone's life. Then they must consider how each machine interacts with one another in a complex production cycle that, in many cases, runs twenty-four hours a day.

Finally, there is the human element. People are maddeningly unpredictable. They improvise on the job, they break rules, they put themselves in unexpected places and create unforeseen hazards. Koch fought against these factors in two ways: by updating the equipment and updat-

ing the thinking and behavior of its workforce. At a large gypsum factory outside Savannah, Georgia, for example, Koch installed new fencing
around dangerous machines and changed long-standing practices
that put employees in harm's way. Bright yellow barriers were erected
throughout the factory to keep workers away from spinning parts and
other barriers.

Koch's largest transformational efforts to improve safety were cultural. Across the company, employees learned about Market-Based Management and how it could be used to prevent accidents. They learned
about the Ten Guiding Principles and the five dimensions of MBM, and
were told that this belief system would help them simultaneously ramp
up production while remaining safer. Maybe more importantly, workers were bombarded with the message of 10,000 percent compliance and
repeatedly encouraged to shut down machines if they considered conditions to be unsafe.

During the lull in production after the housing crash, worker injuries
declined. An internal Koch report showed that there were 730 reportable injuries at Georgia-Pacific in 2005, before the acquisition. Koch had
cut that number by 20 percent. Still, one worker was killed every year at
Georgia-Pacific, except for 2007, when four workers were killed on the
job.

By 2010, Koch Industries managers believed that they had put systems and practices in place that would lock in these safety gains. Between
2010 and 2011, the number of recordable injuries fell from 579 to 545.

In 2011, the housing market and the economy began to recover. The
number of new homes being built rose about 21 percent over the year,
until there were 697,000 new home starts in December. This upward
march in home construction would continue for years, and it increased
demand for plywood, gypsum board, insulation, and other building
materials. Orders started pouring in to Georgia-Pacific.

Koch's newly renovated operations at Georgia-Pacific were put to the
test. The system was an unmitigated success in one respect: the factories and mills were more efficient and more productive. Profit margins
increased, revenue increased, and Koch Industries began aggressively
paying down Georgia-Pacific's debt. Before Koch bought the company,
Georgia-Pacific's debt was rated as being junk bonds, meaning there
was a high risk it would not be repaid. But the debt ratings increased

steadily as Georgia-Pacific's factory hummed with new precision. In 2016, Georgia-Pacific's debt was rated A+ by Standard & Poor's, meaning that it was high-investment grade. Profits roughly doubled. The year before Koch bought Georgia-Pacific, the company earned $623 million in net profit. By 2016, Koch had increased that to an average of more than $1 billion.

This improvement made Georgia-Pacific's CEO, Jim Hannan, a rising star within the company. Hannan had been on the scouting team that first inspected Georgia-Pacific in the early 2000s. After taking the helm of the company, he behaved as the quintessential Koch man. He was relentless, focused, projected humility, and delivered positive results. He spoke fluent MBM, and attributed the company's success to its operating philosophy rather than to his personal attributes.

But one stubborn problem emerged in the shadow of the rising profits. Between 2011 and 2012, workplace injuries jumped from 545 to 584. This would have been displeasing to Charles Koch, who prided himself on running clean operations that were both safe and profitable. But the small gain could have been easily dismissed as a fluke. The number of injuries fell slightly from 2012 to 2013.

Then, after 2012, housing starts rose more sharply, and working conditions became more unsafe year after year at Georgia-Pacific. Deaths began to rise, and the number of injuries rose in almost perfect tandem with the numbers of orders that came through the door between 2012 and 2014.

Injuries jumped sharply between 2013 and 2014, from 527 to 644. Nine employees that year lost limbs or body parts. One hundred and fifty-four employees suffered heat burns, up from 134 the year before and 126 the year before that. The number of electrical shocks jumped to nineteen in 2014 from one the year before. In 2013, two workers were killed on the job.

In many ways, the increasing harm to workers made no sense. Koch was continuing to reinvest in the factories. Managers were told to hammer home the message of 10,000 percent compliance and "safety first." The rhetoric was unambiguous. But more people were hurt all the time.

Most alarmingly, it wasn't just the number of injuries that rose. The *rate* of injuries also increased. This destroyed the argument that perhaps more people were getting hurt just because more people were working more hours, increasing the odds of an accident. The accident rate, as measured by OSHA, climbed steadily each year from 2013 to 2017, rising 44 percent during that period. It was increasingly dangerous for employees to show up for work.

Between March 17 and 18, 2014, Hannan joined a group of senior executives for a team meeting in Atlanta to discuss the safety concerns.

"The last six months is unacceptable," Hannan said, according to notes of the meeting that were taken by someone who observed it. Hannan referred to accidents and deaths at Georgia-Pacific as "learning events," the idea being that each accident taught the company better ways to be safe. But the company was failing to learn. Hannan emphasized that the corporate culture would play a critical role in solving the problem. "We need to have a culture of values and not tolerate individual or organizational risk. We must learn from one another. Work on the items with the most risk."

"Build on an MBM®-based* culture," the notes read. Hannan suggested that the future of the company was on the line. "If we can't keep safe, why invest?" Hannan asked. Market-Based Management should be solving this problem. But it was not.

During this period, Koch Industries changed the way people worked on factory floors across Georgia-Pacific. The company managed to cut the number of unionized workers in half, from 22,000 in 2005 to roughly 11,800 in 2016. This gave Koch flexibility and allowed it to avoid the type of onerous work rules that Charles Koch opposed since he took over the Pine Bend refinery in 1972. These changes were evident at Georgia-Pacific's sprawling mill outside Savannah, one of the largest tissue and paper towel mills in the United States.

The mill was highly mechanized, and its cavernous interior was clean and pleasant to walk through. The space resembled an industrial Santa's workshop; a complicated maze of automatic machines that rolled, spun, and packed countless rolls of toilet paper. Automated forklifts drove

---

* Appending an *R*, for registered trademark, to *MBM* seems to be the preferred style for Koch Industries executives. Charles Koch used the abbreviation in his own writing, and it also appeared in internal memos.

between the machines, guided by lasers beams aimed at the floor in front of them. Employees monitored the machines and fixed them when there was a problem. One of those employees was Dana Blocker, a muscular and intense man who had worked at Georgia-Pacific since the 1990s.

Until Koch bought the company, employees like Blocker had worked with specific job descriptions and were assigned to oversee specific machines. A person was a winder operator, for example, or a wrap operator, or a case pack operator. After Koch took over, those distinctions were dissolved. Blocker's job title became "reliability technician," meaning that he oversaw a wide variety of machines and processes.

"Now you're a technician, expected to go out and run all the equipment on the line. So, no one is tied to one piece of equipment. You have to run the entire process," Blocker said. "When people ask me now, what's my job, what do I do? I run the entire line. I don't have one specific job. Whatever needs to be done, that's what you're going to do."

Blocker's coworker, Mark Caldwell, said this created a new flexibility in the workforce. "You probably couldn't tell who the manufacturing engineer is, or the mechanic, or the technician. You wouldn't be able to distinguish who does what role, because we all flow to the work. We all do what needs to be done."

Both men praised the new system. Blocker said that it helped foster teamwork and galvanized him to think like an entrepreneur rather than a simple factory hand. "That seemed to help everybody out. There's no blaming or finger-pointing at anyone for running something a certain way. You're all trying to help each other out to get the best product," he said. Both men also emphasized that their managers encouraged them to shut machines down in the event of hazards. Safety came first.

While unions seemed stubborn in clinging to work rules and job designations, the tradition of doing so traced its roots back to unsafe working conditions in the early 1900s. Being confined to a certain job helped workers reinforce their expertise not just on a specific process but also on a specific machine. The equipment inside Georgia-Pacific was of a scale that demanded such intimate expertise. Some machines were the size of a small house and ran giant, spinning roles of paper that weighed two thousand pounds. Knowing the quirks and dangers of such machines was vital. But Georgia-Pacific employees were increasingly put into situations where they were learning on the job.

Koch Industries tried to mitigate these safety risks by imposing a complex set of rules and regulations on the daily life of workers. The regulations and standards were codified in a series of papers accessible through the company's internal computer network. Employees were told to learn the rules, but this was not easy. One "work standard" paper dictated how employees should conduct themselves when taking on "nonroutine" work outside their typical operating procedure, and the document was more than twenty pages long. Another work standard, dictating how employees should shut down machines to repair them, was about twenty-five pages long. One employee estimated that the total number of work standards reports were a thousand pages combined. Workers were expected to follow these standards, and could be cited for violations if they did not.

In 2014, this was the system in place when a wave of deaths swept across Georgia-Pacific.

On August 11, 2014, a forty-one-year-old man named Robert Wesson was working at Georgia-Pacific's paper mill in Crossett, Arkansas. He lived in the nearby town of Hamburg with his wife, Lisa. Wesson had a thin and angular face, short-cropped black hair, and a finely trimmed beard that traced his sharp jawline. He was working with a large paper winder that day: a machine that spun industrial-sized rolls of paper weighing thousands of pounds.

As the big rolls went down the conveyor line, Wesson applied tape to the "tails" so that the rolls would remain tightly coiled when they were shipped.* For reasons that remained unclear, Wesson left the area where he was supposed to stand and walked farther down the line to apply more tape to the rolls, perhaps because the first application wasn't working. His movements could be described as "nonroutine" by Georgia-Pacific's standards. If Wesson was trying to compensate for a problem with the taping process, then Koch's voluminous work standards might have recommended that he follow a procedure that employees called LOTO or "Lock-out, Tag-out." The LOTO would have

---

* The "tail" of a paper roll is the last section of paper that flaps loose, like the outside tab of paper on a toilet paper roll.

required Wesson to lock the machine down by stopping it, and then record the reasons for doing so before verifying again that the machine was in fact turned off. Georgia-Pacific's LOTO work standard paper was roughly twenty-five pages long. Wesson did not follow the LOTO procedure, and he approached the rolls instead to apply the tape. Production ran smoothly.

As Wesson approached a paper roll, he failed to take into account the movements of a large piece of machinery called a "kicker," a giant metal arm that shoved the heavy rolls down the assembly line. As Wesson stood near the roll, the kicker engaged and smashed his skull, killing him. His coworkers later discovered his body.

Wesson's death was the fifth fatality at Georgia-Pacific in 2014.

A few months earlier, in March, when Hannan attended the safety meeting in Atlanta, no workers had yet died that year. Hannan had reported this piece of good news to the team, but it turned out to be an anomaly. Accidents and the injury rate were sharply higher by the end of the year.

Roughly a month after Hannan's presentation, a contractor named Sam Southerland was working at Georgia-Pacific's plant in Pennington, Alabama. He was not intimately familiar with the facility. Southerland, who went by the name Sambo, was twenty-nine years old and married to his childhood sweetheart, Michele. He had a son named Carson, and a newborn daughter named Caylin. Southerland was something of a country boy, with a broad smile, who loved to hunt and play baseball with his son. On April 15, Southerland was inside the Georgia-Pacific factory, holding the bottom of a twenty-eight-foot extension ladder. He stepped backward, perhaps trying to find a better place for the ladder, when he fell into a hole in the floor. He plunged thirty feet into a cauldron of noxious chemicals that is called a "digester," an apparatus that processes raw materials for the paper-making process. Southerland sustained multiple bone fractures from the fall, along with chemical and thermal burns on his body from the digester, and was killed.

Less than two weeks later, at Georgia-Pacific's plant in Corrigan, Texas, a fire broke out in a tall silo that captured wood dust. Employees rushed to the location to put the fire out, many of them apparently floor workers who were not trained firefighters. Some bags inside the silo were blocking a group of vents designed to release flames and pressure inside the silo in case of emergency. Pressure built up, and then the silo vents released, engulfing the employees in flames. Different news accounts said between seven and nine employees were burned and transported to local hospitals. Some of them languished in burn wards for weeks. On May 30, a fifty-six-year-old Georgia-Pacific employee named Charles Kovar died from his wounds. About one week later, fifty-eight-year-old Kenny Morris died in the hospital. Both men left behind wives and children. Kovar's obituary suggested that he had lived a full life that was enriched by his Christian faith: "He had just experienced his best Easter ever where he cleaned out the bowl of Aunt Diane's famous banana pudding," the obituary said.

On July 24, a sixty-three-year-old Georgia-Pacific employee named Lydia Faircloth was leaving her shift at the company's mill in Cedar Springs, Georgia. Just two years earlier, Faircloth had been featured in an internal Georgia-Pacific safety bulletin. She had coined a phrase to promote safety awareness: "LET OTHERS SEE SAFETY IN YOU," according to the bulletin. It was close to midnight when Faircloth was leaving. She cut through an area where industrial loader trucks were transporting big loads of product. She crossed the floor in a crosswalk marked for pedestrians, but was hit by a truck driven by her coworker and died from severe internal injuries.

It was less than a month after this that Wesson was killed at the mill in Crossett. Roughly ninety days after that, a contractor named Bobby Creech at the Crossett mill was performing lawn maintenance at the mill while riding an off-road four-wheel vehicle. When Creech traveled over a hill, the vehicle rolled over and killed him. This contractor's name was spelled variously in internal Koch documents as Bobby Creech and Bobby Creach, but there is scant documentary evidence of his death.

By Christmas 2014, six workers had been killed in Georgia-Pacific. And the injury rate and total number of injuries continued to climb. The accident rate jumped 18 percent from the year before. The total number of reportable injuries jumped by 22 percent.

Between 2015 and 2017, accidents and injuries continued to climb each year, along with the rate of injuries. The increasing danger at work seemed tightly linked to increasing production: the upward trend of injuries still mirrored the upward trend in new home construction and economic growth.

The chart below documents recordable injuries, drawn from Koch's own internal tracking system, TRAX. The total number of accidents increased by 30 percent between 2010 and 2017:

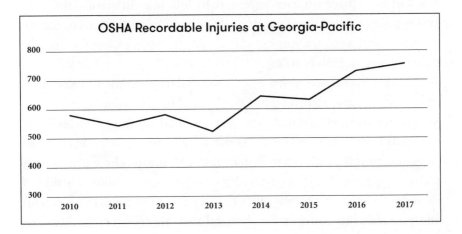

The injury rates rose even more sharply during this period. Koch's TRAX system recorded two injury rates: the "OSHA Rate," which tracked injuries, and the "DART Rate," which basically tracks lost work time due to injuries. The OSHA rate increased by 45 percent, and the DART rate increased by 57 percent:

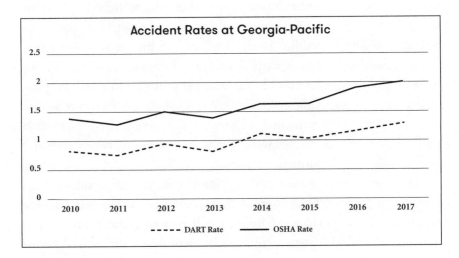

Koch Industries needed to change the way it did business at Georgia-Pacific. But it wasn't clear how it would do so. In the past, Koch changed dangerous procedures after strict government enforcement, coupled with publicity of the company's wrongdoing. In the 1990s, the raft of criminal charges and civil fines for environmental violations prompted Charles Koch to develop the 10,000 percent compliance doctrine. The crisis of workplace injuries appeared to follow a different path. Federal regulators ruled that Koch Industries had violated dozens of federal worker-safety regulations at its Georgia-Pacific facilities, but the fines for doing so were relatively paltry.

Georgia-Pacific was fined $5,000 for violations related to the death of Robert Wesson, according to OSHA records. The company was fined $14,000 for violations related to the burn-related deaths of Charles Kovar and Kenny Morris. It was fined $35,050 for a series of violations dubbed "serious" by OSHA related to Lydia Faircloth's death. These deaths were scattered around the country and garnered little mention outside of local media accounts, which often characterized the deaths as accidents and provided little information beyond that. By contrast, the EPA and the Department of Justice fined Koch $30 million for a series of pipeline leaks and other violations in 2000, grabbing national media attention because it was the largest such fine in history.

In the absence of headlines and fines, Koch Industries responded to the Georgia-Pacific safety crisis by reemphasizing the need of employees to follow the guidelines of Market-Based Management. An internal Koch Industries presentation prepared in 2017 referred to the crisis in terms that military commanders might use to describe a large-scale insurgency. The "Headline Discussion" of the presentation said that Koch needed to "Engage Hearts & Minds" of employees to reverse the increasingly dangerous conditions. "Are we putting too much emphasis on 'we are improving' versus we are not satisfied with where we are and our rate of improvement?" the presentation asked. The presentation noticed that serious injuries were "flat to increasing" between 2016 and 2017, in spite of the company's efforts.

The presentation noted that Georgia-Pacific was more unsafe than Koch's competitors. One internal chart showed that Georgia-Pacific's safety metrics ranked in the bottom half of paper and pulp companies in the United Statets. Significantly, Georgia-Pacific ranked below its three major US competitors: Weyerhaeuser, International Paper, and Pratt Industries. The only companies that ranked below Georgia-Pacific were relatively obscure and sometimes small firms, such as Deltic Timber Corporation, Flambeau River Papers, and Turners Falls Paper.

This chart was a challenge to Koch's senior leadership. None of the companies that ranked ahead of Koch subscribed to Market-Based Management, yet they all did better than Koch. The numbers challenged the company's orthodoxy.

Koch's response was to renew its commitment to Charles Koch's philosophy and to reduce risk by "applying 5 MBM® dimensions throughout the organization." The leadership team set out an ambitious goal. It sought to achieve "zero significant incidents" at Georgia-Pacific in the future. One chart showed a "Georgia-Pacific Safety Risk Glide Path" that would gradually reduce accidents to a level near zero by the year 2035. A different chart noted that every 10 percent decrease in serious incidents would yield between $5 million and $25 million for the company.

Another chart, entitled "Georgia-Pacific 20 Year Bet," was written in the classic style of Market-Based Management materials. It featured colored boxes connected by dark lines in a wheel-and-spoke formation. The box in the center said, "Critical Risk Focus Areas," and the connected boxes listed various Georgia-Pacific operations and risk hazards like "Combustible Dust" and "Electrical Safe Work Practices." (Electrical shocks had skyrocketed at Georgia Pacific, rising from one in 2010, to twenty-three in 2015, and to thirty-one in 2017.) The chart said that risk could be reduced by changing "hearts and minds" in the workforce. It said the company workers must change their mind-set and "Go from Have To—To Want To" in terms of staying safe. In spite of this approach, workplace accident rates continued to accelerate that year.

In past decades, worker safety was a top priority for labor union negotiators. Industrial accidents were a driving force behind unionization in the early years of the New Deal. By 2016, however, unions were so marginalized and overpowered that they were playing a defensive game, simply trying to hold on to what benefits they had left.

This was the reality faced by the Dodger and the Hammer as they prepared to negotiate a new contract with Koch in 2016. Hammond knew that this would likely be the last contract he negotiated on behalf of the IBU, his last chance after nearly a decade to make things better.

Before negotiations even began, Georgia-Pacific sent powerful and ominous signals to the IBU. In 2015, Koch Industries told the IBU that it was pulling Georgia-Pacific's representatives off the board of trustees that oversaw both the IBU's pension and the health care trust. It was common for companies to help oversee the funds, and Koch's withdrawal seemed like the first step toward ending all support for the pension and health care plans.

The Dodger was alarmed. "All the sudden, I'm thinking, *Are they going to pull out of the health trust completely and shove this up our ass?*" he said.

The IBU team reached out to Jackie Steele, a labor relations expert at Georgia-Pacific who was their new negotiating partner. Steele sent a message: Georgia-Pacific might be able to let the workers keep their pension and health care, or it might be able to give them a raise. But it seemed impossible that the company could do both.

Dodge and Hammond conveyed this message to the rank-and-file union members. The union members weren't having it. They wanted to keep their benefits, and they needed to get a raise on top of it. The raises hadn't been keeping up with the cost of living for years. "The guys want more, more, more, more," Dodge said in exasperation. "They don't know what you've got to go through!"

The IBU members were not inclined to listen to Hammond and Dodge. In fact, they were not inclined to the listen to the union at all. This became painfully clear in early 2016, a presidential election year. The IBU and the Longshoremen unions endorsed the Democratic candidate Bernie Sanders. When Sanders lost his primary battle, unions across the country asked their members to switch their support to what they considered the next best thing: the Democratic nominee, Hillary Clinton. Many IBU warehouse workers, for the first time that anybody could remember, said they planned to vote against the wishes of union leadership. They wanted to vote for a Republican. And their grievances were about to be further enflamed.

———

Once again, the Dodger and the Hammer arrived at the Red Lion hotel to negotiate with Koch's team. The IBU members took their assumed seats in the familiar conference room with the view of the river, just next door to the lavishly catered room where Koch's team of negotiators sat staring at their laptops. It was like watching the same movie for the third time. At least this time around, the process was mercifully short.

On the second day, they discussed the money. Dodge said that the IBU workers wanted to keep their IBU health care and their IBU pension. They also wanted annual raises to compensate them for roughly six years of stagnant pay.

"I said, 'Is there any chance on that, and what do you think?'" Dodge recalled. "Steele says: 'Yeah, we may be able to work something out.'"

Steele left the room. He returned with bad news. The company wasn't going for it. If the IBU wanted to keep its pension and health care, then Georgia-Pacific would not offer them annual raises. The company would offer an annual bonus payment instead.

Bonuses were anathema to workers because a bonus didn't compound in value every year the same way that a wage hike did. Raises had been a ladder for middle-class prosperity for decades. But since the economic crash of 2008, US employers started to abandon annual wage increases. Even as recently as 1991, bonuses and temporary awards accounted for only 3.1 percent of all compensation paid by US companies. Annual wage hikes, by contrast, accounted for 5 percent of all compensation that year. This ratio had flipped by 2017, when bonuses accounted for 12.7 percent of compensation spending, and raises accounted for just 2.9 percent.

The Dodger said he wasn't having it. If he didn't walk out of the Red Lion with a contract that promised annual raises, then his union members would vote down the contract.

"Work with me, Jackie!" Dodge recalled saying.

By the end of that day, the Dodger and the Hammer had relented. They agreed to the 2 percent raises for two of the years and $1,000 annual bonuses for the other two years of the contract. "The worst contracts I've ever negotiated—all of my G-P contracts," Dodge said bitterly. "There's no leverage. There's no fucking leverage."

In all, the contract negotiation took less than a week of bargaining. Dodge told Jackie Steele that if Georgia-Pacific wanted the contract passed, then they should help him hold the vote as soon as possible. The company agreed to release its employees from work hours early so they could drive down to the union hall for the vote. "The only way I'm gonna pass this piece of shit is to have them all here," Dodge said.

The IBU members filed into the big Longshoremen's union hall, just downstairs from Hammond and Dodge's office. Ballot boxes had also been prepared for the day's vote. The workers gathered around a stage at the far end of the big room, a slightly elevated platform with an American flag and a podium that was emblazoned with the Longshoremen's crest.

Steve Hammond looked out over the crowd of workers, who were already grumbling. As he looked around the room, he saw symbols that reflected the power of organized labor. There was the big mural showing the labor strife and the solidarity of the old days. On another wall hung the banner of the Jack London poem "The Scab." And next to that was a big glass display case full of old handheld cargo hooks. The place looked like a museum of union power. The totems, the banners, the mural. All of it had a tainted, aging quality. Like paper that was yellowing.

Word had spread through the crowd that they would not get annual raises. It was inconceivable, to many members, how something like this could have happened. Why were they paying union dues, if the contracts just seemed to get worse? Why were they constantly told that their warehouse performed far better than most warehouses in the Georgia-Pacific system, yet none of the improvements translated into a significant pay raise?

Why hadn't Hammond bargained harder? Why hadn't Dodge bargained harder? Why couldn't they ever seem to win?

"Guys were pissed off. Guys in the warehouse were screaming bloody murder. And: 'No way!'" Dodge said. "They got loud and vocal."

Steve Hammond took the stage. And, for the first time that anybody could ever recall, he completely lost his shit.

Hammond upbraided the gathered union members. He scolded them. He insulted them. He told them, in so many words, that they had expected him and Dodge to do exactly the one thing that labor negotiators could not do: win a deal with their silver tongues.

Union power came down to bargaining leverage, and the IBU had no leverage. The warehouse employees couldn't afford to strike, and every-body knew it, including Koch Industries.

David Franzen listened to the speech, slightly awed to see Hammond lose his temper. "He's saying, 'This is it guys. This is your best offer. You're not going to strike anyway,'" Franzen recalled. "'If you didn't do it last time, what makes you think you're going to do it this time? None of you guys did anything about it. We told you to get ready in four years, and you didn't get ready.'"

Then Hammond made the comment that everyone remembered for years: "You guys are nothing but a bunch of Trump lovers. Go ahead—vote for him," Franzen recalled Hammond saying.

Hammond was finished, and he got off the stage. Dodge didn't quite know what to think. Hammond had actually turned into the Hammer, but against his own union members. "He basically told them off and told them: 'Vote no on the fucking thing. Dodger and I will sit back down and talk some fucking more with them.'"

The union members cast their vote in an election that felt like a fore-gone conclusion. The contract passed with over 65 percent of the vote. And that's how Steve Hammond retired from the IBU.

Hammond sobered up after he retired in March of 2016. He spent months just sitting in his home, trying to process what had happened.

Hammond didn't have much to complain about, personally. He retired with his full pension—$3,000 a month—plus Social Security. His two daughters were grown and happy, and he visited with them fre-quently. He was remarried and happy. What made him sad was thinking of the IBU members he'd left behind. He had joined a raucous, militant union, and he had left a splintered, moribund union. And what he saw at the IBU seemed to be happening across the country.

"I think that we kind of fucked ourselves, to tell you the truth," Ham-mond said in his living room, near a big window that let in soft light and offered a view of imposing cedar trees and rolling green grass. "I think that our forefathers—just using that [warehouse] as an example—worked their asses off to get these great contracts and stuff. And then got these great jobs for their kids, and nephews, and little brothers, and stuff like that. And we had all this: Work forty hours a week. Work five days a week. If you worked Saturday and Sunday it was time and a half for Saturday and double time for Sunday. And all that great stuff, you know?

"And we came in, us kids of theirs, and just pissed it away. We just took it all for granted that this was ours."

During the final months of 2016, the members of the IBU turned their attention to another election, for president of the United States. The real estate magnate, reality television star, and Republican candidate Donald Trump campaigned tirelessly throughout the fall. He settled on a consistent theme: the election was rigged. It was controlled by dishonest forces that were allied against working families. And Hillary Clinton, "Crooked Hillary," was the face of a thieving elite.

This story line resonated with many IBU members, like David Franzen. For all his adult life, Franzen had been hitting the "Democrat" button when he voted, but his life did not seem to be improving in material ways. His union told him to vote for Hillary, and for the first time, he wasn't going to listen.

Trump's candidacy was also disrupting Charles Koch's plans. In April of 2015, Charles Koch had given a rare interview to *USA Today* to outline his political strategy for 2016. Koch planned to be more engaged than usual in Republican politics. His donor network would, for the first time, give money to influence the field of Republican primary candidates. The network planned to spend $900 million, an amount that rivaled the Republican National Committee's spending. Roughly one-third would be donated directly to candidates, with the rest going toward "educational" efforts and other activities. Koch told *USA Today* that his network had selected five contenders who might win the money: Wisconsin's governor, Scott Walker; Florida's former governor Jeb Bush; and three US senators: the libertarian-leaning Rand Paul and conservatives Ted Cruz and Marco Rubio.

Koch had carefully set up the game table. Then Trump came along and flipped it over. Over several months, Trump forced every candidate backed by Charles Koch out of the race. To everyone's surprise, Donald Trump became the frontrunner. Rather than back a losing candidate, or risk failure if he confronted Trump directly, Koch retreated to the margins of political attention. On November 8, 2016, Donald Trump won the presidential election. His victory rested on Hillary Clinton's collapse in a group of heavily unionized states that Democrats referred to as the "Blue Wall": Michigan, Wisconsin, and Pennsylvania.

In many ways, Donald Trump posed a greater political threat to Charles Koch's political agenda than Barack Obama. Trump was not seeking to fight American conservatism as much as he sought to transform it from the inside. Charles Koch tried to bend the Republican party toward a libertarian view; now Donald Trump was bending it toward a nationalist, populist philosophy that Charles Koch found abhorrent. Trump's policies aimed to benefit specific populations of Americans, rather than to solely limit government interventions in the marketplace.

Shortly after Trump's election, congressional Republicans scurried to reorient themselves around Trumpism. Many Congress members knew that Trump won their home districts with more votes than they had. They were not about to oppose him. If Donald Trump was president for eight years, it would almost certainly abolish Charles Koch's political project. The Republican Party would be the party of Trump, not Hayek or von Mises. Koch Industries' retreat from the 2016 election cycle had been well publicized, and members of the Trump administration were quick to point out that the Koch network's political influence was diminishing, almost certainly for good.

Charles Koch took a different point of view. He was conditioned to thrive in volatile environments. He thought about the long term, and tended to avoid the wall of noise and media controversy that emanated from the White House each day. Charles Koch worked on a longer political horizon and that gave him an advantage. He had spent more than forty years building a densely connected network of political operatives and institutions in the nation's capital. Donald Trump had not.

When Trump arrived in Washington, Charles Koch was ready.

CHAPTER 24

Burning

(2017–2018)

Springtime came early to the nation's capital in 2017. In early February, the air was unseasonably warm and the trees were starting to get their buds. Brightly colored flowers bloomed in Lafayette Square park, just north of the White House, with early tulips pushing up from their beds and cherry trees frosting themselves with pink and white blossoms. In the suburbs, the forsythia exploded in vibrant yellow flowers and the redbud trees were covered in purple. The riotous colors of spring, usually celebrated in the capital city, were out of place and disquieting, like flashing signals on a dashboard. Across the country, springtime arrived weeks early, with the zone of blooming advancing farther north than usual. The election year of 2016 was the hottest year on Earth since reliable record keeping began around 1880. NASA compared Earth's average surface temperatures against a period in the mid-1990s, and found the average temperature rose steadily each year. Sixteen of the seventeen warmest years on record occurred after 2001, peaking in 2016. Eight of twelve months in 2016 broke records as the hottest months ever recorded. Scientists at NASA did not dispute what caused the warming. It was "a change driven largely by increased carbon dioxide and other human-made emissions into the atmosphere," the agency said. In the winter of 2017, carbon concentrations in the atmosphere reached 407 parts per million, far past the limit where most scientists considered radical climate change unavoidable.

The political seasons in Washington, DC, were being disrupted as well. On January 20 Donald J. Trump stood on the grand dais in the shadow of the Capitol dome, put his hand on the Bible, and took the president's oath. No candidate in US history had risen to the White House like the real estate mogul had done. He was backed by no party, supported by no discernable outside interests, and had no previous experience in government or military service. The usually stable networks of political influence were torn apart in 2017. No one knew who was in or out of Trump's political circle. No one knew what he really wanted—what was hyperbole and what was an actual campaign platform. The lobbyists at Koch Companies Public Sector and other companies had adapted to political shocks before, but this time was different. The Trump administration saw itself as a revolutionary force, independent of both political parties. One person close to the administration, and who also had been close to the Koch's political operations, said that the Trump administration viewed Washington, DC, as a chessboard on which three opponents were doing battle. One opponent (and the weakest) was the Democratic establishment: "Team D." Another was the Republican establishment: "Team R." Finally, there was the Trump administration, "Team T," which planned to beat everyone else.

When Trump delivered his inaugural address, he made it clear that he was upending the political order. His voice was booming and severe.

"Today we are not merely transferring power from one administration to another, or from one party to another—but we are transferring power from Washington, DC, and giving it back to you, the American people," Trump said. His vision was near-apocalyptic, and he talked about "American carnage" that only his administration could stop. He managed to offend and alienate virtually every politician and former president sitting in the gallery behind him.

"For too long, a small group in our nation's capital has reaped the rewards of government while the people have borne the cost," he said. "Washington flourished—but the people did not share in its wealth. Politicians prospered—but the jobs left, and the factories closed. The establishment protected itself, but not the citizens of our country."

Charles Koch was considered part of this establishment. And everything Trump stood for was a threat to Charles Koch's entire political project. Donald Trump's presidency had the potential to destroy everything Charles Koch had built. Charles Koch's political blueprints called for the federal government to retreat from virtually any intervention in the marketplace. But if Donald Trump had an underlying political philosophy, it was that the tools of government should be used aggressively to steer economic activity toward the benefit of the people who voted for him. Trump promised to tear up trade deals and impose tariffs to protect the white, working-class, and affluent voters who put him in office. Trump spoke in favor of punitive taxation on companies that thwarted this vision, and spoke favorably of entitlement programs that were funded by taxes on the rich. Alarmingly, Trump also lashed out in personal ways, at business leaders who antagonized him, using Twitter as his weapon of choice. Trump singled out as targets Jeff Bezos, CEO of Amazon, and the Carrier air-conditioning company, claiming that their economic decisions harmed America. It was clear that this same vindictive power could be used against Charles Koch. Based on Trump's campaign rhetoric, it seemed entirely plausible that Trump would be willing to squeeze Koch Industries with all the available levers of government power, from the IRS to the EPA to the simple use of the White House Twitter account.

Charles Koch responded to this threat with a strategy that bore his hallmarks: patience, persistence, and a reliance on his competitive advantages. To counter Trumpism, the Koch political machine employed a strategy that could be called "block-and-tackle." Charles Koch would "block" Trump when Trump deviated from Koch's wishes—when he imposed tariffs, raised taxes, or supported entitlement programs, for example. But Koch Industries would help Trump "tackle" the things that Charles Koch wanted to see demolished, helping the Trump administration when they did such things as dismantle regulatory agencies, cut taxes, or nominate economically conservative judges to the federal bench and the Supreme Court.

For this strategy to work, however, Charles Koch needed to prove that his political machine was still relevant and still powerful within Donald Trump's Washington. As luck would have it, Koch got the opportunity to do this very early in Trump's tenure, just two months into the life of the Trump administration.

In March of 2017, Donald Trump had no choice but to venture into territory where Koch Industries had the upper hand. It was time for Trump to turn his campaign promises into reality and to show that he really was the deal maker who could solve Washington's dysfunction. This appeared entirely feasible—Republicans controlled the House, the Senate, and the White House. There was nothing standing in the way of Trump's agenda. But to pass the agenda, Trump had no choice but to work through Congress. He had to engage in the complicated, maddening process of writing and passing laws. This is the terrain where Koch Industries was waiting for him.

The first fight was to repeal Obamacare. Republicans had been trying to do this for more than six years and now they had their chance. This seemed like the ideal project for Charles Koch to support. Obamacare, just as Charles Koch had feared, had become a massive government program that redistributed wealth from the very rich to the working class and the poor. The government estimated that Obamacare raised the tax bill of the top 1 percent of American earners by about $21,000, steering about $16 billion from the richest Americans to the poorest, largely in the form of health insurance subsidies.

Throughout his campaign, Trump promised to both repeal the hypercomplex law and replace it with something else. And this is where the problem lay. In Charles Koch's eyes, Donald Trump did not seem sufficiently dedicated to the job of tearing this system out, root and branch, and replacing it with nothing. Trump seemed open to compromise.

Trump made statements along these lines that were particularly worrisome to libertarians, showing that his allegiance to free markets was questionable. After taking office, Trump made promises that were too large to fill without significant government intervention, promises more grandiose than even Barack Obama would have dared to make.

"We're going to have insurance for everybody," Trump told the *Washington Post* during an interview in January. "There was a philosophy in some circles that if you can't pay for it, you don't get it. That's not going to happen with us."

While potentially offensive to Charles Koch, Trump's statements were firmly grounded in political reality. Millions of people depended on Obamacare. The Congressional Budget Committee estimated that even a limited repeal of the law would take health insurance away from fourteen million people the first year, and twenty-four million more people the following decade. Trump and other Republicans sought to avoid such a political calamity. They planned to seek a middle ground that would retain some benefits and subsidies for the working class and the poor.

There was another reason for Trump to compromise. It would help the Obamacare repeal effort move quickly. Trump wanted to achieve a legislative storm of greatness during his first hundred days in office that would rival FDR's. He would repeal Obamacare, then pass tax reform, then pass an infrastructure bill, then pass an immigration law that included construction of a wall along the border with Mexico. With these accomplishments behind him, Trump would emerge as the most effective president of modern times.

Charles Koch helped ensure that this agenda was derailed. The Koch political network would attack the effort to repeal Obamacare, and in doing so it would win a second victory by proving its power and ensuring a place at the bargaining table for Charles Koch.

On March 6, the House of Representatives unveiled a plan to repeal and replace Obamacare with a bill called the American Health Care Act. The next day, Americans for Prosperity mobilized against the plan, just as it had mobilized against Obama. Large tour buses, chartered and paid for by Americans for Prosperity, arrived in Washington, DC, on March 7, unloading hundreds of passengers at an intersection near Union Station, within view of the Capitol dome. The crowd looked like tourists at Disney World. Most of them were older, congenial, and clearly enjoying the free trip to the nation's capital. They were directed down the sidewalk by helpful employees in AFP windbreakers, who led them into the quiet, marble-tiled lobby of an upscale office building. The volunteers were ushered into elevators and sent to the building's rooftop, where they walked into a lavish event space, covered by a party tent, with a beautiful view of the city. As they entered, the volunteers were given glossy placards with a sleek logo for the day's event, reading "You Promised." The message of the day was that these voters had been let down by Congress members who were balking on their years-long promise to repeal the health care law.

The attendees sat in rows of chairs, in front of a stage that was bordered by large-screen televisions. The crowd was shown video testimonials, made by AFP, from everyday people who were purported victims of the ravages of Obamacare. The victim-impact statements were somewhat incoherent, from a policy standpoint. Most of their complaints were that health care was too expensive, or only available intermittently, problems that other industrialized nations had solved by nationalizing the health care industry. But the overall tenor was consistent—Obamacare was a terrible burden, and Congress wasn't doing enough to repeal it.

After the presentation, the crowd was led out onto a terrace in the delightful spring weather and given free boxed lunches. They milled around and talked, and were later led to Capitol Hill where they met with congressional staffers and representatives to share their demands. The popular revolt against the American Health Care Act had begun.

Inside the US House of Representatives, resistance to Trump's plan was led by the House Freedom Caucus, the group of lawmakers most aligned with Charles Koch's worldview. Koch Industries was the second-largest contributor to Freedom Caucus members, according to *Politico*, ranking only behind the Club for Growth (which was partially funded by Koch's political network). The caucus declared that the American Health Care Act was an unacceptable compromise of conservative principles.

Mark Meadows, the North Carolina congressman who chaired the Freedom Caucus, led an effort. On the day the bill was introduced, Meadows published an editorial on the Fox News website, declaring his principled opposition to it. "We call on congressional leaders to keep their word to the American people, to push a real repeal of Obamacare, and to do it now," Meadows wrote. The sin of the AHCA, as it was called, was the inclusion of tax breaks that would help millions of people pay for health insurance—"families will be given up to $14,000 of other people's money," Meadows complained. He pointed out that the bill also forced insurance companies to fine their customers if they dropped their health insurance, a sneaky way to perpetuate Obamacare's mandate to purchase insurance. The bill also included subsidies to insurance companies approaching $100 billion, Meadows said. It was one thing for the Freedom Caucus to obstruct the Obama agenda. Now the caucus was obstructing its own party, its own president, and the bigger Republican agenda.

Weeks dragged on, and Donald Trump began to look just as ineffective as Barack Obama had been. He couldn't move the Freedom Caucus. The obstructionists in Congress knew that time was on their side; the longer the bill was delayed, the weaker Trump's hand became. A left-wing resistance movement emerged, modeled on the Tea Party, that confronted Congress members at town hall meetings in school gymnasiums and auditoriums. New studies emerged showing the deep damage the bill might do by kicking millions off their insurance. With each day, the bill became harder to pass.

The halting effort to pass it was carried forward by Paul Ryan, the Wisconsin Congressman who was the Speaker of the House. Ryan conducted his duties with the enthusiasm of a funeral director, impeccably dressed, unmovably calm, but with a deeply morose look in his eyes. He gave reasoned speeches and laid out the necessity of passing the AHCA quickly out of the House. He couldn't move the Freedom Caucus.

The crisis came to a head during the week of March 20. Ryan wanted to put the bill to a vote in the House. It wasn't clear that the bill had enough votes to pass, but it seemed imperative to move it to the Senate before time dragged on much longer. Donald Trump made bold gestures to support the bill. He traveled to Capitol Hill and cajoled lawmakers. He said that they needed a win at all costs and needed to prove they could govern. Trump singled out Meadows in person and threatened to bring down the weight of the White House upon him if he wouldn't bend. "I'm going to come after you," Trump warned Meadows with a smile, according to media reports of the closed-door meeting.

Nevertheless, Meadows persisted. That week, Trump gave the group an ultimatum—either they passed the health care bill, or he would abandon the effort altogether and lay the blame at their feet.

This is when Charles and David Koch stepped in, to fortify the caucus. They did so in a way that was unprecedented. For forty years, Charles Koch prized his discretion in politics, funding candidates and lobbying groups through obscure cutout organizations with names like 60 Plus Association, Corner Table LLC, and PRDIST LLC. But on March 22, Charles and David Koch went public with their desire to change a legislative outcome. Americans for Prosperity and Freedom Partners (a clearinghouse organization for many of Koch's donations) announced that they would support any member of Congress who voted against the health care bill. If the Freedom Caucus stood up against Trump, the Koch network would be there to protect them afterward. The two organizations announced they were compiling a "seven-figure reserve fund" that obstructionist Congress members could draw on if they voted no. "Republicans have been promising to fully repeal Obamacare since it became law. This bill doesn't do that," James Davis, the executive vice president of Freedom Partners, told *Politico* when the fund was announced.

This tactic carried risks. When the US Supreme Court handed down its decision in Citizens United, the court emphasized that it was still illegal to engage in quid pro quo corruption, meaning the explicit trade of money for a vote. If the announcement from Freedom Partners and Americans for Prosperity was not a promise of money for a specific vote, then it is unclear what it was. Regardless of the risks, the Koch's support stiffened the spines of the Freedom Caucus members. In a private meeting with Donald Trump at the White House, the members said they still were not ready to support the bill. On Friday, March 24, Paul Ryan admitted defeat. He pulled the bill and cemented Donald Trump's failure.

The bill showed passing signs of life over the summer as it was revived and changed in a minor way that ultimately won the support of Meadows and his caucus.* When the bill passed the House, Donald Trump hosted a televised celebration of the victory, alongside a smiling Paul Ryan and other House leaders. But the bill would meet a similar destiny as the cap-and-trade bill in 2010. It was sent to the Senate, where it languished. Eventually the bill was forced to a vote, even though support was weak and the leadership could only hope to pass it by the narrowest of margins. The bill was defeated by the Arizona Senator John McCain, who voted no.

Donald Trump had been hobbled in the Congress. And once he was hobbled, the Koch network pressed its advantage. The fight over health care had been a proxy war, a way for the Koch network to prove its strength. The real fight was still looming.

After he abandoned the Obamacare repeal, Donald Trump moved on to reforming the nation's tax code. Trump had specific ideas about the ways to do this, and many of them ran counter to Charles Koch's inter-

---

* The change that appeared to win over Meadows and the Freedom Caucus was curiously minute. An amendment introduced by Republican congressman Tom MacArthur allowed states to request a waiver from certain obligations imposed by Obamacare, essentially punting hard decisions about cutting health care coverage to state governors. A Brookings Institution analyst speculated that the MacArthur Amendment made the bill palatable in part because it allowed the House to pass the bill on to the Senate, making it the upper chamber's problem.

ests. The Koch network was ready for the fight. Once again, Americans for Prosperity chartered buses and paid for volunteers to travel to Washington, this time to protest against Donald Trump's tax plan.

The Republican party had a once-in-a-generation chance to rewrite the American tax code. It controlled all three branches of government, giving it the freedom to write a tax bill that was true to Republican orthodoxy and untainted by the Democratic impulse to raise taxes and support the social safety net programs.

Orchestrating the task fell to Paul Ryan. He made the mistake of helping write a bill that reflected Republican orthodoxy, but ran counter to the interests of Charles Koch.

Paul Ryan's mistake was caused by seemingly good intentions. He partnered with the Texas Republican Kevin Brady, head of the powerful House Ways and Means Committee. They wrote a bill that would dramatically cut income taxes for US corporations and middle-class families, while also remaining "revenue neutral," meaning that it would not increase the national debt. This might have seemed eminently practical because lowering the debt had been the campaign platform of Republicans for at least seven years. But the approach was fundamentally flawed in Charles Koch's eyes.

This flaw arose because Paul Ryan was trying to do three things at once: avoid adding to the US deficit, cut corporate tax rates, and meet the desires of Republican voters who elected Donald Trump. Ryan thought he could meet all of these needs by using an obscure tax provision called the Border Adjustment Tax (technically it was a border adjustment to the federal income tax, but it became widely known as the Border Adjustment Tax, or BAT), which became a vital pillar of Ryan's tax plan. The BAT is what drew the Koch network's opposition.

It is easy to see why Paul Ryan would have been seduced by the logic of the BAT. A similar adjustment was already in place in more than 140 countries and wasn't exotic or particularly controversial.* There was

---

* This similar tax was called a Value Added Tax on sales inside a country. While not exactly the same as the border adjustment proposed by Paul Ryan, the widely used VATs frequently included border adjustments, allowing economists to study their impact.

strong evidence that the BAT would accomplish one of Donald Trump's most important campaign platforms—boosting economic growth inside US borders and discouraging companies from shifting their factories overseas. Creating a BAT would also help raise money to offset the massive cuts in corporate income tax that Ryan proposed, taking the rate from 35 percent down to 20 percent. If the corporate tax rate was cut with no other changes, it would dramatically increase the deficit. The BAT provided an elegant solution. It would allow the government to raise money—roughly $1 trillion over a decade—that could shore up the budget.

The BAT would do this by making a seemingly subtle shift to the US corporate income tax system that had tremendously large effects. Under the current tax code in 2017, US companies were taxed based on the profits they earned from things that they *produced* in the United States. Under the BAT, companies would be taxed on profits from the things they *sold* in the United States. This difference, although it seemed obscure, would upend the economic logic that enticed companies to send their factories to Mexico and China. In essence, the BAT was a big tax break for exporters.* Under the BAT, exporters who made things in the United States and sold them overseas would not be taxed on income from the sale. Conversely, if a company produced goods in China and sold them in the United States, the company would pay a 20 percent tax on the profit.

The end result of this tax shift was decidedly Trumpian. Most experts predicted that the BAT would encourage companies to locate their factories in the United States and make things to sell overseas. The change wouldn't be dramatic, but it would move the country closer to Donald Trump's vision of "America First." The existing US tax code of 2017 did the opposite—it encouraged companies to move their production to low-cost countries like China (because the United States didn't tax profits from overseas production) and sell them in the United States. For this reason, Ryan began to call the existing tax code the "Made in America Tax." He bolstered his case for the BAT with poll numbers—the

---

* The BAT wasn't expected to be *all* good for exporters. Most experts expected that a BAT would eventually strengthen the dollar, making US products more expensive overseas. But the tax structure would still most likely benefit exporters over firms that shipped production overseas.

new surge of Trump voters supported the idea of a BAT overwhelmingly. They wanted to do anything they could to bring factories back to Wisconsin and Michigan.

Charles Koch opposed the BAT for two reasons. The first was ideological—the BAT would impose a new tax, and Koch's network opposed all new taxes. The second reason was more central to Koch Industries' business. The BAT posed a grave threat to the company's profits. In December of 2016, before Donald Trump was inaugurated, Koch's lobbying office funded a study by a consulting firm called the Brattle Group. Unlike other groups that published Koch-funded studies, the Brattle Group clearly acknowledged Koch's support in the beginning of the report. Kevin Neels, a coauthor of the study, said that Koch initially insisted that its support remain secret. But hiding Koch's financing would have violated the Brattle Group's policies, so Koch eventually agreed to let Brattle disclose it.

The study showed why Koch might have deep concerns with the BAT. The tax could carry a high cost for energy companies that imported crude oil or other fuels from overseas. The Brattle Group report claimed that the BAT, by imposing a 20 percent tax on imported oil sold inside the United States, would raise gasoline prices by about 13 percent, or roughly 30 cents per gallon. This could be a nightmare for oil refineries that imported crude and sold it domestically. The damage could potentially be twofold and severe. First, it might cut into the refineries' profit margins. Second, and most dangerous, the tax might dampen demand for gasoline by raising prices. If that happened, it would stoke demand for alternative energy sources, compounding the long-term problem of peak demand for gas.

Koch Industries would later insist that it opposed the BAT only for purely ideological reasons. The company argued that it would have actually benefited if the border adjustment was imposed because the tax would raise consumer prices for gasoline and other products Koch sold. But the effect of a BAT on Koch's business would be complicated. There was strong evidence that the tax could pose a threat to Koch Industries' oil refinery in Pine Bend, which was still considered to be the company's "crown jewel." After decades, Pine Bend still benefited from occupying a stunningly profitable bottleneck in the US energy system. Cheap oil from Canada's tar sands piled up at the US border without many buyers except Koch, and Koch could still sell its refined gasoline into midwestern markets where prices were relatively high thanks to a lack of refining capacity. Pine Bend was largely depending on imports, and the BAT would make those imports more expensive.

In the month of February of 2017 alone, Koch Industries bought 9.55 million barrels of Canadian crude oil at Pine Bend. The average price at that time was $39.41 a barrel. If the BAT was imposed, the government would be entitled to $75.3 million in new taxes on products Koch made from that oil, for just one month of production. More importantly, the new tax might wipe out some of the price advantage that Koch had long realized by purchasing Canadian crude. Once the BAT was imposed at 20 percent, the cost of Canadian crude would be $47.29. That was still an advantage over the cost of a barrel under the WTI* contract in Texas (which was $53.47), but far less of an advantage than before. And this change would be permanent. The crown jewel might be tarnished, and long-term sales would be hurt by the higher cost of gasoline.

Koch's public relations team claimed that the Pine Bend refinery could actually benefit from the BAT, because the tax would raise gasoline prices. It was difficult to disprove this hypothetical argument, but three former Koch commodities traders said that it was almost inconceivable that a BAT would benefit Pine Bend. One oil trader, intimately familiar with the economics of Pine Bend, said there was "no scenario" under which the refinery would benefit from a border tax. Another pointed out that any 20 percent increase in the cost of inputs could hurt a refining operation, even if gasoline prices rose. Regardless of the hypothetical scenarios from which the Pine Bend refinery might benefit, there was no doubt that a BAT could be disruptive to Koch's refinery business.

The Koch political network moved against this threat hard and early. The network launched its attack on the BAT in December and January, before Trump's inauguration and before the public, or even most Congress members, started thinking about the measure. The goal seemed clear: to kill the BAT in the crib, before a public debate could even begin.

The attack was well fashioned by Koch's political team. After the Brattle Group report was released in December, Koch Industries did not talk in detail about the harm that the BAT posed to its oil business. Instead,

---

* West Texas Intermediate

the company's political proxy groups framed the issue with different arguments. Americans for Prosperity started talking about the US tax code in terms of "crony capitalism" and a "rigged economy." The group presented BAT as an odious corporate giveaway. Corporations were getting a tax cut, the group said, because the corporate tax rate would fall from 35 percent to 20 percent. But consumers would pick up the bill because prices for imported goods—like toys, gasoline, and electronics—would rise. This was a mischaracterization of what the BAT would do. More than a hundred countries had imposed the BAT (or a similar tax) and data showed that the tax caused consumer prices to rise, but only temporarily. The reasons for this were complicated, but they derived from the fact that a BAT strengthened the value of the home country's currency. The incentive for domestic manufacturing would add to this effect, creating jobs and raising wages. The real entities that were harmed by a BAT were companies that sought to shift jobs overseas, and also the richest Americans who owned stocks in such companies. A Tax Foundation report estimated that the financial burden of the BAT would fall primarily on the richest 1 percent of Americans.

In the winter months of January and February, while most public attention was focused on the fight over Obamacare, Americans for Prosperity fully mobilized to defeat the BAT. In May, the group launched a high-profile campaign called "Un-Rig the Economy," which made defeating the BAT a centerpiece of its efforts. AFP released a statement saying that "72 percent of Americans feel that our 'economy is rigged to advantage the rich and powerful.' And the biggest contributor to our country's rigged economy is the US tax code."

In fighting the BAT, Koch Industries seemed out of step with Republican voters. Koch had successfully grafted the fight against a cap-and-trade bill to the Tea Party movement, but it was more difficult to graft opposition to the BAT to a conservative movement that had just voted for an America First president. The Freedom Caucus, which was Koch's strongest ally in Congress, was slow to pick up Koch's cause. When the caucus met privately in January to discuss the BAT, the group was split. Some members supported the notion of cutting tax rates and shifting jobs back onshore.

After the closed-door meeting, Mark Meadows sounded open to the idea of supporting the BAT, even if he had some reservations. "The border adjustment thing is at twenty percent, so that would make sense," Meadows told *CQ Roll Call.*

The weekend after Meadows made his comments, Americans for Prosperity sent a letter to Kevin Brady, chair of the Ways and Means Committee, making AFP's opposition to the BAT clear, claiming that the BAT would hurt low-income Americans by making imports more expensive. That weekend, AFP's president, Tim Phillips, gave a stirring speech at a donor conference in California, saying that the group would pour its resources into defeating the BAT because it was unprincipled. Within weeks, Meadows changed his view of the BAT. He began to say that he wouldn't support it. But his opposition was still tepid. "Let's go ahead and pass [a tax bill] without border adjustment, assuming that we can lower corporate [taxes] to twenty percent, flatten the rate out for individuals," Meadows told the media outlet Axios.

Paul Ryan was unbending. He stubbornly insisted that the BAT was a necessary part of tax reform, even though his support meant that he was now fighting one of the Republican Party's largest donor groups. "I obviously think border adjustment is the smart way to go," Ryan said during a news conference in May. "I think it makes the tax code the most internationally competitive of any other version we're looking at. And I think it removes all tax incentives for a firm to move . . . their production overseas."

Americans for Prosperity brought its volunteers and employees to Washington, DC, to lobby against the BAT. They met with lawmakers from Ohio, North Carolina, Florida, and Virginia. The group ran ads attacking the BAT. "It's safe to say it's been a seven-figure effort in total, so far," Tim Phillips told *Congressional Quarterly.*

If Ryan was fighting for the BAT, it was in part because of the issue of deficits. He had campaigned, for years, on the promise of reducing deficits. Now the Koch network was pushing Ryan to advocate a tax plan that would make the debt balloon. This was not hypocritical on the part of Koch's network. It revealed, in fact, the network's long-term goals and values. It revealed Charles Koch's real thinking about government financing and the role that tax cuts should play.

This thinking was reflected in the political strategy articulated in 1977 by Murray Rothbard, Charles Koch's partner in funding the libertarian Cato Institute.

In a confidential memo entitled "Toward a Strategy for Libertarian Social Change," Rothbard said that the goal of cutting taxes was not to just stimulate economic growth. The goal was to fight oppression in the form of state-sanctioned robbery. Libertarians, Rothbard wrote, should not be concerned about creating budget deficits by cutting taxes. The deficits weakened "the enemy," as Rothbard referred to the state, and strengthened the libertarian's power to demand that the state reduce its spending and shrink its role in society. Deficits and debt were useful, in other words, because they weakened the state.

Both Republicans and Democrats squabbled about the level of taxation, Rothbard wrote. He continued:

> The libertarian, in contrast, should always and everywhere support a tax cut as a reduction in State robbery. Then, when the budget is discussed, the libertarian should also support a reduction in government expenditures to eliminate a deficit. The point is that the State must be opposed and whittled down in every respect and at every point: e.g., in cutting taxes, or in cutting government expenditures. To advocate for raising taxes or to oppose cutting them in order to balance the budget is to oppose and undercut the libertarian goal.

If Paul Ryan felt that Koch's political network turned a deaf ear to his pleas for fiscal responsibility in the form of a Border Adjustment Tax, he was correct. The effect of the Koch network's efforts was not to balance the budget but to attack the state itself.

As Americans for Prosperity was pressing its case publicly, the group was holding private meetings with the Trump administration to help shape the tax bill. One of the most important points of contact between the Koch network and the White House was a forty-seven-year-old official named Marc Short. He had a long history with Koch and a close working relationship with AFP president Tim Phillips. Short joined the Koch network in 2011, where he helped fund Freedom Partners, a nonprofit institution that acted like a clearinghouse for Koch's donor network. Freedom Partners collected donations and disbursed them to Koch-

funded groups. Few people knew the inner workings of the Koch political network better than Short.

Short was the White House director of legislative affairs, the key liaison between Trump and Capitol Hill. He saw firsthand how Americans
for Prosperity hindered the Obamacare repeal. He said the administration had learned its lesson by the time the tax bill came around—Short
would bring aboard third-party groups like AFP early. He met several
times with Tim Phillips in the Executive Office Building, next door to
the White House.

Short had worked closely with Phillips over the years. They had a
warm rapport. During their meetings, Phillips said that AFP had a
handful of key goals with the tax plan. One was to remove the BAT. The
other was to remove the slew of personal deductions that had been written into the tax code over decades, allowing people to get tax breaks
for their children, home offices, and other expenses. These deductions
were the closest thing that middle-class families had to a shell company
in the Cayman Islands. They were a key way to reduce the tax burden,
and many families depended on them to claim tax returns. The tax code
needed to be simplified, Phillips said.

Short took Phillips's concern back to the White House. Trump was
willing to abandon the BAT, even though it was in line with his "America
First" doctrine, Short recalled. Trump felt the BAT was too complicated
to explain. He didn't feel like he could rally political support for the measure. He was also willing to sign a bill that removed deductions.

Tim Phillips was invited with a handful of other conservative movement leaders to a meeting with Trump in the White House. The tone was
friendly. When Trump saw Phillips, he quipped, "You're the Koch guy,
right?" Short recalled. Phillips said that AFP was happy with the tax bill.
Trump could count on the AFP foot soldiers to get out and support it. It
was understood that the BAT was gone.

On July 27, Paul Ryan and Kevin Brady released a statement saying that
the BAT proposal was dead and would not be included in the Republican tax reform bill. Koch had won the fight over the BAT before the public fight began.

Now, with the BAT off the table, the Koch network deployed the second half of its block-and-tackle strategy. After it had blocked the Trumpian Border Adjustment Tax, the political network would help Congress, and President Trump, tackle any opposition to passing a tax cut bill that conformed more closely to Charles Koch's vision.

On July 31, AFP released a statement crowing about its achievement: "AFP's Defeat of the Border Adjustment Tax Clears the Way for Principled Tax Reform." Other interest groups had fought the bill, led by retailers such as Walmart and Best Buy that relied on imports for their sales. But none of the groups, and none of the companies, had a political network that could rival Charles Koch's. None had armies of volunteers, or a network of wealthy donors who could fund attack ads.

On August 8, Americans for Prosperity rented out a large event space in the Newseum, on Pennsylvania Avenue in downtown Washington, DC. The group brought its charter buses from small towns throughout Virginia. Volunteers arrived from North Carolina and Ohio. They filed into a conference room and were handed glossy placards demanding that lawmakers "unrig the economy" by passing tax cuts.

Mark Meadows was the keynote speaker. If he was tepid in his opposition to the BAT before, he was fervent about it now.

"There are some who have said: 'Well, you know, those special interest groups, they want that border adjustment tax,'" Meadows said. "Well, I can tell you that Americans for Prosperity were leading the charge, many times, to say: 'What this is going to be is a new tax on the American people.' When we talk about revenue neutral, what that means is that we're going to cut your taxes in one place and we're going to add them someplace else. There is no benefit from that."

Meadows encouraged the crowd to get out and fight for the new tax cut plan that was working its way through Congress. He warned them that speed was now of the essence—the bill had to be passed before opposition could build. Meadows, who had led the charge to obstruct Trump's agenda, said the time for obstruction was over.

"We've got a president in the White House who is not going to take any excuse. He's saying that we've got to get this done. We've got to deliver. And quite frankly, it's members in the Senate and the House that have kept him from accomplishing his agenda already!" he said.

Meadows framed the debate over tax reform in populist terms. He rallied the volunteers by assuring them that if they helped pass the tax cut bill, they'd be helping reduce corruption in Washington.

"For far too long, it's been the well connected or the people that are well paid that actually get the biggest benefit in terms of our tax code," he said. "That is going to change this year, when we actually start giving you back the money that you earned."

The tax bill passed Congress in December, and was signed into law before Christmas. The most significant portion of the bill was an income tax cut for corporations, permanently reducing their tax rate from 35 percent to 21 percent, a cut that amounted to roughly $1 trillion over a decade. The bill also cut the income tax rate for the richest Americans from 39.6 percent to 37 percent.

Without a border adjustment, the tax cut for corporations increased the federal deficit, making it difficult to pass the bill through the Senate. The reasons for this were complicated. The Republicans planned to use a process called "budget reconciliation," which required only a bare majority vote. This allowed them to avoid a filibuster. But a bill passed through reconciliation could only add so much money to the deficit, and, without the BAT, the current tax cut plan added far too much. To accommodate for this fact, the Republicans came up with a simple maneuver. They made the tax cuts for middle-class families temporary. Those cuts would begin to expire in 2022 and be fully repealed by 2027, leaving many families with a tax increase. The middle class had been given a smaller tax cut, for a few years, in order to make the math work.

In the end, the bill looked very much like the typical tax bill that Mark Meadows described at the Americans for Prosperity event in August. It primarily benefited the highest earners and the best connected. The richest 20 percent of Americans got 65.3 percent of the value of the tax cuts. Middle-income Americans got zero benefit from the tax cuts after their temporary cuts expired.

Starting in 2027, the biggest tax breaks under the plan would go to the richest 5 percent of Americans, while taxes would slightly increase for the poorest Americans, according to an analysis of the cuts by the Tax Policy Center. Using a number of assumptions about the profit margins at

Koch Industries, a liberal policy group called Americans for Tax Fairness estimated that the tax cuts would save David and Charles Koch more than $1 billion annually in taxes.

By the summer of 2017, Koch's block-and-tackle strategy was paying dividends. Koch had proved its power in the Obamacare fight, and had reshaped the tax reform legislation from a Trumpian bill to a Koch bill. With these victories in hand, the Koch network could turn to a more helpful role. As it turned out, the Trump administration and the Koch network shared one important goal. Both groups wanted to ensure that greenhouse gases were not regulated in any way, and that the fossil fuel industry would retain its predominant role in America's energy system. Koch Industries had a knack for positioning itself to exploit good luck, and Donald Trump's election proved extraordinarily lucky in this regard. Trump waged a war on climate change regulation across the federal government, from the US Department of Agriculture to NASA and the Pentagon. Koch Industries was on hand to assist the effort.

Ground zero for the fight happened to be the headquarters of an agency that had antagonized Koch Industries for decades—the EPA.

When the Trump administration's transition team arrived at EPA headquarters, the transition officials described their effort in military terms. After the election, Trump sent a self-described "landing team" of transition officials to the EPA. They were followed by a "beachhead team" of twelve officials who would assume control of the agency. The officials in the beachhead team were designated as "Wave 1," suggesting that backup forces might be arriving behind them.

Before the invasion, however, there had been silence. The career employees of the EPA expected a team of Trump officials to arrive the day after the election, which was standard procedure. But no one arrived. On the second day, no one arrived. At the end of the first week, no one had shown up. And it wasn't at all clear who would be arriving or when. The EPA career staffers, like soldiers on an empty beach, waited in silence for the landing team.

Then, on November 22, the Tuesday before Thanksgiving, the first member of the Trump transition team arrived at EPA headquarters in downtown Washington, DC. He was an older man with graying hair, congenial and talkative. His name was Myron Ebell, and much of his adult life seemed aimed squarely at destroying the EPA.

Ebell was a senior scholar with a DC think tank called the Competitive Enterprise Institute, funded by Koch Industries, ExxonMobil, and other corporations. The CEI, as it was called, was libertarian and studied the growing burden of the federal government. The think tank put out a popular annual report, called "Ten Thousand Commandments," one of the few reliable sources that tracked the steady creation of new federal rules and their costs for the private sector. Ebell earned a name for himself as a leading intellectual opponent not just of the EPA, but of any regulations that might constrain carbon emissions and the use of fossil fuels. He was a key voice in Washington to cast doubt on the reality of human-created climate change and what he called "global warming alarmism" a new religion. He said in 2012 that the consensus around climate change was a political consensus, not a scientific consensus.

By 2016, Ebell had acknowledged that human activity was causing climate change, but he told the *Climatewire* news service that holding this belief didn't mean that climate change was "a serious problem or that the policies to address it will actually do anything or that you are willing to pay the costs of those policies."

Needless to say, this put Ebell directly at odds with the career staff at the EPA. After Congress failed to pass the cap-and-trade bill in 2010, the effort to regulate greenhouse gas emissions quietly moved into the EPA headquarters. The same team of people who had toiled with Jonathan Phillips in the basement of the Longworth Building—namely, Joel Beauvais, Michael Goo, and Shannon Kenny—moved straight to the EPA to continue the effort there. The team quickly realized that the EPA's authority to do anything was limited. Only Congress could pass the type of sweeping legislation that could significantly curtail carbon emissions. But this limitation was counterbalanced by good news. The fracking boom had replaced coal-fired power plants with natural gas–fired power plants, reducing America's carbon emissions. The economics of cheap natural gas essentially doomed coal as a major energy source. But the EPA team, including Beauvais and Goo, took a "rear-guard action" to ensure that coal wouldn't make a comeback and boost carbon emissions again. This rear-guard action took the form of an EPA rule called the Clean Power Plan, which required states to meet targets for cutting back carbon emissions for power plants. The rule aimed to cut emissions by about one-third by the year 2030, compared with 2005 levels. The Clean Power Plan was only part of the EPA's effort to limit carbon emissions. On an upper floor of the agency's headquarters was the home office of the Climate Change Division, a sprawling office of cubicles where the agency collected data on greenhouse gas emissions that were a vital tool in controlling them.

When Myron Ebell finally arrived at the EPA, he was greeted by two senior EPA officials who sat down with him to discuss how the Trump team might lead the EPA. The officials were Matt Fritz and Shannon Kenny, who were tasked with helping the transition. Ebell was an unremarkable-looking man, with the manner of a soft-spoken college professor. He wore round-framed, deeply unstylish eyeglasses with conservative suits and neckties. He was almost overly polite, even courtly, like an English gentleman who would never say anything to offend. This didn't mean that his charm won over the EPA officials. The career officials developed a nickname for him—"Creepy Grandpa"—that reflected both their disdain and mistrust.

It appeared, at least in the eyes of EPA officials, that the disdain ran both ways. As the weeks wore on and Ebell interacted with more EPA employees, he remained strenuously cordial, but they perceived that he was almost gleeful about what was to come. "He was always very polite, but he has this sort of sadistic grin," one employee recalled. "He wants to be sure that you know he knows he's fucking you over."

When Donald Trump arrived in Washington, he had no connections and no political network from which to draw the hundreds of people he needed to staff positions across different government agencies. Charles Koch, by contrast, had spent forty years building political networks in Washington. He had cultivated experts and operatives through years of employing them at think tanks, lobbying offices, and funded university chairs. When Donald Trump went out to hire people, he almost necessarily hired people who were sympathetic to Charles Koch's point of view, if not directly beholden to Charles Koch's largesse.

This influence was apparent in the beachhead team that arrived at the EPA. The team wasn't selected by Koch, but it was stacked with people who understood Koch and sympathized with it. Myron Ebell was the most obvious connection, but not the only one. There was also Charles Munoz, the beachhead team's White House liaison, who helped organize the Nevada chapter of Americans for Prosperity. There was David Kreutzer, a senior research fellow at the Heritage Foundation, which was funded in part by Koch Industries. There was Justin Schwab, an attorney who would help craft EPA legal doctrine; he was previously an attorney at the firm BakerHostetler, where one of his clients was Big River Steel, of which Koch Industries was the majority stakeholder.

One of the most significant members of the beachhead team was David Schnare. He was a former EPA employee of more than thirty years who had left the agency to teach law and work for the Energy & Environment Legal Institute, which was funded in part by the Donors Trust, a group that was funded in part by the Koch network.

Schnare was an imposing presence, both physically and personally. He had a silver goatee and a deep voice and his sentences were honed with lawyerly precision. He also had a deep knowledge of the EPA and the workings of power in Washington. His job was to write a detailed plan for the Trump administration to carry out its campaign promises at the EPA. It became clear, very quickly, that the plan was not to run the agency in the tradition of previous administrations. Someone "in authority, said to me: 'You have to come up with a plan to get rid of it,'" Schnare recalled. In this case, "it" was the entire EPA. "And I said: 'You can't do that. There are laws and all, you know. [EPA] can't just go away,'" Schnare said. His boss was not moved. "They went: 'Read my lips. You have to come up with a plan to get rid of it.'"

So Schnare came up with a plan to get rid of it. He estimated that the entire agency could be cut up into component parts and its functions handed over to other agencies or abandoned altogether. This could be completed by the sixth year of the Trump administration. It couldn't happen fast, but it could happen.

The beachhead team moved into the north building of the EPA headquarters, a stately, stone office building built during the New Deal era, just south of the White House off Pennsylvania Avenue. The building was shaped in a semicircle, embracing a stone courtyard full of picnic tables where office workers with lanyards around their necks ate lunch while packs of sightseers walked past, many of them, in the early winter of 2017, wearing red "Make America Great Again" baseball hats. Inside the front door, the EPA lobby was majestic and full of echoes, like a giant bank lobby, with marble floors and stone walls and hallways with vaulted ceilings. A large spiral staircase, with bannisters of wrought iron emblazoned with ornate designs, led from the lobby up to the third floor, which housed the agency's executive offices.

David Schnare's office was on this floor, near the administrator's office. This was where he worked on the detailed transition plan. Schnare's plan was revealing in what it emphasized. The EPA imposed burdens on American businesses both large and small. Its many rules affected farmers, small business owners, and midsized manufacturers, and all of them complained about regulations over dust pollution, cleanup efforts at Superfund sites, and other matters. But the Trump team's priority was not attacking or changing these rules. The priority was focused, almost entirely, on rules that were a burden for the fossil fuel industry.

A copy of Schnare's forty-seven-page transition plan, entitled "Agency Action Plan," began with an overview of the agency. The next heading was "Priority Change Initiatives." The first priority for change read: "STOP. Obama climate agenda, including Clear Act greenhouse gas regulations for new (NSPS) and existing (ESPS, or the "Clean Power" Plan) coal and natural gas power plants, CAFE Standards, Methane rules and others." These priorities could accurately be called Koch Industries' top priorities. The CAFE standards, for example, referred to the federal fuel efficiency mandates that reduced demand for gasoline. The Clean Power Plan was the closest thing to carbon regulation that the Obama administration had been able to achieve.

The plan then listed a timeline for change. The first item on the timeline read: "Day One—Issue directives to comply with Executive Orders to rescind climate change directives, including greenhouse gas emissions rules for new and existing power plants, suspend for review (withdraw from OMB) all major final rules that have not been published. . . ." The focus on eliminating climate change rules came from a simple source— Donald Trump's campaign speeches. "Myron Ebell always said, 'Go look at the president's speeches and the president's website . . . that's the basis for what we put together in the transition plan," Schnare recalled.

It is difficult to pinpoint the source of Donald Trump's driving fixation with fighting climate change regulation. The fixation was apparent in his campaign speeches, and then in his administration's actions across virtually every federal department. From the USDA to the Departments of Energy and Interior and the EPA, a mandate was handed down to roll back climate change efforts.

One plausible explanation of Trump's fixation was that he responded to the political realities of the modern Republican voting base. If Trump had a genius, it was the genius of reading a crowd and telling people what they wanted to hear, even before they knew they wanted to hear it. He had a sensitive radar for applause lines, and he built on the lines that worked the best. In this way, Trump's focus on denying the reality of climate change could be seen as an echo of Koch Industries' years of work to politicize the issue by casting doubt on the science and portraying carbon emission rules as a government conspiracy against liberty. The politics that Koch stoked in 2010 became the policies that Trump enacted in 2017.

The new EPA administrator would carry out these policies. To fill that role, Trump selected Scott Pruitt, the attorney general of Oklahoma, where oil interests dominated the political landscape. A number of Koch funded groups signed an open letter to US Senators, urging that they confirm Pruitt. Pruitt won confirmation with a vote of 52 to 46. Only one Republican senator, Susan Collins of Maine, voted against him.*

Pruitt arrived for work in the spring of 2017. One of the first people Pruitt met when he arrived at EPA headquarters was David Schnare. "I met him at the door," Schnare said. "I handed him a book, which contained all the statutes that EPA has to implement. It's about three, three and a half, inches thick. And I said: 'Welcome aboard, sir, here's the operating manual.'"

The gift was more than a good-hearted joke. It was also a warning. Schnare knew Pruitt's job was to dismantle the EPA. But dismantling the agency wouldn't be as easy as Trump might have suggested on the campaign trail.

Almost immediately after he arrived in his new office at EPA headquarters, Scott Pruitt apparently became convinced that a lot of people inside and outside the building wanted to kill him.

---

* In 2018, Americans for Prosperity attacked Collins with a campaign of Internet ads, direct mail, and radio spots as she sought reelection.

He requested that a security guard be posted outside his office door, behind a bulletproof desk. The desk would presumably act as a barricade if someone came in the office shooting. Pruitt also requested a bulletproof SUV for his personal transport, complete with bulletproof seats. He dramatically expanded the size of his security detail, building a team that could protect him around the clock. He swept the administrator's office for listening devices and ordered the EPA security department to build a soundproof booth inside his office, where he could make phone calls outside the hearing of career EPA staffers, at a cost to taxpayers of $43,000.

It was common for new EPA administrators to hold town hall meetings with the career EPA staff to meet the team and lay out priorities. But Pruitt rarely interacted with any staff members, including senior staffers. He became something of a curious figure inside the EPA. He rarely saw the staffers, rarely talked to them, and when he did pass employees in the hallway, the effect was sometimes off-putting. He said hello, cheerfully, and quoted Bible scripture without solicitation or apparent relevance to the situation. In one instance, Pruitt recited a long quote about toiling in the fields, which left staffers wondering what he meant. Two staffers suspected the quote was from the Old Testament, but they weren't brushed up on their Scripture and couldn't confirm it. One day, word raced through the office that Pruitt was making a rare public appearance and standing by a bank of elevators, handing long-stemmed roses to women as they arrived for work, for reasons that were unclear.

While Pruitt's personality was a puzzle, his policy stances were well known. When he became attorney general of Oklahoma, Pruitt was extraordinarily close to the state's fossil fuel companies. In 2011, lawyers with Devon Energy drafted a letter complaining to the EPA about air pollution regulations. Pruitt pasted the letter onto an official state document with the official seal of the state's attorney general and sent it to the EPA. After Pruitt sent the letter, a Devon lobbyist named William F. Whitsitt sent Pruitt an e-mail that said: "Outstanding!" Devon Energy's involvement in sending the letter was not made public until 2014, when it was uncovered by *New York Times* reporter Eric Lipton. This was one example among many.

Pruitt's political career had been carefully nurtured in Oklahoma's political culture. But when he arrived in Washington, it seemed that he wasn't prepared for what awaited him. He was particularly unsuited to deal with criticism. In the spring of 2017, Pruitt attended a conference at the Mayflower Hotel in Washington, DC, hosted by the Environmental Council of the States, or ECOS, a nonprofit group representing state-level environmental regulators. Two protestors attended the event. They were women, carrying baskets of oranges with stickers on them, highlighting the use of a pesticide called chlorpyrifos. Pruitt's administration had recently allowed the pesticide's continued use, even though it was shown to harm human health. The women shouted, and were led out of the conference hall. This was standard fare in Washington, where Senate hearings were often staffed by protestors in wait.

When he returned to EPA headquarters, however, Pruitt seemed deeply shaken by the women with the oranges. During a meeting in his office on an unrelated topic, Pruitt kept returning to the protestors and the threat they posed to him. He seemed to suggest that the conference organizers were complicit in letting the protestors in the building.

"He treated it as if he'd been shot at. He wouldn't let it go . . . he was furious at the conference organizers for not protecting him," recalled one person in the room. Pruitt often fixated on what he saw as threats to his safety, this person said. "He becomes obsessed. I think he truly believes that he is sort of on God's mission, and people are out to get him."

Pruitt's new leadership team consisted largely of loyalists from Oklahoma. They barricaded themselves off from the rest of the agency and held hours-long meetings each morning without any EPA staff present. David Schnare attended those meetings, and he became frustrated with Pruitt's refusal to meet with EPA staff. It was hindering Pruitt's ability to understand the agency and to mobilize the people who worked there.

"Let's put it this way. He didn't want anyone to tell him that he couldn't do something. He only wanted to be able to tell people to go do things and sometimes someone has to stand up and say you can't do that. And those people didn't last," Schnare said.

There were other problems with Pruitt. Schnare began to doubt that Pruitt, for all his close ties to energy companies, might be a reliable conduit for the effort to thoroughly dismantle the legal basis for climate change regulation. Schnare discussed the transition plan with Pruitt, and explained the importance of attacking climate rules. But Pruitt seemed uninterested. Instead, Pruitt asked his staff to come up with quick initiatives that could garner headlines and give him a chance to visit states for public events.

"If he had an agenda, the agenda was: promote Scott Pruitt for the next job," Schnare said. "He looked for opportunities that gave him the chance to go out into the states—especially Iowa and New Hampshire."

Schnare quit the EPA that spring. Pruitt's inner circle became tighter. The morning meetings went long—three hours sometimes—and Pruitt's team began issuing policy proposals that were fully formed, without any input from the EPA's staff. In the course of a year, Pruitt's team issued orders to repeal or roll back forty-six rules and regulations. Many of these were major rules. Pruitt's team issued a proposal to repeal the Clean Power Plan and to strip away the CAFE standards for fuel efficiency.

In June, Pruitt attended a ceremony at the White House Rose Garden, where he introduced President Trump. The event was to announce America's withdrawal from the Paris Climate Accord agreement to reduce global greenhouse gas emissions. It was the third global treaty to combat climate change abandoned by the United States. Pruitt was a vocal proponent of the withdrawal, and his argument won out over officials who believed that international obligations should be honored from administration to administration.

The withdrawal was characteristic of the Trump administration's approach to governing and conformed with Charles Koch's views. Trump and his advisors considered the Washington bureaucracy to be a parasitic population, feeding off the American economy. To combat these parasites, the administration left jobs unfilled, transferred career employees considered disloyal into dead-end jobs, and failed to appoint staff members to the one review board that considered employee complaints. This slow corrosion of the civil service melded smoothly with Charles Koch's goals. There would be no harm in letting the administrative state recede.

Still, it wasn't clear how effective Pruitt was in his effort to dismantle, or permanently hobble, the EPA. His efforts to repeal the Clean Power Plan and other measures would face legal challenges. Pruitt also seemed to be stalling on the tedious and time-consuming work of chopping up the EPA's functions and delegating them to other agencies, as Schnare had suggested. Finally, Pruitt became fatally distracted—by mid-2018, he was the focus of eleven federal investigations for his spending on security and relationships with lobbyists. He asked one of his staffers, for example, to reach out to Chick-fil-A to win Pruitt's wife a franchise location.

In July of 2018, Pruitt resigned. He was temporarily replaced by his deputy, Andrew Wheeler, a former coal industry lobbyist. In certain circles, there was hope that Wheeler would be more focused and more disciplined in carrying forward some of the goals outlined in Schnare's transition plan.

Even within the chaos of Pruitt's tenure, he achieved important victories for Koch Industries. The effort to regulate greenhouse gas emissions had been purged from the EPA, at least temporarily, pushing back the date when carbon emission limits might harm Koch's oil refining and trading operations.

The Trump administration also did something that seemed impossible—it politicized the issue of climate change even further than it had been in 2010. It seemed inconceivable, in the Trump era, that any Republican or conservative Democrat could even broach the topic of combating climate change. The real-world effects were measurable. When George W. Bush was elected president, atmospheric concentrations of carbon were 375 parts per million, far exceeding the record level of human history. When Barack Obama pushed for the cap-and-trade bill in 2010, carbon dioxide levels were 393 parts per million. In 2018, the concentrations reached 410 parts per million, a new record.

In late 2017, Charles Koch's political network released a memo to its donors. The memo touted two big achievements that year. The first was the "comprehensive tax reform bill," which the memo said was the network's top priority. The second was the regulatory rollback administered by cabinet members like Scott Pruitt, including the proposed repeal of the Clean Power Plan and the withdrawal from the Paris Climate Accord.

The Koch network couldn't claim credit for these accomplishments. The group had shaped the Trump agenda but had not written it. The balance of power between the Trump administration and the Koch network was still uncertain. Koch claimed some victories, but it was clear that Donald Trump was determined to go his own way. Trump abandoned a major trade deal in Asia and imposed tariffs on goods from Europe and China, policies that Charles Koch vehemently opposed.

Inside the Trump administration, there was disdain for Charles Koch because he was considered too ideological, inflexible, and out of touch with American voters. Trump's influential policy advisor, Steve Bannon, made this disdain public during an interview with the *New York Times Magazine*, published in March of 2017. Bannon, indirectly praising Donald Trump's brilliance, disparaged the Democratic Party. Then he took a shot directly at Charles Koch: "And then the Republicans, it's all this theoretical Cato Institute, Austrian economics, limited government—which just doesn't have any depth to it. They're not living in the real world."

It seemed that the Trump administration and the Koch network were like opposing chess players who couldn't clear the board. There was no clear winner. But Charles Koch pressed his advantage. His donor network announced that they would spend between $300 million and $400 million during the 2018 midterm elections, helping shape the most important political contest of Trump's presidency.

The Koch network maximized its influence with this money by forging a connection with the one senior member of the Trump administration with whom Charles Koch had a long relationship—Vice President Mike Pence. As an Indiana congressman, Pence was a close ally of Americans for Prosperity, a relationship that lasted after Pence entered the White House. In June of 2017, while Charles Koch attended a meeting with his donor network in Colorado Springs, Koch took a detour to hold a private meeting with Pence and a handful of Pence's staff members at the Broadmoor Hotel. The meeting lasted roughly an hour, and was not on Pence's official schedule for that day. Koch and Pence discussed Trump's legislative agenda, including the tax cuts and health care reform. Pence was later given responsibilities for helping manage Trump's strategy for the 2018 midterms. Trump said that if the Democrats won control of the House or Senate, their first order of business would be impeachment proceedings, which would disrupt the presidency. The contest was vital, and Charles Koch ensured he would be a major player in it.

With this money hanging in the balance, Charles Koch traveled to Palm Springs in January of 2018 to host the meeting of his donors. As the event got underway, Charles Koch took the stage, standing behind the podium as an evening breeze blew through the luxury resort. He wore a suit jacket and blue shirt, with no tie. He looked profoundly confident, and told his colleagues that they were making great progress in the Trump era.

"I'm more excited about what we're doing and about the opportunities than I've ever been," he said. "We've made more progress in the last five years than I had in the previous fifty."

In typical fashion, Koch then made a joke at his own expense, pointing out that some people might have wondered what he was doing all those fifty years, if he hadn't achieved great results. The comment drew light laughter. But it was clear enough what he had been doing. He had been building a political network with a reach and influence that was arguably stronger than any other in corporate America. Only the CEO of Koch Industries could call upon a massive lobbying operation, an army of grassroots activists, a donor network with contributions in the billions of dollars, and a universe of political front groups and donor vehicles nearly impossible for outsiders to map. If the CEO of General Electric or any other publicly traded company tried to build a similar machine to influence public policy, and dedicated as much time and money to it as Charles Koch, then that CEO would almost certainly be curtailed by a board of directors. Thanks to his efforts to retain such tight control over Koch Industries, Charles Koch did not face this dilemma. His political network was enduring, and massive. And it would almost certainly outlive the Trump administration.

Charles Koch possessed an attribute that seemed to elude Donald Trump—he possessed almost limitless patience, and a time horizon that was measured in decades.

After the laughter passed during his speech, Charles Koch explained that his fifty years of work in politics had a clear directive, even if the results were slow in coming.

"You've got to build the foundation before you build the house," he said. "That's what I claim I was working on."

CHAPTER 25

Control

(2018)

It was about six in the morning, in the middle of winter, when dawn started to break over Charles Koch's family compound in Wichita. Behind the compound's tall walls, treetops became visible in the faint light, their branches bare and sharp. The sky turned faintly purple, then pink. Outside the compound, a man sat alone in a large black Chevy Tahoe with tinted windows, apparently watching the walls. The man sat patiently. He looked down at his phone and waited, the light of its screen making his face glow. His headlights were extinguished and he was all but invisible to the morning traffic that passed by. Then, a little bit before six thirty, the man in the Tahoe flipped on his headlights and drove forward. At the same time, another black SUV emerged from Charles Koch's compound, pulling out from an entrance that was partly obscured by shrubbery. The man in the Tahoe pulled out into traffic, his timing impeccable, and fell into line behind the other black SUV. Both cars headed north, toward Koch Industries headquarters.

Part of the myth about Charles Koch was that he drove himself to work every day, parking in front of Koch Industries headquarters and walking up the stairs to his office. His reality was different now. It was an open secret in Wichita that Charles Koch rode to work in a convoy of armored vehicles, chaperoned by armed security guards. This was seen as pragmatic. Since he had become politically active, Charles Koch was a magnet for death threats. He was a private man, little understood and widely hated. He was now also one of the richest men on earth, so security was necessary. Charles Koch's great skill was analyzing and mitigating risk.

Traffic was light this early in the morning. The black SUVs drove past strip malls as they headed north. The sky continued to lighten, but only slightly. At this time of day, the commute to Koch headquarters lasted only a matter of minutes. The Koch Industries campus was visible from miles away. The Tower sat at the center of the campus, still the tallest building within several miles. The first rays of the morning sun glinted off the dark brown granite walls and the opaque windows. The parking lots around the Tower were still illuminated, this early in the morning, by bright lights that hung from the top of tall black poles. The lights made the campus look like a self-contained universe, a splendidly isolated pool of shining stars, surrounded by a wall. It was a beautiful sight in the morning. Kochland.

When he arrived at work, Charles Koch's car pulled into a special parking garage with high security. The lot was near the bombproof chamber where mail was sorted before entering the building. Here was a universe that he, primarily, had authored. The people he encountered spoke a language he invented, worked in business units he oversaw, and granted him the kind of deference enjoyed by national leaders. When he entered the hallways of his office building, Charles Koch could take the elevator up to the third floor, or walk there through the spacious and well-lit stairwell.

The hallways were hushed in the morning. The décor of the third floor, which housed Koch's executive suites, had barely changed in twenty years. The doorway to the executive suite was near the elevator bank. Walking inside that door, Charles Koch passed into a spacious lobby. There was a couch, a table, and a small bookcase across from the desk where his assistant sat. Beyond the desk was the doorway to his office. And to the left, on the other side of the lobby, was the entrance to the corporate boardroom, the site of countless strategy sessions and battles over the decades.

As he walked to his office, Charles Koch passed a sculpture. It was a bust of his father's head, mounted on a tall pedestal, surrounded by decorative plants. It looked like a monument to a nation's founder. It had been fifty years since Fred Koch died and Charles took over the family company. Fred Koch, that difficult and driving man, was now safely enshrined in the form of a memorial, a silent bust. The man who had encouraged his sons to wear boxing gloves and fight one another, the man who forced Charles Koch to dig weeds in the family yard with a spoon, the man who sent Charles to military school, who used guilt to drag Charles back home to Wichita to run the business, that man was gone. There was only the memory of him—a memory that was shaped and cultivated by his son Charles. Every year in September, Charles Koch hosted the "Founder's Day" memorial event, where he talked about his father's legacy. He wrote about his father and produced videos about his father. He controlled the narrative. And one part of the narrative that Charles Koch didn't emphasize, maybe because he didn't have to, was that Charles's achievements had surpassed his father's. Fred Koch left behind a company that was a motley assortment of assets—a cattle ranch, a share in an oil refinery, a gas-gathering business. Charles Koch fused them together. Charles was the one who invented Koch Industries. Fred Koch published a political tract and sold it through mail order. Fred Koch cofounded the John Birch Society, a paranoid, marginal political group that dissolved into obscurity. Charles Koch wrote his own political tracts and two books on Market-Based Management, one of which was a national bestseller. Charles Koch built a political network that was arguably more influential than any other in corporate America. Reporters and authors traveled from around the country, seeking an audience with Charles Koch. His political pronouncements made the evening news.

Everything Fred Koch accomplished, Charles Koch surpassed.

And while he might not admit to this fact, Charles Koch must have been aware of it, on some level, as he passed that bust of his father. He walked past the receptionist's desk and into his familiar office. He walked past the small leather couch and coffee table, past the walls with their built-in bookshelves that held his personal library. His desk was still in the same spot, over by the window. It was not uncommon for Charles Koch to arrive at his desk just after dawn.

When he sat down, Charles Koch could turn his head to take in a sweeping view of the Kansas horizon. This view had changed over the last decade or so. It wasn't all empty space now. There was a public-school building just north of Koch headquarters and some suburban neighborhoods to the northeast. But the landscape changed only because Charles Koch had allowed it to change. He owned virtually all the land he could see, out to the horizon. He had purchased the acreage over time, at reasonable prices. He donated the land on which the public school sat to clear the way for its construction. When Charles Koch gazed out his window, he saw a landscape that he controlled.

If this control was like a gravitational field—shaping everything within it—then the epicenter of the field was the Koch Industries campus. The campus extended north, surrounded by the large wall that bowed out in a horseshoe shape with trees planted along its length. Within the wall was the vast parking lot, which started to fill with cars very early in the morning. Charles Koch could sit at his desk and watch the employees get out, filing into the entrance of the underground pedestrian tunnel that brought them into the Tower. As they walked through the tunnel, the employees passed the mounted collages with black-and-white photos of the Koch family history. When they reached the elevator bank below the Tower, they stood near the large portrait of Charles Koch, smiling. The portrait was composed of tiny photos of Koch Industries employees, as if Charles Koch himself incorporated all of them.

Every quarter, the business leaders from Koch's various divisions came to the Tower to report to Charles Koch. When it was time for such meetings, Charles could rise from his desk and walk across the small lobby into the boardroom, where the senior leadership team was seated around the large circular table. The boardroom was still spartan in its decoration. The puffy leather office chairs were unremarkable. The only extravagance was the leather coasters placed at each seat at the table, emblazoned with the company logo. Extra chairs lined the outside wall of the windowless room, providing seats for any support staffers.

Charles Koch sat and listened as his business leaders explained their most recent quarter. He interrogated them and looked for soft spots in their presentations. It was always understood that chaotic market forces were slamming against their front door, and everyone would be accountable for their reactions. If a division lost money, the division's president needed to provide a detailed vision for regaining profits over the long term.

In 2018, as he listened to the division heads make their presentations, Charles Koch oversaw a corporation that seemed to vindicate his every belief. Entire, massive, profitable units of the company did not even exist in 2000, when Charles Koch launched a turnaround effort after the disasters of the 1990s. Georgia-Pacific, for example, was generating over $1 billion in annual profits, on average. The Koch Fertilizer division, the result of one risky bet in 2003, was delivering billions in revenue each year. Then there was Molex, the microchip company, and Guardian Industries. Charles Koch could make the case that his company wasn't just perpetually growing, but perpetually transforming as well, entering new industries, abandoning the old, always searching for the next opportunity. And bolstering these experimental efforts were the reliable cash cows. The Pine Bend refinery, still refining cheap crude and selling expensive gasoline, throwing off cash around the clock. And now Corpus Christi, repeating the same trick thanks to the fracking revolution. And the trading division, still selling derivatives, still trading in markets where it had an unparalleled view into real-time shipments and inventories.

Charles Koch's beliefs would have been validated in another way during these meetings. Senior leaders at Koch Industries phrased everything they said in the vocabulary of Market-Based Management. One of Charles Koch's indisputable accomplishments over the preceding thirty years was creating an organization where every employee—to a person—publicly subscribed to the same intricately encoded philosophy. Division heads who came to Wichita spoke in terms of mental models and discovery processes and the five dimensions. They talked about integrity. Decision rights. Challenge processes. Experimental discovery. Virtues and talents. These weren't dog whistles or catchphrases. They were the internal vocabulary of Kochland. Learning them was the first condition to winning a seat at the table. Downstairs, on the first floor of the Tower, the hallways were lined with classrooms where new recruits sat around circular tables during daylong learning sessions, memorizing this vocabulary and learning the rules of MBM. As Charles Koch himself put it, the new recruit either subscribed to this philosophy entirely, or they left Koch Industries. There was no halfway.

The real-world verdict about MBM's efficacy was less clear than Charles Koch's faith in it. In 2018, as Charles Koch listened to a parade of business leaders describe their operations, there were signs of trouble within Koch Industries. If MBM really was the code of achieving prosperity, then prosperity was necessarily an uneven and volatile thing.

Invista, for example, was deeply troubled. Depending on one's point of view, the Invista acquisition in 2004 was either a disappointment or a disaster. In the spring of 2018, the Invista wing of the Koch Industries headquarters was like a ghost town of empty cubicles. In 2017 alone, Invista cut fifty-two jobs in Athens, Georgia, sold a plant in Tennessee, and sold another one in Derry, Ireland. It seemed that MBM couldn't fix whatever ailed Invista and the global market in synthetic fabrics. Similarly, MBM seemed inadequate to reduce workplace injuries inside Georgia-Pacific. The injury rate fell slightly during the first few months of 2018, but was still at the elevated levels that began in 2012. Jim Hannan and his team were still trying to solve the problem, but it stubbornly persisted.

There were also signs that Koch Industries, in spite of strict adherence to MBM, was repeating some of the mistakes of the 1990s. The company's acquisition spree had once again saddled it with wildly diversified units that seemed like an unnatural fit with one another—glass, steel, computer sensors, greeting cards, and advanced fertilizers, all under one roof. Molex, the microchip and sensor company, was already delivering mixed results. In 2017, a Molex plant in Minnesota laid off 136 employees.

The economy itself was shaky in the spring of 2018. The stock market swung wildly, rising and falling with volatility that hadn't been seen in years. There was speculation that the economy had overheated, thanks in part to the kind of government intervention Charles Koch despised. The Federal Reserve Bank had kept interest rates at zero for several years after the crash of 2008, pumping global markets with easy money. This was compounded by a program called Quantitative Easing, which essentially pumped more than $3.5 trillion of new US dollars into the economy. If this radical monetary policy caused asset bubbles to appear in different pockets of the US economy, those bubbles might soon pop. When that happened, Koch's corporate structure would be tested in ways it hadn't been tested in a decade. The weaker divisions might suffer massive losses.

If the economic future was uncertain, Charles Koch seemed supremely calm during the winter and spring months of 2018. This might have been due to that fact that even in the worst-case economic scenarios, there was seemingly no plausible scenario in which Koch Industries actually failed. There might be layoffs. The company might have to sell some divisions at fire-sale prices. But the Koch Industries entity itself, the core business that executives referred to as KII, seemed impervious to failure. There was simply too much cash in the company, and too little debt, to envision it going under. Koch's bread-and-butter assets—the oil refineries, the fertilizer plants, the paper mills, the commodities trading desks—were part of the machinery that provided life's necessities. People would buy gasoline and fertilizer during any recession, and it was unlikely that big companies could swoop in and build multibillion-dollar facilities to steal Koch's share of the business. Koch's business was also protected by the masterfully constructed corporate veil, the massive, multichambered legal nautilus shell that walled off various parts of the company from one another. Divisions could fail and be sued, but the damage would never penetrate to the heart of KII.

Charles Koch had other reasons to be supremely calm during 2018. If Koch Industries was impervious to bankruptcy, then Charles Koch was outright immune to it. If ever there was evidence for his faith in his own abilities, and the power of MBM, then it was in the size of his private fortune.

In 1991, *Fortune* magazine estimated that Charles and David Koch were worth a combined $4.7 billion, putting them among the wealthiest people in the world. This fortune was the estimated value of Charles and David's roughly 80 percent ownership stake in Koch Industries, which the brothers split evenly.

The policies of the Clinton presidency did not diminish this fortune. During the 1990s, the Kochs' family fortune almost doubled. In 2002, *Forbes* magazine estimated that Charles and David Koch were worth a combined $8 billion.

The fortune exploded during the Bush years, against a backdrop of growing government, uneven economic growth, and overseas military campaigns. In 2007, Charles Koch alone was worth an estimated $17 billion. He and his brother were worth a combined $34 billion, the third-largest fortune in the United States behind Warren Buffett's.

During the Obama years—the years when Americans for Prosperity warned repeatedly about the threat of creeping socialism—Charles and David Koch's fortune more than doubled once again. At the end of the Obama administration, Charles Koch was worth $42 billion. Together, Charles and David were worth $84 billion, a fortune larger than Bill Gates's $81 billion. By 2018, Charles Koch's fortune amounted to $53.5 billion.

Charles Koch was so rich in part because he fought so hard, for so many years, to keep his company private. The vast majority of Koch Industries' ownership wasn't spread among thousands of shareholders, but only two. The employees at Koch Industries—including its senior executives—could not earn a real equity stake in the firm, no matter how hard they worked. They earned, instead, the right to shadow stock, essentially a derivatives contract based on the company's performance. They also earned onetime merit bonuses.

This ownership structure, while rare in corporate America, reflected the US economy in 2018. Charles Koch's household was part of an exclusive club—about 160,000 households in America were in the wealthiest 0.1 percent of the population. This group prospered just like Charles Koch. In 1963, the top 0.1 percent of households possessed 10 percent of all American wealth. By 2012, they possessed 22 percent. This gain came as the vast majority of Americans' lost ground. The bottom 90 percent of Americans possessed about 35 percent of the nation's wealth in the mid-1980s. By about 2015, their share had fallen to 23 percent.

The American labor market resembled the labor market inside Kochland. For more and more Americans, employment and income were now contingent, temporary, and reflected the volatile swing of market conditions. Labor unions, which had shielded workers from financial volatility for decades, were a negligible sideshow of the American economic scene. Militant unions like the OCAW at the Pine Bend refinery were a novelty found in history books. Even the modern, relatively powerless unions like the IBU in Oregon were vanishingly rare. Full-time jobs were increasingly replaced by contract jobs and part-time work. Pensions were replaced by 401(k) plans, whose value rose and fell with the markets. Pay was not steady and was increasingly tied to bonuses rather than annual raises. Across America, the ownership of wealth reflected the ownership structure of Koch Industries. The vast majority of Americans owned shadow stock in the American enterprise.

This disparity in American wealth reflected the disparity in political power. The rich and well connected shaped policy in America. It helped, in 2018, to have several hundred million dollars at your disposal and a large lobbying office, coupled with think tanks and a grassroots army, to have your policy preferences recognized. In 2014, a group of political scientists at Princeton studied the policy outcomes on 1,779 issues between

1980 and 2002. They found that no group in America had a surefire hold over policy making. But the rich—a group they called the "economic elite"—had, by far, the best chance of turning their policy choices into a reality. The second most-powerful entities in Washington were special interest groups like lobbying organizations, which had a lower success rate than the economic elite, but still held significant sway. Significantly, the impact of median-income Americans, meaning the majority, on policy outcomes was "near zero." The study concluded, succinctly: "When a majority of citizens disagrees with economic elites or with organized interests, they generally lose."

In many ways, however, politics were a sideshow for Charles Koch. There was another, more important campaign underway for leadership within Koch Industries. After Charles's son, Chase Koch, took himself out of the fast-track lane to become CEO, something like a three-way race emerged to select Charles Koch's immediate successor. There were three executives who seemed primed to take the job, and Charles Koch could evaluate each one as the business grew.

The contours of this race were defined in 2017, when Koch Industries was overhauled in the most significant restructuring since 2000. This time, the company was redrawn into two divisions: Koch Enterprises and Koch Resources. The Enterprise division included Georgia-Pacific, Molex, and Invista—basically any part of Koch Industries that produced a consumer product or piece of a consumer product. The resources division contained Koch's legacy operations in fossil fuels and other extractive businesses, including Flint Hills, Koch Minerals, Koch Ag & Energy Solutions (which included the fertilizer division), and the commodities trading arm, Koch Supply & Trading.

Jim Hannan was promoted from CEO of Georgia-Pacific to CEO of Koch Enterprises. Brad Razook was promoted from CEO of Flint Hills to CEO of Koch Resources. In these roles, the two executives were engaged in an unspoken competition. Each division reported its results to Charles Koch. He could measure their progress and determine who might be best suited to take over the firm. Then there was David Robertson, the president of Koch Industries, which acted like a holding company over both Enterprises and Resources. Robertson had quietly made his way to the most senior spot beneath Charles Koch over many decades of work. Robertson was soft-spoken, direct, and a consummate MBM man. He knew how to achieve great things and appear to not take any credit for it. If Charles Koch made a bet that his corporate culture could replace him as the charismatic CEO, then David Robertson was a fitting vehicle to carry that bet forward.

If any of these men became CEO, however, they might be taking the job in a caretaker's role, because Chase Koch was still the heir apparent. After working for a while in the specialty fertilizer division, Chase Koch invented a new role for himself. He was spending a lot of time with venture capitalists who wanted Koch to fund their projects, and he became intrigued with many of their ideas. He talked it over with his father when the two of them had dinner at Chase's childhood home. Chase told his dad that Koch Industries was missing out on the future by not getting more involved with venture capital firms making risky bets on new technologies. They mulled over this idea, and came up with a new division of Koch called Koch Disruptive Technologies. Chase was named head of the new division. He would help Koch identify the next wave of big businesses to invest in. One of the group's first investments was in an Israeli medical devices company. Chase's division moved to a newly constructed wing of the Koch headquarters campus. In early 2018, the KDT offices were still a blank slate, a set of cubicles and small offices under construction. In a small meeting room near the space, Chase sat at the head of the table, leading his group through a meeting. His bearing was somewhat stiff, but authoritative. After many years, he seemed comfortable in his own skin. When asked if he would be CEO some day, Chase said it was certainly a possibility. He said he would only fill the right job at the right time.

One day, Charles Koch sent his son a small folder of old papers, with a handwritten note attached. The note was written on a small piece of yellow paper with a simple letterhead: "Charles Koch." Charles Koch's neat, cursive script read:

Chase,

I'm going through my old files for the book project. I found these notes on your Aristotle paper.

Pop

The papers attached were notes that Charles and Chase had written while working on Chase's elementary school assignment about Aristotle. Aristotle believed that people strived to accomplish things, and that is what gives their life meaning. From that meaning flows happiness. This was the message he passed on to his son.

If Charles Koch found meaning during his working days in 2018, that meaning seemed to derive largely from the "book project" he mentioned in his short note to Chase. People close to Charles Koch said he was drawing away from the business, at least somewhat, to work on this book project, which was his private passion. Charles Koch's close friend Leslie Rudd said Charles was finally exhibiting something that was very rare in his life: a sense of contentment. "I think Charles, now, is doing just exactly what he wants to do, which is trying to do good," Rudd said.

Charles Koch had already published two books about Market-Based Management, which he argued was the ultimate solution for running a prosperous business. But even within those books, he had hinted that Market-Based Management was more than a business philosophy. In this new book, Charles Koch planned to show the final dimension of Market-Based Management. He would show that it was a guidebook not just for operating companies, but for operating entire societies. The proper shape of American society was the shape of Kochland.

Charles Koch had no illusions that America would instantly adopt his creed when his new book was eventually published. The path would be long and contentious. He had been cutting the path for fifty years already. But he had always worked on a very long timeline, measuring his success on a scale of years, even decades.

His plan, so long in the making, was still just in its early stages.

ACKNOWLEDGMENTS

So many people helped produce *Kochland* over so many years that it is impossible for me to properly thank them all.

I am deeply grateful to all the current and former employees of Koch Industries who spoke with me for this book. It would have been simply impossible to understand the institution without them. The hardest part of being a reporter is trying to weigh both the good and the bad, and to produce a narrative that is as fair and close to the truth as humanly possible. It's impossible to even try to do it without good sources, and I am deeply indebted to everyone who helped me along the way. Thank you.

This book was only possible because of the guidance, leadership, and tireless support of my editor, Priscilla Painton. She has been unwavering even as the years stretched on and one deadline after another passed by. At every step, I relied on Priscilla's judgment, her ethics, her patience, and her amazing eye for the right word. I am so grateful that we have editors like Priscilla to keep this important work alive. I am also grateful to the entire team at Simon & Schuster for their support. Jonathan Karp gave me great insight and pushed me to ask the right questions early on. Sophia Jimenez and Megan Hogan were vital teammates. Dana Trocker and Larry Hughes have been invaluable, over many years, in helping me communicate these ideas to a broader audience. Samantha Hoback and her team did a miraculous job of improving and polishing up this manuscript under deadline. Edward Klaris and Alexia Bedat at Klaris Law are the best kind of allies a reporter can have: smart, hardworking attorneys who are committed to upholding press freedom. Their rigorous review and feedback made this book much stronger.

My agents, Lauren Sharp and David Kuhn, are the best I could hope for. They are diligent, honest in their critiques, and always willing to put in the extra hours to improve the work. They instantly supported the idea for *Kochland*, even in the face of long odds in the market. I couldn't navigate this business without them.

When I conceived the idea of writing *Kochland* in late 2011, two people came along at just the right moment and helped transform my life as a writer: Steve Coll and Andrés Martinez. They gave me a fellowship at the New America Foundation, and I am grateful every day for the opportunity they provided. I can never repay the gift, but I will keep trying. Thank you. This book wouldn't have happened if you didn't give me that break.

At New America, I was assisted over several years by the most remarkable people. Becky Shafer contributed in countless ways, as a friend and colleague, from researching oil refineries and the EPA's "new source review" process to helping me navigate archival research. Kirsten Berg is one of the most exceptional and diligent reporters I have ever worked with. She unearthed mountains of files on Koch Industries that I never would have found, illuminating everything from US oil policy in the 1970s to Cayman Islands tax schemes in the 2000s. I am so grateful for her help, from the earliest days of the book until the end. Rachel White was a tireless champion for New America and for my work—I won't ever forget it. Jeff and Cal Leonard were incredibly generous and supportive.

My time at New America was possible thanks to support from the 11th Hour Project of the Schmidt Family Foundation, a nonprofit foundation based in Palo Alto. The foundation funded my work through the new model of nonprofit journalism—providing money to an institution that, like a newsroom, allows reporters to pursue their work without outside interference or influence. In this regard, the team at 11th Hour has been a dream. They hold a long-term view and a visceral understanding of the importance of independent journalism. No one at the 11th Hour Project saw any material for this book as I prepared it, tried to influence it in any way, or sought to steer my inquiries in the slightest degree. I deeply appreciate the total independence. I am so grateful to the leadership team at 11th Hour: Wendy Schmidt, Amy Rao, and Joseph Sciortino. I am deeply indebted to Sarah Bell, an incredible person and an incredible ally. Thank you so much for all the hard work, the support, and the patience. I am also so grateful for the help from Ellyn Peabody, Michael Roberts, Christina Vrachnos, Lauren Davis, Jamie Dean, Melody

Gonzales, and Jake Mogan. It has been a joy to know all of you. I am particularly grateful to the other grantees of the 11th Hour project whom I have had the chance to meet—I am inspired by your idealism, your iconoclasm, and your efforts to make the world a better place.

At just the moment when I needed it most, I was given a lifeline from the J. Anthony Lukas Work-In-Progress award in 2017. I am so grateful that such an award exists. Books are vitally important to our public debate, and writing books isn't possible without grants like the Lukas prize. Thank you for being there to give writers hope and support. Thank you to Jonathan Alter and Ann Marie Lipinski. I am indebted to the prize judges: John Duff, Martha Levin, and Sarah Toubourg. I will not forget that you gave me a chance to complete this book. Thank you so much for your vote of confidence before this book was even finished.

At New America, I benefited tremendously to learn from a lot of people who are way smarter than I am. Lina Khan, Sabeel Rahman, Yascha Mounk, Mark Schmitt, and Michael Lind were generous with their time, helping me talk over history and political economics. I learned so much from them. Lee Drutman, one of the best political scientists of our time, taught me about lobbying and threw in something more: while talking in the file room one day, he came up with the title for this book. I wanted to call it *The Republic of Koch*, and he told me the real title was *Kochland*. Thanks for saving me. Barry Lynn, as always, is a great teacher about corporate power and monopolies. Konstantin Kakaes is an incredible guy to help clarify your thinking and demolish weak arguments. Phil Longman, a fantastic student of history, helped me work through so many ideas on this book and always helped me to see the bigger picture. Jesse Eisinger was a great reminder of how real reporters should conduct themselves. He also read through the early chapters of this book and gave me invaluable feedback. Rania Abouzeid is inspiring in her bravery and her skill. Azmat Khan has been so remarkably kind and always pushes me to be better through her example. Anand Gopal, my first friend at New America, had better not quit writing books because he does it better than almost anyone and we are counting on him. Gabriel Sherman taught me so much about reporting and persistence, and I often relied on his advice and example. Alex Holt is such a sharp mind and a great sounding board and friend. Chayenne Polimédio helped me think through the politics. Josh Freedman was generous with his time and brilliance and was invaluable in helping me think about America's political system. Fuzz Hogan, Lauren McCarthy, and Cathy Bryan were wonderful friends and advisors who made it all work. Peter Bergen was a tremendous support as head of the fellows program and always kept his eye on the big picture. Albert Ford was always ready with a smile and a great question. Awista Ayub was a gracious supporter and colleague. Rebecca A. and Laura K. were so kind and so generous in helping me see what I missed—I owe you so much. Louie Palu is a great friend and inspiration. Sue Bencuya rigorously fact-checked this book and was invaluable in correcting errors and clarifying the language. Thank you.

Steve LeVine has been an incredible friend and mentor since I arrived in Washington. Steve generously read through an early version of this book and helped me make it better throughout. His own books and his advice are signposts that show the right way, and I benefited immensely from his wisdom. I will keep trying to follow the path.

I am so grateful for my friend and mentor William T. Vollmann. While I was writing this book, Bill gave me an invaluable piece of advice and a benediction. The advice: "Don't let Koch Industries, or your editor, push you around." The benediction: "It makes me happy when you work every day."

I am gratified that Seymour Hersh humored me and gave advice. He kept asking me why I wanted to hang around, and the real answer is that it makes me feel better to know that there are reporters like him in the business—I am trying to watch and learn.

As I reported this book, I was lucky to work with great editors at newspapers and magazines who helped me publish work that furthered my inquiries into Koch. Brian O'Keefe at *Fortune* magazine gave me the all-important chance to write my first profile of Koch Industries. He was not just smart and incisive, but also steadfast when Koch pushed back. I am so grateful to have worked with him. Romesh Ratnesar, Brad Wieners, Jeremy Keehn, and Matthew Philips at *Bloomberg Businessweek* have been incredible to work with—thank you so much for your support. Andy Serwer at Yahoo! Finance gave me the chance to write about Koch and land an interview with Charles Koch, for which I am forever grateful. Kelly Johnson at the *Washington Post* was a joy to work with, and she masterfully shaped the story on Georgia-Pacific.

Pete, Tina, and the Farrelly boys were incredible hosts who gave me shelter and kinship in Portland, Oregon, during my long reporting trips there. Thank you! You made a lonely job fun.

Jane Mayer and Daniel Schulman are two fantastic reporters who preceded me in writing books about the Koch brothers. One could question why another book was needed, but I hope that I brought something new to the public domain. I am so grateful for the kind support they gave me as I was working on this.

After I left New America in 2017, I was so lucky to find a home (once again) at the University of Missouri School of Journalism, where we hope to open doors for more books and more reporters. I am so grateful for the support of Dean David Kurpius, who has his eyes on the future. Thank you so much to Randy Picht for your guidance, help, leadership, and support. Shannon Burke-Kranzberg has been tireless in her efforts and essential to making the idea real. Randall Smith hatched the idea and brought me in—thank you, neighbor. Mark Horvit has been a tireless ally and a great inspiration, and Earnest Perry has been a vital leader, even if he still scares me a little bit because he used to be my editor. Thank you so much to Colin Kilpatrick and Martha Pickens for the countless hours you've invested to make this happen. Sky Chadde and Uliana Pavlova at Missouri helped me research Koch's Fertilizer business and political activities, respectively. They were both tireless reporters and I look forward to seeing what's next.

All of my people in Kansas City have been there for me the whole time, even though I have been away. I can honestly say that I miss you every day. Thank you so much to the Robertsons, the Leonards, the Launders, the Spradleys, the Kienes, the Fogels, the Zimmers, the Eckels, the Wolbachs, the Dickeys, the Mauros, the Moores, and to all the other families who made me who I am. From the bottom of my heart: thank you. To all my friends in St. Louis: the Andreses, the Diekempers, the Riches, the Dobsons, the Higdons, the Lanes, the Wolfs, and the Berzons: I am really sorry that we had to leave. Saying good-bye to you was one of the hardest things I've ever had to do. I haven't gotten over it.

They say you can't pick your in-laws, so I guess I was just extremely lucky. John and Joan Miller have been the best, most supportive parents-in-law that a person could have. They have helped this project from the beginning, and made it better along the way through their questions, comments, and perspectives. Thank you. And thanks to Claire, Drew, and Mary Ellen for all the happy times when we got to take a break.

David, Blythe, and Mom: I owe you everything. I don't know how to say it except: thank you.

Dad: I hope you like this book. You were there at my desk the whole time.

Josie: There's a reason you're always the first person to read what I write. I don't just trust your judgment—I can't manage without it. You have been with me through seven punishing years of ups and downs on this project. While we were raising a family, you also helped me navigate the punishing terrain of the journalism business, where almost nothing can be counted on. I know I can always count on you. Without you, none of it is possible.

And to the kids: all of it is for you.

APPENDIX

Alphabetical Directory of Significant Characters in *Kochland*

Antrich, Darrell. Former electricity trader for Koch Energy Trading. Antrich was involved in Koch's "parking" trades during the energy crisis in California in 2000.

Ballen, Ken. Attorney hired by the US Senate to investigate Koch's theft of oil in Indian reservations during the 1980s. Ballen uncovered extensive evidence of the theft and referred it to the US Attorney's office in Oklahoma City.

Barnard, Don. Labor negotiator for Georgia-Pacific. He represented the company in drawn-out negotiations that were among the first after Koch Industries purchased Georgia-Pacific.

Beckett, Melissa. Koch Industries commodities trader. Beckett traded gasoline and fuel products, learning the "contango storage play" and other strategies. She later shifted to the Koch Energy Trading desk, where she traded megawatt-hours in the California market. She finally went to the fertilizer trading group, where she worked for Chase Koch.

Bingel, Kelly. Democratic lobbyist who represented Koch Industries as it sought to derail the cap-and-trade bill in 2010.

Brady, Maria. Tea Party activist from Boiling Springs, South Carolina. Brady became politically active after receiving a revelation from God. Her group helped unseat Republican Congressman Bob Inglis. Her Tea Party chapter's efforts were promoted by Americans for Prosperity.

Bucknum, Gary. Former local labor union president at the Inland-boatmen's Union, or IBU, at Georgia-Pacific's warehouse in Portland, Oregon. Bucknum didn't work for Georgia-Pacific but joined the union from a different company it represented. He joined in 2008, at the same time as Steve Hammond. Bucknum negotiated one drawn-out negotiation against Georgia-Pacific and did not seek reelection. Also known as "Gary the Anarchist."

Cordes, Don. Koch Industries' general counsel throughout the 1980s and 1990s. During that time, he was vice president of legal and the corporate affairs chief legal officer. He joined the company's board of directors in 1996. Cordes was Charles Koch's legal advisor as the US Senate investigated Koch's oil theft in Oklahoma and as Bill Koch waged a multiyear legal war against Charles Koch.

David, Steve. Manager of environmental engineering at the Pine Bend refinery in the mid-1990s. Oversaw the work of whistle-blower Heather Faragher during the period when Pine Bend released ammonia into the surrounding environment.

Davis, Gray. Governor of California during the electricity crisis of 2000. The crisis ended Davis's political career.

Dodge, Brian. Local labor union president at the Inlandboatmen's Union, or IBU, at Georgia-Pacific's warehouse in Portland, Oregon. Dodge was Steve Hammond's boss and was elected to the position after his predecessor, Gary Bucknum, resigned. Dodge negotiated multiple labor contracts with Koch Industries but felt that he had no leverage. Also known as "the Dodger."

Dubose, Phil. Longtime Koch employee who joined the company in 1968. Dubose spent many years as an oil gauger, collecting oil for Koch's pipeline system. Dubose used the Koch method of oil collection, in which he intentionally mismeasured the oil supplies for Koch's benefit.

Ebell, Myron. Scholar with the Competitive Enterprise Institute, a think tank funded by Koch Industries and other energy companies. Ebell has spoken out against "climate hysteria" and regulatory efforts to reduce greenhouse gas emissions. Ebell led transition efforts at the EPA for the Trump administration.

Ellender, Philip. President and CEO of Koch Industries' lobbying office, called Koch Companies Public Sector. Ellender began as a lobbyist in Louisiana and transferred later to Washington, DC. He was unusual among lobbyists because of his embrace of Koch's MBM theories. He was known as a "Wichita guy," rather than a Washington guy. Helped lead Koch's lobbying efforts to derail the cap-and-trade bill in 2010.

Elroy, James. Special agent of the FBI, based in Oklahoma. He was the primary FBI investigator into Koch's oil theft in Oklahoma, surveilling the company's employees. Elroy later assisted the US Attorney's office in Oklahoma City as it investigated the theft. After leaving the FBI, Elroy was employed by Bill Koch as Koch pursued a civil suit against Koch Industries for oil theft.

Estes, Ruth. Assistant safety chief at the Pine Bend refinery in the mid-1990s, intimately involved in decision-making around the release of ammonia into the environment.

Feilmeier, Steve. Chief financial officer of Koch Industries from the mid-2000s until present day. Feilmeier held that position during many of Koch's major acquisitions and helped train Chase Koch when Chase joined the company after college.

Franklin, Cris. Koch Industries trader. Franklin began in Koch's pipeline division, helping design software systems to manage complex gas flows. He later shifted to trading financial products. He was on a financial products trading desk during the crash of 2008.

Franzen, David. Warehouse worker at Georgia-Pacific's warehouse in Portland, Oregon. Longtime member of the Inlandboatmen's Union, or IBU. He was on the committee that negotiated a labor contract with Georgia-Pacific, and believed that doing so forever tainted his reputation with managers. He was known as something of a brawler.

Hall, Bradley. Longtime Koch Industries employee who joined the firm in 1975. Hall rose up through the ranks of finance and deal making at Koch, eventually running the corporate development group, which evaluated potential acquisitions. He later became CFO of Koch Supply & Trading before leaving the company in 2004.

Hammerschmidt, Joseph. Militant leader of the OCAW labor union at the Pine Bend refinery who led the strike against Koch in 1972.

Hammond, Steve. Union official with the Inlandboatmen's Union, or IBU, at Georgia-Pacific's warehouse in Portland, Oregon. Hammond was from Portland and worked at the warehouse since graduating from high school. He ran for election as a union leader after his work life at the warehouse became increasingly miserable. Hammond was the deputy negotiator in several contract negotiations with Koch, each one less successful than the last. He retired in 2016, after negotiating a contract that was deeply dissatisfying to the union members. Also known as "the Hammer."

Hanna, Bill. Former president of Koch Industries during the late 1980s and a close associate of Charles Koch's.

Hannan, Jim. Koch Industries executive who joined the company in 1998 as a finance executive. Hannan later joined a deal-making group and was instrumental in the Georgia-Pacific acquisition, the largest in Koch's history. He joined Georgia-Pacific and became CEO of the company. He was later promoted to CEO of Koch Enterprises, a large division of the company that includes Georgia-Pacific, Invista, Molex, and other assets. He is seen as a candidate to become CEO after Charles Koch leaves the company.

Hoffmann, David. Senior compliance attorney at Koch Industries' Invista division from 2005 to 2010. Hoffmann helped implement Charles Koch's 10,000 percent compliance doctrine at Invista's facilities. Hoffmann later transferred to Koch's lobbying office in Washington, DC, where he attended strategy sessions to defeat the cap-and-trade bill.

Howell, Ron. Longtime Koch Industries employee who began as a gasoline trader with the company. He oversaw an expansion and transformation of Koch's trading operations in the early and mid-1980s as electronic trading emerged. Howell later retired and entered politics, becoming a Koch Industries lobbyist in Oklahoma. He led the political effort there to combat the legal case against Koch's oil theft.

Inglis, Bob. Republican congressman from South Carolina. Inglis was once an ally of Koch Industries and took campaign donations from the company. His stance on global warming, however, turned the company against him. Koch Industries funded an opponent to challenge Inglis in a primary election during 2010 and helped unseat him.

Jones, Jeremy. Koch Industries executive who ran the venture capital group called Koch Genesis. Jones worked closely with Charles Koch but left the company when Koch Genesis was shut down after the crash of 2008.

Jones, Nancy. Assistant US Attorney in Oklahoma City who oversaw the office's investigation into Koch's oil theft. Jones says she developed evidence showing that multiple managers at Koch Industries directed the theft. She quit her job as she was pursuing evidence against senior Koch executives. After she left, the case was dropped.

Jones, Wesley. Georgia-Pacific manager whom Koch promoted to run the company's pulp mill division. Jones was later promoted again to become executive vice president over operations. He saw firsthand how G-P's operations changed under Koch, and was allowed to reinvest in the company with far less bureaucracy than before.

Koch, "Bill" William. Charles Koch's younger brother and David Koch's twin. Bill Koch led an attempted coup to unseat Charles Koch as CEO in the 1980s. After the coup failed, Bill Koch launched a legal battle against his brother that lasted for years. He eventually ran his own, smaller company, called Oxbow.

Koch, Charles. CEO and chairman of Koch Industries. Charles Koch took over the company in late 1967 after his father, Fred, died, and has run the firm ever since.

Koch, Chase. Charles Koch's son, born in 1977. Chase began working for the family company as a teenager and joined it full-time a few years after graduating from college. He rose through the ranks to become president of Koch Fertilizer before leaving the position to eventually launch the Koch Disruptive Technologies division. Chase is widely viewed as an heir apparent who might one day succeed his father as CEO.

Koch, David. Bill Koch's twin brother and Charles Koch's younger brother. David Koch joined the family company after graduating from

MIT and splits ownership of the firm equally with Charles Koch. Longtime Koch executives describe David as a "silent partner" who largely deferred to Charles Koch's vision. David Koch retired in 2018 due to health problems.

Koch, Elizabeth. Charles Koch's daughter, born in 1975. While she holds seats on many Koch boards, she has not held significant positions inside Koch Industries. She runs a publishing company in New York.

Koch, Fred. Founder of Koch Industries. Fred Koch was raised in a small town in Texas. Over many years, he built a small corporate empire with holdings in refining, oil transportation, and ranching. He died of a heart attack in 1967.

Koch, Frederick "Freddie," Jr. The oldest of the four Koch brothers, named after his father. Freddie, as he is known, avoided the family company and moved to New York.

Koch, Liz. Charles Koch's wife of more than forty-five years. She is involved in Koch's community efforts and philanthropies.

Leonard, Timothy. Former US Attorney in Oklahoma City who oversaw the criminal investigation into Koch's theft of oil. Leonard was appointed to become a federal judge and dropped the case against Koch Industries before he took the job on the bench.

Lonegan, Steve. The New Jersey state director of Americans for Prosperity. Lonegan was one of the first paid directors hired to run a chapter of the activist group. He helped stoke opposition to the cap-and-trade bill and punished Republicans who voted for it.

Markel, F. Lynn. Koch's former chief financial officer, serving in that position during Koch's period of explosive growth in the 1990s. Markel was hired as an accountant and rose through the ranks as Koch transformed its financial control systems. He left the company in 2000 after twenty-four years.

Markey, Ed. Democratic senator from Massachusetts. When he was a congressman from that state, he helped lead the effort to pass a cap-and-trade bill to control greenhouse gas emissions. Markey led a select subcommittee that spent years crafting the measure.

Mawer, Steve. President of Koch Supply & Trading from 2000 until 2014. Mawer held a social event at his home to host Charles Koch, who gave a salon-style talk to traders about politics and economics.

McKinney, Travis. Forklift driver at Georgia-Pacific's warehouse in Portland, Oregon. He was grateful to get the job, and started just as G-P implemented its Labor Management System. He was an active member of the the Inlandboatmen's Union, or IBU, as its power declined.

Meadows, Mark. Republican congressman from North Carolina and leader of the House of Representatives' Tea Party–aligned Freedom Caucus during 2017. Meadows was often caught in the middle of policy differences between the Koch network and the Trump administration.

Nesmith, Tom. Salesman with the utility company Public Service Company of New Mexico (PNM). Nesmith pitched the "parking" strategy to Koch Energy Trading, which allowed Koch to game electricity markets in California. PNM's participation was vital to making the parking strategy succeed.

Obama, Barack. The forty-fourth president of the United States, elected in 2008 and reelected in 2012. Obama ushered in a liberal political wave that Charles Koch considered dangerous to the nation's future.

O'Neill, Brenden. Koch Industries derivatives trader who earned millions of dollars during the natural gas price spike. O'Neill was an engineer in Koch's oil refinery in Corpus Christi before he shifted to the trading group. He was briefly Chase Koch's boss when Chase worked at the Corpus Christi refinery.

Osbourn, Wes. Energy and gasoline trader with Koch Supply & Trading in Wichita and Houston. Osbourn traded physical gasoline supplies in Wichita and traded paper products like futures contracts in Houston.

Packebush, Steve. Former president of Koch Fertilizer. Packebush was on the team of Koch Nitrogen employees who executed the 2003 acquisition of Farmland Industries' fertilizer plants. He later became president of the new division. He was a key mentor to Chase Koch, bringing him into the fertilizer business and encouraging Chase to later become president.

Paulson, Bernard. Oil refining executive hired by Charles Koch to oversee the Pine Bend refinery in the early 1970s. Paulson led the efforts to break the OCAW labor union there during the strike of 1972–73. He was later promoted to oversee Koch's oil refining operations from Wichita, where he worked closely with Charles Koch.

Peace, Steve. The California state senator who was widely seen as the "father" of the state's electricity deregulation bill, which he cosponsored. Peace shepherded the bill into law and later tried to warn regulators that the system was being manipulated by companies like Enron and Koch Industries.

Phillips, Jonathan. Congressional staffer who helped draft key parts of the Waxman-Markey cap-and-trade bill. Phillips, a Harvard graduate, came to see global warming as a fundamental threat to the environment.

Phillips, Tim. National president of Americans for Prosperity. Phillips was an activist in conservative religious groups before joining AFP. He led the group during a period of explosive growth during the Tea Party movement of 2010.

Pruitt, Scott. Former attorney general of Oklahoma who was EPA administrator from 2017 to mid-2018. Pruitt carried forward many deregulatory efforts long sought by the energy industry and Koch Industries.

Quinn, Joseph. Member of the OCAW labor union at Pine Bend who participated in the nine-month labor strike of 1972–73.

Razook, Brad. Former CEO of Koch's oil products division, Flint Hills Resources. Razook played a key role in helping Koch exploit the fracking boom in the Eagle Ford Shale region of Texas. He was later promoted to CEO of Koch Resources, a large division that includes Flint Hills and other natural resource companies. Razook is seen as a candidate to become CEO of Koch Industries after Charles Koch leaves the company.

Robertson, David. Koch Industries' current president. He joined the company in 1984. Robertson oversaw large parts of Koch's disastrous foray into the beef and agribusiness during the 1990s. He later moved to Koch's oil refining division. Robertson is seen as a strong contender to replace Charles Koch as CEO.

Roos, Brian. Manager, or "process owner," of the Utilities Profit Center division of the Pine Bend refinery during the mid-1990s. Oversaw the wastewater facilities that released ammonia into nearby wetlands.

Roskind, Herbert. Manager of Koch Industries' chemical trading division who hired Bill Koch. Roskind oversaw Bill Koch's early trading activities and tried to diminish the tension between Bill and his brother Charles.

Rothbard, Murry. Libertarian activist who cofounded the Cato Institute with Charles Koch.

Rudd, Leslie. Longtime friend of Charles Koch and the Koch family in Wichita. Rudd encouraged Chase Koch to join the family company after he graduated from college. Rudd died on May 3, 2018, at the age of seventy-six.

Ryan, Paul. Republican congressman from Wisconsin who was Speaker of the House in 2017 and 2018. Ryan was often caught in the middle of policy differences between the Koch network and the Trump administration.

Schnare, David. Longtime EPA employee who later became a critic of what he called the agency's regulatory overreach. Schnare helped lead the Trump administration's transition efforts at the EPA and helped draft a transition plan for the agency that aligned with Koch Industries' interests.

Seibert, Walter. Father of twelve-year-old Zachary Seibert, a pedestrian killed in a 1993 car accident involving Chase Koch, who was driving. Walter Seibert spoke with Chase Koch after the accident, at the urging of Liz and Charles Koch.

Sementelli, Tony. Chief financial officer at Flint Hills Resources who played a critical role in helping the company exploit the fracking boom in the Eagle Ford Shale region of Texas.

Sharp, Jeff. Communications director for the House select subcommittee that wrote the cap-and-trade bill in 2010. Sharp was among the first to notice the Tea Party activism that eventually derailed the effort.

Sobotka, David. President of Koch Energy Trading from 1997 through 2001. Sobotka came to Koch from Lehman Brothers, and he brought Wall Street practices to Koch's trading floor. He promoted a new compensation model that gave derivatives traders a bonus based on a percentage of their profits.

Soliman, Sam. Former head of trading operations at Koch's trading desk in Houston. Soliman became CFO of Koch Industries in 2000 and was replaced by Steve Feilmeier when Soliman left the company.

Sollers, Wick. Assistant investigator to Ken Ballen in the US Senate. Helped oversee the Senate's investigation into Koch's oil theft in Oklahoma. Traveled to Wichita with Ballen to depose Charles Koch.

Trimm, Dennis. Manager at Georgia-Pacific's warehouse in Portland, Oregon. Trimm was a manager when Koch Industries took over and watched the company implement its new policies. He told employees during meetings that Koch could shift their work to nonunion facilities. He was later fired for committing a safety violation.

Tromberg, Ernie. Onetime member of the OCAW labor union at Pine Bend who later left the union to join the ranks of Koch management at the refinery, where he spent his entire career.

Trump, Donald. The forty-fifth president of the United States, elected in 2016. Trump was never close with Charles Koch and operated outside of Koch's political network.

Varner, Sterling. Longtime Koch Industries employee and protégé of Fred Koch. Varner was a father figure to Charles Koch in the late 1960s and is credited with deeply influencing Koch's corporate culture. Varner became president of Koch Industries in 1974 and held that position for thirteen years. He retired as vice chairman of Koch's board of directors in 1989 but remained active in the company and advised Charles Koch.

Voyles, James. Koch Industries attorney involved with the pollution case at the Pine Bend refinery in the mid-1990s. Voyles undermined whistle-blower Heather Faragher as she tried to contain illegal pollution at the refinery.

Watson, Dean. A rising star at Koch Industries who was put in charge of Koch's rapid expansion into the agribusiness sector. Watson oversaw the failed Purina Mills acquisition and was later fired.

Williams, Roger. One of the earliest executives at Koch Industries hired by Charles Koch. Williams oversaw Koch's sprawling pipeline division.

Winn, Abel. Leader of Koch's experimental economics lab, run in partnership with Wichita State University, which tested the tenets of Market-Based Management. Winn ran a large-scale experiment to find ways to beat "holdouts" who bargained for higher prices.

NOTES

The following notes establish sources for the information in *Kochland*. Some facts are cited to a single source when, at times, they came from multiple sources that reinforced the given fact. For the sake of clarity, the author chose to cite the primary and most reliable sources for these facts, rather than listing every interview or comment that supports it. Fred Koch's domineering personality, for example, was related by dozens of interviewees and written sources, but only a select few sources were chosen as citations.

A handful of sources agreed to be interviewed for this book only on the condition that they remain unidentified. Information that they provided was only included in this book if it could be verified by another source or documents independently obtained by the author. When information from those sources is used, it is identified as being from a source speaking on background.

PREFACE: THE FIGHTER

1   *On May 18, 1981 . . . Wichita, Kansas*: Morgan Stanley interoffice memorandum, May 20, 1981, marked confidential.

1   *Charles Koch was forty-five years old*: Analysis and description of Charles Koch based in part on author interviews with Charles Koch and dozens of current and former Koch Industries executives and managers who worked with him at various times between 1975 and 2018. Physical description of Charles Koch in 1981 based on photo in article "Wichita's Koch a Private Man with Money," *Wichita Eagle*, April 30, 1978.

1   *"He does not want this cash"*: Morgan Stanley interoffice memorandum, May 20, 1981, marked confidential.

2   *"Certain of [Koch's] commodity traders"*: Ibid.

2   *Secrecy was a strategic necessity for Koch Industries*: Analysis of Koch Industries based in part on notes from reporting in Wichita and several other locations between 2013 and 2018, and author interviews with Charles Koch and dozens of current and former Koch Industries executives and managers.

2   *When he was challenged by his own brothers*: See endnotes, ch. 5 and ch. 7.

2   *When he was challenged . . . first years as CEO*: See endnotes, ch. 3.

2   *When the FBI . . . criminal investigation*: See endnotes, ch. 1 and ch. 7.

2   *When a liberal Congress*: See endnotes, ch. 19 and ch. 20.

2   *After prevailing . . . true to his vision*: Author interview with Charles Koch, 2015; also author interviews with Roger Williams, F. Lynn Markel, Bradley Hall, Bernard Paulson, Herbert Roskind, Dean Watson, Randy Pohlman, Steve Feilmeier, David Robertson, Chase Koch, Jim Hannan, Steve Packebush, and other current and former Koch Industries executives between 2013 and 2018.

2   *An internal think tank and deal-making committee*: See endnotes, ch. 9, ch. 11, and ch. 14.

3   *In 2003 . . . bought a group of money-losing fertilizer plants*: See endnotes, ch. 14.

3   *This strategy laid . . . decades of continuous growth*: Charles Koch, *The Science of Success: How Market-Based Management Built the World's Largest Private Company* (Hoboken, NJ: John Wiley & Sons, 2007); Charles Koch, *Good Profit: How Creating Value for Others Built One of the World's Most Successful Companies* (New York: Crown Business, 2015); Christopher Leonard, "The New Koch," *Fortune*, December 19, 2013.

3   *It specialized in the kind of businesses that are indispensable*: Leonard, "The New Koch."

3   *Charles Koch and his brother . . . Koch Industries*: Bryan Horwath, "Charles and David Koch Jointly Named 5th-Richest Americans," *Wichita Eagle*, October 15, 2015; court transcripts and exhibits, *William I. Koch et al. v. Koch Industries Inc. et al.*

3   *Together the two men are worth $120 billion*: *Forbes* Billionaires list, 2018.

4   *His portrait hangs . . . his videotaped speeches*: Notes from reporting in Koch Industries headquarters, Wichita, in 2013, 2015, and 2018; author interviews with dozens of current and former Koch Industries employees.

4   *America operated under . . . the New Deal*: Political analysis based on interviews and research including: David M. Kennedy, *Freedom from Fear: The American People in Depression and War, 1929–1945* (New York: Oxford University Press, 1999); Arthur M. Schlesinger Jr., *The Age of Roosevelt*, vols. 1–3 (Boston: Houghton Mifflin 1957–1960); Glenda Elizabeth Gilmore and Thomas J. Sugrue, *These United States: A Nation in the Making, 1890 to Present* (New York: W. W. Norton, 2015); Jacob S. Hacker and Paul Pierson, *American Amnesia: How the War on Government Led Us to Forget What Made America Prosper* (New York: Simon & Schuster, 2016).

5   *Koch Industries . . . lobbying operations in the United States*: Center for Responsive Politics, Lobbying Database, Koch Industries Lobbying Disclosures, Office of the Clerk, US House of Representatives; author interviews with Koch Industries Lobbyists, including Philip Ellender, 2014–18.

5   *Charles Koch frequently derides the current political era*: Charles Koch, "Corporate Cronyism Harms America," *Wall Street Journal*, September 9, 2012.

5   *The entire economy depends on refined oil*: See endnotes, ch. 21.

6   *The legacy oil refiners . . . exploited arcane sections of the law*: See endnotes, ch. 21.

6   *In 2018, the company's headquarters . . . resembled a fortified kingdom*: Author's
      notes, observations, and photographs reporting at Koch Industries headquarters,
      2018.

7   *Adherence to the creed is nonnegotiable . . . at Koch Industries*: Author interviews
      with current and former Koch Industries employees and executives, 2013–14;
      Charles Koch, *The Science of Success*.

7   *Readers will meet*: Paulson, Watson, Heather Faragher, Philip Dubose, Steve Ham-
      mond, Brenden O'Neill, interviews by author, 2013–18.

8   *One of those people is . . . James Elroy*: James Elroy, interviews by author, 2014–16.

CHAPTER 1: UNDER SURVEILLANCE

11   *FBI special agent James Elroy stood on . . . pastureland*: Elroy, interviews by author,
      2014–16; *Final Report and Legislative Recommendations: A Report of the Special
      Committee on Investigations of the Select Committee on Indian Affairs, United States
      Senate*, November 20, 1989; James Elroy, Testimony, Public Hearings of the Select
      Committee on Indian Affairs, May 9, 1989.

11   *For a long time, it was just Elroy . . . all alone*: Elroy, interviews by author, 2014–16.

12   *Elroy's new bosses in the Senate were increasingly*: Elroy, Kenneth Ballen, Senator
      Dennis DeConcini, interviews by author, 2014–17; *Final Report and Legislative
      Recommendations*, November 20, 1989.

12   *Elroy's photos were developed in a darkroom*: Elroy, interviews by author, 2014–16.

13   *Elroy wasn't the typical FBI man*: Oliver Revell, former FBI agent in charge, Okla-
      homa City, interview by author, 2014; Elroy, interviews by author, 2014–16.

13   *The Senate had gotten a tip that Koch Oil was stealing*: FBI internal memoran-
      dum, "Koch Industries Incorporated, Wichita, Kansas; CRIME ON AN INDIAN
      RESERVATION—THEFT; RACKETEERING INFLUENCE AND CORRUPT OR-
      GANIZATION," July 26, 1989; Elroy, Ballen, interviews by author, 2014–16; *Final
      Report and Legislative Recommendations*, November 20, 1989.

14   *It seemed that nobody in either the Senate*: Elroy, Ballen, interviews by author,
      2014–16.

14   *David Koch, one of the company's primary owners and executives*: Nicholas Confes-
      sore, "Quixotic '80 Campaign Gave Birth to Kochs' Powerful Network," *New York
      Times*, May 17, 2014.

15   *Elroy visited their houses in the evenings*: Elroy, interviews by author, 2014–16.

16   *Koch managers never told their employees to . . . steal*: James Elroy, Testimony, Pub-
      lic Hearings of the Select Committee on Indian Affairs, May 9, 1989; Gene Poteet,
      James Spaulding, James Elroy, Testimony, Public Hearings of the Select Committee
      on Indian Affairs, May 9, 1989; Elroy, interviews by author, 2014–16.

16   *Instead, the company put relentless pressure*: Doyle Barnett, Dubose, Elroy, interviews

by author, 2014; further insight into Koch Oil management practices were derived from the sworn statements of senior Koch Oil managers and executives, taken during depositions by US Senate investigators on April 24, 1989. The depositions transcripts, labeled "Confidential," were made public for the first time to the author. The account in this book draws on the depositions of Charles Koch, Bob Dix, Steven Scates, Keith Langhofer, Wesley Stanford, Donnie Alsobrook, William Hougland, Jack Chism, Darrell Brubaker, Thomas Kivisto, Gary Baker, and David Nicastro.

17　*It was almost an accident . . . Elroy's efforts*: DeConcini, Ballen, interviews by author, 2014–16.

17　*The story was the first in a series*: Chuck Cook, Mike Masterson, and M. N. Trahant, "Fraud in Indian Country," *Arizona Republic,* October 4, 1987; Mike Masterson, interview by author, 2014.

17　*The looting happened in a complicated and insidious way*: Chuck Cook, Mike Masterson, and M. N. Trahant, "Honor System License to Loot," *Arizona Republic,* October 4, 1987.

18　*In particular, the series . . . Dennis DeConcini*: "Senate Panel to Begin Probe of Indian Affairs Bureau," Associated Press, October 16, 1987; DeConcini, interview by author, 2014.

18　*By the late 1980s, the results . . . were truly ruinous*: *Final Report and Legislative Recommendations,* November 20, 1989.

19　*In Washington, the Senate Select Committee*: "Senate Panel to Begin Probe of Indian Affairs Bureau," Associated Press, October 16, 1987; "Committee Approves Funding of Indian Affairs Investigation," Associated Press, October 30, 1987.

19　*In the spring of 1988, Ken Ballen walked*: Ballen, interviews by author, 2014–16; scenery description taken from author's notes reporting in Washington, DC, 2014.

20　*Early in the investigation, Ballen knew*: Ballen, Revell, interviews by author, 2014.

21　*In the beginning, Ballen decided*: Ballen, interviews by author, 2014–16.

21　*With his subpoenas, Ballen was able to*: Ibid.; *Final Report and Legislative Recommendations,* November 20, 1989.

21　*The large oil purchaser Kerr-McGee*: *Final Report and Legislative Recommendations,* November 20, 1989; Ballen, interviews by author, 2014–16.

22　*The oil companies also pointed out*: Ballen, interviews by author, 2014–16.

23　*This time the villain was the public*: Daniel Yergin, *The Prize: The Epic Quest for Oil, Money & Power* (New York: Simon & Schuster, 1990).

23　*This was a message that was delivered*: Ballen, interviews by author, 2014–16.

24　*Ballen's case grew stronger after he took a trip*: Ballen, Elroy, interviews by author, 2014–16.

24　*The story was convincing, but it also made Ballen uneasy*: Ballen, interviews by author, 2014–16; FBI internal memorandum, "Koch Industries Incorporated, Wichita, Kansas; CRIME ON AN INDIAN RESERVATION—THEFT; RACKETEERING INFLUENCE AND CORRUPT ORGANIZATION," July 26, 1989.

25   *Ballen's team narrowed its subpoenas*: Ballen, Elroy, interviews by author, 2014–16; *Final Report and Legislative Recommendations*, November 20, 1989.

26   *Even more confusingly, the firm was*: Ballen, interviews by author, 2014–16.

26   *Ballen turned to the oil majors for help*: Ibid.

27   *It is almost awe-inspiring to fly*: Notes from reporting in Wichita, Kansas, 2013.

27   *On April 24, the two Washington attorneys*: Ballen, interviews by author, 2014–16; Charles Koch deposition with US Senate investigators, transcript, April 24, 1989.

28   *They passed through a metal detector*: Ballen, interviews by author, 2014–16.

28   *When Charles Koch entered the room*: Ibid.

29   *"Could you please state your full name for the record?"*: All quotes from this exchange are taken directly from a transcript of the deposition of Charles Koch, April 24, 1989.

30   *For a prosecuting attorney like Ballen*: Ballen, interviews by author, 2014–16.

31   *"I don't think there is such a thing as an exactly accurate measurement"*: Ibid.

33   *At one point during the hearings*: Transcript of the Public Hearings of the Select Committee on Indian Affairs, May 9–11, 1989.

CHAPTER 2: THE AGE OF VOLATILITY BEGINS

34   *It was a Friday in mid-November*: Dick Dilsaver, "Fred Koch, Industrialist, Dies in Utah," *Wichita Eagle and Beacon*, November 18, 1967; ibid., November 19, 1967.

34   *Fred Koch was a large man . . . forceful personality*: Bryan Burrough, "Wild Bill Koch," *Vanity Fair*, June 1994; Charles Koch, video presentation to Koch employees, "Lessons of My Father," 2008, 1:05, uploaded to YouTube by Kochfacts TV on April 13, 2012, www.youtube.com/watch?v=3U3NyKoMrlw; Charles Koch, *Good Profit*, 21–33.

34   *He was a cofounder of a right-wing political group*: "Birch Society Leader Warns of Red Danger," *Wichita Eagle*, October 16, 1960; Carl T. Bogus, *Buckley: William F. Buckley Jr. and the Rise of American Conservatism* (New York: Bloomsbury Press, 2011), 198.

35   *The ranchlands spoke to Fred Koch in a special way*: John Lincoln, *Rich Grass and Sweet Water: Ranch Life with the Koch Matador Cattle Company* (College Station: Texas A&M University Press, 1989), 7.

36   *One of Charles Koch's earliest memories*: Charles Koch, interview by author, 2015.

36   *Charles Koch was not completely surprised*: Ibid.

36   *During the summers . . . access to the Wichita Country Club*: Charles Koch, panel discussion, Wichita Metro Chamber of Commerce, November 2, 2015, www.youtube.com/watch?v=f6UHTCdPLzY&t=1253s; Charles Koch, *Good Profit*, 30; descriptions of Wichita country taken from reporting trips to Wichita, 2013, 2015, 2018; Markel, Dean Watson, interviews by author, 2013–16.

37   *But Charles Koch was denied that kind of summer*: Charles Koch, *Good Profit*, 31.

37   *Fred implored Charles to come home*: Roy Wenzl and Bill Wilson, "Koch Relentless in Pursuing His Goals," *Wichita Eagle*, October 14, 2012.

38   *"I thought, My God"*: Ibid.

38   *Over the years, Fred Koch gave Charles increasing authority*: Charles Koch, interview by author, 2015; Charles Koch, *Good Profit*, 34–37; Guy Boulton, "Koch and His Empire Grew Together," *Wichita Eagle*, June 26, 1994.

38   *On Monday, November 20, 1967*: "Industrialist Fred Koch Dies on Hunting Trip," *Wichita Eagle and Beacon*, November 19, 1967; Daniel Schulman, *Sons of Wichita: How the Koch Brothers Became America's Most Powerful and Private Dynasty* (New York: Grand Central Publishing, 2014), 73–74.

39   *But Frederick, or "Freddie," as everybody knew him*: Daniel Schulman, "The 'Other' Koch Brother," *Vanity Fair*, May 19, 2014.

40   *He worked with an intense purpose*: Charles Koch, Williams, Paulson, Markel, interviews by author, 2013–16; Dick Dilsaver, "Koch Report Shows Firms Rank Among 'Big Ones,'" *Wichita Eagle*, June 27, 1968. This article quotes an anonymous source close to the Koch family as saying of Charles: "It's not easy to be a rich man's son and build a reputation of your own."

40   *The first pillar of the plan*: Pete Wittenberg, "Koch Building Cornerstone Falls on Walk," *Wichita Eagle*, August 14, 1967.

40   *The second pillar of Charles Koch's plan*: Williams, interview by author, 2014; Steve Sells, "Koch Companies Renamed: Sales Hit $250 million," *Wichita Eagle*, June 27, 1968.

40   *The third pillar was personal*: Brad Hall, Markel, Paulson, Williams, interviews by author, 2013–16; Guy Boulton, "Straight-shooting to the Top: Varner Quietly Helped Koch Prosper," *Wichita Eagle*, June 26, 1994.

41   *Charles Koch relied on Sterling Varner*: Markel, Hall, Paulson, Williams, interviews by author, 2013–16; Boulton, "Straight-shooting to the Top."

41   *"It's an orderly world"*: Charles Koch, interview by author, 2015.

41   *Koch read the work of Karl Marx*: Charles Koch, interview by author, 2015; Wenzl and Wilson, "Koch Relentless"; Jim Tankersley, "'I Don't Like the Idea of Capitalism': Charles Koch Unfiltered," *Washington Post*, August 1, 2016.

42   *In Hayek's view*: Jerry Z. Muller, *The Mind and the Market: Capitalism in Western Thought* (New York: Knopf, 2002), 347–87. Selected readings from Friedrich Hayek, including *The Constitution of Liberty* (Chicago: University of Chicago Press, 1960), and *Law, Legislation, and Liberty* (Chicago: University of Chicago Press, 1976).

43   *Roger Williams was an engineer*: Williams, interviews by author, 2014–16.

44   *Charles Koch wasn't wild about the idea*: Ibid.

44   *When he was in Wichita, Roger Williams*: Ibid.

45   *Varner was "opportunistic"*: Ibid.; Markel, Hall, interviews by author, 2014–16.

45   *A ritual was formed at these meetings*: Williams, Markel, Hall, Watson, background sources, interviews by author, 2014–16.

46 *The company directives that came out of Wichita*: Dubose, interviews by author, 2014–15.

46 *In 1968, Phil Dubose was working in a grocery store*: Ibid.

47 *Koch Industries hired Dubose*: Ibid.; Renee Ruble, "Koch Brothers Head Back to Federal Court in Latest Squabble," Associated Press, October 1, 1999, featuring court testimony from Dubose; Asjylyn Loder and David Evans, "The Secret Sins of Koch Industries," *Bloomberg Markets*, November 2011.

48 *The Koch method for oil measurement*: Dubose, interviews by author, 2014–15; Gene Poteet, James Spaulding, James Elroy, Testimony, Public Hearings of the Select Committee on Indian Affairs, May 9, 1989.

49 *At the end of each month, Koch tabulated*: Dubose, interviews by author, 2014–15.

49 *"You wanted to keep your company operating for sure"*: Barnett, interview by author, 2015.

49 *Keith Langhofer . . . Texas and New Mexico*: Keith Langhofer, deposition with US Senate investigators, transcript, April 24, 1989.

49 *It was clear to Dubose*: Dubose, interviews by author, 2014–15.

50 *Since the late 1950s, Fred Koch had owned*: Charles Koch, *Good Profit*, 33; court transcripts and exhibits, *William I. Koch et al. v. Koch Industries Inc. et al.*

50 *But the Pine Bend refinery . . . had a secret source of profits*: Richard H. K. Vietor, *Energy Policy in America since 1945: A Study of Business-Government Relations* (Cambridge, MA: Cambridge University Press, 1984), 128–30.

50 *Pine Bend was one of only four*: Ibid., 129.

50 *In 1969, Charles Koch executed a secret plan*: Charles Koch, *Good Profit*, 44–47.

51 *Workers at the Pine Bend refinery . . . the 1950s*: Paulson, Ernie Tromberg, Joseph Quinn, Lowell Payton, interviews by author, 2015.

51 *Paulson was living in Corpus Christi*: Paulson, interviews by author, 2015.

52 *In 1971, Paulson joined Koch Industries*: Ibid.; "Bernard A. Paulson, Executive Profile," *Bloomberg*; "Bernard A. Paulson Presented with the Albert Nelson Marquis Lifetime Achievement Award by Marquis Who's Who," Marquis Who's Who press release, September 7, 2018.

CHAPTER 3: THE WAR FOR PINE BEND

53 *Bernard Paulson arrived for his first day*: Paulson, interviews by author, 2015; physical descriptions of Pine Bend refinery from notes from reporting at Pine Bend, March 2015.

53 *Good-paying jobs were scarce*: Quinn, Payton, Tromberg, Jim Grotjohn, interviews by author, 2015.

54 *At the base of the giant towers . . . squat office building*: Notes from reporting at Pine Bend, March 2015.

55 *Bernard Paulson often wore cowboy boots*: Paulson, interviews by author, 2015.

55   *Oil arrived . . . giant, white tanks*: Payton, Quinn, Grotjohn, interviews by author, 2015; notes from reporting at Pine Bend, March 2015.

56   *After the oil is heated up, it undergoes a series*: Morgan Downey, ch. 7, "Refining," in *Oil 101* (Echo Park, CA: Wooden Table Press, 2009), 143–65.

56   *Paulson knew this business very well*: Paulson, Quinn, Payton, Tromberg, interviews by author, 2015.

57   *Men took an oath when they joined the OCAW*: Quinn, Payton, interviews by author, 2015.

57   *The union president . . . quantities of alcohol*: Ibid. (Joseph Hammerschmidt could not be interviewed for this book because he was killed in a roadside accident before reporting on the book began. Coworkers said he had pulled his car over to the side of the road, exited the vehicle, and was struck down by an oncoming car in the highway. Descriptions of Hammerschmidt are taken from his coworkers, including Bernard Paulson.) *The Facts Involved in the Strike Between Local 6-430, Oil, Chemical and Atomic Workers, AFL-CIO, and Red Wing Potteries, Inc.* (pamphlet, OCAW, 1967).

58   *During the . . . Pine Bend refinery*: Quinn, Payton, Tromberg, Grotjohn, Paulson, interviews by author, 2015.

59   *Paulson talked often to Charles Koch*: Paulson, interviews by author, 2015.

59   *Hammerschmidt, apparently, did not want to work on Easter*: "Refinery Union Leader's Dismissal Is Upheld," *Minneapolis Tribune*, June 26, 1973; Paulson, Quinn, interviews by author, 2015.

60   *In the late fall and early winter of 1972*: Quinn, Payton, Tromberg, Paulson, interviews by author, 2015; "Oil Refinery Workers Walk Out of Refinery to Defend Seniority," *Bulletin: Weekly Organ of the Workers League*, January 22, 1973.

61   *On January 9, 1973, at four in the afternoon*: "300 Workers Strike at Area Fuel-Oil Firm," *Star Tribune*, Minneapolis, January 10, 1973; "Plant Struck at Pine Bend," *Pioneer Press*, St. Paul (MN), January 10, 1973; Quinn, Payton, Tromberg, Paulson, interviews by author, 2015.

61   *Joseph Quinn, for example*: Quinn, interviews by author, 2015.

63   *Others showed up to get picket signs*: B. Wills, "Twin City Labor Rallies to Defend Oil Strikers," *Bulletin: Weekly Organ of the Workers League*, March 12, 1973; Quinn, interviews by author, 2015.

64   *On a typical day at the refinery, about two hundred*: Jim Jones, "Pine Bend Pickets Can Only Watch Oil Trucks Roll Along," *Star Tribune*, September 19, 1973.

64   *Paulson was prepared*: Paulson, interviews by author, 2015.

65   *Many members of this new workforce*: Quinn, Payton, Tromberg, Paulson, interviews by author, 2015; "Scabs Attack Oil Strikers," *Bulletin: Weekly Organ of the Workers League*, February 12, 1973.

66   *On the first night of the strike*: Paulson, Tromberg, interviews by author, 2015.

67   *Weeks passed*: "Strike Continues at Koch Refinery," *Star Tribune*, January 11, 1973;

Robert Hagen, "Two-Week Strike Hampers States Largest Refinery," *Star Tribune*, January 22, 1973.

67   *Ernie Tromberg, an OCAW employee*: Tromberg, interviews by author, 2015; "Scabs Attack Oil Strikers"; "Both Sides Take Shots at Sheriff," *Star Tribune*, January 24, 1973.

67   *Koch Refinery hired a private company called Wackenhut*: Mike James, "OCAW Strikers Defy Koch's Private Army," *Bulletin: Weekly Organ of the Workers League*, April 9, 1973; Payton, Tromberg, Quinn, interviews by author, 2015.

68   *When the workers got violent*: "Restraining Order Limits Pickets at Refining Plant," *Star Tribune*, January 25, 1973; Paulson, interviews by author, 2015.

68   *On Friday night, February 23*: "3 Charged in Violence at Refinery," Associated Press, February 28, 1973; "Koch Strikers' Case Continued," *Pioneer Press*, March 6, 1973; Paulson, interviews by author, 2015.

69   *Around this time, Bernard Paulson's wife*: Paulson, interviews by author, 2015.

69   *On the night of March 15*: Paulson, Quinn, Tromberg, Payton, interviews by author, 2015; "Train Run into Struck Refinery," *Star Tribune*, March 16, 1973; "Reward Set in Refinery Derailment," *Pioneer Press*, March 17, 1973.

72   *Charles Koch traveled to Pine Bend*: Paulson, interviews by author, 2015.

72   *After the crash . . . the OCAW*: Paulson, Quinn, interviews by author, 2015; "Koch, Union Talks Planned," *Pioneer Press*, March 26, 1973.

73   *On the night of April 17, an OCAW man was driving*: "Gunshots Fired Near Refinery, Police Hold Suspect," *Star Tribune*, April 18, 1973; "Plant-Shooting Suspect Held," *Star Tribune*, April 18, 1973; Grotjohn, Paulson, Payton, Tromberg, interviews by author, 2015.

73   *On June 2, 1973, John Kujawa traveled to Washington*: Hearings before the Subcommittee on Consumer Economics of the Joint Economic Committee, Congress of the United States, 251; Paulson, interviews by author, 2015.

74   *Koch Refining Company offered a $25,000 reward*: "Reward Set in Refinery Derailment," *Pioneer Press*, March 17, 1973.

74   *But Bernard Paulson and Charles Koch seemed to understand*: Paulson, Payton, Quinn, Tromberg, interviews by author, 2015.

75   *John Kujawa . . . did not talk about work*: Martha Ann Kujawa, interview by author, 2015.

76   *Paulson said that he was prepared to break*: Paulson, Payton, Quinn, Tromberg, interviews by author, 2015.

76   *On the evening of September 17*: "Koch Workers Reject Offer," *Pioneer Press*, September 18, 1973; "Koch Refining Strikers to Vote on Pact," *Star Tribune*, September 22, 1973.

76   *After the vote, Paulson gave the Teamsters an ultimatum*: Paulson, Payton, Quinn, Tromberg, interviews by author, 2015.

77   *On the evening of September 23*: "Employees End Koch Strike," *Pioneer Press*,

September 24, 1973; "Koch Refining Workers Going Back to Work," *Minneapolis Star*, September 24, 1973.

77   *OCAW workers like Ernie Tromberg and Joe Quinn*: Paulson, Quinn, Tromberg, interviews by author, 2015.

77   *The OCAW agreed . . . Koch Refining*: Paulson, Payton, Grotjohn, Quinn, Tromberg, interviews by author, 2015. Changes to the OCAW after the 1973 strike were also described by two sources, speaking on background, who currently work for the United Steelworkers union, which absorbed the OCAW many years after the strike of 1973. Sources also provided two labor contracts for the purpose of comparison with earlier agreements: USW Labor Agreement with Flint Hills Resources: November 3, 2006–June 13, 2011; and USW Labor Agreement with Flint Hills Resources: October 17, 2012–June 17, 2016. The sources provided a copy of the current USW labor contract for workers at Pine Bend, which could be compared with the 1972 contract as described by retired employees.

78   *Decades later . . . a sense of admiration, and almost awe*: Markel, Hall, Paulson, and three former senior Koch Industries sources speaking on background, interviews by author, 2013–17.

79   *Charles Koch didn't have any time to celebrate*: Charles Koch, *Good Profit*, 53–54.

79   *On September 24, the St. Paul* Pioneer Press: "Nixon Asks Wide Energy Power," *Pioneer Press*, November 26, 1973.

CHAPTER 4: THE AGE OF VOLATILITY INTENSIFIES

80   *The trouble started on October 6, 1973*: Yergin, *The Prize*, 606–9.

81   *The price shock caused a calamity*: Charles Koch, *Good Profit*, 53–54; Hall, interviews by author, 2013–15.

81   *Charles Koch . . . profit from them*: Koch, Markel, Hall, Paulson, Williams, background sources, interviews by author, 2013–17; Leonard, "The New Koch."

82   *Even in the face of a downturn . . . long-term profitability*: Paulson, interviews by author, 2015; court transcripts and exhibits *William I. Koch et al. v. Koch Industries Inc. et al.*

82   *Bernard Paulson moved to Wichita*: Paulson, interviews by author, 2015.

84   *Charles Koch quickly grasped the potential*: Paulson, Hall, interviews by author, 2013–15.

85   *The strategy worked*: *William I. Koch et al. v. Koch Industries Inc. et al.*, Jury Trial Transcript, vol. 52, 5011.

86   *Koch Industries' own confidential financial documents . . . company's fortunes*: Koch Industries Consolidated Income Summary, 1981–1982, presented at Koch Industries Board of Directors Meeting, March 15, 1983.

86   *Bernard Paulson was often contacted*: Paulson, Hall, interviews by author, 2015.

86   *Information analysis was only part of the strategy*: Paulson, Markel, Hall, interviews by author, 2013–15.

87   *When Markel arrived at the club*: Markel, interviews by author, 2013–14.

88   *Charles Koch told Markel that he was sorry*: Ibid.

89   *Like many other people at the company, Markel*: Markel, Hall, and former senior Koch Industries source speaking on background, interviews by author, 2013–14.

91   *Koch made full use of this strategy*: Williams, interviews by author, 2014.

91   *During this time . . . thinkers like Hayek and von Mises*: Charles G. Koch, "Anticapitalism and Business," address to the Institute for Humane Studies, April 27, 1974.

92   *On November 7, 1973 . . . sweeping government response*: Vietor, *Energy Policy in America since 1945*, 238–52; Joseph P. Kalt, *Economics and Politics of Oil Price Regulation: Federal Policy in the Post-Embargo Era* (Cambridge, MA: MIT Press, 1981), 9–15; Rick Perlstein, *The Invisible Bridge: The Fall of Nixon and the Rise of Reagan* (New York: Simon & Schuster, 2014), 162–63.

92   *"It will be essential . . . to live and work in lower temperatures"*: Richard Nixon, address to the nation, November 8, 1973, www.youtube.com/watch?v=iuvEVwox5L8.

92   *FDR's actions were a response to decades of economic stagnation*: Michael Lind, interview by author, 2014; Joshua Waimberg, "*Lochner v. New York*: Fundamental Rights and Economic Liberty," *Constitution Daily* (blog), National Constitution Center online, last modified October 25, 2015; Doris Kearns Goodwin, *The Bully Pulpit: Theodore Roosevelt, William Howard Taft, and the Golden Age of Journalism* (New York: Simon & Schuster, 2013); Arthur M. Schlesinger Jr., *The Age of Roosevelt*, vol. 1, *The Crisis of the Old Order* (Boston: Houghton Mifflin, 1957).

93   *When FDR was elected in 1932 . . . the hands-off era came to an end*: Kennedy, *Freedom from Fear*; Arthur M. Schlesinger Jr., *The Age of Roosevelt*, vol. 2, *The Coming of the New Deal* (Boston: Houghton Mifflin, 1958); Hacker and Pierson, *American Amnesia*.

94   *The council put a hard cap on "old" oil of $5.25 per barrel*: CAW, "National Energy Goals and FEA's Mandatory Crude Oil Allocation Program," *Virginia Law Review* 61, no. 4 (May 1975): 903–37.

94   *This incensed Charles Koch*: Koch, "Anti-Capitalism and Business," April 27, 1974; Charles G. Koch, letter in support of the Libertarian Party, addressed to "Dear Rocky Mountain Oilman," dated December 23, 1975.

95   *He owned a small bookstore . . . conservative literature*: "Two Birch Society Members Open Book Store," *Wichita Eagle*, July 15, 1975.

95   *He attended and gave money to the Freedom School*: Jane Mayer, *Dark Money: The Hidden History of the Billionaires Behind the Rise of the Radical Right* (New York: Doubleday, 2016), 44–46.

95   *In April of 1974, Charles Koch gave a speech at a gathering in Dallas*: Koch, "Anti-Capitalism and Business," April 27, 1974.

97   *By 1975 . . . not going to go under*: Hall, Markel, Paulson, interviews by author, 2013–15; Charles Koch, *Good Profit*, 54–56.

97   *Standing before the gathering of his brain trust*: Paulson, interviews by author, 2015.

97   *To a remarkable extent . . . pushed out*: Paulson, Markel, Hall, Williams, Watson, interviews by author, 2013–15.

CHAPTER 5: THE WAR FOR KOCH INDUSTRIES

99   *Bill Koch became a full-time Koch Industries employee in 1975*: William I. Koch et al. v. Koch Industries Inc. et al., Jury Trial Transcript, vol. 56, 5468; Roskind, interviews by author, 2015.

99   *Koch's trading division . . . virtually every American*: Howell, Roskind, Hall, background sources, interviews by author, 2013–16; *The Global Source for Commodities: Koch Supply & Trading*, company overview brochure, 2013; Charles Koch, *The Science of Success*, appendix A: "Products Traded," 167.

99   *Bill came across . . . graduated from MIT*: Roskind, Hall, interviews by author, 2013–15; Burrough, "Wild Bill Koch."

100   *As a trader, Roskind . . . industrial chemicals*: Roskind, interviews by author, 2015.

101   *Roskind went to Wichita . . . met Bill Koch's older brother*: Ibid.

102   *Roskind's office opened at eight thirty . . . trading began almost immediately*: Ibid.

103   *Chemical trading wasn't a simple matter of buying low and selling high*: Roskind, Howell, Hall, background sources, interviews by author, 2013–16.

104   *Like all senior executives at Koch Industries . . . provide updates*: Herbert, Hall, Markel, Paulson, background sources, interviews by author, 2013–16.

104   *After his successes . . . Bill Koch got a promotion*: Roskind, Hall, interviews by author, 2013–16; William I. Koch et al. v. Koch Industries Inc. et al., Jury Trial Transcript, vol. 21, 1999.

104   *One of Bill's staffers . . . Brad Hall*: Hall, interviews by author, 2013–18.

105   *Bill Koch became enamored of the kind of data-driven analysis*: Ibid.

106   *Early in the afternoon, Bill Koch called the office to check in on Hall's progress*: Ibid.

106   *Hall finished the Monte Carlo simulations*: Ibid.

107   *Like all vice presidents . . . battery of probing questions*: Ibid.; William I. Koch et al. v. Koch Industries Inc. et al., Jury Trial Transcript, vols. 21, 23, 24, and 28.

108   *Bill's requests . . . started to take an accusatory tone*: William I. Koch et al. v. Koch Industries Inc. et al., Jury Trial Transcript, vols. 52–59.

108   *There was a problem at a Koch Industries office in Denver*: William I. Koch et al. v. Koch Industries Inc. et al., Jury Trial Transcript, vol. 57, 5494–546.

108   *Bill Koch was doing more than asking questions*: William I. Koch et al. v. Koch Industries Inc. et al., Jury Trial Transcript, vol. 52, 5089; vol. 54, 5263–72; vol. 57, 5506.

109   *On April 27, 1980 . . . a handwritten note*: William I. Koch et al. v. Koch Industries Inc. et al., Jury Trial Transcript, vol. 52, 5089; vol. 54, 5271.

109   *On June 12, 1980, he sent a memo to Charles*: William I. Koch et al. v. Koch Industries Inc. et al., Jury Trial Transcript, vol. 52, 5089; vol. 54, 5274.

110   *In a lengthy interview with* Vanity Fair: Burrough, "Wild Bill Koch."

110   *Charles called Bill at the end of June*: William I. Koch et al. v. Koch Industries Inc. et al., Jury Trial Transcript, vol. 52, 5089; vol. 59, 5731–34.

110   *The memo was ten pages long, single-spaced*: William I. Koch et al. v. Koch Industries Inc. et al., Jury Trial Transcript, vol. 54, 5284.

111   *In early July, Koch Industries held an emergency meeting*: William I. Koch et al. v. Koch Industries Inc. et al., Jury Trial Transcript, vols. 21 and 54.

112   *Starting in 1980 . . . political activity*: Confessore, "Quixotic '80 Campaign."

112   *Chris Hocker, wrote Charles Koch a thank-you letter*: Chris Hocker, letter to Charles Koch, dated July 14, 1978.

112   *Charles Koch advised . . . over the years*: Charles Koch, letter to Chris Hocker, dated February 13, 1978.

112   *He wrote a Libertarian campaign letter in 1975*: Charles G. Koch, letter in support of the Libertarian Party, addressed to "Dear Rocky Mountain Oilman," dated December 23, 1975.

113   *While Charles Koch . . . David Koch contacted the Libertarian Party*: Confessore, "Quixotic '80 Campaign."

114   *Charles wanted to share his thoughts on two issues*: William I. Koch et al. v. Koch Industries Inc. et al., Jury Trial Transcript, vol. 54, 5306.

115   *"I said, 'Bill, what? Why are you doing this?'"*: William I. Koch et al. v. Koch Industries Inc. et al., Jury Trial Transcript, vol. 54, 5314.

116   *The day after Thanksgiving, Charles got a call from David*: William I. Koch et al. v. Koch Industries Inc. et al., Jury Trial Transcript, vol. 55, 5322.

116   *Charles Koch boarded a private jet Thanksgiving weekend*: William I. Koch et al. v. Koch Industries Inc. et al., Jury Trial Transcript, vol. 55, 5327–40.

117   *When they were children . . . polo mallet*: Burrough, "Wild Bill Koch."

117   *There was a board meeting on December 5*: William I. Koch et al. v. Koch Industries Inc. et al., Jury Trial Transcript, vol. 55, 5334–42.

118   *Charles pressed his case . . . a convincing one*: William I. Koch et al. v. Koch Industries Inc. et al., Jury Trial Transcript, vol. 52, 5085–86.

118   *Bill and Fred Koch . . . Charles and David*: Brian O'Reilly and Patty De Llosa, "The Curse on the Koch Brothers," *Fortune*, February 17, 1997; Boulton, "Koch and His Empire."

119   *When it came time to close the deal . . . Brad Hall*: Hall, interviews by author, 2013–14.

CHAPTER 6: KOCH UNIVERSITY

120   *In the early 1980s . . . Charles Koch began to reveal*: Markel, Hall, Paulson, Dubose, interviews by author, 2013–15.

121   *These teachings—the "classic Sterling" guidelines*: Ibid.; Boulton, "Straight-shooting to the Top."

122   *W. Edwards Deming was not simply a business consultant*: David Halberstam, *The Reckoning* (New York: William Morrow, 1986), 311–18.

122   *"Deming's passion was for making better products"*: Ibid.

122   *After rising through the company ranks*: Dubose, interviews by author, 2014–15.

124   *All the while, he was in contact with managers from Wichita*: Ibid.

124   *One of the most important elements . . . the need to expand*: Markel, Hall, Paulson, Watson, background sources, interviews by author, 2013–15; Leslie Wayne, "Pulling the Wraps Off Koch Industries," *New York Times*, November 20, 1994.

125   *Brooks was part of a small cadre . . . in the mid-1980s*: Markel, Hall, interviews by author, 2013–14; Wayne, "Pulling the Wraps Off"; Boulton, "Koch and His Empire."

125   *Over time . . . blue-sky studies*: Hall, interviews by author, 2013–14.

126   *The development group made its first major deal*: Paulson, interviews by author, 2015.

127   *In September of 1981, Koch Industries paid $265 million*: Phillip Wiggins, "Sun to Sell a Refinery to Koch," *New York Times*, September 25, 1981.

128   *In 1987, Phil Dubose got the promotion*: Dubose, interviews by author, 2014–15; "Koch Brothers Head Back to Federal Court in Latest Squabble," Associated Press, October 1, 1999; Loder and Evans, "The Secret Sins of Koch Industries."

CHAPTER 7: THE ENEMIES CIRCLE

130   *The issue of oil theft . . . focused exclusively on Koch Industries*: Transcript of the Public Hearings of the Select Committee on Indian Affairs, May 9, 1989; Ballen, Elroy, DeConcini, background source, interviews by author, 2014–16.

131   *This legal threat coincided with another attack from Bill Koch*: O'Reilly and De Llosa, "The Curse"; Burrough, "Wild Bill Koch."

132   *the federal investigation . . . federal prosecutor named Nancy S. Jones*: Nancy Jones, Timothy Leonard, Elroy, interviews by author, 2014–18; details of the investigation are also based on the FBI case file, released for the first time in 2018 to the author, with minor redactions, including several hundred pages of internal FBI memos and interview transcripts.

132   *Jones was skeptical, at first*: Nancy Jones, interviews by author, 2015–2016. During interviews for this book, Jones refused to discuss what the grand jury learned, or the specific evidence presented to it, due to confidentiality rules. She refused to say whom the jury called as witnesses, or what documents it might have obtained. But the confidentiality rules allowed her to discuss her strategy in the case and how the case progressed over the months.

133   *As Jones pressed her case from the US Attorney's office*: *United States of America ex rel. William I. Koch and William A. Presley, Plaintiffs, v. Koch Industries, Inc., et al., Defendants*, Order, August 6, 1998, 7.a.

133 *Koch Industries responded by circling the wagons*: United States of America ex rel. William I. Koch and William A. Presley, Plaintiffs, v. Koch Industries, Inc., et al., Defendants. Order, August 6, 1998.

133 *The standards of conduct said*: Ibid., 5.a–c.

134 *On July 11, 1988, Koch's president, Bill Hanna*: Ibid., 5.d.

134 *Bill Koch only fed into the company's sense of embattlement*: Elroy, Dubose, interviews by author, 2014–15; FBI internal memorandum, "Koch Industries Incorporated, Wichita, Kansas; CRIME ON AN INDIAN RESERVATION—THEFT; RACKETEERING INFLUENCE AND CORRUPT ORGANIZATION," July 26, 1989; Burrough, "Wild Bill Koch."

135 *Charles Koch did more than circle the wagons*: "Before the Special Committee on Investigations, Select Committee on Indian Affairs, United States Senate: Statement by Koch Industries, Inc.," submitted June 7, 1989.

135 *But when faced with . . . Koch redirected his political efforts*: Howell, interviews by author, 2015–16; Phillip L. Zweig and Michael Schroeder, "Bob Dole's Oil Patch Pals," *Bloomberg Businessweek*, April 1, 1996.

136 *Koch's first tactical goal . . . issue of oil theft*: Howell, interviews by author, 2015–16; Zweig and Schroeder, "Bob Dole's Oil Patch Pals."

136 *One of the primary victims . . . Osage tribe in Oklahoma*: Charles O. Tillman, interview by author, 2015.

137 *Tillman and other Osage leaders went public*: "Osages Deny Tribe Swindled in Oil Deals," *Tulsa Tribune*, March 21, 1990; Bob Vandewater, "Osage Royalties Probe Calls Oil Payments Fair," *Daily Oklahoman*, March 21, 1990.

138 *Koch Industries deepened its relationship with Kansas senator Bob Dole*: Bob Dole, interview by author, 2016; Zweig and Schroeder, "Bob Dole's Oil Patch Pals."

138 *Dole helped Koch delegitimize the issue*: "Investigation of Indian Oil Purchase," Bob Dole submission to US Congressional Record, March 26, 1990.

138 *As senators fought . . . Koch put another piece of its plan into place*: Howell, interviews by author, 2015–16; John J. Fialka, "How Koch Industries Tries to Influence Judicial System," *Wall Street Journal*, August 9, 1999.

139 *Michael Corrigan attended a Koch-sponsored seminar*: Fialka, "How Koch Industries Tries."

139 *The Law & Economics Center claimed*: Law & Economics Center website, https://masonlec.org.

140 *Jones and Elroy . . . Koch's internal documents*: Nancy Jones, Elroy, interviews by author, 2014–16.

140 *Nicastro was no ordinary document courier*: David Nicastro, deposition with US Senate investigators, transcript, April 24, 1989; United States of America ex rel. William I. Koch and William A. Presley, Plaintiffs, v. Koch Industries, Inc., et al., Defendants, Order, August 6, 1998, 45.b.i.

140 *When the Oklahoma grand jury . . . Nicastro apparently made a special trip*: Nancy

Jones, interviews by author, 2015–16. David Nicastro declined to be interviewed. He left Koch Industries after these events and became president of Secure Source International, an independent corporate security firm. On his website, Nicastro claims to be able to penetrate even the most sophisticated corporate security systems, as a way to show clients how those systems are vulnerable.

141   *Then something happened that punctured a hole in the case:* Elroy, Nancy Jones, interviews by author, 2014–15.

141   *In Elroy's absence . . . Koch's favor:* FBI "302" reports summarizing interviews with Koch gaugers in in Oklahoma and Texas, 1990; FBI internal memorandum, Subject: "Koch Industries," August 20, 1990; FBI internal memorandum, 196B-OC-48271: "[L]eads assigned in June 1991 have been put on hold until further notice."

142   *one gauger was interviewed in a Dairy Queen parking lot:* FBI 302 report (REV. 3-10-82), June 18, 1991.

142   *The FBI was searching . . . shakeup at the US Attorney's office:* Nancy Jones, Leonard, Don Nickles, interviews by author, 2015–2018; Zweig and Schroeder, "Bob Dole's Oil Patch Pals."

142   *She said there was lukewarm enthusiasm . . . the Koch case:* This account is based on Nancy Jones's recollection of events. Arlene Joplin refused to discuss the meeting or anything having to do with the Koch Industries investigation.

143   *In April of 1991 . . . Nickles nominated Timothy Leonard:* Nancy Jones, Leonard, Nickles, interviews by author, 2015–18.

143   *Leonard's decision raised suspicion:* Zweig and Schroeder, "Bob Dole's Oil Patch Pals"; Mayer, *Dark Money*, 133–34.

143   *The FBI's case file . . . not to file charges:* FBI internal memorandum, Subject: "Koch Industries," August 20, 1990. The memo states, in part: "During this sixty (60) day period the writer has received eighteen (18) FD-302's from interviews of Oklahoma guager, relief gaugers and gauger/drivers. All of these interviews, with the exception of one, have been negative concerning alleged violations. The only positive information . . . attributes this practice to laziness on the part of the gauger." FBI internal memorandum, 196B-OC-48271: "[L]eads assigned in June 1991 have been put on hold until further notice."

153   *it was assistant US Attorney H. Lee Schmidt:* FBI internal memorandum, Subject: "Koch Industries, Inc., Wichita, Kansas' Fraud by Wire," February 12, 1992.

144   *During an interview in his home:* Leonard, Nickles, interviews by author, 2018.

145   *case went to trial in Tulsa in late 1999:* "Judge Finds Sufficient Evidence to Take Koch Lawsuit to Trial," Associated Press, August 10, 1999.

145   *During the trial, Koch officials admitted:* Ruble, "Koch Brothers Head Back to Federal Court in Latest Squabble." Story included the statement "Koch Industries officials concede the company made about $10 million in profit per year from the overages. But they say that was only a small amount of the company's overall intake."

145   *Jack Crossen, a district gauger for Koch*: Ruble, "Former Employees Testify at Federal Trial of Koch Industries," Associated Press, October 5, 1999, and October 6, 1999.

145   *Ricky Fisher said he rationalized stealing oil*: Renee Ruble, "Former Measurement Supervisor Takes Stand," Associated Press, October 12, 1999.

146   *The fines for Koch could have been enormous*: Danny M. Boyd, "Penalty Against Koch Approaches Settlement," Associated Press, October 26, 2000; *United States of America ex rel. William I. Koch and William A. Presley, Plaintiffs, v. Koch Industries, Inc., et al., Defendants*, Verdict Form 1, Verdict Form 2, December 23, 1999.

146   *The deep changes . . . Reagan presidency*: Budget figures drawn from United States Budget, 1981–1988, *Inside Government*, Office of Management and Budget.

147   *The trend continued under Bill Clinton*: Gimore and Sugrue, *These United States*, 576–95.

147   *the overall size and burden of the federal government continued to grow*: Clyde Wayne Crews Jr., *Ten Thousand Commandments: A Policymaker's Snapshot of the Federal Regulatory State* (Washington, DC: Competitive Enterprise Institute, 1996).

148   *There was . . . between government and private enterprise*: Hacker and Pierson, *American Amnesia*.

148   *But a loophole . . . apply only to new oil refineries*: Dianne M. Shawley, former senior counsel, Environment and Natural Resources Division, US Department of Justice, interviews by author, 2016. Shawley participated in a federal effort to enforce the new source review process of the Clean Air Act, resulting in settlements with Koch Industries and other oil refiners. Also Shi-Ling Hsu, "What's Old Is New: The Problem with New Source Review," *Regulation*, Spring 2006; Jonathan Remy Nash and Richard L. Reeves, "Grandfathering and Environmental Regulation: The Law and Economics of New Source Review," *Northwestern University Law Review* 101, no. 4 (2007).

149   *Oil companies expanded . . . gaming the New Source Review program*: Shawley, interviews by author, 2016; Suzanne Gamboa, "Refiner Agrees to Pollution Controls," Associated Press, December 22, 2000.

149   *After the Watergate scandal of the early 1970s*: Zephyr Teachout, interview by author, 2017; Zephyr Teachout, *Corruption in America: From Benjamin Franklin's Snuff Box to Citizens United* (Cambridge, MA: Harvard University Press, 2014).

150   *In 1996 . . . Economic Education Trust*: Glenn R. Simpson, "New Data Shows That Koch Firm Funded GOP TV Ads in '96 Races," *Wall Street Journal*, June 1, 1998.

150   *In October of 1996, the Economic Education Trust gave $1.79 million*: "Investigation of Illegal or Improper Activities in Connection with 1996 Federal Election Campaigns," *US Senate Report* 5, no. 167 (1998): 6309.

150   *Triad was . . . had a strange business model*: Ibid., 6289–313; *US Senate Report* 4, no. 167 (1998): 4603.

150   *One of Triad's consultants . . . designed specifically to shield the wealthy*: US Senate Report 5, no. 167 (1998): 6311.

151   *"Most disturbing, Triad is poised to become a model"*: Ibid., 6290.

151   *Koch Industries' political operations . . . inside the company*: Markel, Hall, interviews by author, 2013–14; Boulton, "Koch and His Empire"; Boulton, "Straight-shooting to the Top."

151   *Charles Koch's office was located on the third floor*: Notes and photos from reporting at Koch Industries headquarters and Charles Koch's office, 2015.

152   *Charles Koch liked to tell people that "true knowledge results in effective action"*: Boulton, "Koch and His Empire."

152   *One of the first things Charles Koch did . . . get the rules written down*: Wayne Gable and Jerry Ellig, *Introduction to Market-Based Management* (Fairfax, VA: Center for Market Progress, 1993).

152   *The words of Market-Based Management were not simple slogans*: Dozens of current and former Koch Industries executives and employees, Markel, Hall, Watson, interviews by author, 2013–18.

CHAPTER 8: THE SECRET BROTHERHOOD OF PROCESS OWNERS

154   *Heather Faragher . . . winter of 1995*: Heather Faragher, interviews by author, 2015; Heather Faragher, transcript of interview with Minnesota Pollution Control Agency (hereafter cited as MPCA) investigators, December 19, 1997.

154   *The empty fields . . . sky was often slate gray*: Notes from reporting at the Pine Bend refinery in March 2015.

154   *Faragher joined the company*: Faragher, interviews by author, 2015; Heather Faragher, transcript of interview by MPCA investigators, December 19, 1997.

155   *It would be inaccurate to describe . . . corporate training*: Faragher, and dozens of other current and former Koch Industries employees, interviews by author, 2013–18.

156   *She watched while her bosses and coworkers broke the law*: Accounts in this chapter are based in part on transcripts of lengthy interviews that the primary actors gave to investigators with the MPCA in 1997. Citations of interview transcripts often include a page number corresponding to germane sections of the interview in question, but those pages are not the only source for information in this narrative—details of each episode are often reinforced by statements elsewhere in the interview and by interviews with other participants. It is the overlapping accounts of all the interviews, in full, that undergird the narrative in this chapter. The interview transcripts are supplemented by interviews with participants, newspaper accounts, and court filings.

156   *Faragher's experience . . . problems at Koch Industries during the 1990s*: Loder and Evans, "The Secret Sins of Koch Industries."

157   *Heather Faragher . . . small town of Bayport, Minnesota*: Faragher, Lawrence, interviews by author, 2015; US Census data on Bayport, Minnesota.

159   *In 1992, Koch launched . . . make cleaner fuels*: "Koch Begins Construction on Clean Fuels Project," PR Newswire, March 24, 1992.

159   *In 1995, Koch was considering a new $300 million project*: "Koch Refining Eyes Building 250-MW Petroleum-Coke Fired Unit in Minn.," *Industrial Energy Bulletin*, May 19, 1995.

159   *The production capacity . . . during this time*: "Annual Refining Capacity," *Oil & Gas Journal*, March 18, 1985; ibid., March 18, 1986; ibid., March 18, 1995; ibid., March 18, 1996.

160   *The rapid expansion created strains*: Faragher, interviews by author, 2015; Faragher, Brian Roos, Steve David, Tim Rusch, Larry Barnett, Terry Stormoen, Joseph Butzer, Charlie Chadwell, Gary Ista, Todd Aalto, Karen Hall, Ruth Estes, Eric Askeland, Rick Legvold, transcripts of interviews by MPCA investigators, December 19, 1997; "Whistleblower Trial Against Koch Refinery Begins in Federal Court," Associated Press, January 4, 2000.

160   *Karen Hall oversaw the division*: Karen Hall, transcript of interview by MPCA investigators, November 4, 1997.

160   *Faragher's glass-walled office was located next to Hall's*: Faragher, interviews by author, 2015.

160   *The refinery pumped . . . every day*: Roos, transcript of interview by MPCA investigators, November 17, 1997, 64; Faragher, interviews by author, 2015.

161   *There was, in fact, a stark division of power*: Faragher, interviews by author, 2015. Safety officials like Faragher are considered as working for "nonprofit" centers at Koch Industries, while managers who operate the facilities are considered "property owners." Koch sought to contain expenses within its "nonprofit" functions. Gable and Ellig, *Introduction to Market-Based Management*, 41–46.

162   *Karen Hall explained . . . the operations people*: Karen Hall, transcript of interview by MPCA investigators, November 4, 1997, 14.

162   *The operations team that Faragher reported to was run by . . . Brian Roos*: Faragher, interviews by author, 2015; Roos, transcript of interview by MPCA investigators, November 17, 1997, 64.

162   *The refinery at Pine Bend was divided into five groups*: Faragher, interviews by author, 2015; Karen Hall, transcript of interview by MPCA investigators, November 4, 1997, 19–20; Roos, transcript of interview by MPCA investigators, November 17, 1997, 5–6.

163   *Environmental engineers . . . nonprofit groups*: Gable and Ellig, *Introduction to Market-Based Management*, 41–46.

163   *Heather Faragher spent a lot of time walking*: Faragher, interviews by author, 2015.

164   *One of the operators . . . Todd Aalto*: Todd Aalto, transcript of interview by MPCA investigators, November 6, 1997.

164 *When inspecting . . . the concrete floor*: Ibid., 50.

164 *In this case, the decision would have gone up to Karen Hall's boss*: Steven David, transcript of interview by MPCA investigators, November 19, 1997.

164 *Faragher proposed new investments and upgrades . . . those investments were delayed*: Faragher, interviews by author, 2015; Faragher, transcript of interview by MPCA investigators, December 19, 1997.

165 *"If the payback of the investment was going to be less"*: Faragher, interviews by author, 2015.

165 *At the Pine Bend refinery, Koch was allowed to expel*: WWTP Spec Sheet, Pine Bend refinery, May 1995; Faragher, interviews by author, 2015.

166 *One day, Steve David . . . Koch method of wastewater treatment*: Notes and drawings of charts at meeting, made extemporaneously and provided later to author; Faragher, interviews by author, 2015.

166 *Things started going wrong around June 1, 1996*: Timothy Rusch, plant manager, transcript of interview by MPCA investigators, November 18, 1997, 22–23; Karen Hall, transcript of interview by MPCA investigators, November 4, 1997.

167 *Doing so would require a partial outage*: Roos, transcript of interview by MPCA investigators, November 17, 1997, 59.

167 *The fine for doing so would have only been about $30,000*: Rusch, transcript of interview by MPCA investigators, November 18, 1997, 30.

167 *Brian Roos discussed this problem*: Roos, transcript of interview by MPCA investigators, November 17, 1997, 44, 66–67, 74.

167 *From the control room . . . water that was flushed*: Aalto, transcript of interview by MPCA investigators, November 6, 1997.

168 *In June of 1996, operators like Aalto . . . detention ponds*: Roos, transcript of interview by MPCA investigators, November 17, 1997, 74; Rusch, transcript of interview by MPCA investigators, November 18, 1997, 22.

169 *As water kept stacking up . . . a novel idea*: Roos, transcript of interview by MPCA investigators, November 17, 1997, 44.

169 *Roos downplayed the risk*: Ibid.

169 *Nobody told Heather Faragher*: Faragher, transcript of interview by MPCA investigators, December 19, 1997, 23–25.

169 *Every weekday morning at seven*: Faragher, interviews by author, 2015; Faragher, transcript of interview by MPCA investigators, December 19, 1997, 23–25.

171 *On October 24, 1996, Heather Faragher sent a memo*: Faragher, transcript of interview by MPCA investigators, December 19, 1997, 40; Roos, transcript of interview by MPCA investigators, November 17, 1997, 62–63; Estes, transcript of interview by MPCA investigators, October 31, 1997, 41.

171 *Todd Aalto . . . at the wastewater plant*: Aalto, transcript of interview by MPCA investigators, November 6, 1997, 24–28; Roos, transcript of interview by MPCA investigators, November 17, 1997, 63–64; Rusch, transcript of interview by MPCA

investigators, November 18, 1997, 24; David, transcript of interview by MPCA investigators, November 19, 1997, 95.

171 *"I hope these moves prove sufficient"*: Roos, transcript of interview by MPCA investigators, November 17, 1997, 64.

171 *Estes was the shift supervisor on duty*: Estes, transcript of interview by MPCA investigators, October 31, 1997, 44–45.

172 *At seven o'clock . . . to the hydrants*: Ista, transcript of interview by MPCA investigators, October 31, 1997, 31–36, 54; Russ Hawkinson, transcript of interview by MPCA investigators, December 19, 1997, 8, 17; Aalto, transcript of interview by MPCA investigators, November 6, 1997, 20.

172 *On the morning of November 4 . . . detention ponds*: Faragher, interviews by author, 2015; Faragher, transcript of interview by MPCA investigators, December 19, 1997, 24.

172 *Estes later told state investigators*: Estes, transcript of interview by MPCA investigators, October 31, 1997, 35–38.

173 *They reached Jim Voyles . . . in Wichita*: Faragher, interviews by author, 2015; Faragher, transcript of interview by MPCA investigators, December 19, 1997, 25–28.

173 *Faragher reported directly to the Minnesota Pollution Control Agency*: Faragher, interviews by author, 2015; Faragher, transcript of interview by MPCA investigators, December 19, 1997.

174 *Ruth Estes was the shift supervisor on Saturday*: Estes, transcript of interview by MPCA investigators, October 31, 1997, 32–61; Roos, transcript of interview by MPCA investigators, November 17, 1997, 42; Faragher, transcript of interview by MPCA investigators, December 19, 1997, 31–37; Karen Hall, transcript of interview by MPCA investigators, November 4, 1997, 49–52.

176 *Aalto walked along a tree line that bordered an empty field*: Aalto, transcript of interview by MPCA investigators, November 6, 1997, 20.

176 *Heather Faragher returned . . . glass-walled office*: Faragher, interviews by author, 2015; Faragher, transcript of interview by MPCA investigators, December 19, 1997.

177 *On January 17, Faragher . . . dozens of employees*: Heather Faragher to Pine Bend supervisors and employees, memo, January 17, 1997.

178 *Before she sent the letter to the state*: Faragher, draft letter, 1997.

178 *Voyles deleted that entire paragraph*: Faragher, interviews by author, 2015; edited version of Faragher draft letter, 1997.

179 *Faragher spilled her story*: Ibid.

180 *On February 18, Brian Roos sent a memo*: Roos, transcript of interview by MPCA investigators, November 17, 1997, 82–85.

180 *Koch Industries opened the fire hydrants and spewed ammonia-laden water*: Faragher, transcript of interview by MPCA investigators, December 19, 1997, 142–44; Roos, transcript of interview by MPCA investigators, November 17, 1997,

74–77; Ista, transcript of interview by MPCA investigators, October 31, 1997, 45–46; Chadwell, transcript of interview by MPCA investigators, November 20, 1997; Stormoen, transcript of interview by MPCA investigators, November 6, 1997.

180 *This was just one . . . during the 1990s*: Grotjohn, background sources, interviews by author, 2015.

181 *Longtime employees like Charlie Chadwell wanted*: Chadwell, transcript of interview by MPCA investigators, November 20, 1997; Dennis Lien, "Koch Casts Doubt on Whistle-Blower's Motives; His Mental State and Conduct Are Scrutinized," *Pioneer Press*, January 12, 2000; Dennis Lien, "Former Koch Employee Says She Was Subjected to Retaliation; Engineer's Testimony Supports Whistleblower," *Pioneer Press*, January 11, 2000; Charles S. Chadwell v. Koch Refining Company, United States Court of Appeals, Eighth Circuit ruling, May 17, 2001.

181 *On April 8, 1997, Steve David*: Faragher, interviews by author, 2015; Faragher, transcript of interview by MPCA investigators, December 19, 1997, 147–51.

183 *David would later say that he hid the fact*: David, transcript of interview by MPCA investigators, November 19, 1997, 73–79.

184 *This was how Koch Industries wanted it*: Tromberg, interviews by author, 2015.

184 *On May 12, Faragher called Kriens*: Faragher, interviews by author, 2015; Faragher, transcript of interview by MPCA investigators, December 19, 1997.

184 *Faragher kept her mouth shut at work*: Faragher, interviews by author, 2015; Faragher, transcript of interview by MPCA investigators, December 19, 1997; Lien, "Former Koch Employee Says"; Lien, "Koch Casts Doubt."

186 *On March 18, 1998, Faragher was home*: Faragher, interviews by author, 2015; copies of business cards, John Bonhage and Maureen O'Mara.

187 *In 1998, the Minnesota Pollution Control Agency fined Koch Industries*: "Koch Refinery Hit with Fines," *Oil & Gas Journal*, October 11, 1999; United States of America and the State of Minnesota v. Koch Petroleum Group, Consent Decree.

187 *Koch did not retaliate against Faragher by firing her*: Faragher, interviews by author, 2015; Lien, "Former Koch Employee Says."

188 *Terry Stormoen, the other shift worker*: Interview attempt with Stormoen by author, 2015.

188 *Not everyone did so poorly*: Online job descriptions, résumés, Koch Industries employee listings.

188 *The illegal activity at Pine Bend was not an isolated incident*: Loder and Evans, "The Secret Sins of Koch Industries."

CHAPTER 9: OFF THE RAILS

191 *Koch Industries executives gathered . . . in Wichita*: Watson, Hall, interviews by author, 2013–16; John Pitinger, Participant Profile, Aspen Institute, Communica-

tions and Society Program; "Innovation: Everyone's Job," *Discovery: The Quarterly Newsletter of Koch Companies*, October 2016.

193 *Dean Watson joined . . . twenty-two years old*: Watson, interviews by author, 2016.

194 *Watson wasn't shy about challenging the people around him*: Watson, Hall, interviews by author, 2013–16.

194 *Koch's fertilizer plant was basically an oil refinery*: Joe Hise, former fertilizer plant manager in Enid, Oklahoma, interviews by author, 2013; insight into the American food system derives in part from the author's previous reporting as national agribusiness reporter for the Associated Press between 2008 and 2012.

195 *fertilizer business itself was a platform for growth*: Watson, Packebush, interviews by author, 2013–16; Bruce Upbin and Brandon Copple, "Creative Destruction 101," profile of Koch Industries and Koch Agriculture, *Forbes*, December 14, 1998.

196 *Koch Agriculture first branched out into the beef business*: Watson, Perry Owens (feedlot manager), interviews by author, 2016.

197 *If the motivations . . . the tactics Bill employed were even darker*: Douglas Frantz, "Journalists, or Detectives? Depends on Who's Asking," *New York Times*, July 28, 1999; Burrough, "Wild Bill Koch."

197 *The* Wall Street Journal *published a front-page story*: Robert Tomsho, "Blood Feud: Koch Family Is Roiled by Sibling Squabbling over Its Oil Empire," *Wall Street Journal*, August 9, 1989.

197 *During the late 1990s, Charles Koch found himself consumed*: Hall, interviews by author, 2013–14; O'Reilly and De Llosa, "The Curse."

198 *There was . . . dedicated to expanding the company*: Hall, Markel, interviews by author, 2013–14.

199 *The largest animal feed maker in America*: Watson, Hall, interviews by author, 2013–16; Traci Carl, "Koch Agriculture Buys Purina Mills," Associated Press, January 13, 1998.

200 *The pig industry was emblematic of this shift*: Christopher Leonard, *The Meat Racket: The Secret Takeover of America's Food Business* (New York: Simon & Schuster, 2014), 253–69.

200 *The company operated fifty-eight giant feed mills*: Purina Mills, 10-K filing with the Securities and Exchange Commission, Fiscal Year Ended December 31, 1996.

200 *But 1996 was a down year for Purina Mills*: Ibid.

200 *This didn't mean . . . excited about selling it*: Arnie Sumner, interviews by author, 2016.

201 *Koch's ambitions for Purina were vast*: Sumner, Watson, Hall, interviews by author, 2016.

201 *Koch ended up borrowing . . . two massive sources of debt*: Purina Mills, SEC Filing, form 10-12G, section 2, "Financial Restructuring Developments," describing indebtedness as of March 31, 1998, and March 23, 2000.

202   *One of Dean Watson's first and most important jobs*: Sumner, Watson, interviews by author, 2016.

204   *Things started to go south . . . government policy*: Watson, Hall, interviews by author, 2016; E. C. Pasour Jr. and Randal R. Rucker, *Plowshares and Pork Barrels: The Political Economy of Agriculture* (Oakland, CA: Independent Institute, 2005).

205   *Before the deal . . . warned about Purina's pig business*: Watson, interviews by author, 2016.

205   *In 1998, the US hog market experienced a shock*: Leonard, *Meat Racket*, 329–33.

206   *Purina Mills should have been insulated*: Watson, Hall, interviews by author, 2016; Purina Mills, SEC Filing, form 10-12G, "Management Discussion and Analysis," March 23, 2000.

206   *Watson was named CEO of Purina Mills*: Watson, interviews by author, 2016; "Purina Mills Names New CEO," PR Newswire, December 21, 1998.

207   *The hog market crisis raced forward faster . . . could respond*: Dean Watson, Hall, interviews by author, 2016; Purina Mills, SEC Filing, form 10-12G, section 2, "Financial Restructuring Developments," March 23, 2000.

207   *Brad Hall was dispatched from Wichita to St. Louis*: Hall, interviews by author, 2013–16; Purina Mills, SEC Filing, form 10-12G, "Management Discussion and Analysis," March 23, 2000.

208   *Charles Koch was just returning his full attention*: Leslie Wayne, "Zero Is the Verdict in $2 Billion Koch Family Feud," *New York Times*, June 20, 1998.

208   *Most people . . . have never seen him get angry*: Cris Franklin, Markel, Paulson, Hall, interviews by author, 2013–16.

208   *When Brad Hall explained what was happening*: Hall, interviews by author, 2016.

209   *Watson was in Wisconsin*: Watson, interviews by author, 2016.

211   *There was only one way that Purina Mills might survive*: Sumner, Hall, interviews by author, 2016.

211   *"True knowledge results in effective action"*: Boulton, "Koch and His Empire."

211   *In late August of 1999 . . . no extra money from Wichita*: Purina Mills, SEC Filing, form 8-K, November 9, 1999, 22.

212   *Koch appeared to have . . . protected it from the bankers' claims*: Koch's use of the corporate veil as a financing structure was first discussed with the author by two sources requesting anonymity; both sources were directly involved with Koch Industries' financial activity and strategies. Koch's use of the corporate veil was confirmed by a third source, a financier working for a bank that lent Koch money for the Purina Mills acquisition who also requested anonymity. Also Purina Mills, SEC Filing, form 8-K, November 9, 1999, 27–28, 102–3.

213   *Lawyers working for the banks . . . first hurdles of a lawsuit*: Source directly involved in the matter, background interview by author, 2016.

213   *Koch finally agreed to pay $60 million*: "Purina Mills: Tentative Agreement for $60 Million from Parent," *Troubled Company Reporter*, November 12, 1999.

214 *After the banks were paid off, Charles Koch began to dismantle*: Hall, interviews by author, 2016; "Economic Downturn Leads to Layoffs at Koch Industries," Associated Press, April 13, 1999.

CHAPTER 10: THE FAILURE

215 *Charles Koch drove himself to work every day*: Charles Koch's habit of driving his own car to work every day, and arriving very early, was described by several current and former Koch Industries employees, many of them making a special note of it because his car was in the employee parking lot before they arrived. His habits later changed, as noted in ch. 20.

215 *The previous decade had been a public embarrassment*: See endnotes, chs. 1–9.

216 *This mattered to Charles . . . company's conduct*: Charles Koch deposition with US Senate investigators, transcript, April 24, 1989.

216 *Charles Koch said . . . difficult times of his life*: Charles Koch, interview by author, 2015.

216 *Charles Koch was in a position to see the seeds of strength*: The following passage summarizes the strengths of Koch Industries based on reporting outlined in endnotes for chs. 1–9.

217 *"I just work harder"*: Charles Koch, interview by author, 2015.

CHAPTER 11: RISE OF THE TEXANS

221 *Over the course . . . reinvented Koch Industries*: Details about Koch Industries' strategic overhaul effort after the debacles of the 1990s were provided to the author by a source with direct knowledge of events who requested anonymity. Many granular details of the overhaul were included after being confirmed by external sources— Charles Koch's decision to fire many company presidents, for example, created an external footprint of news releases announcing personnel changes. Broad outlines of the overhaul were also confirmed on the record by senior sources at Koch such as Brad Hall and F. Lynn Markel. (Markel left during the transition but witnessed its aftereffects.)

221 *The revolution began with a purge*: "Koch Industries Names New Vice Chairman, President; New President Only Fourth in Company's History," BusinessWire, August 3, 1999; Corliss Nelson, biography and work history, Ryder System; Mike Sutten, biography and work history, Royal Caribbean Cruises; Rex Clevinger, biography and work history, Reliant Energy; Jim Imbler, announcement of replacement by David Robertson, January 24, 2000; Seth Vance, executive profile, *Bloomberg*; Pedro Haas, departure announcement, Kosa, July 24, 2000; Markel, LinkedIn profile, interview by author, 2016.

222 *The change in personnel was only the beginning*: Source with direct knowledge of events speaking on background to author, 2016.

223   *This change . . . ushered in a decade of unprecedented growth*: See endnotes, chs. 11–17; Leonard, "The New Koch."

223   *During this decade . . . impervious strength of its corporate veil*: The use of the corporate veil strategy was first revealed to the author by a source with direct knowledge of Koch's legal and financial strategies. It was later confirmed by a second senior source at Koch Industries with direct knowledge of the matter. Finally, the strategy can be seen by the footprint it leaves at Koch companies, which indeed are operated with a level of autonomy that can seem, at times, to be curiously redundant for a company so focused on efficiency.

224   *Koch Industries . . . institutionalized this drive to expand*: Charles Koch, Hall, Feilmeier, Packebush, Hannan, current and former Koch Industries employees, interviews by author, 2013–16; Leonard, "The New Koch."

224   *Koch was seen by outsiders . . . was seen quite differently*: Charles Koch, Hall, Feilmeier, O'Neill, Packebush, Hannan, current and former Koch Industries employees, interviews by author, 2013–16; Leonard, "The New Koch."

226   *In Washington . . . bitter rain and gray skies*: George W. Bush inauguration coverage, January 20, 2001, ABC News.

226   *The broad, national political consensus . . . no new consensus at all*: Readings include: Hacker and Pierson, *American Amnesia*; Mounk, *The People vs. Democracy: Why Our Freedom Is in Danger and How to Save It* (Cambridge, MA: Harvard University Press, 2018).

227   *Bush ran as a . . . "compassionate conservative"; Gore ran as a right-leaning liberal*: Gimore and Sugrue, *These United States*, 591–95.

229   *In fact . . . Koch Industries built a financial trading desk*: Accounts of Koch's trading operations are based in large part on interviews with senior executives inside Koch's trading operations, including Brad Hall, who was CFO of Koch Supply & Trading. Senior traders also offered insight, including Brenden O'Neill, Wesley Osbourn, Cris Franklin, Melissa Beckett, and Adam Glassman. Three former senior sources in Koch's trading division described its operation in detail, on the condition that they not be identified. Also, "Koch Supply & Trading," *Discovery: The Quarterly Newsletter of Koch Companies*, January 2009; "Koch Smooths Volatile Waters," Risk.net, November 10, 2003.

229   *Koch began trading crude oil . . . in the 1970s*: Howell, Hall, interviews by author, 2013–16.

229   *In the late 1970s, Ron Howell made one of the most significant investments*: Howell, interviews by author, 2016.

230   *In fact, there was no global market for oil*: This key insight into the structure of oil markets was first provided in a 2016 interview with Matthew Burkley, CEO of Genscape, which provided real-time intelligence on energy supplies to commodities traders. The insight was bolstered by interviews with Hall, Howell, Osbourn, Beckett, Glassman, and former senior Koch traders speaking on background between 2013–16.

232   *This supervaluable information . . . Koch Industries had access to*: Hall, Howell, senior Koch trading executives speaking on background, interviews by author, 2013–16.

233   *Other traders began dropping into the room*: Howell, interviews by author, 2016.

234   Merc . . . *also called the NYMEX for short*: Emily Lambert, *The Futures: The Rise of the Speculators and the Origins of the World's Biggest Markets* (New York: Basic Books, 2011), 151–163, 181–187.

234   *At first . . . a threat to Koch's business model*: Howell, interviews by author, 2016.

235   *Koch Industries . . . expertise in trading over the years*: Hall, Howell, senior Koch trading executives speaking on background, interviews by author, 2013–16.

236   *In the stock market, it is illegal to trade on inside information*: Nancy Doyle, general attorney at the Commodity Futures Trading Commission; Bart Chilton, former commissioner at the Commodity Futures Trading Commission; source speaking on background, interviews by author, 2016.

236   *Koch exploited this advantage*: Hall, Howell, senior Koch trading executives speaking on background, interviews by author, 2013–16.

237   *Koch Industries . . . in energy futures markets*: Former senior Koch trading official speaking on background, interview by author, 2016; Saule T. Omarova, "The Merchants of Wall Street: Banking, Commerce, and Commodities," Cornell Law Faculty Publications, Cornell Law School, 2013.

237   *"We kept getting approached by banks"*: Former senior Koch trading executive speaking on background, interview by author, 2016.

238   *Throughout the 1990s . . . derivatives trading*: Gimore and Sugrue, *These United States*, 583–84.

239   *After analyzing the McKinsey report, Koch Industries decided*: Three former senior Koch trading employees speaking on background, Hall, interviews by author, 2013–16.

240   *Naturally, the consolidated office . . . was based in Houston*: Monica Perin, "Koch Investment Group Moves Base from Kansas to Houston," *Houston Business Journal*, June 17, 2001.

CHAPTER 12: INFORMATION ASYMMETRIES

241   *It was still dark when Brenden O'Neill drove*: O'Neill, interviews by author, 2016.

241   *There was no single morning for a commodities trader*: Glassman, former Koch Industries derivatives trader, interviews by author, 2014.

242   *The headlights . . . as he approached*: O'Neill, interviews by author, 2016; notes from reporting at Koch Supply & Trading office, 2016; historic weather reports for Houston.

242   *The interior lobby . . . like a geode hidden inside a black stone*: Notes, photos, and video from reporting in lobby of 20 Greenway Plaza, 2016.

242   *Koch's trading floor . . . several thousand square feet*: Photos of trading floor taken from David Barboza, "Energy Traders Continue to Prowl the Floor That Enron

Helped Build," *New York Times*, December 6, 2001; other photos of trading floors taken from LinkedIn profile pictures of Koch Supply & Trading employees; descriptions of trading offices taken from Franklin, O'Neill, Osbourn, two sources speaking on background, interviews by author, 2013–16.

242 *Koch's in-house meteorologist was hard at work*: Former employee of Koch Supply & Trading meteorologist team speaking on background, interviews by author, 2016.

243 *O'Neill settled into his desk and turned on his computer*: O'Neill, interviews by author, 2016.

245 *overseen by a man named Sam Soliman*: Franklin, O'Neill, Hall, Lou Ming (former Koch Industries quantitative trader), interviews by author, 2013–16; Perin, "Koch Investment Group Moves Base."

248 *Koch maximized the advantage . . . other assets*: Hall, Beckett, Osbourn, three former senior Koch Industries trading executives (executives in this case, including senior managers of the rank of vice president or higher), interviews by author, 2013–16.

250 *On the first day he reported to work*: O'Neill, interviews by author, 2016.

250 *Koch purchased these pipelines and the company that owned them*: Larry Foster, "United Flashes New Wealth—and New Faces—After Koch Takeover," *Inside FERC*, November 16, 1992; "Koch Industries Buys United Gas Pipeline," PR Newswire, November 9, 1992.

250 *Prior to the first Bush administration . . . wasn't too different*: Paul W. MacAvoy, *The Natural Gas Market: Sixty Years of Regulation and Deregulation* (New Haven, CT: Yale University Press, 2000), 1–120.

251 *Senior managers . . . the growing natural gas marketplace*: Hall, O'Neill, former senior Koch Industries trading executive speaking on background, interviews by author, 2013–16.

252 *Koch went so far as to fold its origination group*: Former senior Koch Industries trading executive speaking on background, interviews by author, 2016.

253 *O'Neill spent his day on the phone*: O'Neill, interviews by author, 2016.

253 *Koch's traders often got off work early . . . after US market trading ceased*: O'Neill, Osbourn, Franklin, interviews by author, 2016.

254 *Inside, the bar was pleasingly dim and cave-like*: Notes and photos from author's reporting trip inside the Ginger Man bar, 2016. Comparison with the Coates Bar taken from notes and photos from author's reporting trip inside Coates Bar, 2015.

254 *Koch had hired engineers to staff its trading desk*: O'Neill, Osbourn, former senior Koch Industries trading executive speaking on background, interviews by author, 2016–17.

255 *It might have been disappointing . . . wasn't an easy path to riches*: O'Neill, interviews by author, 2016.

255 *Sam Soliman stretched his top traders*: O'Neill, Franklin, Ming, interviews by author, 2016.

256   *Here is a brief description of a derivatives contract*: The author is indebted to Nancy Doyle, general attorney for the Commodities Futures Trading Commission, for letting him audit her class at Georgetown Law School, entitled Complex Derivative Transactions, during the spring semester of 2013. This class was absolutely invaluable in helping the author grasp the complex world of futures, derivatives, and swaps markets and the regulatory framework around them. The author was also assisted by his auditing classmate Lina Khan, who helped him work through complex issues during many long discussions. The author answered only one question during the class, which he answered incorrectly (which is mortifying to do in front of a group of competitive Georgetown Law students), but Doyle was exceedingly generous in taking time in and out of class to help clarify important elements of these opaque markets.

256   *O'Neill started experimenting*: O'Neill, interviews by author, 2016.

258   *He was on an e-mail list . . . WinterSkinny*: Koch Industries internal e-mail, subject line: "WinterSkinny.xls," from Patrick Ferguson to Koch Industries traders including O'Neill, December 23, 2002.

258   *Other internal reports, such as the* Daily Analysis: Koch Industries internal e-mail, subject line: "Daily Analysis.xls," including attachment and report, May 7, 2001.

258   *These reports were coupled with . . . Plant managers*: Former senior Koch Industries trading executive speaking on background, Hall, interviews by author, 2013–14.

259   *In 2000, two Koch analysts . . . "Natural Gas Point of View 2000–2001"*: Wayne Knupp and Blake Hill, Internal Koch Industries report, *Koch Energy: Forecasts and Strategies—Focus on Gas. Natural Gas Point of View 2000–2001.*

259   *The assessment matched what O'Neill was seeing*: O'Neill, interviews by author, 2016; historic natural gas prices taken from database of TradingEconomics.com.

259   *In early 2000 . . . mistaken assumption*: O'Neill, interviews by author, 2016; "Koch Fully Acquires Natural Gas Asset Management Company; Koch Energy Trading Increases Ownership Interest in IMDST to 100 Percent by Buying Out IMDCI," BusinessWire, May 1, 2000.

260   *Senior executives . . . no longer pay their traders like engineers*: O'Neill, former Koch Industries trading executive speaking on background, interviews by author, 2016.

262   *It was a cold winter in 2000. Demand for electricity was strong*: O'Neill, interviews by author, 2016; historic natural gas prices taken from database of TradingEconomics.com; *Natural Gas: Analysis of Changes in Market Price*, GAO report to congressional committees and members of Congress, December 2002.

263   *the entire pipeline company of Koch Gateway*: Income figures, "Koch Gateway Pipeline Company Annual Report Form No. 2," June 4, 2011, 114.

264   *After the books were closed . . . time for O'Neill to get his bonus*: O'Neill, interviews by author; O'Neill's income figures were confirmed by a former senior Koch Industries trading executive speaking on background, interview by author, 2016.

264   *With a single paycheck... economic life*: O'Neill, interviews by author, 2016; figures on houses taken from housing deeds and Realtor.com databases.

CHAPTER 13: ATTACK OF THE KILLER ELECTRONS!

266   *Koch's trading division was always expanding*: Beckett, Hall, former Koch Industries trading executives speaking on background, interviews by author, 2013–16. Documents from Federal Energy Regulatory Commission (FERC) proceedings detailed below.

266   *The new commodity in this market was called a megawatt-hour*: Bethany McLean and Peter Elkind, *The Smartest Guys in the Room: The Amazing Rise and Scandalous Fall of Enron* (New York: Portfolio, 2003), 264–83; Toni Mack, "Power Players," *Forbes*, May 19, 1997.

267   *The company selected . . . the megawatt markets*: Darrell Antrich's account is based in part on prepared testimony he provided to federal regulators. It will be referred to in these endnotes as "FERC testimony." For the first citation, the full document name is provided: "Prepared Testimony of Darrell W. Antrich on Behalf of Koch Energy Trading Inc., Before the Federal Energy Regulatory Commission, in Regard to San Diego Gas & Electric Co. v. Sellers of Energy and Ancillary Services into Markets Operated by the California Independent System Operator Corporation and the California Power Exchange," October 25, 2011, 3.

267   *Antrich helped build a team of traders*: Antrich, FERC testimony, October 25, 2011, 3–7.

268   *Darrell Antrich would end up getting engulfed by this disaster*: Descriptions of Antrich's personality from Beckett, speaking on background, interviews by author, 2016; Antrich, FERC testimony, October 2, 2003, December 3, 2003, September 17, 2009, October 25, 2011.

269   *It is significant that the disaster began in Sacramento*: Notes and photographs from author's reporting trip to Sacramento, 2016.

269   *That isn't to say that Stephen Peace didn't try*: Stephen Peace, interviews by author, 2016.

269   *Peace was put in charge . . . energy committee*: Ibid.; Ron Russell, "Dim Bulbs," *SF Weekly*, March 7, 2001; Chris Kraul, "Radical Changes in Power Industry Pass Legislature," *Los Angeles Times*, September 1, 1996.

270   *It only became apparent years later that* Attack of the Killer Tomatoes! *was prophetic*: Peace, interviews by author, 2016; notes from watching *Attack of the Killer Tomatoes!*, 2016.

271   *When Peace held public hearings . . . minuscule*: Timothy P. Duane, "Regulation's Rationale: Learning from the California Energy Crisis," *Yale Journal on Regulation*, no. 2 (2002); "Historical Look at California's Restructuring of Electricity Regula-

tion: Influences Leading to the Legislature's AB 1890 of 1996," California Senate Office of Research.

273 *Again, this is an excruciatingly dull story that nobody wanted to hear about*: Peace, interviews by author, 2016; Dan Morain, "Assembly OKs Bill to Deregulate Electricity," *Los Angeles Times*, August 31, 1996; Mark Gladstone, "Gridlock Gives Way to Teamwork in Legislature," *Los Angeles Times*, September 2, 1996.

273 *ALEC was an umbrella group . . . the nation*: Bonnie Sue Cooper, former ALEC executive director, and Lisa Graves, executive director of the Center for Media and Democracy, interviews by author, 2014–16; *Corporate America's Trojan Horse in the States: The Untold Story Behind the American Legislative Exchange Council* (New York: Natural Resources Defense Council and Defenders of Wildlife, 2002).

274 *By the time Peace arrived . . . promoting electricity deregulation*: Peace, Cooper, interviews by author, 2016; "Electricity Industry Restructuring: History and Background," *The State Factor*, ALEC report, November 1996; ALEC Model Bill: "Electric Industry Restructuring Act"; *Corporate America's Trojan Horse in the States.*

275 *During the 1990s . . . key members of the ALEC task force*: Stuart Eskenazi and Mike Ward, "Lawmakers' Corporate Classmates," *Austin American-Statesman*, November 2, 1997; Eskenazi and Ward, "2 Learning Styles: Seminars and the Golf Course," *Austin American-Statesman*, November 2, 1997; *Corporate America's Trojan Horse in the States.*

275 *Even though . . . Peace remained uneasy*: Peace, interviews by author, 2016.

276 *Peace and Brulte passed the bill in August of 1998*: Dan Moran, "Deregulation Bill Signed by Wilson," *Los Angeles Times*, September 24, 1996.

276 *Koch Industries had constructed its own intelligence network*: O'Neill, Beckett, speaking on background, interviews by author, 2016.

276 *Traders on the electricity desk analyzed the new marketplace*: Antrich, FERC testimony, October 25, 2011, 5–6.

276 *Darrell Antrich helped lead . . . West Power Clearing Model*: Beckett, interviews by author, 2016; Antrich, FERC testimony, December 3, 2003, 1; photos of Beckett and Antrich from Barboza, "Energy Traders Continue to Prowl."

277 *The bill created a new market . . . buy and sell megawatt-hours*: Peace, interviews by author, 2016; McLean and Elkind, *Smartest Guys*, 264–83; Russell, "Dim Bulbs."

278 *When Melissa Beckett started her day*: Beckett, interviews by author, 2016; photos of Beckett's desk and surroundings from Barboza, "Energy Traders Continue to Prowl."

279 *West Power Clearing Model began to produce some very strange numbers*: Beckett, interviews by author, 2016; Antrich, FERC testimony, October, 25, 2011, 7.

280 *The thinking of Enron traders was captured in recorded phone calls*: "Blackout: The California Crisis," *Frontline*, 2001; "Enron Traders Talking About Grandma Millie,"

video, 2:11, uploaded to YouTube by irwinmcraw on March 17, 2009, www.you
tube.com/watch?v=DOLNWF5QMxY.

280   *It would be up to the traders . . . make the markets work*: Beckett, interviews by author, 2016; Antrich, FERC testimony, October 25, 2011, 7.

281   *Antrich wasn't . . . met with Tom Nesmith*: Beckett, interviews by author, 2016; Antrich, FERC testimony, December 3, 2003, 3–6, and October 25, 2011, 6; Gary Taylor, FERC testimony, February 27, 2004, 60.

281   *Antrich and his team . . . information-sharing agreement*: Consulting agreement between Koch Energy Trading and PNM, dated to take effect January 2001. The KET
representative on the document is David Owens, vice president of Koch Energy
Trading, while the PNM representative is Duane Farmer, director of Wholesale
Power Marketing.

281   *Enron traders . . . while the power from California was not*: The author is grateful
to energy consultant Gary Taylor, who served as an expert witness for federal authorities investigating illegal trading schemes in California, for his detailed and
patient explanations of the parking trade. Readers with more interest in the topic
are urged to pick up the thorough and well-researched book he coauthored, *Market Power and Market Manipulation in Energy Markets: From the California Crisis
to the Present* (Reston, VA: Public Utilities Reports, 2015); Taylor, interviews by
author, 2016; Taylor, FERC testimony, January 31, 2005, 33–35, and February 27,
2004, 64–82.

282   *Once PNM learned . . . it started pitching the service to trading companies*: Taylor,
FERC testimony, February 27, 2004, 64–82; transcript of Nesmith phone call in
ibid., 76–78.

282   *On February 28, 2000, Koch Energy . . . in the coming months*: Contract between
Koch Energy Trading and PNM, dated February 22, 2000, and signed February 28,
2000.

282   *"I am excited about practicing"*: Darell Antrich to Tom Nesmith, e-mail, May 5,
2000.

282   *On May 22, 2000 . . . parking transactions*: Date and volumes of parking transactions taken from "Response of Koch Energy Trading, Inc., to Order to Show
Cause," filed with FERC, July 31, 2003, 5–6; Antrich, FERC testimony, December 3,
2003, 8; a detailed overview of Koch's "parking" activities is also provided in Taylor's testimony to FERC, February 27, 2004, 82–89.

283   *The state was facing a shortage . . . Independent System Operator*: Nancy Rivera
Brooks and Zanto Peabody, "Heat Triggers Moderate Power Emergency," *Los Angeles Times*, May 23, 2000.

283   *Koch's parking arrangement . . . desperation*: "Response of Koch Energy," filed with
FERC, July 31, 2003, chart breakdown of May 22 parking transaction, chart 1-1;
Antrich, FERC testimony, October 25, 2011, 9–11.

283   *Of the 650 megawatt-hours that Koch parked with PNM*: Ibid.

283   *Gaming the system was creating dire, real-world effects*: Rivera Brooks and Peabody, "Heat Brings Outages and Emptied Offices."

284   *On June 14 Koch's traders executed . . . complex parking transaction*: "Response of Koch Energy Trading," filed with FERC, July 31, 2003, chart breakdown of May 22 parking transaction, chart 2-2.

284   *Darrell Antrich e-mailed . . . Brian Arriaga*: Antrich to Arriaga, e-mail, June 15, 2000.

284   *On June 14 and 15, temperatures rose above 100 degrees*: Mara Dolan, "California and the West: S.F. Cools Off but Outages Persist," *Los Angeles Times*, June 16, 2000.

284   *Lights blinked . . . inside the cavernous control room*: Images from ISO office control room taken from ABC News reports of blackouts.

284   *By the afternoon of the fourteenth . . . fall short*: Nancy Rivera Brooks and Charles Piller, "Bay Area Heat Wave Strains Power Grid," *Los Angeles Times*, June 15, 2000.

285   *Throughout the autumn . . . incomprehensibly complex schemes*: McLean and Elkind, *Smartest Guys*, 264–83.

285   *Steve Peace . . . knowing more than anybody*: Peace, interviews by author, 2016.

286   *a similar fatalism playing out at the ISO offices*: Ibid.; ABC News report on blackouts; "Blackout: The California Crisis."

287   *Gray Davis was a popular, if somewhat bland, governor*: John Balzar, "Bright Days for Gray Davis," *Los Angeles Times*, July 7, 2006.

287   *The weekend of January 12, 2001*: Peace, interviews by author, 2016; Lynda Gledhill, "Davis to Seek State Role in Energy Pricing," *San Francisco Chronicle*, January 15, 2001; Nancy Vogel, Bob Drogin, and Nicholas Riccardi, "Energy Players Deeply Divided on Rescue Plan," *Los Angeles Times*, January 15, 2001.

287   *Davis quickly discovered . . . Market prices were nonnegotiable*: Nancy Vogel and Miguel Bustillo, "Power Firm Demands Utilities Pay Bills Now," *Los Angeles Times*, January 16, 2001.

288   *FERC also refused to compromise*: Peace, interviews by author, 2016; Steve Johnson and Mark Gladstone, "Federal Panel Blasted over Emergency Moves, Davis Calls Commissioners 'Pawns' of Electricity Sellers," *San Jose Mercury News*, December 16, 2000; Bart Jansen, "Davis Asks FERC to Order Refunds for Power Customers," Associated Press, November 9, 2000; Jon Sarchie, "Western Governors Turn Up Pressure for Electricity Price Cap," Associated Press, December 20, 2000.

288   *Mike Bowers steered his semitruck off the freeway*: Peace, interviews by author, 2016; Seth Rosenfeld, Janine DeFao, and Jaxon Van Derbeken, "Capitol Suspect 'Flopped'—Mom Says Prison Mental Health Systems Failed Him," *San Francisco Chronicle*, January 17, 2001; Jim Williams and Alison Stewart, "California's Energy Crisis Forces Governor to Declare State of Emergency; Truck Driver Who Hit California Capitol Was Ex-Convict," ABC News, January 18, 2001.

289   *a story line emerged about the electricity crisis*: Russell, "Dim Bulbs"; McLean and Elkind, *Smartest Guys*, 264–83; Wendy Zellner, "Enron's Power Play," *Bloomberg Businessweek*, February 12, 2001.

289 *This narrative was misleading*: Peace, interviews by author, 2016; Timothy P. Duane, "Regulation's Rationale: Learning from the California Energy Crisis," *Yale Journal on Regulation*, no. 2, 2002; "Historical Look at California's Restructuring of Electricity Regulation," California Senate Office of Research; Morain, "Assembly OKs Bill"; Gladstone, "Gridlock Gives Way to Teamwork."

290 *On November 20, 2000, Koch Industries . . . in California*: Antrich, FERC testimony, December 3, 2003, 3.

290 *Koch walked away from*: Unsigned consulting agreement between KET and PNM, dated November 20, 2000, and addressed to Melissa Beckett.

290 *Other firms ramped up . . . got more expensive*: FERC Opinion No. 536, "Order Affirming Factual Findings, Directing Compliance Filing and Ordering Refunds," November 10, 2014, 62; Enron activities, McLean and Elkind, *Smartest Guys*, 264–83.

290 *Back in 1968, when the oil gauger Phil Dubose*: Dubose, interviews by author, 2014–15.

291 *Koch's priorities in the winter of 2000 were telling*: Antrich, FERC testimony, October 2, 2003, 3; Antrich to Nesmith, e-mail, May 5, 2000. Antrich wrote: "Remember when you commit to a date to insist on golf for an afternoon." Meeting agenda with heading: "PNM/KET Knowledge Alliance Meeting," September 13, 2000. Agenda items include: "Tour of Trading Floor," "Risk Management and Controls," "Trading Alliance Discussion," and "Power Trading Capabilities." Also KET internally produced slideshow for PNM, dated April 26, 2000. Slides include: "Power Trading Profitability," "Competitive Advantages of Koch Power Trading Group," and "Potential Business Opportunities."

291 *The California crisis ended in April*: Taylor et al., *Market Power and Market Manipulation in Energy Markets*, 79–83; FERC Final Report on Price Manipulation in Western Markets, March 2003.

292 *Enron declared bankruptcy in December of 2001*: Case file, *San Diego Gas & Electric Co. v. Sellers of Energy and Ancillary Services*; FERC Opinion No. 536, Order Affirming Factual Findings, Directing Compliance Filing and Ordering Refunds, November 10, 2014, 62; FERC Order Approving Uncontested Settlement with Koch Energy Trading and others, October 8, 2015.

292 *Steve Peace's life in politics was also ended*: Peace, interviews by author, 2016.

293 *After the electricity markets cooled . . . never quite so white hot again*: Beckett, speaking on background, interviews by author, 2016–17; Taylor et al., *Market Power and Market Manipulation in Energy Markets*, 79–83.

CHAPTER 14: TRADING THE REAL WORLD

294 *To the private equity world . . . a game board*: Eileen Appelbaum and Rosemary Batt, *Private Equity at Work: When Wall Street Manages Main Street* (New York: Russell Sage Foundation, 2014); Daniel Souleles, interviews by author, 2017; Souleles, *Songs of Profit, Songs of Loss: Private Equity, Wealth, and Inequality* (Lincoln: University of Nebraska Press, 2019).

294   *$91 billion in private deals at the dawn of the century*: Appelbaum and Batt, *Private Equity at Work*, 35–36.

294   *Koch Industries . . . put itself aggressively into the hunt*: Feilmeier, Hall, Packebush, Chase Koch, interviews by author, 2013–18.

295   *Charles Koch sat on the Corporate Development Board*: Charles Koch, Feilmeier, Hall, Markel, Jeremy Jones, Packebush, former senior Koch Industries executive speaking on background, interviews by author, 2013–14.

296   *If going before the board . . . doubly intimidating to Steve Packebush*: Packebush, Watson, interviews by author, 2013–16.

297   *But in 2003, Steve Packebush . . . made an appointment*: Packebush, interview by author, 2013.

297   *The Koch Nitrogen team . . . took their places*: Ibid.; background on development board meetings: Hall, Feilmeier, Jeremy Jones, interviews by author, 2013–14.

298   *Koch Industries . . . since at least the 1990s*: Watson, interviews by author, 2016; Joe Hise, former Farmland Industries fertilizer sales manager in Enid, Oklahoma, interviews by author, 2014–15.

299   *Farmland would, in fact, collapse . . . destroyed it*: Bob Terry, former Farmland Industries CEO, interview by author, 2013; "Farmland Industries Files for Protection Under Chapter 11," GrainNet, last modified May 31, 2002; David Barboza, "Facing Huge Debt, Large Farm Co-op Is Closing Down; Farmland Industries Battled Major Food Conglomerates," *New York Times*, September 16, 2003.

300   *Packebush and his team . . . identified something that no one else saw*: Packebush, interview by author, 2013.

301   *he and the development board considered the plan*: Hall, Markel, Charles Koch, interviews by author, 2013–15.

301   *The development board . . . all three of these criteria*: Packebush, interview by author, 2013; Leonard, "The New Koch."

302   *The timing was perfect. Farmland's CEO, Bob Terry*: Bob Terry, interview by author, 2013.

302   *The delegation . . . mild spring day*: Packebush, interview by author, 2013; weather conditions from historic weather database; Nancy Seewald, "Koch Wins Farmland's Fertilizer Assets," *Chemical Week*, April 2, 2003; Barboza, "Facing Huge Debt"; images of Farmland mural taken from online archive.

303   *The American economy in 2003*: Souleles, interviews by author, 2017; Appelbaum and Batt, *Private Equity at Work*, 18–21.

303   *Between 2000 and 2012 . . . took companies private*: Applebaum and Batt, *Private Equity at Work*, 37.

304   *There was a large table*: Packebush, Terry, interviews by author, 2013.

304   *Agrium was the largest . . . producer*: Robert Westervelt, "Full-Year Earnings Disappoint," *Chemical Week*, May 21, 2003; Seewald, "Koch Wins."

305   *The glossy photos . . . were taken down*: Packebush, interview by author, 2013; notes from Packebush's office, 2013.

305   *Koch Nitrogen was renamed Koch Fertilizer*: Packebush, Beckett, interviews by au-
      thor, 2013–16; notes from reporting at Koch Fertilizer offices, 2013; Leonard, "The
      New Koch."

                    CHAPTER 15: SEIZING GEORGIA-PACIFIC

307   *This time . . . dispatched to Atlanta*: Hannan, Wesley Jones, interviews by author,
      2016; Christopher Leonard, "An Inside Look at How Koch Industries Does Busi-
      ness," *Washington Post*, July 1, 2017.

308   *The team from Koch . . . Georgia-Pacific tower*: Hannan, Wesley Jones, interviews
      by author, 2016; notes and photos from reporting at Georgia-Pacific tower, 2016;
      Georgia-Pacific, 10-K filing for fiscal year 2003.

309   *When they arrived . . . a hushed cocoon of luxury*: Hannan, Wesley Jones, inter-
      views by author, 2016; notes and photos from reporting at fifty-first floor of
      Georgia-Pacific Tower, 2016.

309   *Georgia-Pacific was founded in 1927 . . . lumber yard*: Doug Monroe, *The Maver-
      ick Spirit: Georgia-Pacific at 75* (Old Saybrook, CT: Greenwich Pub. Group, 2001);
      Claudia H. Deutsch, "Georgia-Pacific to Acquire Fort James," *New York Times*, July
      18, 2000.

310   *Georgia-Pacific's stock price was still struggling*: Hannan, Wesley Jones, interviews
      by author, 2016.

311   *After their trip to the Pink Palace . . . pulp mills*: Hannan, interview by author, 2016;
      "Koch Cellulose and Subsidiaries Acquire Fluff, Market Pulp Business," Business-
      Wire, May 10, 2004; Roxana Hegeman, "Koch Industries to Buy Georgia-Pacific's
      Pulp Operations," Associated Press, January 29, 2004.

311   *This acquisition . . . was just a down payment*: Hannan, Wesley Jones, interviews by
      author, 2016; Charles Koch, *Good Profit*, 48–50.

312   *In November of 2003, Koch agreed to buy DuPont's synthetic fiber plants*: Hannan,
      interview by author, 2016; "Koch Industries Subsidiaries to Purchase Invista,"
      BusinessWire, November 17, 2003; Randall Chase, "DuPont Sells Textile Unit to
      Koch Industries," Associated Press, November 18, 2003; "Koch Completes Acquisi-
      tion of Invista Textile Business," Associated Press, May 1, 2004.

313   *Invista became a laboratory*: David Hoffmann, interviews by author, 2016–17.

313   *After Koch bought Invista . . . compliance attorneys*: Ibid.

314   *Hoffmann worked in the new Invista headquarters*: Ibid.; reporting notes from In-
      vista headquarters, 2013, 2018.

315   *Koch Industries backed up the philosophy with drastic actions*: Hoffmann, interviews
      by author, 2016–17; *Invista B.V. et al. v. E.I. Du Pont de Nemours and Co.*, Com-
      plaint, March 26, 2008.

316   *The Brunswick pulp mill . . . southern charm with a futuristic*: Wesley Jones, inter-
      views by author, 2016; reporting notes and photos from Brunswick mill, 2016.

318 *Karen Marx, a logistics manager*: Karen Marx, interview by author, 2016; reporting notes from Savannah mill, 2016.

318 *Charles Koch gained confidence*: Charles Koch, *Good Profit*, 48–50; Georgia-Pacific 10-K filing for fiscal year 2005; Michael Arndt, "Koch: Very Private, and a Lot Bigger," *Bloomberg Businessweek*, November 15, 2005; Dennis K. Berman and Chad Terhune, "Koch Industries Agrees to Buy Georgia-Pacific," *Wall Street Journal*, November 14, 2005.

319 *To make a debt-fueled deal work*: Souleles, interviews by author, 2017; Souleles, *Songs of Profit, Songs of Loss: Private Equity, Wealth, and Inequality* (Lincoln: University of Nebraska Press, 2019).

319 *A key part of making the whole strategy work*: Former Koch Industries senior finance employee speaking on background, interviews by author; Appelbaum and Batt, *Private Equity at Work*, 45.

319 *Koch Industries . . . largest acquisition in its history*: Arndt, "Koch: Very Private"; Berman and Terhune, "Koch Industries Agrees"; Hannan, interviews by author, 2016; Georgia-Pacific, 8-K filing, November 13, 2005.

320 *Georgia-Pacific . . . roughly $8 billion in debt*: Charles Koch, *Good Profit*, 221–22; Georgia-Pacific, 8-K filing, November 13, 2005; Arndt, "Koch: Very Private"; Berman and Terhune, "Koch Industries Agrees."

320 *When Koch bought Georgia-Pacific . . . seventeen employees*: Hannan, Wesley Jones, interviews by author, 2016.

321 *The desk, the furniture, and the art on the walls were replaced*: Reporting notes from Georgia-Pacific Tower, 2016.

321 *Hannan moved to Atlanta and bought a house*: Hannan, interview by author, 2016; descriptions of Hannan's office and Dunkin' Donuts cup from notes during interview with Hannan in his office, 2016.

322 *Hannan led a $200 million acquisition*: Hannan, interview by author, 2016; "Insulair Announces Agreement with Georgia-Pacific," BusinessWire, June 29, 2006.

CHAPTER 16: DAWN OF THE LABOR MANAGEMENT SYSTEM

323 *When Koch Industries . . . giant paper mills and timber operations*: Notes, photos, and video from reporting at Georgia-Pacific mills in Portland, Oregon, 2014, 2017.

323 *Steve Hammond was embroiled in this battle*: Hammond, interviews by author, 2013–17.

324 *The Georgia-Pacific warehouse . . . squealing tires*: Notes, photos, and video, Georgia-Pacific mills, 2014, 2017.

324 *Hammond was hired at the warehouse in 1972*: Hammond, interviews by author, 2013–17.

325 *The union guys tended to give each other nicknames*: Hammond, Brian Dodge,

Adam Smith, Travis McKinney, David Franzen, Dennis Trimm, interviews by author, 2013–17.

326   *Hammond started hanging around with a pretty girl named Carla Hogue*: Hammond, interviews by author, 2017.

328   *One of Hammond's close friends . . . to become a manager*: Hammond, Trimm, interviews by author, 2017.

328   *As the warehouses and their timber mills . . . chain of CEOs*: Trimm, interviews by author, 2017.

329   *In one video . . . sitting in front of a black screen*: Charles Koch video address, viewed by author.

330   *some of the employees expressed their concerns*: Trimm, interviews by author, 2017.

331   *Increasing the bottom line became Trimm's prime directive*: Ibid.

331   *Just when Koch bought Georgia-Pacific . . . software system in its warehouses*: Hammond, McKinney, Franzen, Trimm, interviews by author, 2013–17; "Georgia-Pacific Selects North American Transportation Solution Provider," *Supply & Demand Chain Executive*, August 19, 2005; "Georgia Pacific Cuts Distribution Centre Overheads by 22% with Warehouse Management System from Red-Prairie," BusinessWire, October 16, 2007, https://www.businesswire.com/news/home/20071015006673/en/Georgia-Pacific-Cuts-Distribution-Centre-Overheads-22.

333   *The LMS tracked workers . . . the pallets*: Hammond, McKinney, Franzen, Trimm, Dodge, Smith, interviews by author, 2013–17.

333   *the forklift drivers arrived for work*: Hammond, McKinney, Franzen, Trimm, Smith, interviews by author, 2013–17.

334   *McKinney was hired in 2004, shortly before the LMS went live*: McKinney, interviews by author, 2017.

334   *People were clamoring to be a forklift driver . . . had all but disappeared*: Ibid.; Jacob S. Hacker, *The Great Risk Shift: The Assault on American Jobs, Families, Health Care and Retirement and How You Can Fight Back* (New York: Oxford University Press, 2006), 63, 68–70.

336   *Trimm, their supervisor, monitored the drivers*: Trimm, interviews by author, 2017.

336   *On pa day . . . Nicolai Street Clubhouse*: McKinney and Franzen, interviews by author, 2017. Descriptions of the Nicolai Street Clubhouse taken from notes and photos during reporting trip in 2016. The establishment has since been converted from a strip club to a bar and grill. Photos of neon signs behind the old stage are taken from outdated Google Maps photos. Descriptions of stripping are taken from interviews and notes from reporting at Annie's Saloon in Astoria, Oregon, an establishment with the same stage setup and floor plan.

338   *LMS accrued huge volumes of data on each employee*: Trimm, Hammond, McKinney, Dodge, Smith, interviews by author, 2017.

338   *This system seemed harsh*: Charles Koch, *The Science of Success*, 89–93.

339 *Life at the warehouse . . . LMS rankings*: Trimm, Hammond, McKinney, Dodge, Smith, interviews by author, 2017.

339 *Alt lived in the red zone*: Kerry Alt, Shirley Alt, Trimm, interviews by author, 2017; Charles Koch, *The Science of Success*, 90.

340 *The drivers weren't the only employees who were ranked*: Trimm, interviews by author, 2017.

341 *The warehouse could not get rid of Travis McKinney*: McKinney, interviews by author, 2017; Erin El Issa, "2016 American Household Credit Card Debt Survey," NerdWallet, accessed 2017.

342 *Hammond often felt sick when he arrived*: Hammond, interviews by author, 2013–17; Harvey Schwartz, *Solidarity Stories: An Oral History of the ILWU* (Seattle: University of Washington Press, 2009).

CHAPTER 17: THE CRASH

344 *David H. Koch was in a charitable mood*: Robin Pogrebin, "Billionaire Pledges $100 Million to New York State Theater," *New York Times*, July 10, 2008; Gary Weiss, "The Price of Immortality: Does Charity Bring Status? Ask the Second-Richest Man in New York. How David Koch Is Changing Big Philanthropy," *Condé Nast Portfolio*, October 15, 2008; David Koch net worth figures taken from *Forbes'* lists of world's richest people, 2002, 2008.

346 *The first signs of trouble . . . trading floor*: Franklin, Jeremy Jones, interviews by author, 2013–16; "Dealing with Difficulty," *Discovery: The Quarterly Newsletter of Koch Companies*, January 2009.

346 *Cris Franklin, the young trader in Houston*: Franklin, interviews by author, 2016.

347 *The risk extended all the way into the foundation*: Debt figures from Alan S. Blinder, *After the Music Stopped: The Financial Crisis, the Response, and the Work Ahead* (New York: Penguin Press, 2013), 49–50.

347 *debt was carried in the form of home mortgages*: Blinder, *After the Music Stopped*, 19. Insight into the economic crash also derived from the author's time as a national business reporter for the Associated Press from 2008 to 2012, when he was covering unemployment, the labor market, and the Great Recession.

348 *Then the loans were packaged into . . . CDOs*: Michael Lewis, *The Big Short: Inside the Doomsday Machine* (New York: W. W. Norton, 2010); Adam Tooze, *Crashed: How a Decade of Financial Crises Changed the World* (New York: Viking, 2018).

348 *All of these derivatives bets were opaque*: Doyle, Georgetown Law School class, "Complex Derivative Transactions," spring semester of 2013.

348 *a Clinton Administration regulator named Brooksley Born*: Peter Coy and Silla Brush, "Top Clinton Aides Blew a Chance to Avert the Financial Crisis," *Bloomberg Businessweek*, May 1, 2014.

349　　*The black box financial system swelled*: Blinder, *After the Music Stopped*, 59–65.

349　　*Lehman Brothers declared bankruptcy*: Carrick Mollenkamp, Susanne Craig, Serena Ng, and Aaron Lucchetti, "Lehman Files for Bankruptcy, Merrill Sold, AIG Seeks Cash," *Wall Street Journal*, September 16, 2008.

350　　*The losses on Cris Franklin's trading desk*: Franklin, interviews by author, 2016.

351　　*others who worked with Charles Koch saw him behave in the same way*: Franklin, Jeremy Jones, interviews by author, 2013–16.

352　　*Jeremy Jones came into frequent contact with Charles Koch*: Jeremy Jones, interview by author, 2013.

353　　*His venture fund, Koch Genesis, was shut down*: Ibid.; "Naturally Advanced Technologies Appoints Industry Veteran VP to Advisory Board; Industry Veteran Jeremy K. Jones to Consult on Partnership and Business Development Initiatives," PR Newswire, March 2, 2009; Jefferson Weaver, "Georgia-Pacific Plant to Close Dec. 1," *News Reporter* (Whiteville, NC), October 6, 2008; Gary Haber and Dan Shortridge, "Invista to Lay Off 400 at Nylon Plant," *News Journal* (New Castle, DE), October 15, 2008; Geoff Folsom, "Flint Hills Closing: Vest Vows to Find Use for Plant," *Odessa American* (TX), November 7, 2008; Geoff Folsom, "Flint Hills ESOP," *Odessa American* (TX), January 28, 2009; Jeff Amy, "Monroeville Area to Lose 300 Jobs," *Mobile Register Press* (AL), November 12, 2008; "Invista Will Halt Nylon Production in Waynesboro, Vice Mayor Says It's a 'Strong Blow' to City," *News Virginian* (Waynesboro, VA), December 10, 2008; Dan Heath, "70 to Lose Jobs at Georgia-Pacific," *Press-Republican* (Plattsburgh, NY), December 11, 2008; Jimmy LaRoue, "Invista Cuts Debt by 63 Percent," *News Virginian*, February 10, 2009.

353　　*The bloodletting at Koch . . . was mild*: National job-cut figures compiled from historic database of the US Bureau of Labor Statistics.

353　　*Many of the jobs lost in 2008 never came back*: Blinder, *After the Music Stopped*, 10–14.

354　　*Things looked very different from Charles Koch's office*: Charles Koch, Hall, Beckett, Markel, Feilmeier, interviews by author, 2013–16.

355　　*It's difficult for outsiders to even understand . . . a contango market*: Beckett, former senior Koch Industries trading executives speaking on background, interviews by author, 2013–16.

355　　*When the market goes into contango . . . to profit*: Ibid.; Robert Tuttle and Alexander Kwiatkowski, "In Troubled Times, Stockpiling Crude May Be the Way to Hit a Profit Gusher," *Bloomberg News*, December 9, 2008; "Pricing for Oil, Gas Seems Peculiar," *Times Record News* (Wichita Falls, TX), February 8, 2009; Guy Chazan and Russell Gold, "Big Oil Still 'Printing Money' Despite Slump in Crude Prices," *Wall Street Journal*, April 30, 2009; "Hoarding Crude Boosts Futures Prices: Companies Stockpiling in Supertankers," *Bloomberg News*, December 9, 2008.

356　　*Outsiders . . . were denied*: Steve Everly, "Speculators Profit by Locking in Higher Oil Prices," *Kansas City Star* (MO), February 10, 2009.

357 *even David Koch was forced to adjust his behavior and his outlook*: Mike Spector, "Big Players Scale Back Charitable Donations," Associated Press, November 25, 2008.

357 *One evening in Houston . . . an exclusive social event*: Franklin, interviews by author, 2016.

359 *First came a giant federal bailout plan*: David M. Herszenhorn, "Bailout Plan Wins Approval: Democrats Vow Tighter Rules," *New York Times*, October 3, 2008; Edmund L. Andrews, Michael J. de la Merced, and Mary Williams Walsh, "Fed's $85 Billion Loan Rescues Insurer," *New York Times*, September 16, 2008.

360 *What was unspoken . . . was that all of this would also mean more taxes*: "Charles Koch: Perspective," *Discovery: The Quarterly Newsletter of Koch Companies*, January 2008.

360 *This moment was dangerous, in Charles Koch's view*: Ibid., January 2009; Bill Wilson and Roy Wenzl, "The Kochs' Quest to Save America," *Wichita Eagle*, October 13, 2012; Jake Tapper, "Billionaire Conservative Activist Charles Koch on 2012 Election: 'We Have Saddam Hussein, This Is the Mother of All Wars,'" ABC News online, last modified September 6, 2011; Charles G. Koch, "Anti-Capitalism and Business," address to the Institute for Humane Studies, April 27, 1974.

361 *After these crashes . . . the American people blamed capitalism*: "Charles Koch: Perspective," *Discovery: The Quarterly Newsletter of Koch Companies*, January 2009.

362 *message found a receptive audience in Steve Mawer's living room*: Franklin, interviews by author, 2017.

363 *On the wall . . . painting that was quite unpleasant*: Notes and photos from reporting in Charles Koch's office, 2015.

CHAPTER 18: SOLIDARITY

367 *In the early morning hours . . . Koch Industries' headquarters*: Notes from reporting at Koch Industries headquarters, 2015; current and former Koch Industries employees, interviews by author, 2013–18.

368 *training began . . . a certain kind of employee*: Pohlman, Charles Koch, Hall, Markel, interviews by author, 2013–15; Charles Koch, *Science of Success*, 77–94.

368 *Koch began training them immediately*: Notes from guided tours at Koch Industries headquarters, 2013, 2018; Abel Winn, Andrew Methvin, Hoffmann, interviews by author, 2013–16.

368 *The unity among Koch Industries' employees*: General analysis based on interviews with dozens of current and former Koch Industries employees, 2013–18.

369 *One of the true believers . . . Abel Winn*: Winn, interviews by author, 2013.

370 *Winn helped design a large laboratory*: Ibid.; Amy Geiszler-Jones, "New Center to Teach Successful Koch Industries Strategy," *Inside WSU*, September 22, 2006; Michael D. Parente and Abel M. Winn, "Bargaining Behavior and the Tragedy of the

Anticommons," *Journal of Economic Behavior and Organization* 84 (November 2012): 475–90.

371   *Hammond . . . worked in a crummy little office*: Hammond, Gary Bucknum, Franzen, Dodge, Smith, interviews by author, 2013–17; descriptions of IBU office from notes, photos, and video taken during reporting trips, 2013, 2017.

372   *The size of the task . . . more severe than many of them understood*: These figures and analysis are based on copies of IBU labor agreements for workers at the warehouse dating back to 1975, excluding several contracts during the 1980s and 1990s. The contracts from the 1970s provided a historic baseline, while more recent contracts showed the trajectory of working conditions since 2000. During this time, ownership of the warehouse changed several times, but the facility and the IBU remained constant. IBU labor contracts: 1975, 1978, 2000, 2005, 2010 (the first contract negotiated with Koch Industries), 2014, 2016.

373   *economic stagnation . . . Georgia-Pacific warehouse workers*: Lawrence Mishel, Elise Gould, and Josh Bivens, "Wage Stagnation in Nine Charts," Fig. 2: "Workers produced much more, but typical workers' pay lagged far behind," Economic Policy Institute, January 6, 2015 (analysis of data from the Bureau of Labor Statistics and Bureau of Economic Analysis); "Real Median Family Income in the United States," data from the Federal Reserve Bank of St. Louis: https://fred.stlouisfed.org/series/MEFAINUSA672N.

373   *Hammond and Bucknum were elected*: Hammond, Bucknum, Franzen, Dodge, McKinney, Smith, interviews by author, 2013–17.

373   *Abel Winn closely scrutinized the data he developed*: Winn, interviews by author, 2015; Parente and Winn, "Bargaining Behavior."

374   *Hammond and Bucknum negotiated*: Hammond, Bucknum, Franzen, Dodge, McKinney, Smith, interviews by author, 2013–17; LinkedIn data from LinkedIn website search.

375   *the university dispatched Lynn Feekin*: Lynn Feekin, Ron Teninty, Bucknum, Hammond, Franzen, interviews by author, 2017; descriptions of union hall meeting room from notes and photos taken inside the room during a reporting trip, 2017; Joseph A. McCartin, *Collision Course: Ronald Reagan, the Air Traffic Controllers, and the Strike That Changed America* (New York: Oxford University Press, 2011); Stanley Aronowitz, *The Death and Life of American Labor* (Brooklyn, NY: Verso, 2014).

376   *The first negotiating meeting was held*: Hammond, Bucknum, Franzen, Ken Harrison, interviews by author, 2017; IBU labor contracts, 1975, 1978, 2000, 2005, 2010; internal IBU memos and negotiation proposals from the 2010 period, including nearly twenty IBU bargaining proposals.

380   *Don Barnard reported . . . to a man named Ken Harrison*: Harrison, Hammond, Bucknum, interviews by author, 2017.

381   *Harrison earned degrees . . . career at Georgia-Pacific*: Harrison, interview by author,

2017; Pohlman, interview by author, 2013. Pohlman, a former Koch Industries HR executive, confirmed that Koch's use of a "caucus" room and deep data analysis during labor union negotiations dated back to at least the 1990s.

382 *IBU set up a large stage . . . in downtown Portland*: Hammond, Bucknum, Franzen, McKinney, Harrison, interviews by author, 2017; descriptions of the rally and its attendees are taken from dozens of photos provided by the IBU.

383 *The rally . . . stoked energy*: Hammond, Bucknum, Franzen, McKinney, Harrison, interviews by author, 2017; descriptions of union hall taken from notes and photos during reporting trip, 2017.

384 *Winn put the final touches on his study*: Winn, interviews by author, 2013; Parente and Winn, "Bargaining Behavior."

384 *IBU workers faced outside competition*: Trimm, Hammond, Bucknum, Franzen, McKinney, interviews by author, 2017.

386 *This is what the IBU would get*: Teninty, Hammond, Bucknum, Franzen, Smith, Dodge, McKinney, interviews by author, 2017; IBU labor contracts, 2005, 2010, 2014; internal IBU memos and negotiation proposals from the 2010 period, including nearly twenty IBU bargaining proposals.

387 *Franzen . . . ready to encourage his coworkers to go on strike*: Hammond, Bucknum, Franzen, Smith, Dodge, McKinney, Alan Cote, Harrison, interviews by author, 2017.

388 *IBU's struggle was not for nothing*: This passage is based on an analysis of IBU labor contracts between 1975 and 2016 conducted by Ron Teninty, who does similar analysis for clients who engage him to help in labor negotiations. He compiles pay and benefit figures from the contracts, adjusts for inflation and other factors, and collates it into a unified spreadsheet for analysis.

389 *Franzen went back to driving a forklift*: Franzen, Harrison, interviews by author, 2017.

389 *Charles Koch had been disturbed . . . ascendancy of progressive politics*: Former senior political operatives with Koch Industries speaking on background, interviews by author, 2014–17; Wilson and Wenzl, "Kochs' Quest."

CHAPTER 19: WARMING

392 *Charles Koch hosted a private party at his home*: This event was described by two former senior political operatives with Koch Industries speaking on background, who attended the annual party; Koch PAC spending figures from the Center for Responsive Politics database.

394 *There was a belief . . . could put the company out of business*: Hoffmann, two former senior political operatives with Koch Industries speaking on background, interviews by author, 2014–17.

394 *Koch was caught unprepared when the US Senate investigated oil theft*: Koch lobby-

ing expenditures compiled from Koch Industries quarterly lobbying disclosures, Office of the Clerk, US House of Representatives; Koch Industries lobbying database, the Center for Responsive Politics.

395 *Even these expenditures . . . Koch's political machine*: Charles G. Koch Charitable Foundation, Claude R. Lambe Charitable Foundation, 990 Disclosure Forms from the IRS, 2001–10.

396 *Phillips could have ended up as a Koch Industries employee*: Jonathan Phillips (former US Senate senior staffer), Jeffrey Sharp (former congressional staffer), speaking on background, interviews by author, 2017; description of Longworth Building and committee offices taken from notes and photos during reporting trips to the office, 2017.

396 *The Committee on Global Warming . . . one of Nancy Pelosi's first official acts*: Phillips, Sharp, interviews by author, 2017; analysis of Congress based on interviews with lobbyists, congressional staffers, political scientists, and previously cited books on politics; John Heilprin, "Pelosi Shaking Up House Fiefdoms to Draft Global Warming Proposal," Associated Press, January 17, 2007; "Speaker Pelosi Announces Creation of Select Committee on Energy Independence, and Global Warming," *US Fed News*, January 18, 2007; Darren Samuelsohn, "Climate: Pelosi to Create Special House Committee for Global Warming," *Environment and Energy Daily*, January 17, 2007; Cathy Cash, "Key Lawmakers See Reasons to Push for Vote on Climate Bill in '08; Will 'Work It One-on-One,'" *Electric Utility Week*, December 24, 2007; "Pelosi Creating Global Warming Panel; Dingell Shrugs," *National Journal's Congress Daily*, January 17, 2007; Susan Davis, "Dingell Gives Warming Panel Tepid Reception," *Roll Call*, January 18, 2007; John Dingell, US House of Representatives, financial disclosure statement for calendar year 2005.

397 *Ed Markey built a team . . . bank heist*: Phillips, Sharp, interviews by author, 2017.

398 *began to smolder sometime around the year 1800*: This account is based on multiple sources about climate change and energy. Two of the most valuable sources were Bill McKibben, ed., *The Global Warming Reader* (New York: Penguin Books, 2011); and Joseph Romm, *Climate Change: What Everyone Needs to Know* (New York: Oxford University Press, 2016). Also Daniel Yergin, *The Quest: Energy, Security and the Remaking of the Modern World* (New York: Penguin Press, 2011), 426–504.

399 *Carbon is a curiously durable element*: Nicola Jones, "How the World Passed a Carbon Threshold and Why It Matters," *Yale Environment 360*, January 26, 2017.

399 *When a barrel of crude oil . . . invisible carbon*: Jim Bliss, "Carbon Dioxide Emissions per Barrel of Crude," *The Quiet Road* (blog), March 20, 2008; Johannes Friedrich and Thomas Damassa, "The History of Carbon Dioxide Emissions," World Resources Institute online, last modified May 21, 2014; carbon, parts per million in atmosphere, taken from National Oceanic and Atmospheric Administration database.

400 *In 1988 . . . Intergovernmental Panel on Climate Change*: Reports available at IPCC online, www.ipcc.ch.

401 *Koch Industries, ExxonMobil, and other firms . . . "alternative" view*: *Koch Industries: Secretly Funding the Climate Denial Machine* (Washington, DC: Greenpeace, March 2010); Connor Gibson, "Koch Industries, Still Fueling Climate Denial," PolluterWatch.com, last modified May 9, 2011; Seminar Agenda for "Global Environmental Crises: Science or Politics?" June 5–6, 1991, Cato Institute.

401 *ExxonMobil eventually abandoned this strategy, but Koch Industries persevered*: Ellender, interviews by author, 2014–17; Steve Coll, *Private Empire: ExxonMobil and American Power* (New York: Penguin Press, 2012), 534–56.

401 *Koch Industries officials were even more dismissive*: Former senior Koch Industries executive speaking on background, Hoffmann, interviews by author, 2017.

402 *This is what lent the sense of desperation*: Phillips, Sharp, interviews by author, 2017.

402 *Markey's committee realized . . . a more provocative step*: Ibid.; "Rep. Markey Announces Revolutionary Global Warming Bill," press release, May 28, 2008; "Rep. Edward J. Markey Delivers Remarks on Global Warming Legislation at the Center for American Progress," press release, May 28, 2008; "Rep. Markey: G8 Global Warming 'Goal' Doesn't Reach the Goal Line," press release, July 8, 2008; information on George H. W. Bush and cap-and-trade law for acid rain, Yergin, *The Quest*, 476–79.

404 *Koch Industries' lobbying office . . . majestic stone building*: Hoffmann, interviews by author, 2016–17; descriptions of Koch Industries' lobbying office from notes taken during tour of office and interview of Ellender in its conference room, 2014.

405 *Koch's lobbying efforts had been fragmented*: Former senior Koch Industries political operatives speaking on background, interviews by author, 2014–17; Koch Industries and related companies Lobbying Disclosure Reports, Office of the Clerk, US House of Representatives, 2005–10.

405 *Hoffmann led an internal committee at Koch*: Hoffmann, interviews by author, 2016–17.

406 *Koch's team of lobbyists gathered*: Ellender, Hoffmann, Kelly Bingel, former senior Koch Industries political operatives speaking on background, interviews by author, 2014–17; descriptions of meeting room taken from notes, 2014.

407 *For all the talk about ideological purity, Ellender's operation reflected a more complicated reality*: Ellender, Hoffmann, Bingel (speaking on background), Phillips, Sharp, Lee Drutman, interviews by author, 2013–17; Drutman, *The Business of America Is Lobbying: How Corporations Became Politicized and Politics Became More Corporate* (New York: Oxford University Press, 2015) 4–40; Koch lobbying expenditures drawn from Koch Companies Public Sector Lobbying Disclosure Reports, Office of the Clerk, US House of Representatives; Koch lobbyist database, Center for Responsive Politics.

408 *Ellender's team was small, considering the size of their job*: Koch Industries and related companies Lobbying Disclosure Reports, Office of the Clerk, US House of
Representatives, 2005–10; Koch Lobbyist database, Center for Responsive Politics.

409 *One of the lobbyists . . . Kelly Bingel*: Bingel, Alex Vogel (former senior Koch Indus-
tries political operative speaking on background), interviews by author, 2016–17;
Koch Industries expenditures to Mehlman Vogel Castagnetti drawn from Koch
Companies Public Sector Lobbying Disclosure Reports, Office of the Clerk, US
House of Representatives; Koch lobbyist database, Center for Responsive Politics.

410 *There were two ways . . . attention of a politician*: Bingel, former congressional staffers speaking on background, two former senior Koch Industries political operatives speaking on background, interviews by author, 2015–17.

411 *David Hoffmann worked for months*: Hoffmann, interviews by author, 2016–17.

412 *The meeting convened*: Ibid.; chart on "carbon allotments" under Waxman-Markey
entitled "Allocation of Cumulative Pollution Allowances in ACES Cap and Trade
Program 2012–2025," produced by the Breakthrough Institute, 2009.

414 *the carbon allotment provision . . . was written by Jonathan Phillips*: Phillips, interviews by author, 2017.

414 *the long-held liberal dream . . . starting to look like a reality*: Phillips, Sharp, interviews by author, 2017; John M. Broder, "Waxman Advances in Struggle to Wrest
Committee from Dingell," *New York Times*, November 19, 2008; John M. Broder,
"Obama Urges Passage of Climate Bill," *New York Times*, June 23, 2009; Teryn Norris and Jesse Jenkins, "Climate Bill Analysis, Part 1: Waxman-Markey Gives Nearly
5 Times More to Polluters Than to Clean Energy," Breakthrough Institute, May 15,
2009; John M. Broder, "House Republicans Draft Energy Bill with Heavy Focus on
Nuclear Power," *New York Times*, June 10, 2009.

415 *The committee invited conservative Democrats to negotiate*: Phillips, Sharp, interviews by author, 2017; Norris and Jenkins, "Climate Bill Analysis, Part 1."

416 *His view was not shared by Koch Industries' lobbyists*: Hoffmann, two former senior
Koch Industries political operatives speaking on background, interviews by author, 2014–17.

416 *Inglis was a reliably conservative Republican*: Bob Inglis, former senior Koch Industries political operative, interviews by author, 2017; Louise Radnofsky and Michael
M. Phillips, "As US Political Divide Widened, a Friendship Fell into the Rift," *Wall
Street Journal*, November 9, 2010; "Raise Wages, Cut Carbon Act of 2009," text of
bill H.R. 2380.

418 *Inglis was closely aligned with Koch Industries*: Inglis, speaking on background, interviews by author, 2017; Koch Industries expenditures to Inglis drawn from Koch
Industries campaign finance database, Center for Responsive Politics.

418 *The pressure intensified . . . Waxman-Markey bill was passed*: Inglis, Phillips, interviews by author, 2017.

419 *Inglis raised cash . . . office on Capitol Hill*: Inglis, interviews by author, 2017.

420 *Jonathan Phillips stood in the gallery*: John M. Broder, "House Backs Bill, 219–212, to Curb Global Warming," *New York Times*, June 27, 2009; vote tally details from "H.R. 2454 (111th): American Clean Energy and Security Act of 2009," GovTrack .us; Ed Markey and Mike Pence comments during vote taken from C-Span archival footage.

422 *Koch held meetings in the company boardroom*: Former senior Koch Industries political operative speaking on background, interviews by author, 2017.

424 *Phillips and the other members of the Global Warming Committee*: Phillips, Sharp, interviews by author; quotes from Mike Castle town hall event taken from "Mike Castle Confronts Right Wing Hatred," video, 5:33, uploaded to YouTube by climatebrad on July 21, 2009, www.youtube.com/watch?v=lbQKry5Z_ok.

CHAPTER 20: HOTTER

427 *Inglis was standing in an auditorium*: Inglis, interview by author, 2017; footage of Inglis town halls taken from "US Congressman Bob Inglis Questioned at Tea Party," video, 9:50, uploaded to YouTube by ElectionFastFacts on April 25, 2010, www.youtube.com/watch?v=G_OHCGnZZAo; and "Healthcare Bill to Put Embedded Chips in Everyone?," video, 2:24, uploaded to YouTube by Jonathon Hill on August 25, 2009, www.youtube.com/watch?v=4Ots4zUQZg8.

429 *heated protests . . . Fourth of July weekend of 2009*: Steve Lonegan, former senior Koch Industries political operatives speaking on background, interviews by author, 2017; footage of Fourth of July Americans for Prosperity rally taken from "Taxpayer Tea Parties Sponsored by Americans for Prosperity New Jersey," video, 4:09, uploaded to YouTube by trinnj on July 6, 2009, www.youtube.com /watch?v=qSM2rD0alMo; Americans for Prosperity financial details and state chapter listings taken from Americans for Prosperity, 990 Disclosure Forms with the IRS, 2003–10.

435 *Bob Inglis's congressional district . . . Boiling Springs*: Maria Brady, Inglis, interviews by author, 2017.

436 *Tea Parties . . . national conversation*: Maria Brady, interview by author, 2017; Rick Santelli, archival CNBC footage, www.youtube.com/watch?v=zp-Jw-5Kx8k.

437 *Maria and Michael Brady . . . helped form the Boiling Springs Tea Party*: Description of Michael Brady's costume taken from photo of Boiling Springs Tea Party rally.

437 *This time Maria and Michael had help*: Archival Americans for Prosperity websites taken from the Internet Archive; Michael Brady's contact information from AFP South Carolina blog: "July 4th Tea Party Rallies in South Carolina," July 1, 2009; address and time of Bob Inglis town hall taken from AFP page "Visit Your Representatives and Senators!," September 1, 2009.

438 *disagreement between Tea Party activists and . . . Charles Koch*: Maria Brady, interview by author, 2017; Vanessa Williamson, Theda Skocpol, and John Coggin, "The

Tea Party and the Remaking of Republican Conservatism," *Perspectives on Politics*, March 2011.

439   *Glenn Beck was the most prominent voice*: Nellie Andreeva, "Is Glenn Beck's Popularity Fading?," *Deadline* online, last modified February 2, 2011; Dana Milbank, *Tears of a Clown: Glenn Beck and the Tea Bagging of America* (New York: Doubleday, 2010); Glenn Beck, "The world is on fire;" from "Glenn Beck: The Antichrist Revealed," clip, www.youtube.com/watch?v=gpWPfY9hYC8; clips of Beck doubting climate change and criticizing the Obama administration's renewable-energy programs, www.youtube.com/watch?v=xquohKzR8QI; www.youtube.com /watch?v=JJwmi9IqUyg; www.youtube.com/watch?v=ZKlfXtqnG_w; www.you tube.com/watch?v=I4HdyRovA1o.

439   *Americans for Prosperity helped promote this point of view*: Phil Kerpen, guest appearance on Glenn Beck, www.youtube.com/watch?v=dJpPktn4f0M.

440   *Beck's show informed Maria Brady's self-education*: Maria Brady, interview by author, 2017.

441   *When Bob Inglis . . . Brady and her compatriots were prepared*: Inglis, Maria Brady, interviews by author, 2017; exchange about Glenn Beck from "Crazy Teabaggers & Retirees Boo Rep. Bob Inglis (R-SC) for Suggesting They 'Turn Glenn Beck Off,'" video, 1:15, uploaded to YouTube by chinacreekpj on August 8, 2009, www.you tube.com/watch?v=wPbs0ozEVBc.

442   *Koch Industries' activities . . . one piece of a broader strategy*: Lonegan, Hoffmann, former senior Koch Industries political operative speaking on background, interviews by author, 2017.

442   *Republican lawmakers who voted for the Waxman-Markey bill*: Lonegan, interviews by author, 2017; Jim Lockwood, "N.J. Activists Protest Against 'Cap-and-Trade' Law Aimed at Fighting Global Warming," *Star-Ledger* (NJ), July 20, 2010; Paul Mulshine, "Here's the Lonegan Letter," *Star-Ledger* (NJ), July 13, 2009; Matt Friedman, "Von Savage Calls Shaftan 'Reckless': Lonegan Backs Primary Challenges to Three Congressmen," *New York Observer*, June 30, 2009; Derek Harper, "Energy Vote Has the Right Angry with LoBiondo: Republican Voted for Cap-and-Trade Bill," *Press of Atlantic City* (NJ), July 3, 2009.

443   *Harry Reid . . . manipulating the political process*: Phillips, speaking on background, interviews by author, 2017; quotes and descriptions of US Senate hearings taken from archival C-Span footage; Ryan Lizza, "As the World Burns," *New Yorker*, October 11, 2010; "Democrats Feel the Heat from the Heartland, Push Back Timeline on Global Warming Legislation," Congressional Documents and Publications, Senate Environment and Public Works Committee, July 9, 2009; Darren Samuelsohn, "Boxer, Baucus Headed for Turf War over Cap-and-Trade Bill," *Environment & Energy Daily*, August 7, 2009; "Hunt for Health Compromise Continues as Deadline Looms," *National Journal's Congress Daily*, July 20, 2009, accessed 2018; Josef Hebert and Dina Cappiello, "Senate Climate Bill Tougher Than House Ver-

sion," Associated Press, September 29, 2009; "Boxer Readies Carbon Bill Amid
Competitive Issues," *Electric Power Daily*, July 17, 2009; Darren Samuelsohn,
"Dems Want Global Warming Law by December," *Environment & Energy Daily*,
July 9, 2009; "Senate Democrats Further Delay Climate Bill," *Clean Air Report*, September 3, 2009.

445   *The strategy originated . . . Koch had been building for almost forty years*: Two former senior Koch Industries political operatives speaking on background, interviews by author, 2014–17; *Koch Industries: Secretly Funding the Climate Denial Machine*.

446   *In 2007, for example, Koch Industries quietly funded . . . Third Way*: This account is based on two sources with direct knowledge of the transaction between Koch Industries and Third Way, speaking on background, interviews by author, 2017. The sources spoke independently and represented both sides of the transaction. A third source, a former Koch political operative who was not directly involved with the transaction, confirmed the broad outlines of the incident. Also Anne Kim, John Lageson, and Jim Kessler, "Why Lou Dobbs Is Winning," Third Way report, November 2007.

447   *To produce the report . . . American Council for Capital Formation*: This account is based on one source with direct knowledge of the matter, speaking on background, interview by author, 2017.

447   *Koch network had funded . . . Claude Lambe Charitable Foundation*: Claude Lambe Charitable Foundation, 990 Disclosure Forms with the IRS, 2006–10; *Analysis of the Waxman-Markey Bill "The American Clean Energy and Security Act of 2009,"* a report by the American Council for Capital Formation and the National Association of Manufacturers.

448   *The study was announced*: Erin Streeter, "State-by-State Analysis of Waxman-Markey Cap and Trade Legislation Paints Dour Picture for Nation's Economy: NAM-ACCF Study Concludes Bill Will Cost 2.4 Million Jobs," press release, National Association of Manufacturers, December 3, 2009.

448   *Once the ACCF's study was published . . . echo chamber system*: Source with direct knowledge of the matter speaking on background, interview by author, 2017; "The ACCF/NAM Estimate of Waxman-Markey," statement on the Institute for Energy Research website, August 13, 2009; Lee Fang, "Charles Koch Personally Founded Group Protecting Oil Industry Hand-Outs, Documents Reveal," Republic Report, August 29, 2014.

449   *After the study . . . another Koch Industries–affiliated think tank*: Source with direct knowledge of the matter speaking on background, interview by author, 2017; Thomas Pyle, Lobbying Disclosure Reports, Office of the Clerk, US House of Representatives; American Energy Alliance, "Fact Sheet: AEA Radio Ad 'Waxman-Markey Energy Tax'"; American Energy Alliance, "Fact Sheet: AEA TV Ad 'Turned Off.'"

450   *"It's pretty clear the costs outweigh the benefits"*: Margo Thorning, testimony to US

Senate Finance Committee, "Climate Change and Jobs," November 10, 2010, archival footage from C-Span.

450   *Inside Koch Industries . . . a tremendous victory*: Source with knowledge of reaction
inside Koch Industries speaking on background, interview by author, 2017.

450   *Koch Industries wasn't the only company to use these tactics*: Koch Industries: Secretly
Funding the Climate Denial Machine.

450   *The efforts to undermine popular support . . . were effective*: Dina Cappiello, "Poll:
Americans' Belief in Global Warming Cools," Associated Press, October 22, 2009.

451   *Koch Industries applied yet more pressure*: Lonegan, former senior Koch Industries
political operative speaking on background, interviews by author, 2017.

451   *Bob Inglis . . . challenged by one of Koch's candidates*: Bob Inglis, former senior Koch
Industries political operative speaking on background, interviews by author, 2017;
Koch Industries donations to Trey Gowdy taken from campaign finance disclosure
reports, "Trey Gowdy for Congress," 2010; campaign finance database, Center for
Responsive Politics; Rudolph Bell, "Spartanburg Prosecutor May Challenge Inglis,"
Greenville News (SC), May 24, 2009; Bell, "Critics Blast Inglis," *Greenville News*
(SC), September 17, 2009; Bell, "Republican Field Narrows in 4th District Race,"
Greenville News (SC), July 11, 2009; "Republican Congressional Races Take Shape,"
State (Columbia, SC), June 14, 2009; Radnofsky and Phillips, "As US Political Di-
vide Widened."

451   *Inglis and Gowdy met . . . tent next to a highway*: "Landrum Debate Part 12," video,
6:09, uploaded to YouTube by ThomasforCongress on May 24, 2010, www.you
tube.com/watch?v=O8z2XsDR2qo.

452   *As it pressured . . . built a hard wall of "no" votes*: Carbon pledge figures taken from
Americans for Prosperity website: "No Climate Tax," archived pages from 2009–10,
the Internet Archive.

453   *As Koch Industries encircled . . . passing Obamacare*: Phillips, Sharp, interviews by
author, 2017; Lizza, "As the World Burns."

453   *Bob Inglis was fighting in a primary election against Trey Gowdy*: Inglis, interviews
by author, 2017.

454   *It is difficult . . . to declare its final defeat*: Phillips, interviews by author, 2017; Lizza,
"As the World Burns"; "Hunt for Health Compromise Continues as Deadline
Looms," *National Journal's Congress Daily*, July 20, 2009.

455   *Americans for Prosperity . . . strongest position ever*: Lonegan, interviews by author,
2017.

455   *As AFP solidified . . . change it from within*: Theda Skocpol and Alexander Hertel-
Fernandez, "The Koch Network and Republican Party Extremism," *Perspectives on
Politics* 14, no. 3 (September 2016): 681–99.

455   *In November . . . destroyed the Democratic majority*: Jeff Zeleny, "GOP Captures
House, but Not Senate," *New York Times*, November 2, 2010.

456   *The magnitude of this victory was immense*: Charles Lewis, Eric Holmberg,

Alexia Fernandez Campbell, and Lydia Beyoud, "Koch Millions Spread Influence Through Nonprofits, Colleges," *Investigative Reporting Workshop*, last modified July 1, 2013.

456   *One of the earliest . . . Select Committee on Energy Independence and Global Warming*: Phillips, Sharp, interviews by author, 2017.

456   *In the absence . . . continued to soar*: Data from Center for Climate and Energy Solutions Carbon Dioxide Emissions database, www.c2es.org/content/international-emissions; International Energy Agency, "Global Energy & CO2 Status Report," 2017; Romm, *Climate Change*; carbon, parts per million in atmosphere, taken from National Oceanic and Atmospheric Administration database, accessed 2018.

457   *After he left politics, Bob Inglis . . . climate change*: Inglis, interview by author, 2017.

458   *Charles Koch still felt threatened*: Charles Koch to donors, September 24, 2010.

458   *Security around the donor conference was intense*: Former senior Koch Industries political operative speaking on background, interviews by author, 2017; Kate Zernike, "Secretive Republican Donors Are Planning Ahead," *New York Times*, October 19, 2010; Rich Connell and Tom Hamburger, "Hundreds March Outside Koch Brothers' Retreat," *Los Angeles Times*, January 31, 2011; Jesse Marx, "Charles Koch to Indian Wells Donors: 'I'm Still Here,'" *Desert Sun* (Palm Springs, CA), January 30, 2016.

458   *The events had grown . . . since 2006*: Charles Koch donor network agenda and brochure for gathering in Aspen, Colorado, June 27 and 28, 2010, "Understanding and Addressing Threats to American Free Enterprise and Prosperity."

459   *The publicity culminated in August of 2010*: Jane Mayer, "Covert Operations," *New Yorker*, August 30, 2010.

459   *The whale . . . harpoons began to fly*: Connell and Hamburger, "Hundreds March"; descriptions of protests taken from amateur video of event; Charles Koch quote taken from leaked audio from event.

460   *"I remember talking to him . . . victims of the system"*: Former Koch Industries senior political operative speaking on background, interview by author, 2017.

461   *Charles Koch's net worth doubled*: *Forbes* Billionaires list, 2008–16.

CHAPTER 21: THE WAR FOR AMERICA'S BTUS

462   *In the winter of 2010 . . . a series of business deals*: Brad Razook, Tony Sementelli, interviews by author, 2018; "Koch Pipeline Company Expanding South Texas Crude Oil Pipeline Capabilities; Flint Hills Resources to Process Additional Supplies of Eagle Ford Production," *ENP Newswire*, November 30, 2009.

462   *Koch's series of deals accelerated*: Razook, Sementelli, interviews by author, 2018; "Koch Pipeline and Arrowhead Pipeline Add to South Texas Crude Oil Capacity," *ENP Newswire*, September 29, 2010; "Koch Pipeline Company and NuStar Logistics Finalize Agreement on South Texas Crude Oil Pipeline Capacity to Move Eagle

Ford Crude to Corpus Christi," BusinessWire, October 18, 2010; "Koch Pipeline Company to Begin Building 16-Inch Crude Oil Pipeline in Texas," Koch Pipeline Company online, last modified December 16, 2010; "Flint Hills Resources Adding Oil Shipping Capacity," BusinessWire, February 17, 2011; "New Pipeline from Pettus to Corpus Christi Will Aid Eagle Ford Shale Production," *Victoria Advocate* (TX), April 10, 2011.

463 *The puzzling part . . . oil supplies that didn't seem to exist*: Eagle Ford region production and drilling rig figures taken from US Energy Information oil production database.

463 *The wells . . . were the face of an energy revolution*: Meghan L. O'Sullivan, *Windfall: How the New Energy Abundance Upends Global Politics and Strengthens America's Power* (New York: Simon & Schuster, 2017), 1–107.

464 *The first signals emerged . . . around 2009*: Razook, Sementelli, interviews by author, 2018; US natural gas production figures taken from US Energy Information gas production database.

465 *This was the start of the fracking revolution*: Michael Levi, *The Power Surge: Energy, Opportunity, and the Battle for America's Future* (New York: Oxford University Press, 2013), 20–49.

465 *The earliest waves . . . Koch's leadership team*: Feilmeier, Razook, Sementelli, interviews by author, 2013–18; US natural gas prices taken from US Energy Information gas price database.

466 *Razook and other senior executives . . . top story of the Tower*: Razook, Sementelli, interviews by author, 2018; descriptions of Flint Hills offices based on notes and photos from reporting trip, 2018.

467 *One reason . . . fracking had been around since the 1970s*: Meghan L. O'Sullivan, *Windfall: How the New Energy Abundance Upends Global Politics and Strengthens America's Power* (New York: Simon & Schuster, 2017), 21–26.

468 *In 1980 . . . tax break for natural gas supplies*: Alex Trembath, Jesse Jenkins, Ted Nordhaus, and Michael Shellenberger, "Where the Shale Gas Revolution Came From: Government's Role in the Development of Hydraulic Fracturing in Shale," Breakthrough Institute online, last modified May 2012; Michael Shellenberger and Ted Nordhaus, "A Boom in Shale Gas? Credit the Feds," *Washington Post*, December 16, 2011.

468 *Brad Urban and his team canvassed the industry*: Razook, Sementelli, interviews by author, 2018; Eagle Ford region production and figures taken from US Energy Information oil production database.

470 *Koch Industries' boardroom . . . Koch's office*: Razook, Sementelli, interviews by author, 2018; descriptions of boardroom taken from notes and photographs during reporting trip, 2018.

471 *The Eagle Ford region . . . July of 2010*: Eagle Ford region production and figures taken from US Energy Information oil production database; "Eagle Ford Takes

Flight," *Discovery: The Quarterly Newsletter of Koch Companies*, October 2011; O'Sullivan, *Windfall*, 1–107.

472   *Along the Gulf Coast of Texas ... oil refineries*: Notes and photos from reporting trip to Gulf Coast and Flint Hills facility near Port Arthur, Texas, in 2016.

473   *Nobody had built ... since 1977*: Anthony Andrews et al., *Small Refineries and Oil Field Processors: Opportunities and Challenges* (Washington, DC: Congressional Research Service, August 11, 2014).

473   *The primary obstacle to building a new refinery was the Clean Air Act*: "The Petroleum Industry: Mergers, Structural Change, and Antitrust Enforcement," Federal Trade Commission Bureau of Economics, Staff Study, August 2004; Anthony Andrews and Robert Pirog, *The US Oil Refining Industry: Background in Changing Markets and Fuel Policies* (Washington, DC: Congressional Research Service, December 27, 2012); Andrews, et al., *Small Refineries and Oil Field Processors*; Robert Bradley and Thomas Tanton, "US Petroleum Refining: Let the Market Function," Institute for Energy Research, December 19, 2005; *Energy Market: Effects of Mergers and Market Concentration in the US Petroleum Industry* (Washington, DC: US General Accounting Office, May 2004).

473   *Between 1991 and 2000, there were 338 mergers*: Ibid., 7; Diana L. Moss, "Competition in US Petroleum Refining and Marketing: Part 1—Industry Trends," working paper, American Antitrust Institute, January 2007.

473   *In 2002, there were ... By 2012, there were only 115*: *The US Oil Refining Industry*, 1.

474   *Arizona Clean Fuels attempted to build*: Andrews, *Small Refineries and Oil Field Processors*, 8; Joyce Lobeck, "3 Major Yuma-Area Projects Have Stalled, *Yuma Sun* (AZ), September 4, 2011; Michele Linck, "It's No Race, but Arizona Clean Fuels Is Ahead, for Now," *Sioux City Journal* (IA), September 4, 2009.

474   *Fewer and fewer companies ... larger and larger facilities*: Andrews and Pirog, *The US Oil Refining Industry: Background in Changing Markets and Fuel Policies* (Washington, DC: Congressional Research Service, December 27, 2012), 4–5.

474   *By 2004 ... "imperfectly competitive"*: *Energy Market*, 113–14.

474   *By the time the Eagle Ford tsunami ... full tilt*: John R. Auers, interview by author, 2018; "US Refined Product Exports Developments, Prospects and Challenges," presentation by John R. Auers, to 2017 EIA Energy Conference, Washington, DC, June 27, 2017, slide 6.

474   *The bottleneck was severe ... catastrophic price increases*: Alison Sider, "Refinery Woes Stall Gasoline Price Drops," *Wall Street Journal*, August 23, 2015.

475   *In this environment ... breathtaking*: Auers, interview by author, 2018; "The Refining Cup: US 'Trumps' the World—but Challenges Abound," presentation by John R. Auers, to AFPM Annual Environmental Conference, October 17, 2016, slide 19.

475   *The profit margins fell sharply after 2011*: Auers, interview by author, 2018; "The Refining Cup," slide 19.

475   *Koch enhanced the profitability ... in Houston*: Osbourn, interview by author, 2016;

Energy Market; Moss, "Competition in US Petroleum Refining and Marketing";
Christopher Leonard, "A Blade Strikes Steel, and the Blast Shocks a Nation's Energy System," *Bloomberg Businessweek*, November 23, 2016.

476   *Koch traded around Corpus Christi*: Osbourn, Razook, Sementelli, interviews by
author, 2016–18; Ben Fox Rubin, "Koch Industries to Buy PetroLogistics in $2.1
Billion Deal," *Wall Street Journal*, May 28, 2014.

477   *Obama administration failed to pass a carbon regulation bill*: Michael Grunwald,
The New New Deal: The Hidden Story of Change in the Obama Era (New York:
Simon & Schuster, 2012); Brad Plumer, "A Closer Look at Obama's '$90 Billion for
Green Jobs,'" *Washington Post*, October 4, 2012.

477   *In 2007 . . . all the BTUs consumed in America*: "Primary Energy Consumption by
Source," table 1.3, US Energy Information Administration, *Monthly Energy Review*,
January 2018; "US Primary Energy Consumption by Source and Sector, 2016," US
Energy Information Administration, *Monthly Energy Review*, April 2017.

477   *Even as Koch refined . . . emerging across America*: Auers, interview by author, 2018;
"US Refined Product Exports Developments," slide 13.

478   *Like twenty-nine states . . . 10 percent of their power*: Andy Marso, "Koch Works Behind Scenes on Renewable Energy Bill," *Topeka Capital-Journal* (KS), February 26,
2013; Todd Wynn, "ALEC to States: Repeal Renewable Energy Mandates," *Master-
Resource*, November 1, 2012.

478   *Many Kansas state lawmakers were like Tom Moxley*: Tom Moxley, interview by
author, 2018; Alan Claus Anderson et al., *The Economic Benefits of Kansas Wind
Energy* (Kansas City, MO: Polsinelli Shughart and Kansas Enegry Information
Network, November 19, 2012).

479   *In 2013 . . . remove the renewable-energy mandates*: Moxley, interview by author,
2018; Marso, "Koch Works Behind Scenes."

481   *Koch's efforts . . . push back renewable-energy subsidies*: Moxley, interview by author, 2018; *Attacks on Renewable Energy Standards and Net Metering Policies by
Fossil Fuel Interests & Front Groups 2013–2014* (San Francisco: Energy and Policy
Institute, May 2104); Juliet Eilperin, "Climate Skeptic Group Works to Reverse
Renewable Energy Mandates," *Washington Post*, November 24, 2012; Tim Dick-
inson, "The Koch Brothers' Dirty War on Solar Power," *Rolling Stone*, February
11, 2016.

481   *ALEC's efforts bore fruit*: Moxley, interview by author, 2018; Bryan Lowry, "House
OKs Ending Renewable-Energy Tax Break for Businesses," *Wichita Eagle*, May 14,
2015; "Tomblin Approves Energy Act Repeal," Associated Press, February 3, 2015.

482   *By 2014 . . . corporate culture at Koch Industries*: Notes from reporting at Koch Industries headquarters, 2013; Rhoda Miel, "Koch Buys Stake in Guardian," *Crain's
Detroit Business*, October 7, 2012; "Koch Industries Acquires Guardian Industries Corp.," press release, Guardian Industries, November 21, 2016; David Smith,
"Koch Industries Called Steel Mill's Largest Investor," *Arkansas Democrat-Gazette*,

February 2, 2013; Andrea Murphy, "Weiss Family to Take American Greetings Private with Help from the Koch Brothers," *Forbes*, April 1, 2013; "Molex Incorporated Agrees to be Acquired by Koch Industries, Inc. for $38.50 Per Share in Cash," press release, Molex Inc., September 9, 2013.

483 *The sense of mastery . . . expanded and renovated the company headquarters*: Notes, photos, and video from reporting trips at Koch Industries headquarters, 2013, 2015, 2018; "Koch Industries, Inc., Announces Plans to Expand Wichita Headquarters," press release, Koch Industries, December 13, 2012; Daniel McCoy, "Koch Industries Unveils Expansion," *Wichita Business Journal*, June 17, 2015.

CHAPTER 22: THE EDUCATION OF CHASE KOCH

486 *When he was a young boy, Chase Koch might have seemed unteachable*: Chase Koch, interview by author, 2018; "Charles Koch: On Parenthood," Koch Industries video, June 15, 2017.

487 *Those plans . . . the first day Chase Koch was born*: Hall, interviews by author, 2018.

487 *Charles and his wife . . . in their children*: Chase Koch, Hall, interviews by author, 2018; "Charles Koch: On Parenthood," Koch Industries video, June 15, 2017.

488 *Things weren't as easy for Elizabeth*: Elizabeth Koch, "The World Tour Compatibility Test: Back in Tokyo, Part 1," *Smith Memoirville*, March 30, 2007; "The World Tour Compatibility Test: Back in Tokyo, Part 2," *Smith Memoirville*, April 17, 2007; "The World Tour Compatibility Test: Back in Tokyo, Grand Finale," *Smith Memoirville*, May 3, 2007.

488 *Every year . . . sent out as a Christmas card to Koch Industries employees*: Charles and Liz Koch family Christmas card, undated. Inscription reads: "My family joins me in wishing you all the joys of the holiday season throughout the year." Signed by Charles Koch; Elizabeth Koch, "World Tour Compatibility Test, Grand Finale."

488 *Spending time . . . Chase Koch's life*: Chase Koch, interview by author, 2018.

489 *By the time he was in middle school . . . difficult to sustain*: Ibid.

491 *"Aristotle taught . . . use your natural ability"*: Note from Charles Koch to Chase Koch, undated.

491 *Chase enrolled . . . Wichita Collegiate School*: Chase Koch, interview by author, 2018. Descriptions of Wichita Collegiate School based on notes from reporting trips at the school, 2013, 2018.

491 *The tennis courts . . . Dave Hawley*: David Hawley, interview by author, 2018; "Junior Championships, Results," Associated Press, March 25, 1991; Taylor Eldridge, "Boys Tennis: Collegiate's Dave Hawley Wins His 50th Tennis State Championship," *Wichita Eagle*, May 13, 2017.

492 *Chase Koch's style of play . . . two primary strengths*: Hawley, interview by author, 2018.

493 *Chase Koch could never beat Matt Wright*: Ibid.; "Boys State Tennis Champions," *Kansas State High School Activities Association Championship History*, 2018.

493 *On the evening of Saturday, September 18, 1993*: Robert Short, "Teenage Driver Ran Red Light, Police Say," *Wichita Eagle*, September 21, 1993.

493 *That evening, a woman named Nola Foulston*: Bill Hirschman, "Special Prosecutor Enters Koch Case," *Wichita Eagle*, November 2, 1993.

493 *Zachary Seibert was out for a jog*: Walter Seibert, interview by author, 2018; Short, "Teenage Driver Ran Red Light"; Jennifer Comes Roy, "Loss of 12-Year-Old Zac Pains Family, Classmates," *Wichita Eagle*, September 21, 1993.

494 *Zachary Seibert . . . HCA Wesley Medical Center*: Seibert, interview by author, 2018; Short, "Teenage Driver Ran Red Light"; Bill Hirschman, "Chase Koch Charged in Fatal Auto Accident," *Wichita Eagle*, November 4, 1993.

495 *Charles Koch . . . one of the city's economic engines*: Short, "Teenage Driver Ran Red Light."

495 *Charles and Liz . . . Zac's parents in their home*: Seibert, interview by author, 2018.

496 *Charles, Liz, and Chase Koch attended Zachary Seibert's funeral*: Seibert, interview by author, 2018; Boulton, "Koch and His Empire."

496 *Nola Foulston recused herself . . . in the case*: Hirschman, "Chase Koch Charged"; Hirschman, "Special Prosecutor Enters."

497 *Walter Seibert said . . . justice had been served*: Seibert, interview by author, 2018.

497 *Chase Koch would never be able to escape what he had done*: Chase Koch, interview by author, 2018.

497 *During the second half . . . found his place on the tennis court*: Chase Koch, Hawley, interviews by author, 2018.

498 *After Chase Koch's senior year . . . Koch Industries' oil refinery*: O'Neill, interview by author, 2016.

499 *Fred Koch went to MIT*: Schulman, *Sons of Wichita*, 50–57.

499 *Chase majored in marketing*: Chase Koch, interview by author, 2018.

500 *In 2003 . . . with his family*: Chase Koch, Leslie Rudd, interviews by author, 2018.

500 *Chase Koch began a rotation . . . Koch Industries' modern business*: Chase Koch, Hall, interviews by author, 2013–18.

501 *Chase's first assignments was to Koch's development group*: Chase Koch, interview by author, 2018.

501 *The first principle . . . state-sanctioned theft*: Murray N. Rothbard, "Toward a Strategy for Libertarian Social Change," memo obtained by author, April 1977, 13.

502 *These two competing ideas*: Three sources speaking on background; Alexandria Robins and Michele Surka, *Picking up the Tab 2016: Small Businesses Bear the Burden for Offshore Tax Havens* (Boston: MASSPIRG Education Fund, November 2016); Will Fitzgibbon and Dean Starkman, "The 'Paradise Papers' and the Long Twilight Struggle Against Offshore Secrecy," International Consortium of Investigative Journalists online, last modified December 27, 2017, www.icij.org/in

vestigations/paradise-papers; "The Panama Papers: Exposing the Rogue Offshore Finance Industry," International Consortium of Investigative Journalists online, last modified April 3, 2016, www.icij.org/investigations/panama-papers.

502 *Charles Koch . . . is listed as an employee or director*: Nexis database, business entities.

502 *Koch Industries, like many US companies*: Two sources speaking on background; Grand Cayman business registries; Floyd Norris, "The Islands Treasured by Offshore Tax Avoiders," *New York Times*, June 5, 2014; Laura Davison, "Corporate America Flees Zero-Tax Caribbean Havens After Crackdown," *Bloomberg News*, November 15, 2018; Steve Lohr, "Where the Money Washes Up," *New York Times Magazine*, March 29, 1992.

502 *Koch Industries had a surprisingly diverse*: American Bridge report, "How the Kochs Avoid Paying Their Fair Share," 2016.

503 *The ways in which Koch could employ*: Alison Fitzgerald Kodjak and Marina Walker Guevara, "Latest 'Lux Leaks' files obtained by ICIJ disclose secret tax structures sought by 'Big 4' accounting giants for brand name international companies," Center for Public Integrity, December 9, 2014; Alison Fitzgerald, Marina Walker Guevara, and Colm Keena, "Koch Industries Implicated in Luxembourg Leaks," *Irish Times*, December 10, 2014.

504 *When Chase Koch . . . gripped a tennis racket*: Chase Koch, interview by author, 2018.

504 *Chase got a view . . . most traders never got to see*: Chase Koch, Hall, interviews by author, 2013–18.

504 *a job opened up in Koch Fertilizer*: Chase Koch, interview by author, 2018.

505 *Chase grinded it out . . . in an up-close and granular way*: Chase Koch, Osbourn, interviews by author, 2016–18.

506 *Elizabeth, followed in the footsteps of her uncle Freddie*: Elizabeth Koch's lack of participation in the business was confirmed by several current and former Koch Industries employees. It was also confirmed by what they didn't say: during five years and dozens of interviews about different divisions of the business, no one mentioned Elizabeth's participation in any business venture. She was brought up only in reference to the family, and one source mentioned her involvement with the family's foundation. Also, Jennifer Maloney, "A Literary Koch Launches New Publishing House," *Wall Street Journal*, September 10, 2015.

506 *Elizabeth's contact with Charles Koch was both limited and strained*: Elizabeth Koch, "You Don't Say," *Guernica*, February 24, 2008.

507 *Chase Koch got a promotion*: Chase Koch, interview by author, 2018; Kathy Huting, "Taking Nitrogen Technology to the Next Level," *Farm Industry News*, October 7, 2013; "Precision Agriculture," *Discovery: The Quarterly Newsletter of Koch Companies*, October 2011; Gary DiGiuseppe, "Snake Oil or Silver Bullet," *Cattleman*, February 1, 2013.

507   *Packebush . . . offered Chase the biggest break of his career*: Chase Koch, interview by author, 2018; "Koch Fertilizer Announces New Holding Company and Leadership Changes," press release, Koch Industries, December 5, 2013.

508   *Chase would be the public face of Koch Industries*: Chase Koch, interview by author, 2018; "Koch Industries Breaks Ground on Single Largest Project in Company History," *Wichita Business Journal*, October 10, 2014; "Koch's Largest Project: Enid Expansion," *Discovery: The Quarterly Newsletter of Koch Companies*, February 2015.

508   *It was an awful day to make a speech*: Video of groundbreaking on expansion of Koch Fertilizer plant in Enid.

509   *Chase Koch's confidence . . . changes in his personal life*: Chase Koch, Rudd, interviews by author, 2018; "2010 Year in Review," *Discovery: The Quarterly Newsletter of Koch Companies*, January 2011.

509   *Chase and Annie . . . their home*: "Buyer of 70 Acres Is Newlywed Chase Koch," *Wichita Eagle*, June 10, 2010.

510   *wasn't what most people might think it would be*: Chase Koch, interview by author, 2018.

CHAPTER 23: MAKE THE IBU GREAT AGAIN

513   *Steve Hammond volunteered to become a union official*: Hammond, interviews by author, 2013–17.

513   *This question was at the heart of . . . Koch Industries in 2016*: Ibid.; for worker fatalities citations, please see this chapter's endnotes p. 646–48.

514   *Hammond still worked . . . Longshoremen's union hall*: Hammond, Dodge, interviews by author, 2013–17; descriptions of office from notes and photos taken during reporting trips, 2014, 2017.

514   *In 2015 . . . biggest challenge of their new partnership*: Hammond, Dodge, Smith, Franzen, McKinney, interviews by author, 2013–17.

516   *The discontent throughout Georgia-Pacific went beyond economic concerns*: Georgia-Pacific employee speaking on background, interview by author, 2017–18.

516   *When Koch . . . inherited a new monitoring system at the company*: Ibid.; Georgia-Pacific internal TRAX reports, 2008–18. Ten years' worth of TRAX data, and other documents listed here, were provided to the author by a Georgia-Pacific insider in the summer of 2017 and early 2018. When Koch Industries was given a chance to respond to this material in early 2019, the company provided its own set of TRAX data which differed slightly from the data the author previously obtained. Koch explained that the deviation was due to updates made to the data over time as new cases were added or old ones eliminated. This explanation seemed reasonable. The data showed the same patterns over time, although Koch's new data showed the problem was worse than indicated earlier—accident rates had increased more steeply and reached a higher level than was evident in 2017 or 2018. The author

chose to use Koch's newly provided data for this book because it was more recent and because the deviations were small.

516 *Between 2005 and roughly 2009, the TRAX data set was spotty*: Georgia-Pacific employee speaking on background, 2017–18; Georgia-Pacific TRAX report, 2010.

517 *Georgia-Pacific was reporting six worker deaths a year across the country*: Internal Georgia-Pacific safety presentation, slide 4: "Hearts and Mind: Averaging 2 Fatalities a Year Since 2007." The presentation is undated but includes data through the first quarter of 2017.

517 *Koch Industries was delivered something of a reprieve*: Ibid.; analysis of safety procedures at Georgia-Pacific is based on tours of Georgia-Pacific plants in Savannah and Brunswick, Georgia, and interviews with current and former Georgia-Pacific managers and employees named in this chapter.

518 *During the lull . . . injuries declined*: Georgia-Pacific TRAX reports, 2007–11.

518 *In 2011, the housing market . . . began to recover*: Housing-starts data taken from historic database of US Census Bureau, Department of Commerce, "New Residential Construction," 2005–17.

518 *Koch's newly renovated operations . . . were put to the test*: Notes and interviews at Georgia-Pacific facilities, 2016; debt ratings from Thomas J. Nadramia and Maurice Austin, "Summary: Georgia-Pacific LLC, Standard & Poor's Rating Services, Corporate Credit Rating: A+/Stable/A-1+"; earnings from Georgia-Pacific 10-Filing, 2005; Hannan, interview by author, 2016.

519 *Jim Hannan, a rising star within the company*: Hannan, interview by author, 2016.

519 *But one stubborn problem emerged in the shadow of the rising profits*: Georgia-Pacific TRAX reports, 2011–14.

519 *Injuries jumped sharply between 2013 and 2014*: Ibid., 2013–14.

519 *Most alarmingly . . . rate of injuries also increased*: Georgia-Pacific TRAX reports, 2013–17.

520 *Hannan joined a group of senior executives*: Notes from "Health and Safety Conference," March 17–March 19, 2014.

520 *Koch Industries changed the way people worked*: Dana Blocker, Mark Caldwell, interviews by author, 2016.

522 *Koch Industries tried to mitigate these safety risks*: Georgia-Pacific employee speaking on background, interview by author, 2017–18.

522 *a forty-one-year-old man named Robert Wesson*: Occupational Safety and Health Administration inspection report and accident summary, August 12, 2014; Georgia-Pacific employee speaking on background, interview by author, 2017–18; "Hamburg Man Killed in Plant Accident," KTVE online, last modified August 13, 2014; Patty Wooten, "Hamburg Man Killed in Accident at Georgia Pacific," *Seark Today* (AK), last modified August 13, 2014; internal Georgia-Pacific safety presentation, slide 7, "The Heart," list of Georgia-Pacific fatalities.

523 *Wesson's death was the fifth . . . in 2014*: Safety presentation, slide 7, "The Heart."

523   *Sam Southerland was working . . . in Pennington*: OSHA inspection report and accident summary, April 16, 2014; obituary of Samuel Eugene "Sambo" Southerland Jr., April 2014.

523   *at Georgia-Pacific's plant in Corrigan, Texas*: OSHA violation detail and accident summary, September 23, 2014; OSHA inspection detail, April 27, 2014; Jessica Cooley, "2nd Plant Explosion Victim Passes Away," *Lufkin Daily News* (TX), June 6, 2014; "7 Injured in Texas Plant Explosion," Associated Press, April 27, 2014; Bailey Woolum, "Nine Injured in Paper Plant Explosion," KFOR online, last modified April 27, 2014; Gary Bass, "Lawsuit Filed to Determine Cause of Georgia-Pacific Plant Explosion," KTRE online, last modified August 5, 2014; obituary of Kenneth W. "Kenny" Morris, June 2014; obituary of Charles Wayne Kovar, May 2014.

524   *Georgia-Pacific employee named Lydia Faircloth*: OSHA inspection report and accident summary, July 25, 2014; internal Georgia-Pacific safety memo, "Safety Awareness for Everyone," April 20, 2012; Susan Vernon-Devlin, "Colquitt Woman Killed in Tragic Accident at Georgia-Pacific," *Miller County Liberal* (Colquitt, GA), July 30, 2014; Lance Griffin, "OSHA Investigating Georgia Pacific Workplace Fatality," *Dothan Eagle* (AL), July 28, 2014.

524   *Wesson was killed at the mill in Crossett*: Georgia-Pacific employee speaking on background, interview by author, 2017–18; safety presentation, slide 7, "The Heart."

524   *six workers had been killed in Georgia-Pacific*: Safety presentation, slide 4, "Hearts and Mind: Averaging 2 Fatalities a Year."

524   *accidents and injuries continued to climb each year*: Georgia-Pacific TRAX reports, 2010–17.

526   *Koch Industries needed to change . . . how it would do so*: Notes from "Health and Safety Conference," March 17–March 19, 2014.

526   *Georgia-Pacific was fined $5,000*: OSHA violation detail, January 20, 2015; OSHA volation detail and accident summary, September 23, 2014.

526   *Koch Industries responded . . . by reemphasizing the need of employees to follow the guidelines*: Georgie-Pacific internal safety presentation, slides 1, 2, and 3. The presentation is undated but includes data through the first quarter of 2017.

526   *Georgia-Pacific was more unsafe than Koch's competitors*: Safety presentation, slides 5 and 6, "2016 AF&PA Member Company TCIR Quartiles" and "2016 AF&PA Member Company DART Quartiles."

527   *Koch's response . . . reduce risk*: Safety presentation, slides 1, 9, 10, 11.

527   *Another chart, entitled "Georgia-Pacific 20-Year Bet"*: Safety presentation, slide 9.

527   *This was the reality faced by the Dodger and the Hammer*: Hammond, Dodge, Smith, Franzen, McKinney, interviews by author, 2013–14.

529   *Once again, the Dodger and the Hammer . . . Koch's team*: Hammond, Dodge, interviews by author, 2013–14; descriptions of Red Lion hotel taken from notes and photos during reporting trip in 2017.

529   *Bonuses were anathema to workers . . . the same way that a wage hike did*: Patricia Cohen, "Where Did Your Pay Raise Go? It May Have Become a Bonus," *New York Times*, February 10, 2018; *US Salary Increase Survey 2017/2018* (London: Aon Hewitt, 2017).

529   *The Dodger said he wasn't having it*: Hammond, Dodge, interviews by author, 2013–17.

530   *IBU members filed . . . Hammond and Dodge's office*: Hammond, Dodge, Smith, Franzen, McKinney, interviews by author, 2013–14; descriptions of union hall meeting room from notes and photos taken inside the meeting room during a reporting trip, 2017.

531   *Hammond sobered up after he retired*: Hammond, interviews by author, 2013–17.

532   *During the final months . . . another election*: Hammond, Dodge, Smith, Franzen, interviews by author, 2013–17.

532   *Trump's candidacy . . . disrupting Charles Koch's plans*: Fredreka Schouten, "Charles Koch: We Like 5 GOP Candidates in Primaries," *USA Today*, April 21, 2015; Fredreka Schouten, "Charles Koch: We're Not in Politics to Boost Our Bottom Line," *USA Today*, April 24, 2015.

532   *Koch had carefully set up . . . flipped it over*: Matt Flegenheimer and Michael Barbaro, "Donald Trump Is Elected President in Stunning Repudiation of the Establishment," *New York Times*, November 9, 2016.

533   *Shortly after . . . Republicans scurried to reorient themselves around Trumpism*: Former senior US Senate staffer speaking on background, interview by author, 2017.

CHAPTER 24: BURNING

534   *Springtime came early . . . in 2017*: Notes reporting in Washington, DC, 2017; Jeremy White and Henry Fountain, "Spring Came Early: Scientists Say Climate Change Is the Culprit," *New York Times*, March 8, 2017; "NASA, NOAA Data Show 2016 Warmest Year on Record Globally," press releasee, NASA, January 18, 2017; carbon, parts per million in atmosphere, taken from National Oceanic and Atmospheric Administration database.

534   *political seasons . . . were being disrupted*: Descriptions of Trump's inauguration taken from C-Span archive.

535   *The Trump administration saw itself as a revolutionary force*: Trump political operative speaking on background, interview by author, 2017.

536   *Koch responded . . . with a strategy that bore his hallmarks*: This analysis is based on interviews with political operatives in both the Koch and Trump spheres and observations of Koch's political actions during 2017 and 2018. "Block-and-tackle" is my own phrase that I believe captures the Koch strategy.

537   *The first fight was to repeal Obamacare*: Jeff Stein, "Obamacare Jacked Up Taxes on the 1 Percent, Gave $16 Billion Annually to Poor," *Washington Post*, March 28,

2018; Veronica Stracqualursi, "How the GOP Health Care Bill Failed Without a Vote," ABC News online, last modified March 24, 2017.

537 *Trump promised to both repeal . . . and replace*: Robert Costa and Amy Goldstein, "Trump Vows 'Insurance for Everybody' in Obamacare Replacement Plan," *Washington Post*, January 15, 2017; Stracqualursi, "How the GOP Health Care Bill Failed."

538 *another reason for Trump to compromise*: Transcript of "Trump's Takeover," *Frontline*, April 10, 2018.

538 *On March 6 . . . plan to repeal and replace Obamacare*: Description of Americans for Prosperity event taken from reporting notes, 2017; Robert Pear and Thomas Kaplan, "House Republicans Unveil Plan to Replace Health Law," *New York Times*, March 6, 2017; Haeyoun Park and Margot Sanger-Katz, "The Parts of Obamacare Republicans Will Keep, Change or Discard," *New York Times*, March 6, 2017.

539 *Inside the US House of Representatives . . . Freedom Caucus*: Rand Paul and Mark Meadows, "Senator Paul, Rep. Meadows: Let's Fully Repeal ObamaCare, Then Have an Open Debate on How to Replace It," FoxNews.com, last modified March 6, 2017; Bob Bryan, "Conservatives Just Dealt 'Trumpcare' a Significant Blow," Business Insider, March 15, 2017; Isaac Arnsdorf, "Club for Growth and Koch Nurtured Freedom Caucus," *Politico* online, last modified October 22, 2015.

540 *The halting effort to pass it was carried forward by Paul Ryan*: Transcript of "Trump's Takeover," *Frontline*; Alana Abramson, "Read Paul Ryan's Response to the Republican Health Care Bill Failure," *Time* online, last modified March 24, 2017.

540 *Charles and David Koch stepped in*: Kevin Robillard, "Koch Network Pledges to Defend Republicans Who Vote Against GOP Health Bill," *Politico* online, last modified March 22, 2017; "Maze of Money," visual map of Koch Industries political financial network, Center for Responsive Politics, last modified January 7, 2014.

541 *This tactic carried risks*: Teachout, interview by author, 2017; Zephyr Teachout, *Corruption in America: From Benjamin Franklin's Snuff Box to Citizens United* (Cambridge, MA: Harvard University Press, 2014).

541 *The bill showed passing signs of life*: "White House Officials Offer Change to Failed Healthcare Bill—But Is It Enough?," Associated Press, April 4, 2017; "House Freedom Caucus Announces Support for House AHCA Bill with MacArthur Amendment," statement from House Freedom Caucus, April 26, 2017; Elizabeth Mann Levesque and Molly E. Reynolds, "The AHCA's MacArthur Amendment: Unusual Politics, Unusual Policy," Brookings Institution online, last modified May 12, 2017; Thomas Kaplan and Robert Pear, "House Passes Measure to Repeal and Replace the Affordable Care Act," *New York Times*, May 4, 2017.

542 *Ryan's mistake was caused by seemingly good intentions*: Rachael Bade and Josh Dawsey, "Ryan Bucks White House, Setting Up Clash on Taxes," *Politico* online, last modified May 22, 2017; Michelle Fox, "Border Adjustment Tax Is 'Critical' Part of Tax Reform, Chief GOP Tax Writer Says," CNBC.com, last modified May 25, 2017.

542   *It is easy to see why Paul Ryan would have been seduced*: Stephen Ohlemacher, "GOP Running into Opposition from GOP on Tax Overhaul," Associated Press, February 3, 2017; Matt O'Brien, "Tax Cuts Are Easy; Tax Reform, and Not Losing Revenue, Is the Tough Part," *Washington Post*, March 29, 2017; Scott Greenberg and Scott A. Hodge, "FAQs About the Border Adjustment," Tax Foundation online, last modified January 30, 2017; Kyle Pomerleau, "What Is the Distributional Impact of a Destination-Based Cash-Flow Tax?," Tax Foundation online, last modified January 18, 2017; "Trump Eyes Border Tax on Imports to Pay for Wall," *Congressional Quarterly News*, January 26, 2017.

544   *Charles Koch opposed the BAT*: Philip K. Verleger Jr. et al., "Border Adjustment Import Taxation: Impact on the US Crude Oil and Petroleum Product Markets," white paper, Brattle Group, Cambridge, MA, December 16, 2016.

544   *BAT posed . . . Koch Industries' oil refinery in Pine Bend*: Liz Hampton and Catherine Ngai, "Border Tax Ideas Roil Oil Markets, Favor Gulf Coast Refiners," Reuters, January 27, 2017; "US Oil Lobby 'Concerned' About Import Tax Plan," *Oil Daily*, January 5, 2017; "Koch-Backed Group Pledges to Fight Controversial Border Tax," *Daily Oil Bulletin*, January 31, 2017; Jim Geraghty, "Koch Network Ready for a Fight on the Border Adjustment Tax," *National Review*, January 29, 2017.

545   *Koch Industries bought 9.55 million barrels of Canadian crude*: Oil import figures taken from Energy Information Administration database, "Company Level Imports." The author is deeply grateful to Liz Hampton, energy reporter at Thomson Reuters, for steering him to this database when he called for help. Tar sands oil prices are taken from the database of Alberta government, "Oil Prices." Also Nick Cunningham, "Canadian Oil Prices Plunge to $30," OilPrice.com, last modified December 16, 2017; Verleger et al., "Border Adjustment Import Taxation."

545   *The Koch political network moved against*: "Koch Kicks Off Lobbying Salvo Against GOP Tax Proposal," *O'Dwyer's* 31, no. 5 (May 2017): 84; "How the Koch Network Is Derailing House GOP's Border Tax," *Congressional Quarterly News*, May 19, 2017; Nicholas Confessore and Alan Rappeport, "Divide in G.O.P. Now Threatens Trump Tax Plan," *New York Times*, April 2, 2017; "Spending Surges in Lobbying's Top 50," *Hill*, August 2, 2017; "US Oil Lobby 'Concerned'"; "Koch-Backed Group Pledges to Fight"; Geraghty, "Koch Network Ready for a Fight."

545   *The attack was well fashioned*: *Comprehensive Tax Reform: Un-Rigging the US Economy* (Arlington, VA: Americans for Prosperity, May 2017); Americans for Prosperity, "The Problem with a Border Tax," video, 1:12, February 17, 2017; Pomerleau, "What Is the Distributional Impact?"

546   *In fighting . . . out of step with Republican voters*: Jonathan Swan, "Inside the Freedom Caucus Meeting on Border Adjustment," Axios, last modified February 7, 2017; "Interview with North Carolina Congressman Mark Meadows," *CEO Wire*, February 7, 2017; "Trump Eyes Border Tax."

547   *after Meadows made his comments . . . Kevin Brady*: "Koch-Backed Group Pledges

to Fight Controversial Border"; Caitlin Owens, "Rep. Meadows Likely a 'No' on Border Adjustment Tax," Axios, last modified February 13, 2017.

547 *Paul Ryan was unbending . . . tax reform*: Bade and Dawsey, "Ryan Bucks White House"; "How the Koch Network Is Derailing."

547 *This thinking . . . articulated in 1977 by Murray Rothbard*: Rothbard, "Toward a Strategy," 13–14.

548 *As Americans for Prosperity . . . to help shape the tax bill*: Marc Short, interviews by author, 2018.

549 *Paul Ryan and Kevin Brady released a statement*: Damian Paletta, "Speaker Ryan Admits Defeat, Giving Up on Border Adjustment Tax," *Washington Post*, July 27, 2017.

550 *AFP released a statement, crowing about its achievement*: "AFP's Defeat of the Border Adjustment Tax Clears the Way for Principled Tax Reform," statement from Americans for Prosperity, July 31, 2017; "The Koch Brothers Put a Knife in Border Adjustment," *Congressional Quarterly News*, June 1, 2017.

550 *Americans for Prosperity rented out a large event space*: Notes and audio recording from Americans for Prosperity event, 2017.

551 *The tax bill passed . . . signed into law before Christmas*: Thomas Kaplan and Alan Rappeport, "Republican Tax Bill Passes Senate in 51–48 Vote," *New York Times*, December 19, 2017; Heather Long, "The Final GOP Tax Bill Is Complete. Here's What Is in It," *Washington Post*, December 15, 2017; Danielle Kurzleben, "Charts: See How Much of GOP Tax Cuts Will Go to the Middle Class," NPR online, last modified December 19, 2017; "Tax Cuts Will Cross All Income Lines but Disappear by 2027," CBS News and Associated Press, December 19, 2017; Tom Kertscher, "House Tax Plan: Permanent Tax Cuts for the Rich, Eventually Tax Hikes for All Middle-Class Families?," PolitiFact, last modified December 15, 2017.

551 *the bill looked very much like the typical tax bill that Mark Meadows described*: *Distributional Analysis of the Conference Agreement for the Tax Cut and Jobs Act* (Washington, DC: Tax Policy Center report, December 18, 2017); Borys Krawczeniuk, "Congressional Candidates Talk Tax Cuts, Jobs," Associated Press, October 21, 2018; *Analysis: Koch Brothers Could Get up to $1.4 Billion Tax Cut from Law They Helped Pass* (Washington, DC: Americans for Tax Fairness, January 24, 2018).

552 *Koch's block-and-tackle strategy was paying dividends*: Michelle Ye Hee Lee, "Paul Ryan Credits Koch Network for Supporting GOP's Tax Overhaul," *Washington Post*, January 28, 2018.

552 *the Trump administration's transition team . . . described their effort in military terms*: Two senior EPA officials speaking on background, interviews by author, 2017–18; EPA "Landing Team" roster, reviewed by author, 2018.

552 *the Tuesday before Thanksgiving . . . arrived at EPA headquarters*: Two senior EPA officials speaking on background, interviews by author, 2017–18; Gayathri

Vaidyanathan, "How to Get a Skeptic to Believe in Climate Change? Scientists Are Studying That," *ClimateWire*, last modified August 8, 2016.

553 *this put Ebell directly at odds with the career staff at the EPA*: Senior EPA official speaking on background, interviews by author, 2018.

554 *When Myron Ebell finally arrived . . . two senior EPA officials*: Ibid.

554 *This influence was apparent . . . at the EPA*: Two senior EPA officials speaking on background, interviews by author, 2017–18; EPA "beachhead" roster reviewed by author, 2018.

555 *Schnare was an imposing presence*: David Schnare, two senior EPA officials speaking on background, interviews by author, 2017–18.

555 *Schnare came up with a plan to get rid of it*: Schnare, interviews by author, 2018. Descriptions of EPA headquarters taken from notes and photos during reporting trip, 2017.

556 *Schnare's office was on this floor*: Schnare, two senior EPA officials speaking on background, interviews by author, 2017–18.

556 *Schnare's forty-seven-page transition plan*: "Agency Action Plan": US Environmental Protection Agency. This document is undated but was provided to the author in 2017.

557 *The new EPA administrator would carry out these policies*: "How Senators Voted on Scott Pruitt for EPA Administrator," *New York Times*, February 17, 2017.

557 *Pruitt arrived for work*: Schnare, two senior EPA officials speaking on background, interviews by author, 2017–18.

557 *Almost immediately after he arrived . . . Pruitt apparently became convinced*: Two senior EPA officials speaking on background, interviews by author, 2017–18; Liam Stack, "Scott Pruitt's Wish List: Private Jets, Fancy Furniture, 24-Hour Security," *New York Times*, April 6, 2018; Ethan Sacks, "EPA Chief Scott Pruitt's $43K Soundproof Phone Booth Violated Federal Spending Laws, GAO Says," NBC News online, last modified April 16, 2018.

558 *Pruitt's . . . policy stances were well known*: Eric Lipton, "Energy Firms in Secretive Alliance with Attorneys General," *New York Times*, December 6, 2014.

558 *Pruitt's political career . . . Oklahoma's political culture*: Two senior EPA officials speaking on background, interviews by author, 2017–18; Kevin Bogardus, "EPA Protesters Deemed Threat to Pruitt, Triggered Probe," *Greenwire*, last modified January 23, 2018.

559 *When he returned . . . Pruitt seemed deeply shaken*: Senior EPA official speaking on background, interview by author, 2018.

559 *Pruitt's new leadership team . . . loyalists from Oklahoma*: Schnare, former Pruitt staffer speaking on background, two senior EPA officials speaking on background, interviews by author, 2017–18.

559 *There were other problems with Pruitt*: Schnare, interviews by author, 2018; Harvard Law School Regulatory Rollback Tracker database, 2018.

560   *Pruitt attended a ceremony . . . where he introduced President Trump*: Video of Rose
      Garden press conference taken from C-Span archive.

560   *The withdrawal . . . conformed with Charles Koch's views*: Evan Osnos, "Trump vs.
      the Deep State," *New Yorker*, May 21, 2018.

560   *it wasn't clear how effective Pruitt was*: Juliet Eilperin and Brady Dennis, "Amid
      Ethics Scrutiny, EPA's Pruitt Also Finds His Regulatory Rollbacks Hitting Bumps,"
      Washington Post, May 20, 2018.

561   *In July of 2018, Pruitt resigned*: Coral Davenport, Lisa Friedman, and Maggie
      Haberman, "EPA Chief Scott Pruitt Resigns Under a Cloud of Ethics Scandals,"
      New York Times, July 5, 2018; carbon, parts per million in atmosphere, taken from
      National Oceanic and Atmospheric Administration database.

561   *Koch's political network . . . touted two big achievements that year*: Koch seminar
      group memo: "Efforts in Government: Advancing Principled Public Policy." This
      memo is undated and was first revealed by Lee Fang and Nick Surgey, "Koch Doc-
      ument Reveals Laundry List of Policy Victories Extracted from the Trump Admin-
      istration," *Intercept* online, last modified February 25, 2018.

562   *Inside the Trump administration, there was disdain for Charles Koch*: Source speak-
      ing on background, interviews by author, 2017–18; Robert Draper, "Trump vs.
      Congress: Now What?," *New York Times Magazine*, March 26, 2017.

562   *the Trump administration and the Koch network were like opposing chess play-
      ers*: James Hohmann and Matea Gold, "Koch Network to Spend $300 Million to
      $400 Million on Politics, Policy in 2018 Cycle," *Washington Post*, January 28, 2017.

562   *The Koch network maximized its influence*: Lisa Mascaro, "Vice President Mike
      Pence Stops In for an Unscheduled Chat with Billionaire Charles Koch," *Baltimore
      Sun*, June 24, 2017; Kenneth P. Vogel and Eliana Johnson, "Trump's Koch Admin-
      istration," *Politico* online, last modified November 28, 2016; John Frank, "Koch
      Brothers' Conservative Network to Hold Retreat in Colorado Springs This Week-
      end," *Denver Post*, June 23, 2017.

562   *Koch traveled to Palm Springs*: Video of Charles Koch speech provided by Koch In-
      dustries, "Charles Koch: Opening Remarks (Palm Springs 2018)," video, 3:29, up-
      loaded to YouTube by the Seminar Network on January 28, 2018.

CHAPTER 25: CONTROL

564   *Charles Koch's family compound in Wichita*: Notes and photographs from report-
      ing trip to Koch Industries headquarters and entryway to Charles Koch's office,
      2018; descriptions of Charles Koch's office and the view from his desk taken from
      notes and photos taken in, 2015.

567   *the business leaders from Koch's various divisions came . . . to report to Charles Koch*:
      Packebush, Feilmeier, Hall, Markel, Koch Industries employees and executives
      speaking on background, interviews by author, 2013–18.

567   *as he listened to the division heads make their presentations*: See previous endnotes. Georgia-Pacific profits taken from interview with Jim Hannan, 2016.

568   *Koch's beliefs would have been validated in another way*: Current and former Koch Industries employees and executives, interviews by author, 2013–18.

569   *Invista, for example, was deeply troubled*: Former Koch Industries executive speaking on background, interviews by author, 2018; notes and photos taken at Invista headquarters, 2018; "Plant Shut-Downs, Closings & Layoffs Profile—Invista," taken from Nexis database, "Plant Shut-Downs, Closings & Layoffs," November 27, 2017; Thad Moore, "In Winnsboro, One of South Carolina's Oldest Surviving Textile Mills May Close," *Post and Courier* (Charleston, SC), August 20, 2017; Casey White, "On the Chopping Block," *Shelby Star* (NC), July 19, 2017; "New Owner for Derry Lycra Plant," *Irish News* (Belfast, Ire.), October 31, 2017; Mike Pare, "Kordsa Slated to Acquire City's Invista Plant," *Chattanooga Times Free Press* (TN), April 1, 2017.

569   *The economy itself was shaky*: Analysis based on general reporting by the author during 2018.

570   *Charles and David Koch were worth a combined $4.7 billion*: "The Billionaires 1991," *Fortune*, September 9, 1991; all Charles and David Koch net worth figures are taken from *Forbes'* list of the four hundred richest people and billionaires, 2002, 2005, 2009, 2013, 2016, 2018; existence of shadow stock confirmed by current and former Koch Industries employees.

571   *This ownership structure . . . reflected the US economy*: Emmanuel Saez and Gabriel Zucman, "Wealth Inequality in the United States since 1913: Evidence from Capitalized Income Data," *Quarterly Journal of Economics* 131, no. 2 (May 1, 2016): 519–78; Christina M. Gibson-Davis and Christine Percheski, "Children and the Elderly: Wealth Inequality Among America's Dependents," *Demography* 55, no. 3 (June 2018): 1009–32.

571   *American labor market resembled the labor market inside Kochland*: Analysis based on reporting cited in earlier chapters.

571   *This disparity . . . reflected the disparity in political power*: Martin Gilens and Benjamin I. Page, "Testing Theories of American Politics: Elites, Interest Groups, and Average Citizens," *Perspectives on Politics* 12, no. 3 (September 2014): 564–81.

572   *Koch Industries was overhauled in the most significant restructuring since 2000*: Koch Industries executive speaking on background, interview by author, 2018; Daniel McCoy, "CEOs of Georgia-Pacific and Flint Hills Resources Take On Larger Roles Within Koch Industries," *Wichita Business Journal*, March 3, 2017; "Fischer Named GP CEO, Hannan to Assume New Role," press release, Georgia-Pacific, March 2, 2017; Jim Hannan executive bio, Koch Industries newsroom, 2017; Brad Razook, executive bio, Koch Industries Newsroom, 2017.

573   *If any of these men became CEO, however*: Analysis based on Chase Koch, Koch Industries executive speaking on background, interviews by author, 2018; descrip-

tions of Koch Disruptive Technologies offices taken from notes and photos during reporting trip, 2018.

573 *Charles Koch sent his son a small folder of old papers*: Chase Koch, interview by author, 2018; photo of undated note from Charles Koch to Chase Koch.

574 *If Charles Koch found meaning . . . seemed to derive largely from the "book project"*: Rudd, Koch Industries executive speaking on background, interviews by author, 2018.

INDEX

ABOUT THE AUTHOR

Christopher Leonard is a business reporter whose work has appeared in the *Washington Post*, the *Wall Street Journal*, *Fortune*, and *Bloomberg Businessweek*. He is the author of *The Meat Racket* and *Kochland*, which was the recipient of the J. Anthony Lukas Work-in-Progress Award. A graduate of the University of Missouri School of Journalism, Leonard lives outside Washington, DC.